1917

1917

WAR, PEACE, AND REVOLUTION

DAVID STEVENSON

OXFORD
UNIVERSITY PRESS

OXFORD
UNIVERSITY PRESS

Great Clarendon Street, Oxford, OX2 6DP,
United Kingdom

Oxford University Press is a department of the University of Oxford.
It furthers the University's objective of excellence in research, scholarship,
and education by publishing worldwide. Oxford is a registered trade mark of
Oxford University Press in the UK and in certain other countries

First Edition published in 2017

Impression: 1

Published in the United States of America by Oxford University Press
198 Madison Avenue, New York, NY 10016, United States of America

British Library Cataloguing in Publication Data
Data available

Library of Congress Control Number: 2017932564

ISBN 978-0-19-870238-2

Printed in Great Britain by
Clays Ltd, St Ives plc

Preface and Acknowledgements

> The responsibility of those who needlessly prolong such a War is not less than that of those who needlessly provoke it.
>
> > (Lord Lansdowne to the British Cabinet, November 1916)[1]
>
> I am making this statement as an act of wilful defiance of military authority because I believe that the war is being deliberately prolonged by those who have the power to end it.
>
> > (Siegfried Sassoon, 'Finished with the War: A Soldier's Declaration')[2]

This book focuses on a single year of the First World War, coinciding with the months from January to November 1917. It is one of the best-established benchmark dates in modern history. What follows does not cover everything that happened in these pivotal months. It centres on the war's transformation under the impact of the Russian Revolution and American intervention: events that between them marked the most significant turning point since the opening campaigns had bogged down into stalemate in the autumn of 1914. Yet still the conflict continued, despite its having developed into something that at its outset was scarcely foreseeable or even credible. And that it did continue would have repercussions to the present.

Many paths approach the centre of this labyrinth. The main one followed here runs via an analysis of decision-making, reconstructing it in depth, placing it in national and international context, and showing how decisions interacted. Lord Lansdowne and Siegfried Sassoon began from very different vantage points: as a former Foreign Secretary practised in the ways of Whitehall and a disenchanted officer who hurled his Military Cross into the Mersey. But both perceived the First World War, and the accompanying havoc, as prolonged not by blind impersonal forces but through deliberate will. The conflict was *constructed*. This is not to say the decision-makers' choices were either easy or unconstrained. They generally emerged from complex and protracted bureaucratic processes. By 1917 the debates preceding them were often fractious and left copious records. Alternatives existed, and made responsibility more agonizing. Still, the choices taken were to prolong and escalate the violence. Even Vladimir Lenin, perhaps the war's most visceral critic, sought to transcend it not through peace but through a life-and-death struggle against the bourgeoisie.

To focus on decision-making is to adopt an elite perspective. Historians have analysed intensively the conflict's outbreak in summer 1914 but much less the decisions that propelled it forward and sustained its momentum. The intention is in no way to disparage the alternative—and for long unjustly neglected—approaches to the conflict's history that in recent years have drawn so much attention. We should investigate not only why governments and high commands gave orders but also why soldiers of all ethnicities obeyed them (or by 1917 increasingly did not) and why men and women on the home fronts gave or withheld their consent. None the less, understanding how the crucial decisions were taken provides an indispensable key to also understanding *why* they were taken and how far they displayed incompetence or prescience. The English philosopher Bertrand Russell, who helped draft Sassoon's protest, remarked 'This war is trivial, for all its vastness. No great principle is at stake, no great human purpose is involved on either side.'[3] Yet as statesmen at the time well recognized, the elite decisions really mattered, and on their outcome might turn tens of thousands of lives. By 1917, moreover, at both elite and popular levels, the war was controversial as never before. Much of what follows therefore concentrates on why costlier and riskier options were pursued instead of other courses, apparently less perilous and less painful.

A purely chronological survey of these developments might convey the whirlwind atmosphere of the time yet lack coherence. Instead the material is organized thematically, in three sections. The first, or 'Atlantic Prologue', starts with Germany's decision for unrestricted submarine warfare. It was the precondition for American intervention. It gambled on the U-boats throttling Britain so quickly that US entry would not matter, but this calculation proved unfounded, in large part because Britain countered with the convoy system. The first three chapters therefore travel from Berlin via Washington to London. The second section transfers from the oceans to the Continent, and to Europe's suicidal military and political impasse. If the submarine gamble led to Germany's defeat and temporary eclipse, its enemies' actions likewise scarred them for decades. Tsar Nicholas's abdication derailed the Allies' spring campaign, and highlighted the revolutionary threat. These warnings notwithstanding, the French persisted with the calamitous Nivelle offensive. The Russian Provisional Government similarly authorized the Kerensky offensive, to the ruin of the country's liberals and moderate socialists. Scarcely less dispiriting are the origins of Britain's ill-starred Third Battle of Ypres, and those—arising also from spring and summer offensives—of Italy's rout at Caporetto. Against this backdrop, attention returns to Austria-Hungary and Germany's peace feelers, and to those feelers' rejection. In the third section the horizon widens. By 1917 the conflict's global repercussions included new war entries (not only by America but also by Greece, Brazil, Siam, and China), and Britain's backing for 'responsible government' in India and a Jewish national home in Palestine. The conclusion links to developments in 1918, via Russia's October Revolution, Germany's decision for an all-out Western Front offensive, and America's intensification of its war effort. These developments concluded the transition that had begun in late 1916, and opened the struggle's end-game: in its way a simpler story, during which first the Germans and then their enemies launched culminating offensives, and the latter prevailed.

Much of this book rests on contemporary records, both published and archival. It cites them liberally. It highlights the arguments presented by contemporaries, who in 1917 were all too aware of inhabiting turbulent times. It also draws on work by fellow historians: often of the highest calibre, albeit not previously synthesized in the form adopted here. In particular Ian Kershaw's *Fateful Choices* has provided a model, although the analogous period in the Second World War (1940–1) came in its opening rather than its closing months.[4] Much contemporary testimony—including unsung masterpieces such as Edward Spiers's *Prelude to Victory*—is also rich. I have benefited enormously from working in the International History Department at the London School of Economics & Political Science, and I am grateful to my colleagues and students as well as to the School for the sabbatical leave that made research and writing possible. Three years as Vice-Chair of the LSE Appointments Committee gave practical decision-making experience. My thanks go to Michael Hemmersdorfer and Charles Sorrie for visiting the German and French archives, and to Kevin Matthews and Andrea Heatley for hospitality in Washington. Nick Bosanquet supplied encouragement and bibliographical recommendations, and Anthony Heywood was very helpful over Russian railways. Among the libraries and archives consulted, I should make specific mention of the British and the American National Archives, the Manuscripts Division of the Library of Congress, the British Library of Political and Economic Science, the British Library (including its Manuscript

Contents

PART IV. CONCLUSION

List of Illustrations, Maps, and Table

Illustrations

Maps

Table

List of Abbreviations

AA	Auswärtiges Amt (German Foreign Ministry)
AC	Austen Chamberlain papers, Cadbury Research Library, Birmingham
ADM	Admiralty papers, TNA
AEF	American Expeditionary Force
AFGG	*Les Armées françaises dans la Grande Guerre* (Paris, 1922–37) [French official history]
AOK	*Armee Oberkommando* (Austrian-Hungarian High Command)
AR	Akten der Reichskanzlei, Bundesarchiv, Berlin
BA-MA	Bundesarchiv-Militärarchiv, Freiburg-im-Breisgau
BEF	British Expeditionary Force
BL	British Library
CAB	Cabinet papers, TNA
CAS	Chief of Admiralty Staff
CFC	Conjoint Foreign Committee
CGS	Chief of the General Staff
COS	Chief of Staff
CND	Council of National Defense
CPI	Committee on Public Information
CQG	Grand quartier-général
DAMS	Defensive Arming of Merchant Ships
DVP	*Deutsche Vaterlandspartei*
EEF	Egyptian Expeditionary Force
EZF	English Zionist Federation
FO	Foreign Office papers, TNA
FRB	Federal Reserve Board
FRUS 1917	*Foreign Relations of the United States 1917*
FRUS LP	*FRUS The Lansing Papers, 1914–1920* (1939)
GAC	*Groupe d'armées du centre*
GAN	*Groupe d'armèes du nord*

GAR	*Groupe d'armées de la rupture*
GHQ	General Headquarters (British High Command)
GNP	Gross National Product
GOI	Government of India
GQG	*Grand Quartier-général* (French High Command)
HNKY	Hankey papers, Churchill Archives Centre, Cambridge
INC	Indian National Congress
LGP	Lloyd George papers, Parliamentary Archives, London
LHCMA	Liddell Hart Centre for Military Archives, King's College London
LOC	Library of Congress, Washington
MECA	Middle East Centre Archive, St Antony's College, Oxford
MEF	Mesopotamia Expeditionary Force
MOFB	James Edmonds, *Military Operations, France and Belgium 1914–1918* (1933–48) [British official history]
MOI	James Edmonds, *Military Operations: Italy, 1915–1919* (1949)
MOM	Cyril Falls, *Military Operations: Macedonia* (1933–5)
MRC	Military-Revolutionary Committee
MT	Ministry of Transport papers, TNA
NARA	National Archives and Record Administration, Washington DC
NLS	National Library of Scotland, Edinburgh
NMM	National Maritime Museum, Greenwich
OHL	*Oberste Heeresleitung* (German High Command)
ÖULK	Edmond Glaise von Horstenau and Rudolf Kiszling (eds), *Österreich-Ungarns Letzter Krieg, 1914–1918* (1929–35) [Austrian official history]
PRO	Public Record Office papers, TNA
PSI	*Partito Socialista Italiano*
PWW	Arthur Link (ed.), *The Papers of Woodrow Wilson* (1966–94)
RMA	*Reichsmarineamt* (German Navy Ministry)
SFIO	*Section française de l'Internationale ouvrière* (French Socialist Party)
SHAT	*Service historique de l'armèe de terre*, Vincennes
SPD	*Sozialdemokratische Partei Deutschlands* (German Socialist Party)
TNA	The National Archives, Kew
WK	Reichsarchiv, *Der Weltkrieg 1914 bis 1918* (1925–56) [German official history]
WO	War Office papers, TNA
WPC	War Policy Committee

List of Principal Personalities

Unless otherwise indicated, the responsibilities indicated are those held by the relevant individual during 1917. Please refer to list of abbreviations.

Albert I	King of the Belgians
Alekseyev, Mikhail	Russian CGS (until May)
Arz von Straußenberg, Arthur	Austro-Hungarian CGS
Alexander, David	President, Board of Deputies of British Jews
Allenby, Sir Edmund	British commander in Egypt/Palestine (from June)
Alston, Beilby	British *chargé d'affaires* in China
Amery, Leo	British Unionist MP and member of the Lloyd George government
Aosta, Duke of	Italian Third Army commander
Armand, Count Abel	French intelligence officer and participant in Armand–Revertera conversations
Asquith, Herbert Henry	British Liberal leader; prime minister (1908–16)
Augusta Victoria, Queen	Wife of Wilhelm II
Bacon, Reginald	Commander, Dover Patrol
Badoglio, Pietro	Commander, Italian IV Corps
Baker, Newton Diehl	US war secretary
Balfour, Arthur James	British Foreign Secretary
Barbosa, Ruy	Brazilian Senator
Barnes, George	British Labour politician and War Cabinet member
Barrère, Camille	French ambassador in Italy
Barthou, Louis	French foreign minister (October–November)
Bauer, Hermann	Commander of German High Seas Fleet U-boats

Bauer, Max	OHL representative in Berlin
Beatty, Sir David	Commander, British Grand Fleet
Beliaev, Mikhail	Tsarist Russian war minister
Below, Otto von	Commander of Austro-German Fourteenth Army
Benedict XV	(Giaccomo della Chiesa) Pope
Benson, William Shepherd	US Chief of Naval Staff
Bernstorff, Joachim-Heinrich, Count von	German ambassador in the United States
Besant, Annie	Head of Indian Home Rule League
Bethmann Hollweg, Theobald von	German chancellor (until July)
Bissolati, Leonida	Italian socialist and minister
Bliss, Tasker Howard	US Army Deputy COS; then COS (from September)
Bonar Law, Andrew	British Chancellor of the Exchequer and Unionist leader
Boroević, Svetozar	Austro-Hungarian commander on Isonzo Front
Boselli, Paolo	Italian premier (until October)
Brandeis, Louis	US Supreme Court Justice
Braz, Wenceslau	Brazilian president
Briand, Aristide	French premier (until March)
Broqueville, Charles de	Belgian premier
Brugère, Joseph	Chair of Nivelle offensive inquiry commission
Brusilov, Aleksei	Commander, Russian South-West Front; then CGS (May–July)
Bryan, William Jennngs	US Secretary of State (1913–15)
Buchanan, Sir George	British ambassador in Russia
Burián, Istvan	Austro-Hungarian foreign minister (1915–16)
Cabot Lodge, Henry	Chair, Senate Foreign Relations Committee (from March)
Cadorna, Luigi	Italian commander-in-chief
Caillaux, Joseph	Former French premier
Cambon, Jules	Secretary-general, French Foreign Ministry
Cambon, Paul	French ambassador in Britain

Capelle, Eduard von	German navy secretary
Capello, Luigi	Italian Second Army commander
Carranza, Venustiano	Mexican president
Carson, Sir Edward	British First Lord of the Admiralty (until July)
Castelnau, Curières de	French Army Group commander
Caviocchi, Alberti	Commander, Italian XXVII Corps
Cecil, Lord Robert	Parliamentary under-secretary, British Foreign Office
Chamberlain, Austen	British Secretary of State for India (until July)
Charteris, Sir John	Chief Intelligence Officer, GHQ, BEF
Chelmsford, Viscount	Viceroy of India
Chernov, Viktor	Socialist Revolutionary leader; Russian agriculture minister
Chkheidze, Nikolai	Menshevik; Chair of Petrograd Soviet
Chiozza Money, Leo	British Shipping Ministry official
Churchill, Winston	British minister of munitions (from July)
Clemenceau, Georges	French premier and war minister (from November)
Constantine I	King of Greece
Coppée, Baron Evence	Belgian industrialist, intermediary between von der Lancken and Briand
Craddock, Reginald	Member of Indian Executive Council
Cramon, August von	German plenipotentiary at AOK
Creel, George	Director of Committee on Public Information (United States)
Curzon, George Nathaniel Lord	British War Cabinet Member
Czernin, Ottokar Count	Austro-Hungarian foreign minister
D'Alenson, Colonel	Chef de cabinet to Nivelle
Dall'Olio, Alfredo	Italian armaments minister
Dan, Fyodor	Menshevik and leading member of Petrograd Soviet
Daniels, Josephus	US navy secretary
Davidson, Sir John	BEF GHQ Chief of Operations
Delmé-Radcliffe, Charles	British military attaché in Italy
Derby, Edward Stanley, Earl of	British Secretary of State for War

Dering, Herbert	British minister in Siam
De Salis, John	British minister to the Vatican
Devonport, Lord	British Food Controller
Dewrawangse, Prince	Siamese foreign minister
Diaz, Armando	Italian commander-in-chief (from October)
Duan Qiriu	Chinese premier (previously war minister)
Doumergue, Gaston	French colonial minister (until March)
Duff, Sir Alexander	Head of British Admiralty Anti-Submarine Division
Eckhardt, Heinrich von	German minister in Mexico City
Enver Pasha	Turkish war minister
Erzberger, Mathias	Deputy leader, German Centre Party
Evert, Aleksei	Russian Western Front commander
Falkenhayn, Erich von	German CGS (1914–16)
Feisal, Prince	Son of Sharif Hussein
Franchet d'Espérey, Louis	Commander, French Northern Army Group
Franz Joseph I	Austro-Hungarian emperor (1848–1916)
Freycinet, Charles de	Former French premier and minister in Briand government
Galt, Edith	Second wife of Woodrow Wilson
Gandhi, Mohandas Karamchand	Indian nationalist leader
Gasparri, Cardinal Pietro	Vatican Secretary of State
Gatti, Angelo	Italian army staff historian
Geddes, Sir Eric	British First Lord of the Admiralty (from July)
George V	British king
Gerard, James Watson	US ambassador to Germany
Giardino, Gaetano	Italian war minister
Giolitti, Giovanni	Former Italian premier
Gokhale, Gopal Krishna	Indian nationalist leader
Golitsyn, Prince Nikolai	Last Tsarist Russian premier
Goubet, Lt. Col.	Head of French General Staff intelligence (Second Bureau)
Gough, Sir Hubert	British Fifth Army commander
Graham, Ronald	British Foreign Office official

Grey, Sir Edward — British Foreign Secretary (1905–16)

Grimm, Arthur — Swiss socialist

Guchkov, Aleksandr — Russian Octobrist leader; war minister (March–May)

Gurko, Vasily — Acting Russian CGS (1916–17)

Haig, Sir Douglas — BEF commander-in-chief

Hall, Sir Reginald — British Director of Naval Intelligence

Hankey, Maurice — Secretary to British War Cabinet

Harding, William — Chair, US FRB Board of Governors

Hardinge, Sir Arthur — British ambassador in Spain

Hardinge of Penshurst, Baron — Viceroy of India (to 1916); permanent under-secretary, British Foreign Office

Harington, C. H. — COS to Plumer

Helfferich, Karl — German secretary for the interior (until October)

Henderson, Arthur — British War Cabinet member and Labour leader

Henderson, Reginald — British Admiralty official

Herbillon, Emile — Liaison officer between Poincaré and GQG

Hertling, Georg von — German chancellor (from September)

Hindenburg, Paul von — German CGS

Hoffmann, Robert — Swiss foreign minister

Hohenlohe-Schillingsfürst, Prince Gottfried von — Austro-Hungarian ambassador in Germany

Holtzendorff, Henning von — German Chief of the Admiralty Staff

Hötzendorff, Franz Conrad von — Austro-Hungarian CGS; from March commander on the Tyrol front

House, Edward Mandell — Adviser to Woodrow Wilson

Houston, David Franklin — US agriculture secretary

Hughes, Charles Evans — Republican presidential candidate, 1916

Hussein bin Ali, Sharif — Ruler of Mecca

Jagow, Gottlieb von — German foreign minister (1913–16)

Jellicoe, Sir John — British First Sea Lord

Joffre, Joseph — French CGS/commander-in-chief (1911–16)

Jusserand, Jules — French ambassador in the United States

Kamenev, Lev	Bolshevik Central Committee member
Karl I	Austrian emperor
Kato, Count Komei	Japanese foreign minister (1914–15)
Kerensky, Aleksandr	Justice minister in first Russian Provisional Government; then (from May) premier/war minister
Khabalov, Georgi	Commander, Petrograd Military District
Kiggell, Sir Launcelot	BEF CGS
Kitchener, Lord	British Secretary of State for War (1914–16)
Knox, Alfred	British liaison officer in Russia
Kolyschko, Josef	Russian representative in talks with Erzberger
Kornilov, Lavr	Commander, Russian Eighth Army, then commander-in-chief (July–September)
Krafft von Delmensingen, Karl	COS to Austro-German Fourteenth Army
Kuhl, Hermann von	CGS to Rupprecht of Bavaria
Kühlmann, Richard von	German foreign minister (from July)
Kuhn, Joseph	Head of War College Division
Lancken-Wakenitz, Baron Oscar von der	Head of the Political Department of the German occupation administration in Brussels
Lansdowne, Lord	Unionist peer and former Foreign Secretary
Lansing, Robert	US Secretary of State
Lema, Marqués de	Spanish foreign minister
Long, Walter	British colonial secretary
Lenin, Vladimir	Russian Bolshevik leader
Leslie, Norman	British Shipping Ministry official
Levetzow, Magnus von	Chief of Operations, German High Seas Fleet
Li Yuan-hang	Chinese president
Lloyd George, David	British prime minister
Lockhart, Robert Bruce	British Consul General in Moscow
Long, Walter	British colonial secretary
Loβberg, Friedrich von	German Fourth Army COS

Ludendorff, Erich	German First Quartermaster-General
Lvov, Prince Georgy	Premier, First Russian Provisional Government
Lyautey, Hubert	French war minister
McAdoo, William Gibbs	US treasury secretary
MacDonough, George	British Director of Military Intelligence
McKenna, Reginald	British Chancellor of the Exchequer (1914–16)
MacLay, Sir Joseph	British Shipping Controller
McMahon, Sir Henry	British High Commissioner in Egypt
MacMullen, Norman	Officer in BEF GHQ Operations Section
Mangin, Charles	Commander, French Tenth Army
Margerie, Pierre de	Political Director, French Foreign Ministry
Martin, William	Director of Protocol, French Foreign Ministry
Maude, Sir Frederick	British commander in Mesopotamia
Mazel, Olivier	Commander, French Fifth Army
Mérode, Countess Pauline de	Intermediary between von der Lancken and Briand
Messimy, Adolphe	Former French war minister
Meston, Sir James	Lieutenant Governor of United Provinces (India)
Metaxas, Ioannis	Greek CGS
Michaelis, Georg	German chancellor (July–September)
Micheler, Alfred	Commander, French Breakthrough Army Group
Mikhail, Grand Duke	Brother of Nicholas II
Milyukov, Pavel	Russian Kadet leader; foreign minister (March–May)
Milner, Alfred Lord	British War Cabinet member
Moltke the Younger, Helmuth von	German CGS (1906–14)
Monro, Sir Charles	Commander-in-chief, Indian Army
Montagu, Edwin	British Secretary of State for India (from July)
Montefiore, Claude	President, Anglo-Jewish Association
Motono, Baron Ichiro	Japanese foreign minister

Müller, Georg von	German Chief of the Naval Cabinet
Müller, Lauro	Brazilian foreign minister (until May)
Murray, Sir Archibald	British commander in Egypt/Palestine (until June)
Neilson, J. F.	British liaison officer in Russia
Nicholas II	Russian emperor
Nitti, Francesco	Italian finance minister (from October)
Nivelle, Robert	French commander-in-chief, Western Front (Dec. 1916–May 1917)
Orlando, Vittorio	Italian minister of the interior; then premier (from October)
Pacelli, Eugenio	Papal nuncio in Munich
Page, Walter Hines	US ambassador in Britain
Payer, Friedrich von	Deputy to Hertling
Paléologue, Maurice	French ambassador in Russia
Peçanha, Nila	Brazilian foreign minister (from May)
Pershing, John J.	Commander, AEF
Pétain, Philippe	Commander, French Army Group Centre, then CGS (April), then French commander-in-chief, Western Front (from May)
Picot, François Georges–	French diplomat and colonial lobbyist
Plumer, Sir Herbert	Commander, British Second Army
Poincaré, Raymond	French president
Polk, Frank	Counsellor, US State Department
Porrò, Carl	Deputy to Cadorna
Protopopov, Aleksandr	Tsarist Russian interior minister
Rama VI	King of Siam
Rasputin, Grigori	Russian faith healer and mystic
Rawlinson, Sir Henry	Former commander of British Fourth Army
Redfield, William Cox	US commerce secretary
Reinsch, Paul	US minister to China
Renouard, Georges	Head, French GQG Third Bureau
Revertera, Count Nikolaus	Austrian participant in Armand–Revertera conversations
Ribot, Alexandre	French finance minister, then premier (March–September)

Riezler, Kurt	Secretary to Bethmann Hollweg
Rittikh, Aleksandr	Tsarist Russian agriculture minister
Robertson, Sir William	British CIGS
Rodd, Sir Rennell	British ambassador in Italy
Rodzianko, Mikhail	Speaker of Russian Duma
Rothschild, Baron Walter	British banker and Zionist supporter
Runciman, Walter	President of the British Board of Trade (to December 1916)
Rupprecht of Bavaria, Crown Prince	German Army Group commander
Ruszky, Nikolai	Russian Northern Front commander
Sacher, Harry	Manchester-based journalist and Zionist
Sakharov, Vladimir	Russian Romanian Front commander
Samuel, Sir Herbert	President of the British Local Government Board (1914–15)
Sarrail, Maurice	Commander, Allied armies in Macedonia
Sassoon, Siegfried	British army officer
Scheer, Reinhard	Commander, German High Seas Fleet
Schlieffen, Alfred von	German CGS (1890–1905)
Schulenburg, Friedrich Count von der	COS to Crown Prince Wilhelm
Scott, Charles Prestwich	Editor, *The Manchester Guardian*
Scott, Hugh	US CGS
Sims, William	Head of US naval mission to UK
Sixte de Bourbon, Prince	Intermediary in spring 1917 peace contacts
Smuts, Jan–Christiaan	Former South African defence minister; British War Cabinet member
Sokolow, Nahum	Zionist activist, based in London
Sonnino, Sidney	Italian foreign minister
Spiers (from 1918 Spears), Edward	British liaison officer in France
Spring-Rice, Sir Cecil	British ambassador in the United States
Stone, William	Chair, Senate Foreign Relations Committee (to March)
Stürmer, Boris	Russian premier and foreign minister (1916)
Sun Yat-sen	Chinese nationalist leader
Sykes, Sir Mark	British MP, officer, and diplomat

Taft, William Howard — US president (1909–13)

Tchlenov, Yehiel — Russian Zionist leader

Tereschchenko, Mikhail — Russian foreign minister (May–November)

Thomas, Albert — French socialist; armaments minister

Tilak, Bal Gangadhar — Indian nationalist leader

Tirpitz, Alfred von — German Navy Secretary (1897–1916)

Trepov, Aleksandr — Penultimate tsarist Russian premier

Trotsky, Leon — Chair of Military-Revolutionary Committee (September–November)

Tsereteli, Irakli — Menshevik; Russian minister of posts and telecommunications (May–August)

Tumulty, Joseph — Secretary to Woodrow Wilson

Valentini, Rudolf von — German Chief of Civil Cabinet

Venizelos, Eleutherios — Greek premier (from June)

Verkhovsky, Aleksandr — Russian Provisional Government war minister

Villa, Pancho — Mexican revolutionary leader

Villalobar, Marqués de — Spanish representative in the Low Countries

Vittorio Emmanuel III — King of Italy

Waldstätten, Alfred von — CGS to Arz von Straußenberg

Webb, Sir Richard — Director of British Admiralty Trade Division

Weizmann, Chaim — President of the English Zionist Federation

Wetzell, Georg — German OHL Chief of Operations

Wilhelm, Crown Prince — Son of Wilhelm II; German Army Group commander

Wilhelm II — German emperor

Wilson, Woodrow — US president

Wise, Rabbi Stephen — US Zionist leader

Wiseman, William — British secret service agent in the United States

Wolf, Lucien — Secretary to the Conjoint Foreign Committee

Xavier de Bourbon, Prince — Brother of Sixte de Bourbon

Yrigoyen, Hipólito — Argentinian president

Yuan Shikai — Chinese president (to 1916)

Zaimis, Alexandros	Greek premier (until June)
Zimmermann, Arthur	German foreign minister (November 1916–July 1917)
Zinoviev, Grigori	Bolshevik Central Committee member
Zita, Empress	Wife of Karl I

Map 1. Europe in 1917

Map 2. The British Isles

Map 3. The Eastern Front

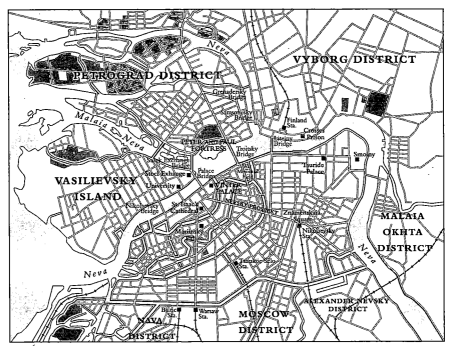

Map 4. Petrograd

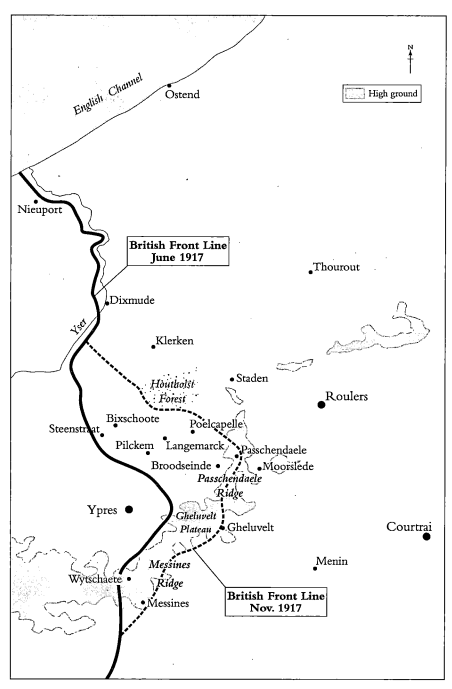

Map 5. Flanders

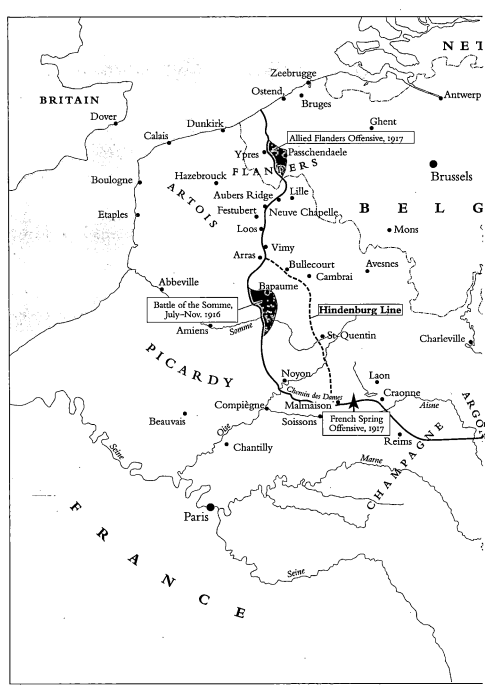

Map 6. The Western Front

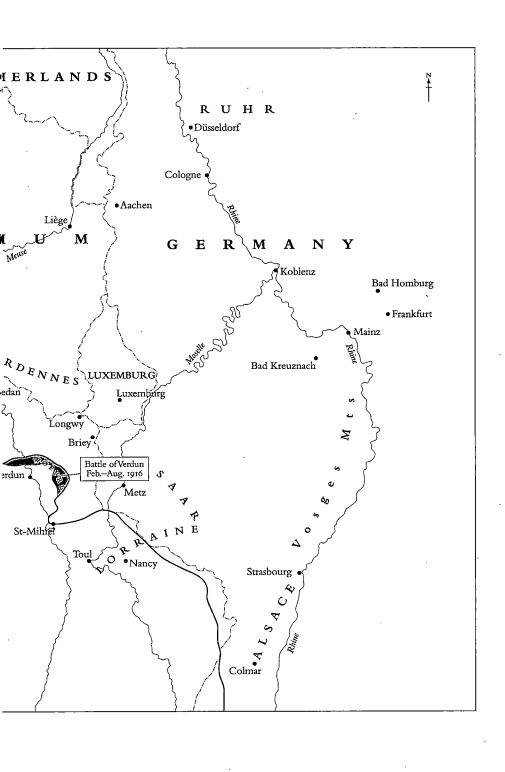

NETHERLANDS

N

RUHR

●Düsseldorf

Cologne ●

●Aachen

Liège ●

BELGIUM

Meuse

GERMANY

Rhine

●Koblenz

Bad Homburg
●

●Frankfurt

●Mainz

Rhine

Moselle

Bad Kreuznach
●

ARDENNES

LUXEMBURG

Sedan

Luxemburg
●

Longwy
●

Briey ●

Battle of Verdun
Feb.–Aug. 1916

Verdun ●

SAAR

Metz ●

St-Mihiel ●

LORRAINE

Toul ●

●Nancy

Vosges Mts

Strasbourg ●

ALSACE

Rhine

●Colmar

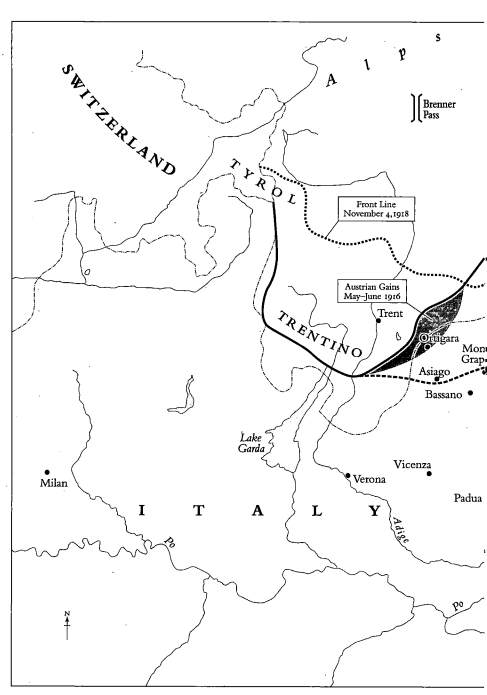

Map 7. The Italian Front

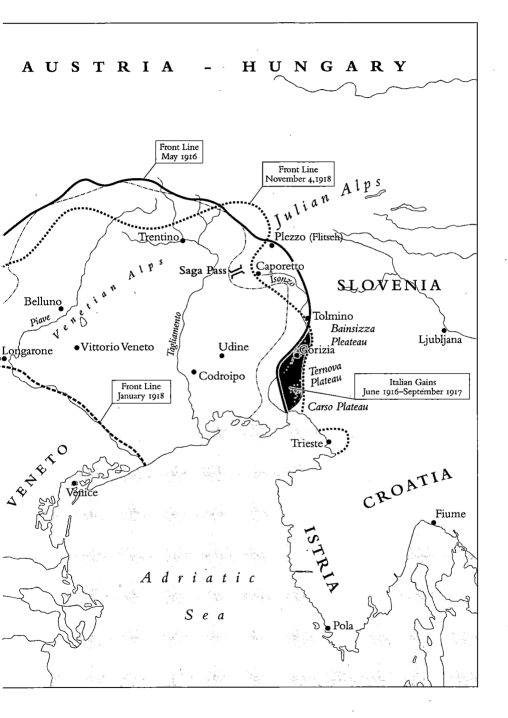

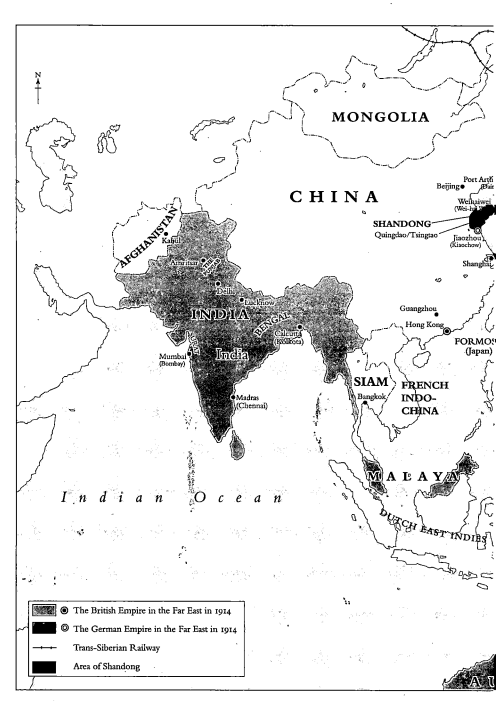

N

MONGOLIA

CHINA

Port Arth
Beijing●   ♭ait
Weihaiwei
(Wei-h̶
SHANDONG
Quingdao/Tsingtao   Jiaozhou
(Kiaochow)

Shanghai

AFGHANISTAN
●Kabul

Amritsar ●THE PUNJAB

●Delhi
●Lucknow

INDIA

BENGAL

Calcutta
(Kolkota)

Guangzhou
●
Hong Kong●

FORMOS
(Japan)

Mumbai
(Bombay)   India

●Madras
(Chennai)

SIAM   FRENCH
Bangkok   INDO-
CHINA

M A L A Y A

I n d i a n   O c e a n

DUTCH EAST INDIES

A U

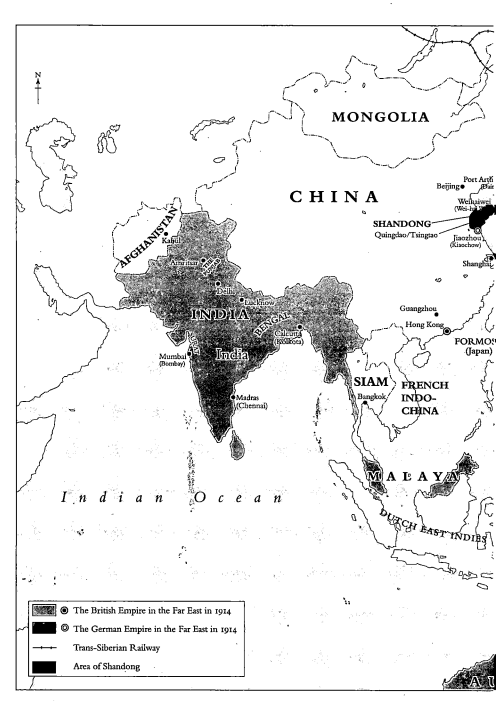

▨ ◉ The British Empire in the Far East in 1914
■ ◎ The German Empire in the Far East in 1914
—+—   Trans-Siberian Railway
■   Area of Shandong

Map 8. East and South Asia

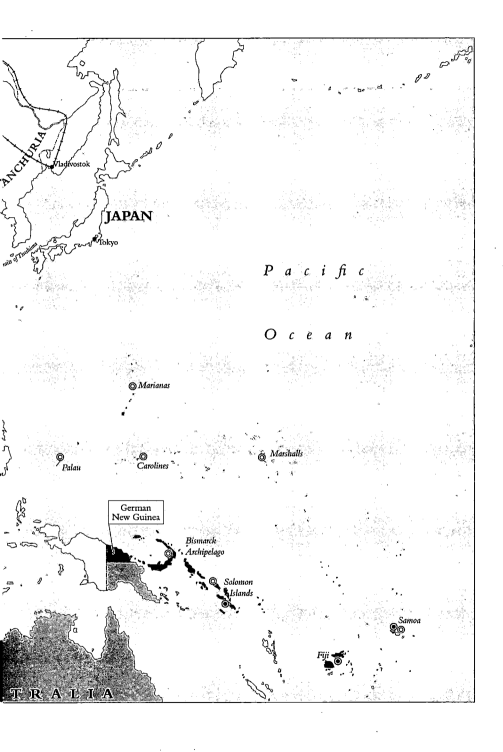

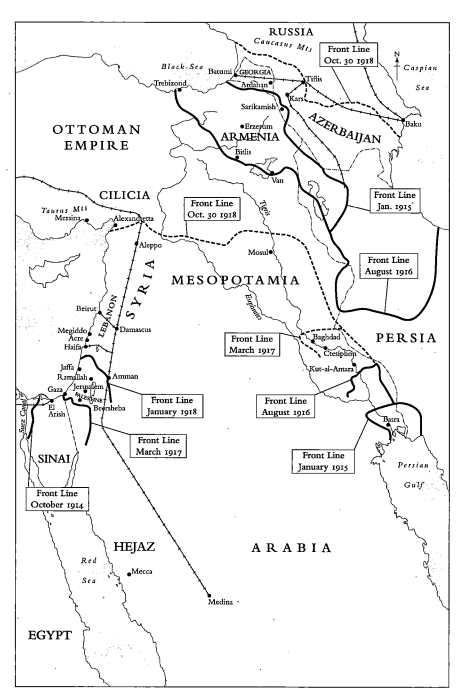

RUSSIA

Caucasus Mts

Black Sea Batumi GEORGIA

Trebizond Ardahan Tiflis

Sarikamish Kars

Erzerum

OTTOMAN ARMENIA

EMPIRE Bitlis

Van

AZERBAIJAN

Baku

Front Line
Oct. 30 1918

N

Caspian

Sea

Front Line
Jan. 1915

CILICIA

Taurus Mts

Mersina Alexandretta

Aleppo

Mosul

MESOPOTAMIA

Tigris

Front Line
August 1916

Front Line
Oct. 30 1918

Beirut

Megiddo Damascus
Acre
Haifa

Jaffa
Ramallah Amman
Gaza Jerusalem
PALESTINE
El Beersheba
Arish

Euphrates

Baghdad

Ctesiphon

Kut-al-Amara

PERSIA

Front Line
March 1917

Front Line
January 1918

Front Line
August 1916

Basra

SINAI

Front Line
March 1917

Front Line
January 1915

Persian

Gulf

Front Line
October 1914

HEJAZ

Red

Sea

Mecca

ARABIA

Medina

EGYPT

Map 9. The Middle East

Introduction

The 1916–17 winter was among the harshest in European memory. It descended on a continent in deep war.[1] Since 1913 German and British government spending—mostly military—had risen more than tenfold,[2] and the opposing armies now approached their maximum strengths.[3] During 1916 the fighting at Verdun and on the Somme in France, and during Russia's Brusilov offensive in Poland, became prototypes for a new type of battle, lasting for months and inflicting hundreds of thousands of casualties. As Lord Lansdowne warned the British Cabinet, 'We are slowly but surely killing off the best of the male population of these islands.'[4] According to Cyril Brown of the *New York Times*, 'As seen at close range it seems inaccurate to call the German attack at Verdun a drive, except in the sense that one speaks of driving a tunnel through solid rock by slow blasting and boring operations... [It] resembles the humdrum and well-organized production of a great engineering enterprise.' Both sides in the Somme campaign experienced it as a mechanized mass slaughter, devoid of drama or romance.[5] Outpourings of money and of lives that three years earlier would have been unimaginable had become routine.

This deadlock was so intractable because its roots lay deep. The six strongest European states were Austria-Hungary, Britain, France, Germany, Italy, and Russia. By Christmas 1916 the Central Powers comprised Austria-Hungary, Bulgaria, Germany, and Turkey; the principal Allies were Belgium, the British Empire, France, Italy, Japan, Montenegro, Portugal, Romania, Russia, and Serbia. Territorial rivalries between these coalitions' members reached back decades. In 1870–1 Germany had been reunified, defeated France, annexed its provinces of Alsace and northern Lorraine, and displaced it as the leading Western European power. Russia and Austria-Hungary, two multi-ethnic empires ruled by the Romanov and Habsburg dynasties, clashed over Russia's sympathy for Slav nationalism. By 1894 Russia was allied to France in response to Germany's 1879 alliance with Austria-Hungary. Italy's leaders eyed the Italian-speaking territories under Austrian rule, and although between 1882 and 1915 it formed a Triple Alliance with Austria-Hungary and Germany, this arrangement was one of expediency. Britain, in contrast, which in the 1880s and 1890s had competed in Asia and Africa with France and Russia as well as Germany, reached understandings with the French and Russians in 1904 and 1907 and supported them against the Central Powers, partly because of the menacing battle fleet that Germany was building across the North Sea.

A key development was the Russo-Japanese War of 1904–5, which disabled Russia after its armies and navies were defeated and an economic crisis prompted strikes and peasant unrest. Germany tried to reshuffle Europe's alliances by creating a German–French–Russian bloc. France and Russia rejected its overtures, and France and Britain opened secret military talks. With London, Paris, and St Petersburg aligned, and Rome unreliable, Berlin and Vienna now occupied a seemingly built-in minority position that Germany's and Austria-Hungary's leaders decried as 'encirclement'. Hence the pre-war decade witnessed mounting tension. In two crises over Morocco in 1905–6 and 1911 Britain backed France against Germany; in two over the Balkans in 1908–9 and 1912–13 Germany, though more fitfully, backed Austria-Hungary against Russia. Coming in ever closer succession, and each more acute, the crises helped precipitate a land arms race between the Austro-German and Franco-Russian blocs, which after 1912 superseded the Anglo-German naval contest as Europe's most dangerous military rivalry. It entailed not only higher spending but also conscripting more young men. Pre-war developments therefore heightened public awareness of international affairs, while polarizing views between the labour and socialist movements (which would accept war only in self-defence) and right-wing nationalist and militarist leagues. By the time hostilities broke out, public opinion had to some extent been prepared.

The circumstances of that outbreak allowed both sides to claim they were responding to enemy aggression. The 1914 crisis began with the assassinations on 28 June of the heir to the Austro-Hungarian throne, the Archduke Franz Ferdinand, and his wife, Sophie Duchess of Hohenberg, by Gavrilo Princip, a Bosnian Serb who wanted unity and independence for the South Slavs, including those under Habsburg rule. As Serbian military intelligence had armed and trained the conspirators, the Austro-Hungarian authorities had grounds for drastic demands on Belgrade. But they devised an ultimatum that would trigger war, and they received a 'blank cheque' from the German emperor, Wilhelm II, and his chancellor, Theobald von Bethmann Hollweg, who promised support if Austria–Hungary used force, whatever the consequences. Wilhelm and Bethmann knew Russia might well back Serbia, and as well as willing a Balkan war they risked a wider European one. Although the latter may not have been their preference, it was so for the Chief of the German General Staff (CGS—the leading military planner and de facto wartime commander) Helmuth von Moltke the Younger. Once Serbia received the ultimatum on 23 July, and accepted most but not all of it, events moved rapidly. Austria–Hungary declared war on Serbia on 28 July, but already from the 26th Russia had started military preparations, and it ordered general mobilization (calling up reservists and placing its armed forces on a war footing) on the 31st. When Russia disregarded a German ultimatum to desist, Germany declared war on 1 August. But German strategy (the Schlieffen–Moltke war plan) assumed that war with Russia meant also war with Russia's ally, which was best conducted by sending most of the army westward, invading France not directly across its fortified border but indirectly via neutral Belgium. Victory depended on speed, and when France refused to pledge neutrality (i.e. to repudiate its Russian alliance) Germany declared war on a fabricated pretext that French aircraft had bombed Nuremberg. When Belgium refused peaceful passage to German forces they invaded. This action violated the 1839 Treaty of London that guaranteed Belgian neutrality and independence, and Germany ignored a British warning to respect it. Belgium became the grounds for Britain to declare war, although the London Cabinet's inner circle saw the crucial issue as being that if Germany defeated France, Britain might be next.[6]

This sequence of events still seems bewildering. Yet it deepened the chasm between the opposing blocs, and rallied support for their governments. Germany's Social Democratic Party or SPD, the largest in the Reichstag (the elected lower house of parliament) and a champion of democratization, accepted that the mobilization by the Russian autocracy meant Germany went to war in self-defence. Tsar Nicholas II roused patriotic enthusiasm for defending Serbia and repelling Teutonic aggression. Still more did the French government, which seemed an innocent victim of provocation. And although Britain did not face invasion, that of Belgium gathered Liberal backbenchers, Labour, trade unions, and Irish nationalists behind the government, while the Unionist[7] opposition viewed Germany as a rival that must not dominate Europe. Hence political truces and national unity initally characterized what was expected to be only a brief emergency. Governments deferred to the military chiefs who implemented the mobilization and concentration[8] plans, which entailed attacking rapidly and with the maximum force. Armies many times larger than in 1870, conveyed to the frontiers by strategic railways, let loose with magazine rifles, machine guns, and quick-firing artillery. Yet this prodigious fire power, amplified by difficulties in controlling and supplying the forces once they passed the railheads, made the opening offensives impossible to sustain. After the battle of the Marne in September the Germans retreated from the Paris approaches, while still occupying north-eastern France and most of Belgium. They halted a Russian invasion of East Prussia at the battles of Tannenberg and the Masurian Lakes. By Christmas not only on the Western Front in France and Belgium but also in the Balkans and on the Eastern Front in Poland the initial plans had failed. Instead, trench lines on the Western Front extended for 475 miles, and more than twice as far in the east. They soon became thicker and more densely garrisoned. Autumn 1914 was the first great moment of transition in the conflict, spring 1917 being the second. The question after both transitions was what to do next.

If the two sides had been divided enough even before 1914, hundreds of thousands of dead now barred the road to a compromise. Instead, the fighting expanded. Japan, allied to Britain since 1902, treated a request from London for naval assistance as a pretext to enter the war on 23 August. After overrunning Germany's Chinese and North Pacific possessions, Japan presented its 'Twenty-One Demands' to Beijing.[9] In contrast, in November the Ottoman Turkish Empire joined the Central Powers, its leaders expecting Germany to win and to protect them against Russia, and hoping to reverse a century of decline. Turkey's entry made its Caucasus border with Russia and its Sinai border with Britain's protectorate in Egypt into new fighting fronts: when Italy joined the Allies it added another. The Italians expected the Allies to win quickly, and they could offer Italy Austro-Hungarian territory, including not only Italian-speaking areas round Trento and Trieste but also the German-speaking South Tyrol and the Slovenes and Croats of Istria and Dalmatia. The April 1915 secret Treaty of London that promised Italy these gains also brought it into the September 1914 Pact of London, which had bound Britain, France, and Russia to make no separate peace. But the results were disappointing, as a new line formed between Lake Garda and the Adriatic, along which Italian soldiers struggled uphill in the harshest of conditions. Repeated assaults along the Isonzo river made negligible headway.

Instead during 1915 the Central Powers enjoyed their best year of the war. During the quieter winter months both sides planned for the forthcoming spring and summer. In Berlin during the 1914–15 winter Generals Paul von Hindenburg and Erich Ludendorff, the Tannenberg victors, prevailed over Erich von Falkenhayn, who had replaced Moltke as CGS. Germany deepened its Western Front defences but reinforced its field army in Poland, to assist the Austrians and herd the Russians eastwards in the hope Nicholas II would break the Pact of London and sign a separate peace. Germany and Austria-Hungary conquered Russian Poland and Lithuania and took over a million prisoners. Yet Nicholas spurned their feelers, and continued doing so when they overran Serbia, aided by Serbia's rival, Bulgaria, which in September joined the Central Powers. An Allied expedition to Salonika landed too late to assist. Instead another stalemated front emerged in Macedonia, between Bulgaria and an Allied force of French, British, Russians, Italians, and Serbs. Although during 1915 France and Britain also attacked on the Western Front, the Allies' efforts were disjointed. Whereas early in the year their prospects had seemed fair and Austria-Hungary near collapse, by its end progress was disappointing. The main British Empire operation had been a bid to invade the Gallipoli peninsula and seize Constantinople, but the landing force advanced little beyond its bridgeheads. While Italy attacked on the Isonzo and France sought to liberate its territory, the British Secretary of State for War, Lord Kitchener, came to accept that the British Expeditionary Force (BEF) must attack on the Western Front to support France and Russia, even accepting 'very heavy losses indeed'.[10]

For 1916 the Allies planned better coordination. At his headquarters (*Grand quartier-général* or GQG) at Chantilly in December 1915, the French commander-in-chief, Joseph Joffre, convened a conference of military leaders. They envisaged a concerted sequence of summer offensives on all the European fronts. The French and British would attack side by side astride the River Somme, where they would break through and wheel northwards. Although the French had already suffered nearly a million casualties and were running short of men, the British, Russian, and Italian armies were still growing and all the Allies had boosted armaments production. There seemed grounds for optimism.

In the event, it was Germany and Austria-Hungary who struck first. At Verdun, starting on 21 February, the Germans staged the first of the months-long battles that became a hallmark of the war. As Falkenhayn lacked numerical superiority he envisaged a limited advance that imperilled the French position—a fortified complex charged with symbolic and strategic significance—and would force Joffre's soldiers into counter-attacks that Germany's heavy guns would pulverize. The French government indeed insisted on holding Verdun, and some 70 per cent of French soldiers eventually rotated through it; but the battle became almost as much a prestige issue for the attackers. Although German casualties were lower they too were enormous, and when the fighting subsided they remained short of their objectives. In May, moreover, the Austro-Hungarian commander, Franz Conrad von Hötzendorff, launched a 'punishment expedition' against the Italians in the Trentino, and the latter appealed for help. The Russians responded by bringing forward into early June their Chantilly attack, known after its commander as the Brusilov offensive, against depleted Austrian forces in Galicia. Brusilov used innovative, surprise tactics and some half of the Habsburg forces on the Eastern Front were killed, wounded, or captured, obliging Germany to rush in reinforcements. Fighting then dragged on into the autumn, costing the tsarist army another million casualties, and leaving many Russians doubting how the war could ever be won.[11] Such doubts grew stronger after Romania, promised Austro-Hungarian territory as Italy had been, entered the war in August, only to be overwhelmed in its turn with half its territory falling under occupation.

Although the Central Powers contained their crisis, Austria-Hungary never recovered militarily from the Brusilov offensive, and increasingly its forces came under German command. In summer 1916 a sense of emergency possessed Berlin. Wilhelm replaced Falkenhayn as CGS by Hindenburg, who brought Ludendorff with him as his First Quartermaster-General. Although the Allies' Somme offensive began calamitously, as it continued it pressed the Germans harder. It eased the situation at Verdun, and in its later stages British tactics improved and the fighting was more evenly matched. For the first time the German infantry faced better-equipped antagonists, and by November the battle had claimed some 420,000 British and 200,000 French but also 500,000 German casualties.[12] Ludendorff was determined to spare his men a 'second Somme'.[13]

At a further Chantilly conference in November, the Allied commanders judged they had made progress and planned more synchronized attacks in early 1917. This prospect encouraged one of Hindenburg and Ludendorff's rashest judgements: to support the German navy's lobbying for an unrestricted submarine campaign. Thus far the war at sea had also seemed a stalemate, Britain and Germany's battleships avoiding contact except for twenty minutes during the Battle of Jutland on 31 May 1916. This caution was no accident, the British Grand Fleet commander (Admiral Sir John Jellicoe) fearing the hazards of an action in which Britain might forfeit its superiority; whereas the Germans, though willing to sally out under the aggressive leadership of Admiral Reinhard Scheer, were under political direction not to risk their High Seas Fleet (which might prove a bargaining asset at the peace conference) against greater numbers. At Jutland the Germans inflicted double the losses that they suffered, but the underlying balance remained unaltered. As the Allies had eliminated Germany's surface forces outside Europe, they commanded most of the seas and could draw upon their empires for manpower and on the neutrals—above all the United States—for manufactured goods, food, and raw materials, even if their efforts to stifle their enemies' imports worked dishearteningly slowly. None the less, the combination of a tightening Allied blockade with the High Seas Fleet's inactivity fuelled agitation within Germany to unleash its submarines, untrammelled by conventions that they should surface and give warning before sinking their victims. In fact until late 1916 the U-boats were too few to inflict really damaging losses, but that the American President Woodrow Wilson restrained them by insisting on his interpretation of maritime law caused intense frustration. It did so all the more because American supplies made possible the rain of high explosive that descended on the German army on the Somme.[14]

Behind the Chantilly offensives lay a build-up of manpower and materiel. In 1916 Britain introduced conscription (to prevent volunteers leaving strategic industries as well as to maintain drafts into the army); while tsarist recruiting dredged up middle-aged family men and triggered an uprising in Central Asia. In munitions and especially in heavy artillery, the essential weapon against trenches, the Germans held an early advantage, but the Allies narrowed it. In all the belligerents taxation covered only a fraction of war costs, the bulk of which were covered by borrowing (mainly via war bonds sold to the middle class, though also from abroad, which for the Allies meant principally from the United States). The balance was met by printing money, especially in poorer belligerents such as Turkey and Russia, where by 1916 inflation was soaring. Nowhere, however, could such expenditure be sustained indefinitely.

Economic mobilization was facilitated by private initiative and individual choices. Hundreds of thousands of women entered munitions plants or took over farms and businesses. But it also needed government direction, two highlights being David Lloyd George's 1915 creation of the British Ministry of Munitions and Hindenburg and Ludendorff's counter-project, the 1916 Hindenburg Programme of armaments production. Even the first of these initiatives was less successful than its proponents claimed, however; and the second fell behind its targets and exacerbated civilian hardship. Even so, to recruit volunteers, sell war bonds, and save on food consumption, governments could draw on a groundswell of patriotism, most of it not generated by state propaganda, though the press, nationalist lobbyists, and community leaders all fostered it. That each side blamed the conflict on the other sustained the process, as did governments' insistence that the struggle was defensive, and victory alone could spare future generations from facing a rerun. Each side also blamed the other for atrocities, especially during 1915, when German wrath over the blockade matched Allied outrage over Zeppelin raids, U-boats, poison gas, and the genocidal massacres directed by the Ottomans against the Armenians.[15] For maintaining pro-war consensus it helped that during the first two years at least Germany, France, and Britain enjoyed full employment, relatively stable prices, and mostly adequate food supplies. Finally, both sides had grounds for confidence: the Central Powers because of the German army's martial reputation and its string of successes, the Allies because of their greater manpower and resources. Moreover—and this was fundamental—the 'short-war illusion' that victory lay around the corner did not end in 1914. Both civilians and soldiers still believed (or professed to believe) that the next offensive could bring triumph. In these circumstances patriotic socialists still had answers for their detractors who demanded a negotiated solution or who (like Lenin) denounced the conflict as a project of imperialist aggression.

None the less, by 1916 consensus grew more fragile. In France and Germany disaffection on the left was growing; in Italy the government could not claim the war was defensive, and most socialists and many Catholics opposed it. In Russia strikes and even mutinies were frequent. The disappointing 1916 harvests and the severe ensuing winter made food scarcer; while the passage of another campaigning season with so little visibly accomplished rekindled debate over how the struggle could ever be won and whether it was worth the sacrifice. It also raised the question of what the war was being fought for. Governments had indeed remained ambiguous about their war aims, fearing precision would cause dissension. None the less, coded phrases such as 'guarantees of security' veiled the formulation of more concrete objectives. Bethmann Hollweg had initialled in the conflict's opening weeks a 'September Programme' for security through buffer states on Germany's borders, indemnities, and a Central European customs union, as well as colonial expansion.[16] The Russian government hoped to advance its frontiers towards Berlin and Vienna by absorbing Germany's and Austria-Hungary's Polish-inhabited areas, and to annex Constantinople and the Turkish Straits. By 1916 Austria-Hungary intended via annexations and buffer states to dominate the western Balkans.[17] Most of these ambitions stayed secret, as did the Allies' promises to Italy and their agreements to carve up Germany's African and Pacific colonies and the Ottoman Empire. Within Europe the French government publicly claimed reparations and the return of Alsace-Lorraine, and prepared confidentially to secure a strategic frontier on the Rhine. In contrast Britain was vaguer about its European than its extra-European objectives, not least because it feared that weakening Germany would strengthen Russia and France. It was clear that Belgium—for strategic as well as altruistic reasons—should regain its independence and integrity, but beyond that few conclusions were reached. Even so, any peace talks would face formidable obstacles. Britain, France, and Germany were divided over Belgium and Alsace-Lorraine; Germany, Austria-Hungary, and Russia over Poland; and Italy and Austria-Hungary over the Alps and Adriatic. It was true that the Germans tried to split their enemies. By attacking Russia in Poland in 1915 and France at Verdun in 1916, they hoped to force Petrograd or Paris into concluding a separate peace. The Allies, however, were bound by treaty and by national interest to stay together. Neither side could lightly present their peoples with a compromise when so many families were bereft of husbands and sons. The European nations had dug themselves into a war trap, and on one level the story of 1917 is of their efforts to escape it. According to the Italian army staff historian, Angelo Gatti, 'today the atmosphere of melancholy, of heaviness, of nihilism that weighs on all of us in Europe depends on this sole fact: that no exit can be seen from what we are doing'.[18] Hindenburg and Ludendorff looked to submarine warfare as an alternative to new Verduns and Sommes, while French and British ministers sought less costly substitutes for the Chantilly strategy. The new Austrian emperor, Karl hoped to save his monarchy by combining peace diplomacy with internal liberalization. And whereas Nicholas II claimed that renewing the Chantilly offensives would speedily bring victory, the Provisional Government that replaced him came to hope that a new attack, linked to cooperation with

PART
I

Atlantic Prologue

I

Unleashing the U-boats

The castle of Pless (Zamek w Pszczynie) today belongs to Poland. But before 1945 it was German. Subjected in the 1870s to a pseudo-Renaissance refurbishment, its amenities included a hall of mirrors. Here in 1915 Wilhelm II established his general headquarters, close to Germany's Eastern Front commanders yet accessible from Berlin. And here, on Monday and Tuesday 8–9 January, the first critical 1917 decisions were taken.

At Pless the German leadership—emperor, chancellor, and army and navy chiefs—resolved to embark from 1 February on 'unrestricted' submarine warfare. In a 'prohibited zone' around the British Isles and France almost all vessels risked being torpedoed without warning, be they Allied or neutral, merchantmen, passenger liners, or hospital ships, with no inspection to check for contraband, nor perhaps time for the passengers to clamber into the boats. In the Allied countries this action seemed profoundly shocking, an affront to civilized norms. It was virtually certain to cause hostilities with the United States. Chancellor Bethmann Hollweg likened Pless to 'a second decision for war'.[1] If they got this wrong, feared Interior Secretary Karl Helfferich, Germany would be 'lost, lost for centuries',[2] and Bethmann's secretary Kurt Riezler felt 'We are in so novel a situation that all the old thoughts and methods fail'.[3] Yet if some approached the decision with foreboding, for others it meant release, as if Germany had unsheathed its sharpest sword. And this time, in contrast to the scramble in 1914, the leadership had debated unrestricted warfare repeatedly, and a year earlier had rejected it. The crucial shift came between March 1916 and January 1917. Its context was the growing ascendancy of Germany's high command, as part of the war's broader metamorphosis into a contest between autocracy and democracy.

By 1917 U-boat warfare had divided Berlin from Washington for two years. Having stumbled into confrontation, both struggled to disengage. At one level the conflict was over maritime law. In 1914 the Allies and the Central Powers had promised to abide—more or less—by the 1909 Declaration of London, though Britain had never ratified it. The Declaration permitted remarkably unimpeded seaborne trade, except in weapons and goods with a direct military purpose. In practice the British soon extended the contraband list, mined the Channel, and declared the entire North Sea a war zone. The Germans rightly viewed these measures as meant to sever their overseas commerce, even if not officially a blockade.[4] Geography helped Britain to intercept enemy and neutral shipping, and Germany had few means of retaliation. Under Navy Secretary Admiral Alfred von Tirpitz it had built a fleet for fighting warships rather than for raiding commerce. In June 1914 the U-boat fleet commander proposed using his vessels against shipping, but found no approval.[5] Their mission was to protect the battle fleet.

Modern submarines had entered service with the Royal Navy only in 1901 and with the German in 1906. They operated primarily on the surface, where they used a diesel engine and recharged their batteries; beneath the waves their endurance was limited. At first they carried typically just half a dozen torpedoes and a small deck-mounted gun. Yet the sinking by U-9 in September 1914 of three British cruisers, the *Aboukir*, the *Cressy*, and the *Hogue*—with the loss of over 1,400 lives—showed how dangerous submarines could be. The German navy saw a means of compensating for the surface fleet's inaction. It lobbied for a spring offensive when Britain most needed grain imports before the harvest. Yet Germany at first had barely twenty U-boats, only a third of which could patrol the Western Approaches to the British Isles at any one time.[6] Physical destruction of the Allied merchant fleet was impossible: the steamers must be terrorized.

Torpedoing while submerged would protect the submarines. A surfaced U-boat was highly exposed, and if its hull was pierced it could not dive. Yet according to customary law, before sinking a merchantman a raider should inspect its bills of lading for contraband (if neutral), and if not rescuing the crew at least allow time to man the boats. These guidelines, known as 'cruiser rules', derived from the surface warfare of a more leisurely epoch.[7] But the Germans argued Britain's legal violations gave them a right of reprisal, which they used to declare a zone of unrestricted submarine warfare round the British Isles in February 1915.[8] They warned neutrals to keep clear, and— given the U-boats' paucity—sinkings were likely to be few. Bethmann Hollweg raised no moral or humanitarian objections, protesting rather that the action was premature, though expecting opposition primarily from the

European neutrals. He and the Foreign Ministry under-estimated the risk of friction with America: the first of many such misjudgements.[9]

The United States reacted much more sharply to submarine warfare than it had to Britain's blockade of Germany, warning that it would hold those responsible to 'strict accountability'. The sinking of the British liner *Lusitania* in May 1915 with 1,201 dead—128 of them American—opened a year of crisis. During these months, which also witnessed the torpedoing of the liner *Arabic* in September 1915 and the Channel steamer *Sussex* in March 1916, President Wilson demanded not only that the U-boats respect neutral vessels and all passenger liners, but also that they desist from unrestricted warfare altogether. After the *Sussex* case he warned that unless Germany stuck to cruiser rules he would break off diplomatic relations, which the Berlin leaders interpreted as a threat of war. Actually scant enthusiasm existed in America for armed intervention in the conflict, but Wilson enjoyed backing from most of his administration and from much of the media and Congress for a firm line, and his position was one that he considered national interest, prestige, law, and morality all dictated.

Bethmann was taken aback. His guideline became to conduct as much submarine warfare as was possible without breaking with Washington. He had support from CGS Erich von Falkenhayn, as he did from Wilhelm, who shrank from war against America and expressed revulsion against killing women and children. Years of bureaucratic in-fighting had estranged Tirpitz from Bethmann, and the admiral's over-investment in scarcely useable battleships had antagonized Wilhelm, who rejected Tirpitz's requests to resign in protest against concessions to America. On the contrary, Admiral Gustav Bachmann, the Chief of the Admiralty Staff (CAS)—the chief naval strategic planner—*was* dismissed for harping on the topic, and a previous Tirpitz adversary, Admiral Henning von Holtzendorff, replaced him. By the end of 1915 attacks on neutral ships and passenger liners had been suspended. Most sinkings now followed customary rules.[10]

When debate resumed, the navy was better placed. Each winter the U-boat advocates pressed for decisions before the spring, when calmer waters returned with longer days and better visibility, and British grain stocks dwindled. Tirpitz, who had mobilized press and parliament behind his pre-war battleship programmes, now did likewise for the U-boats.[11] Civilian ministers distrusted him as an unscrupulous intriguer. Yet despite being appointed as a check on Tirpitz, Holtzendorff came over to him.[12] The navy had more U-boats (up from twenty-seven in January 1915 to forty-one in January 1916), and an improved distribution, with fourteen now stationed near Bruges in Flanders (exiting via Ostend or Zeebrugge), and roaming the Channel and the southern North Sea.[13] Under Holtzendorff the Admiralty Staff turned to experts on global cereals markets and shipping. Apparently more reasonable than Tirpitz, he still claimed he could start in March and succeed in four months: and both men talked to Falkenhayn,[14] who considered an unrestricted campaign a necessary complement to his Verdun spring offensive. Because the Eastern and Balkan fronts had stabilized, the risk of Balkan countries intervening had lessened. And time was working against him, as he expected Austria–Hungary and Turkey not to last beyond the autumn.[15] Actually the U-boat camp overstated the submarines' potential, and was over-hasty in dismissing alternatives; yet still, there was a dilemma. An unrestricted submarine campaign might bring in America, whereas refraining might doom Germany to exhaustion.

In the interim, in February 1916 Germany began 'intensified' U-boat warfare against armed merchantmen. This failed to still the controversy, and Wilhelm delayed a ruling.[16] He felt responsibility before God for the method of waging war, but also responsibility not to sacrifice lives by rejecting military recommendations.[17] He hated arbitrating in faction fighting and lamented his advisers' abrasiveness.[18] In these circumstances Bethmann turned to Helfferich, with whom he had compatible working methods— both, according to Foreign Minister Gottlieb von Jagow, liked 'long dialectical discussion of every question'. Helfferich had financial expertise, forensic skills, and relished statistics, and he helped Bethmann prepare a counterblast.[19] The resulting document became the chancellor's testament.

Bethmann's 29 February memorandum refuted the navy point by point. It noted that Holtzendorff and Tirpitz differed over predicted shipping losses; and that they made no allowance for Allied counter-measures. Even if Holtzendorff's 4 million-ton figure proved accurate, Britain would still control 9 million tons of its own and 4–5 million tons of neutral shipping. It might introduce convoys; and would resist to the last man and coin. Unrestricted warfare would bring in the United States, encouraging the Allies while disheartening the public and Germany's partners. America would send more supplies and hundreds of thousands of volunteers, making victory impossible. Yet the Central Powers could still prevail without the submarines, and Germany's circumstances did not yet justify a 'break-the-bank game'. Its objective should remain the maximum U-boat warfare possible without breaking with Wilson.[20]

At the climactic Charleville Crown Council on 4 March, Bethmann reasserted this case, knowing beforehand that Wilhelm agreed. The emperor acted (which he did not always) as a constructive chair.[21] Bethmann was 'very passionate', insisting American involvement meant a 'war of exhaustion', the loss of Germany's Great Power status, and the fall of the Hohenzollern dynasty. If Germany was circumspect it could hold on, whereas the Allies might break up, thus letting it survive as Frederick the Great's Prussia had done in the Seven Years War, through the disunity of its enemies. Although the meeting ended without recording the outcome, and deferred a decision, unrestricted submarine warfare was now off the agenda. The more tractable Eduard von Capelle succeeded Tirpitz (though continued to liaise with him). For the moment, with Wilhelm's tacit encouragement, the chancellor had overwhelmed his critics, by cogency of argument and strength of conviction. Moreover, after the *Sussex* incident, Bethmann provided Wilson with the '*Sussex* pledge' in May 1916. Germany would suspend unrestricted warfare, but expected America to act against the British blockade. This time Capelle and Falkenhayn accepted it was prudent to yield.[22] The crisis had resulted partly from insubordination by U-boat commanders, who exceeded their instructions. Indeed, the frequent amendments to their complex guidelines heightened the risk (which Bethmann perceived) of a single error plunging Germany into a transatlantic war. But after the *Sussex* pledge the Flanders U-boats called off operations against merchant shipping, as did those coming under the High Seas Fleet in the North Sea. Scheer, the High Seas Fleet commander, considered only an unrestricted campaign would justify the risks to the submarines' crews.[23] If not all, it would be nothing.

From the Charleville council and the *Sussex* pledge several points emerge. The kaiser led effectively and the navy was divided. Wilhelm's Chief of the Naval Cabinet (his household naval adviser), Admiral Georg Alexander von Müller, disagreed with the Holtzendorff–Tirpitz line. Falkenhayn proved erratic and inconsistent whereas Bethmann was determined and well prepared. None the less, the chancellor had reached his peak. Much of his position rested on the navy's implausibility while the U-boats were so few. In addition, he had maintained that Germany's predicament was less desperate than Holtzendorff portrayed it. But over the next twelve months U-boat numbers would grow and Germany's situation deteriorate, while Holtzendorff continued to lobby, the army command changed hands, and the military and naval leaderships converged, whereas the Reichstag and the emperor lost patience with Bethmann's stalling. The bases of resistance would crumble one by one.

One reason for restraint was that the navy had an alternative strategy. After taking command of the High Seas Fleet, Scheer conducted North Sea sorties in the hope of engaging at least part of the British Grand Fleet on favourable terms. He needed U-boats to screen his capital ships, rather than for commerce raiding. In fact submarines played little part in the Battle of Jutland on 31 May, which opened with a clash between the German and British battle-cruisers, both running ahead of their main fleets. When Scheer's battle fleet pursued the British battle-cruisers and ran up against its British counterpart, however, it turned away, escaping back to port during the night. German publicity emblazoned Jutland as challenging the Trafalgar mystique of British invincibility, but Scheer judged privately that he had narrowly avoided a disastrous encounter with stronger forces. He reported that 'as things now stand, even the unlikely case of a most favourable outcome in a fleet battle could not in itself give a decisive turn to the war against England'. He reverted to advocating unrestricted submarine warfare, and was willing to release his U-boats from their current role.[24] Scheer did not represent the navy in dealings with the government: that task devolved on Holtzendorff.[25] None the less, the Jutland aura strengthened Scheer's and his officers' authority; and Holtzendorff feared for his position if he failed to speak for them.

When the Charleville council met the Verdun offensive was two weeks old. It remained unclear that it had failed, and the Central Powers retained the initiative. In contrast, during summer 1916 synchronized blows descended on them as the Chantilly plan for a concerted Allied onslaught unfolded. While Austria-Hungary attacked the Italians in the Trentino, its front in Poland collapsed before the Brusilov offensive. On 1 July the Anglo-French Somme offensive began. Although the German army chiefs were confident they could cope with it, they shut down Verdun. Finally, when both main Central Powers were tightly stretched, Romania joined the Allies and invaded Austria-Hungary, forcing the latter's partners to assist. When Holtzendorff proposed an unrestricted submarine campaign in the English Channel, therefore, he argued it could sever Somme reinforcements. None the less, at a meeting on 8 August Bethmann blocked the idea. He questioned whether such attacks would have much impact (no cross-Channel troopships had yet gone down), and they were virtually certain to cause a rupture with Washington, the danger of which seemed disproportionate to any gain. Once again Wilhelm supported the chancellor, whereas neither Müller nor Capelle supported Holtzendorff.[26] At this stage the governmental system still worked reasonably well. Even so, aspects of the episode were disquieting. Capelle argued for going all-out in spring 1917, when Germany had more U-boats and Britain's grain stocks would be lower, rather than confronting America now over a more limited campaign.[27] Helfferich agreed it would be better to wait until the spring, as Britain had four and a half months of reserves. Bethmann noted that Germany was less vulnerable now its harvest was in, and spring 1917 would be the optimum time—'should the war last so long, so in all probability we can and must in the winter of next year grasp the *ultima ratio* of U-boat war'—and the U-boats were best conserved for such an effort.[28] Not only the more moderate elements in the navy, but also the political leaders, were looking to the spring. It was harder now for the civilians to show optimism, and their objections to unrestricted warfare were losing purchase.

By 1916 public opinion was polarizing, as food grew scarcer and rumours spread about the government's expansionist war aims. The Allies tightened the blockade, notably through the 'Agricultural Agreement' restricting Dutch exports to Germany.[29] The struggle seemed less defensive, and more of the SPD pressed for moderate objectives and a negotiated settlement. Yet among the majority of the public that seems still to have supported the war,[30] a harsher mood was evident, attitudes towards the submarine question becoming a litmus test. The U-boats offered a method of striking back, and the navy mobilized a formidable agitation, with cross-party support and spearheaded against Bethmann.[31] During the spring 1916 debate the National Liberal leader, Ernst Bassermann, joined the Conservative leader, Ernst von Heydebrand, in opposing the chancellor, while the pro-submarine press attacked not only Bethmann but implicitly also Wilhelm, branding them as Anglophile. Wartime censorship—which was controlled not by the central government but by the Deputy Commanding Generals ruling Germany's military districts—did little to muzzle it.[32] Committees formed in many cities, and Professor Dietrich Schäfer organized petitions—one with 30,000 signatures in March 1916[33]—while pro-submarine correspondence flooded into government offices.[34] Tirpitz's resignation little weakened the agitation, which he continued to feed. On the other hand, wartime experience had mellowed Bethmann, who liaised with and respected the Socialists and Progressives while becoming estranged from the Conservatives and National Liberals.[35] He and Helfferich avoided plenary sessions of the Reichstag, the Bundesrat (the federal upper house), and the Prussian lower chamber, the Landtag, though at the price of greater dependence on the Reichstag Budget Commission and the Bundesrat Foreign Affairs Committee.[36] When in autumn 1916 the issue came to a head, the Catholic Centre Party held the Reichstag balance of power between the Conservatives and National Liberals and the Socialists and Progressives; but this party itself was divided, its leader, Martin Spahn, inclining to the submarine lobby, whereas Matthias Erzberger, who was more sympathetic to Bethmann, acquiesced for the sake of unity in a resolution passed on 7 October that a decision would 'have to be supported basically by the conclusion of the Supreme Command'.[37] Henceforth a Reichstag majority would support the chancellor only while the army leadership did likewise.

The chancellor was appointed and dismissed by the emperor rather than depending on a majority in the legislature, but it was part of Bethmann's function to manage the latter, and that he was losing control enfeebled him. Moreover, the Centre Party resolution reflected broader trends: as Germany's military-political plight worsened so caution seemed less attractive, and the new army high command of Paul von Hindenburg and Erich Ludendorff expanded its influence. This latter development formed the most important single contrast between spring 1916 and spring 1917. Within the German governmental system the Prussian war minister was responsible for supplying men and equipment: over strategy he had little say. Wilhelm's Chief of the Military Cabinet advised primarily on personnel. Hence the emperor's principal adviser on strategy was the CGS, whom he appointed and who reported to him direct, rather than to the civilian government. Wilhelm intervened in land operations less than in naval matters, and the CGS was de facto the army commander. Under Falkenhayn this had mattered less. Although his personal relations with Bethmann were fractious, he agreed with him that Germany could not defeat all its enemies, and it needed to divide them. Yet the conquest of Poland and Serbia had not forced Russia to negotiate, and Verdun had not broken France's will. Instead, in summer 1916 Germany faced its worst emergency since war began, Müller characterizing the situation as a 'grave crisis'.[38] Bethmann, who agreed with Falkenhayn that emerging with a draw would be tantamount to victory,[39] felt Germany should seek peace negotiations. But such a step risked a firestorm of protest that the monarchy itself might not withstand, and it was with this danger in mind, as well as the military emergency, that Bethmann wanted Hindenburg and Ludendorff to replace Falkenhayn. Wilhelm, in contrast, feared Hindenburg and detested Ludendorff, and Falkenhayn had warned that if they took over Wilhelm would become an emperor in name only. Wilhelm acquiesced in their appointment, but as the Tannenberg victors they commanded more prestige than he did. Whereas in a confrontation between Bethmann and Falkenhayn the emperor could adjudicate independently, in one between Bethmann and Hindenburg he was likely to support the latter.

The duo replaced Falkenhayn in late August at the OHL (*Oberste Heeresleitung*, or Army Supreme Command), Hindenburg becoming CGS and Ludendorff First Quartermaster-General. Ludendorff's latest biographer reaffirms that he provided the energy and intellect, drafting most of the letters issued under Hindenburg's name.[40] Yet the pair in many ways were complementary. They brought command experience and Ludendorff's pre-war planning expertise, but lacked understanding of manpower and economic questions, as well as of foreign policy and naval matters.[41] They were in contact with Tirpitz, with whom they instinctively sympathized. Although they had worked with Bethmann against Falkenhayn, and at first showed the chancellor deference, this cordiality would dissipate as they extended their political reach. Bethmann hoped to use them, but he disparaged Ludendorff's commoner background and lack of social graces, referring to him as 'Kanaille'.[42] Just days after Hindenburg and Ludendorff arrived, moreover, the German authorities held their most important discussion of submarine warfare between March 1916 and January 1917. It took place on 31 August at Pless, and although Wilhelm did not chair it, the principal political, military, and naval officials attended. Such machinery for coordinating strategy had previously been lacking, and Hindenburg and Ludendorff used it to impinge on maritime strategy without the naval leadership reciprocating. Thus although the conference assembled when the Romanian crisis was at its height, it arose from yet another attempt by Holtzendorff to revive the U-boat issue.

In a new memorandum, Holtzendorff argued from a calculation of Britain's food stocks and freight capacity that it could be forced to capitulate 'in a few months'. The time to start was now, as although U-boat numbers would rise over the next six months, so would Britain's anti-submarine capacity. Once all its merchant steamers were armed, only sub-surface attacks would be feasible. The American president had had long enough to challenge the British blockade as the *Sussex* pledge envisaged, and American naval assistance to Britain would make no difference. Even if the United States sent over volunteers, they would at present worry Germany little, but would become a bigger concern once Germany's manpower surplus was exhausted.[43] Germany faced a 'grave defensive battle' and a 'war of exhaustion' until its food and raw materials ran out: it was a 'question of living or going under for the German Empire and people', and only unrestricted submarine warfare would avert slow strangulation. But if Holtzendorff had gained confidence, the chancellor was more tentative, saying he suspended judgement until he knew the OHL's assessment of Romania's intervention. To start an unrestricted campaign just after Romania's entry would signal desperation: although 'nobody doubts that U-boat war is to be expected'. He remained unconvinced by Holtzendorff's projections, pointed out that Britain might take counter-measures, and insisted unrestricted warfare would mean hostilities with the United States. He put his stress, however, on the danger of the *European* neutrals—Holland and Denmark—coming in, lengthening Germany's battlefronts when its forces were already stretched. Holtzendorff countered that Germany still had leverage over the neutrals (for example by withholding coal supplies) that would lessen as its economy weakened. But the key point was that Bethmann had linked his position to Hindenburg and Ludendorff's military appraisal. Indeed, he said the moment to decide on unrestricted warfare would be when the new OHL judged the circumstances ripe—which meant they would determine the timing, not the substance, of that decision, but it was understandable that they should misinterpret the statement. Still, for the moment they remained cautious. They favoured unrestricted submarine warfare in principle, but the situation in south-eastern Europe was uncertain and they had no spare divisions: nor could they risk denuding Germany's northern borders. This ruling settled the matter for now, and Bethmann got a declaration to reassure the Reichstag, but his parliamentary position was becoming dependent on Hindenburg's willingness to cover it, and once the fighting fronts had stabilized he faced the danger of a stronger naval/military combination than the one he had beaten down at Charleville. Moreover, both Bethmann and Helfferich were less sure of their ground, and both had grown more open to agreeing unrestricted warfare in the spring, when there would be additional U-boats, the danger from the neutrals might be lower, and Britain more exposed.

It was therefore ominous that in the following weeks, while the Central Powers overran Romania, OHL/Chancellery relations deteriorated. Hindenburg and Ludendorff foresaw fresh Allied offensives, and needed more equipment and more men. Hindenburg wrote to Bethmann that 'it will be a decision between the existence and the non-existence of the German people'.[44] Equipment would come, they hoped, from the extraordinarily ambitious 'Hindenburg Programme' of armaments production, agreed with the government in September, but which proved unrealizable, helping to paralyse fuel supply and transport.[45] Manpower would come from a new Auxiliary Service Law, but Bethmann rejected compulsory service for women and the Reichstag amended the bill to strengthen the trade unions, so that when implemented it transferred hundreds of thousands of soldiers to home production. Further manpower came from deporting thousands of Belgian civilians: a programme that caused an international outcry, particularly in America, and eventually was halted. Finally the OHL hoped to aid recruiting by proclaiming 'independence' (in practice much circumscribed) for the German- and Austrian-occupied areas of former Russian Poland: a step that obstructed a separate peace with Russia and elicited just a trickle of volunteers. In short, Hindenburg and Ludendorff's opening political initiatives were not just failures but actually counter-productive, and unrestricted submarine warfare formed part of a pattern. Bethmann bemoaned an increasing militarization of politics, and Müller now saw him bearing a 'corpse-bitter expression'.[46] According to Riezler, 'The Emperor has fled completely into the two soldiers' shadow—swimming spineless [willenlos] in their wake', while according to Bethmann, 'the two are saving us the present but most gravely burdening the future'.[47]

Developments at sea also favoured the U-boat lobby. Allied anti-submarine warfare was ineffective: five U-boats were lost from all causes in 1914, twenty-three in 1915, and twenty-three in 1916.[48] Tirpitz had adopted a submarine construction programme belatedly, and initially Krupp was the near-monopoly builder. After war began, orders went more widely. In 1915 they were placed for 'UCII' vessels with an eight-month building period, and these boats made the biggest difference. Yet the Navy Office did not treat them as war-winners. Although the navy (unlike in Britain) came second for resources behind the army, Tirpitz ordered thirteen battleships and battle-cruisers during the war, mostly never completed, whereas after September 1915 submarine orders paused, and after Jutland the priority was to repair the surface ships.[49] Even so, submarine numbers rose from forty-one in January 1916 to 103 in January 1917, peaking at 140 in October.[50] Although big ocean-going submarines could take eighteen months to build, the arrival of dozens of short-range vessels in Flanders enhanced German striking power.

On 6 October Wilhelm authorized a resumption of restricted submarine warfare, the Flanders boats operating in the southern North Sea while the High Seas Fleet boats switched to commerce raiding. Some of the surface fleet's most pugnacious officers transferred to them, while twenty-four destroyers moved to Zeebrugge to safeguard the U-boats' passage through the Dover Straits.[51] The campaign targeted Britain's coal shipments to France, iron ore from Spain, and grain from Argentina, India, and Australia.[52] Cruiser rules were still to be followed, but if a steamer was clearly Allied there was no need to view its papers.[53] In practice the submarines indeed mostly followed cruiser rules, and most crews seem to have preferred the more humanitarian procedure. Even so, sinkings more than doubled, and maintained that level.[54] This very success pointed to a middle way, inflicting grave shipping losses while avoiding conflict with America, and perhaps for this reason Scheer omitted reference to it in his memoirs. President Wilson reacted relatively mildly to the torpedoing in this period of the *Marina* and the *Arabia*, and it was not the U-boat commanders who demanded unrestricted warfare. That demand came rather from the public at large and from the navy's upper echelons, and it derived partly from the symbolic value of matching the blockading enemy's ruthlessness.

The chancellor had one more possibility: that of seeking peace. He had long been willing for compromise over war aims in order to reduce Germany's adversaries, whereas for Ludendorff not winning outright would be tantamount to defeat. To launch a peace process, Bethmann looked to Wilson—whom he had met in 1911[55]—despite experience having taught him that the president was pro-Allied and held objectives such as open diplomacy and disarmament that the German leaders opposed. Earlier in 1916 Bethmann had resisted American mediation, but the pressure for unrestricted submarine warfare brought him round to it, although he still objected to US involvement in territorial discussions.[56] Warned by Joachim-Heinrich, Count von Bernstorff, the ambassador in Washington, that an American initiative was likely, Bethmann replied he was willing to accept in order to get negotiations going, though the peace terms must be settled between the belligerents, the United States being involved only in a subsequent congress on the broader issues.[57] After the 31 August Pless conference Bethmann asked Bernstorff if mediation could succeed if Germany pledged to restore limited independence to Belgium, though warned that if mediation failed Berlin must seriously consider unrestricted submarine warfare.[58] A design was emerging: US mediation to enable Germany to disengage

from the war relatively unscathed; but otherwise a submarine campaign that
could be blamed on the Allies, and perhaps—a holy grail—would not bring
in the Americans. Bethmann knew, however, that the clock was ticking,
and Wilson repeatedly delayed. During September Bethmann consulted
Wilhelm, Holtzendorff, and Hindenburg and Ludendorff—military involvement again being new—over Bernstorff's instructions, which called for
Wilson to be asked to appeal for talks unaccompanied by a ceasefire and
starting without delay.[59] On 5 October Bernstorff reported Wilson was
unlikely to act before the November presidential election, but now an alternative materialized: a proposal from the Austro-Hungarian Foreign Minister
István, Baron von Burián for a peace offer by the Central Powers once
Romania had been beaten.[60] The German leaders had just conducted a
deeply pessimistic discussion about their ally,[61] but such forebodings were
not the only reason why Bethmann seized on the idea. It offered a new
chance to get the Allies talking, from a position of relative German strength,
although he rejected Burián's wish to summarize the Central Powers' peace
terms in a declaration. However, they would, he agreed, formulate a confidential negotiating programme.[62]

The peace offer therefore prompted the first comprehensive war aims
discussion between the Central Powers, and war aims were among the issues
on which Hindenburg and Ludendorff felt most strongly. Wilhelm was
enthusiastic about the offer, which stirred his quixotic impulses: 'The purpose to make peace is a moral act...Such an act is the province of a ruler
who has a conscience and feels himself responsible to God, who has a heart
for his own people and those of the enemy, and the will to free the world
from its suffering.'[63] Yet he expected rejection, seeing it alternatively as a
ruse to embarrass the enemy: 'We've got the English and French governments in a nice predicament, trying to explain to their people why they
don't make peace.'[64] Hindenburg and Ludendorff disliked the peace note,
and tried to stipulate that if it failed unrestricted submarine warfare would
begin in January, which Bethmann resisted.[65] Ludendorff did insist, however, on the offer being delayed until the fall of Bucharest and the approval
of the Auxiliary Service Law—and the timing, together with its boastful
tone, diminished any prospect of the Allies treating it seriously. Expecting a
refusal, the OHL's priority was to avoid any semblance of weakness that
might damage national unity and the troops' fighting spirit.[66] All the same,
even the possibility of negotiations forced a war aims discussion not only
between the Central Powers but also between the army, the navy, and the

civilians in Berlin, treating each other as quasi-sovereign entities. On almost every detail Bethmann yielded to the OHL's demands: whereas he proposed exchanging territory with France, he finally accepted that Germany would annex part of the Longwy-Briey iron ore basin and cede nothing in return; unless it could negotiate 'guarantees' with Belgium it would annex Luxemburg and Liège and a strip of Belgian territory protecting the Ruhr; as well as annexing territory on the eastern border of a nominally independent Poland, both Poland and Belgium being economically subordinated to Germany with their railways under German control.[67] Holtzendorff listed the navy's requirements, the foremost being the Bruges–Ostend–Zeebrugge triangle as an advance base 60 nautical miles from Britain, but including also the Courland coast in the Baltic and overseas bases from the Faeroes to the Azores, Dakar, East Africa, Madagascar, New Guinea, Tahiti, and Valona.[68] As the submarine debate approached its climax, the army wanted Germany to form the hub of buffer-state systems in Western and Eastern Europe, and the navy to acquire a chain of naval bases, menacing British command of the seas and of communications not just in European waters but also globally.

The final significance of the Central Powers' peace offer—published on 12 December—was that the Allies rebuffed it. In a note of 31 December drafted primarily by the French, they slammed the door on negotiations and gave only the vaguest indication of their objectives.[69] Even before this, a series of separate rejections by Allied spokesmen prejudiced the chances for the American peace note when Wilson published it on the 18th. Although the president had foreseen this danger and warned the Germans against pre-empting him, they went ahead regardless and created the misleading impression that the two initiatives were concerted. Wilson asked the two sides to spell out their war aims, but Germany's reply omitted to detail Berlin's goals, and although the Allies' reply on 10 January did publish a list, it included territorial claims on Germany and Austria-Hungary that neither of the latter could contemplate. By this point, in any case, Germany had already decided for unrestricted submarine warfare, and Allied intransigence confirmed to Wilhelm that the negotiating road was closed, while Bethmann's personal authority was weakened as were his grounds for counselling delay. After Bucharest fell on 6 December, moreover, the dangers from Dutch and Danish intervention lessened and Hindenburg and Ludendorff grew still more assertive. The final confrontation would soon follow.

Once again Holtzendorff led. He acted partly due to pressure from Scheer and the High Seas Fleet, but he drew encouragement from the Channel campaign, and he concentrated on the OHL.[70] He now had many more submarines available, and told Hindenburg they would deploy as many as possible for the maximum terror effect, so that fourteen or fifteen would operate off the west coast of the British Isles, nine or ten off the east coast, and six in the Channel, though the numbers would settle down at between eight and nine, seven and eight, and three and four respectively.[71] To prevent the British from accumulating food stocks, he wanted no warning. His staff expected unrestricted warfare to raise average monthly sinkings from 400,000 to 600,000 tons and to frighten off at least half the neutral vessels, while the British crews might refuse to sail. The offensive would cut off Britain's Spanish and Swedish iron ore and Swedish timber (vital for pit props), forcing London to terms within five months.[72] He summarized these arguments in the 'Holtzendorff Memorandum', which went to Hindenburg and Ludendorff on 22 December, but to Bethmann only on 6 January.[73] Totalling fifty-eight pages, it insisted on ending the war quickly, as an indecisive outcome based on all parties' exhaustion would be 'fatal'. Because of the poor 1916 harvests, America, Canada, and Argentina could supply Britain with little after February, forcing reliance on the longer voyages from Australia and India. The available shipping tonnage would drop by 39 per cent within five months: food was short already and Britain lacked the administrative expertise and public support needed for rationing. Continuing with the cruiser rules campaign would achieve only an 18 per cent reduction, which was too slow, and the 'panic' and 'terror' spread by unrestricted warfare were crucial. Although doing everything possible to avert American intervention, Germany must if necessary accept it. And even if America came in, it would provide the Allies with few extra vessels; the German freighters trapped in its ports would be sabotaged; and American money would help little. In short, Germany must seize its opportunity; and Holtzendorff invoked a spurious mathematical precision. His arguments seemed fortified by the growth in U-boat numbers and the Channel campaign, and by the poor northern hemisphere harvests, which created an argument for acting now, as did Britain's strengthening anti-submarine defences. And *not* to act would condemn the Central Powers to progressive asphyxiation.

Following the fall of Bucharest and the signs that the Central Powers' peace offer would fail, the high command's attitude hardened. By December a string of disputes—from Poland to the Auxiliary Service Law—had soured its relations with the chancellor, whom Hindenburg and Ludendorff rightly suspected of wanting to postpone unrestricted warfare indefinitely. Although Ludendorff confessed to being a 'non-expert' on naval questions, he thought it time to repudiate the *Sussex* pledge,[74] and he and Hindenburg pressed their right to a voice in what had previously been considered political questions for the kaiser, Foreign Ministry, and Chancellery.[75] Retrospectively Ludendorff testified to scepticism about Holtzendorff's claims, envisaging Britain's defeat might take a year rather than five months, but at the time he voiced no reservations.[76] He was particularly influenced by a visit to the Western Front—undertaken after a French attack had retaken most of Germany's Verdun gains and captured thousands of prisoners—when several commanders told him their troops were worn out.[77] On 22 December Lersner, the government representative at the OHL, warned that Ludendorff had reiterated that 'without unrestricted U-boat warfare we will lose the campaign ... The Field Marshal [Hindenburg] could no longer take responsibility for the outcome of the campaign if the government did not take this course.'[78] Hindenburg was threatening resignation, and when Bethmann visited the OHL on 29 December his reception was icy.[79] Although the chancellor insisted they must wait until the diplomacy connected with the Central Powers' and American peace notes was completed, he and Helfferich concluded 'that in the question of unrestricted U-boat warfare they must now give way, as otherwise open conflict would break out between the OHL and the government. That would shake the emperor, people, and fatherland to their foundations. They, as the weaker party, must set aside their own better convictions for the sake of internal peace.'[80] Privately Bethmann feared that the 'foundation of the entire situation relates to a dictatorial quest for mastery and the consistently pursued objective of militarizing the entire life of the state'.[81] None the less, he was prepared to yield even before he received the Holtzendorff memorandum. Holtzendorff offered at least a chance of victory and securing the war aims that the OHL deemed essential, whereas Bethmann offered slow defeat, and a spring renewal of the Allies' offensives with no certainty of the munitions and manpower needed to resist. Certainly Ludendorff told the navy he had run risks in his career but always calculated risks,[82] and the OHL delayed until Romania's defeat secured the borders. But remarkable was both armed services' indifference to the United States. Although it possessed one of the world's most modern fleets, Holtzendorff said its naval contribution would make no difference, Capelle telling the Reichstag it would be 'zero'.[83] The Holtzendorff memorandum considered the Americans lacked the tonnage to send many volunteers, and could send few more munitions than they were doing already.[84] The army had little modified its 1913 assessment that the Americans could assemble a first-line land force of just 100,000 soldiers at low readiness. On 15 January Hindenburg wrote to Conrad von Hötzendorff that the Americans could not add much to Allied shipping and munitions, their men were untrained, and their country lacked food. Whereas Bethmann and Helfferich insisted that American intervention might condemn Germany to defeat, Hindenburg believed American forces would be 'not decisive'.[85] The OHL's world-view was continental rather than global, Ludendorff summing up derisively that 'I whistle at America.'[86]

Meanwhile the chancellor's backing further dissipated. Foreign Minister Gottlieb von Jagow had quietly assisted in the U-boat debates and helped Bernstorff keep the lid on tension with Washington.[87] But in November 1916 Arthur Zimmermann replaced him, a quicker but more superficial figure with poor judgement, who was more acceptable to the OHL. However, the Foreign Ministry mattered less than did the emperor. During summer 1916 Wilhelm had endured prolonged depression over whether the war could be won.[88] He had not wanted Hindenburg and Ludendorff. His wife, Augusta Victoria, supported Tirpitz, as did the Crown Prince. And the Allies' dismissal of the Central Powers' peace offer enraged him.[89] Further, Wilhelm relied heavily on von Müller, who enjoyed regular access and advised on matters well beyond his remit, the chancellor using him to influence the emperor.[90] Müller detested Tirpitz and had supported Bethmann before the Charleville Crown Council, but although he also disagreed with Holtzendorff he was on better terms with him and inclined towards the Admiralty Staff's modified case. The correlation of forces therefore shifted not just because of Hindenburg and Ludendorff's overbearing personalities. Even more moderate figures, such as Müller, Helfferich, and Bethmann himself, recognized the balance of argumentation had altered.

The end came swiftly. Holtzendorff was stung when on 4 January he met Magnus von Levetzow, a former protégé who was now Scheer's Chief of Operations. Levetzow voiced his personal disappointment in Holtzendorff's failure to obtain unrestricted warfare, as well as the fleet's lack of confidence.[91] Afterwards Holtzendorff told Hindenburg he would ask Wilhelm for a ruling, adding that Hindenburg's support would carry decisive weight.[92] On the 5th he forwarded his memorandum to Bethmann, who, unlike in March 1916, would have little time to analyse and counter it before the new conference scheduled for Pless on 9 January. On the 8th Bethmann met Levetzow, who told him the High Seas Fleet would neither guarantee it could sink American troopships nor specify how long it would take to defeat Britain, so that although the fleet certainly wanted unrestricted submarine warfare it did not necessarily endorse Holtzendorff's prognoses. But whereas previously Helfferich might have made hay with such information, this time Bethmann went to Pless without his deputy. Helfferich did prepare a rebuttal of the Holtzendorff Memorandum, but whether the chancellor used it, or even took it, is uncertain.[93] And whereas the chancellor prepared less thoroughly than usual, Holtzendorff held a succession of prior conversations, through which he cemented a united front.[94] On the morning of 8 January he met Müller, who now switched into the submarine camp, saying the Allies' rejection of the peace offer had prepared the terrain politically. Müller found that Wilhelm shared this view, and was willing to remove Bethmann, saying (in contrast to previous practice) that this was a military domain in which the chancellor should have no say.[95] When Holtzendorff met Hindenburg and Ludendorff, he said if Bethmann refused to go along then Hindenburg should become chancellor, but Hindenburg said he could not manage the Reichstag. None the less, Hindenburg added, 'We reckon with war and have made all preparations. Things cannot get worse. The war must be shortened with every means.' War against America, Hindenburg wrote later, was inevitable, and the public was angry about Britain's blockade and US shell deliveries. When Helfferich told Holtzendorff, 'Your way leads towards catastrophe', the CAS rejoined, 'You are letting us be drawn into catastrophe.'[96]

When Bethmann arrived at Pless on the following day, therefore, 'very agitated and depressed', the cards were stacked. Although he seems to have planned to fight, he was weary, Müller telling Bethmann of his change of view.[97] In a morning meeting with Hindenburg and Ludendorff, or so Bethmann said afterwards, he set out all the arguments, but the record (which is disputed) suggests he actually conceded a large part of the case, even saying the chances of success were 'very favourable'. The rejection of the Central Powers' peace offer meant the European neutrals were more likely to keep out, Germany had more submarines than previously, and Britain's economic situation was precarious. Hindenburg wanted to shorten the war (although Bethmann feared prolonging it) and Ludendorff to spare his troops a second Somme. The generals wanted to seize the opportunity, while Bethmann acknowledged the prospects had improved and deferred to the military judgement.[98] At 6.00 p.m. Hindenburg, Ludendorff, Holtzendorff, and Bethmann met finally with Wilhelm. The emperor's Chief of the Civil Cabinet, Rudolf von Valentini, penned a portrait: the participants standing round a large table, on which the emperor ('pale and emotional') rested his hand. Holtzendorff, 'exceedingly conscious of victory', reiterated that the Americans did not frighten him, and anyway Britain would be beaten in six months, before the Americans arrived. Bethmann again set out his position but said he would not maintain it, and Wilhelm, dismissive of his chancellor, signed the orders to prepare.[99] According to the emperor, 'He reckoned absolutely with an American declaration of war.'[100] The chancellor had not only submitted, he had been humiliated: and yet, he wrote later, he felt that he was talking to men who were no longer amenable to reason.[101]

Bethmann had further bitter pills to swallow. Holtzendorff detested the chancellor, but preferred to keep him in post. Hindenburg asked Wilhelm to dismiss him but the emperor refused: it would create 'the worst possible impression'. The generals responded that although the present moment was inappropriate, they had lost confidence in Bethmann (whom Hindenburg found incorrigibly indecisive) and could work neither with him nor Helfferich nor even Zimmermann.[102] So far from their initial restraint, they challenged Wilhelm's prerogative over top appointments.[103] From now on, Bethmann held office on sufferance.

This, however, he was prepared to do so. Rather than altering his opinions, he repressed them, prophesying on the night of 9 January that American entry would cause 'a boundless prolongation of the war' and that Holtzendorff's scenarios were utopian. He considered resigning but shrank from a display of disunity.[104] He told Müller that Wilhelm had corrupted the German people with vanity and chauvinism. The Allies would negotiate only after driving Germany back to the river Meuse, and it would have to accept a 'very, very modest peace'.[105] He likened the submarine campaign to classical Athens's disastrous Sicilian expedition.[106] And yet in a secret session of the Reichstag Budget Commission on 31 January he defended the outcome. He explained that he had never opposed unrestricted warfare on principle (whatever method ended the fighting fastest was the most humane) and blamed the Allies for expanding the conflict. He admitted to continuing uncertainty about whether Britain could be starved, but since spring 1916 Germany had built more U-boats and Allied food supplies diminished, while the European neutrals were less likely to intervene and now he even considered that America might stay out.[107] Helfferich similarly had decided against resignation,[108] and told the Commission how although Germany could supply itself through 1917, British and American grain reserves were low and Britain's shrinking tonnage threatened its coal exports and iron ore imports. He too had apparently internalized Holtzendorff's theses.[109] Yet the Commission took the two men's statements well, perhaps the more because they had previously opposed unrestricted warfare. By staying on they helped manage public opinion, though at the risk of strengthening the reaction if Holtzendorff proved wrong.

Holtzendorff wanted not just secrecy but also terror and shock. It was essential to his concept that during the three-week preparation period the decision remain confidential (although in fact British intelligence got wind of it).[110] Hence the diplomatic exchanges consequent on Wilson's peace note continued, the Allies' reply on 10 January prompting an American request for Germany to forward its terms. Eventually it did, though communicating simultaneously that it was about to break the Sussex pledge. This ham-handedness dashed any American trust in Berlin's good faith,[111] and when Bernstorff tried to postpone the campaign he was told the submarines were heading towards their battle stations and it was too late. In the interim the navy deployed every available U-boat in the combat zones. This effort might be sustainable for five months, but the crews would tire and their boats need overhaul, though no new submarines were being laid down, the Navy Ministry fearing being encumbered with a surplus if the war ended as rapidly as projected. But as the priority for the U-boat high command was to accelerate the destruction, the submarines were to use the Channel (despite its minefield barrage) to reach the Western Approaches, rather than sail round Scotland. According to the commander of the High Seas Fleet submarines, Hermann Bauer, they must be 'sharp' and 'speedy'. They were expected still to use gunfire (which was cheaper than torpedoes, and enabled more sinkings per voyage), but to dispense with warning shots. They must be ruthless, and the respect for crews and passengers common previously now had no place.[112]

Kurt Riezler, as often, was among the most perceptive commentators. The decision had been taken, he observed, before Bethmann reached Pless, and although Germany had three times more U-boats than previously the

Figure 1. Photograph of Imperial German Army Headquarters, 1917. From left
to right: Hindenburg, Wilhelm II, Bethmann Hollweg, King Ludwig III of
Bavaria, Ludendorff, and Holtzendorff

key consideration had been that 'militarily only more defensive [warfare
was] possible, but in 1917 a further deterioration [was] to be expected'. The
decision was a 'Leap in the dark. We have the sense that this question hangs
over us like a Fate.' Yet now at least the German people would know the
answer, and discover how unrestricted submarine warfare would play out.[113]
The 'last card', as Bethmann dubbed it, was played to avoid an inexorable
wearing down.[114] In the background—though curiously absent from the
documents—lay the privations of the 1916–17 'turnip winter'. Similarly, the
German General Staff's official history maintained that in the light of what
was known to Hindenburg and Ludendorff the alternative was a purely
defensive posture—leaving the initiative to Germany's enemies—from
which victory could emerge only by luck.[115] As Ludendorff put it, 'Otherwise
it is not foreseeable how we should terminate the struggle'[116] and, as
Hindenburg wrote later, they faced assaults in the east and west by stronger
forces while the Hindenburg Programme had yet to deliver: unrestricted
submarine warfare was the only means available to offset an Allied material
advantage that on the Somme was all too evident. Of the Russian Revolution,
he had no premonition: on the contrary, Russia was creating new divisions.[117] Yet actually both Bethmann and other observers had said Russia was

unstable, without predicting when its collapse would come.[118] Nor did they foresee the French army mutinies or appreciate Britain's financial difficulties in America, despite briefings from their Washington embassy.[119] Ironically also, Germany was already causing consternation in London by destroying 400,000 tons of shipping a month, and although sinkings rose from February this was primarily due to the additional U-boats committed rather than the freedom to torpedo without warning.[120] The record confirms that it would have been possible to increase British losses while avoiding a confrontation with the United States, whereas the Allies' spring 1917 disasters—Nicholas II's abdication and the failure of France's Nivelle offensive, not to mention a British foreign exchange crisis—would have happened anyway, crippling Allied strategy without the consolation of American war entry. In short, Germany should have waited, as Bethmann and Helfferich had counselled. The submarine lobby was correct that U-boat numbers had grown (and could have grown more with different building priorities), and also correct that Britain's tonnage was stretched and its cereal reserves were low. Holtzendorff predicted accurately how much could be sunk, at least initially, and that neutral shipping could be frightened off (though on the extent of the latter phenomenon he was over-confident). But he overstated Britain's closeness to starvation and underestimated its capacity for counter-measures, above all through convoying, which Bethmann and Helfferich, as well as Müller, had foreseen.[121] Finally, both the navy and the army gravely underrated how much America could help the Allies, even within six months, although it would indeed need longer to field a mass army. Even so, tonnage losses did not prevent it from doing so, or interdict crucial deliveries of oil, wheat, and steel.

It was no accident Bethmann felt a sense of déjà vu. Unrestricted warfare was a 'dice throw' and Germany would be seen as a 'mad dog'.[122] Once again, it gambled on a strategic plan—the Schlieffen–Moltke plan in 1914 and now the Holtzendorff plan—though in 1914 the civilian leaders had been readier to acquiesce, and debate had been perfunctory. In 1916–17, in contrast, debate was thorough and searching. The submarine lobby prevailed in part because the evidence seemed to lean its way. Even so, the play of personalities was crucial, and had Hindenburg and Ludendorff not succeeded to the high command a compromise based on the October 1916 cruiser rules campaign would have been more likely to carry assent. And had it done so, it seems likely that Germany by late 1917 would have secured not a crushing military victory but at least a favourable draw in negotiations with a demoralized and fissiparous opposing bloc. It was not to be, and as Bethmann foresaw, the Pless decisions prolonged the conflict until Germany retreated to the Meuse. The preconditions for that outcome were that unrestricted submarine warfare indeed brought in America, but failed to starve out Britain. To that conjuncture we must now turn.

2

Enter America

The German leaders knew that unrestricted submarine warfare almost certainly spelt war with the United States. They misjudged not whether America would enter but that entry's impact. Yet the mere announcement of unrestricted warfare was insufficient to bring America in. During 1916 Woodrow Wilson's relations with the Allies had become more strained than with the Central Powers, and two months elapsed before he made up his mind. The war aversion of both the president and the public is among the story's most arresting features. None the less, the pattern of American neutrality before Germany's announcement set the context for developments afterwards. It worked against the Central Powers, and encouraged them to gamble. Its form was moulded through successive phases, whose consequences were not clearly foreseeable. The cumulative outcome, however, has been termed a 'revolution' in American foreign relations,[1] and meant that when a decision came, the choice to fight was likeliest. Even so, America's route to war was indirect and incremental. Although Wilson resolved that Germany must be beaten he wanted no smashing Allied triumph, and this circle, once in the war, he still tried to square.

American policy formed in layers. From August 1914 until May 1915 the key issues were trade and blockade. Between May 1915 and May 1916 Berlin and Washington were in confrontation over submarine warfare, while American war exports gathered momentum. Wilson heightened American preparedness, while seeking to mediate. Between May 1916 and February 1917, in contrast, the U-boat issue receded. Wilson knew it might return, and partly for this reason he delivered his December 1916 peace note and his January 1917 'Peace without Victory' speech. For a moment he supposed that peace was close at hand and Germany would cooperate. The submarine announcement left him feeling disoriented and betrayed.

Figure 2. Photograph of US President Woodrow Wilson from 1917

According to the British ambassador, Sir Cecil Spring-Rice, the American government was more autocratic than in Germany, Russia, or Turkey.[2] Yet public opinion and Congress counted for more than he allowed, and advisers helped shape Wilson's speeches and writings. Wilson entered politics when aged fifty-three.[3] The son of a Presbyterian minister, and a former professor of history and political science at Princeton who admired British constitutional practice, he met his Cabinet relatively frequently and at first was tolerant of disagreement. He worked with the Democratic Party in Congress, over which as the only Democrat and Southerner to become president since the Civil War, he held considerable ascendancy. On foreign policy, however, he consulted less, despite lacking experience of it. His White House staff was tiny, and he typed out himself most of his diplomatic notes. Edith Galt, who in 1915 became his second wife, went daily through his correspondence with him, and seems to have favoured a hard line against Germany. So did his secretary, Joe Tumulty, who dealt primarily with legislative and political management. Wilson's leading policy adviser during the neutrality period was the Texan businessman and political fixer, 'Colonel' Edward Mandell House, who held no official position. The two men had a close rapport, of fluctuating strength. House was at his apogee after Wilson's first wife, Ellen, died in 1914, but in spring 1915 and spring 1916 he made long visits to Europe, and the second Mrs Wilson resented him. He was a sympathetic, sometimes obsequious, sounding board, who altered points of substance in the president's declarations but whom Wilson also overrode. For although House had hoped to organize a Great Power condominium, including Germany, to manage world affairs, after war broke out he was consistently pro-Allied, or at least pro-French and especially pro-British, fearing a German–Russian–Japanese combination. If Britain lost, he warned, 'our turn would come next'.[4] He contrasted with William Jennings Bryan, Wilson's Secretary of State until 1915. As a former presidential candidate, Bryan commanded party affection. He was loyal to the president, but Wilson used him to offer public mediation while House operated independently behind the scenes. Still, for the first ten months Bryan remained a senior figure who warned against compromising even-handedness or risking involvement. After Bryan's State Department number two, Robert Lansing, replaced him, however, Wilson's officials formed a pro-Allied phalanx.

The initial neutrality decision was uncontroversial. The American tradition, epitomized in George Washington's Farewell Address, was of non-involvement in European politics. In 1914 no one in Congress or the press demanded intervention, and most abhorred the violence. Yet Wilson asked Americans to observe neutrality not only in deed but also in thought, which was more challenging. When canvassed in November, two-thirds of newspaper editors declared themselves to be impartial.[5] But 15 per cent of the population had been born abroad, mostly in Europe.[6] Neither Irish Americans (whose ancestors had suffered at Britain's hands) nor Jews (who had suffered at Russia's) had reason for pro-Allied sympathies, and German-Americans were the biggest ethnic minority. In 1910 out of a US population of 92 million, 2.5 million were German-born and 5.8 million of the native-born had one or both German-born parents.[7] Although Wilson believed 90 per cent of America's people were strongly pro-Allied, he had grounds to fear that rival allegiances would breed civil strife.[8]

The traditional corollary to political abstention was unimpeded commerce. Exporting to belligerents was unobjectionable, the more so as America was in recession and the fighting expected to be brief. But demands for artillery, munitions, steel, machine tools, chemicals, and food and raw materials rose far higher than anticipated, fuelling one of the strongest upsurges in US history. In the winter of 1914–15 German-Americans backed a proposal in Congress to embargo arms exports, but Wilson prevented the move as 'a foolish one, as it would restrict our plants'.[9] Commerce secretary, William Cox Redfield, and the Treasury secretary, William Gibbs McAdoo, urged the boom must be sustained, Redfield advising that exports were at record levels,[10] and McAdoo using the extra revenue to pay off debt. Between 1915 and 1917 exports to Britain, Canada, France, Italy, and Russia grew from $3,445 million to $9,796 million (184 per cent); those of wheat by 683 per cent; and of copper by 277 per cent;[11] but whereas pre-war trade with the Central Powers had been one-fifth of that with the Allies, now it shrank to 1 per cent.[12] The Allies could find the shipping to transport their purchases and the cash or credit to pay for them; the Central Powers could find neither, so whatever stance America took would benefit one side. Britain had the world's biggest merchant navy in 1914 (43 per cent of world tonnage—and the Allies in total 59 per cent, against the Central Powers' 15 per cent).[13] As the Allies converted to military production, however, they had less to export, and were less able to pay. The Wall Street banking giant, J. P. Morgan & Co., became the British government's purchasing and financial agent and permitted it a growing overdraft, and in the summer of 1915 it advised the Allies to attempt a bond flotation. Following convention, Wilson had prohibited loans to belligerent governments. But McAdoo warned that 'to maintain our prosperity we must finance it. Otherwise it may stop, and that would be disastrous.'[14] Finally Wilson approved the bond issue, and even if the primary motive was to sustain the boom and the yield proved disappointing, American policy had clearly altered to the Allies' advantage. In 1915, 75 per cent of US exports went to the Allies or to countries that had broken relations with Germany and between 1913 and 1916 America's percentage of French imports rose from 10 to 30.[15] By 1916 bottlenecks on the railroads into New York stretched back for miles.

Central to the British, and later the American, government's justification for involvement in the conflict was the duty to uphold international law.[16] Conversely, Germany charged the Americans were one-sided; and Wilson's protests against the Allied blockade were indeed much milder than those against the submarines. From Washington's perspective, the blockade might entail confiscation of American property which could be compensated by agreement or by arbitration; the U-boats destroyed not just shipping and cargo but also lives. Thus Wilson distinguished between Britain's 'violation of neutral rights' and Germany's 'violation of the rights of humanity'.[17] Yet from Berlin's perspective the blockade killed far more civilians than the U-boats, with no stronger legal basis. The law of the sea gave only imprecise guidance. The fundamental text was the 1856 Declaration of Paris, which stipulated that to be legal a blockade must be 'effective'—not just declaratory—and which protected neutral goods on belligerent vessels and belligerent goods on neutral vessels, provided neither were contraband. The 1909 Declaration of London narrowed the definition of contraband, thus assisting traders rather than blockaders. But neither Britain nor America ratified the London Declaration, although in 1914 Wilson called on both sides to honour it. Whereas the Germans said they would reciprocate if the Allies did, Britain agreed only with reservations.[18] It tried to stop all goods not only from entering German ports but also from reaching Germany via the neutrals. It mined the North Sea exits so as to leave only cleared channels for neutral merchantmen, thus obliging them to accept inspection in British harbours. It argued that because German government agencies might use some food imports Britain was entitled to stop all food reaching Germany, and a March 1915 Order in Council invoked the right of reprisal against Germany's first unrestricted submarine campaign to justify suppressing all commerce with the Central Powers. The British were now violating the Declarations both of Paris and of London, but both sides argued that the other's transgressions entitled them to breach convention.[19]

Bryan knew little of international law, but he supported Lansing's protests to London. Wilson himself, however, toned down the American notes.[20] The administration argued that the British were following precedents set by the Union side in the American Civil War, although actually it knew the circumstances differed.[21] A more influential precedent was the War of 1812, when, in Wilson's understanding, British encroachments on neutral rights had forced President Madison into hostilities.[22] The upshot was that although America condemned British actions, it did not insist they cease, or threaten sanctions. It reserved the right to compensation, rather than forcing the issue. Conversely, British Foreign Secretary Sir Edward Grey, in mirror image of Bethmann Hollweg, sought the tightest blockade possible without a breach with the United States.[23] He responded politely but evasively. He too remembered 1812,[24] and both governments held the disagreement below danger point. Wilson was more guarded in his pro-Allied sympathies than were House and Lansing, feared Russia, and considered the best outcome would be a draw, although an Allied victory would not harm American vital interests.[25] Hence America supplied the Allies with ammunition,

food, and raw materials, while acquiescing in the Allies' efforts to starve
out their enemies.

Such was the context for the clash over U-boats. When the Germans
announced their first unrestricted campaign, Wilson reacted slowly. Perhaps
he understood the submarines could not maintain a traditional blockade.
However, from the start American language was stronger than against the
Allies, Bryan warning the United States would hold Germany to 'strict
accountability', and take any steps necessary to safeguard American lives
and property and the rights of American citizens on the high seas.[26] The
crisis following the torpedoing of the *Lusitania* on Friday 7 May 1915 then
committed American prestige. It has been likened to Pearl Harbor and 9/11
as an event so devastating that years later people still recalled where they had
learned of it.[27] It followed hard on other shocks: Germany's first use of poison gas, Zeppelin raids on London, and the report by the Bryce Commission,
chaired by a former British ambassador to Washington, on German atrocities in Belgium. However, American outrage centred on the eastern sea-
board and soon subsided; and when the New York newspapers asked editors
across the country how to respond, only six out of a thousand favoured
intervention.[28] Hence, Wilson confessed to Bryan, 'I wish with all my heart
that I saw a way to carry out the double wish of our people, to maintain a
firm front in respect of what we demand from Germany and yet also do
nothing that might by any possibility involve us in the war.'[29] His mother had
taught him to refrain from fighting,[30] and as he said to Tumulty 'I will not be
rushed into war, no matter if every last Congressman and Senator stands up
on his hind legs and proclaims me a coward.'[31] Yet he felt impelled to do
something; though Bryan urged the alternative of avoiding all risk of conflict
and warning Americans against travel on belligerent liners, such acquiescence, considered Wilson, would be 'both weak and futile. To show this sort
of weak yielding to threat and danger would only make matters worse.'[32]
As well as courting further challenges, it would strip America of any influence on the peace settlement: a consideration that House emphasized. Instead
the president hoped that 'firmness may bring peace'. He embarked upon a
middle road, of making demands on Germany without using force, which
for two years served him well but in 1917 reached its limit.[33]

The president also disregarded Bryan on another point: preserving
impartiality by combining protests to Berlin with protests to London. Instead,
Wilson's guideline was to conduct one confrontation at a time, as antagonizing

Britain and Germany simultaneously would be 'folly',[34] and Germany's transgressions were more heinous. Bryan found himself isolated in the Cabinet, whose other members favoured firmness, and although he acquiesced in the president's first Lusitania note, he resigned over the wider demands of the second. Lansing, who replaced Bryan, was treated ungenerously by Wilson. Lansing was a New York lawyer, and unlike his predecessor had no political following. He managed the State Department more as a civil servant, generally tolerating House's encroachments. He viewed autocracy (as represented by Germany) as the biggest threat to global peace. His successor as State Department Counsellor, Frank Polk, was a House nominee: so from now Wilson faced a largely interventionist State Department as well as Cabinet, although he was strong willed enough to ignore them.

Wilson's preferred instrument was a public exchange of notes. His critics derided it, as text succeeded text without eliciting concessions. Still, his first Lusitania note asserted the 'practical impossibility' of using submarines to destroy commerce without violating cruiser rules. It called on Germany to disavow sinkings that caused American casualties, make reparation, and prevent a recurrence.[35] Following a tardy and unsatisfactory response, his second note sought more protection of non-combatants on non-resisting merchant ships, and sureties that neutral merchantmen (unless carrying contraband) were respected. Although his third note refocused on disavowal of the Lusitania sinking,[36] he was gravitating towards insistence that submarines must follow cruiser rules, and denial that the right of reprisal legitimated infringements on neutral rights.[37] Moreover, on 19 August another British liner, the Arabic, was torpedoed with forty-four dead, including three Americans, despite the third note having warned that such behaviour would be 'deliberately unfriendly'.[38] Wilson hesitated, fearing to lose the influence that a neutral America might exert over the peace settlement, but Ambassador Bernstorff was so alarmed that on his own responsibility he publicly pledged that Germany would respect cruiser rules for liners, and disavowed the Arabic sinking, promising compensation. His superiors reproved but did not repudiate him, and in September 1915 they secretly called off the submarine campaign.[39] After months of exchanges Germany had finally made real concessions. House understood that in Berlin hawks and doves were competing, but it is less clear that Lansing and Wilson did, and Germany's erratic conduct deepened their suspicions. The 1915 context therefore helps explain the vigorous American reaction against 'intensified' U-boat warfare in spring 1916, culminating on 24 March when the steamer *Sussex* was torpedoed in the English Channel with several Americans injured and some eighty passengers dead.

The *Sussex* crisis came just after Wilson had quelled a revolt in Congress, where resolutions had been introduced to warn Americans against sailing on belligerent ships. He insisted on the resolutions being withdrawn, and wrote to William Stone, the chair of the Senate Foreign Relations Committee, that if the government acquiesced in any abatement of its citizens' rights 'the whole fine fabric of international law might crumble under our hands piece by piece'.[40] This was an extreme statement, perhaps sharpened in vain hopes of discouraging Germany from the spring U-boat offensive, but when the *Sussex* was hit both Lansing and House believed action, in the shape of breaking off relations, was now needed. Wilson, in contrast, saw breaking relations as a staging post towards hostilities, and objected that if America entered the conflict no one would be left to mediate.[41] Characteristically, he waited for fuller facts, but soon no doubt remained that an unarmed passenger vessel had been torpedoed without warning. Hence Lansing prepared another note, which Wilson strengthened at House's suggestion, calling on Germany to halt at once its submarine warfare against passenger ships and merchantmen, or America would break off relations.[42] Bethmann called off the intensified campaign, and in the '*Sussex* pledge' of 4 May agreed to follow cruiser rules though warning that Germany expected America to act against the blockade. Wilson, conversely, insisted Germany's obligations should remain distinct: 'Responsibility in such matters is single, not joint: absolute, not relative.'[43]

The *Sussex* pledge set the trip-wire that in 1917 Germany crossed. House was surprised at how the president advanced from passivity to intransigence.[44] In the name of international law Wilson not only asserted American rights but also told the Central Powers how to conduct hostilities. He again refused to link protests against German methods with protests against British ones, while in spring 1916 he also authorized House to launch a decidedly pro-Allied peace initiative. He had set his course in response to the *Lusitania* sinking, partly to satisfy the 'double wish' for action without commitment, and partly because this year of tension strengthened the impression that Germany was duplicitous. German embassy involvement in propaganda and in sabotage within America would further reinforce that impression.[45] Finally, both House and Lansing impressed on Wilson that his handling of the submarine dispute would determine America's peace conference leverage, and the president seems to have shared that view.[46]

With the *Sussex* crisis Wilson (at least implicitly) threatened war over European issues. This development was revolutionary in American foreign relations, the more as it accompanied a military and naval build-up. In 1914–15 Wilson had authorized only modest rises in defence spending, despite demands for military 'preparedness' from the National Security League (based in New York City with wealthy Republican backers) and the Military Training Corps Association (which trained Ivy League students in officer summer camps, and wanted training to be universal). Opposition came from the American Union against Militarism, as well as from Mid-Western and Southern farmers, pacifist and women's groups, and Jewish, Irish, and German Americans.[47] None the less, after the *Lusitania* sinking Wilson asked his War and Navy Secretaries to prepare proposals. Although he had no plans to fight, he could no longer be sure of keeping America out.[48] McAdoo found money by postponing tariff cuts,[49] and Navy Secretary Josephus Daniels, although a Cabinet dove, agreed with his advisers on the principle of a navy second to none.[50] The resulting bill was weighted towards large capital ships through the construction of four battleships and four battle-cruisers, as well as four escort cruisers, twenty destroyers, and twenty-seven submarines. As a three-year programme that needed preliminary adaptation of the navy yards, however, it was oriented towards the long-term expansion of American power and influence rather than the needs of anti-submarine warfare and of shipping protection if America joined the Allies.[51]

The army bill was more disputed. War Secretary Lindley Garrison was an interventionist, and Wilson had reservations about his plan not just to strengthen the regular army but also to replace the National Guard as the ready reserve by a new 'Continental Army'. Congress resisted the idea on grounds of cost and the challenge to the National Guard, and Wilson scrapped it, resulting in Garrison's resignation. However, Garrison's successor, Newton Diehl Baker, combined idealism with administrative effectiveness, and for passing the measure it also helped that the Mexican revolutionary Pancho Villa raided Columbus, New Mexico, in March 1916. The War Department sent an expeditionary force to chase him and deployed the National Guard along the border. None the less, Wilson wanted a larger army for broader purposes. He told a delegation from the American Union against Militarism that 'This is a year of madness. It is a year of excitement, more profound than the world has ever known before, and the world is seeing red. No standard we had obtains any longer.' If other nations regarded America as helpless, it would be treated as negligible, including in the peace settlement; and in a post-war 'joint effort to keep the peace' the world would expect it to contribute.[52] Even so, the 1916 National Defense Act provided only for modest forces. The regular army would be nearly doubled over five years to 175,000 (with a war strength of 298,000); the National Guard would rise over six years to 450,000.[53] These were leisurely schedules, and by 1917 little progress had been made.

Wilson's backing for preparedness coincided with a tilt in favour of a post-war international organization, as well as a peak in sympathy for the Allies. The best evidence comes from the discussions surrounding the secret 'House–Grey Memorandum' of 22 February 1916.[54] The memorandum emerged from Anglo-American correspondence in autumn 1915, followed with a visit by House to Europe. It envisaged that, at a moment selected by France and Britain, Wilson would convene a peace conference, and if Germany objected America would 'probably' declare war. If Germany attended but the conference failed because Berlin was 'unreasonable', America, once again, would intervene—an eventuality Wilson qualified with a second 'probably' but still approved, even though the text recorded that House had favoured peace conditions that restored Belgium's independence, returned Alsace-Lorraine to France, and secured for Russia a sea outlet. America would mediate at a juncture that suited the Allies and would offer them a peace incorporating several of their crucial demands, or continued war with America now a partner.[55]

The memorandum disregarded domestic politics. While it was negotiated Wilson faced a Congressional revolt over much smaller issues, and it is scarcely credible that the legislature would have voted for war in the circumstances envisaged. Negligible support as yet existed for military intervention, as the British ambassador rightly reported.[56] Wilson's 'probablies' indicated his awareness of the limits set by Congress and by public opinion, and he had actually warned House to avoid territorial questions and to concentrate on principles such as arms limitation and the freedom of the seas.[57] He saw the House–Grey project not as a step to war but as emphasizing 'the possibilities in the direction of peace',[58] and he soon had second thoughts.[59] It was fortunate for him politically that the British refrained from taking it up, diverting the blame on to the French; and when House visited Paris he found Aristide Briand's government hostile, at a moment when the Verdun battle seemed to be moving against Germany and the summer campaigning might turn the war round. The French opposed compromise and the British did not press them.[60] Several members of Herbert Asquith's coalition government were appalled by the war's expense and sceptical about the forthcoming Somme campaign, but the doubters (who were mostly Liberals) hesitated to confront the military and the Unionists.[61] Moreover, the British were intercepting American cables, and may have known that Wilson was not fully behind House.[62] The Cabinet's War Committee was indecisive, which amounted to a negative and a gamble on the Somme delivering victory before the Allies faced ruin. The episode damaged Anglo-American relations, especially when Wilson gave a speech on 27 May that professed indifference as to who had caused the war.[63] Yet the speech had actually been intended to encourage Britain, by declaring America's willingness to join a post-war security association.[64] Tumulty advised Wilson that this initiative would be popular in an election year, and it linked the president with internationalist Republicans such as William Howard Taft, despite his disagreements with them over how such an association would operate.[65] Both the 27 May speech and Wilson's earlier comments to the American Union against militarism suggest experience had convinced him that America must play a bigger global role, with stronger armed forces, and this conviction influenced him in the final crisis.

Yet Wilson had actually reached an anti-German and pro-Allied extreme, and was about to row back. Between May 1916 and January 1917 American neutrality traversed a third and less pro-Allied phase. While Germany for the time being honoured the *Sussex* pledge, Wilson prepared a more open and less partisan mediation. After winning a second term in the November presidential election he issued his peace note, and in the light of the responses set out a blueprint for the settlement in his 'Peace without Victory' speech. He combined public diplomacy with secret contacts with Germany and Austria-Hungary and it was when he seemed close to success that the submarine bombshell exploded. All of these developments further contributed to the decisions to break off relations and to declare war.

Bethmann had warned the *Sussex* pledge was contingent on action against the Allied blockade. It was predictable that once the confrontation with the Germans eased, Wilson would put more pressure on their enemies. But relations with London also deteriorated for other reasons.[66] The Easter Rising by Irish Republicans in Dublin and the subsequent executions of its leaders inflamed Irish Americans. Washington protested against new British powers taken to read the mail on intercepted neutral ships in order to gain intelligence, but London paid little heed. Instead it published a 'blacklist' of neutral, including American, firms that British companies were forbidden to contact because they were suspected of trading with the enemy. This ban meant, for example, refusing access to Britain's worldwide bunker-coal facilities. Finally, the Allies ceased any pretence of operating within the 1909 Declaration of London. Wilson wrote to House that he was 'about at the end of my patience with Great Britain and the Allies', and the blacklist was 'the last straw'.[67] Anglophobia (which pervaded the US navy's senior ranks) was one reason for the navy bill, Wilson telling House, 'Let us build a navy bigger than hers and do what we please', while a Shipping Act was passed to lessen dependence on foreign carriers. Finally, the September 1916 Revenue Act, besides paying for military preparedness, gave the president discretion to deny clearance in US ports to vessels that discriminated in acceptance of cargo.[68]

Wilson refrained from using these powers, and the Anglo-American relationship did not degenerate into a spiral of retaliation. Had it done so, American intervention on the Allied side would have been much harder. The British conceded little, although agreeing that only neutral vessels proceeding voluntarily to British ports would have their mail inspected. Commerce Secretary Redfield warned that America depended on the British Empire for essential imports. But in addition reports were arriving by September that the Germans might soon renew submarine warfare, and until November Wilson was preoccupied with re-election. Pressure on the British eased until after his victory.

Had Wilson not been re-elected, his Republican challenger, Charles Evans Hughes, would probably also have taken America in. The Republicans generally were more anti-German and interventionist, although Hughes's foreign policy statements were few and ambiguous.[69] Assuming that the Germans would have resumed unrestricted submarine warfare in any event, Hughes might have responded faster but found it harder than Wilson to unite the public and Congress, though once in the war he would have conducted it in a less independent and a more pro-Allied fashion. The election mattered rather for how the United States fought the war and concluded the peace than for whether it entered. In fact the contest was among the closest in American history, Wilson obtaining 9,127,595 votes to Hughes's 8,533,507 (and 277:254 in the Electoral College). He owed his victory partly to his domestic reforms, though he also got inserted into the Democratic Party platform a provision that America should join an association of nations to preserve the freedom of the seas and prevent wars of aggression.[70] The phrase, 'He kept us out of war' became a Democratic hallmark, plastered on billboards across the country,[71] though Wilson disliked it, warning Daniels that 'any little German lieutenant can put us into war at any time by some calculated outrage'.[72] All the same, he allowed himself to be represented as a peacekeeper, and observers still found negligible demand for the United States to intervene.[73] Moreover, although the result was a personal triumph for Wilson, the Republicans reduced his majority in the House of Representatives and almost eliminated it in the Senate, and during the campaign the situation in Berlin had worsened.

Over the summer the German moderates lost ground. Wilson did not take his ambassador in Berlin, James Watson Gerard, very seriously, but Gerard, like House, had a sense of the German bureaucratic battles. In October Bethmann warned Gerard that the military party was getting the upper hand. He had advised Bernstorff that Wilson should act before it was too late. When Bernstorff reported that Wilson had postponed mediation until after the election, Wilhelm personally prepared a warning that Germany might resume its freedom of action unless the president acted soon, which Bernstorff conveyed to House.[74] On 14 November Wilson told House that he must urgently appeal for peace, or the United States would inevitably drift into war over the U-boats. Indeed he considered that their new Channel offensive already violated the *Sussex* pledge, and the United States should be breaking off relations, but he wanted to try for peace first.[75] By 27 November he had drafted a note, as usual working alone. House preferred to let the German–American confrontation develop and thought the timing wrong; he cautioned against reiterating that the causes of the war were obscure, but the president insisted on saying so. Lansing too would have preferred to do nothing. He feared an impossible position if the Allies responded less satisfactorily than the Central Powers.[76] Finally Wilson decided to call on both sides to declare their war aims rather than demand they make peace. He published his note in haste on 18 December, because the Central Powers had published their peace offer on 12 December. Although the Americans insisted the two texts were unrelated, Wilson feared a vehement Allied reaction to the Germans would bar all prospects for his own initiative unless he acted at once.[77]

By the time the note was sent, the administration had applied pressure. On 28 November the Federal Reserve Board warned members of the Federal Reserve System to be cautious about locking up funds in long-term loans or in short-term ones that repeatedly had to be renewed until normal conditions returned; it was destabilizing if foreign governments issued securities faster than investors could absorb them, and against America's interests for members to invest in foreign Treasury bills, which would reduce capacity for domestic lending. Even private investors (who fell outside the FRB's remit) were warned against unsecured loans. The war had raised America to a level of financial power that would otherwise have taken a generation, and 'We must be careful not to impair this position of strength and influence.'[78]

America was two years into a tremendous boom. McAdoo wrote to Wilson that 'Our economic strength, and particularly the financial part of our economic strength is so great, being in fact the greatest of any Nation in the world, that we have a paramount advantage...'.[79] Yet he shared the Board's 'apprehension' that American banks were 'loading up too heavily' with European loans.[80] In 1916 exports accounted for 11 per cent of US GNP, or more than double the pre-war proportion,[81] and the authorities had reason to doubt the growth was sustainable. During 1915–16 Britain took on the financing of American imports for the entire Allied coalition, borrowing with growing difficulty and at increasing interest.[82] In November the British Treasury warned that of £5 million spent daily on the war, £2 million had to be found in North America, which the Munitions Ministry considered indispensable for oil, petroleum, processed meat, cotton, military raw materials, and grain.[83] According to Chancellor of the Exchequer Reginald McKenna, by June 1917 the American president would be able to 'dictate his terms to us': Britain was exhausting its collateral in gold and securities, and would need to borrow $200 million a month although it was struggling to raise $80 million.[84] In these unpromising circumstances J. P. Morgan prepared in December 1916 to issue unsecured British Treasury bills, to be bought by US banks and repeatedly renewed, for up to $1.1 billion. Morgan's were too perfunctory over the prior consultation with the FRB, but the 28 November warning was unprecedented, and before issuing it William Harding, the chairman of the FRB governors, consulted Wilson, who not only welcomed the statement but wanted it strengthened and the private investor included.[85] The damage to British credit was immediate, the new loan was abandoned, and the British Treasury and the Foreign Office considered the situation extremely grave.[86] The incoming Lloyd George government had the American exchanges near the top of its agenda. It agreed that US purchases must be restricted, and did not know how to finance them into the New Year.[87]

This was the situation when Wilson issued his peace note. He had deleted earlier references equating British navalism with Prussian militarism, but he maintained that the two sides' war aims as publicly declared seemed virtually the same. He sought specific statements on 'what definitive results, what actual exchanges of guarantees, what political or territorial changes or readjustments, what stage of military success even, would bring the war to an end'.[88] He hoped the rival objectives were more reconcilable than they seemed, and given his knowledge that a break with Germany might be looming, it suited him to show he had explored every alternative. None the less, his apparent equating of the belligerents predictably infuriated the Allies, and that he acted only a week after the Central Powers reinforced the impression of concertation.[89]

The Allies' response might therefore have impeded American intervention. It did not. An Anglo-French conference in London on 26–28 December approved a French draft that indignantly rebutted the Central Powers while offering only generalities about the Allies' goals. Though the British had misgivings, they let it go forward.[90] But the French also wanted the response to Wilson to refer him to the reply to the Central Powers as a summary of Allied objectives, thereby evading the essence of the American request. They took this line despite their dependence on American food, steel, explosives, and shells, as their Foreign Ministry judged America unlikely to impose an arms embargo and wanted to nip any peace process in the bud.[91] But the British Cabinet, which the Treasury had advised to conciliate Washington, took a different line, and in the note that the Allies published on 10 January 1917 they included a paragraph that tried to satisfy Wilson, even if Lloyd George did not feel bound by it. Belgium, Serbia, and Montenegro should regain their independence and integrity; France, Russia, and Romania be evacuated and receive reparations; the Italians, Slavs, and Romanians freed from 'foreign domination'; and the Turks' subject peoples liberated. Alsace-Lorraine (implicitly) would return to France, and 'appropriate international arrangements' would 'guarantee land and sea frontiers against unjustified attack'; the document also supported a League of Nations.[92] The guiding principles were self-determination (without using the phrase) at the expense of Austria-Hungary and the Ottoman Empire, reversing the Central Powers' conquests, and providing safeguards against future aggression. The note was more detailed than any previous Allied declaration, whereas the Central Powers' reply to Wilson gave no detail whatever. When Wilson offered confidential mediation in a follow-up note, Bethmann personally was willing to outline Germany's territorial claims, but he deferred to a vaguer Foreign Ministry text.[93] And although we have no record of how Wilson judged the two sides' responses, during January the financial authorities became more accommodating towards Britain, and Wilson alluded favourably to the Allies' reply in his Peace without Victory speech.

The speech was delivered to the Senate on 22 January. It formed a coda to the peace note. But Wilson told House his real audience was European public opinion, and he hoped that appealing to that public could help peace even though the governments were more divided than he had realized.[94] Both the French Socialists and the British Labour Party had wanted a detailed Allied reply to Wilson, and reports about British progressive opinion may have encouraged him.[95] According to a 'very sober and significant' letter from the Independent Labour Party, all sections of British society wanted to end the war at once and establish a League of Nations.[96] Further, House had made contact with William Wiseman, a British intelligence agent who bypassed the British ambassador and was more in tune with radical thinking. Wiseman misleadingly suggested that his government would accept a peace conference, and Wilson may again have overestimated his initiative's likely results.[97]

Wilson ignored Lansing, who advised against the 'Peace without Victory' phrase.[98] The president wanted to be specific (as he had invited the belligerents to be); but when he ruminated over the issues with House their thinking resembled the pro-Allied inclination of the House–Grey Memorandum. Although they were 'not quite sure' about Alsace-Lorraine, Belgium and Serbia should be restored, and House thought Russia should get a warm water port. They wanted to highlight Poland, as Russia and Germany had indicated willingness to free it, and the Polish National Committee representative, the pianist Ignacy Paderewski, had impressed both men.[99] In the end, however, the speech stuck largely to the general conditions on which the American people would be willing to participate in 'some definite concert of power' secured by 'the organized major force of mankind'. To be durable, the peace must be between equals, with no vengeful loser, and based on the freedom of the seas, arms limitation, and transcending the balance of power system. It should rest on the principles that governments derived their just powers from the consent of the governed and no nation should extend political control over another. It should rest, in other words, on democracy and on self-determination, although Wilson did not use the latter phrase and that Poland should regain autonomy and independence was the only specific example given.[100]

The speech had a mixed reception. In Congress Democrats mostly welcomed it and Republicans were mostly hostile, including Henry Cabot Lodge, who in the post-election Senate would replace Stone as chair of the Foreign Relations Committee and had previously favoured a League of Nations but had now changed his mind.[101] The press acknowledged Wilson's idealism but doubted the practicality, and pro-Allied papers disliked the Peace without Victory phrase.[102] Wilson's ability to keep broad support was reaching its limits. But private exchanges after the speech confirmed that the administration's thinking was veering back towards the Allies. Neither Germany nor Russia really wanted an independent Poland: both pursued a nominally autonomous buffer state that would expand at their opponent's expense. Wilson's speech, Bethmann told Ambassador Gerard, showed the president had embraced the Allies' 10 January reply, and meant Poland gaining sea access through German territory located only two hours from Berlin.[103] Yet the Americans still hoped to mediate, which misapprehension Bernstorff encouraged. Even after being told that unrestricted submarine warfare was impending, he advised Berlin that US intercession could bring better terms than a U-boat offensive, which Wilson would consider a 'slap in the face' and would bring America in—whereas if Germany accepted mediation Wilson would find it very difficult to declare war.[104] On 24 January Wilson told House that 'if Germany really wants peace she can get it, and get it soon, if she will but confide in me and let me have a chance'.[105] However, he stressed that Berlin's requirements must be reasonable, whereas Bethmann briefed Gerard that Germany must hold the forts of Liège and Namur, continue occupying Belgium and control its ports and railways, obtain frontier rectifications in northern France and 'very substantial' territorial changes in the east, regain its colonies, and receive indemnities.[106] Bethmann communicated similar conditions to Bernstorff, which on 31 January were delivered simultaneously with the news that unrestricted submarine warfare would recommence the following day. Within a week Wilson was transported from lingering hope to precisely the slap in the face that Bernstorff had foreseen, while House dismissed Bethmann's proposals as 'no proposals at all'.[107] Moreover, during the weeks of peace diplomacy Wilson had refrained from protests against either the submarines or the blockade, and the anti-Allied emphasis of his diplomacy since the *Sussex* crisis practically came to an end.[108]

None of this, however, predetermined Wilson's eventual response to what Lansing described as 'the gravest crisis presented since the war began'.[109] Between Germany's submarine announcement and America's declaration of war, US policy moved through four phases: breaking off relations; armed neutrality; the reaction to the Zimmermann Telegram; and the final decision.

Wilson's breach of diplomatic relations was regretful but swift, and easier because he did not deem it irrevocable. It was true that Germany's conduct had grown more brutal,[110] one of the president's correspondents denouncing 'an insolent threat of ferocious terrorism'.[111] Wilson was shocked, angered, and humiliated, telling House he felt 'as if the world had suddenly reversed itself'. The colonel found Wilson 'deeply disappointed at the sudden and unwarranted actions of the German Government' when they had expected that within a month the belligerents would be talking peace: 'I am merely trying all day to think, and not to form any hasty judgement.'[112] Lansing, in contrast, had long expected something similar. He agreed with his officials that America should break off relations, urging that the breach was inevitable and unless America led, it would lose respect as a 'great nation'.[113] Even so, Wilson paused. If it was in America's interest to stay neutral, he would bear the criticism and abuse. He believed the supremacy of 'white civilization' depended on America's remaining intact to rebuild the belligerents: 'he was willing to go to any lengths rather than have the nation actually involved in the conflict'.[114] He had told House that the United States alone among the 'great white nations' remained at peace, and it would be a 'crime against civilization' to go in.[115] Although Germany was 'a madman that should be curbed',[116] it would be 'a crime for our Government to involve itself in the war to such an extent as to make it impossible to save Europe afterwards'. His instinct was to stay aloof, and he consulted with an unusually open mind.[117] On 2 February he met with a group of senators and with his Cabinet. The senators were all Democrats (supposedly the Congressional pages could find no Republicans), and although Senators Stone and Lewis wanted to wait until Germany sank American ships, the others (all of whom had previously supported neutrality) believed the United States should break relations at once and their constituents would support it.[118] The Cabinet outcome was similar. Wilson admitted feeling unable to trust his own or anyone's judgement, and 'abhorrence' at joining either side.[119] If it was better to do nothing and preserve the white man's position against the yellow, he would shrug off accusations of weakness and cowardice.[120] Lansing suspected none the less that Wilson was following his wont by playing devil's advocate, and not unwilling to be pushed. And a push he received, only two Cabinet members wanting to delay.[121] McAdoo led those who favoured acting now, supported by Houston (Agriculture), who felt no concern about the Yellow Peril.[122] Although Daniels agreed that 'we are the trustees of the civilization of our race', he and Baker both favoured breaking off relations. As was also his usual practice, Wilson closed the meeting without giving his view, but on the following morning he told Lansing he would break off relations, and address Congress at 2.00 p.m.[123]

What motivated him? In addressing Congress he invoked the *Sussex* correspondence. Now Berlin had violated its assurances, no alternative to breaking relations was compatible with honour and dignity. Yet America desired no conflict and had no selfish ends, desiring merely the right to liberty, justice, and an unmolested life.[124] He refused to believe that Germany would do what it had said, and only 'actual overt acts' would convince him, though if they happened he would ask Congress to authorize necessary steps. He left the option for the Germans to retract, though also for further escalation. In fact House's and Lansing's notes suggest Wilson had agreed in principle on the first day to break off relations, but he wanted to test out the objections. Wilson was concerned with Japanese expansion, and in early 1917 the navy's General Board was reviewing its War Plan 'Orange' for conflict against Tokyo,[125] but the president subordinated such anxieties. He winced when House insinuated that America was letting others fight its battles, but insisted he was determined to keep out if possible.[126] He had listened to but seemed less convinced by Lansing's case that peace and civilization depended on spreading democratic institutions, which necessitated breaking Prussian militarism's hold on Germany.[127] He was more receptive to the argument that firmness would earn influence at the peace conference, and his ambitions to refashion international politics eased his path. Thus he produced for Lansing a sketch of the 'Bases of Peace', setting out the principles of a mutual guarantee of independence and integrity and protection against economic warfare, and of limiting armaments to what was needed to enforce these arrangements. No permanent international institutions would be needed at first, however, and he avoided greater detail so as to give no handle to his critics.[128] But in the first instance he was defending America's neutral rights and national honour and interest, and if the Germans had confined their targets to *belligerent* vessels he might have stood aside.[129] On this basis he obtained support in Congress, including

from Republicans,[130] and senators voted 78:5 in favour of his speech, while
the press, too, was outraged, and its backing almost unanimous.[131]

Wilson still hoped to avoid war. Perhaps with 1914 in mind, he took care
to supply no pretext or provocation. The War Department ensured its
priority access to the cable and telephone systems and liaised with the
railways, but Baker prohibited any troop movements that suggested 'we are
mobilizing', as this 'might be gravely misconstrued'.[132] The CGS, Hugh
Scott, confirmed the army was doing nothing that might be misinterpreted
as mobilization.[133] Similarly, the Navy's General Board took precautions to
protect the fleet in the Chesapeake, and reviewed its War Plan 'Black' against
Germany, but it avoided warship movements,[134] and Admiral Benson (the
Chief of Naval Staff) refrained from mobilizing.[135]

During February the United States therefore lingered in a curious limbo.
Bernstorff had been sent packing, and although the Germans remained
willing for conversations they refused to suspend unrestricted warfare,
which Wilson made a precondition.[136] On the other hand he left it open
for Berlin to back down, and although Austria–Hungary participated in
the submarine campaign, he maintained relations with Vienna.[137] Indeed
the Austro–Hungarian Foreign Minister Ottokar Count Czernin told the
Americans that his country was fighting for Peace without Victory, and
pressed for the Allies to abandon the objective—stated in their 10 January
note—of dismembering the Dual Monarchy.[138] Wilson was willing to explore
this opening, informing the British that if given assurances to Austria–
Hungary he could end the war on Peace without Victory lines. Lloyd
George replied that peace with Austria–Hungary was against the Allies'
interest, because it might mean losing Italy, and Austria–Hungary was a
liability to Germany. But after consulting his Cabinet he confirmed that
Britain would consider a peace proposal. Czernin, however, demanded
guarantees that Austria–Hungary would remain intact, and in any case
envisaged only a general and not a separate settlement.[139] By the end of
February the negotiating road was barred, not only with Germany but also
with its ally.

The State Department tried to rally the other neutrals into breaking off
relations,[140] but the response was slight; and when China expressed interest
the Americans discouraged it, fearing further Japanese encroachment on
the country.[141] Similarly Wilson took only tentative steps towards rapprochement with the Allies, and the latter too were wary. Lloyd George
sent a message that he wanted America in, but less for military assistance than

for help at the peace conference.[142] The French sent to Washington the philosopher Henri Bergson, who found Wilson suspicious of both sides and over-optimistic about the German people overthrowing their regime, but although America was headed for war the president would not decide for it until he was sure the country was united. The best policy was restraint and letting the situation develop.[143] Until March 1917, in fact, the French desired American benevolent neutrality rather than intervention.[144] The British ambassador Spring Rice was similarly low-key, reporting that although the newspapers were beginning to shift, the public remained far from a pro-war consensus.[145] And although in February the British floated an issue of $250 million worth of Treasury bills, the interest rate (6 per cent) was high and it would not help for long.[146]

Even so, America was inching towards armed neutrality. The Council of National Defense, established in 1916 to encourage government–business cooperation, agreed to consult industry chiefs on the essential steps in the event of war, specifying that the guideline should be what was necessary to supply an army of one million men and provide munitions for ninety days of active service.[147] The General Staff's War College Division (its planning arm) laid down that for the first year of a war against the Central Powers the entire regular army would be needed to train the recruits: 'It should, therefore, be our policy during this year to devote all of our energies to raising sufficient numbers to exert a substantial influence in a later stage of the war and during the necessary period of organization and training we should refrain from using any of our troops in "active operations".'[148] Similarly, Scott saw war against Germany as a 'providential' chance to ready a force, 'and if we never fire a shot in Europe it will strengthen the country in the view of Japan and other predatory nations'.[149] The army prepared intellectually rather than taking concrete steps, and saw no urgency to help the Allies. Although the president's advisers undertook no systematic assessment of the military balance, they too misunderstood how beleaguered the latter were.[150] McAdoo believed 'Germany's economic condition is getting worse every day, although we get very little accurate information.'[151] Scott suggested that 'It will take a year at least for us to get any kind of force to the other side, and we hope that by that time the war will be so nearly over that we will not have to kill off all our people to enter it.'[152] House told Wilson the struggle was in its final phase, and if unrestricted submarine warfare and the Allies' spring offensives failed, both sides would be willing to negotiate: no more lives would be lost if America entered than if it stayed neutral, while the chances of a 'wholesome' settlement would enormously increase. If America showed a united front and Britain could minimize the submarines' impact, Germany would soon go to pieces, leading to 'a general collapse'.[153] The advice to Wilson was that the war was nearing its end, the Allies would win, and the USA could husband its strength for a leading contribution at the finish.

On one count action was more urgent. After the submarine announcement, American ship-owners kept their freighters in port, and in New York most shipping halted.[154] Three-fifths of American exports went to Western Europe, and practically all were now at risk; the New York stock exchange tumbled, as did wheat and cotton prices, while shipping insurance rates rose 25–33 per cent.[155] Coastal as well as transatlantic trade was interrupted, as were food and fuel supplies to eastern cities,[156] the more so as America's railroads were suffering extreme congestion.[157] On 20 February women protesting over price rises led hunger riots in New York,[158] while Wilson's Cabinet agonized over what to do. On 6 February it agreed to tell ship-owners they could arm their vessels, but it became clear they would only sail if given government assistance.[159] On 13 February McAdoo urged that ships be armed, provided with gun crews, and preferably put in convoy.[160] But Wilson believed such action might lead to war, and needed Congress's approval; he did not wish to force the legislature's hand, and he believed the public still favoured caution. The 19 February meeting remained indecisive, most of the Cabinet feeling humiliated, but still awaiting overt acts.[161] On 23 February McAdoo pressed again for action, if necessary without Congress, Houston warning that if Germany took Britain's fleet and colonies Berlin would become 'mistress of the world'.[162] The meeting became animated, Wilson accusing the hawks of leading the country into a war it was unwilling to risk.[163]

By this point, however, Houston felt the president was again playing devil's advocate, and the administration sensed that Congress was turning.[164] The next day Wilson sent McAdoo a draft Congressional resolution empowering the government to provide 'defensive' armament and ammunition for merchant ships: he would seek $100 million for this purpose and for war risks insurance. Thus on 26 February he asked Congress not only to request credit and authority for arming merchant ships but also to take other steps. Although they were defending the rights of humanity, his stress was still on protecting American commerce and lives. For that purpose armed neutrality might now be needed, although clear-cut 'overt acts' were still absent, and he did not wish to use force or contemplate war.[165] Although two US merchant vessels had gone down, neither loss seemed unambiguously due to unrestricted submarine warfare. None the less, by late February American freighters were sailing towards the war zone,[166] which meant 'overt acts' were just a matter of time, and Wilson acknowledged that only luck had so far prevented them. He was reconciled, in other words, to measures that were virtually certain to lead to shooting war, and primarily in defence of US citizens and commercial interests. What remained unclear was how far public opinion would support him, how extensive America's participation would be, and how far it would concert with the Allies.

During the following month the answers crystallized, and in the first instance due to the Zimmermann Telegram. Its origins are inseparable from the continuing revolutionary upheaval in Mexico, in which Wilson had already twice intervened. American forces had landed at Veracruz in 1914, and the casualties had preyed on his memory, while for months during 1916 US troops had pursued Pancho Villa across the north of the country. Germany, conversely, assisted the Constitutionalist movement of President Venustiano Carranza.[167] Zimmermann had been involved in this effort and his expertise in subversion was one reason he became foreign minister. However, the idea of a Mexican alliance came from a junior Foreign Ministry official, Hans Arthur von Kemnitz.[168] That of linking an approach to Mexico with one to Japan also had a lineage, extending back to German–Japanese contacts in Stockholm during 1916. Zimmermann and Bethmann approved the scheme with little discussion, and Ludendorff also endorsed it. It testified to the Germans' cynicism, as they were quite unable to give Mexico serious help and an air of the absurd hung over the enterprise. Regardless, in its finalized form on 13 January the telegram instructed the German envoy in Mexico City, Heinrich von Eckardt, to propose an alliance to Mexico as soon as American entry into the war was considered imminent; to offer financial support and German acquiescence in Mexico's acquiring territory lost to the United States in Texas, New Mexico, and Arizona in 1848; and to suggest that Carranza invite Japan to join the combination.[169] The telegram went to Bernstorff to forward to Eckardt, which he did on 19 January. As the British had cut the Germans' transatlantic cables it could be sent only because the United States—ironically in the interests of facilitating peace negotiations—had permitted Germany to use American diplomatic wires. But as the British were intercepting the communications of the American embassy in London, the message came to

Room 40, the decrypting and decipherment unit of the Naval Intelligence Division in the Old Admiralty Building in Whitehall. Initially the proposal was presented as a contingency plan, to be pursued if America entered the war, but in a follow-up message on 5 February Zimmermann authorized Eckardt to consult the Mexicans as soon as he thought appropriate. A partially decoded version of the initial telegram went to Admiral Sir Reginald Hall, the Director of Naval Intelligence, as early as 17 January, but Hall delayed before forwarding the information to the Foreign Office, for fear the Americans learned that Britain was reading their traffic. It was Hall's idea that Balfour should give the decoded text on 23 February to the American ambassador, Walter Hines Page, by which stage the British had obtained a further copy in Mexico City and Balfour could obscure the real source with the half-truth that it had been 'bought in Mexico'.[170]

What matters here is less the telegram's provenance than its consequences. Page reported it on 24 February. It showed that even when the Germans had seemed open to American mediation they had already decided for unrestricted submarine warfare and were plotting an anti-American alliance.[171] Wilson once more masked his emotion, writing 'These are days when none of us can feel absolutely certain of a correct judgement because there are so many things to stir passion and so many things to distress the mind and throw it off its right balance.'[172] But he said to House the telegram was 'astounding', and told a delegation of peace activists that if they had the information he possessed they would not ask him for further peaceful dealings with the Germans.[173] He seems never to have doubted the text's authenticity, thanking Balfour for information 'of such inestimable value' and 'so marked an act of friendliness'.[174] Though he felt 'much indignation' and wanted to publish at once, he delayed until 1 March and after a few anxious days Zimmermann acknowledged the telegram was genuine.

None the less, State Department inquiries elicited that Mexico had not, in fact, received an alliance offer,[175] and obtained a Japanese assurance that the scheme was 'absurd'.[176] The telegram did not presage an imminent threat, though it rekindled Wilson's anger over German bad faith. It also encouraged better relations with the Allies. Wilson told French Ambassador Jules Jusserand that by 'Peace without Victory' he meant a 'scientific peace' that entailed no more Alsace-Lorraines, which Jusserand interpreted as being favourable.[177] On 6 March Wilson approved a message from House to Wiseman that although Ireland was an obstacle and there existed no mass pro-Allied feeling, the administration had understood the causes of the war

and was sympathetic. 'There is a feeling among the Americans that if they
tolerate too much they will lose their prestige and authority as a world
power', and they would probably intervene 'to uphold America's rights and
her dignity as a nation'.[178] House told Spring Rice that Wilson planned an
appeal on the necessity of 'putting an end to methods of Prussian military
clique, which are a return to the Stone Age'. Spring Rice responded that
the first priority was to reverse the effects of the Federal Reserve Board
declaration,[179] but this was already in hand. Page had alerted Wilson and
Lansing on 5 March to 'an almost immediate danger' of the dollar shortage
compelling the Allies to minimize their American orders. Only by becoming a belligerent could the US government lend direct to them: 'Perhaps
our going to war is the only way in which our present preeminent trade
position can be maintained and a panic averted.'[180] Wilson, Lansing, and
McAdoo discussed Page's message, and after McAdoo spoke to the FRB the
latter announced it had no objection to foreign loans and that gold reserves
had so expanded that US banks could safely invest abroad.[181] This step
reversed the November warning, and although only American war entry
could more permanently alleviate the Allies' financial predicament, McAdoo
was preparing for that eventuality also.[182]

In other respects the telegram's impact was more limited. Wilson had
already decided to arm merchant ships, although he published Zimmermann's
message in part to bring round Congress.[183] The House of Representatives
passed the armed ships bill by 403:14 on the day the telegram hit the
newsstands.[184] In the Senate, however, although a large majority would
have been willing to approve, a filibuster by its opponents talked out the
bill until the Congressional session expired.[185] Opposition came from a
curious combination of anti-capitalist and anti-militarist isolationists from
the Midwest and South with east-coast Republicans who thought Wilson
too mild. However, the president deemed he could act even without
Congressional endorsement. On 9 March he approved a set of rules of
engagement prepared by Daniels, though these were still defensive. Armed
US merchantmen were neither to seek out submarines (indeed they
should avoid them) or take aggressive action, but could open fire if within
the war zone a U-boat approached within 4,000 yards.[186] Daniels felt this
might prove 'the death warrant for young Americans' and bring the
United States into the war.[187] But on 4 March the breathing space allowed
by Germany for neutral ships expired, and they too were now subject to
unrestricted attacks.

Zimmermann's telegram mattered less than developments on the high seas. It swayed the Senate less than it did the House of Representatives, and the filibusterers received hundreds of supporting letters from their constituents, even if Wilson and most newspapers condemned them.[188] For the first time, indeed, significant portions of the press now advocated war.[189] But Spring Rice reported that the 'vast majority' of Americans still wanted peace,[190] and the uproar proved a flash in the pan. By mid March coverage had almost disappeared, and in April few newspapers highlighted it as a reason for intervention.[191] It was true that thanks to the telegram Wilson for the first time could reckon on a significant minority for war entry, not least in western and south-western states that had thought themselves remote from the conflict; but isolationism and pacifism remained vigorous and, although opinion had become divided, American belligerency had no overwhelming support. The president's personal intervention would be crucial.

Between 7 and 20 March, Wilson worked towards a solitary decision. He consulted neither House nor his Cabinet, and papers piled high on his desk.[192] In the outside world, Nicholas II abdicated and Bethmann prepared a 'New Orientation' for constitutional liberalization in Germany.[193] Berlin made no effort, however, to avert a confrontation: on the contrary, Wilhelm agreed with Holtzendorff that it was impossible to call off the submarines, and Bethmann told the Reichstag that if America declared war Germany would not be responsible.[194] While armed American merchantmen set sail,[195] on 18 March the press reported the sinking of three American vessels, one of them, the *Vigilancia*, losing fifteen of its crew after being torpedoed without warning.[196] Polk, the State Department Counsellor, was sure the sinking of another US ship, the *Algonquin*, constituted an 'overt act': and for part of the press America was in a state of war already.[197] On 19 March the navy decided to recruit 27,000 more personnel and build 260 'submarine chasers'.[198] Yet on the same day Wilson told Daniels that he still hoped to avoid declaring war.[199] He had a difficult conversation with Lansing, who said war was inevitable and America should declare it, as Germany would not do so and the public was becoming restive; but the president was unconvinced the latest incidents justified hostilities.[200] Shelving personal jealousies, Lansing urged House to write to Wilson, which the colonel did, saying America should not raise a big army but instead become 'a huge reservoir to supply the Allies with the things they most need', and that de facto 'we are already in the war, and that if we will indicate our purpose to throw all our resources against Germany, it is bound to break their morale and the Washington Departments were preparing as fast as they could, while Admiral William Sims left for London on a secret naval liaison mission.[207] The administration raised its target for the land forces from 1 to 1.5 million,[208] aiming first to reinforce the regular army, then the National Guard, and then recruit up to 500,000 volunteers.[209] It belatedly resolved to ask Congress for conscription, but this was to head off the political threat of ex-President Theodore Roosevelt leading a volunteer force to France, as well as to ensure that military recruitment did not absorb skilled workers needed at home. Wilson was concerned that in Britain voluntary recruitment had generated poisonous propaganda, and conscription was a means of regulating the war effort.[210] Meanwhile, shipping losses continued, the oil tanker *Healdton* going down on 21 March, again without warning, and with twenty-one dead.[211] Even so, again little is known of Wilson's thinking while he prepared his war message, although he did confer with House on 27 March. They agreed the message would differentiate between the German people and their rulers, though not appeal directly for revolution.[212] The president feared—unfairly—that the Cabinet would have 'picked to pieces' his text,[213] though he did ask them about public opinion, which they believed would support a declaration of hostilities.[214] Fortified by this assurance (although to House appearing nervous), he went before Congress on Monday 2 April.

The war message was one of Wilson's finest rhetorical achievements, delivered in an expectant silence to a packed and sombre legislature.[215] It reviewed the history of the submarine controversy and insisted Germany had violated the laws of war; and whereas property seizures could be compensated, loss of life could not. It was common prudence to seek out the U-boats as soon as detected, and armed neutrality gave neither the rights nor the effectiveness of belligerent status. America would not, therefore, choose the path of submission (and at this point the audience burst into applause), and he asked his listeners to deem Germany's actions as amounting to war against the United States, which should become a belligerent and use all its resources to bring Berlin to terms. His stress was on Germany's *actions*, and he followed House and Lansing in framing the issue as democracy against autocracy, self-government being at the heart of a future League. America had no quarrel with the German people, but Germany's leaders had launched a long-planned enterprise of aggression (a charge the president had previously withheld), broken bargains, conducted spying and sabotage, and fathered the Zimmermann Telegram. Defeating them and making the world safe for democracy was not just in conformity with American interests but was also to champion the rights of mankind, and encouraging the Russian Revolution would constitute an additional benefit. Hence he underlined the consistency of purpose with his Peace without Victory speech and with his earlier addresses. And although the means selected now might seem more forceful, they remained limited. America would lend to the Allies, supply as much as possible, mobilize its economy, and build up its navy; but conscript only half a million men. While cooperating with the Allies, it would retain its diplomatic independence.

The press and both political parties received the speech warmly.[216] Yet Congress was short of unanimous. In the Senate eighty-two voted to enter the war and six against; in the House the figures were 373:50. House speakers concentrated on U-boats and American economic interests; only a minority referred to the League and few envisaged a big expeditionary force. The opposition came primarily on ethical grounds from Republican Midwestern Progressives and Bryanite Southern Democrats,[217] foreshadowing an isolationist bloc that would survive for two decades. Anti-war feeling was ideological rather than pro-German.[218] The British Foreign Office was still briefed that the mass of the population knew little about the war, and the Mid- and Far West cared little.[219] Still, the majorities were convincing, and supported by most religious and ethnic community leaders, as well as by business and by labour unions.[220] The president had not achieved a complete consensus, but he had obtained a wide one.

Wilson had insisted that it was neither ethical nor practical to intervene without the widest possible support. Appearing pushed into hostilities suited this purpose.[221] Yet he slapped down suggestions that he should merely track opinion: 'I do not care for popular demand. I want to do right, whether popular or not.'[222] After the Zimmermann Telegram a portion of the press—and Republican east-coast rallies—advocated intervention, but the president was disdainful of New York,[223] and anti-war rallies provided balance.[224] Many Congressmen suppressed their doubts about declaring war because the president gave a lead, and he could probably have taken them in either direction, although it was becoming more divisive to stay out than to go in.[225] Wilson's idealism (and his modest assessment of the US contribution) helped less hawkish legislators and the public to support him, as well as reflecting his personal views.

Fundamentally, as House put it, 'I feel that he had taken a gamble that there would be no war and he had lost.'[226] Since the *Lusitania* crisis Wilson had sought a middle ground of neither acquiescing in unrestricted submarine warfare nor using force. Once the Germans violated the *Sussex* pledge and especially once they sank American ships he had to choose. He had tried to escape from this dilemma through his peace initiatives and hoped that Germany would not follow through, but unlike previously Berlin showed no disposition to meet halfway. Yet American national security faced no immediate danger: on the contrary, Wilson's advisers' military assessment, such as it was, predicted that the Allies would win. The Russian Revolution was interpreted as pro-Allied and patriotic and Allied weakness understated, and although it was reported that French civilians were very war weary, it was also said that America's breach of relations raised French troops' morale.[227] Nor does it seem that American economic interests weighed particularly heavily. William Durant, the head of General Motors, hoped Wilson would keep America out.[228] Except in Page's 5 March telegram, such considerations rarely figured in Wilson's circle, though he was well aware of the war trade boom and believed he must promote American prosperity.[229] Yet as late as November 1916 he and the FRB were trying to rein the boom in, and they changed tack for non-economic reasons. Finally Wilson's war message assumed America had a case in international law, and the State Department experts apparently agreed, although probably over-estimating its strength.[230] None the less, fundamental for the president was his obligation to protect American lives and commerce; and by stages he engaged his country's prestige and Great Power status. He moved closer to the Allies in early 1917 while remaining suspicious, telling his Cabinet that both sides' methods were 'abhorrent'.[231] Even so, the diplomacy during the winter suggested the obstacles to cooperating with the Allies were less than those between America and the Central Powers.

Although a pro-intervention consensus was forming by spring 1917 it was shallow, especially beyond the east coast. Wilson's declared intention to fight a limited war therefore mattered. The United States would cooperate with the Allies but keep its distance; and it is striking how little discussion occurred between Washington and Paris and London. America would give economic aid, on credit. US naval assistance would be vital, but America was poorly prepared for a land effort. Its regular army was small and dispersed,[232] and it lacked modern heavy equipment,[233] military intelligence, and experienced commanders and staffs.[234] None the less, Wilson hoped, this contribution would buttress the German democrats and hasten Allied victory, as well as assuring full representation at the peace conference instead

3

Britain Adopts Convoys

With unrestricted submarine warfare Germany took a break-the-bank gamble. Its leaders had not foreseen the Russian Revolution—at any rate not at this time—and had they done so they might have shown more caution.[1] But they had foreseen American intervention, and reconciled themselves by assuming that if Britain were defeated the war was won. Whether American entry offset the impact of the Russian Revolution would depend on whether Britain survived the U-boat onslaught.

British leaders understood the gravity. For Maurice Hankey, the secretary to Lloyd George's War Cabinet, the U-boats were the one thing that gave him sleepless nights.[2] Admiral Sir John Jellicoe, who in November 1916 moved from Grand Fleet commander to First Sea Lord at the Admiralty in order to respond to the challenge,[3] considered it 'the gravest danger which has ever faced the empire'.[4] And for the premier, 'the submarine was the crucial problem on which the issue of the war would depend'.[5] The year 1917 was the one in which the British Empire's relative contribution to the Allied cause was at its greatest, and if Britain had indeed been starved into submission, France and Italy and Russia would have had to follow suit, and America been rendered powerless to intervene.

The British Isles depended on seaborne imports. The Victorians had ended tariff protection and bought food where it was cheapest, and on the eve of war two-thirds of the UK's nutrition by calorific value came from overseas, including all the sugar, three-quarters of the cheese, and two-thirds of the bacon and wheat, as well as two-thirds of the barley, oats, and oil cake fed to its livestock. In 1911, 35 per cent of its wheat imports came from the Black Sea area (Russia, Turkey, and Romania), 30 per cent from Canada and the United States, 14 per cent from India, 13 per cent from South America (principally Argentina), and 8 per cent from Australia and New Zealand.[6] The Board of Trade advised the Cabinet that in peacetime four-fifths of

Britain's wheat, half its iron ore, and almost all its textile raw materials were imported.[7] As Turkey's war entry closed off the Black Sea, Holtzendorff was right that Britain needed long-haul supplies.

Although the British Empire in 1914 had far the world's largest merchant navy, only two-thirds of UK imports were conveyed by British vessels,[8] and Britain's merchantmen had other duties. Arthur Salter, an official who dealt with shipping allocation, estimated that in late 1916 seventy vessels were earmarked for transporting troops; 335 for provisioning overseas forces; 350 brought in raw materials for the munitions and army clothing industries; thirty fuelled and provisioned the navy; 500 supplied Britain's allies, and only 750 remained for the home population.[9] According to the Board of Trade, of a total mercantile tonnage of 14.838 million in October 1917, 3.763 million was servicing the army and navy, 1.626 million Britain's allies, 692,000 the colonies, 1.275 million was permanently committed abroad, and the residual for Britain's own trade was just 6.469 million.[10] Most Red Ensign tonnage supplied coal to France and Italy, or worked for the Admiralty, Ministry of Munitions, and War Office.

Britain therefore struggled to satisfy its food requirements even before the intensified submarine campaign. Moreover, summer 1916 saw cool weather and disappointing wheat harvests across the Northern Hemisphere. The Royal Commission on Wheat Supplies (which the government had made sole purchaser of overseas wheat) bought in Australia, but this source was three times more remote than North America, and few orders there were ever delivered. The wheat imported between November 1916 and March 1917 totalled 2.13 million tons, or 380,000 tons below the agreed target (a shortfall equivalent to three weeks' supply).[11] This shortfall the Royal Commission attributed directly to the shipping shortage, and as a consequence stocks were dangerously low.[12]

Until summer 1916 the impact of German surface raiders, mines, and submarines had been shocking but small. This was just as well, as British shipbuilding slumped in output as its workers volunteered for the forces and the top priority for steel became shell production. But during 1916, U-boats entering service far outnumbered those lost, and the newer boats carried bigger guns and more torpedoes. With greater range and endurance they could patrol far out into the Atlantic. From October 1916, when the submarines started their intensified campaign under cruiser rules, the Admiralty and the Board of Trade warned the government's War Committee that Britain faced an emergency. Unrestricted warfare from 1 February 1917

Table 1. Shipping losses, 1916–17: Gross merchant
shipping tonnage lost

1916	British	World total
August	43,354	162,744
September	104,572	230,460
October	176,248	353,660
November	168,809	311,508
December	182,292	355,139
1917		
January	153,666	368,201
February	313,486	540,006
March	353,478	593,841
April	545,282	881,207
May	353,289	596,629
June	417,925	687,505
July	364,858	557,988
August	329,810	511,730
September	196,212	351,748
October	276,132	458,558
November	173,560	289,212
December	253,087	399,111
Total	3,729,785	6,235,878

From John Terraine, *Business in Great Waters: the U-Boat Wars,*
1916–1945 (1999), p. 766.

raised losses even higher. Not only Germany and Russia but also Britain
confronted a supply crisis (see Table 1).

Anti-submarine warfare was in its infancy. The defensive arming of
merchant ships—or DAMS—worried Holtzendorff but progressed slowly,
mainly due to a shortage of guns.[13] The minefield laid across the Straits of
Dover hindered but did not prevent the submarines' passage.[14] Nor were
efforts to mine the Helgoland Bight successful, because German mine-
sweepers quickly cleared the fields and British mines were ineffective.[15]
Jellicoe expected a better 'horned' mine (copied from its German counterpart) to be widely available only from June 1917.[16] Efforts to bombard the
U-boats' Flanders sea exits at Zeebrugge and Ostend did little damage, and
their bases on the German coast were still less accessible, being protected
both by minefields and by shore batteries with longer ranges than the Royal
Navy's guns.[17] Similarly, Q-ships, or decoy ships (merchantmen whose cannon remained concealed until U-boats drew alongside) had successes against

surfaced submarines but could do little if the U-boats fired their torpedoes while submerged, and during 1917 they were withdrawn.

However, the key anti-submarine vessel was the destroyer, which was faster than a surfaced U-boat and whose shallow draught made it difficult to torpedo. In July 1917 Britain had 212 modern and seventy-six older destroyers, though only the former were suitable for anti-submarine patrolling. But even though the German High Seas Fleet no longer put to sea, its continuing presence tied up almost half of Britain's destroyer force.[18] A total of 100 were assigned to the Grand Fleet at Scapa Flow, twenty-four to Harwich, and twenty-five to Dover, but as the Harwich vessels escorted merchant sailings to Holland and those at Dover protected troop ferries, substantial numbers could be stationed in the Western Approaches only by immobilizing part of the Grand Fleet, which as 1917 went on was in practice what happened.[19] But more fundamental was the sheer difficulty of locating and destroying U-boats. The hydrophone, developed to detect the sound from submerged submarines, remained experimental, and whereas submarines could spot destroyers from up to 15 miles, destroyers could sight a U-boat periscope from at most 4 miles.[20] Typically a patrol vessel could take eight hours to reach the vicinity of a sighting, by when the submarine might be 100 miles away.[21] Similarly, although depth charges were introduced in 1916, for another year destroyers typically carried only two of them. Until well into 1917 the crews simply rolled the charges over the side, as they lacked throwers to catapult them away from the ship.[22] Thus during one week in September 1916 three U-boats operating in the Channel sank between them over thirty merchant ships, despite being hunted by forty-nine destroyers, forty-eight torpedo boats, and 468 auxiliary vessels.[23] By February 1917 two-thirds of the destroyers were engaged in anti-submarine warfare, and in June the Grand Fleet devoted nine days to a massive submarine-hunting exercise round northern Scotland. Yet although it sighted U-boats sixty-one times and attacked twelve times, none were destroyed or even damaged.[24]

Given Jellicoe's other priorities—including the Mediterranean and hospital ships, which the unrestricted campaign made targets—in the seas west and south-west of Ireland in spring 1917 the destroyers never exceeded fifteen and at times numbered four or five. Whereas the Allied naval authorities reckoned that a destroyer could cover 1 square mile of ocean, the Queenstown flotilla had to cover 25,000. Although between northern Ireland and Brest only between eight and ten U-boats were normally operational, and at most fifteen,[25] their destructiveness was disproportionate, and this in good measure because of the system the British had devised. Troopships and the fleet enjoyed destroyer escorts but the Admiralty resisted them for merchant shipping, claiming dispersal was the best protection,[26] combined with patrolling to seek out predators. This combination succeeded against German cruisers in 1914, and was adequate against small numbers of short-range submarines in 1915; but in 1916–17 it was arguably counter-productive. The Admiralty ran an 'approach route' scheme of 'patrolled lanes', whereby incoming vessels from the South or North Atlantic funnelled through four cones that converged on Falmouth (via the Scillies), Berehaven (via the Fastnet Rock), Inistrahull (via Tory Island), and Kirkwall.[27] Before entering the cones merchantmen received directions, but as most lacked wireless it took up to fourteen days to alter the recommended route for departing vessels, while the patrols were distributed so thinly that they had negligible chances of detecting U-boats and may actually have alerted them to the course the unescorted steamers pursued.[28]

Even the restricted U-boat campaign from October 1916 raised freight rates and rang alarm bells for Asquith's coalition government.[29] Jellicoe saw a 'serious danger' that by summer 1917 shipping losses would compel an unfavourable peace. Previously successful methods were less effective, and new solutions urgent.[30] Asquith communicated this message to the War Committee,[31] while the Admiralty warned 'we must be content for the present with palliatives', and Walter Runciman, the president of the Board of Trade, predicted 'a complete breakdown in shipping would come before June 1917'.[32]

Although the government was surprised by the speed with which the threat developed, it had not been asleep at the wheel. It had centralized wheat procurement for Britain and its allies, and by late 1916 state purchases accounted for more than three-quarters of the calorific value of Britain's food imports.[33] In addition, the authorities had requisitioned most of Britain's tramp steamers, although not yet its cargo liners.[34] None the less, when in December the Lloyd George government took office, shipping and food supply were among the issues on which it acted most forcefully.

Lloyd George brought in two sets of administrative innovations. The first was the War Cabinet, a five-man executive, most of its members without departmental responsibilities, which met in almost continuous session. Besides the premier it included Alfred Lord Milner, George Nathaniel Curzon, and the Chancellor of the Exchequer, Andrew Bonar Law, as well as the Labour leader, Arthur Henderson. The Foreign Secretary, Arthur

Balfour, was a frequent attender. Its composition was mainly Unionist in sympathy, although the coalition had parliamentary support from about half the Liberals (the other half remaining loyal to Asquith), and most of Labour, as well as of the Unionists. It would be assisted by a new Cabinet secretariat under Hankey, who was not only an organizer and minute-taker but also had Lloyd George's ear and took the initiative in proposing policy changes. In fact the War Cabinet functioned poorly at first, and Hankey became frustrated when it drifted off its agenda.[35] Still, it had the authority to set priorities and insist on changes, and increasingly it got a grip.[36] Lloyd George's second innovation was creating new ministries, modelled on the 1915 Ministry of Munitions, which brought in technicians and businessmen alongside officials under the leadership of non-parliamentarians. The latter included Sir Joseph Maclay, a Glasgow shipowner who headed the new Ministry of Shipping, a man who knew his brief and whom the premier respected. Maclay became a critic of the Admiralty, and functioned along-side Hankey as an alternative source of advice. At the Admiralty itself, however, Sir Edward Carson became First Lord and, although an independent and strong-minded Unionist who played a key role in Lloyd George's replacement of Asquith, Carson chose not to second-guess his advisers, Jellicoe being pre-eminent among them. As First Sea Lord, Jellicoe issued orders on the distribution, movements, and operations of the navy's warships. He imported officers from the Grand Fleet, most notably Rear Admiral Sir Alexander Duff, who headed a new Anti-Submarine Division, tasked by Jellicoe with finding 'new <u>methods</u> of dealing with them [the U-boats] <u>offensively</u> and also defensively'.[37] Duff, Jellicoe, Hankey, and Lloyd George would be the central protagonists in convoying's introduction.

Although convoying was the most conspicuous element in Britain's response to the crisis, on its own it would not have sufficed. But character-istic of the Lloyd George government was its openness to multiple solu-tions. It soon concluded that the war would last through 1917 and into 1918,[38] which meant medium-term measures would have time to take effect. One such measure was import restriction, which a subcommittee under Curzon kept under review.[39] Another was raising home food produc-tion. Lloyd George investigated rushing in extra food, but was advised that neither surplus cereals nor tonnage were available.[40] The Food Controller, Lord Devonport, opposed rationing but appealed for voluntary cuts in con-sumption: an approach that scored some success. To provide more shipping, a similarly composite approach was taken. The government exempted shipbuilders and marine engineers from military service,[41] while to release shipbuilding steel the Ministry of Munitions was asked to cut artillery and shell production, and the Admiralty to suspend work on three battle-cruisers and five cruisers.[42] Whereas in 1915–16 the priorities had been to support the Grand Fleet against the High Seas Fleet and equip the BEF, now the Admiralty needed smaller vessels, while shell and gun production for the army reached a plateau. Additionally Maclay ordered merchant vessels in Canada, Japan, and the United States, although after entering the war the American government took over the latter. More immediately, existing tonnage needed to be deployed more efficiently, for which the prerequisite was state control over the rest of the merchant fleet. Although shipping charges had risen dramatically and caused an outcry against company profits, the government accepted Maclay's recommendation against nationalizing the liner fleets. They were, however, requisitioned at state-regulated rates, enlarging the spare capacity available for most urgent needs.[43]

These dispensations could not staunch the shipping losses. Between February and April over 2 million tons of British, Allied, and neutral shipping

Figure 3. HMHS *Gloucester Castle* sinking after being torpedoed by UB-32, 31 March 1917

were sunk, and another 320,000 tons were damaged.[44] More U-boats were now at sea (between 12 and 15 in January, 23 and 32 in February, 27 and 30 in March, 21 and 28 in April, 18 and 29 in May, 27 and 40 in June, 20 and 31 in July, 25 and 34 in August, 29 and 45 in September, and 31 and 38 in October), and their tactics altered.[45] Whereas between October 1916 and January 1917 most losses occurred in the Channel and the Irish Sea, now they were concentrated on the South-Western Approaches to Ireland, sometimes over 200 miles from land.[46] The heaviest toll came among inbound vessels (therefore laden with cargo), including oil tankers, and whereas before January most sinkings were by surface gunfire, by April two-thirds were by torpedo.[47] If the crews escaped their foundering vessel, they faced days in winter seas in open boats. When the *Alnwick Castle* was torpedoed on 19 March (already bearing survivors from another wreck), 139 people took to the lifeboats 300 miles from land. When the captain's boat was picked up four days later only twenty-four of the 139 remained. During the Napoleonic Wars both sides had regularly rescued their opponents from drowning, even—as at Trafalgar— risking their own lives in the process. But a strand of calculated cruelty had always run through U-boat warfare and now it intensified. It sought to terrorize crews and owners as much as to sink ships. When the *Torrington* was torpedoed its master was taken prisoner, but twenty of his men were forced to stand on the U-boat's deck while it submerged, abandoning them to drown, and when the *Cairndhu* went down the submarine rammed a life- boat. Whereas in February 355 seafarers lost their lives, in April 997 died.[48] Remarkably, no British ship failed to put to sea due to inability to find a crew, and volunteers came forward even after being repeatedly 'submarined'. But from October 1916 departures were delayed when U-boat activity was reported, and every postponement diminished the rate at which cargoes were landed. And although the British and Allied steamers still put to sea, Holtzendorff's additional target was the neutrals. In February Norwegian arrivals in Britain halved, while other neutral traffic almost halted. In February and March together neutral arrivals in British ports totalled only a quarter of those a year before.[49]

The government therefore faced an emergency. Although the War Cabinet was kept informed through February and March, it reacted tardily. But in the second half of April losses peaked, forcing the issue to the Cabinet's attention while confidence between Cabinet and Admiralty broke down. In these circumstances the Cabinet resolved to give convoy a trial. Only the Admiralty—and Jellicoe in particular—could give the orders, and its motives for doing so have long been disputed, especially how far the change of heart was due to Cabinet intervention. That intervention seems to have hastened a decision that was coming anyway, but that even so was implemented slowly and whose immediate—as opposed to longer-term—significance has been overestimated.

Convoy had been used as early as the sixteenth century, and routinely in the Napoleonic Wars. It was absent from the Admiralty's pre-war planning, which focused on surface rather than submarine raiders. The initial approach of scattering merchant traffic while the navy hunted the predators betrayed a certain offensive bias: that the warships, rather than escorting, should seek out the enemy.[50] When Jellicoe warned the Asquith government about shipping losses, he still focused on new attack methods rather than convoying.[51] Yet convoy had had its advocates since early in the conflict, and as losses mounted they spoke more loudly. Once the Admiralty was challenged, it set out objections that it would maintain into 1917. They seemed solid enough. When Vice-Admiral Reginald Tupper proposed a trial in the Channel, arguing that a compact mass of merchant ships would be less vulnerable, his superiors said no escorts were available. Admiral Sir Richard Webb, the Director of the Admiralty Trade Division, advised that merchant ships were more numerous and headed for more varied destinations than in Napoleonic times, and convoying would actually reduce carrying capacity: gathering the steamers would cause delay, and unloading would be slower because they arrived en masse.[52] When Lloyd George and Bonar Law raised the issue in the Asquith government's War Committee, Jellicoe said the merchantmen would straggle and convoys offer too big a target, while Runciman said they would waste tonnage and congest the ports.[53] The objections were partly technical (the freighters would not 'keep station' and would be more exposed, especially as too few escorts were available) and partly logistical (convoying meant that ships could no longer sail at their own speed and be unloaded singly). At a time when Britain's docks and railways were overstretched, cargo might be handled less efficiently and shipping shortages exacerbated. The Board of Trade and many shipowners agreed with the Admiralty that convoy was 'inadvisable except as a last resort'.[54]

Neither the change of government nor the unrestricted submarine campaign immediately altered matters. In contrast to the Board of Trade, Maclay and his Shipping Ministry were more supportive. They quizzed the Admiralty about why convoying could not be implemented. It replied that it already protected freighters by patrolling, through the recommended routes, and through Defensive Arming of Merchant Ships. Whether to do more remained 'continuously under consideration'.[55] A week into the unrestricted campaign, however, Hankey noted that 'The submarine warfare has become frantic...Everyone rather disturbed about submarine losses.'[56] He drafted for the premier a memorandum setting out the convoy case, which formed the basis of a 13 February breakfast meeting (one of Lloyd George's characteristic means of doing business) between Hankey, Lloyd George, Carson, Jellicoe, and Duff.[57] Although Hankey had previously accepted the Admiralty's arguments, he now felt it was time for 'a system of scientifically organized convoys', to which all available escorts would be committed. The fall in imports would ease pressure on the harbours; and merchant ships were inactive already when held in port by U-boat sightings. Merchant ships could be trained to keep station, and attacking a protected convoy would be more difficult than sinking isolated vessels.[58] Although on all of these points Hankey (by background a Royal Marine and self-confessed amateur) would prove correct, he reviewed the arguments in principle rather than the operational practicalities, and was unclear about where the escorts would come from. He also felt intimidated in addressing officers of such seniority. At the breakfast meeting the Admiralty representatives insisted that a convoy must travel at the speed of the slowest ship; that if a U-boat located one member it would sink many; that merchant ships could not keep station and fog would cause chaos; and there were too few escorts.[59] Hence the discussion was inconclusive, and its principal follow-up a further meeting on 23 February, this time between Jellicoe, Duff, Webb, and ten merchant steamer masters. Jellicoe convened it hastily, and its attendees were later criticized as representing coastal rather than ocean-going traffic, while Lloyd George suspected they were liner masters who disdained tramp steamers. Whatever the reason, they were unanimous that merchant ships could not keep station in close convoy columns. Especially at night, maintaining formation and zig-zagging to present the U-boats with a more elusive target would be 'quite out of the question...The Masters...would prefer to sail alone rather than in company or under a convoy.' Jellicoe told the US Navy representative, Sims, that 'the merchantmen themselves are the chief obstacle to the convoy'.[60]

During March the War Cabinet's attention turned to the forthcoming Western Front offensive. Hankey could not redirect Lloyd George towards the U-boats, which the premier viewed less apocalyptically than did the Cabinet secretary.[61] The patrolled approaches system continued. None the less, a series of developments undermined the Admiralty's opposition. The first was running convoys towards Holland, France, and Scandinavia; the second was American intervention; and the third was the dreadful losses during April, which precipitated a civilian challenge that proved to be pushing on an open door, in part because the Admiralty had reassessed its escort requirements.

The first regular escorted convoys for merchant ships were the 'Beef trips' to the Netherlands. Beginning in July 1916, the Dutch convoys were protected by destroyers from Harwich, and losses were low. They were linked to the 'Agricultural Agreement' whereby Britain supplied Holland while the latter restricted exports to Germany,[62] but they set less of a precedent than did the French coal convoys. By 1916 nearly half of France's seaborne imports were coming in British or British-chartered ships.[63] In peacetime two-thirds of its coal needs were imported, mainly from Belgium and Germany (which were no longer accessible) and from Britain. British coal supplies were essential both for war production and for civilian needs.[64] Yet the autumn 1916 U-boat offensive sank many Channel colliers and by December neutral ships leaving British ports for France had fallen by nearly two-thirds, while reported submarine activity led to 30–40 per cent of vessels being refused permission to leave harbour.[65] The French sent a naval officer, Commandant Vandier, who urged that convoy was coming and the Admiralty should trial it with the coal trade.[66] Even so, by the time convoys were introduced in February coal deliveries had fallen from 2 million tons per month to 1.2 million, and the French premier, Aristide Briand, warned that arms factories were closing down and France faced 'an extremely grave crisis'.[67] The new system (which the Admiralty dubbed 'controlled sailings') consisted of intensified patrolling and night crossings by groups of vessels accompanied by armed trawlers, following routes that could be altered rapidly. Although this innovation again reduced losses, Duff felt the circumstances differed from those of ocean convoys, even if some of his subordinates disagreed.[68]

For Scandinavian shipping the Admiralty made an exception because of the significance of Scandinavian supplies and of keeping neutral shipping at sea.[69] Here, too, it began in February with 'protected sailings', from Lerwick to Bergen. But at 25 per cent, losses still proved high.[70] According to the coal adviser to the British Legations, over half of Norway's shipping was 'engaged in trades that are vital to us', including nitrates, carbide, timber, and iron and steel, and unless it was protected convincingly 'I foresee the whole fabric which is based upon our use of Norwegian shipping needlessly collapsing, with disastrous consequences.'[71] Hence a naval conference at Longhope in the Orkneys on 4 April recommended using 'the convoy system... in preference to the scheme of continuous stream of traffic', and with prodigious levels of protection: between twenty-three and twenty-eight destroyers and submarines and fifty to seventy trawlers for convoys whose average size would be fourteen.[72] In approving, Duff noted that 'the convoy system is one on which very different opinions are held',[73] but until German surface raiders attacked the Scandinavian convoys in the autumn the new arrangements drastically reduced losses, though they meant seconding destroyers from the Grand Fleet and could not be extended more generally. Indeed, Duff and Jellicoe contended that if a partial system left the remaining shipping routes unguarded it might be worse than no escorting at all.[74]

A second new factor was American entry. Duff in retrospect placed weight on convoys now being able to assemble and to rendezvous with their escorts in American ports, whereas previously for the United States to have tolerated such activity would have bordered on being un-neutral, while forming up on the high seas was impracticable.[75] More important, however, was that the Americans could lend destroyers, even though the American naval authorities were as suspicious of convoying as were the British. It was fortunate that Sims was an Anglophile who got on well with Jellicoe. 'I hope to get a good deal out of USA', Jellicoe told Admiral Sir David Beatty, his successor as Grand Fleet commander.[76] Sims found the situation far worse than Washington had supposed and that the Admiralty had no answer to it, telling Daniels that the U-boat issue was 'the real crisis of the war'.[77] He obtained the urgent dispatch to Ireland of six destroyers, though these were still for patrolling rather than as convoy escorts. American entry facilitated change rather than precipitating it.

The further facilitating element was a reworking of the statistics. The submarine crisis was largely invisible to the British public. The tables published by the Admiralty suggested losses were small in relation to the 4,000–5,000 vessels entering and leaving the ports each week.[78] They also suggested it was out of the question to provide a comprehensive escort. Actually the tables were partly for reassurance, and the Admiralty's internal calculations may have established by January that the number of ocean-going steamers (exceeding 1,600 gross tons) engaged on long-haul voyages was much lower.[79] None the less, the Admiralty's retrospective technical history admitted the scale of the task had been overestimated, as Duff later acknowledged to Lloyd George.[80] Although the Admiralty repeatedly invoked the escort shortage, it appears not until January 1917 to have tried to calculate what was needed.[81] A leading role was played by Commander Reginald Henderson, who had responsibility under Duff for the French coal sailings. The work brought him into contact with Norman Leslie in the Shipping Ministry, and the two established that the ocean-going vessels entering and leaving Britain's ports weekly numbered 120–140.[82] Additionally Henderson belonged to a group of younger officers who were feeding Hankey and Lloyd George with a pro-convoy viewpoint at variance with that of their superiors, a viewpoint that Beatty also voiced to the premier.[83] Jellicoe became aware of Henderson's involvement only after the war.[84] He viewed such conduct with distaste, and criticized Lloyd George for by-passing established channels;[85] whereas Lloyd George felt that practical experience had saved Henderson from 'hardening of the professional arteries'. The premier's habit of a lifetime had been to seek out and interrogate the best-informed on particular questions, and as the man now ultimately responsible for naval matters, of which he lacked previous knowledge, he continued doing so.[86]

The climax came in April, when the Admiralty decided on a trial for ocean convoy at the moment when the Cabinet lost patience. The common concern was the shipping losses, which during the 'black fortnight' in the second half of the month became completely unsustainable. As before, the action centred on the Western Approaches, far out to sea, and on torpedo attacks delivered without warning. The U-boats may have grown more ruthless because American entry meant Germany had less to lose.[87] From 24 to 29 April between seven and nine merchant ships were lost each day, and over the month Britain lost 120 ocean-going vessels.[88] Between February and April the net tonnage reduction at an annualized rate was 23 per cent, and the chance of a ship being lost on its outward or return voyage reached one in four.[89] The Shipping Ministry kept ministers briefed,[90] and Jellicoe warned of 'the most serious results' if such trends continued beyond a few days. Britain must rush in food supplies, for 'until means can be found and provided for a more extended attack on submerged enemy submarines, the only palliative exists in the provision of a sufficient number of small craft to keep them submerged and so cramp their activities'.[91] His focus continued to be intensified patrolling until such time as more effective anti-submarine offensive weapons became available, and in a further paper backed by the entire Board of Admiralty he became almost insubordinate: 'the Admiralty can no longer accept responsibility for conducting the war on its present basis . . . our present policy is headed straight for disaster' either through starvation in Britain or through the non-delivery of coal and other essentials to its allies. Although Jellicoe agreed to release warships for protecting 'convoys . . . bringing essentials in the way of food and munitions, we should be very hard pressed to it unless the United States help us to the utmost of their ability'. Hence he called for saving shipping by withdrawing British forces from Salonika, for a crash programme of food imports, and for ruthlessly eliminating all non-essential import requirements.[92]

Indeed April was a month of crisis not only for shipping losses but also for food stocks, which dwindled to the lowest level of the war. Sir John Field Beale, the first secretary to the Food Ministry, warned on 12 April that wheat reserves were down to 5.491 million quarter hundredweights or nine weeks' consumption and, if they fell below eight weeks, 'local famines' might occur. Argentina had banned wheat exports, India also had railway difficulties, congestion on the US railroads had lowered shipments, and Paris had 'grave shortages'.[93] According to Devonport, wheat shipments since November had fallen 15 per cent below target and should now be an absolute priority for available tonnage, while the Royal Commission on Wheat Supplies warned that Britain would run out of oats (essential for its horses) in four weeks.[94]

The Cabinet faced, therefore, interconnected crises in shipping, food, and supplies to Britain's allies. A visit to France enabled Hankey to work on Lloyd George, who by 22 April 'at last seemed to have grasped the danger of the submarine question'.[95] When the Cabinet discussed it on the following day, however, Jellicoe still resisted convoy, saying it remained under consideration.[96] He had little regard for the War Cabinet, and sat mute through its discussions, writing to Sir Frederick Hamilton during the 25 April meeting that 'There are no destroyers at all to carry it [convoy] on the Western Approaches; but some day I may be able to carry it out, and the arrangements for doing so are being prepared.'[97] The Cabinet's exasperation coloured Hankey's minutes: 'Ministers felt that they had not been sufficiently informed about the submarine menace, and there was not enough co-ordination in these matters.' They agreed that while Milner chaired a committee to reconsider shipping priorities, in order to accumulate food stocks, Lloyd George would visit the Admiralty to investigate its anti-submarine warfare methods. According to Lloyd George's memoirs, he had decided on 'peremptory action'.[98]

On the following day, however, 26 April, Duff submitted a memorandum proposing a trial with ocean-going convoys that one day later Jellicoe approved.[99] The Admiralty was at least now willing to experiment. Duff set out the kernel of the scheme eventually adopted for regular Atlantic convoys, including realistic estimates of the merchantmen needing escort and of the accompanying warships: destroyers in the danger zone around the British Isles and other vessels (such as cruisers) for the passage across the ocean.[100] Duff accepted that a scheme was needed because of the large and sudden increase in losses and the imperative of safeguarding food supply. The balance of risks had altered. He also noted the successful experiment with French coal convoys and that American entry had alleviated some of the difficulties. Writing afterwards to Jellicoe, he highlighted the shipping losses as the reason for his memorandum and 'the assured prospect of additional naval forces becoming available as the organisation developed'. None the less, had it not been for the surge in sinkings 'the risk would not in my opinion have been justified until the measures in course of development had been brought into use'. Jellicoe concurred: afterwards he remembered Duff telling him that even a disaster to a trial convoy could not be worse than the losses now being sustained.[101] Duff's memorandum was too elaborate to have been prepared as an overnight response to Lloyd George's pending visit, and it seems the Admiralty was already reconsidering. But there is no doubt that the political pressure—coming not just from the premier but also from the War Cabinet collectively—imposed an urgency still lacking in Jellicoe's letter to Hamilton of 25 April. In a private letter Duff acknowledged that 'the [convoy] system is regarded by the Cabinet as our salvation, and we are being forced into giving it a <u>partial trial</u>'.[102]

Hence the April crisis would end in civilian–naval rapprochement. Already in the Cabinet on 26 April Jellicoe conceded that 'the intention of the Admiralty was to introduce a system whereby groups of merchant ships would be convoyed by a cruiser across the Atlantic, if the necessary cruisers could be provided, and as they entered the submarine danger zone (whether outward or homeward bound), they would be escorted by destroyers when the required number became available'—although at present none were, unless the USA sent extra.[103] And when Lloyd George descended on the Admiralty on the 30th and met its principal officials, the tone was constructive, Hankey recording that the day passed 'very pleasantly' and the premier played with Jellicoe's young daughters.[104] None the less, Lloyd George spelled out that the Admiralty's organization was unsatisfactory and statistical recording must improve, as must liaison with the Shipping Ministry. He found Duff willing to experiment, because of the prospect of additional American escorts, because the existing system was not giving protection, because even a 'great disaster' to a convoy would not be worse, and because 'as a result of investigations in concert with a representative of the Shipping Controller, he finds that the number of ships for which convoy will have to be supplied is more manageable than he had thought'.[105] Although Duff left no diary of his thinking, his note of 26 April and his statements to Lloyd George broadly corroborate.[106]

The decision reached was only for a trial. On 30 April the Admiralty warned it would take time, and Lloyd George did not hide his impatience. Even if convoys were adopted and losses staunched, he prophesied, 'the position a year hence is likely to be very grave'.[107] Duff and Jellicoe maintained their doubts about station-keeping and their fears of a massacre, and still needed to find the escorts.[108] The British were fortunate that in May the sinkings diminished, although they remained far higher than prior to unrestricted warfare and the respite was largely due to Germany relaxing its effort.[109] In June the losses increased once more. Although the War Cabinet turned back to the Western Front, the shipping crisis was little alleviated and the Admiralty response still slow. The first experimental convoy (inbound from Gibraltar) sailed on 10 May: the station keeping was satisfactory, it sighted no U-boats, and suffered no losses: two weeks later a second sailed from Hampton Roads. This time two ships fell behind and one was sunk, but four more convoys left Hampton Roads during June, with no losses. The Admiralty set up a Convoy Committee, which drew up a detailed Atlantic scheme by 6 June, and Duff, Jellicoe, and Carson approved it.[110] The decision to convoy inbound North Atlantic traffic had now been taken. The trials had shown that merchant captains could keep station and not collide at night, and the system was workable. Even so, its introduction was incremental. Lloyd George believed the Admiralty was dragging its feet,[111] but once convoys promised minimal losses without unacceptable delays, the shipowners moved in favour. This became evident from a devastating analysis by Sir Norman Hill (the secretary of the Liverpool Shipowners' Association) that went to the Cabinet on 21 June. At this stage the system of approach cones was still operating, and Hill damned the losses in the Fastnet zone as 'appalling'. They proved 'either that the Admiralty theory is unsound in principle, or that in practice the force employed has been entirely inadequate to secure protection'.[112] Hill protested of the Admiralty 'that by forcing us to concentrate in areas which are admittedly inadequately protected, the lives of our men, our ships, and the essential supplies of the country have been and are being thrown away'.[113] Similarly Maclay advised that whereas the pre-war monthly weight of imports had been 4.9 million tons, in the first five months of 1917 it had averaged 2.9 million, and on present trends would reach the 'irreducible minimum' early in 1918.[114] On 26 June Duff wrote that the Cabinet 'count on convoy as the only salvation to a very critical position, and great pressure will be brought to extend the system at once'.[115] Fortunately a parallel reconsideration was proceeding in Washington, after Sims urged on Daniels that convoy was essential and the trials' success helped overcome professional scepticism. By August the Americans had seconded thirty-seven destroyers, or almost half their total, while the Royal Navy's sloops increased to ninety-one in July and 170 by December.[116] Bit by bit, the escort shortage was alleviated.

Although Duff still felt convoy's benefits had been oversold,[117] and Jellicoe agonized over where to find destroyers, Jellicoe came to recognize 'the vital importance of the complete introduction of the convoy system'.[118] By 21 July the Shipping Ministry felt 'considerable progress has been made in arranging for the protection of merchant steamers bound for this country by convoy'.[119] Down to October, the convoy round-trip loss rate was 1.23 per cent, or about one twentieth of that during the April 'Black Fortnight', and by the autumn sinkings were reducing sharply and Lloyd George and the Cabinet more reassured.[120] In the longer term, convoying was vital for husbanding the tonnage needed for American forces and equipment to be delivered to Europe. As a converted Duff acknowledged in retrospect, 'The institution of a general system of mercantile convoy is commonly regarded as the turning point in the submarine campaign and the salvation of the country.'[121] And yet its slow and piecemeal implementation renders it insufficient as an explanation of Britain's survival. It succeeded only in conjunction with the wider measures that the Asquith government had initiated and which Lloyd George's followed through.

Not all these measures worked at first. The government acted too late to raise farm output much in 1917, and although merchant shipbuilding recovered to pre-war levels, it remained below replacement rate. Neutral merchant shipping availability permanently diminished, although a secret agreement with the Norwegian shipowners kept half of Norway's merchant navy in Allied service in return for Britain delivering coal and other essentials.[122] But as the available tonnage dwindled, of critical importance were steps to boost the 'carrying power' of what remained. The Cabinet cut back bulky imports such as timber, more of which was felled at home or (for trench warfare) in France. To alleviate port congestion, a battalion of transport workers was deployed to the points of greatest need. Probably most significant was concentrating the merchant navy on the shortest supply routes, principally from North America, at the expense of those to Australasia and East Asia. Leo Chiozza Money in the Shipping Ministry worked out the principle, which the War Cabinet approved,[123] and already between January and May 1917 although ship numbers entering British ports fell by 10 per cent the weight of cargo showed a 4 per cent increase.[124] However, as the Shipping Ministry put it, 'the concentration of shipping on the short North Atlantic route is primarily a method of getting more work out of a given amount of shipping. But since the time spent in the danger zone is correspondingly increased, this method would also use the ships up more quickly unless the Admiralty were enabled (by the fact of concentration) to render that route appreciably safer than other routes. This really is the crux of the problem.'[125] In the longer term, route concentration would save tonnage and sustain the Allies until replacement building revived, but in the short term it made stemming the losses more essential than ever, which was what convoying accomplished.

Two further measures helped Britain through. One was food shipments. In April–May food stocks reached danger levels, and the authorities were anxious about Ireland and East London.[126] In May, the biggest labour unrest of the war spread through the engineering industry, and Devonport proposed bread rationing, but Lloyd George ruled against it and the government agreed instead, despite Treasury opposition, to subsidize the bread price. It could do so partly because cereal stocks recovered from less than seven weeks' supply in early May to thirteen by 1 August, which in turn reflected a Cabinet decision to divert tonnage to North American food deliveries.[127] The Royal Commission on Wheat Supplies recorded 'very satisfactory arrivals' during May and June, and wheat and flour imports in summer 1917 exceeded those in summer 1916.[128] By July the Shipping Ministry reported a 'striking increase' generally in imports landed and a 'great increase in shipping on the North Atlantic route'. Britain's 1917 imports were predicted to be not much lower than had been expected prior to unrestricted submarine warfare, which underlines that the crucial variable was neither the number of U-boats being sunk nor even the toll of merchant vessels but rather the quantity of goods entering Allied ports.

It was the wider steps taken to maintain supply that enabled British leaders by the autumn to feel more confident.[129]

A final area of concern was oil. Whereas the Victorian navy had burned coal and Germany's largely did so still, Britain's most modern battleships were oil-fired, as were its destroyers. The biggest pre-war oil producers were America and Russia, and in wartime conditions neither Russian nor Romanian oil was available. Oil, unlike coal, was found neither in the British Isles nor in most of the empire, nor in Britain's pre-1917 allies. Hence here too the North Atlantic corridor was crucial; but tankers' design made them conspicuous targets, and they took a long time to replace. By 1 June the Admiralty was down to three months' supply.[130] Beatty advised Jellicoe that 'I am taking steps to minimize the consumption of oil fuel', ordering the navy to steam at three-fifths speed.[131] Once again, emergency American shipments were needed to raise stocks, while freighters were converted to carry oil in the 'double bottoms' of their ballast tanks.[132] By August, the Admiralty's anxiety had eased.[133]

Even though the U-boat numbers at sea rose during the spring and reached their wartime peak in the autumn, the sinking rates per submarine diminished.[134] Whereas in the spring the Admiralty feared it had no answer to the U-boats, by the autumn the submarines had no answer to the convoys, which were both hard to locate and dangerous to attack. A U-boat first sighted an Atlantic convoy only in mid July.[135] The inward-bound convoys proved so successful that the U-boats turned against the outward-bound vessels, often empty and therefore less attractive, but from August these too were escorted, as was shipping from the South Atlantic. The submarines then shifted again, towards the Mediterranean and to British coastal waters, but from the winter these also received convoy protection, while coastal vessels were generally smaller and closer to safety, which alleviated the strain on the crews. At each stage the prey became less valuable. From summer 1917 American destroyers were assisting and the Admiralty found more escorts by reducing its patrols, while the destroyers were more likely to carry depth charges and depth charge throwers, and the Royal Navy at last deployed an efficient mine. Hence the numbers of U-boats lost increased, and their crews were tiring, as a campaign promised to last for five months of supreme effort now dragged out longer, and Allied captures found the prisoners increasingly demoralized. After the submarines switched in February to more ruthless tactics and to sinking usually by torpedoes, they became less innovative. In contrast the Allied merchant seamen—all civilian volunteers, and many not even from the UK—continued signing up for further voyages, so that one thing never worrying the Allies was whether the freighters would be crewed.

Winston Churchill wrote in 1931 (in a *Daily Telegraph* article that infuriated Duff and Jellicoe) that over convoy the 'politicians were right, and admirals wrong', the amateurs with searching minds had prevailed over the professionals, and 'no story of the Great War is more remarkable or full of guidance'. He contrasted British experience with the German civilians' capitulation to their admirals, backed by the OHL.[136] By implication, here was an object lesson in the superiority of liberal over autocratic governance. There is something in the case, even if the Germans in January and the British in April took different kinds of decision. Unrestricted submarine warfare, by bringing in the USA, had irrevocable consequences far beyond the war at sea, and was an offensive rather than a defensive gesture. But if the submarine campaign now seems a desperate gamble, at the time adopting convoy looked riskier than it does in retrospect. Even a convoy supporter such as Sims noted that its proponents lacked knowledge of the technical difficulties.[137] Sims—a thoughtful observer—contrasted Lloyd George, forever cheerful, always laughing and joking, with Jellicoe, the diligent, seemingly unemotional professional who never raised his voice.[138] The two protagonists were equally conscious of their differences. Jellicoe disparaged the premier as 'impressionable' and a 'hopeless optimist', who got figures from any source and dashed off at tangents;[139] Lloyd George and Hankey regarded Jellicoe as defeatist and pessimist, the prime minister's memoirs pouring scorn on a 'palsied and muddle-headed' Admiralty: 'In an emergency the able but unimaginative expert is a public danger.'[140] Jellicoe's memoirs, as befitted the man, showed more restraint, but his bored irritation in War Cabinet sessions betrayed his feelings. Because he had the power to give orders, and to that extent would bear responsibility if convoying led to massacre on the high seas, and given the transformation of seamanship since the Napoleonic Wars, the Admiralty rightly viewed convoy not as restoring an old system but as creating a new one. The French and Scandinavian convoys helped break down their resistance, as did American entry, but Duff yielded primarily to 'Black Fortnight', which discredited the existing dispositions and made the War Cabinet insistent. Even so, convoy was adopted as a trial, and only gradually accepted. Despite the Admiralty's understandable reluctance to jump prematurely, many of its objections proved unfounded, and by delaying it acquiesced in continuing forfeiture of ships and lives. By remaining wedded to patrolling it diverted potential convoy escorts, and it overestimated the number of escorts needed.[141] This was a different kind of responsibility from that of the Western Front generals, though the admirals shared with them a bias in favour of seeking the initiative and of taking the war to the enemy. Hence they tarried, while the politicians hesitated to force the issue. When the losses started falling, and Whitehall could breathe more easily, it was still unclear why and even whether the corner had been turned, and many—from Lloyd George downwards—still feared the turn had come too late. None the less, Britain's survival was critical in the prolongation and transformation of the conflict, from which so many of the other epoch-making events of 1917 would follow. When the new First Lord of the Admiralty, Sir Eric Geddes, told the Commons in November that after three years of fighting the country must still prepare for 'a long war', the containment of the U-boats made that sobering eventuality at least possible to contemplate.[142]

PART
II

Continental Impasse

4

Tsar Nicholas Abdicates

1917's Atlantic prologue had set a time bomb ticking under the course of the war. Germany's leaders gambled on starving Britain before America intervened in force. Britain's convoy decision made it likely that this gamble would fail. By now, however, a second time bomb had been planted, in the shape of Russia's February Revolution, an insurrection in the Russian capital, Petrograd, that culminated in Tsar Nicholas II's abdication.[1] But whereas much of the popular movement was—if not overtly pacifist—directed against the burdens of the war, the parliamentarians and commanders who pressed the tsar to go did so in part because they considered him an obstacle to victory. They hoped the Allies' spring offensives would enable Russia to emerge triumphant before undertaking internal reform. Whether the February Revolution would be a pro-war movement (like the Bourbons' overthrow in 1792, to use the French analogies so current in 1917), or an anti-war one remained contested for months. Most of the Russian army remained at the front, attempted a summer offensive, and continued holding down the Central Powers' forces. Only after the second Russian Revolution, the Bolshevik seizure of power in November, did a government emerge in Petrograd that would accept any terms available. From here on the question became whether the Central Powers could close down the Eastern Front before the Americans transformed the balance in the west, and the answer would be partially, but not enough.

The February Revolution grew out of a subsistence crisis. The first of the 'February Days', Thursday 23 February (8 March by the Gregorian calendar used in most other countries), was International Women's Day. None of Petrograd's revolutionary parties had planned a major effort to mark it. Regardless, women workers in the textile factories of the city's Vyborg district held illegal meetings and marched through the streets demanding bread. They reached the adjoining metal factories, where male workers decided—it seems quickly and unanimously—to join them.[2] Once the men, supported by the revolutionary parties' factory committees, joined in, the slogans became more political. But the spark came from the women. Since 1914 they had grown as a proportion of the city's labour force from 25.7 to 33.3 per cent.[3] Many were supporting families without their husbands, working ten-hour days before queuing—often fruitlessly—in the cold and dark outside the bakeries.[4] Since 1915 subsistence riots had spread from central Russia, in which army wives featured prominently, the more so when subsidies for dependants were unpaid.[5] The Okhrana (the secret police) warned in October 1916 that Russia stood on the break of revolution, and on 22 February/7 March a policeman in the Vyborg district reported that 'almost all the police officers hear every day complaints that they [the workers] have not eaten bread for two, three days or more. Therefore it is easy to expect major disturbances.'[6]

General Sergei Khabalov, the commander of the Petrograd Military District, tried reassurance. He proclaimed that flour deliveries and baking were proceeding as before, so any shortages were due to hoarding.[7] Although this flew in the face of working-class experience, it was true that the problem was less of production than of distribution.[8] In the non-occupied provinces of European Russia grain production rose from 4,304 million poods (1 pood = 16.38 kg) in 1914 to 4,659 million in 1915 before falling to 3,916 million in 1916 and 3,800 million in 1917.[9] The decline was serious, especially as army demand rose from 85 million poods in 1913–14 to 600 million in 1915–16 before falling to 485 million in 1916–17, although a collapse in exports from 640 million poods in 1913–14 to fewer than 3 million in 1916–17 offset it. By 1917 Russia's farms had lost a tenth of their horses to the army, and equipment and fertilizer supplies had deteriorated, though the horse shortage was manageable and Russia used less fertilizer than did Western Europe. The key problem was the fall in the marketed portion of the harvest from 1,700 million poods in 1914 to 794 million in 1916, of which more than half went to the army and less than 300 million to Russia's cities.[10] A two-thirds reduction in hired labourers hit particularly the gentry estates that accounted for 12 per cent of total grain production and 22 per cent of the marketable surplus. For the dominant feature of Russian agriculture was peasant family farms, many of whose menfolk were with the colours while women—alongside men too old, too young, or too infirm to serve—replaced them. As inflation took a grip, villages relapsed into self-sufficiency.

Before 1914 Russia had run a comfortable budget surplus, but it had greater difficulty financing the war than did any Western European belligerent, which its build-up before the 1916 Brusilov offensive exacerbated. In 1914 income per head averaged $44, compared with $146 in Germany, $185 in France, and $243 in Britain:[11] Russia's poverty limited both taxing and borrowing capacity, the more so as the state deprived itself of a principal revenue source by banning sales of alcohol. Russia's wartime deficit totalled 30 billion roubles, of which half was covered by domestic and foreign borrowing and half by issuing paper currency. More than elsewhere, the government paid by increasing the supply of printed money available. By January 1917 prices had almost quadrupled,[12] as resources shifted towards the war effort at civilians' expense. The process resulted in fewer consumer goods for which peasants might be willing to sell their grain, and depreciated the currency they received for doing so. Given the inflexibility of army demand, the cities bore the shortfall.

The government's response was ineffectual. At first it foresaw no special difficulty, given the scale of Russia's grain exports, but it underestimated both the army's needs and the strain on transport. Ministry of Agriculture commissioners purchased for the armed forces, while civilian consumers fended for themselves. In 1915–16 the authorities tried to fix prices first for military grain and then more generally, but setting a price for supplies to the flour mills caused months of wrangling, the producers opposing ceilings on their income while their costs remained uncontrolled. Farmers hesitated to market grain when the return was so uncertain, and in summer 1916 the market was paralysed. In September prices were set and a new and energetic agriculture minister, Aleksandr Rittikh, came to office. He increased purchases for soldiers and defence workers, but left still less for other civilians. Reports that the government was introducing rationing spurred panic buying in the capital, and on the first day of the disturbances Rittikh indeed authorized rationing, but too late.[13]

It was scarcely feasible to cover the shortfall by importing. From autumn 1914 Russia suffered a 'dual blockade' as Germany barred its Baltic Sea outlet and Turkey closed the Dardanelles. The remaining ports were Vladivostok and those in the Arctic, but Archangel was ice-free only six months in the year and Murmansk lacked a railway to Petrograd.[14] Moreover, from December 1916 the winter overwhelmed the railway system. Russia was more sparsely settled than Western Europe, and its roads were primitive. Nor could its waterways—which in winter mostly froze—serve as arteries like the Rhine. Its railways were indispensable. Yet three-quarters of the lines were single-track, and many locomotives wood-burning. The system was designed to carry coal, grain, and oil from the south and south-east to the central and northern cities, rather than for east–west traffic between the interior and the Front, and after Romania's defeat a longer front line added to the strain.[15] During the war the quantity of rolling stock and length of track increased, but much of the expanded labour force was unskilled, and maintenance suffered: by 1917 one in four locomotives were out of service.[16] Although the railways conveyed 20 per cent more freight in 1916 than in 1914,[17] military goods moved rose from 152 million poods in 1913 to 2,625 million in 1917 whereas civilian goods fell by more than a third.[18] Even so, the worst deterioration came after, not before, the revolution. The problem in February was a temporary disruption due to exceptional cold and snowfall. Snow blocked the tracks while boilers froze, the authorities restricting passengers in order to prioritize freight. Because of the confusion during the summer, grain reserves had fallen: by December to four-fifths less than a year earlier.[19] In that month Petrograd needed 3,740,000 poods of grain and received 524,000; in January it received forty-nine wagonloads a day but needed eighty-nine, while Moscow and the central provinces received less than a third of requirements.[20] As of 14/27 February the Petrograd authorities had enough food only for twenty days, and in the provinces matters were worse.[21] By autumn 1916, Nicholas knew 'the people are beginning to starve', and between December and February basic foodstuff prices rose 25 per cent while many foods became unobtainable.[22]

During January and February the temperature in Petrograd averaged −12.1 centigrade. But during the February days it suddenly grew warmer: +8 degrees.[23] If food shortages ignited the movement, it was never simply a bread riot. As unrest spread from the women protesters to the metal and armaments plants, demonstrators progressed from factory to factory, turning out those who wished to continue working, and denouncing the autocracy and the war. Even compared with the many previous strikes in Petrograd, this one was remarkable for how fast it spread and for its politicized ardour, the insurgents targeting the city centre. When the police blocked the Liteinyi bridge, they crossed the River Neva on the ice. On the first day, according to police estimates, some 78,000 workers from fifty factories took part, mostly in the Vyborg and Petrograd districts. By the second day (24 February/ 10 March) the figures were 158,000 workers from 131 factories; and by the third day over 200,000 workers. By now the movement had reached all parts of Petrograd, was practically general among manufacturing employees, and was widening to embrace students, teachers, and white-collar employees, while public services and transport halted.[24] In places the protesters looted and smashed bakeries; factory yards became mass-meeting spaces, foremen were carted out on wheelbarrows, and the chief executive of the giant Putilov arms plant was murdered.

Petrograd had one of the most militant workforces in Europe. Its central districts, with government buildings, theatres, and restaurants, recalled Vienna or Paris. But round them lay grim factories and tenements, where no lights shone at night, roads were unpaved, and basic sanitation was absent. It was Russia's biggest urban area, its population growing from 1.9 million in December 1910 to 2.3 million in November 1915 and 2.42 million in April 1917. In peacetime it had sucked in country dwellers; in 1915 thousands of refugees joined them. Between 1913 and 1917 the number of factory workers rose from 243,600 to 382,628.[25] This population was young (most factory workers were under 40), bachelors outnumbered husbands, and the majority were literate.[26] In contrast to the Paris of the 1790s, moreover, whose revolutionary epicentre lay among the craftsmen of the inner ring, Petrograd was a city of giant enterprises. In 1917, 70 per cent of factory workers were employed in plants with over 1,000 operatives.[27]

Between 1895 and 1916 an average of a quarter of the factory workforce went on strike each year.[28] The revolutionary upsurge of 1905–6 had marked a first peak, the pre-war period in 1912–14 a second, and in July 1914 barricades had paralysed much of Petrograd. After war broke out unrest subsided, but from September 1915 a third wave of stoppages began. An incident at Kostroma, where the police fired on workers, provided the spark, but summer and autumn 1915 were a time of broader political crisis.[29] Henceforth real wages for most industrial workers deteriorated sharply: by 1916 even those for the skilled metal and chemical employees who were most needed for the war effort lagged behind living costs. Numbers striking returned to 1914 levels, and the motives were increasingly political. Two strikes called for 9/22 January 1917 (to commemorate 'Bloody Sunday' when troops had fired on protesters in 1905) and for 14/27 February (coinciding with the reconvening of the Russian parliament) exemplified the trend.

Even so, organizing the workforce was difficult. The Okhrana had infiltrated the factories. When war broke out civil liberties were suspended and ringleaders arrested. The trade unions, the working-class press, and the socialist and revolutionary political parties all suffered, and were cut off from their exiled comrades. The main revolutionary parties were the Socialist Revolutionaries and the Social Democrats, both socialist but the latter more steeped in Marxism, the SRs being strongest in the countryside and the SDs divided between the Bolsheviks and the more gradualist Mensheviks. Both SRs and SDs, in fact, ranged from uncompromising class hatred to willingness to work with the liberal opposition; but the exiled Bolshevik leader Vladimir Lenin opposed all cooperation with the bourgeois parties. The outbreak of war superimposed further divisions. Lenin's defeatism—that it was better if Germany were victorious and the struggle must be converted into an international civil war between proletariat and bourgeoisie—won few adherents, and some enthusiastically backed the war effort, but the majority position was one of conditional support that rejected annexationism, and the Russian Left was always more guarded in its patriotism than were its British, French, and German counterparts. The ideological fissures between the revolutionaries in exile mattered less among the some 4,000 activists in the factory and district committees who formed the driving force behind the workers' movement in Petrograd.[30] It was the Vyborg factory committees that backed the women protesters, and each evening they and the district committees confirmed plans for the following day. The February Revolution may have been 'spontaneous' at the outset, but it soon became more organized, and the activists saw a chance to stage the long-awaited revolution. Nor does their role of leadership invalidate the evidence that the protests had enormous popular support.

Before a protest movement could become a revolution, it must overcome the forces of order. Responsibility for Petrograd's internal security lay in the first instance with Khabalov, who answered to the war minister, Mikhail Beliaev, although the interior minister, Aleksandr Protopopov, closely followed developments. Neither Khabalov nor Beliaev had command experience, and both had poor relations with General Nikolay Ruszky, the commander of the Northern Front.[31] The contingency plans envisaged that repression initially would lie with the police, who numbered only 3,500 and were much hated, but would refrain from using firearms. In a second stage cavalry (primarily Cossacks) should support the police, who could fire in self-defence, but only in a third phase would the infantry and guards let loose with rifles and machine guns. At this stage the authorities would be turning to the Petrograd garrison, a huge contingent of reserve military units: some 180,000 quartered in the city and another 200,000 in its environs. They seem not to have foreseen that it would mutiny, but that it did proved crucial.[32]

At first Khabalov and Beliaev showed restraint, and Protopopov encouraged them to be non-provocative.[33] But as the demonstrations grew, hostility to the police deepened: some were hurt, some killed, and their stations torched, yet the Cossacks failed to support them, and on 25 February/10 March they assailed them,[34] while members of the garrison refused to fire on the crowds. At this point an evening telegram from the tsar ordered that 'tomorrow the troubles in the capital, inadmissible in time of war, are put an end to'. Khabalov and Beliaev had been slow to brief the high command, where Nicholas was stationed, and he underestimated how difficult the disturbances would be to repress, but it is significant that he cited the war as justification.[35] Interrogated later, Khabalov said he had tried to avoid bloodshed and the telegram had been a 'bludgeon stroke to the head'; but the contingency plans were manifestly failing. That evening Khabalov told the guards commanders that if the next day's crowds were small and peaceful the cavalry could disperse them, but if they were aggressive the troops, having given warning, should fire.[36]

Therefore 26 February/11 March became the 'Bloody Sunday' of the February Revolution, as troops with rifles and machine guns took up position and when the protesters again entered the central districts the soldiers fired in four major incidents and on Znamenskaya Square dozens were killed. Although crowds stayed on the streets, they were more subdued, and both the authorities and the revolutionaries surmised that the government was regaining control. They were mistaken. During the 1905 revolution the government could generally rely on soldiers to shoot protesters, but now it could not. Already on the 26th the men of the Fourth Company of the Pavlovsky Regiment would not open fire and the Preobrazhensky Regiment refused to repress their comrades. Overnight in the city-centre barracks of the Volinsky Regiment a still more serious protest began, led by young NCOs. According to Sergeant Kirpichnikov, 'enough blood has been shed. It is time to die for freedom.' The men resolved no longer to obey orders, and in the morning they fanned out to other barracks, seizing weapons and shooting officers, while advertising their new allegiance by tying red ribbons to their bayonets. They converged with a workers' detachment from the Vyborg district, who brought makeshift weapons. Like the strike before it the mutiny disseminated quickly: from 10,200 participants on the morning of 27 February/12 March to 66,700 by the evening, 127,000 by the evening of 28 February/13 March, and by the afternoon of 1/14 March to almost the entire garrison.[37] The troops had crossed the Rubicon in no uncertain fashion, for if discipline were restored they would face the death penalty. And now the movement crossed over into insurrection, as soldiers and workers seized weapons, opened prisons, and attacked police stations. Although some army officers were killed, most, surprised, did not resist. By the evening of 27 February/12 March the remaining loyal troops were out-numbered and running short of ammunition, while the police melted away and the Council of Ministers, left defenceless, resigned. The government had lost control of its capital.

The war's economic effects had caused the food supply crisis. Its impact on the army lay behind the mutiny. Although Russia had boosted military spending between 1909 and 1914, during the previous decade spending had stagnated. The 1914 army in some ways resembled the British rather than the French or German as, although composed of conscripts (in contrast to the British), it was relatively small and well equipped. The reverse of the coin was that barely a third of each age cohort had done service, so when casualties proved far higher than expected Russia ran out of trained men. Despite its bigger population than France or Germany, it called up similar numbers of conscripts:[38] during the war it mobilized only 5 per cent of its population for active duty, against France's 16 per cent and Germany's 12 per cent.[39] By 1917 14.6 million men had enlisted and over 5.5 million become casualties, 2.4 million of them as prisoners. At least 1 million returned to service after being wounded, and fatalities may have totalled 1.6–1.85 million.[40] In 1914 the government sent to war the standing army and those who had served between 1904 and 1910. Subsequently it called up all the trained men of the 1896–1910 cohorts and many untrained members of the 1914–18 cohorts,[41] but by 1916 it was recruiting men who were not only untrained but also in their forties, with jobs and families, and resistance mounted, leading in Central Asia to open revolt against being enlisted in labour corps.[42] Even so, during the Brusilov offensive and its follow-on attacks Russian casualties may have reached another 2 million, of whom 1 million lost their lives.[43] From the autumn the army was calling up its last reserve, including previously exempted sole breadwinners. Recruiting them led to riots in the villages and to wives mobbing induction points, and to mass protests in Petrograd.[44]

Military censors read the soldiers' letters, whose mood was ugly. By 1916 they betrayed deep hatred of the war and despair about winning it, con-doned fraternization and mass surrender, and were desperate for a speedy peace, the Brusilov offensive exacerbating the discontent.[45] Repeated defeats and superior enemy weaponry had dashed any early confidence, and the authorities were held to have betrayed their men.[46] By the autumn, moreover, the army ate less and poorer-quality food. Daily bread rations were cut by a third or even two-thirds, or replaced by unpalatable lentils.[47] Brusilov complained that on his South-Western Front the miserably inadequate provisions demoralized his troops,[48] and between October and December over twenty mutinies broke out, including refusals to attack or to move up.[49] Troops called out to quell a disturbance at Kremenchug refused to shoot, and the French ambassador learned to his dismay that during a strike in Petrograd soldiers had fired on the police. The authorities no longer placed their most reliable units in the cities, whose garrisons included the middle-aged and convalescents. Since 1916, moreover, strikers had been conscripted. Yet although the Petrograd commanders knew some men held revolutionary views, they had no plans to replace them.[50] Khabalov insisted the garrison was reliable and resisted Protopopov's pressure to move some out, while General Vasily Gurko, the acting CGS in early 1917, refused a request from Nicholas himself to second two cavalry regiments to the capital, which might have dispersed the early protests.[51] Instead the demonstrators confronted rank-and-file troops who only recently had been civilians themselves, and whose officers and NCOs might be equally disaffected. Between 1914 and 1917 the officer corps expanded from 40,590 to 145,916, despite officer losses by January 1917 that totalled 67,847. Some 170,000 men became officers, only 10 per cent of whom by early 1917 were pre-war regulars. Russia had fewer reserve officers than France or Germany, and the bulk of the replacements came from accelerated promotion and a training that for the infantry averaged just four months. Perhaps over 80 per cent had peasant or urban lower-class backgrounds. Even so, many regiments lacked their full officer complement, while NCOs were still less distinguishable in class, education, and training from the men.[52] In short, although the mutiny of the guards reserve regiments caught the authorities unawares, warning signs had been plentiful. And once the mutiny had started and officers had lost their lives, the perpetrators would remain unsafe until they forestalled reprisals by overthrowing the regime.

By the evening of Monday 27 February/11 March the Romanov double-headed eagles were being torn from Petrograd's buildings and tossed into the canals. The crowds and mutinous soldiers knew more clearly what they opposed than what they wanted. The revolution began not as a seizure of power but as a disintegration of authority, creating a void into which others

Figure 4. Royal emblems thrown onto the canal ice after Nicholas II's abdication, Fontanka Canal, Petrograd, March 1917

gingerly stepped. The outcome was a dual power (*dvoyevlastiye*), shared between the Petrograd Soviet and the Provisional Government. The Soviet, or Council of Workers' and Soldiers' Deputies, had an antecedent in the Petrograd Soviet of 1905, which inspired those (primarily Mensheviks) who called for a successor. Discussion began on the third day of the protests,[53] and an appeal went out at 2.00 p.m. on 27 February/11 March, the day the government lost control of the city. Elections proceeded quickly and the Soviet began assembling that evening. It was an unwieldy body, several hundred strong, which occupied the same building (the Tauride Palace) as the lower house of the Russian parliament, the Duma. The Soviet elected an executive committee, which the Mensheviks dominated, but they did not intend to form a government themselves, instead setting conditions for and monitoring whatever government emerged. Their line derived partly from Marxist ideology—Russia was not yet ripe for a socialist revolution and needed an interim phase of bourgeois rule—but also reflected their lack of administrative experience and fear of civil war.[54] It left the field to the Duma liberals, who formed a Temporary Committee to act as an executive. The committee carried little weight with the workers' and soldiers' delegates flooding the Tauride Palace, but it controlled the cable and rail links with the rest of the country, and could communicate with the Stavka (the high command).[55] In succession to the Temporary Committee, from 2/14 March a Provisional Government, eight of whose fourteen members were Duma deputies, emerged. This, too, was primarily a liberal enterprise, and its main concerns were to limit the revolution and maintain the war effort.

The liberals had not desired this outcome. According to one of their leaders, Pavel Milyukov, 'We did not want the revolution. We did not wish particularly that it would come at the time of the war. And we had desperately struggled so that this would not happen.' According to the Okhrana they had dreaded it.[56] Before 1914 the regime had faced two challenges. One was the gulf between the tsarist political institutions and the mass of ordinary Russians and subject nationalities. It characterized not only the cities but also the countryside, where most people still lived. On the eve of the revolution the villages were quiet, but observers noted that deference towards the dynasty was fading.[57] Agriculture was prospering, but hunger for the gentry's land persisted, and the peasant soldiers' disenchantment filtered home. The second and more visible challenge, however, was the schism between the tsarist autocracy and the propertied and educated. Its roots lay in Russia's social and political divergence from Western Europe. Since the 1880s the authorities had faced an underground revolutionary movement, with both liberal and socialist elements. After the 1905 Revolution, when Nicholas had conceded limited civil liberties and an elected lower house of parliament, the liberals had formed into open and legal parties: the Octobrists, the Progressives, and the Kadets. The Octobrists (led by Aleksandr Guchkov) were broadly satisfied with the 1905 concessions; the Kadets (led by Milyukov) wanted something closer to a constitutional monarchy. But they too tempered their ambition for reform with fear of revolution or even anarchy, particularly in the midst of a war.

The tsarist government could not work with a Kadet-dominated chamber, and in 1907 it staged a partial counter-revolution, maintaining the Duma but with a more restricted franchise. Even so, after 1912 relations again neared breakdown. Ministers were hardly ever Duma members, and rather than their being responsible to the legislature the tsar appointed and dismissed them, though they needed Duma endorsement for legislation and for budgets.

In 1914 the government took emergency powers to rule by decree, and the Duma met only occasionally, but during the war's opening months most of its members accepted the curtailment of their powers in the hope of an early victory. To begin with, many educated Russians felt patriotic enthusiasm.[58]

In 1915 the honeymoon ended. From May the Central Powers were advancing into Poland and the Baltic provinces, killing, wounding, or capturing some 2 million Russian soldiers, and uprooting hundreds of thousands of refugees. One response was citizen involvement in delivering weapons, supplies, and medical care via the newly established Union of Zemstvos (district councils), Union of Towns (municipalities), and War Industries Committee (representing business enterprises especially in Moscow). By 1917 these organizations were very substantial employers and producers, with whom the authorities managed to coexist.[59] But a second response was the 'Progressive Bloc', which constituted a Duma majority and demanded a 'government of confidence': not necessarily composed of deputies, but one that the legislature could support. Nicholas rejected this demand, and in September 1915 he took over in person the role of commander-in-chief. Even if in practice the higher direction of the war would fall to the CGS, General Mikhail Alekseyev, the tsar would now be absent for long periods at the Stavka, hundreds of miles from Petrograd, and day-to-day supervision of government business would fall to Empress Alexandra. Not only the Duma but also most of Nicholas's ministers opposed this step, but again he had his way.[60]

The critics' forebodings were borne out. Alexandra expanded her role, and ministers and provincial governors were replaced with disconcerting frequency. Under Boris Stürmer, who in 1916 became premier and then also foreign minister, the government became more reactionary. The liberals and the Allied ambassadors suspected him of seeking reconciliation with Germany, though he denied it.[61] The empress was emotionally dependent on the peasant healer and religious mystic Grigori Rasputin, in part because of faith that he could manage the haemophilia of Prince Aleksei, the heir to the throne. Allegations that 'occult' forces were the government's puppet masters became stock charges not just of the liberals but much more widely, Alekseyev warning Nicholas that all the soldiers' letters were gossiping about Rasputin and the empress.[62] By autumn 1916, after the high hopes raised by Brusilov's offensive had been dashed, the British ambassador, Sir George Buchanan, had never been so depressed. Pro-German influence was growing, the impression gaining ground that continuing the struggle was useless and that Russia (unlike Britain) had nothing to gain from doing so.[63] The liberals displayed a new intransigence, born of desperation, when in the Duma on 1/13 November Milyukov implied Stürmer was guilty not only of incompetence but also of treason (a charge Milyukov knew he could not substantiate).

By now the most arresting development was the autocracy's alienation not only from the liberals but also from conservatives, aristocrats, and other members of the royal family.[64] The most melodramatic evidence was Rasputin's assassination in December by a circle of conspirators that included a Romanov grand duke. The British consul-general in Moscow, Robert Bruce Lockhart, noted how even Nicholas himself was publicly disparaged in a fashion previously inconceivable.[65] The State Council (the upper legislative chamber, half of whose members were appointees) denounced 'hidden irresponsible forces', as did the Petrograd nobility.[66] It was true that in November Nicholas replaced Stürmer (over Alexandra's protests) by Aleksandr Trepov, whose honesty and competence were respected. But by now the lightning conductor for Duma criticism was Protopopov, a former Octobrist who had been appointed minister of the interior, and whom the liberals deemed reactionary and traitorous. Protopopov was indeed considering holding fresh elections or simply suppressing the Duma, and he had met with a German representative in Stockholm in 1916, although he made light of the episode. When Trepov sought to drop Protopopov as the precondition for working with the Duma, Nicholas accepted Trepov's resignation rather than consent, and although the next and last tsarist premier, Prince Nikolai Golitsyn, also wanted to remove Protopopov, Nicholas insisted on keeping him. If anything, Rasputin's death made the government more intransigent.[67] In early 1917 it prorogued the Duma for weeks, replaced the speaker of the State Council, and arrested the workers' representatives on the War Industries Committee (who came from the more moderate wing of the working-class movement). The liberals were so concerned about the gulf between the government and the rest of society that they refrained from protest.[68] Some of them, including the Octobrist leader, Guchkov, were plotting a palace coup to replace Nicholas and Alexandra by more pliable Romanovs. But primarily because they lacked senior military backing, none of these schemes came to fruition.[69] Other liberals, including Milyukov and the Duma speaker, Mikhail Rodzianko, opposed them. None the less, because the idea of forestalling revolution by removing Nicholas was already current, it was easier to stage such a manoeuvre when the crisis came.

A day before the protests began, Nicholas had left his palace at Tsarskoye
Selo for the Stavka, 200 miles distant at Mohilev. Protopopov assured him
that the political situation was under control. Nicholas had not been
intended for the throne, which had been earmarked for his elder brother
who died young. He had been well educated, but his greatest pleasures
came from physical exertions such as shovelling snow, and above all from his
wife and children. In the French ambassador's damning judgement, Nicholas
was devoted to his family but lacked empathy with his people.[70] Public
administration was a burden, which he accepted dutifully. An introverted
melancholic, by 1917 he had laboured under difficult decisions for too long.
He impressed observers by his lack of feeling and his disengagement.[71]
Nicholas was not unremittingly intransigent, but he regretted the 1905
reforms and he had found concessions encouraged more demands. Hence
he often seemed inconsistent, veering between compromise and firmness.
Deeply pious in his way, and a Russian patriot, he felt a responsibility to
uphold the autocratic rights that God had granted him, and bequeath them
to his son. In contrast Alexandra was effusive where her husband was laconic.
She distrusted his ministers, loathed the Duma, and wanted to assert authority
so the people could 'feel the whip'. She dismissed the Petrograd disturbances
as 'a *hooligan* movement'.[72] Nicholas's telegram to Khabalov on 25 February/
9 March shows his instinct too was to repress them as wholly unacceptable in wartime. Yet just two days later, it was evident that Beliaev and
Khabalov had lost control.[73] Even so, when Speaker Rodzianko warned that
'Humiliation and chaos threaten Russia, because the war cannot be conducted victoriously under such conditions', and pleaded once more for a
government enjoying public confidence, the emperor ridiculed the idea. He
disregarded similar pleas from the elected members of the State Council,
from his younger brother Grand Duke Michael, and from the head of the
Allied military mission.[74] Instead Nicholas ordered General Nikolai Ivanov,
who had helped suppress the 1905 revolution, to replace Khabalov and
readied loyal troops to accompany Ivanov to Petrograd, where he would
exercise plenary powers.[75] At the same time Nicholas decided to rejoin
his family at Tsarskoye Selo, where he would again fall under Alexandra's
influence, as well as it being only 15 miles from the epicentre of revolt.

At this point the revolution had spread little beyond Petrograd, and
one possible prognosis was for civil war, reminiscent of the 1871 suppression
of the Paris Commune, as front-line units approached the capital. Actually
the front commanders doubted their men were reliable; but in any case their

loyalty was not tested. Instead Nicholas was eased out of power by the army leaders, whose loyalty was outweighed by their concern for order, in the interests of continuing the war. Nicholas had enjoyed his military service as a young man, he liked watching parades and wearing uniform, and felt more comfortable at the Stavka than with politicians and officials.[76] Alekseyev, who after his illness had resumed his role as CGS, was temperamentally similar to Nicholas, and exerted quiet influence over him.[77] According to Maurice Paléologue, the French ambassador to Russia, Alekseyev was patriotic, energetic, upright, and hardworking, though narrow.[78] It therefore mattered considerably that, possibly due to intervention by the Duma's Temporary Committee, Nicholas's train was diverted while en route to Tsarskoye Selo, ostensibly because insurgents blocked the way.[79] The emperor spent the following days not with Alexandra but with his entourage at Pskov, under the protection of the Northern Front commander, General Ruszky. Like Woodrow Wilson two weeks later, he made his critical decision alone.

Ruszky was the most politically liberal of the front commanders. Although he had steered clear of the plots against Nicholas, he had scant respect for him. Moreover Alekseyev, who remained in communication with Ruszky and with the liberal politicians in the capital, began aligning himself with the latter. Whereas the high command might have been willing to try force against the Petrograd Soviet (especially given the Soviet's indifference to the war effort), once the Duma seemed likely to form a pro-war government it became easier to support a power transition, which should be as smooth as possible.[80] On 1/14 March, the day Nicholas reached Pskov, Alekseyev concluded that for the sake of national unity and victory Nicholas should appoint a government under Rodzianko, around which the country could rally. On the same day the revolution spread to Moscow and to the Baltic fleet at Kronstadt, where the sailors murdered dozens of their officers, rendering imminent the prospect of the movement reaching the front-line troops.[81] In a telegram Alekseyev warned Nicholas about the risks of anarchy, the disintegration of the army, and the impossibility of carrying on the war, whereas a Rodzianko government could still stop the rot: 'the fate of Russia, the honour of our heroic army, the welfare of our people, the whole future of our beloved fatherland demand that the war should be brought to a victorious end at all costs'.[82] Assuming the liberals were taking over, concession rather than repression would better serve the larger purpose of defeating the enemy.[83] And on the same day the Stavka, with Nicholas's consent, suspended Ivanov's expedition.[84]

Two days followed of pressure from the high command. Alekseyev and Ruszky were not openly insubordinate, and did not threaten disobedience. But they were insistent. Alekseyev had independent information about the developments in the capital, and he responded to Rodzianko's prompts on what was needed to contain them. As Rodzianko later admitted, he used the army as a lever to gain a responsible government.[85] In fact the liberals and the Stavka overestimated the chances of regaining control, though it is likely that attempting repression would have spread the revolutionary contagion faster. The demolition of the autocracy went through three phases: Nicholas's agreement to a constitutional monarchy; his abdication in favour of Grand Duke Michael; and Michael's abdication. The first phase was the most diffi-cult. In a heated discussion late on 1 March Ruszky urged the emperor to concede the constitutional monarchy he had always resisted, Nicholas at first maintaining it was a matter of conscience and he was answerable 'before God and Russia'. But after Alekseyev's supporting telegram arrived the tsar gave way, and Ruszky thought that otherwise he would not have prevailed on Nicholas, who reflected ruefully that he had accepted a responsible min-istry because Alekseyev and Ruszky, who could hardly agree on anything, both favoured it.[86] The point is crucial because of the key weight Alekseyev placed on military considerations, and also because once Nicholas had agreed to responsible government he had signed up to a different concep-tion of monarchy, and ruling as a constitutional sovereign was harder for him than to abdicate.

Abdication was the course that almost immediately was urged on him. In the small hours of 2/15 March Ruszky and Rodzianko held a cumbersome conversation via a primitive teleprinter, the Hughes apparatus. Rodzianko said the situation on the streets had worsened (although actually Rodzianko was losing ground in the Duma committee to those who wanted a republic). Nicholas's willingness to appoint a Cabinet responsible to the legislature had come too late. The Duma Committee would form a government committed to victory and supply the army with what it needed, yet 'the hatred towards the dynasty has reached extreme limits, but all the people, all with whom I have spoken when coming out to the crowds and to the troops, have firmly decided to continue the war until its victorious end'. The price of victory now was that Nicholas should step down in Aleksei's favour, with Grand Duke Michael acting as Regent, Nicholas himself having become impossibly divisive.[87] And once again, when the liberals raised their demands the army leadership backed them; and this time more collectively and emphatically.

On Thursday 2/15 March, therefore, the previous day's scenario was replayed, but this time the outcome was abdication. Alekseyev's response to the Ruszky/Rodzianko conversation was that Nicholas must be woken, and he asked to tell Ruszky of 'my deep conviction that there is no choice and that abdication should take place'.[88] He conveyed the same message to his front commanders: 'It is necessary to save the active army from disintegration: to continue the fight against the external enemy to the end; to save the independence of Russia and the fate of the dynasty. It is necessary to put this in the foreground, even at the price of expensive concessions.' He urged them, if they agreed, to petition Nicholas via Ruszky.[89] Alekseyev was now unambiguously intervening in high politics, and setting a line for his subordinates, whose responses were speedy. Vladimir Sakharov, commanding the Romanian Front, was outraged by Rodzianko's 'criminal and shocking' statement, but acknowledged that Nicholas's abdication might be 'the least painful solution for the country and for preserving the possibility of fighting the external foe'.[90] Brusilov, the South-West Front Commander, also supported a speedy abdication to contain the revolution and keep Russia in the war. He considered Nicholas an unfortunate monarch. And Aleksei Evert, the Western Front commander, believed the troops were no longer dependable for repression and a decision was needed to check disorder and keep the forces intact to combat the enemy. Alekseyev forwarded Brusilov's and Evert's view to Nicholas, urging he should step down now for Russia's independence, integrity, and unity, whereas otherwise revolution would spread from Petrograd, Moscow, and Kronstadt, leading to defeat, shame, and disintegration.[91] In fact the Stavka was pushing at an open door. On the morning of 2/15 March Nicholas was morose but inclined to go. He said he was born for unhappiness and had brought unhappiness to his country.[92] After hearing the commanders' responses (which Ruszky and his Chief of Staff, Yuri Danilov, supported), he thought for a few moments and then affirmed that he would abdicate in favour of his son. He wrote in his diary that 'The essence is that in the name of saving Russia and maintaining calm in the army it is necessary to take this step. I agreed.'[93]

The decision was therefore taken before the arrival that evening of two delegates from the Duma Temporary Committee, Vasily Shulgin and Aleksandr Guchkov, the latter of whom had only weeks earlier been plotting Nicholas's overthrow. Guchkov had long believed that for Russia to have a chance of victory Nicholas and Alexandra must step down, and the revolution convinced him that if Nicholas stayed it meant civil war. When they met on the evening of 2/15 March, Guchkov warned of the threat of a social republic; the Petrograd garrison was out of control and the Soviet monitored everything the Duma did; the moderates might be swept aside. Ruszky confirmed no units could be relied on to suppress the revolution. Shulgin, a former monarchist, said the Duma Committee was working in a 'madhouse...We are going to have to begin a decisive battle with leftist elements, and we need some sort of basis to do this.' Nicholas again said little, beyond that in order better to care for his son he preferred to abdicate in favour not of Aleksei but of Grand Duke Michael. The Duma delegates accepted, and an act of abdication was hastily prepared and signed,[94] Nicholas travelling the next day to Tsarskoye Selo as a private citizen. Guchkov suspected the tsar was so disengaged that he failed to appreciate what was happening; according to General Voiekovo, the commander of the royal household, Nicholas was 'very disheartened, sad, very sad'.[95] Nicholas recorded in his diary that he left Pskov 'with a heart heavy from suffering...all around is treachery, cowardice, and deceit'.[96] He resented the pressure, but his abdication document reproduced the wording Alekseyev had drafted: that internal disturbances threatened a 'calamitous' impact on a struggle in which Russia was close to victory. 'The destiny of Russia, the honour of our heroic army, the welfare of the people, the whole future of our beloved fatherland demand that the war be carried to a victorious conclusion whatever the cost.' The ex-tsar's final manifesto to his soldiers repeated the message.[97]

All parties to the abdication—army, politicians, and emperor—invoked victory's primary importance. Yet despite the liberals' insinuations that Stürmer and Protopopov were Germanophile and the (unfounded) allegations that Alexandra sympathized with the enemy, Nicholas's commitment to that victory was undoubted. In 1914 he had agreed to general mobilization, reluctantly but—as he saw it—in response to Austro-German provocation. He had rejected overtures for a compromise peace. He had supported ambitious war aims for reunifying the German and Austrian parts of Poland with the Russian portion to form a buffer state under Russian sovereignty, as well as for annexing Armenia, Constantinople, and the Turkish Straits.[98] In the winter of 1916–17 the Allies made public their support for the latter, and Nicholas and his ministers reaffirmed their commitment to absorb the

Figure 5. Photograph of Russian Emperor Nicholas II from 1917

whole of Poland, although the military feasibility was now questionable.[99] Since the disastrous battle of Lake Narocz in March 1916, followed by further failures in the autumn, the Russian army seemed incapable of ousting German, as opposed to Austro-Hungarian, soldiers from prepared defences.[100] None the less, Nicholas's New Year imperial rescript reiterated his solidarity with the Allies, rejected peace before final victory, and awaited the decisive battle.[101]

In January 1917 the Russian army was better equipped than ever before, and the Allies generally seemed to be widening their superiority.[102] The November 1916 Chantilly conference had agreed to further synchronized offensives where those of summer–autumn 1916 had left off. It was true that Alekseyev preferred an operation whereby forces from Salonika and Romania would converge on Bulgaria, forcing it to surrender and separating the Ottoman Empire from Austria-Hungary and Germany. The scheme did not win favour, and the setback fed resentment that Russia had made sacrifices for the common cause but received no consideration in return.

Moreover, Romania's defeat left the Russian army with a 270-mile addition to a 1,650-mile front, in a sector poorly connected by rail.[103] The Stavka estimated that it needed 300,000 new men each month for six months in order to make good losses, which it simply could not manage.[104] For these reasons, and for others including the weather, whereas the other Allies wanted the Chantilly II offensives to start in February the Russian commanders decided to postpone their contribution until May at earliest. They also approved a radical reorganization (reducing each infantry division from four to three regiments while creating and equipping fifteen new divisions) that would delay their readiness. They envisaged that Brusilov's South-Western Front would again take the lead (and therefore strike primarily against the Austrians), with support from the other sectors.[105] However, they were very conscious that France and Britain were better equipped, and they hoped for massive Western resupply before attacking again. This concern became the central issue at the February 1917 Petrograd Conference, where high-level Italian, French, and British delegations spent two weeks in wordy and not particularly productive sessions with their Russian counterparts. The British delegate, Milner, observed 'the chaotic way in which public business is at present conducted in Russia—where extreme slowness and infinite delays are diversified by occasional acts of great precipitation'.[106] Admittedly the meeting agreed on a 4.25 million tonne programme of deliveries, including heavy artillery, aircraft, and railway track and rolling stock, but the Western Allies won little reassurance that Russia would use the material efficiently or remedy its transport failings, while the discussions on strategy rambled.[107] However, the alliance agreed to launch a synchronized offensive between 1 April and 1 May, with Russia the last to leave the starting blocks.[108] Despite the 'feeling of considerable discouragement' in Russia—which took Milner aback—there were grounds for hoping that if it hung on for a little longer it might yet emerge victorious.[109] Both Ruszky and Brusilov told their troops that victory was approaching, and according to Nicholas in February, 'I know the situation is very alarming, and I have been advised to dissolve the State Duma . . . But I can't do this . . . In the military respect we are stronger than ever before. Soon, in the spring, will come the offensive and I believe that God will grant us victory, and then moods will change.'[110] Two days before the abdication, Buchanan lamented that Protopopov's policy had brought revolution 'just as we were approaching decisive phase of the war'.[111] Conversely, as Rodzianko put it later,

'Revolution is a dangerous business. We tried, somehow, to hold on until the spring offensive—to crush the Germans. After that we could revolutionize as much as we wanted and get all the freedoms.'[112] Both the government and the opposition placed their faith in the offensive, and both were disappointed.

The combination behind the revolution was disjointed and brittle. The war would soon divide it. Although the initial protest had been over bread, once the strike developed the protestors' banners also targeted the war, though other demonstrators opposed the anti-war banners. According to the Okhrana the workers denounced the war, whereas the bourgeoisie wanted a change of government to achieve victory.[113] The Petrograd Soviet's early declarations concentrated on the struggle against the tsar and for democracy, calling on soldiers to join the people but maintain their discipline. It was notably silent about the war and about Russia's allies.[114] Conversely, the Duma liberals wanted a constitutional monarchy or Nicholas's removal not only as a matter of principle but also to combat the Central Powers more efficiently. Once revolution had broken out, their previous reluctance to force the issue during wartime changed into determination to act quickly, in order to contain the popular movement and maintain military discipline. Rodzianko conveyed this message to Ruszky and Alekseyev, and on this basis previously apolitical generals applied the pressure that succeeded—where the Duma and the insurrection had not done—in driving Nicholas to abdicate.

The army was sold a false prospectus. Alekseyev apparently believed the Duma politicians were re-establishing order so that the war could continue. Rodzianko and Guchkov conveyed contradictory messages that they were taking control but their authority was threatened. In fact it was too late for either a responsible government or Nicholas's abdication to enable Russia's elites to continue as previously. It was true that on 2/15 March the Provisional Government came into being, consisting of Duma members headed by Prince Georgy Lvov, whom in one of his final acts Nicholas approved as premier. But the government was more left-wing than the Temporary Committee that preceded it, being composed primarily of Kadets and including two socialists, Nikolai Chkheidze and Aleksandr Kerensky. Even in this form, it exerted no authority over the insurgents without the backing of the Petrograd Soviet, which resolved not to enter the government but to endorse it on the basis of a list of conditions negotiated during the night of 1–2/14–15 March. The terms were set by the Soviet but mostly accepted by the Duma side, and included an amnesty, free expression and organization, and the election of a constituent assembly to draft a constitution. However, abolishing appointed provincial governors and replacing the police by militias risked destroying governmental control over the provinces, and conceding civil liberties was risky against the background of an economic and political crisis and a desperate war. Moreover, although the Duma side resisted a proposal that the army should elect its officers, it conceded that off-duty soldiers should enjoy the same rights as all Russian citizens, and the Petrograd garrison would neither be removed from the city nor disarmed.[115] Hence the government would remain vulnerable to the Soviet and the insurgent soldiers, and the agreement did not mention foreign policy or the war. The omission might seem remarkable, but the Soviet was primarily concerned with internal politics,[116] and it endorsed a Cabinet whose majority (including Milyukov as foreign minister and Guchkov as war minister) advocated fighting until victory and achieving territorial expansion.[117]

In this respect the outcome justified the Stavka's expectations. In others it did not. Nicholas abdicated in favour not of his son but of his brother, which Guchkov and Shulgin had accepted although it contravened the law of succession. But Grand Duke Michael was unenthusiastic, and the monarchy's survival even in this form antagonized the Tauride Palace crowds. Most Duma leaders opposed Michael's accession and, before matters reached a head, Rodzianko repeated the tactic of contacting Ruzsky, warning it would inflame the situation and 'touch off a merciless destruction of everything'.[118] Alekseyev now suspected Rodzianko of brandishing the revolutionary menace in order to steer the army into successively more radical positions. He tried to call a halt, proposing a conference of Front commanders under the ex-tsar's uncle Grand Duke Nicholas. But Brusilov and Ruzsky saw no need, and Grand Duke Nicholas refused to attend. They might not like the Duma politicians, but they were willing to back them. Hence the military were out of the picture when Michael met with members of the Temporary Committee and the future Provisional Government on 2/15 March. Although he heard arguments both for and against his taking the throne, the majority pressed him not to do so and could not vouch for his personal safety. After leaving the room to consider, he announced he would stand down, thus creating a vacuum that meant the end of the Romanov dynasty. By default, Russia had become a republic, and the assumptions on which Alekseyev had withheld support for repression and for the Ivanov Mission had been undermined.[119] They were undermined still more by 'Order No. 1', drafted by the Petrograd Soviet's Executive Committee on the night of 1/14 March, under pressure from soldiers' representatives and in response to an order from Rodzianko that troops should accept their officers' authority and return to barracks.[120] The Soviet's newspaper, *Isvestia*, published Order No. 1 on 2/15 March. It provided for elected soldiers' committees in all units above company level, which should send representatives to the Soviet; for the committee to control each unit's weapons and not issue them to officers; for military units to be subordinated to the Soviet in all political actions; and for them to obey orders from the Duma's Military Commission only if such orders did not contradict the Soviet's.[121] Order No. 1 was drafted independently of the Soviet/Temporary Committee agreement about the formation of the Provisional Government, which the order fundamentally modified. And although it supposedly applied to the Petrograd garrison, it circulated rapidly and soldiers' committees were soon elected across much of the army. Officers remained unelected, but their authority increasingly rested on cooperation with the committees.[122] Although most of the army stayed in place and violence against officers was rare, military authority had been compromised and Russia's ability to keep fighting and launch a spring offensive would now depend substantially on ordinary soldiers. To judge from the petitions submitted after the revolution to the Provisional Government and the Soviet, opinions were divided. Working-class petitions most frequently supported a democratic republic and constituent assembly, and better pay and conditions, especially an eight-hour day. Foreign policy comments were rarer, and divided between support for a defensive war and support for a peace without annexations and indemnities. Peasant petitions called for a democratic republic but also for an early and equitable peace (and the countryside was where most soldiers lived). Soldiers' petitions were less pacifist and their main demand was to end officers' disciplinary powers, although garrisons in the rear were more likely to demand peace negotiations and others inclined towards peace because they feared that officers hoped through war to restore control.[123] The petitions bear out the evidence from the February Days that although lower-class Russians were rarely unconditionally pacifist they were less warlike than were the military, business, and parliamentary

5

France Attacks

It is time to enter the trenches. If the Germans chose a naval offensive that cost them their last best chance of victory, the Allies jeopardized their prospects by French, Russian, British, and Italian land attacks. The same few crowded months in 1917 also witnessed the most sustained and serious efforts to settle the conflict by negotiation. Their failure meant that by the autumn both sides now prepared for even greater violence. Between them, the belligerents so slighted European strength and civilization that the repercussions lasted decades.

The opening Allied 1917 campaign was the Franco-British Western Front assault usually known collectively as the Nivelle offensive (after the French commander-in-chief). It climaxed in the 16 April attack against the Chemin des Dames ridge lying north of the River Aisne. The campaign was intended *not* to emulate the 1916 attrition battles, but even so it claimed some half a million casualties. It was also, from the French perspective, an almost unmitigated disaster. It not only wrecked Nivelle's reputation but was also the precondition for army mutinies in May and June, and it opened months of political crisis. Although the damage was contained, and the French army remained crucial in defeating Germany, for the rest of the year it was reduced to relative inactivity. The debacle also set back inter-Allied strategic harmonization, which in 1916 had made progress. For decades the Chemin des Dames was consigned to the attic of French historical memory, being neither much written about nor memorialized. And yet the offensive is well documented, not least because like Pless (see chapter 1) and Caporetto (see chapter 8) it prompted a commission of inquiry. It underlines how French strategic judgements were no longer delegated to the high command but reflected close political involvement. More deliberation meant greater opportunity to assess American intervention and the Russian Revolution, albeit eventually to disregard them. Broadly the story passed through four phases: the inception of the Nivelle Plan and its acceptance by the French government; its elaboration and approval by the British; the doubts stirred by the February Revolution and Germany's withdrawal to the Hindenburg Line; and the anguished debates preceding confirmation.

By January 1917, nearly a million Frenchmen had been killed, wounded, or captured,[1] yet little French territory had been reconquered and the Germans remained ensconced some 50 miles north-east of Paris.Throughout the war the French army garrisoned by far the longest section of theWestern Front, and in 1917 it remained twice the size of the British Expeditionary Force (BEF).[2] Yet French endurance was nearing its limits, and the discussions preceding the offensive assumed it was imperative to win in 1917 and that new methods were needed.The government headed by Aristide Briand had tried to improve Allied coordination, one consequence being the scheme for synchronized 1916 offensives agreed at the December 1915 Chantilly conference. By attacking at Verdun the Germans had upset the Chantilly schedule, and the French feared something similar in 1917. Even so, in retrospect Ludendorff considered the summer of 1916 one of Germany's most testing moments, and he and Hindenburg did their utmost to prepare against a renewal of the synchronized attacks. Joseph Joffre, the French CGS since 1911 and commander-in-chief since the outbreak of war, indeed envisaged such a strategy, starting operations earlier to head off new pre-emptive moves. But whereas the 1916 campaign had delivered 'a serious blow', he told the Allied commanders that the aim in 1917 should be to decide the war before the Allied peoples tired of it; and the only place where Germany could be beaten was the Western Front.[3] The military chiefs adopted this agenda at a new Chantilly Conference on 15–16 November, which set the foundation for Allied planning down to the Chemin des Dames attack. Views differed about the optimum timing, but the commanders (and subsequently their governments) endorsed the principle that 'To prevent the enemy from any regaining of the operational initiative, the coalition armies will be ready to undertake concerted offensives from the first half of February 1917 with all the means at their disposal.'[4] The attacks would be launched at the earliest date when they could be concentrated within three weeks.[5]

In late 1916 the Allies had little reason to see American entry as imminent. The French leaders feared for Russia's political stability,[6] and it was far from certain that a British-dominated victory would suit French interests. Since summer 1916 the Briand government had taken the precaution, working with President Poincaré, of seeking to define French war aims. In January 1917 a letter from Briand to Ambassador Paul Cambon in London, and intended for discussion with the British, envisaged not only regaining Alsace-Lorraine but also annexing the Saar coalfield, and reserving France's right to decide the future of the German territory west of the River Rhine. Yet it was the Russians whom Briand actually talked to, and in the secret 'Doumergue Agreement' of February–March, Nicholas II promised to support claims to the Saar and to French-occupied buffer states on the west bank in return for France supporting Russia's claims on the German- and Austrian-governed areas of Poland.[7] As the Pless Conference had followed a redefinition of Germany's objectives, so France's commitment to a 1917 offensive complemented an expansion of French political goals.

In the political discussions accompanying the November 1916 Chantilly conference, Lloyd George (still at this stage British Secretary of State for War) pushed for a primary offensive on the Italian Front. His French and Italian counterparts were sceptical.[8] The French intended the Western Front to be the decisive theatre, though not to fight there in the same way as in 1916. When Joffre and his planners in the GQG 3rd (Operations) Bureau began work they envisaged that Picardy, where the Allies had attacked the previous year, would remain the battle-zone. However, this time the British and French would no longer fight side by side but independently, the British between Arras and Bapaume and the French between the Somme and the Oise. And in further contrast to the previous year, Britain would take the larger role. Joffre knew from censorship of his soldiers' letters that their morale had fallen to 'crisis' level: they felt the war's costs exceeded any political gains (many wanting an immediate peace), and that Britain and Italy were not pulling their weight.[9] In addition, France was running out of men. In November Briand's government responded to Germany's Hindenburg Programme—the German armaments programme adopted in 1916—by calling up the 1918 conscript cohort, which the Chamber of Deputies approved but demanded that France's allies take more of a share.[10] To maintain the symbolically important total of French army divisions, Joffre planned to reduce the regiments per division from four to three, though he planned that more artillery and portable machine guns should compensate.[11] The evidence reaching British General Headquarters (GHQ) was that French numbers and morale were ebbing, and although French leaders wanted the starring role in an Allied victory they were not averse to Britain taking more casualties.[12] Joffre told General John Davidson that he had warned his government that the army was 'exhausted' and it would be unwise to strain it unduly, so the principal 1917 burden should fall on Britain.[13]

The British were not unwilling. Thus far they had fought as junior partners, on battlefields mostly selected by Joffre. Sir Douglas Haig's inclinations since becoming BEF commander had been towards an offensive in Belgium; and as losses to the Flanders U-boats mounted he won wider support. Although at a meeting on 29 November he agreed to Joffre's request for a British attack near Arras, to support a French one further south, it was as part of an implicit bargain: if the spring offensive failed he would attack in Flanders in the summer.[14] Joffre duly proposed a Western Front offensive that would be ready, as agreed at Chantilly, by 1 February. The main assault would again come in the Somme sector, but from a wider baseline than in 1916. Fifteen days later a subsidiary French attack would go in north of the Aisne, making possible a pincer movement against the heights north of the river.[15] It seemed that GQG had a plan and GHQ had accepted it.

At this point civilian politics intervened. The 1916 campaigning had imposed extraordinary strain on every belligerent. The results seemed meagre. It was unsurprising that as the year ended political crises erupted in France and Britain, as well as Russia. During the 1914 emergency Joffre had determined strategy with minimal interference. But normal politics reasserted itself, and by now the Marne 'seemed so far away as to belong to another existence'.[16] Much of the French officer corps was monarchist and Catholic, and fear of a coup against the Third Republic had sharpened during the Dreyfus Affair at the turn of the century. Joffre was not a royalist, but the Left in the Chamber of Deputies felt he had unfairly penalized the republican General Maurice Sarrail, who was compensated with the command of the Allied expeditionary force at Salonika. Joffre and GQG were also blamed—with greater justice—for unpreparedness at Verdun, whereas other generals such as Philippe Pétain and Robert Nivelle burnished their reputations during the battle. Briand sensed that Joffre was becoming a liability. Great disappointment was felt over Romania's defeat, and impatience over the creeping progress on the Somme, and Briand accepted a secret session in which parliamentarians could speak freely. During a prolonged and difficult debate between 28 November and 7 December, he acted.[17] He appointed a new war minister, Hubert Lyautey, a royalist lacking parliamentary experience but with a high reputation as a former military governor of Morocco, and he formed a War Committee, modelled loosely on Lloyd George's War Cabinet. Joffre accepted a new position as 'technical military adviser', which he understood to be a coordinating role with real authority, while command on the Western Front went to Nivelle. But soon the orders to Nivelle and to Sarrail were issued direct from the War Ministry and Nivelle struck out on his own, without consulting his predecessor. Realizing the advisory post was meaningless, and compensated with the title of Marshal of France, Joffre resigned.[18]

The Nivelle offensive had many causes, but unbridled militarism was not among them. Joffre's eclipse and Nivelle's rise signalled a reassertion of civilian oversight, which in France recovered as in Germany it crumbled. It was also a choice for boldness: as one politician put it, 'Nivelle means risk.'[19]

Figure 6. Photograph of the Prince of Wales decorating General Robert Nivelle five days after the start of the Nivelle offensive, 21 April 1917

Yet the appointment seemed reasonable. Nivelle spoke English fluently and his English mother was the daughter of an Indian Army officer: these might be assets with the British. He came from a military family and had served in Tunisia and China. He was not a particularly political animal, but he was a Protestant, so more acceptable to the Left, and had been courteous and solicitous with parliamentarian visitors. At 61 he was no young thruster, and the same age as his rival, Pétain. He had, however, risen rapidly. Entering the war as a colonel, by late 1915 he was a corps commander, his units distinguishing themselves by positioning their artillery far forward.[20] Although enjoying Joffre's patronage, he owed his promotion primarily to his Second Army command at Verdun, where two attacks in October and December 1916 regained much of the lost terrain. Facing weary and dispirited opponents, they moved forward rapidly despite foul weather and churned-up ground. They benefited from meticulous preparation and excellent artillery–infantry coordination,[21] as well as innovative use of radio and of machine guns protected by concrete. To some extent all Nivelle did was catch up with German tactics, but he wrote his own instructions and his reputation rested not just on panache and public relations but also on achievement.

As the politicians saw it, the alternatives were a 'Somme school' of step-by-step advance, the infantry remaining behind artillery cover; and a 'Verdun school' of deep and rapid progress on a narrow front, facilitated by intensive prior bombardment.[22] Selecting Nivelle was a choice for the latter. Parliamentarians feared the Somme method was too slow, and France was running out of time, while Germany might regain the initiative. According to the Chamber Army Commission, the attack must start in February and not be forestalled as in 1916: this was 'a question of life or death for France'.[23] Briand was a natural sceptic, not to say cynic, but Nivelle impressed him and he favoured giving the general a try. In contrast, Paul Painlevé, minister for education and military technology, was a disbeliever and wanted to appoint Pétain, so stayed out of Briand's reshuffled government. Painlevé acknowledged, however, that he was in a minority.[24] Finance Minister Alexandre Ribot told the British that 'if before the end of summer [1917] we have not obtained a decision in our favour, peace will be almost inevitable, and we will negotiate it in conditions that we have not chosen. After immense efforts France is arriving at a critical moment when, better organized than ever, it must obtain results without delay. General Nivelle is convinced that operations must be conducted in a new spirit.' Ribot added that the political changes in France and Britain 'have led the governments to affirm more firmly than ever their right in the last resort to take the decisions for which at the end of the day they bear the responsibility'.[25]

Nivelle's powers were intentionally less than those enjoyed by Joffre, and his prestige could never match that of his predecessor. He could not appoint and dismiss army and army corps commanders: this was for the war minister.[26] He had been promoted over other men, and had little experience of senior command. Though eloquent, confident, and at first good-natured, he seems to have understood that he might have climbed too fast. His personality deterioration was one of the tragedies of the following weeks.[27] Although appointed partly for his ability to work with Joffre, he clashed with him and reworked the inherited planning. Like Briand's War Committee, he believed 'The situation is critical, and the peace ideas that are floating in the atmosphere make energetic action more necessary than ever.'[28] He told the British liaison officer, Edward Spiers, that France could not last another twelve months. 'All I care-for is to win the war this year.'[29] He shared—indeed obsessively—Joffre's fear that unless the Allies struck first their enemies would. He was fearful about morale,[30] and that Allied numerical superiority would diminish as the German army created new divisions. France's coal and steel shortages would slow its war production while the Hindenburg Programme forged ahead.[31]

Whereas Joffre had envisaged the main blow coming in Picardy and the hardest fighting falling to the British, Nivelle wanted the BEF and France's Army Group North (Groupe d'armées du Nord—GAN) to draw off German reserves with a diversionary attack before France staged the principal assault on the Aisne (where Joffre had envisaged a follow-up). The Somme sector, Nivelle considered, was 'used up': the river formed a barrier and German guns defended it in strength; the BEF should therefore strike further north. He liked the idea of supporting blows along adjoining sides of a square— the great salient in the German line around Noyon—and he favoured the Aisne in part because he feared a German drive through Switzerland.[32] He also claimed to have a recipe for victory. On bidding farewell to his Verdun command, he wrote, 'The experience is conclusive: our method has proved itself'; he told an officer, 'We have the formula.'[33] He conceived of an advance that in one bound would reach the enemy artillery, achieving a 'rupture in 24–48 hours'. Fresh manoeuvre troops would then pour through and defeat the enemy in open country, herding them northward.[34] Yet although the French held a bridgehead north of the Aisne, the sector was remote and its railways poor. For the advance to progress, it must seize the observation posts along the Chemin des Dames ridge. The offensive would be the first French attack to use tanks, but Nivelle's main ground for confidence was the re-equipping of his mobile heavy artillery with 155 mm short quick-firing cannon and with guns on caterpillar tracks: an upgrade that was incomplete. His tactical formula derived from a four-division attack at Verdun. Its premise was that the French artillery could now destroy the entire depth of the German defences and do so quickly. Whether it would work in an operation many times larger was problematic.[35] None the less, Briand's War Committee approved the scheme, and when Lyautey took over the War Ministry he found a new commander and a new plan, both decided without him.

Nivelle also reorganized the command structure. At GQG he mostly kept on Joffre's staff officers—the 'Young Turks'—though moving them from Chantilly to Beauvais and importing some of his team from Verdun. The most important new arrival was Colonel d'Alenson, an able but brusque and inflexible personal secretary (chef de cabinet), who shielded Nivelle from dissentients.[36] The GAN commander was General Louis Franchet d'Espérey, who though not a Nivelle protégé, cooperated loyally. The Aisne break-through would be led by the Sixth Army under General Charles Mangin (who had commanded under Nivelle at Verdun and had a reputation as a thruster, advocating using Africans as shock troops) and by the Fifth Army under General Olivier Mazel, while the Tenth Army behind them would be the exploitation force, the three being constituted in a new 'Army Group Breakthrough' (Groupe d'armées de rupture—GAR) under General Alfred Micheler. Pétain continued to command the Army Group Centre (Groupe d'armées du centre—GAC), further east, and would later be assigned a supplementary attack round Reims. But he was marginalized.

The most delicate command problem was relations with the British. Whereas Haig had been willing for a leading role in Joffre's scheme, now he was expected to attack in a subordinate capacity and to take over more of the French front, thus thinning his line so that Nivelle could create a larger manoeuvre force. Nivelle needed to win over Haig's GHQ and Robertson's Imperial General Staff, as well as to convince Lloyd George's War Cabinet, although the friction between British generals and politicians would help him. He largely succeeded, at the price of harming both British civil–military relations and Allied strategic cooperation. None the less, Britain as well as France would back him.

Nivelle met Haig on 21 December. Haig found him a 'most straightfor-ward and soldierly man', who planned to gain surprise and to breakthrough in twenty-four hours.[37] Nivelle expected the British to extend their line and undertake the preliminary attack, but if the spring offensive failed Haig could strike in Flanders, and if it succeeded the Germans would lose the Belgian coast anyway.[38] Haig—who was higher in rank than Nivelle—was friendly but non-committal, and when at an Anglo-French conference on 26 December Ribot warned that the health of the alliance might depend on Britain's willingness to cooperate, the British insisted that first they must consult their commander-in-chief.[39]

From this point on, British civil–military relations impinged on the dis-cussion. In 1917 they reached a nadir. Robertson and Haig were disdainful of politicians in general, and Robertson viewed Lloyd George as an oppor-tunist, whom he and Haig had distrusted before becoming prime minister and soon distrusted even more. Yet in the negotiations with the Unionist Party when he formed his government, Lloyd George had been obliged to keep them, and although the premier normally relished working with non-politicians, he looked to men who offered unconventional solutions and a fresh approach. Robertson and Haig, in contrast, who had taken over after the fiasco at Gallipoli, believed in concentrating on the Western Front and in wearing-out offensives on the Somme model. Actually Robertson had serious reservations about Haig's 1916 tactics,[40] but he kept them from the civilians. He was generally loyal to Haig, and blunt and uncommunicative to the Cabinet.[41] Civil–military tensions, however, were not just personal. Although Lloyd George had high political and moral courage, he rarely visited the Front: he accepted the war's necessity but abhorred the manner of its conduct, and did not intend to authorize another Somme. Indeed he was one of the few senior figures on either side to show consistent concern about casualties. Whereas Haig had written in 1916 that 'Three years of war and the loss of one tenth of the manhood of the nation is not too great a price to pay in so great a cause',[42] it was Lloyd George's right and duty to seek less costly means of securing national objectives. In his very first meeting as premier with Robertson and Haig, he voiced doubt about whether victory on the Western Front was possible, at any rate in 1917. He wanted to transfer two divisions from France to Egypt, and 200 heavy guns to Italy. Haig listened, but opposed both proposals.[43]

Lloyd George and the military also differed over Britain's allies. The premier had been impressed by French success in gaining territory for fewer lives; he surmised that French commanders were more competent than British ones. Yet GHQ was unimpressed by French infantry discipline and knew the French were tired,[44] while Robertson's officers doubted whether Nivelle's Verdun formula could be scaled up, whether the French artillery could really destroy the entire German position, and whether a rapid break-through was feasible. Haig and Robertson also had less confidence than under Joffre that they could launch their Flanders campaign, Robertson fearing being sucked into an extended French-led operation.[45] Lloyd George, however, told the War Cabinet that although 'he was inclined to take Field-Marshal Haig's rather temperate view as to its [the Nivelle Plan's] prospects',[46] he feared the damage to Anglo-French relations if Britain seemed obstructive. Backing Nivelle presented an opportunity for French rather than British generals to direct strategy, and might win the war for fewer British lives.

Nivelle visited London on 15–16 January. To constitute his manoeuvre force he wanted the BEF to lengthen its sector by 32 kilometres.[47] As this would complicate the preparations for Flanders, and GHQ had received fewer new divisions than expected, Haig resisted. Hence Nivelle prepared a paper for the War Cabinet. He contended that destroying the enemy's 'principal mass' would decide the war, that 130 of Germany's 200 divisions were on the Western Front, and only France and Britain could defeat them. Taking Trieste, Pola, or even Vienna would have no influence on the out-come of the war. In contrast, his Verdun battles showed that 'We will break the German front when we want, on condition of not attacking at the strongest point and carrying out the operation by surprise and with a sud-den attack in 24 or 48 hours.' The attack should come as soon as possible, before Germany increased its war production and moved divisions from the east, and although France would play the largest part 'There will then be a splendid harvest of glory for the British and French armies' as they reached the Belgian coast, the Meuse, and the Rhine.[48] What impressed Lloyd George was the emphasis on *surprise*, which on the Western Front seemed almost unattainable, but Nivelle would achieve by launching widely separated preliminary attacks so the enemy would not know which one would be the principal. Short but ferocious prior bombardments would also contribute.[49]

In the War Cabinet Nivelle faced close questioning. He warned of France's 'fatigue': decisive operations must come as soon as possible. Ambassador Cambon urged that if the Allies delayed, the military balance would move against them. Haig, in contrast, wanted to wait until May, when he would be better equipped and Russia and Italy more likely to attack simultaneously. Nivelle viewed such considerations as secondary to keeping the initiative. When reminded by Curzon that they had heard promises before of decisive results, Nivelle said he would use different methods. With the mobile long-range heavy artillery he could achieve in a day what had previously needed a fortnight or a month, and although he was still taking delivery he could exploit the guns that he did have by positioning them forward. He would advance so fast that the Germans could not bring up reserves. Lloyd George summed up that 'a decision on which the fate of the war could depend is too important to be taken precipitately',[50] and in fact the Cabinet should have pressed harder, as no guns on caterpillar tracks would arrive by April. But Nivelle had impressed the British, who decided to override Haig and instructed him to implement the agreement 'in the letter and the spirit'.[51] Indeed, beforehand Lloyd George had said to Haig and Robertson that he considered French generalship superior. Afterwards he told Haig the British line would be extended and he must try to make the Nivelle Plan a success.[52] Nivelle, did, however, agree with Haig to delay for more preparation, and the War Cabinet accepted a 1 April start. This concession proved the thin edge of a wedge.[53]

At first Haig made the best of it. He wrote to his CGS, Lieutenant General Sir Lancelot Kiggell, that it was better than the Joffre plan, under which 'we were to do all the fighting'.[54] But on reflection he felt the BEF had lost 'its chance of attacking in force and reaping a decisive success. We willingly play a second rôle to the French... We shall at any rate have heavy losses, with the possibility of no showy successes, whereas the French are to make the decisive attack with every possibility of gaining the fruits of victory.' While he accepted this arrangement was for the general good, 'let the future critics realise that we have accepted it with our eyes open'.[55] What he particularly objected to, however, was being rushed into attacking prematurely. The critical point was the overload of the northern French railway network, which had disrupted supplies to the Somme, and which a report by the railway executive Sir Eric Geddes had recommended remedying through massive injections of British equipment and railway personnel. The problem was genuine, and the weather exacerbated it by freezing the canals;[56] but Haig demanded more rolling stock than the French used for much larger manoeuvres, and their GHQ liaison officer inferred that transport had become a cover for prevarication.[57] The real cause, Lloyd George later alleged, was that Haig required so much capacity because he was preparing for his Flanders scheme.[58]

Matters came to a head at the 26–27 February Calais conference. It became notorious due to Lloyd George's ambush tactics, which rebounded against him. Before the meeting the premier saw the French military attaché, distancing himself from his generals and encouraging the French to propose putting Haig under Nivelle's command.[59] He secured the War Cabinet's general authority to support Nivelle against Haig, but not for more than that, and he took none of its Unionist members with him. Nor did he forewarn Haig and Robertson while they travelled to the hotel at the Calais *gare maritime* where the conference took place. Hence the British military supposed they were discussing transport, but when Lloyd George called on Nivelle to speak freely about his difficulties with Haig, the French produced a text that would have subordinated the BEF to Nivelle's orders, its commanders' authority being reduced to justice and discipline.[60] Hankey cobbled together a compromise, whereby Nivelle's command power applied just for the forthcoming offensive, and Haig could appeal to London if he felt his troops were endangered, and on this basis Haig and Robertson, while still detesting the document, signed. Nivelle distanced himself from the French proposal when speaking to British counterparts, and although Haig accepted his assurances Nivelle emerged poorly, as a political pawn.[61] None the less, with the British premier as well as the French government backing him, he had reached his apogee. From now on, it would be downhill all the way.

The Calais conference had the biggest consequences in Britain, where it would weaken Lloyd George's efforts to veto Haig's Flanders offensive. For the French, it created an additional reason for sticking with the Nivelle Plan even as the plan's premises crumbled. The Russian Revolution began to undermine them, as did a German strategic withdrawal. And still more damaging was evidence that the enemy had been forewarned, alongside growing doubts among Nivelle's subordinates.

The U-boat crisis had relatively little influence on French planning. Nivelle considered the shipping losses another ground for urgency, and well into March the French remained uncertain whether America would come in, their Washington military attaché warning that in any case the US army could do little for a long time.[62] In contrast, French leaders were extremely anxious about Russia even before the revolution, and on 26 March Alekseyev reported his army could not attack before June or July.[63] This development in turn discouraged Italy from attacking, its commander Luigi Cadorna being more concerned about an Austro-Hungarian pre-emptive strike than about participating in the second Chantilly scheme. An even bigger challenge for Nivelle came from the German retreat. Despite the Allies' fear of a spoiling attack, the OHL preferred to stay on the defensive: it lacked trained men, weapons, and horses, and Allied superiority was too great. Ludendorff wanted to be able to hold out if the submarines failed: 'I believe the war will end in 1917, but prepare simultaneously for 1918.' During the winter the Germans called up their 1898 and 1899 conscript cohorts and expanded their army from 199 to 232 divisions.[64] The OHL issued new guidelines on defensive tactics, intended to reduce bombardment casualties by holding the front line lightly, but readying counter-stroke units to recapture lost ground promptly once a labyrinth of machine-gun nests had slowed down the attackers.[65] In addition, detachments up to 370,000 strong built massive defensive lines running parallel to and behind the Western Front,[66] and on 4 February the OHL ordered withdrawal to the new position (the *Siegfried Stellung*—but dubbed by the British the Hindenburg Line), just after the unrestricted submarine campaign began. The retreat did not include the Chemin des Dames but it did relinquish positions that had menaced the Channel and Paris and had been defended at great cost. Although it caused much heart-searching, if victory was imminent it was easier to justify. And at this stage Ludendorff still expected Allied spring assaults, even if he did not yet know where or when. In mid February, however, a French high command directive captured in a German raid detailed the attack methods, while over-flights west of Reims showed aerodrome and store construction and new railway work. Soon the Germans were certain that the French were concentrating reserves south of the Soissons–Reims line, and they too reinforced the sector.[67] Meanwhile the withdrawal to the *Siegfried Stellung* would shorten, straighten, and strengthen the line further west, releasing more divisions for the reserve. Nivelle's concept rested on strategic surprise, and he was losing it.

Neither French nor British intelligence had warned of the withdrawal. GQG did not believe the Germans would abandon ground that they had fought for so tenaciously. The Allies were taken unawares when British forces along the River Ancre found no enemy opposite them.[68] Yet into March GQG remained unconvinced, and rejected Franchet d'Espérey's urgings to accelerate the offensive and catch the Germans on the move. Allied troops picked their way forward, throwing doubt on their capacity

Figure 7. Indian cavalry with lances advancing towards the Hindenburg Line, March 1917

for the rapid manoeuvres Nivelle envisaged, while the Germans fell back unmolested through a booby-trapped wilderness.[69] The preparatory attack assigned to the Franchet d'Espérey's GAN between the Somme and Oise would now strike into the devastated area—which would waste the expensively accumulated stockpile of French shells—or against the formidable and still unreconnoitred Hindenburg Line, while preparing a new battlefront would mean weeks more delay. It was true that GQG maintained the German withdrawal would also release Allied divisions,[70] but Nivelle planned to use them in a supplementary operation in Champagne, east of Reims, to which he transferred divisions from the GAN. There would really now be just one preliminary offensive—Haig's.[71]

Unfortunately the withdrawal also heightened Franco-British tensions. On 27 February Nivelle's staff issued such a peremptory directive to Haig that even Balfour, the mild-mannered British Foreign Secretary, remonstrated against it.[72] Although Nivelle may not have been responsible, he now believed 'a true subordination of the English army to the French command' would be impossible until Haig went.[73] Haig conversely wondered 'how any Frenchman can have the impertinence to think any one of us will allow himself to be commanded by them'.[74] He feared the German withdrawal would release enemy divisions to attack at Ypres and cut him off from the Channel. But under the Calais agreement he had lost control over his reserves, and he demanded still more time to prepare, adding that 'if the situation develops unfavourably for the proposed [Nivelle] offensive it may be necessary to abandon it'. This time Nivelle reacted very strongly indeed, flatly denying Ypres was endangered, and insisting Haig should commit all available forces to the coming attack. He had decided 'not to make any fundamental change in the general plan of operations'. A note to Britain from the French government demanded Haig should be warned to comply without delay.[75] Such bluntness was extremely unusual and underlined how Briand still supported Nivelle. However, the British had gone along with the Nivelle Plan partly to uphold the alliance, and the War Cabinet left the question of the reserves for discussion between the commanders: only if this broke down could Haig appeal for support.[76] Yet another Anglo–French conference held in London on 12–13 March reaffirmed the Calais Agreement.[77] Possibly Haig was reassured by a sort of compact: he would go along with the general offensive (whose failure he expected) in return for Nivelle backing the Flanders plan.[78] For the next month GHQ and GQG concentrated on preparing their assaults. In the end, reflecting the Cabinet's concern that if Nivelle failed Britain should not be blameable, the BEF contribution more than matched up to expectations, with the major reservation that it started late.[79]

Yet as Haig's resistance lifted, doubts surfaced within France. Initially Nivelle's fresh thinking had echoed the mood of the government, the Chambers, and the press. But delay made for second thoughts. André Tardieu, one of France's most prominent columnists, penned an article suggesting the army should stay on the defensive. Although the government censored the piece, many officers voiced similar opinions to journalists and deputies.[80] Lyautey, the new war minister, wanted projects that were 'not from literature', and considered replacing Nivelle, but decided it was impossible. His doubts were fed by an old acquaintance, Colonel Georges Renouard, the head of GQG's Third Bureau,[81] who wrote a letter declining responsibility for the operation, which d'Alenson removed from the file. Disagreements also opened within Nivelle's command team. Whereas Mangin accepted the advance could prevail in a single bound, Micheler wanted a more methodical progress, reaching Laon in three or four days rather than one. Already in January Renouard had to ask Nivelle to arbitrate.[82] These tensions came to a head when in mid March the Briand ministry collapsed, and with it Nivelle's political buttress. Three weeks of agonizing followed, at the end of which the offensive still went ahead, although its authors now knew that it was highly likely to fail.

Briand's majority was fragile, and Lyautey brought the government down by imputing in the Chamber that he could not rely on the deputies to respect confidential information. Perhaps Lyautey was looking for a way out, given his loss of confidence in Nivelle. It took several days before, on 20 March, Ribot formed a new government. Ribot was 75 and had been premier during the negotiation of the Franco–Russian alliance. He was more moderate than Briand over war aims, and his incoming declaration denied France was fighting in a 'spirit of conquest'.[83] It also reconfirmed the civil–military ground rules: 'the government, which has the political direction of the war under the supervision of the Chamber, controls everything pertaining to the organization and maintenance of our armies...But once the government has chosen the chief who ought to lead our troops to victory, it leaves to him full liberty in the strategic conception, preparation, and direction of operations.'[84] In practice Ribot's government would depart considerably from this standard, in good measure due to War Minister Paul Painlevé. Unusually for his portfolio, Painlevé was a civilian, although well qualified. Previously a professor of mathematics at the elite military engineering academy, the *Ecole polytechnique*, he had flown in the first demonstration of the Wright brothers' aeroplane in France and in 1915–16 had been responsible for military innovations.[85] He had often visited the Front. He admired Pétain and agreed with him that France's strategy should be defensive, making only limited and very thoroughly prepared attacks. He believed Pétain should have replaced Joffre. None the less, he promised Ribot that he would respect Nivelle's position, and told Nivelle that he wanted a clean slate.[86] He did ask, however, whether in the light of the Russian Revolution, the German retreat, and American entry, the offensive should be reconsidered. Nivelle insisted the retreat had released more French than German divisions and that his commanders were certain of prevailing with low casualties and taking the key Craonne plateau at the eastern end of the ridge: 'I fear but one thing, that the Germans will retire.'[87]

This was not what Painlevé wanted to hear, and Nivelle's confidence was unrepresentative. Many officers contacted Painlevé with their misgivings, and the Third Bureau itself issued a jeremiad as the new government took office. It had always been clear that the terrain—characterized by marshy rivers, steep slopes, and poor artillery observation—made an assault extremely difficult, but GQG had hoped to enjoy surprise and that diversionary attacks would draw off German reserves. But now the preliminary attacks would be curtailed and the main operation, according to the Third Bureau, was 'hare-brained' (*éventée*). Circumstances had become 'very disadvantageous for an offensive...Our attack will progress slowly, at the price of costly and poorly rewarded efforts.' It is uncertain whether this assessment reached Painlevé, and a subsequent Third Bureau memorandum recommended that the attack should go ahead, Renouard being told to silence his doubts.[88] It was harder, however, to keep down the army commanders, and foremost among them Pétain and Micheler. When Painlevé took over, the concentration of supplies and men on the attack front was well advanced, and the British preliminary bombardment scheduled to start within two weeks. To stop now might demoralize the troops, many of whom hoped for a win-the-war attack, as well as freeing the enemy to retaliate. Painlevé knew the British felt that unless a French attack followed their own, the BEF's sacrifices would be wasted, a British officer telling him 'We don't need the Americans to beat the Germans.'[89] Yet he also got wind of the French commanders' disagreements, Micheler warning Nivelle that the Germans were reinforcing and the enemy withdrawal had completely changed the situation.[90] Micheler prepared a directive to his three army chiefs that the 'strategic exploitation' of the offensive might be not 'a rapid march' but rather a methodical progression, each engagement needing proper artillery support. Nivelle responded that German reinforcements made no difference to the principle that the infantry's arrival in the enemy's third and fourth lines must be rapid and sudden: 'it is necessary...not to say a word that could hamper the attacker's élan'. He 'totally condemned' (and insisted on suppressing) the sentence 'The progress of the infantry will, in all circumstances, be most closely supported by the guns.' He believed 'the general character to impress upon our operations has remained the same', with the emphasis on 'audacity' rather than 'prudence'.[91] In March Nivelle had set a pace for the advance of 100 metres every three minutes.[92] Mangin's and Mazel's soldiers were expected to progress at 1 kilometre per hour, although Mangin's army had no tanks and, whereas Mazel's did, if his tanks fell behind the infantry must keep going.[93] Nivelle assured Micheler—now exasperated with his superior's inflexibility—that 'You will find no Germans in front of you.'[94]

While Nivelle and d'Alenson clamped down on dissent, Painlevé received (via a distinguished former premier and War Minister Charles de Freycinet) a note from a colonel on the GAR staff, purportedly conveying his colleagues' near unanimous view. The attack was insufficiently prepared and its tempo too rapid: now the Germans had brought up their best units, France's might be squandered. Painlevé's response was the unconventional and irregular step of holding individual conversations with the army group commanders in Nivelle's absence. He first met Micheler, who had earlier thought the plan might work but now was very critical: surprise would be difficult and he did not expect to get initially beyond the first two German positions, and even that only with good weather. It would, however, be dangerous simply to cancel. Pétain agreed on the dangers of letting Germany regain the initiative, but the attack could not succeed because the bombardment was targeted over too large and deep an area, and it would be better to concentrate on the first two lines:[95] 'Even the waters of Lake Geneva would have little effect if dispersed over the length and breadth of the Sahara desert.'[96] Finally Franchet d'Espérey doubted his preliminary attack would help, and implied the commander-in-chief was losing his grip.[97] Further, on 2 April Ribot himself joined a dinner arranged by Painlevé that Pétain and Franchet d'Espérey attended but Nivelle did not. Pétain did not believe an offensive 'in depth' would succeed and repeated that the enemy must be worn down by successive attacks. Ribot disliked Pétain's caustic manner, but suspected he was right, though doubted the wisdom of changing the plan when the Germans would probably attack if France did not.[98] Given Nivelle's absence, however, Pétain and Franchet still held back.[99]

Curiously when President Raymond Poincaré (a much more orthodox politician that Painlevé) visited the Front at the start of April, he found Franchet apparently confident and Mangin and Mazel 'very confident', but that Nivelle himself, while 'very sure of a complete tactical success', was 'much less categorical about the possibility of strategic exploitation'.[100] The episode suggests—uniquely—that Nivelle had doubts, vouchsafed to the president but to nobody else. Yet Nivelle became more rigid as his authority was challenged. Mangin later complained that Painlevé had consulted only the generals whom he knew would agree with him,[101] and that the individual army commanders might have been more upbeat. But the upshot was that the commander-in-chief resisted changing tack and the British feared being left in the lurch, yet the army group commanders, while accepting the need to keep the initiative, doubted much would be achieved. Painlevé was left in the delicate position of subverting military authority on the eve of a great offensive: and American entry made his choices still harder. On 3 April (the day after Wilson's War Message) the attack, which had been scheduled for the 8th, was again postponed due to bad weather.[102] On the same day the liaison officer between GQG and Poincaré, Colonel Emile Herbillon, found Painlevé questioning whether it should still be launched on the scale

planned. Russia could not help, Italy would not, and it might be better to
wait until American aid created 'a certain superiority'. A failure might dash
morale, now raised so high, so that at a later stage 'we could no longer
provide the violent effort needed and which would be decisive'. The war
minister was looking to the end game, and the risk that if France weakened
itself now, others would dominate. Without a better than 50:50 chance of
success, he preferred to sit tight.[103]

When Herbillon went on to Ribot the premier similarly asked if there
was a real chance of success and when Herbillon said yes, Ribot noted with
a sceptical smile that he had been told they would reach Laon the first evening. He felt the project was 'very hazardous', and looked out of his window
at the garden, as was his wont when worried.[104] He wondered why Briand's
War Committee had ever approved it. Poincaré warned Ribot about the
dangers of interfering in the military domain, but found the premier 'very
preoccupied' and Painlevé 'very troubled'.[105] As Ribot summarized in his
diary, the terrain was difficult, the retreat to the Hindenburg Line would
justify a cancellation, the secret was out, and the high command always
tended to over-optimism; moreover, by inflating public expectations it had
heightened the risks. He knew that Painlevé agonized over whether it was
his responsibility to stop the offensive, and he felt the war minister was right
to hesitate, although had done so for too long and was wrong to have gone
behind Nivelle's back.[106] Painlevé, however, felt that scrapping the offensive
would also mean scrapping the Calais Agreement and breaking France's
word to the British, who had accepted a position that Haig warned was
dangerous. Nor did it seem right to remove Nivelle without giving him a
chance, only three months after his Verdun victories. Hence Painlevé tried
to re-establish army unity by inducing Nivelle to make modifications.[107]

On the evening of 3 April, a meeting was convened at the War Ministry,
with Nivelle this time attending as well as his army group commanders.
Also present were Ribot; Painlevé; the navy minister, Lucien Lacaze; the
armaments minister, Albert Thomas; and the colonial minister (and injured
hero) André Maginot. The ministers sat in a semicircle facing an enormous
map of the Western Front, Maginot resting his leg on a chair. Painlevé
again asked whether the Russian Revolution, the German withdrawal, and
American entry made it necessary to reconsider, and he read out the
Freycinet memorandum. Nivelle, now less patient, reiterated his confidence.
The Americans would take a long time to come in any numbers and if
Germany remained unmolested it might gather forces from Russia and

attack in the west. Given good weather, he expected to take the first two positions with trifling losses: in no circumstances would he stage another Somme. Moreover—and this was his trump card—not attacking would destroy the laboriously acquired Calais Agreement. The army group commanders did not pursue their criticisms, and none advocated cancellation. Hence Painlevé summed up that Nivelle had authority to go ahead, provided the weather was favourable and the preliminary bombardment did not sacrifice the targeting of the first and second positions in order to strike the third and fourth: in other words that it minimized losses rather than seeking a breakthrough.[108]

Nivelle assumed the matter was now closed. Indeed the bombardment for Britain's Vimy–Arras preliminary offensive started the next day. And yet there would after all be one further round of debate, in the most emblematic of all the troubled 1917 conclaves: the Compiègne conference on 6 April. After the War Ministry meeting Ribot and Painlevé were visited by the presidents of the Senate and the Chamber of Deputies, who had spoken to several generals and gained extremely pessimistic impressions. On 5 April Painlevé received a letter from another of his predecessors as war minister, General Adolphe Messimy, which Messimy claimed had been written at Micheler's virtual dictation. It predicted the attack would gain some guns and prisoners and a narrow strip of territory, but no 'strategic results', and by the time fine weather came France would be paralysed for lack of men. GQG was 'about to commit a grave error which may have irreparable consequences', and the army group commanders must be consulted.[109] In fact Micheler had told Messimy that Nivelle was unlikely to get beyond the second position and the plan should be revised although an attack was still necessary, so Messimy had misrepresented him.[110] Once again, the generals were saying different things to different audiences. But Poincaré found Ribot 'rather agitated' and 'very hesitant', while Painlevé said everyone he had consulted expected a tactical success, but they should wait for good weather and not throw in all the available reserves. On that same day, 5 April, Ribot had spoken in the Chamber to congratulate Woodrow Wilson, and both he and Painlevé felt American entry enabled them to prolong the war: 'It is not the moment to stake everything.'[111] In these circumstances Poincaré proposed yet a further meeting between politicians and commanders. He told Herbillon that 'we must finish with these veiled intrigues … this conference has only one aim: to permit General Nivelle to explain himself and assure himself of the government's confidence'. Painlevé agreed—more ambiguously—that, 'the aim of this meeting is to lance the boil and bring matters to a head', and he too intended to support Nivelle, although less decisively than Herbillon would have wished.[112]

The conference gathered on Good Friday 6 April at 10.00 a.m. The venue was Poincaré's railway carriage, which drew up in Compiègne station under a lowering sky, presaging snow.[113] Those attending were the president, Ribot, Painlevé, Nivelle, the four army group commanders (Micheler, Pétain, Franchet d'Espérey, and Castelnau), Lacaze, and Thomas—so virtually an identical cast to the 3 April meeting, with the important addition of Poincaré, whom Nivelle could expect to back him. Yet Nivelle was 'very nervous' beforehand and complained that his position was being made impossible.[114] Although a similar gathering of generals had preceded Joffre's autumn 1915 offensives, there was no precedent for a commanding general defending himself before his army group chiefs in the presence of France's senior politicians.[115] Yet Compiègne was surprisingly informal, the subsequent parliamentary debate being appalled at its casualness.[116] Poincaré conceived the meeting as an opportunity to exchange views and strengthen Nivelle's position rather than to revisit the principle of the offensive: indeed, the British bombardment had now been proceeding for forty-eight hours, and a million French soldiers were crammed into the attack zone.[117] Yet the discussion meandered, Franchet testifying afterwards that it was 'above all an exchange of ideas, as we had not been advised on its purpose and there were no minutes ... the conversation was at first very confused, the discussions were not directed, no question having being posed we got lost in generalities'.[118] Nivelle had brought two staff officers who could have taken minutes, but they were excluded.

None the less, from eye-witness accounts and the subsequent Brugère commission of inquiry, a reasonably consistent picture emerges. Poincaré gave only a minimal introduction before handing over to Painlevé, who reiterated the calculus of risk. If France were on the verge of being starved out it would be reasonable to attack with everything now; whereas if US troops arrived in force in two to three months it would clearly be right to wait; but as it was an intermediate case the government envisaged a limited offensive. Circumstances had changed since the Chantilly conference last November, and France could not risk sacrificing on a dice throw the young men on whom its military effectiveness depended. He did not oppose any attack, but one that caused 'losses ... disproportionate to the results'. On this operation 'the fate of the country will perhaps be staked'.[119]

When Nivelle responded, participants noted he had lost his habitual equipoise. Having been dragged again from his headquarters, he was tense and his presentation had an embittered edge, though it was as always, according to Franchet d'Espérey, 'theoretical' and citing Verdun, as if Nivelle could not proceed beyond generalities.[120] Most important—and Nivelle said this with passion—'The offensive alone can give victory; the defensive spells defeat and shame.' He invoked again the compact with Britain: 'Bound by these directives, the commander-in-chief has no right to call off the offensive.'[121] Postponement would let Germany force Russia into a separate peace, whereas attacking would give the Provisional Government a respite. Waiting for the Americans meant abandoning all chance of victory in 1917, and the U-boats might prevent essential raw materials from crossing the Atlantic (indeed, the day before, Thomas had warned Nivelle that shipping shortages would curtail munitions output).[122] Time had worked for the Allies but was now working against them: as Germany had forty-three reserve divisions, attacking was less dangerous than leaving it the initiative.[123] No offensive had been better prepared, and troop morale had never been higher, whereas 'we know that the enemy's morale is very low and that he will not stand'. Although if Nivelle broke through he would fight an action 'of long duration',[124] if he did not succeed within two days he would break off: he reiterated that 'I will not, under any pretext, get involved in another battle of the Somme.'[125] What he would not do, however (and did not understand—here he cited Napoleon) was fight a 'half battle'.[126] He offered continuing confidence that he could break through, offset by assurances of halting quickly if he did not. The balance of risks pointed to going ahead. Indeed, according to Poincaré, Nivelle predicted 200,000 prisoners.

Thus far Painlevé and Nivelle had largely reasserted their previous positions. But what happened next was decisive, as Poincaré called on a 'pale and nervous' Micheler, who—immediately interrupted by Nivelle and seemingly drained of confidence—favoured attacking as soon as possible.[127] He thought the first two positions could be taken, but was less sure about the third and fourth.[128] In fairness, Micheler had also said previously that the attack should take place, though he preferred a more modest, step-by-step approach. Yet the contrast between what he said in public before his superior and what were known to be his private views took his listeners aback, and the discussion became desultory. Franchet d'Espérey also said the attack should go ahead though they should not expect too much, but the British were already committed and should not be left in the lurch. Pétain, embarrassed, was laconic, confirming that they would not get beyond the second line. At this point, Nivelle interrupted again to say he must resign, but the politicians huddled round him in a corner and persuaded him to retract. The participants ate a morose lunch, and dispersed.

Painlevé felt the meeting added nothing: 'Minds were too keyed up, animosities too keen, for the controversy to be dispassionate.'[129] In his usual fashion, Pétain asked as they departed, 'In sum, what?'[130] In his memoirs Poincaré recorded that all had agreed on postponement if the weather remained poor; and if they could not break the third line they would desist rather than recommence a Somme-style battle.[131] According to some accounts Poincaré summed up that the attack would go ahead but Nivelle would commit his reserves prudently if there was a breakthrough and halt if there were not; and they would await good weather.[132] The premier spoke to Micheler afterwards for confirmation that the latter felt France should attack, even if not in the fashion Nivelle envisaged.[133] Ribot and Poincaré gave reassurance, in the words of Nivelle, 'that from now on I would be left alone', and when on 7 April the commander again threatened resignation they again dissuaded him, reiterating that he had the government's confidence and would be left in peace.[134] Painlevé, on the other hand, evidently in doubt, wrote to Ribot that the government's 'essential directive' was that France must be able to 'endure'; now its manpower reserves had become 'so weak'. He believed there was agreement that 'it is not a case of pursuing at any cost a battle committing all our forces; but on the contrary the battle would be halted as soon as it seemed to inflict on our army excessive losses, liable to weaken it profoundly for insufficient or risky results'.[135] It is unclear, however, whether this formula was communicated to Nivelle, who might reasonably have supposed from Poincaré's and Ribot's assurances that he held a blank cheque, although he himself had promised to stop if he failed in the first two days. Micheler emerged from Compiègne having forfeited respect, and the conference seemed to have shored up the commander-in-chief. By 6 April it was anyway too late to cancel without compromising relations with the British, whose heavy casualties at Arras would be pointless if no French attack followed. Although Ribot and Painlevé had the gravest doubts about the enterprise's wisdom, they had inherited it at an awkward moment (albeit from a ministry of which Ribot had been a senior member). At Compiègne perhaps the most achievable was to limit the consequences.

The Chemin des Dames ridge was some 24 kilometres long. Its slopes rose 100–200 metres above the River Aisne, too steeply for horse-drawn artillery. Its eastern end was honeycombed with limestone caverns, the so-called *creutes*. From February the Germans were deepening their already strong defences to three or four positions, each comprising two trench lines with concrete blockhouses and machine-gun nests; they considered it one of their strongest Western Front sectors. Nivelle had visited the position, which Pétain thought impregnable.[136] Yet Nivelle had promised to break through on the conditions of *not* attacking at the strongest point, and of obtaining surprise, but security had been lax. When Nivelle visited London in January he discussed his plans with society hostesses;[137] his staffers were no tighter-lipped, and among French parliamentarians information circulated freely. Briefing papers passed well down the army hierarchy early, and the Germans captured sensitive documents in mid February, apparently without GQG realizing. None the less, by mid March it knew secrecy had been lost.[138] Moreover, on 4 April a German raid at Sapigneul captured material showing the order of battle south of the Aisne and objectives for two corps north of the river. According to the French official history, 'It was a document of the highest importance.'[139] Although Micheler told Nivelle, the commander-in-chief apparently decided there was nothing for it but to go ahead, the plans stayed unchanged, and the government was not told of the breach.[140] By the eve of battle the Germans knew French strengths, deployments, and intentions, and on 15 April they received an agent report that the infantry would attack at sunrise on the 16th, which they anticipated with a pre-emptive bombardment.[141] Their Seventh Army, which would bear the brunt, had risen from six divisions in January with two in reserve to nine in March with five in reserve; the adjoining Third Army from three to five divisions. By the end of March the Germans had sixteen divisions in the attack sector and fourteen in reserve. GQG well knew the enemy were reinforcing, and its 2nd (Intelligence) Bureau estimated as of 14 April that the opposing divisions had risen since 15 February from nine to fifteen plus between five and seven reserve divisions in close proximity and six not far away; while the artillery batteries had risen from ninety-two batteries to over 500.[142]

Moreover, the German artillery had not been silenced, and this too was known. The GQG liaison officer with the I Army Corps reported on 14 April that the preliminary bombardment 'is not as one would have hoped, as one expected, there are gaps', and the infantry would face 'great resistance'.[143]

Eleven of the twenty-seven first-line divisions reported that the opposing front line was intact.[144] The heavy artillery had gradually expanded—although the 155 mm and mobile guns Nivelle had banked on were still lacking—and the guns available exceeded those for the successful French bombardment at the opening of the Somme. In contrast, in that battle the British had suffered from Haig's insistence on targeting the entire depth of the German position, and this time Nivelle insisted likewise, despite the fears of Painlevé and others that the barrage would be spread too thin. The artillery was targeting a much larger area than on the Somme, let alone than in Nivelle's Verdun attacks, and German air superiority and atmospheric conditions exacerbated the difficulties. The German positions, concealed in *creutes* or on the ridge's reverse slope, were often invisible to ground observers, nor could French spotter aircraft see them. German fighter aircraft on the Western Front had risen from 144 in July 1916 to 530 in April 1917, and their new DIII Albatros inflicted heavy losses. When Nivelle ordered an operation to shoot down the German observation balloons over the battlefield, it almost totally failed. The French also lacked trained air observers, and in any case the weather permitted air observation for only twenty-three hours during the fourteen days before the attack.[145] At the Compiègne conference the bad weather was mentioned repeatedly. It prevented the aircraft from flying, and impeded ground observers. According to Spiers, early April was 'so incredibly, so unbelievably bad that in any other circumstances it would have been funny'.[146] Because of the weather, on 5 April Nivelle decided to delay the attack to 14 April; on the 10th it was postponed to the 15th; and on the 13th to the 16th. On the 16th itself snow fell together with sheets of rain.[147]

Nivelle did, therefore, take account of the Compiègne debate, and if the operations went ahead despite the weather, it was in large measure to keep faith with the BEF. Essential to the original concept had been a spread of preliminary attacks to keep the Germans guessing. But troop transfers had much reduced Franchet's GAN, and on his front, too, the weather impeded reconnaissance and the bombardment was inadequate. When Franchet's assault went in on 13 April it fell short of its objectives, and in twenty-four hours was over.[148] As Pétain's attack in the Reims sector was scheduled to follow the main offensive, responsibility for drawing off enemy reserves fell almost entirely to Haig, whose infantry jumped the parapet on Easter Monday 9 April. Haig could have treated the battle of Arras as a secondary effort, but his directives envisaged a breakthrough, although his principal

objective was attrition before his Flanders operation. Whereas Nivelle wanted
the battle's centre of gravity to be south of Arras (where it would be closer
to Franchet d'Espérey), Haig insisted on attacking north of the town as well,
and here his forces scored their greatest success, the Canadians seizing Vimy
Ridge on the opening day. In contrast to Nivelle's offensive, the bombardment was on a shorter front than before the Somme, and more intense and
accurate. In addition, the British attacked six days before the Germans
expected, and the latter's reserves were too far back.[149] Even so, the advance
soon lost momentum, as reinforcements doubled German numbers. The
British main effort was redirected south of Arras into piecemeal attacks that
made little headway.[150] By 13 April the main fighting was over, and if Nivelle
lingered the initial success would be a wasting asset.

The French had concentrated at least 1 million men, with 180,000 in
the first wave.[151] This very concentration became another reason for
action—for fear the Germans would pre-emptively assail the forces
spread out beneath them. The army censorship of soldiers' letters reported
that the men were tired but would attack.[152] In fact the infantry went
forward with high but fragile confidence, despite spending the night in
sodden fields, the morning downpour, and the Germans' four-hour
anticipatory bombardment. But failure came quickly. The key obstacle
was the machine guns, concealed in the *creutes* and under concrete, often
scything the attackers from behind. The barrage advanced too quickly,
leaving the infantry exposed. German accounts suggest the situation was
never critical. The tanks became detached from the infantry, and as they
were large, slow, and highly visible, carrying spare petrol in attached
drums, the German gunners turned them into fireballs. The hands of the
Senegalese, whom Mangin intended as shock troops, were so frigid that
they could not use their rifles, and 6,500 of the 10,000 Africans engaged
on 16 April became casualties, many massacred by their own artillery.[153]
Nowhere did the attack pierce the second line, nor in much of the assault
front did it get beyond the first. By the afternoon the Germans were
unleashing counter-attacks, while congestion mounted in the rear and
casualties swamped the medical services. Although Mazel's Fifth Army
had more success than Mangin's Sixth, a pall descended over GQG,
which delayed a communiqué until the evening.[154]

The government, respecting its assurances, did not intervene for the
first week. Nivelle as early as the 17th ordered Mangin to consolidate.
Smaller operations continued until 23 April, after which Nivelle, though

Figure 8. French soldiers (September 1917) re-enact 16 April 1917 attack

evidently not having broken through in forty-eight hours, planned concerted new attacks. By now the parliamentarians near the front had been briefed on the events of 16 April, and Poincaré recorded that 'in the Chamber the disorder of feelings is incredible'.[155] Haig visited to urge on Painlevé that operations should continue, now insisting he had confidence in Nivelle, but the government had had enough.[156] As a first step, Pétain became CGS at the War Ministry, but in May he replaced Nivelle, and Ferdinand Foch took over as CGS from Pétain. As both men broadly agreed with Painlevé, civil–military tension lifted. French strategy became to launch no big offensives until 1918, and to plan for a smaller army with more aircraft, tanks, and guns.[157] Painlevé set out this doctrine publicly to the legislature, and Pétain in his 'Directive No. I' on 19 May told his commanders that the present military balance ruled out 'the rupture of the front followed by strategic exploitation. Our effort should therefore now be directed to wearing out the adversary with the minimum of losses.' This meant localized attacks to seek surprise in quiet sectors, with maximum artillery use, while preparing transport and reinforcements for a defensive campaign. He already looked ahead to the battle that the Allies would fight in 1918,[158] and until then he envisaged only limited operations to revive the soldiers' confidence. Attacks took place alongside the British in Flanders on 31 July; at Verdun on 20 August; and at La Malmaison on 23 October, when a thoroughly prepared assault actually conquered the Chemin des Dames ridge, though only after an enormous bombardment and prodigious expenditure of resources. When the presidents of the two parliamentary chambers urged an all-out autumn offensive, Painlevé refused, and Georges Clemenceau, who became premier in November, also accepted Pétain's doctrine.[159] Had America still been neutral and US Treasury credits unavailable that doctrine would not have been viable and the French economy unable to sustain the re-equipment burden, in which case the April gamble might well have lost the Allies the war.

The change of strategy came none too soon. Pétain, Painlevé, and Foch had already been thinking in such terms, but the mutinies left them little choice. In some units discipline fractured on the opening day, and as the fighting continued soldiers' letters became not just resigned but also angry: the operation had been an incompetent massacre. The mutinies developed from mid May, and reached their paroxysm in early June. Although they followed the Nivelle offensive only after a time lag, and they spread beyond the Aisne, they were concentrated in the attack sector and among the divisions that had participated.[160] The movement was remarkably non-violent and in its way a manifestation of disciplined indiscipline: some men displayed red flags and borrowed the language of soviets, but most would stay in the line if treated with dignity and their conditions improved, and they were spared from botched attacks. Their grievances included miserable food and accommodation, inadequate rest, and too little (and too unpredictable) home leave. Some 30,000–40,000 soldiers may have taken part in two-thirds of the army's divisions,[161] and the peak of the unrest coincided with a broader malaise, including a May–June strike wave. Although the German front commanders had some inkling of developments, the OHL seems to have gained a comprehensive picture only in late June, by which time the movement was subsiding.[162] Pétain's remedy was selective repression (coming largely after officers on the spot had contained the upheaval) combined with better material conditions and the new strategy. But although the acutest stage passed quickly, it was months, if ever, before morale recovered, and during the summer

French *civilians* were deeply depressed,[163] while both Ribot's government and that of Painlevé (who became premier between September and November) lacked safe majorities and lurched from crisis to crisis. Painlevé appointed an investigative commission into the offensive, under General Joseph Brugère, which produced a cautious report that did not satisfy him, though his government fell before it could pursue the matter.[164] The commission judged, none the less, that Micheler and Nivelle had failed in their duties.

Many observers noted the change in Nivelle. He departed into obscurity in a North African command, where his views remained unaltered. He appears a classic example of a man who rose beyond his ability, and lacked the astuteness needed for high office. He brought tactical experience from Verdun, but having devised his scheme became content to reiterate its general principles, more stubbornly as criticism grew. He won and retained authorization for an attack that his Operations Bureau Chief and Army Group Commanders expected to fail. French casualties of 134,000 killed, wounded, or captured in the first ten days[165] were comparable to those in Joffre's 1915 offensives but suffered in a shorter period of time, while the territory gained was smaller than the most pessimistic had foreseen, and expectations now were higher. Painlevé rightly feared the damage to combatant and civilian morale, even though the country seemed to recover. By the armistice the army was intensely weary, and the memory of 1917 contributed both to France's defensiveness and pacifism in the 1930s and to disaster in 1940.

Nivelle had been appointed by the Briand ministry, which endorsed his plans. French politicians regained control of national strategy, and kept it. The British government also approved the Nivelle Plan, in deference to the French though also because Lloyd George lacked confidence in his own military. The complex diplomacy that created these inter-Allied arrangements established a further element of inflexibility. By the time Ribot and Painlevé took over, countermanding the offensive would carry major costs—not least, paradoxically, to relations with London. The debates of early April were exceptionally revealing as deliberations in extreme uncertainty, which despite submarine warfare, the Russian Revolution, and American entry still concluded that the balance of risks favoured going ahead. French leaders faced a lack of obvious alternatives, given the revulsion against the Somme strategy, and that only from April did waiting

6

The Kerensky Offensive

During 1917 one army after another wasted itself in failed offensives. France on the Aisne, Britain in Flanders, and Italy on the Isonzo launched campaigns that tried their soldiers to breaking point. Still more calamitous were events in Russia, where the abortive Kerensky offensive of June/July, falling midway between Nicholas's abdication and the Bolshevik takeover, hobbled the liberals and moderate socialists who governed the country between the two revolutions and helped clear the path for Lenin and the Bolsheviks. By supporting the offensive the Bolsheviks' rivals exposed themselves to charges of wasting lives and of flirting with counter-revolution. They antagonized not only the Russian public but also the troops. Even had the Provisional Government signed a separate ceasefire—or at least stayed on the defensive—its future would have been precarious. But that it took neither course allowed it to be outflanked, and accelerated Russia's trajectory towards anarchy and dictatorship. Even so, by remaining a belligerent, the Provisional Government lent the Western Allies a breathing space during their gravest hour of crisis. The unfolding of the war and the revolution were intextricably interlinked.[1]

The February Revolution grew out of strains on Russia's economy, on its army, and on relations between the Romanovs and the Duma and high command. In the end the liberals carried out a form of coup,[2] pressing Nicholas to abdicate in order to safeguard the empire and its war effort against a more radical upheaval. The Provisional Government inherited an economy headed for hyperinflation in which neither the cities nor the army were adequately supplied. Its troops were mutinous, and their units haemorrhaging from desertion. Yet it also inherited inter-Allied agreements that envisaged a major spring attack. Its strategy and its implements were ill-matched.

The Western Allies' military chiefs wanted to renew their coordinated 1916 offensives as early as possible (see chapter 4). In contrast, the Stavka believed that Russia had sacrificed itself to help its partners by hastening its advance into East Prussia in August 1914 and its attack at Lake Narocz in March 1916, as well as by accelerating its summer 1916 Brusilov offensive. France and Britain had not sufficiently reciprocated during the Central Powers' eastward drive in 1915, and nor had they delivered enough supplies. The Stavka's alternative 1917 strategy—which would strengthen Russia's influence in the Balkans—was to eliminate Bulgaria through pincer attacks by the Russians from Romania and by the Salonika army from Macedonia. When the Allied prime ministers considered this proposal at a November 1916 meeting in Paris, however, they objected that the Central Powers benefited in the Balkans from interior lines of communication and could more than match any Allied deployment. Instead the prime ministers adopted the Chantilly scheme, which meant that Russia would again attack as part of a plan set by the West and one that envisaged a February offensive at a time when operations were scarcely feasible even in normal winters, let alone in one as harsh as 1916–17.

Well before the February Revolution in fact, the weaknesses in the Chantilly scheme became glaring. On 17–18/30–31 December the Front commanders met under Nicholas II's chairmanship. They pleaded that neither the army's equipment nor its manpower would be up to strength in time. Nicholas still approved a memorandum of 24 January/6 February by CGS Alekseyev that envisaged the main offensive being directed, as in 1916, by the South-Western Front armies, towards Lviv and the Galician oilfields. Here the Russians faced mainly Austro-Hungarians, the railways were adequate, and the Russian troop numbers relatively dense, thus reducing preparation time. Other sectors would deliver supporting attacks, particularly the Western Front armies towards Vilnius.[3] (In this chapter the 'Western Front' refers not to France and Belgium but to the group of armies in the central portion of the Russian Front, between the Northern and South-Western 'Fronts'.) At the inter-Allied Petrograd conference opening on 19 January/1 February, however, General Gurko, standing in for Alekseyev, warned that February would be too early. The conference's military committee agreed instead that an Allied general offensive could start during April, with the Russians commencing, at the latest, a month after the West.[4] This was the situation when the Provisional Government took office.

In early 1917 the Russian army still seemed imposing. It was better equipped, partly because a new railway had opened to Archangel, where Allied supplies had accumulated. The British understood that between 1 April 1916 and 1 January 1917 Russian field gun numbers rose from 5,193 to 6,316 and heavy guns and howitzers from 1,183 to 2,066, while munitions output almost doubled.[5] The army was also at record size, though its losses were ever harder to replace. As of 30 April, the Stavka estimated, the active army numbered 7,060,700. Yet since 1914 no fewer than 4,467,800 men had been killed, wounded, or captured, and 4,269,500 had fallen sick. Many units were below regulation strength: the South–Western Front armies by 150,000.[6] Moreover, during the winter a massive reorganization caused more disruption. Paralleling changes in France and Germany, it aimed to increase the number of infantry divisions (and hence rotate them more easily into the reserve) by cutting regiments per division from four to three. Divisional manpower would diminish but machine–gun and artillery provision would rise to compensate. French observers considered the scheme sound, and Nicholas and Gurko approved it, but it would unsettle virtually every unit in the army, and Alekseyev thought it unwise so close to an offensive.[7] Moreover, Russia lacked the artillery to equip the additional divisions, as well as experienced officers to command them. After the revolution many of the new formations became foci of indiscipline.

Several of the factors that plunged the Russian army into crisis therefore pre-dated the change of regime. Demoralization and unrest had spread during 1916, and at the core of the February Revolution was the Petrograd garrison's mutiny. But after the revolution the process intensified, and spread out from the capital. This contradicted the intentions of the Provisional Government, which had taken power to avert political and social breakdown, and appointed a conservative liberal, Aleksandr Guchkov, as war minister. When on 8/21 March (six days after Nicholas abdicated) Nivelle asked for an offensive by mid to late April, Alekseyev replied that the earliest he could manage was 1 May.[8] But he then received a despondent message from Guchkov that the government could do only what the Petrograd Soviet permitted: 'The demoralization of the reserve units of the interior districts has set in and is making progress', and the authorities could neither requisition more horses (which the peasants needed for sowing) nor transport and feed them; nor deliver artillery in time.[9] On 13/26 March Alekseyev advised Nivelle that actually he could not launch a big attack until June or July: the roads were impassable, morale had suffered, and he could not make up either men or horses to regulation strength. When Alekseyev consulted his Front commanders, Brusilov, on the South-Western Front, said his officers believed the army was ready and willing to attack, but the Western Front commander, Aleksei Evert, was pessimistic about morale (though believing an offensive necessary to divert the men from politics); and the Northern Front commander, Ruszky, reported his units were 'sick', below strength, and the officers and men distrusted each other. The contrasting responses mirrored the February Revolution's ambiguity, and the hopes of some like Brusilov that it might stir a patriotic awakening.[10] But at a gloomy Stavka conference on 18/31 March reality set in. Alekseyev's Director of Military Operations, General Aleksandr Lukomsky, reported food supplies were inadequate for the army at its present size, and he must either further cut rations or reduce the number of troops. Weapons and ammunition supply had been disrupted, as had the railways and horse provision. There were 'low spirits among the officers, unrest among the troops, and a great number of deserters'.[11] A spring offensive was impossible. Yet Alekseyev still hoped that, if the army attacked, the soldiers' new passion for politics would subside, and believed that a breakdown in discipline would be more serious if they were defending than if they were advancing. Like Nivelle and Haig, he also feared that inactivity would free the Central Powers to strike at a time and place of their choosing. Finally, he saw danger in disappointing Russia's Allied partners, who might retaliate. The risks of doing nothing therefore exceeded those of going ahead.[12] In short, the Provisional Government had inherited an offensive plan and the high command still wanted to implement it, despite being divided over the timing. None the less, the project hung fire.

A first reason was German strategy. The February Revolution came as a surprise to Ludendorff. He felt that 'A hundredweight burden fell from my heart',[13] although the implications were difficult to appraise. Hindenburg wondered afterwards whether he should have attacked the Russians at once, given the ease with which the Germans would halt the Nivelle offensive. But the OHL remembered how in 1792 a Prussian invasion had galvanized French revolutionary nationalism.[14] Bethmann Hollweg opposed forceful intervention, and the high command as well as the Austro-Hungarian Foreign Minister Ottokar Czernin went along with him.[15] Instead it was agreed to wait while Russia disintegrated, though to assist the process by facilitating the return from exile of revolutionaries such as Lenin—who arrived in Petrograd from Zurich on 21 March/3 April—while local commanders encouraged fraternization. German intelligence officers freely crossed the lines, and the Central Powers lobbed pamphlets and newspapers into the opposing trenches, which were often read without hindrance.[16] Finally, despite much of the front relapsing into a de facto truce, the Germans continued localized attacks, the biggest occurring on the River Stokhod on 21–22 March/3–4 April, when they overran an exposed Russian bridgehead. Bethmann insisted on Ludendorff not trumpeting the victory, but the Stavka was mortified by Germany's capture of 9,000 prisoners in one day.[17]

A second obstacle to an offensive was the Provisional Government's weakness. It lacked legitimacy. Although it received Allied diplomatic recognition it had not taken power legally, and although it was composed of Duma members the Duma ceased to sit. And as the revolution replaced the police by local militias and destroyed the tsar's hierarchical system of local administration, the government lost authority in the provinces and over the subject nationalities, which—particularly in Finland and the Ukraine—soon sought autonomy. The economic difficulties that had sparked the revolution became still more acute: according to the British liaison officer Alfred Knox, coal production in April was 20 per cent down on April 1916 and pig iron production 17.2 per cent.[18] Enormous wage demands (to keep pace with inflation) and strikes for the eight-hour day proliferated.[19] Against a backdrop of sharpening class consciousness, the government shared the capital with the Petrograd Soviet, which though elected by the city's workers and soldiers was composed largely of intelligentsia: more precisely of Socialist Revolutionaries and Mensheviks, who saw February as just a beginning but suspected the government of wanting to put the clock back. Fear of counter-revolution lay behind the Soviet's Order No. 1, whose consequences spread through much of the army. It took symbolic steps such as abolishing compulsory saluting for off-duty soldiers and forbidding officers from using the familiar second person ('ty') when addressing their men. But its key provision was for the lower ranks in all companies, battalions, regiments, batteries, and squadrons (as well as navy warships), to elect committees, and for the committees rather than the officers to control the weapons; while orders from the government should be implemented only in so far as they were compatible with orders and resolutions from the Soviet. Subsequently an Order No. 2 clarified that the soldiers' committees would not elect their officers (although they could object to their appointment), but that to prevent counter-revolution the Petrograd garrison must not be disarmed. The government would remain a hostage in its own capital.[20]

Although the Provisional Government sacked many commanders (and rapid turnover in the upper ranks became endemic), middle and junior officers largely stayed in post. In the navy dozens of officers were murdered, but in the army violence was rarer, though officers were humiliated and old scores settled. In the Fifteenth Army, according to the British Major J. F. Neilson, authority collapsed with bewildering speed, and Order No. 1 was the main instrument, though followed up by agitators from Petrograd.[21] Eyewitnesses commented on the exhilarating sense of liberation. The revolutionary impact was greatest round the capital city, in the Baltic Fleet, and in the Northern and Western Front army groups; the South-Western and Romanian Fronts were less affected. It touched the infantry more than the cavalry and artillery (which had more long-serving officers and men). Nor were soldiers' committees everywhere subversive. Alekseyev quickly accepted them, and in many units they cooperated with the officers. Even so, during April conditions deteriorated, and even Brusilov became less confident.[22] Visitors to his sector were bemused to encounter troops freely reading German propaganda and Bolshevik newspapers, routine tasks neglected, roads not repaired, horses not fed, and front-line men going bathing or sitting smoking and playing cards.[23] Most immediately preoccupying were desertions. Between August 1914 and the February Revolution they totalled some 205,000 but between February and 1 August 1917 an additional 170,000 deserted.[24] Soldiers on leave clogged the trains, sometimes commandeering them and storming the first-class compartments. Moreover, the ordinary troops largely originated in the countryside, and in March and April peasant unrest spread across Central Russia. It led on to seizures of aristocratic land, in which returning veterans participated.[25] Although most front-line soldiers stayed in place, it grew harder to keep units, and especially reserve units, up to strength. Of 22,000 men supposed to move up to replenish the Twelfth Army during May, only 14,353 actually arrived.[26] And if no reservists replaced the troops on active service, the latter feared that they would never escape, hence missing out on the redistribution in their villages.

Many officers blamed this state of affairs on the Provisional Government and on Guchkov. It is true that the government acquiesced in Order No. 1, and abolished the death penalty. Many of its members were humanitarians and idealists, who had suffered from tsarist oppression and abhorred bloodshed. Guchkov played for time, assuring Allied representatives that it was wisest to be patient and avoid draconian measures.[27] The deadlock between

the Soviet and the Provisional Government impeded action, until broken
by a controversy over war aims.

The tsarist government had been at the centre of the inter-Allied web
of secret treaties. As late as February–March 1917, Gaston Doumergue,
who led the French delegation at the Petrograd conference, obtained a
Russian pledge to support France's Rhineland demands in return for
French support for Russia's plans in Poland. The Provisional Government
promised Poland autonomy but in a 'free military alliance' with Russia,
reaffirming the tsarist government's bold commitment to conquering
Poland's German– and Austrian–ruled areas.[28] When the new ministers
learned about the other secret treaties, however, most were shocked and
wanted to revise them. The main exception was Pavel Milyukov, the
Provisional Government's foreign minister, who reassured Russia's partners
that it remained committed to victory.[29] He gave an uncompromising
interview, calling for an independent Czechoslovakia, unification of the
Serbs, and Russian annexation of Constantinople.[30] Under the guise of
self–determination, this was a programme for Russian expansion and for
breaking up both Austria–Hungary and Turkey. It did not reflect the prevailing Cabinet view, and Aleksandr Kerensky, the minister of justice, in a
counter–interview proposed the 'internationalization' of Constantinople
as an alternative.[31] Milyukov and Kerensky were now publicly at odds, and
a statement by the premier, Prince Georgy Lvov, on 14/27 March struggled to reconcile their viewpoints. Russia, it said, must be defended against
invasion, and would observe its obligations to its allies. But it did not aim
to dominate other countries or seize their national possessions, and it sought
a stable peace based on self–determination.[32] War aims, moreover, not only
divided the Cabinet, but also separated it from the Petrograd Soviet.
Already the Soviet had appealed to the world's proletarians to launch a
decisive struggle against their governments, and to German workers to
overthrow the regime in Berlin. The way to end the war was by spreading
revolution and through both sides moderating their objectives.[33] The
Soviet embraced the 'Petrograd formula' of a peace without annexations
or indemnities, based on national self–determination, in contrast with
Milyukov's vision. It pressed harder after the Socialist Revolutionary leader,
Viktor Chernov, returned from exile.[34] Chernov saw a revolution in
Germany as the best means for enabling Russia to exit from the war, and
wanted Russia publicly to scale down its war aims. After Lenin returned,
moreover, although the Bolshevik leaders within Russia repudiated his

extreme anti-war position, the new arrival began to win over the party rank and file.[35]

The struggle over war aims culminated when a political crisis led to Mensheviks and Socialist Revolutionaries from the Soviet entering a new government. The crisis began when the Cabinet bowed to Soviet pressure by forwarding officially to the Allies Lvov's compromise statement of 14/27 March. Milyukov protested that it was ambiguous (as indeed it was), and if Russia's allies thought it meant renouncing annexations and indemnities they might reject it. Hence he accompanied it with a covering note endorsed by his ministerial colleagues. It insisted that the government would defend the motherland and stand by its obligations, while the Allies established 'guarantees and sanctions' against future wars.[36] Since Nicholas's abdication the capital had been surprisingly orderly,[37] but on May Day crowds spilled out into the streets, denouncing the war and demanding Milyukov's resignation. A new coalition was formed. Lvov continued as premier but Mikhail Tereshchenko replaced Milyukov as foreign minister and Kerensky replaced Guchkov as war minster, while the government brought in Soviet representatives, including Chernov as minister of agriculture and a leading Menshevik, Irakli Tsereteli, at Posts and Telecommunications. Tsereteli led a faction, the 'Siberian Zimmerwaldians', who commanded a Soviet majority. While in exile in Siberia they had come to accept that in certain circumstances socialists could support a defensive war.[38]

According to British Ambassador Buchanan, the new government 'offers us last and almost forlorn hope of saving military situation on this side'.[39] Actually the Soviet representatives had conflicting purposes, some seeking to steer the government towards the Soviet's programme, others to stay in the war and avert anarchy. The coalition made the Kerensky offensive possible, but as part of a bargain. Tereshchenko reassured Buchanan that prosecuting the war was 'the end and aim of their policy', but the Soviet wanted further democratization of the army and improvement of its fighting effectiveness, as a complement to an activist foreign policy that sought the speediest possible peace, and negotiations with the Allies to reduce their war aims.[40] The new government declared that it opposed a separate peace but would pursue a general one based on no annexations or indemnities and on national self-determination. As the Allies' defeat would be incompatible with such a peace, however, it believed the army would not let the Central Powers first beat the Western Allies and then turn eastwards in full strength: hence its top priority would be to democratize the army and reinforce its offensive and defensive fighting power.[41] This formulation sidestepped the feeling amongst officers that the army's democratization was precisely what was undermining fighting efficiency, and it left Russia's military strategy open; although by saying the Western Allies should not be crushed it leaned towards attacking. None the less, as Tsereteli's associate, the Menshevik Fyodor Dan, put it, the revolution must end the war before the war destroyed the revolution.[42] The new coalition therefore pursued peace at the same time as preparing the troops: the twin tracks of the 'revolutionary defencism' Tsereteli had espoused since returning from Siberian exile.

It is harder to reconstruct the Petrograd decision-making process than those in Paris or London. The Cabinet kept no minutes, and according to its secretary it had no fixed agendas, was often barely quorate, and exhausted ministers dozed during reports.[43] It remains possible, none the less, to trace the moderate socialists' logic. The coalition suspended domestic reform until the convening of a Constituent Assembly, thus making it all the more imperative to disengage from the war. As the Provisional Government and the Petrograd Soviet both ruled out a separate peace, however, the only way forward was to press the belligerent governments to facilitate a general peace by reducing war aims. Russia should repudiate Nicholas's annexation-ism, and court the international working-class and socialist movements. During the spring and early summer the Russians tried to influence the Western Allies and the Central Powers accordingly, while the Austrian Emperor Karl and his Foreign Minister Czernin acted similarly (though less publicly) on the other side.[44] By June, however, when the Kerensky offen-sive was authorized, diplomacy had reached a dead end, and with it the government's hopes of disengaging without breaking alliance undertakings. Rather than achieve a decisive military breakthrough, the offensive was meant to shake up the situation, strengthen Russia's leverage over its part-ners, and moderate its enemies.

The Central Powers should be taken first. The Berlin Foreign Ministry feared the revolution would strengthen Russia's loyalty to the Western Allies, and even that the British had instigated it.[45] The first Provisional Government indeed rejected a separate peace, and the second did so almost equally emphatically, with backing from the Soviet and all the political parties, even Lenin denouncing any one-sided deal with the German capitalists. Unofficially, however, the Russians were at least willing to sound out their enemies. Yet when Austria-Hungary pressed for the Central Powers to reciprocate by repudiating annexations and indemnities, Germany resisted.

The Austrians, whose provinces of Eastern Galicia and the Bukovina lay under Russian occupation, stood to gain from a mutual renunciation, whereas the Germans planned to dominate Poland, Lithuania, and Courland in perpetuity. Although Bethmann was willing to make a peace gesture, Wilhelm and Ludendorff disagreed, and the government confined itself to an inspired newspaper article.[46] The episode underlined how, since the submarine-warfare decision, Bethmann had lost his freedom of action. Hindenburg and Ludendorff repeatedly complained to Wilhelm about the chancellor, and wanted to pin Bethmann to a new programme of war aims. Conversely, Bethmann wanted to retain the maximum discretion over war aims in order to split the Allies, but when Wilhelm insisted he had to submit.[47]

The outcome was the Kreuznach Programme of war aims, agreed at a conference on 23 April and, when later published, becoming a standing indictment of German militarism. The text approved by Wilhelm drew heavily on a Hindenburg draft. Bethmann initialled it but minuted that he did not consider himself bound and it would be 'laughable' to resign over 'fantasies'.[48] He stressed the programme was attainable only in the extremely unlikely event of Berlin being able to dictate terms. Germany would annex Luxemburg and the French iron-ore basin of Briey-Longwy, as well as the Belgian armaments centre (and strategic river crossing) at Liège. The rest of Belgium would remain German-controlled until ready for a permanent alliance. Poland likewise would fall under Berlin's 'predominance', with German annexations (and population resettlement) on its northern and western borders, while Courland and Lithuania would be annexed. The navy demanded Flemish and Baltic harbours as part of a worldwide network of bases. In essence the Kreuznach Programme was a scheme for western and eastern buffer states, from which to menace Paris, the Thames estuary, and Petrograd.[49] Yet Hindenburg and Ludendorff wanted more, as did Wilhelm, who insisted on clarifying Germany's objectives before opening negotiations with Russia. He envisaged partitioning Belgium, and depriving Russia of Livonia, Estonia, and the Ukraine.[50] Such ambitions were an obstacle not only to a separate peace with Russia, but also to a general settlement.

None the less, a succession of German–Russian contacts occurred, the most sustained being the Erzberger–Kolyschko conversations. Josef Kolyschko was a journalist and state councillor who had worked under Sergei Witte, the pre-war Russian finance minister, and who indicated that he would be serving in the Provisional Government, although exactly what authority it had given him remains obscure. Mathias Erzberger was a deputy leader of

the German Catholic Centre Party and in close contact with the German
and Austro-Hungarian Foreign Ministries. At the first meeting, held in
Stockholm on 26 March, Kolyschko said the Provisional Government
needed an assurance that Germany would not intervene in Russia's internal
affairs and could grant an honourable peace, which a speech by Bethmann
three days later went some way towards satisfying. When Erzberger and
Kolyschko met again, on 19 April, they discussed returning to the 1914
borders with 'frontier corrections', while a plebiscite determined the future
of Poland. Bethmann and Zimmermann were broadly satisfied with this
conversation, and Kolyschko took Erzberger's statements to Petrograd with
a view to preparing a further rendezvous.[51] Ludendorff, however, was outraged at the modesty of the gains envisaged, and Zimmermann admitted
that Erzberger had exceeded his brief. At a further Kreuznach conference,
held on 17–18 May, Austria-Hungary and Germany agreed on Courland
and Lithuania's 'territorial attachment' to Germany and that Poland would
'lean towards' it.[52]

Under the second Provisional Government, moreover, Russian interest
also cooled. When Erzberger returned to Stockholm for a third meeting,
Kolyschko refused to see him, and was later arrested in Petrograd. During
May, German and Austrian Front commanders unavailingly offered armistice talks to their Russian counterparts.[53] General Vladimir Dragomirov's
troops pushed him into talking to the Germans, but when the latter sent
a draft ceasefire they received no reply.[54] The final development was the
Grimm–Hoffmann Affair. Robert Grimm, a Swiss socialist who had travelled to Petrograd, asked the head of the Swiss Foreign Ministry, Arthur
Hoffmann, to obtain a statement of German war aims for use in conversations
with the Russians. Remarkably, given the unorthodox channel, Zimmermann
provided one. The Germans offered non-interference in Russia's internal
affairs and a 'friendly understanding' over Poland, Lithuania, and Courland,
while Russia would return what it had conquered from Austria-Hungary.[55]
As the correspondence was published in Stockholm on 18 June, it was as
well the Germans reserved the interests of Austria-Hungary and of Turkey,
neither of whose governments had they consulted. The contact went no
further—Hoffmann had to resign and Grimm to leave Russia—but it confirmed that the minimum tariff for a separate peace would be loss of Russian
sovereignty over Poland, Lithuania, and Courland, as well as a client relationship with the Central Powers. These revelations came at the same time
as Russian diplomacy vis-à-vis the Allies also reached an impasse.

For a general peace, the two sides' bargaining positions had to be reconciled. Hence the Russians had practical reasons for calling on the belligerents to renounce annexations and indemnities, in addition to their moral and ideo-logical objections to a war of aggrandisement. If the second Provisional Government followed a twin-track policy of seeking peace while readying the Russian army, its diplomacy followed a twin track within the twin track. On the one hand, the Foreign Ministry pursued a conference of the Allied governments, tasked with revising down their war aims; on the other, the Soviet appealed for an international socialist conclave.

Tsereteli and the new foreign minister, Tereschchenko, were agreed the socialist gathering must come first, to work on Allied public opinion before the intergovernmental meeting.[56] They hoped to capitalize on Russia's pres-tige within the European socialist movement. After seeing membership plummet in 1914, that movement was now reviving, galvanized by revulsion against exorbitant casualties and by wartime austerity, and yet it remained divided. On the one hand the patriotic socialists on the Right (or the 'Majority', as they were commonly known), which until 1917 included most of the British Labour Party, the French *Section française de l'Internationale ouvrière* (SFIO), and the German SPD, supported the war effort, voted war credits, and even (in Britain, France, and Belgium) entered the government. On the other, the Centre (or 'Minority'), including the Independent Labour Party in Britain and growing factions within the SFIO and SPD as well as most of the Italian *Partito Socialista Italiano* (PSI), neither voted credits nor entered governments, and wanted to restore peace via negotiation and through popular protest. Finally the Left or 'Zimmerwaldian' wing included revolutionaries such as Lenin who wanted a mass uprising, and its adherents were ready to meet with socialists from the opposing camp. Some of them had done so already, at the Zimmerwald and Kienthal conferences held in 1915 and 1916 in Switzerland. In Russia patriotic socialism was weak and the Zimmerwaldian element strong; although the Mensheviks and Socialist Revolutionaries who drove the policies of the second Provisional Government were aligned with the Centre. The project for an international conference emanated from disparate initiatives, united by ambitions to rebuild the semblance of unity provided by the Socialist International in the halcyon years before 1914.

The first appeal came from Dutch and Scandinavian socialists, working through the vestige of the International known as the International Socialist Bureau or ISB. On 9/22 April they invited the European socialist parties to attend a conference in Stockholm on 15/28 May. On 14/27 April the Zimmerwaldian socialists appealed for a third Zimmerwaldian conference to precede the event. Initial reactions from the Allied majoritarian parties were hostile, the more so because the SPD supported the idea and the German and Austrian governments were willing for their socialists to attend. Although Ludendorff disagreed, Zimmermann hoped to deprive the Allies of a propaganda point and to calm domestic dissension; and he believed that if the SPD attended the minoritarians who had broken away in the newly formed Independent Social Democratic Party (USPD) should go too, or the SPD would appear as stooges. Bethmann quickly agreed.[57] But if the SPD were present, Allied socialists would be meeting Germans in the midst of a life-and-death struggle, and at first the SFIO and the Belgian and British Labour parties all decided not to participate.[58]

At this point the Petrograd Soviet climbed on the bandwagon. The Dutch and Scandinavians sent a representative to Russia, and Tsereteli and his comrades felt a duty to give leadership. On 2/15 May, during the Milyukov crisis, the Soviet appealed for an international socialist conference. It presented the February Revolution as the first stage of a global upheaval that would end the war, and called on all socialists to press their governments to make peace.[59] It joined the Dutch and Scandinavians in a preparatory commission, and clarified that the conference would be open to all elements, but they must liquidate the policy of 'national unity' with imperialist governments.[60] Although the majoritarian Allied socialists remained unenthusiastic, the issue now was whether to make concessions to keep the Russians in the war, and to preserve the Western parties' unity. Further, although the Provisional Government did not publish the secret war aims agreements that it had found in the Russian Foreign Ministry archives, their existence was widely rumoured. The implication was that Allied socialists, in supporting a struggle they had supposed to be defensive, had been duped.

The Allied governments sent representatives of their more patriotic socialists to win the Russians round, but this tactic blew up in their faces. The Belgian socialists were the most intransigent, and given the fate that had befallen Belgium the Soviet respected their position. It was much cooler towards the French and British. However, after Arthur Henderson, the leader of the Labour Party and a member of Lloyd George's War Cabinet, arrived in Petrograd on 20 May/2 June he grew more sympathetic to the moderate Russian socialists, though loathing Bolshevik extremism.

He disliked the Stockholm conference proposal, but decided that if it went ahead then Labour should attend.[61] Henderson's French counterpart was Albert Thomas, a leading SFIO figure, who was also French minister of armaments.[62] Thomas was sent initially to deal with the French ambassador, Paléologue, who had become too identified with the tsarist regime and ill-advisedly threw his weight behind Milyukov and against Kerensky. Thomas replaced him, and Ribot accepted Thomas's recommendation to support the new Russian coalition, as the British government accepted similar advice from Buchanan. But after Thomas was briefed about the Doumergue Agreement, which had been kept secret from the Cabinet in which he had served, he agreed that France must reduce its war aims.[63] Marius Moutet and Marcel Cachin, two SFIO deputies who accompanied Thomas, reacted to the disclosure more strongly. They urged the SFIO to renounce annexations and attend Stockholm, and on 27–28 May the party's National Council agreed to send representatives to a preliminary meeting.[64] This turnabout came at a moment when strikes were spreading through Paris and the French army mutinies were approaching their crescendo.

It was not, however, the socialist parties that would settle the conference's fate. The French government had already secretly decided to refuse passports. At the end of May a weary Ribot was willing to reconsider, but the premier faced a Cabinet revolt and a blunt warning from Pétain that if passports were granted he could not answer for army discipline—as Pétain put it, losing Russia was a lesser danger than a collapse in army morale.[65] Hence on 1 June the government announced its decision to withhold passports, and Ribot defended himself in a long and stormy secret session of the Chamber of Deputies. He distanced himself from the Doumergue Agreement, but stood by the vaguer language of the letter from Briand to Paul Cambon (see chapter 5) which most of the Cabinet (though not the socialists) had accepted, and which envisaged leaving it to France to decide the Rhineland's future. On 6 June the Chamber voted 467:52 for a compromise, the Dumont Resolution, according to which France was fighting for 'the liberation of invaded territories, the return of Alsace-Lorraine ... and the just reparation of damages'. Although opposed to 'conquering and subjugating foreign populations', it desired the overthrow of 'Prussian militarism' and 'lasting guarantees of peace and independence for both large and small nations in an organisation ... of the League of Nations'.[66] The government denied that regaining Alsace-Lorraine constituted an annexation, and that reparations for damage constituted an indemnity, but the Dumont Resolution certainly conflicted with the spirit of the Petrograd Soviet's peace formula and yet was supported not only by the Right and Centre but also by half the SFIO. Ribot did enough, therefore, to divide the socialists, and dealt a body blow to Stockholm. The Italian government followed France's example, and the Americans had already done so.[67] The Socialist Party of America opposed the war, and Wilson considered inter-socialist discussions were 'likely to make a deal of mischief'.[68] Uncertainty lingered only in Britain, where the War Cabinet initially inclined to let the Labour Party attend the Stockholm conference but Labour itself was reluctant. In August, after Henderson returned from Russia, Labour followed the SFIO in reversing itself, but by now the Cabinet too had changed its mind, and denied passports.[69] Although Henderson resigned from the War Cabinet, another Labour representative, George Barnes, replaced him. The Stockholm conference never met.

The other arm of Russia's peace offensive made still less progress. The Tsereteli group intended the Stockholm meeting to prepare the terrain for an inter-Allied governmental conference, and they wanted to act quickly, liquidating the war within months. But Tereshchenko, though less expansionist than Milyukov, was uncommitted to their cause. From a non-party rather than socialist background, he had made a fortune from Ukrainian sugar and had travelled and knew languages but otherwise had few qualifications for his new role, beyond being acceptable to all parties and able to work with Kerensky. He did not seek to annex Constantinople and the Straits, but he was willing to consider neutralizing them, and did not feel unequivocally bound to the Petrograd Soviet's peace formula. Further, he began with the embarrassment of the Allies' responses to Prince Lvov's 14/27 March declaration and the covering letter that Milyukov had forwarded. The replies were tardy and critical, and published only after Tereshchenko managed to tone them down. Even that from the Americans, who shared Russia's distaste for the inter-Allied secret treaties, offered little basis for a Petrograd–Washington axis. Certainly Wilson denied seeking 'aggrandisement' or any 'selfish object', but he emphasized that a return to the pre-1914 status quo was unacceptable, wrongs must be righted, safeguards created, and 'effective readjustments' implemented.[70] Implicit here was the president's new doctrine of seeking peace through victory, not without it, and prosecuting the war more vigorously rather than negotiating now. The European Allies were still more dismissive. The Italians denied seeking conquest or domination. The French refused to discuss war aims, but believed that only victory could be the basis for a lasting peace; they sought the return of Alsace-Lorraine, 'reparatory indemnities', and guarantees against another war. Finally, the British voiced willingness to reconsider their agreements in conjunction with the other Allies, but they denied pursuing conquest, and they noted the Provisional Government's intention to liberate all parts of Poland, an undertaking that by itself excluded any accommodation with the Central Powers.[71] The British Cabinet had just approved a programme of expansion in the Middle East,[72] while the French had only months before adopted the Cambon letter and the Doumergue Agreement, and the Italians stood by the 1915 Treaty of London. On 31 May/13 June Tereshchenko told Thomas that Russia sought a general peace that excluded all imperialist designs, and proposed an early inter-Allied war aims conference, but his note contained neither a date nor an agenda, and nor was it even officially forwarded, thus saving Russia's partners the embarrassment of having to reply.[73]

The disappointing outcome of Provisional Government diplomacy highlighted the obstacles to ending the war by compromise. Partly the issues were territorial: the German government wished to annex portions of Poland and Lithuania and to turn the remainder, with Courland, into buffer states (to which shopping list it would soon add the Ukraine); the Provisional Government had not abandoned hope of neutralizing or internationalizing Constantinople, and expanding Poland at Germany's expense. And even if Bethmann might have been willing to moderate German demands, his influence was fading. Although the Provisional Government would not cede ethnically Russian populations under a separate peace, it would lose great industrial and agricultural wealth and would allow a formidable enemy to reach closer to Petrograd. Yet the quest for a general peace had also failed. The Stockholm conference proposal divided the Western European Left, but its influence on the Allied governments was slight, as the shadow-boxing over Tereshchhenko's conference proposal underlined. Neither France nor Britain would entertain the idea, which Tereshchenko had been pushed into by the Soviet. He and Kerensky were very willing to suspend it. Hence diplomacy seemed unlikely to free the Provisional Government from its predicament, and this increased the temptation to try force. On 1 June Tereshchenko informed his ambassadors that the direction of Russia's foreign policy was linked to the condition of the army and the

Figure 9. Kerensky in the Cabinet room, 1917

possibility of an offensive. He advised the Russian chargé in London that the time for discussing a revision of Allied war aims would be 'after the present efforts of the Provisional Government to restore the situation on our front are crowned with success'.[74]

In contrast to developments in France, Britain, and Italy, the offensive became a politicians' project, although the generals went along with it. At a Stavka conference on 1/14 May the Front commanders told Alekseyev that the army was on the eve of disintegration', but 'regardless, we must go on the offensive'. Alekseyev agreed—the Western Powers took Russia less and less into consideration, and without an offensive 'we will be in a very serious situation as regards further military action or even the conclusion of peace'.[75] The crucial figure, however, was Kerensky as war minister. Even though his nomination was agreed with Alekseyev, the latter privately thought Kerensky a 'nincompoop' and a 'charlatan'; and according to Knox, 'Kerensky ministry are [sic] enthusiastic, honest, and energetic, but he has no administrative experience and probably no idea as to the value of discipline'.[76] Kerensky surrounded himself with younger officers and carried through another purge of senior commanders, including Alekseyev himself, whom he replaced by Brusilov, only weeks before Brusilov's South-Western Front armies were to spearhead the assault. Despite or because of his 1916 success, Brusilov lacked respect in the officer corps and was seen as too much of a yes-man: he proved ineffective. For his part, Kerensky originated from a professional family in the same Volga city of Simbirsk as Lenin; as a law student he became radicalized and defended regime opponents before being elected to the Duma in 1912 as a member of the Trudovik (Labour) faction of the Socialist Revolutionaries. He played a leading role in the February Days, when one of his guiding principles was not to compromise the war effort,[77] and between 1914 and 1917 he had supported a defensive war while upholding his revolutionary ideals, thus differentiating himself from the Progressive Bloc.[78] His rivalry with Milyukov pre-dated their uneasy coexistence in the first Provisional Government, in which Kerensky served as minister of justice while continuing as vice-chair of the Soviet's Executive Committee, the only politician maintaining such a foothold in both camps. He also kept in contact with the British embassy, telling Buchanan that Russia must continue the war and that he wanted internationalization for Constantinople and self-government for Poland, Finland, and Armenia. 'Russian democracy was in favour of war of defence in a political sense but this did not exclude a war of offence in a military sense'. He hoped the February Revolution would change the political situation in Germany, but, in the words of Buchanan, 'If it fails to do so he admits that we must fight until Germany submits to the will of Europe and in any case offensive would not he said be delayed by any attempt to win over German Social Democrats.'[79] Kerensky's logic implied the war must go on; and, if Russia failed to take the initiative, Germany might do, striking either eastwards or against Russia's allies. He told a meeting at Odessa on 16/29 April that 'War and diplomacy are bound together. If you strengthen the front you strengthen the voice of diplomacy. We prosecute the war in order to end it, and to end it quickly it is necessary to prosecute it vigorously.'[80]

The plan prepared by Alekseyev under Nicholas—centred on the South-Western Front, with supporting blows elsewhere—remained on the books, and Kerensky and the Provisional Government did not contest its substance, Russia in this respect resembling Italy rather than France or Britain.[81] They did, however, further postpone the start date (to 18 June/1 July) in order to secure wider political support and to prepare as well as further democratizing the army in order to satisfy the Soviet. Whereas under Guchkov the principal development had been Order No. 1, under Kerensky it was a Declaration on Soldiers' Rights, which Guchkov had refused to sign for fear of undermining discipline. Although Kerensky modified the declaration, it remained a remarkable document to issue in the midst of a war. It allowed all servicemen to belong to any political organization; when off-duty they could freely express their opinions; and all printed matter addressed to them must be delivered; nor, unless in combat, could they be punished without trial.[82] The declaration reaffirmed Order No. 114, which had permitted soldiers to join political organizations despite Alekseyev's warning this would have 'catastrophic consequences' and undermine the army's non-interference in politics.[83] It meant that officers could neither censor subversive literature nor stop their soldiers attending political meetings. Many then used the Soviet's slogan of 'no annexations or indemnities' to resist preparations for an attack.[84]

None the less, during May and June the Russian army's cohesion improved. One sign was that fraternization stopped. Admittedly this was partly because the Central Powers had halted it, judging it was working too slowly, while the Austro-Hungarians feared their Slav contingents might be infected.[85] Still, the units facing the Russians noticed a difference: sending officers across the lines became more dangerous, and aerial overflights and artillery bombardments resumed. These were unmistakable portents of an offensive, and the Front's continuing porousness made it easier to divine when and where it was coming, so that Kerensky's offensive, like Nivelle's, would lack surprise. It was true that the Russians were better equipped than previously, despite interruptions to production and transport. On the South-Western Front Knox thought Russia had a 2:1 artillery superiority with plentiful ammunition, and even air superiority, although Russian gunners were less skilled than their Western Front counterparts in utilizing aerial reconnaissance. The Russians also had a big numerical advantage, which the Stavka estimated at 900,000 Russian troops compared to a third of that number fielded by the Central Powers.[86] None of this would count for much, however, unless the infantry went forward. Kerensky compensated for his lack of military experience with what in the circumstances perhaps mattered more: revolutionary credentials and a talent for melodramatic oratory. He was also—at 37—remarkably young. He visited unit after unit, addressing sometimes recalcitrant audiences and eliciting impassioned promises to attack, even if officers and foreign observers paid tribute to his eloquence but judged its impact to be fleeting.[87] Brusilov told the British military attaché, General Barter, that 'he was on the whole satisfied with his units ... Discipline and fighting spirit had undoubtedly improved, but there were still a large number of soldiers whose sole desire was to go home and enjoy the new liberty in dividing up the land.' He could guarantee nothing, though he hoped for the best; and other commanders warned that the troops did not want to attack.[88]

The Kerensky offensive did not follow agonized high-level deliberations in the manner of the Nivelle offensive and Third Ypres, but there was a public debate. Lenin, writing in *Pravda*, said Russia must choose between two courses: 'One is the programme of the capitalists, adopted by the Chernovs and Tseretelis. This is the programme of the offensive, the programme for continuing the imperialistic war, continuing the slaughter'; the other was the programme of the Bolsheviks and the revolutionary workers of the world, of spreading the fraternization on the Russian front to all the others and then accelerating global proletarian revolution and a truly just, universal settlement. Right-wing newspapers argued an offensive was needed to win the war quickly and without a shameful peace, that the Allies must impress Bethmann and Wilhelm as well as the SPD; and that the timing, with the Russian army well supplied and Germany's best units away in the west, was auspicious. Left-wing papers accepted that the army must attack to defend Russia's territory. The Petrograd Soviet's mouthpiece, *Izvestiya*, supported, as it put it, creating the possibility of an offensive so as to stop Germany moving divisions to the west, arrest the army's disintegration, and help Russia speak as an equal in peace negotiations.[89] The Soviet itself endorsed the offensive,[90] although insisting that it be put to the All-Russian Congress of Soviets' and Workers' Deputies that convened on 3/16 June, where the Bolsheviks and some Mensheviks and Socialist Revolutionaries opposed an attack. Tsereteli's ally Fyodor Dan responded that a strong and active army was needed to assist the Stockholm conference and to pressure the Allies;[91] and on 12/25 June the Congress passed a resolution that the army should be ready for both offensive and defensive action, whether or not to attack being decided on military and strategic grounds. With this in his pocket Kerensky could go to the Stavka and order the operation, the Soviet itself also voting by 472:271 on 20 June/3 July—the third day of infantry combat—to approve.[92]

Kerensky insisted afterwards that the great majority of opinion across the spectrum had supported the offensive, and that even leaving aside the position of Russia's allies, it was 'dictated absolutely by the inner development of events in Russia'. As they knew from the Grimm–Hoffmann Affair that Germany would not attack while a chance of peace with Russia remained, they faced a choice between accepting the Russian army's virtual demobilization—which Kerensky deemed tantamount to capitulating—and taking the initiative, to restore the army's psychological capacity for action that ultimately was necessary also to prevent anarchy. Even without victory, attacking would keep as many German divisions as possible on the Eastern Front with a view to holding on until the Americans arrived in Europe and in strength, a victory in 1917 now being less urgent than it had been when the offensive plan was first adopted in January. But above all, opinion in the officer class and all political parties except the Bolsheviks considered restoring the army's fighting quality was 'demanded by Russia's national consciousness'.[93] Indeed one governmental motive was undoubtedly domestic stabilization, Tereshchenko telling the French military mission that the offensive could be a pretext for ordering members of the Petrograd garrison to the Front, while the finance minister warned that if the war continued and the Allies provided no new credits, Russia's bankruptcy would be inevitable.[94] Financial viability, internal order, and international credibility all pointed in the same direction.

Kerensky delayed the start until he got approval from the All-Russian Congress and to allow him a final visit to the attacking units. But on 16/29 June the two-day preliminary bombardment began, the heaviest yet seen on the Russian Front. Even so, when Kerensky observed the infantry advance on 18 June/1 July, he was unsure whether the grey-clad columns would actually go over the top. The Seventh and Eleventh Armies conducted the main assault in a sector where it had long been planned and the Central Powers had plenty of warning. According to Knox (a jaundiced observer), the infantry advanced to the limit of the bombarded zone. Having reached it they felt they had made their contribution, and it proved extremely difficult to get further units to move up. By the first evening many had returned to their starting positions, while German reinforcements arrived by lorry, and after two more days the operation halted.[95] Further south General Lavr Kornilov's Eighth Army made more progress. It captured Kalush and crossed the River Lumnica, placing the Austrians in difficulties until the arrival of German assistance and of torrential rain, which slowed down both sides. Increasing enemy resistance and supply shortages then forced operations here to halt also. In a reversal of normal practice the subsidiary attacks by the Northern and Western Fronts armies went in later, and suffered even more from refusals to go forward. Both were over in two days, and Austro-German retaliation now forced all the Russian armies to suspend attacks.

The OHL had decided not just to fight defensively but also to deliver a counterstroke and seek a large-scale breakthrough.[96] The chosen sector was

Figure 10. Wilhelm II awarding Iron Crosses after defeat of Kerensky offensive, July 1917

the upper River Siret, where a comparatively small initial effort might yield disproportionate results. After defeating Nivelle, Ludendorff was under less pressure in France, and he moved six divisions eastwards. Preparations were completed by late June, though Kornilov's success forced a delay. After a hurricane bombardment that fired off 90,000 gas rounds, intended to silence the Russian artillery batteries, the attack went in on 6/19 July with eleven divisions, nine of them German, the divisions from France and Belgium being concealed behind Austro-Hungarian ones. On the first day the Central Powers took 6,000 prisoners, while the Russian soldiers' committees decided not to fight, and for a while the Russians retreated so rapidly that their pursuers lost contact.[97] With the Siret on their left, the Central Powers drove south-eastwards, reconquering Eastern Galicia and the Bukovina though not continuing into Romania, in part because Ludendorff needed the men elsewhere. When operations ended on 27 August, the outcome was an 'ordinary' victory, less spectacular than the OHL had hoped for but still virtually clearing Austro-Hungarian territory (thus removing a source of tension between the Central Powers) and pushing back larger forces by up to 120 kilometres on a front 200 kilometres long, while capturing 42,000 prisoners and 257 guns.[98] Kerensky, Tsereteli, and Tereshchenko's illusions that a military triumph could resolve their difficulties collapsed with the defeat.

Disillusionment at the Front coincided with another internal crisis. In early July the Kadet party left the Cabinet in protest against autonomy being granted to the Ukraine. The Provisional Government became more narrowly based on the Socialist Revolutionaries and Mensheviks, and within both parties the coalition with the liberals faced growing left-wing opposition. Prince Lvov resigned as minister-chairman, and Kerensky replaced him while continuing as war minister. He took more than a fortnight to form a new Cabinet, in which Tsereteli, one of the guiding figures since April, no longer served.[99] Hence the reshuffle weakened the Provisional Government's connection with the Soviet. But a second development was the so-called July Days, an abortive insurrection in Petrograd that began on 3/16 July and was prompted by the government's decision to move elements of the First Machine Gun Regiment out of the city and away to the Front, despite the assurances given during the February Revolution. The government had hoped to use the offensive to regain control of the capital, and the rebellion was assisted by revolutionary sailors from Kronstadt and encouraged by radical Bolsheviks. It lacked authorization from Lenin and the Bolshevik leadership, and after heated discussion the party's Central Committee decided it was premature and called a halt, while some of the garrison wavered and others stayed loyal to the authorities. The movement collapsed, the Machine Gun Regiment was disarmed, and while Lenin went into hiding many Bolsheviks were arrested.[100]

The new Cabinet and the failure of the July Days created the conditions for a move to the right, which culminated in the Kornilov Affair. Kornilov's Eighth Army had the best record during the offensive, and after the Central Powers' counterstroke Kerensky made Kornilov CGS. On 16/29 July, an angry meeting took place between Kerensky and the Front commanders, in which General Anton Denikin led the accusations that the Provisional Government's neglect of discipline had caused the debacle.[101] During the retreat Kornilov restored summary executions of offenders. Once the enemy counter-offensive lost impetus, he and his officers started preparations to impose a dictatorship. Although the Kornilov Affair remains one of the most perplexing 1917 episodes, it seems that initially he and Kerensky acted in conjunction. However, by 14/27 August their relations had broken down after Kornilov ordered cavalry under General Aleksandr Krymov to move on Petrograd, ostensibly to counter the threat of a German advance, but also with a counter-revolutionary purpose. At this point Kornilov sent Kerensky a virtual ultimatum, and the government ordered Kornilov's arrest. Fraternization and striking railway workers soon halted Krymov's advance, and the revolt—if such it was—collapsed without violence. Its effect, however, was to reverse the consequences of the July Days, by reviving fears of counter-revolution and rehabilitating the Bolsheviks—thousands of whose supporters were armed by the government as a precaution—and by mid September control of the Petrograd Soviet had passed into their hands. Equally serious was the strain on officer–man relations in the army. Observers and commanders now reported a much uglier mood at the Front, and a determination in any circumstances to avoid another winter campaign.[102]

The Kerensky offensive, via its connections to the July Days and Kornilov's promotion, laid the basis for an attempt to crack down, whose failure left the Provisional Government still more vulnerable. As an effort to restore discipline and internal unity, the offensive failed. But as an effort to revitalize Russian diplomacy, it failed too. The French authorities downgraded their assessment of Russia's future military contribution, and the British Cabinet likewise concluded that the country was unlikely to do more.[103] By August no Allied government favoured the Stockholm conference project, while Kerensky and Tereshchenko told the Allied diplomats that the Provisional Government would not feel bound by it and did not want it to meet—disclosures that to the Russians' embarrassment the British government published.[104] The diplomatic failure undermined the previous solidarity with the Petrograd Soviet, and from now on the Provisional Government was drifting. A separate peace would cost too much, and a general peace seemed still more distant. Yet neither was Russia capable of military action. The other Allies disregarded it when in April they promised Italy a sphere of influence in Asia Minor and when in May they decided to depose King Constantine of Greece.[105] In September Lloyd George seriously considered a peace with the Central Powers at Russia's expense.[106] In spite of everything, until November the Russian army performed an enormous service to its partners by holding down almost as many enemy divisions as in the spring. But by the autumn

Britain, France, and Italy could aspire to victory even without the Russians by waiting for the Americans. Hence both a separate and a general peace were blocked, and the Provisional Government could neither restore order nor alleviate discontent by trying, even in the midst of hostilities, to implement sweeping internal reforms. In this melancholy story, the Kerensky offensive—although not everything can be blamed on it—was the most important single turning point. Before it, the Provisional Government's position was already fragile, but most of the army was in place and substantial portions of it loyal, while the Bolsheviks remained a small (if rapidly growing) minority. By September the government's predicament was much darker. The alternatives to the offensive would have been to sit tight and merely to hold the line or to conclude a separate peace by sacrificing Poland, Courland, and Lithuania. Either course of action would have better served the non-Bolshevik cause. Even so in the summer of 1917 Kerensky's logic—however questionable it may seem in retrospect—seemed to point compellingly to an attack.

7

The Road to Passchendaele

In the spring and summer of 1917 failed offensives brought the French and Russian armies to the brink of disaster. In the autumn they would do the same to the Italians. Britain's leaders were conscious of possessing, as they saw it, the last effective Allied army, Lloyd George fearing that, if it followed the French one, Allied victory—in 1919—would only come by courtesy of the Americans.[1] Yet in the Third Battle of Ypres the BEF was plunged into a campaign that did it terrible damage. Initiated with sweeping objectives, the British advance barely attained the first stage of the GHQ scheme, and the Germans halted it on the line they had pre-planned. On both sides the troops endured even worse conditions than on the Somme. None the less, by most standards of judgement Third Ypres was a grievous British defeat.

Like the Chemin des Dames, Third Ypres was not just a high command project. After an exceptionally painful appraisal, both Lloyd George and the War Cabinet endorsed it. The story ran through three phases: antecedents down to May; debate and decision between May and July; and implementation from July to November. Throughout, this strand in the 1917 narrative was interwoven with others such as the U-boat campaign and the fighting on the French and Italian fronts. The weight of circumstance shaped and restricted the options available, but did not mean no choice existed. Like the French before them, the British leaders opted to do something rather than do nothing, in an environment of extreme uncertainty in which there seemed no risk-free course.

For centuries British policy had striven to keep the coastline opposite the Thames estuary out of a hostile power's control. Germany's invasion of Belgium had triggered Britain's war entry. In October 1914 German forces overran western Flanders, and the BEF moved northwards to confront them at the First Battle of Ypres. In April 1915 a further German attack, in the

Second Battle of Ypres, distinguished by the first use on the Western Front of poison gas, reduced the Allies to a narrow salient east of the city. The troops defending the salient were constantly bombarded by guns concealed behind the higher ground that ringed it, and the high water table impeded them from digging. Ypres took on martyr status, its ruins embodying the Teutonic threat to civilization, and a German advance there would endanger the Channel ports. Conversely, an Allied advance might deprive the Germans of their destroyer bases and submarine outlets at Ostend and Zeebrugge, menace them where their communication lines were longest, and bring Holland into the war.

Planning for a Flanders offensive had a lengthy pre-history. Winston Churchill had advocated one in 1914, as did GHQ in 1915 until Gallipoli took precedence.[2] Haig made his reputation at First Ypres and on becoming commander-in-chief he still looked to a Flanders campaign, as did Sir William Robertson, the Chief of the Imperial General Staff (CIGS) and

Figure 11. Photograph of Sir Douglas Haig with French First Army commander, General François Anthoine

the government's primary strategic adviser.[3] A GHQ memorandum of March 1916 anticipated many features of the following year's operation. Haig rejected a primary advance along the coast because of the flooded area along the Yser estuary, draining which would give the Germans warning. Instead he would break out from the Ypres salient, taking the Passchendaele–Staden ridge, the Gheluvelt plateau, and the Messines–Wytschaete ridge to the south-east. The next stage would be to cut the Roulers–Thourout railway, only after which would a coastal advance be complemented by a landing. At this stage Flanders was intended to be Britain's main 1916 operation, following a preliminary attack on the Somme, but the Verdun crisis forced Joffre to elevate the Somme into an all-out offensive, although Haig maintained his Flanders interest even while the Somme progressed.[4]

Thus far, planning had been by the professionals. But by autumn 1916 U-boat activity in the Channel alarmed the politicians. On 20 November the Asquith government's War Committee discussed the situation as an unprepared agenda item, and without keeping minutes—which the Cabinet secretariat considered 'curious'. Afterwards Asquith wrote to Robertson that the War Committee were unanimous that 'the submarine constitutes by far the most dangerous menace to the Allies at the present' and 'there is no operation of war to which the War Committee would attach greater importance than the successful occupation, or at least the deprivation to the enemy, of Ostend, and especially Zeebrugge'. He asked the General Staff to 'give the matter their closest attention' and report as soon as possible.[5] The circumstances of Asquith's letter were also unusual, as Lloyd George signalled in his memoirs, and a 1934 investigation failed to clarify them. It appears that Asquith did not send it, though Robertson received a copy for guidance. Army leaders subsequently cited it as authorizing the Flanders offensive,[6] but Lloyd George was correct that it was not actually a go-ahead, and Asquith received no General Staff report before he left office. None the less, the War Committee (which Hankey believed Lloyd George must have attended) had attached the highest priority to attacking Ostend and Zeebrugge. Moreover, a paper to the Cabinet by the First Sea Lord and the Chief of the Admiralty War Staff had highlighted that it was 'only by the destruction or capture of the enemy's main and subsidiary naval bases that the [submarine] menace can be practically eliminated', and 'too much stress cannot be laid on the importance of the recapture of the Belgian ports from a naval point of view'.[7] Robertson met with Admiralty representatives and referred to plans for a surprise sea attack on Ostend, a coastal advance to within artillery range of the town, and a larger operation to capture Zeebrugge. The navy was aware of them, though judged it even more important to expel the enemy from their Adriatic submarine bases at Fiume and Pola. Haig, however, opposed diverting men or guns to Italy and said that, whereas in 1916 Verdun had obliged him to fight alongside the French, 1917 would be different. He wanted to press the matter on Joffre.[8]

Although Robertson may have been incautious in now writing to Joffre on behalf of 'my government', therefore, Whitehall would have been virtually unanimous in supporting his request to include the Belgian ports in the 1917 operations.[9] Joffre was accommodating, and sent a draft plan for capturing Ostend and Zeebrugge that was generally acceptable to Haig,[10] while Robertson asked Admiral Reginald Bacon, the commander of the Dover Patrol, to start preparations at once. The most sensitive point was the relationship between the Flanders operation and Joffre's proposals under the November 1916 Chantilly agreement for parallel British and French offensives in Picardy, but these latter would be delivered early and if they failed Joffre was content for Britain to lead the Flanders campaign and for France to assist. During the winter Bacon made preparations to land infantry, guns, and tanks (to cross the sea wall) from pontoons lashed to shallow-draught monitors under cover of a smokescreen. Jellicoe and Beatty were sceptical.[11] Germany's shore batteries might have wreaked havoc, and Haig insisted that the landing could proceed only after the inland advance.[12] After the Chantilly conference he asked the BEF Second Army in Flanders, commanded by Sir Herbert Plumer with Major General C. H. ('Tim') Harington as Chief of Staff, to plan for a 1917 offensive. Second Army responded with a scheme for a step-by-step advance against expected heavy resistance, starting by taking the Messines–Wytschaete and Pilckem ridges to deprive the Germans of their best fields of observation.[13] This was no longer a message, however, that GHQ wanted to hear. After Nivelle replaced Joffre, he and Haig agreed at least on avoiding another Somme-type battle and on seeking rapid breakthrough. Haig's Chief of Staff (COS), Launcelot Kiggell, told Plumer to reconsider and assume a prior French offensive would draw off German reserves. Whereas the Second Army had proposed 'a sustained and deliberate offensive such as has been carried out recently on the Somme Front', which would allow the enemy to bring up reinforcements and build new defence lines, instead 'the plan should be based on rapid action and entail the breaking through of the enemy's defences on a wide front without any delay . . . The object of these operations is to inflict a decisive defeat on the enemy and to free the Belgian coast.'[14] After Second Army captured the Messines–Wytschaete ridge, a separate 'northern army' would take the Roulers–Thourout railway and drive towards the Channel.

A special unit in the GHQ Operations Section under Lieutenant Colonel Norman Macmullen was instructed to draw up a plan for implementation if Nivelle's offensive failed. It was advised that 'the whole essence is to attack with rapidity and push right through quickly'.[15] Macmullen noted that the assault must 'push on with the greatest boldness and resolution, taking considerable risks'.[16] From this point, planning proceeded in parallel in Second Army and at GHQ. When Plumer submitted his revised proposals on 30 January he too stressed surprise and rapidity, with only a brief artillery preparation for the first phase, even though the defences were 'exceptionally strong'; but GHQ still found his efforts too cautious.[17] Both Plumer and General Sir Henry Rawlinson, the Fourth Army chief who had commanded on the Somme, were anxious to take the higher ground in the centre of the attack front, known as the Gheluvelt plateau, before proceeding further; but Macmullen's final memorandum, incorporating Haig's amendments, provided for simultaneous southern, central, and northern assaults, prior to open operations with pursuit troops and cavalry directed towards Roulers, and from now on this document formed the planning basis. It envisaged 'breaking through' on a 30,000-yard line from the Messines–Wytschaete ridge via Gheluvelt and Broodseinde to Morslede, and advancing north-east via Roulers and Thourout in conjunction with an attack from Nieuwpoort and a coastal landing.[18] Measured against Western Front experience these objectives were remarkably ambitious.

The plan would need three months for preparatory railway construction. Underlying much of the Haig/Nivelle tension was Nivelle's resistance to the Flanders scheme.[19] Nivelle told Spiers it was an '*idée fixe*', and Flanders lay too far at the extremity of the German line for an attack there to be decisive: 'To drive the Germans a little way off is no good... you must destroy them.'[20] Because the British government backed Nivelle, however, the BEF had to take over more of the French front, hence reducing its reserve divisions. Haig's efforts to clarify when he could shift from supporting Nivelle at Arras to commencing in Flanders were fruitless, and it remained unclear what aid France would give.[21] None the less, Haig came to see advantages in persisting at Arras, in order to fix the German reserves and to keep them guessing about the next blow.

By late April, when the question arose of how to follow the Chemin des Dames disaster, Haig had gained the advantage. Lloyd George had become prime minister with a record of highly visible success as minister of munitions, and comparative failure as secretary for war, in which position he had reluctantly presided over the Somme and resolved never again to stage anything similar. Yet neither his support for an Italian campaign at the January 1917 Rome conference nor that for Nivelle had been fortunate. By encouraging Nivelle, Lloyd George and the War Cabinet had weakened their ability to second-guess Haig and Robertson, and the premier lost some of his characteristic self-confidence. In Haig he faced a sparring partner whose self-confidence was much greater. On 9 February the War Cabinet agreed on preparations for 'combined operations after the termination of the Franco-British operations', in view of the developing U-boat threat; and on 14 March it authorized Haig to prepare to attack in Flanders if Nivelle failed.[22] Once it became clear that Nivelle had indeed failed, Haig reminded Nivelle that 'if no decisive, or sufficiently useful, results are likely to be gained by the present offensive', British efforts would be redirected to clearing the Belgian coast,[23] while Robertson pressed for the BEF to regain its independence, given that the Calais conference had subordinated it only for the spring campaign. He chafed at the constraints of coalition warfare, telling the Cabinet that Britain had become the Allies' mainstay and yet was the junior partner to an unstable and short-sighted government in Paris. Invoking 'the vital necessity of clearing the Belgian coast before the winter', he concluded 'Our objective is not primarily the direct defence of French soil, but to win the war and secure British interests.'[24] He correctly predicted that the French would now avoid major offensives until American troops arrived in strength in spring 1918, if shipping permitted. Britain should continue preparations to attack in Belgium, though he did not yet recommend that it attack alone. Indeed, he was guarded about the kind of victory to expect. Privately he told Haig that Nivelle's hopes of smashing into open countryside in twenty-four to forty-eight hours had been 'most ridiculous', and that modern firepower made 'audacity and determination' matter less than careful preparation and well-directed artillery. But he agreed the best thing was to continue fighting on the Western Front, in order to inflict more losses on the Germans than the British suffered themselves, and eventually to show the Germans they had more to lose than gain from carrying on. An attack in Belgium was the right course now, rather than letting the enemy regain the initiative.[25]

Figure 12. Photograph of UK Prime Minister David Lloyd George from 1917

It would be harder for Lloyd George to unite his Cabinet than he had done over convoys. In March, Hankey conducted confidential soundings and found no support for sacking Haig.[26] And Hankey himself, who had played a backstairs role against the Admiralty, accepted much of the GHQ case. Although acknowledging Britain might need to continue at least into 1918, he believed it could not wait passively for the Americans but:

> must do the enemy all the damage we can... This can best be done by fighting a great battle with the object of recovering the Flanders coast, which would be the most effective way of reducing our shipping losses... even a battle of the Somme type, in which we would rely mainly on our unequalled heavy artillery, if prolonged throughout the summer, might produce great results. If the enemy retires, he gives us what we want. If he stands, he exposes himself to colossal losses from our heavy artillery.[27]

Several key characteristics of the case for attacking were here: that sitting still was dangerous; that unlike the Somme this campaign would target close and important objectives; and the BEF could exploit its newly strengthened heavy artillery. Moreover, Hankey was a shrewd and independent-minded thinker who was not in the army's pocket, and to whom the premier listened.

Lloyd George also respected Jan Christiaan Smuts, who as a former South African defence minister and commander in German East Africa brought experience both as a statesman and a strategist, albeit in very different circumstances from those at Ypres; Haig and Robertson were less impressed by his expertise.[28] Lloyd George encouraged Smuts's ascension into the government's inner circles, probably seeing him as a counterweight to the Cabinet's military advisers. But in fact Smuts also accepted much of the military case, although expounding it in fresh and imaginative terms.[29] Thus Robertson believed that 'We have reached a critical stage of the war', and told the Cabinet that 'In any great battle a time of extreme stress arrives and the side which sets its teeth the hardest usually wins';[30] while Smuts advised similarly that 'We are approaching the final stages of this long drawn-out struggle, when we cannot afford to make any more mistakes, and when any false move made by either side may well prove decisive and fatal to it.' Like Robertson, Smuts feared this new kind of struggle might not end in the classic decisive fashion. Germany's defeat would not be solely or entirely military, and he had little expectation of a large-scale breakthrough, although a measure of military success was needed and its precondition was 'a process of remorselessly wearing down the enemy', despite this process being slow, costly, and running the risk of exhausting Britain's manpower. He too sought emancipation from French strategic tutelage, and believed 'It will mean much for our future prestige if (as at Waterloo) we are in a position to strike the final blow', but although America's weight might be felt in 1918, 'we may not get there', and he warned against following France and Russia into a passivity that could bring no military successes and might demoralize the public by suggesting the Allies had lost. Smuts provided a political and psychological as much as a strategic rationale for continued activism, but he agreed the Belgian coast was what Britain should seek to recapture.[31] His approach was couched in politicians' language rather than in Staff College terminology, and ranked among the most carefully articulated formulations that the Cabinet received.

The changing balance of forces became evident in a discussion on 1 May, which centred on the line to follow at a forthcoming inter-Allied conference in Paris.[32] The Cabinet considered the recent memoranda from Robertson and Smuts, and a warning from Haig that it would be useless for him to pursue his offensive vigorously unless the French actively supported it. Lloyd George therefore led off by reporting that Alekseyev had said Russia could not undertake a big offensive this year and Pétain opposed another French one. The danger now was that by attacking on the Western Front the Allies 'would exhaust their man-power in an operation offering no prospect of success, thereby weakening their offensive capacity for 1918'. He too was trying to think beyond the present campaigning season, but seeing a summer offensive as inimical to Allied staying power rather than sustaining it. The French could say that Pétain had accurately predicted Nivelle's failure, and they believed in 'repeated surprise attacks designed on a less ambitious scale'. If the Allies had no advantage in the west they would do better to try eliminating Turkey, Bulgaria, or Austria-Hungary. Moreover, 'if Russia collapsed it would be beyond our power to beat Germany', and they could not face with equanimity a peace conference before having at least conquered Mesopotamia and Syria. 'Shipping was at present our weakest flank', and he would not give the army men who were needed to build freighters. Britain lacked sufficient manpower to take on the bulk of the German reserves before the Americans arrived in strength; moreover, 'time after time' Allied generals had voiced similar confidence and it had proved baseless.

Although Lloyd George professed to speak as a devil's advocate, he evidently considered the case for an offensive unconvincing. Yet he did not command the Cabinet's support. Robertson and Smuts both characterized a Pétain policy of small attacks as tantamount to staying on the defensive and freeing up enemy reserves to attack Russia or Italy: 'Even admitting that the Allies had not much chance of breaking the German line this year, it was argued, nevertheless, that by continuing to harass the enemy we might bring them to a frame of mind in which they would agree to a peace on terms acceptable to the Allies.' Moreover, although the Cabinet did not expect the U-boats to cause starvation, Britain might have to divert shipping from the military effort in order to feed its civilians. Because of shipping losses, time (as Nivelle had warned) was no longer necessarily on their side. 'To desist now would be to lose the moment when our own force was at a maximum and when the enemy's anxieties [before the next harvest] were most acute. It was further suggested that to relinquish our efforts at this point of the War would be to deal a fatal blow at the moral [sic] of the Allies.' The minutes recorded this as being the viewpoint of the Cabinet as a whole, but such reasoning came particularly from Smuts, who insisted that if Britain relaxed, 'pessimism and despair' would grow rife. Although they had no chance of breaking the German lines and 'heavy casualties' were inevitable, by hammering away they might bring the enemy to terms: 'though it was a great misfortune, the Western Front was our problem and it could only be solved by this policy'. Conversely, to wait for the US might be disastrous and 'from a purely British point of view, it would be better to attack in Flanders, where very important objects of British policy were to be achieved'. Moreover, doing so would leave the French with the incentive of having to clear their territory themselves, rather than letting the BEF do it for them.

The 1 May discussion indicated the prevailing view was in favour of a Flanders campaign. The British representatives at the Paris conference must press the French to continue their Aisne offensive but 'insist on our freedom of action'. In fact the conference was dominated by pressure from the British to reduce their forces at Salonika, which partly reflected Jellicoe's anxiety about the strain Salonika imposed on shipping, though also reflected British concern to release forces from a French-dominated effort in the Balkans in order to pursue British aims in Palestine.[33] However, a subcommittee of Robertson, Haig, Pétain, and Nivelle advised 'it is essential to continue offensive operations on the Western Front', so as not to let the Germans recover from the exhaustion of their reserves in the recent battles, transfer forces against Russia and Italy, or proclaim that they had fought their adversaries to a standstill, 'which might be fatal to our chances of winning the war'. The Nivelle Plan was 'no longer operative', and it was a question now not of breaking through towards distant objectives but wearing down the enemy's resistance.[34] This text reflected Robertson's thinking, and the conference protocol endorsed it, the two governments undertaking 'to continue the offensive on the Western Front in accordance with the proposals agreed to by Generals Pétain, Nivelle, Robertson, and Field Marshal Haig... and to devote the whole of their forces to this purpose'. In the main sessions Lloyd George 'very emphatically' backed the report, urging 'the importance of pressing Germany with our whole strength this year... We must go on hitting and hitting with all our strength until the German ended, as he always did, by cracking.' Ribot agreed that 'to shut ourselves up on the defensive after three years of war would be reckless and imprudent', but warned that France could not incur 'excessive losses', to which Lloyd George rejoined that 'we were willing to put the full force of the British army into the attack, but it was no good doing so unless the French did the same'.[35] Lloyd George's apparent inconsistency so soon after his scepticism in the War Cabinet may have been because he was representing his colleagues' views;

but also he was doing his best to secure continuing French assistance, whereas Smuts favoured a British offensive whatever France did. In the following weeks this difference of emphasis became critical.

For the moment, the Paris conference had endorsed continuing Western Front offensives, and the politicians left detailed planning to the military.[36] Implicitly, it delivered inter-Allied sanction for the Flanders plan. Haig was 'very pleased' with how the premier had handled things and had 'quite forgiven him his misdeeds up to date'.[37] Lloyd George was trying to put the Calais conference behind them. Yet his backing for an offensive had been predicated on a comparable French effort, and on the objective being to wear the enemy down, whereas GHQ envisaged a rapid breakthrough, and on 30 April Haig had assigned command of the 'northern operations' (i.e. the break-out from the salient) not to Plumer but to the Fifth Army commander, General Sir Hubert Gough. Evidently Haig was dissatisfied with Plumer's concept of successive infantry battles, and Gough was a cavalryman whom Haig had chosen before the Somme to command the mounted troops that would drive through the expected breach. Even so, when Haig wrote to the War Cabinet he played down this emphasis. Only 'hard and continued fighting' could break German resistance; but on the conditions of a French supporting attack and his infantry and heavy artillery being brought up to strength, success was reasonably probable, and 'even if a full measure of success is not gained, we shall be attacking the enemy on a front where he cannot refuse to fight, and where, therefore, our purpose of wearing him down can be given effect to', for the first step 'must always be to wear down the enemy's power of resistance until he is so weakened that he will be unable to withstand a decisive blow'.[38] After the Paris conference, however, Haig could be more definite. To Nivelle he stressed the need for 'a great effort to clear the Belgian coast this summer', depriving Germany of the Belgian ports because of the U-boat campaign and the menace to British sea communications.[39] He told his commanders that 'the objective of the French and British will now be to wear down and exhaust the enemy's resistance by systematically attacking him by surprise. When this end has been achieved the main blow will be struck by the British forces operating from the Ypres front, with the eventual object of securing the Belgian coast and connecting with the Dutch frontier.'[40] Combined with Gough's appointment, this guidance suggests Haig still envisaged not just a wearing-down process but also far-reaching conquests and even a German collapse.

At this stage also, Haig still believed he could obtain substantial French support, and a telegram from Robertson reiterated that the premier and War Cabinet supported Haig's policy 'on express condition the French also play their full part... Cabinet could never agree to our incurring heavy losses with comparatively small gains, which would obviously be the result unless French cooperate wholeheartedly.'[41] Haig took this warning as intended to strengthen his hand with Pétain, to whom he presented his Flanders plan at Amiens on 18 May: 'The objective of the operation is, by surprise and rapidity of movement, to clear the coastline and open up Ostend, after the enemy has been severely shaken by the attack further south and his rear threatened.' Although Haig used Pétain's favoured language, his aspirations were greater. Still, Pétain approved and offered six divisions to take part. Pétain disclosed a schedule for French attacks across the summer, but he regarded the British offensive as the main one, and 'he would do all he could to co-operate with it... he would do his utmost to attract as many hostile divisions as possible'.[42]

Haig now had sufficient assurances to proceed. Though warned by London not to expect big reinforcements, he felt 'that if the ranks of the British army were only kept full up, that they would win the war for the Allies. Indeed our Army is the only one which can do so.'[43] On 5 June he told his army commanders that the German people might reach 'breaking point' this year: if the realization that unrestricted submarine warfare would not achieve its objectives were combined with:

the steady, determined, never-wearying advance of our Armies... the possibility of the collapse of Germany before next winter will become appreciably
greater... even one great and striking success, combined with general activity
and steady progress on the whole front and a secure hold of all that had been
already won, will have far reaching results... one more great victory, equal
to those already gained, may turn the scale finally, and, at the least, will have
even a greater effect than previous victories on Germany and on the world
opinion generally.[44]

The language seems tinged with hubris, which Haig's Chief Intelligence Officer, Brigadier General John Charteris, nurtured with reports of food riots in Germany, of unrest in its army, and of indications the OHL was call-ing up early the 1918 and even 1919 conscript cohorts.[45] Captured enemy correspondence that Haig read on 2 June was 'the most encouraging I have yet read: hunger, want, sickness, riots all spreading in the most terrible manner'.[46] Though the reports were not without foundation, and civilian and even military unrest in Germany was indeed growing, Haig exaggerated its significance. At this point his primary motive for the offensive seems to have been neither to help the French nor to stymie the U-boats but to achieve Germany's collapse before the year ended.[47]

The battle of Messines between 7 and 14 June fortified this confidence. Plumer and Harington had been preparing two years for this operation, which was designed to cover the right flank of the advance and take high ground that afforded the Germans observation over the salient and a reverse slope for their artillery.[48] The twenty-one mines dug deep into the clay, nineteen of which exploded at zero-hour, provided additional shock and surprise, although the artillery fire plan and the exceptionally well-prepared infantry assault might well have taken the ridge anyway. The Germans had known an attack was coming, and the higher command had wanted to evacuate, but the local commanders insisted on staying. Whereas most of the British gains came rapidly and with little cost on the first day, however, Haig insisted on continuing down the eastern side of the ridge, and final Allied casualties were comparable to Germany's. None the less, the British press feted Messines, as earlier Vimy, as showing that even the strongest enemy positions were now vulnerable.[49] Charteris toured the prisoner cages and found more evidence that the Germans were drawing on their youngest age cohorts. New GHQ briefings for the War Cabinet stressed that the enemy was short of men and might have to make peace that year, although there is prima facie evidence that Charteris adapted his analyses to his chief's expectations.[50] In a 12 June memorandum to the Cabinet, Haig was bullish: 'Given sufficient force, and provided no greater transfer of troops is made in time from East to West, it is probable that the Belgian coast could be cleared this summer and the defeats on the German troops entailed in doing so might quite probably lead to their collapse.'[51] He urged the Secretary of State for War, Lord Derby, 'to prevent the Government delaying to take action until the American army is in the field... There is no time like the present... We cannot tell how our Allies will stand another winter.' Robertson, however, withheld the summary of GHQ intelligence from the Cabinet, as it conflicted with a more pessimistic appraisal by Brigadier General George Macdonogh, the Director of Military Intelligence in the War Office, which rightly questioned how far the Germans were running out of manpower and whether their morale was near collapse. Robertson urged Haig 'not to argue that you can finish the war this year or that the German is already beaten but that your plan is the best plan'.[52] Despite his private doubts, however, Robertson maintained a united front with Haig and became GHQ's manager in dealing with the War Cabinet rather than an independent source of governmental advice.

Haig by early June had reached a comparable apogee to Nivelle's after the Calais conference. He had won assent not only from the British government but also from the French, which had acquiesced in its strategic subordination. Plumer and Rawlinson were too loyal to take their differences with Haig to the politicians;[53] but even if they had done, Derby backed his commander and was no Painlevé. Haig had the greater field experience and was senior in rank to Robertson, who deferred to him. When Robertson visited GHQ to urge the danger of big attacks without French support and that by the autumn 'Britain would be without an army!', Haig insisted that:

> the German was now on his last legs and that there was *only one sound* plan to
> follow viz
> 1. Send to France every possible man.
> 2. "   "   "   "   possible aeroplane
> 3. "   "   "   "   gun

and Robertson returned converted to Haig's thinking.[54] None the less, Haig acknowledged the 'northern operation' was not yet decided on,[55] and during June and July the War Cabinet reconsidered its entire politico–military strategy, establishing for this purpose a War Policy Committee (WPC). The committee's proceedings held a comparable position in the run–up to Third Ypres to that of the Compiègne conference before the Nivelle offensive. Although the government had first approved a Flanders campaign in November 1916 and done so again, after the Nivelle interlude, in May, Lloyd George remained in two minds. Once again a major Allied operation would gain final (and half-hearted) approval only on the eve of the preliminary bombardment. Yet although Cabinet approval was conditional, eventually Haig, like Nivelle, received an effective blank cheque. Even after his plan exhibited fundamental flaws, British politicians proved slower than French ones to intervene.

It was Milner who on 7 June identified 'an urgent need of a fresh stock–taking of the whole war situation'. Back in January the Allies had had a coordinated plan but 'the defection of Russia has completely destroyed these prospects'. With this and American intervention they faced 'a wholly new situation', and 'I feel as if we were just drifting': to have some plan was better than none at all.[56] Lloyd George welcomed a chance to reduce dependence on the military and naval professionals, as 'in a large number of instances throughout the war the advice of the experts had proved to be wrong'. Moreover, the resolutions passed at the Paris conference had assumed strong French support, but now this too was in question.[57] The upshot was the War Policy Committee, chaired by Lloyd George and with Milner, Curzon, and Smuts as its core personnel—much the same as the War Cabinet but minus its Labour member. It was to 'investigate the facts of the Naval, Military, and Political situations and present a full report to the War Cabinet',[58] and it began its work on 11 June. Its report, dated 10 August but compiled in mid July, gave the Flanders plan a cautious and conditional go-ahead.[59]

The Allies' strategic situation continued to deteriorate. Although shipping losses fell in May, in June they rose again, and convoying was only just being implemented. Nor was it clear when an American mass army would arrive. Major General Tom Bridges, a British liaison officer, reported that America might have six divisions (120,000–150,000 men) in France by the end of 1917 and eighteen (500,000) by the end of 1918, but most would have to be trained and equipped from scratch.[60] The long term looked very long indeed, and Curzon described this as 'the most depressing statement that the Cabinet had received for a long time'.[61] During May ministers took fright at the repercussions of their abolition of the 'trade card' scheme, enabling more semi-skilled employees to replace workers in private plants so that the latter could be conscripted. Some 200,000 men downed tools before the government yielded, and in July the Cabinet overruled Treasury opposition and approved a bread subsidy.[62] Derby warned Haig that the government was 'really scared' about the mood in the country, and Parliament would resist sending the army more men: the Cabinet had rejected a War Office request for 500,000 soldiers and Lloyd George said shipping and agriculture needed all the manpower available.[63] Robertson told Haig similarly that Lloyd George had warned 'we could not expect to get any large number of men in the future but only scraps'.[64] Indeed, Robertson briefed the WPC that casualties had already neared 100,000 in April and 60,000 in May.[65] The BEF was 20,000–30,000 men below establishment, although 150,000 more would become available by August.[66] The politicians kept it on a tight leash, Hankey noting that 'Although it has never been formulated in the War Cabinet Minutes it is understood that the policy of the Government is first, by keeping the War Office short to compel the soldiers to adopt tactics that will reduce the waste of man-power.'[67]

The biggest change, however, came in France. Until May the fighting on the Chemin des Dames dragged on and, despite Pétain's replacement of Nivelle, the French authorities envisaged continued operations in support of Britain. Yet GQG rightly saw the Flanders plan as signalling that Britain was pursuing its own interests, Pétain now telling Henry Wilson, head of the British Military Mission in Paris, that he was 'opposed to Haig's plans of attack', which were 'certain to fail', while Foch, the CGS, condemned the project as a '"duck's march" through the inundations'.[68] But Wilson seems not to have communicated these opinions to the War Cabinet and when actually meeting Haig, Pétain had undertaken to assist him. Hence Haig could assure the WPC that he had French backing. In late May and early June, however, the French army mutinies reached their climax, and coincided with a wider malaise, as women workers went on strike and Ribot struggled to defend his government after withholding Stockholm conference passports. The French told the British about the mutinies belatedly and minimized them; the British military representatives then reported neither promptly nor accurately, while Robertson and Haig withheld the details from the War Cabinet.[69] But eventually Pétain had to acknowledge that an attack he had agreed to launch on 10 June would now be too risky. He admitted to Haig that discipline was poor and more leave must be granted to his men at once.[70]

The message meant that Pétain was disengaging from the undertaking in the Paris agreements that both armies would continue attacking with all their strength. It was hardly likely he would so act unless the situation was grave. In fact from late April the British embassy got wind of poor French morale, and Charteris learned of 'serious trouble', but only on 6 June did the Director of Military Operations at the War Office tell the War Cabinet of 'serious trouble, practically amounting to mutiny, in a number of regiments'.[71] Henry Wilson expressed 'grave doubts' to the Cabinet as to whether France would hold until effective American assistance arrived,[72] and one of the WPC's first acts was to hear testimony on the French situation from Edward Spiers. Spiers acknowledged there had been a mutiny, though said (wrongly) that it had been confined to two regiments. He thought the French would keep up a 'considerable effort' but not enough to divert enemy reserves. This might seem to weaken the arguments for going ahead; and yet Spiers also warned that 'If the British response ... was to go into winter quarters, so to speak, themselves, the effect on French opinion would be very bad ...' The crisis was not just military but also a political one, as 'there was no good alternative' to the present French government. This was an argument—endorsed by Henry Wilson—that Britain must take action or risk disheartening French *civilians*.[73]

Such was the context when the WPC discussed the Flanders plan. As Robertson briefed the ministers, 'This policy...holds the field until cancelled or modified.'[74] The committee had before it three Haig memoranda, and although Haig was often inarticulate in speech, on paper he could be forceful. The first stressed the division of the operation into phases. 'It will be seen, therefore that my arrangements commit me to no undue risks and can be modified to meet any development in the situation. Meanwhile they enable me to maintain an offensive proportionate to the forces at my disposal, which, in my opinion, is necessary in order to prevent the initiative passing to the enemy.'[75] In the second, he argued that at minimum by capturing the higher ground round the salient he would so reduce 'normal' casualties as to save thousands of lives. The German army was flagging, but relaxing the pressure would let it recover while demoralizing the French (and in his diary he doubted 'whether our allies would quietly wait and suffer for another year').[76] The risks of inactivity exceeded those of attacking and the benefits from attacking might be great: 'Given sufficient force, provided no great transfer of German troops is made, in time, from East to West, it is probable that the Belgian coast could be cleared this summer, and the defeats on the German troops entailed in doing so might, quite possibly, lead to their collapse.'[77] In the third paper Haig urged that capturing the Belgian coast was the best response to air raids against Britain, by forcing enemy bombers to fly greater distances and for longer over hostile territory. This opinion could hardly have been timelier, as German 'Gotha G.IV' aircraft based in Belgium bombed London on 13 June, killing 162 people including eighteen primary schoolchildren in Poplar. Further, the Germans on the Flanders coast might be cut off, as only two trunk railways connected them to the fatherland whereas the British had good rail and sea links to their home base, and in no other theatre were the logistics so favourable.[78]

When the WPC met, Robertson asserted that 'the prevailing view in the British Expeditionary Force was that they could beat the Germans by themselves', and that Haig 'was preparing to do what in November 1916 the War Committee had asked him to do'. But Lloyd George saw few signs that Germany was crumbling: the Allies had been mistaken in attacking their strongest rather than their weakest opponents; and Haig was 'by nature an optimist...What the War Policy Committee wished to avoid was a series of costly operations as the result of which we would have no more to show than after the Somme last year.' In summary the committee 'generally agreed that as a policy of perfection the most hopeful plan would be to clear the enemy out from land bases, but it was pointed out that if this was to involve a loss of hundreds of thousands of men, perhaps without achieving this object, it would not be worth attempting'.[79]

On Tuesday 19 June Haig testified in person, sweeping his hands theatrically across a raised map. Lloyd George memorialized that although he, Milner, and Bonar Law were sceptical, for others 'the critical faculties were overwhelmed'.[80] Much of the meeting consisted of an exchange between the premier—largely unsupported—and Haig and Robertson. Lloyd George asserted that the Allies had only a 10–15 per cent numerical superiority on the Western Front and were outnumbered in heavy guns. Haig said Britain had twice as many guns as on the Somme, and cited intelligence that Germany was short of ammunition and its artillery was deteriorating. Robertson added that the British guns were consistently gaining the upper hand. Moreover, the relatively flat terrain would assist air observation. Haig foresaw casualties of 100,000 per month, the same rate as on the Somme. None the less, he had enough men to begin. He would concentrate forty-two British Empire divisions, six French, and six Belgian, twelve attacking at the outset. They would face thirteen 'fresh' and thirty-five 'used' German divisions: the enemy were running short of men and their morale was 'poor'. Robertson foresaw no difficulties in ammunition supply. Hence the resources were sufficient, and Robertson insisted Haig would 'proceed methodically and consider the situation methodically before making each fresh bound', proceeding only after gaining air and artillery superiority. Lloyd George, however, was doubtful about French support, and feared the BEF would be 'engaged against the main strength of Germany'. Nor did he accept Haig's contention that unless Britain attacked Germany would, so that British casualties would end up much the same.

At this point, other committee members intervened. Smuts seemed broadly to accept Haig's claims. Curzon agreed Flanders was the most favourable point for an attack though feared the British army would be 'practically exhausted for the year', which Haig contested.[81] Milner was more cryptic: 'to get the enemy away from the Belgian coast was worth half a million men', but 'while we were wearing the enemy down he was also wearing us down'. Haig summarized that although nothing in war was certain he was 'quite confident' of reaching the Passchendaele ridge; but Lloyd George believed the Germans would move reserves from Pétain's front, and the question was whether it was feasible to undertake the operation now or better to defer it. Given the strikes and the parliamentary resistance to military drafts, 'We were now reduced to the point where we had to scrape up every man we could.' Britain was 'sustaining the whole burden of the war...it was important not to break the country...He did not want to have to face a Peace Conference some day with our country weakened while America was still overwhelmingly strong and Russia had perhaps raised her strength.'[82]

On the following day, 20 June, discussion shifted to Lloyd George's alternative: sending seventy-five heavy artillery batteries (300 guns) to help Italy capture Trieste and encourage Austria–Hungary to request a ceasefire. The premier had pursued the idea since January, and he knew the Austrian emperor had extended peace feelers.[83] Robertson and Haig may not have shared this knowledge, and Robertson doubted Austria–Hungary would drop out, but in any case whereas in Flanders the Allies' logistics were excellent, in Italy they controlled only two railways to the front against the Central Powers' five, and if the Germans were no longer pressed in the west they might assist the Austrians. Given that 'we must continue to be aggressive somewhere', he saw fewer risks and more to gain in Flanders. He acknowledged that 'Germany may yet take a great deal of beating, and that it is necessary France should be aggressive as well as ourselves. On the other hand, Germany may be much nearer exhaustion both on the fronts and at home, than we imagine...' He therefore rejected the Italian alternative, and Haig was more emphatic. He expected the Germans not to reinforce Flanders from elsewhere, and the Allies to outnumber them at least 2:1 in infantry and by more in guns, ammunition, and air power: 'our wisest and soundest course is to continue to wear down the German forces on the Western Front'. He reassured the WPC that 'we ought not to push in attacks that had not a reasonable chance of success, and that we ought to proceed step by step. He himself had no intention of entering on a tremendous offensive involving heavy losses. His plan was aggressive without committing us too far.' According to Lloyd George this formulation—rather different from Haig's insistence during the army planning on rapid breakthroughs towards distant objectives—had 'a considerable influence on the Committee'.[84]

The premier was therefore losing ground even before a dramatic intervention by Jellicoe, who said the navy faced 'immense difficulties' unless the

Germans were excluded from the Belgian ports by winter, and the position would become 'almost impossible' if they used their Flanders destroyers to assail cross-Channel traffic. Unless cleared out this year, they might stay permanently, as 'he felt it to be improbable that we could go on with the war next year for lack of shipping'.[85] Lloyd George immediately challenged this statement, and according to Hankey, Jellicoe's attitude caused 'great irritation', while other evidence undermines Hankey's later assertion that Jellicoe 'produced an almost decisive effect'.[86] Before listening to Haig the committee had reviewed the shipping position with Jellicoe, Duff, and Maclay, and they were less anxious than in April; Lloyd George summarizing that although Maclay 'took a very grave view it was not a despondent one'. In contrast the Admiralty—and Jellicoe in particular—carried little conviction with ministers.[87] Haig noted that 'No one present shared Jellicoe's view, and all seemed satisfied that the food reserve in Great Britain was adequate.'[88] In fact as of 1 February some twenty-three of the German navy's 105 operational U-boats were based in Flanders, and they accounted for 24.5 per cent of Allied shipping losses between February and May.[89] The submarines stationed there were smaller and shorter-range than those in the High Seas Fleet ports of Kiel and Wilhelmshaven, though could be withdrawn to the latter harbours if Flanders were abandoned (as in 1918 they would be). In summary, Jellicoe's prediction that the war could not be maintained may have influenced Smuts, but not the rest of the WPC. His concern about the Flanders ports was referred to in the WPC's report, but seems not to have tipped the balance of argument. Nor did the two services concert their positions, Haig regarding Jellicoe as an 'old woman!' Although the Admiralty assisted him, Haig saw the projected landing as subsidiary to the main scheme.[90]

The WPC was approaching impasse. On the evening of 20 June Lloyd George held a long discussion with his colleagues. He gave the matter 'many hours of anxious consideration'.[91] On the following day they met with Haig and Robertson again, and he appealed to the generals to reconsider. This was a climactic moment. Yet Lloyd George clarified at the outset that 'it would be too great a responsibility for the War Policy Committee to take the strategy out of the hands of their military advisers'. If after considering his views they still adhered to their position, 'then the responsibility for the advice must rest with them'. He hoped to make them retract, rather than overruling them. He reiterated that 'a most momentous decision now had to be taken. A wrong step forward might bring disaster to the cause of the Allies.'

He had suppressed his misgivings and supported the case in May on the understanding that Britain and France would attack together; but Pétain was no longer offering full support. If Haig did not attain his first objective, all the world would see this as a British failure, benefiting 'the disintegrating forces that were operating in all belligerent countries on both sides, but more especially on the side of the Allies, owing to the position in Russia'. The Germans knew Britain's objective was the Flanders coast, as the *Frankfurter Zeitung* had indicated that morning, and if Britain advanced only 7–10 miles with heavy casualties 'the effect would be very bad throughout the world'. Yet to reach Ostend they must advance 25 miles. They still lacked heavy artillery and although they had more shells, surely the Germans could sustain a defence; moreover, there would be no surprise: 'the chances... were against a success'. He feared the public would be discouraged and the army weakened, and asked the experts to reconsider the alternatives of 'Pétain tactics, namely a punch here and there and a process of wearing down the enemy', or an attempt on Trieste. Conversely, if Russia dropped out and Austria–Hungary stayed in, the Germans could transfer 1.5 million men to the Western Front, outnumbering the 0.5 million expected Americans, and 'we should have no chance of eventual victory'. If Russia left, in fact, he would almost agree with Jellicoe that the war could not be continued next year, and in any event not to 'complete victory'. Even so, 'he would not be willing to impose his strategical view on his military advisers, but he had felt he would not be doing his duty if he concealed his grave misgivings'.

Once again the dynamics of the meeting were curious, Lloyd George's colleagues saying almost nothing. Robertson said he and Haig acknowledged 'this might be the greatest decision of the war', and they did not resent Lloyd George's criticism. But in reality both did, Haig disparaging 'a regular lawyer's stunt to make black appear white!', and Robertson writing that 'The procedure followed...reminded one more of the Law Courts than a Council Chamber. Instead of being received as a military chief, the accuracy of whose views, so far as they were military, were not in dispute, I was made to feel like a witness for the defence under cross-examination, the Prime Minister appearing in the dual capacity of counsel for the prosecution and judge.' Haig saw the intention as getting him and Robertson to underwrite the Trieste plan, and was dismissive of the premier's 'long oration, minimising the successes gained, and exaggerating the strength of the enemy'.[92] Like Nivelle at Compiègne, Haig and Robertson now found themselves in the unwonted position of being rigorously challenged, and Hankey correctly insisted afterwards that the WPC was in its rights.[93] Yet Lloyd George did not claim to speak for his colleagues, conceded that he would not overrule his advisers, and had implausible alternatives to offer. Hence, although his statement was both prescient and a forensic tour de force, he could not persist if the military stood their ground. Robertson had sensed this when he advised Haig simply to insist that his was the best plan and defy the politicians to veto it: 'They dare not do that.' As Hankey summarized, 'Lloyd George felt he could not press his amateur opinions and over-rule them, so he gave in, and Haig was authorized to continue his preparations'.[94]

The 'great argument' ended raggedly. On 25 June the committee reconvened to consider two papers in which Haig and Robertson restated their case. Although they drafted the documents independently they then conferred, Haig telling Robertson he agreed with everything he had written but refusing to co-sign, exhibiting (and not for the only time) a greater punctiliousness than his colleague. In fact it was on Robertson that Lloyd George concentrated his fire. Haig's memorandum was, as usual, concise: he acknowledged 'the momentous effect' of the decision and his 'grave responsibility', but the discussion had 'confirmed me as strongly as ever'. To justify his 'optimistic views', he cited intelligence evidence that Lloyd George had discounted: the German army was running out of men, and its combat effectiveness was fading.[95] Robertson, in contrast, nettled, denied being inconsistent. He did not predict they would reach the coast, but the chances of 'good results' were no smaller than in Italy and the risks lower. As for the prime minister's other alternative, 'Pétain's tactics are to attack on a broad front with limited objectives, and so to wear down the enemy. That is what we are aiming at.' When Lloyd George tried to pin down Robertson on whether he shared Haig's confidence in achieving 'great results this summer', Robertson replied it would depend on whether Russia and France pulled their weight; if so, there was quite a good chance of success, but in any case it was the right plan. Lloyd George wanted authority to tell the French that unless they fought with all available resources, Britain would not do either. But this was not what the committee concluded. Despite Robertson's failure to provide a strong endorsement, the WPC accepted that Haig should carry on preparing while Albert Thomas, with whom Lloyd George had good relations, should try to influence the French government before the next Anglo-French conference.[96] Haig was disappointed with Robertson:

'All he would say was that my plan was the only thing to do',[97] but the WPC was losing its grip and running out of time.

On 3 July Robertson reported on a visit to Paris, where he found the French 'very much dejected'. Foch opposed sending heavy guns to Italy; Pétain was reticent about his future plans.[98] These findings boded well for neither the Flanders operation nor Lloyd George's alternative. Henry Wilson confirmed that the French army was 'downhearted' and although it would help the British it could not launch a great attack. On the following day, however, Lloyd George said he had private information that the political situation was serious and anything might happen, and Smuts agreed that 'the really important situation in France was political rather than military'.[99] In the final stages French politics therefore preoccupied the committee. On 6 July Smuts tried to sum up that if the French attacked decisively Haig would do likewise; but if they did not the committee should look at action against Turkey. Lloyd George, still targeting Robertson, 'asked the Committee to bear in mind that they were asked to sacrifice hundreds of thousands of men on an operation on the success of which our principal Military adviser refused to pledge his military reputation', but at this point the WPC suspended deliberations for over two weeks, then discussed Salonika, and did not reconvene until late September. Robertson wrote to Haig that Smuts wanted to land at Alexandretta, Milner liked the Balkans, and Curzon supported Flanders; while Lloyd George was keener than ever on Italy, 'but I think it will right itself in time, because before long you will be on the point of going off'.[100]

In these unpromising circumstances Hankey drafted a summary of the recommendations.[101] His paper imposed misleading coherence on a disorderly process. It acknowledged that Haig's preparations were in furtherance of policy priorities set out in the November 1916 Asquith note and the May 1917 Paris resolutions. However, the French army was unlikely to draw off Germany's reserves on a scale commensurate with French numerical strength. While there was no 'over-mastering desire in France for peace', this might change—whereas a major military or diplomatic success could halt the drift. The committee was unconvinced that the German army or home front was on the point of collapse; but also doubted if Austria-Hungary would negotiate separately. It would be 'many months' before America could supply 'effective military assistance'—and Britain could not replace 'heavy casualties, immediately after they occur'. The committee had been influenced by 'misgivings' about Britain's 'ability to sustain the war with undiminished strength through 1918', particularly in view of shipping shortages. Its report incorporated Robertson's objections to the Italian plan, whereas it accepted Jellicoe's testimony on the Belgian ports and that naval bombardments would not suffice. It also incorporated Haig's assertions that the operation could be controlled yet also offer big advantages if the railway could be cut, the coastal bases shelled, or Germany forced to abandon Flanders. It could frustrate German air attacks on England, and 'from the point of view of wearing down the enemy' it offered the advantage that the Germans could not retreat. The committee also found, however, that Allied superiority was marginal, the distances to cover were ambitious, and it would be dangerous to use up Britain's manpower. It was dissatisfied about the extent of French support, though it noted Haig's assurances that 'the attacks would be made by definite stages, and a gradual and systematic advance would be aimed at ... The method of attack was also calculated to reduce casualties as far as possible.' It concluded that the preliminary bombardment had now begun and given that the BEF might now have reached its maximum strength, and given also 'the great weight of responsible military advice', it had been decided to recommend going ahead. None the less, 'this offensive must on no account be allowed to drift into protracted, costly, and indecisive operations as occurred in the affair on the Somme in 1916', and progress must be frequently reviewed, so that 'If a degree of success commensurate with the losses is not achieved the offensive should be stopped.' Hence the committee delayed as late as possible before endorsing the battle. It took account of Lloyd George's objections, though paid them less attention than the army's case. It gave much weight to the assurances that the operation might yield a sorely needed success but could be halted if it did not. This formulation resembled the conditional approval given to Nivelle. Yet to monitor the operation as envisaged would require a pertinacity that the War Cabinet—beset with other preoccupations—was scarcely likely to maintain.

On 18 July Robertson told Haig that although he understood the War Cabinet was in favour, he still lacked 'official approval': only Lloyd George held out in opposition. Haig, furious, replied 'the Cabinet does not really understand what preparation for an attack really means'.[102] But three days later Robertson reported that the Cabinet had finally reached a draft conclusion after a 'rough and tumble' meeting in which Lloyd George still favoured Italy or Palestine rather than Flanders. It endorsed the WPC recommendations and backed the Flanders operation on condition it was kept under review. Haig replied that the first objective would be the Passchendaele ridge, and he anticipated severe fighting over several weeks before he controlled it. He gained the impression—as well he might—that he still lacked the War Cabinet's confidence. The latter replied that 'having approved your plans being executed you may depend upon their whole-hearted support'. He responded that even if the operations, contrary to his hope and expectation, did not gain ground, 'we ought still to persevere in attacking the Germans . . . Only by this means can we win . . .'[103]

Lloyd George had failed to win his colleagues' backing or find unassail-able grounds for forbidding the offensive. He had been handicapped by reluctance to override professional advice (in good measure because of his misjudgement in supporting Nivelle), as well as by his ministers' disarray, the unanimity of the naval and military advisers, and the risks entailed in doing nothing, given the time that would elapse before American troops entered the line. But if action must be taken, no alternative had Cabinet backing. Lloyd George's Italian scheme rested partly on secret information about Austria-Hungary's peace feelers, in whose absence there seemed little evidence that Italy could drive the Austrians back, while Robertson's logis-tical objections were cogent. Lloyd George's most plausible alternative was 'Pétain tactics'—surprise short assaults on the Messines model—but he failed to develop this idea, while Robertson rejoined both that it was tanta-mount to staying on the defensive, and that the Flanders plan was a variant of 'Pétain tactics' anyway. Yet the latter contention did not match with GHQ's directives or with Haig's appointment of Gough. Haig hoped in reality to do much more, and even to win the war. While to the poli-ticians he stressed a step-by-step approach, his guidance to the army was less measured.

Gough felt afterwards that his appointment was a mistake: he did not know the salient like Plumer, and this had cost precious time. He believed the forces committed were simply too small.[104] Haig came to realize that Fifth Army staff work was poor: divisions seconded to Gough branded him a 'butcher' and wanted never to serve under him again.[105] None the less, on 10 June Gough took over the attack sector, and Second Army transferred to him eight divisions and more than half its artillery: a very sizeable reorgan-ization that coincided with the mass migration northwards of men, guns, and stores.[106] It also seems that Gough was uncertain of his mandate. On 13 May GHQ advised that he should capture the Passchendaele–Staden ridge and the Roulers–Thourout railway in order to facilitate a landing and gain control of the coast, while his right flank overran the higher ground between Gheluvelt, Broodseinde, and Morslede.[107] On 16 June the V Army Corps commanders were told not to pause on the 'green line' (the second furthest forward of the blue, black, green, and red target destinations), and on 30 June they were told to expect 'a series of organized battles on a grand scale and on broad frontages', with the aim of reaching open country in thirty-six hours.[108] Fifth Army's boldness was underlined when Brigadier General John Davidson, the GHQ Chief of Operations, proposed more modest advances at two- to three-day intervals, each progressing 1,500 to 3,000 yards. This would be better for maintaining communications, moving the artillery forward, resisting counter-attacks, minimizing casualties, and easing the strain on the infantry. But Gough responded that he wanted to benefit as much as possible from the initial bombardment by reaching at least the green line, and if possible the red one. He opposed defining first-day objectives, as he had seen too many operations founder through failing to exploit the opening opportunities.[109] Moreover, Haig had told him that the aim was to capture the Passchendaele ridge before advancing as fast as possible on Roulers and then Ostend: in other words to 'break through'. Gough's COS confirmed 'The break through was the policy', even though Kiggell later doubted whether this was how it had been seen at the time.[110] Between Davidson and Gough, Haig ruled for Gough, and he supervised Gough less closely than he had Plumer before Messines.[111] Whereas after his interrogation in the WPC, Haig had been more subdued, now he reverted to his habitual optimism. In an order to his commanders on 5 July he drew comfort from the Kerensky offensive and from Germany's waning faith in the submarines and in its army's ability to hold supposedly impregnable positions. He foresaw the opening battle was 'likely to entail very hard fighting lasting perhaps for weeks', but subsequent progress would be faster and 'opportunities for the employment of cavalry in masses are likely to offer'. Although they could count on only a comparatively short period of fine weather, 'The general situation is such, however, that the degree of success gained and the results of it may exceed general expectations, and we must be prepared for the possibility of great developments and ready to take full advantage of them.' He emphasized not caution but the chance of reaching Ostend and Bruges before the autumn.[112]

    This emphasis had serious consequences. Haig urged Gough to limit the northward advance until the Gheluvelt plateau was secured. He said the same to Lieutenant General Claud Jacob, whose II Corps would have to take it.[113] But Gough's dispositions distributed his troops evenly rather than concentrating them on Jacob's sector, where the Germans were preparing a quadrilateral of heavily fortified woods and no fewer than seven defence lines. Jacob's corps transferred belatedly from Second to Fifth Army, and its assault force comprised three divisions, of which the key one, the 30th, comprising mainly Liverpool and Manchester battalions, had suffered severely on the Somme and at Arras.[114] But the Gheluvelt plateau was only one of the eminences from which the Germans surveyed the salient, and whereas at Messines the British overlooked the Germans from three sides, this time the positions were reversed, without underground mines to compensate. GHQ knew the Germans understood an attack was coming—as Charteris put it, 'we cannot hope for a surprise; our preparations must have been seen'—and the gap between Messines and the 31 July start date gave them six weeks.[115] Ever since the spring this gap had been accepted, required primarily to move men and equipment from Messines to the Ypres sector and upgrade the infrastructure, but Haig had promised the Cabinet he would prepare thoroughly and thus offset the lack of surprise. The delay was further extended by requests for extra time from General François Anthoine's French divisions, and from Gough himself. After agreeing these extensions, Haig, according to Charteris, was 'very moody', as well he might have been,[116] for the offensive was starting a month later than the Somme and he anticipated weeks of attrition before any more mobile operations. The British also understood the importance of the weather, Haig registering the air pressure and precipitation in his diary, and GHQ having established a meteorological section under a well-qualified civilian forecaster, Ernest Gold.[117] They had consulted statistics for the last eighty years and could hope for only two to three weeks of fine conditions—though it proved to be much less.[118]

The attack would start late, without surprise, with a short time horizon for success, and insufficient focus on the crucial initial objective. To compensate for these deficiencies, it would need to deal an exceptional blow. Thirty-eight British Empire divisions would be allocated, alongside six French and six Belgian ones. Gough's opening attack would be with nine divisions, or some 100,000 men.[119] The British had reason to believe their army was better equipped and trained than in 1916, though this faith depended greatly on the artillery, which had grown in numbers, in quantity and quality of ammunition (duds were fewer, and new 106 fuses could destroy barbed wire) and in accuracy. A principal reason for the catastrophe on the first day of the Somme had been that the bombardment was simply not intense enough for the area of terrain to be covered, but on a similar frontage the BEF now assembled double the field and heavy guns and more than three times the medium-calibre weapons, firing 4,283,550 compared with 1,732,873 shells. The fire plan was modelled on Messines, but now the British were firing out of a salient instead of into one. The German guns mostly lay on reverse slopes round it and were invisible to the British batteries, so all depended on air superiority, which was fiercely contested although by mid July the British generally possessed it. Even so, the bombardment was less effective than at Messines, partly because the Germans moved their batteries frequently and the British overestimated their success in destroying them.[120] Indeed, the Germans counter-bombarded the assembling forces more intensely than before any previous British offensive, including with the first use of mustard gas. In addition, the bombardment broke up the ground. The salient was actually not among the most waterlogged British sectors, but that the gradient was so gentle impeded run-off. Before the bombardment and counter-bombardment the battleground bore the scars from two years of fighting, but the earth remained carpeted with green and villages such as Passchendaele were recognizable as such. Afterwards the terrain was pockmarked with shell-holes, and the drainage system had been smashed. According to the official history, 'No special difficulties were expected as regards the ground', but the advance depended more than ever on good weather, and the terrain was highly unfavourable for the over 100 tanks Haig deployed, as also for the waiting cavalry.[121] The British never used so extended a bombardment again.

During the spring the Germans had believed the BEF sought a breakthrough at Arras, but on 18 May the OHL reported that it expected a big attack in Flanders. In the first instance this meant Messines, but from March/April the Germans noticed increased air and torpedo boat activity off the coast, and the laying of narrow-gauge railways—at astonishing speed—in the interior.[122] Haig was right to think the German army was under strain, but GHQ overestimated its deterioration and underestimated its resilience. Between April and June the *Westarmee* had casualties of 384,000, of whom 121,000 were dead or missing, but at the end of July it was only 16,000 smaller than at the start of April. Infantry battalions averaged 713 men instead of the regulation 750.[123] The German authorities felt their troops' fighting power had diminished since 1916, and a cut in the bread ration (except for combat troops) eroded morale, as did restricted leave, long absences from home, and evidence that the submarine campaign was not proceeding as hoped. Disturbances occurred on troop trains, while discipline in several regiments broke down.[124] And although the number of guns available had risen since 1916 from 5,300 to 6,700, horses were too few in number, which as the battle developed hampered munitions supply. The OHL had expected to spend 1917 on the defensive, had used new tactical regulations successfully against the French in April, and the Flanders defence scheme would be similar. However, the Germans did not contemplate another withdrawal like that to the Hindenburg Line, and Haig was right to expect them to stand and fight.[125] After Messines, the German Fourth Army observed Allied preparations in the sector between the coast and the Lille–Armentières road, which was correctly anticipated to be the next main theatre. Friedrich von Loßberg, the most senior German defensive expert, was moved in as Fourth Army's COS.[126] He agreed with the local commanders on guarding the first lines only lightly, holding the main forces back to protect them from mines and artillery but ready for prompt counter-attacks. Although they were outnumbered, he was confident—'An army has never before been so well placed before a defensive battle'—and Crown Prince Rupprecht, the Army Group Commander, considered 'I can face this offensive in a calm frame of mind, because never before have we deployed along a front under attack such strong reserve forces, which have been so well trained in this role.'[127] During June and July the Fourth Army was reinforced from twelve to seventeen and one-third divisions and its guns from 389 to 1,162.[128] But the core of the defence system consisted of hundreds of concrete pillboxes (many built after Loßberg took over), arranged in six and even seven lines. The Allies would never reach the fifth.[129] Gough's intelligence reported correctly that the Germans had made 'great progress' in improving their defences on the plateau, and front-line units were to hold their positions 'at all costs'.[130]

Between 13 and 27 July the Germans' counter-bombardment inflicted over 13,000 Allied casualties.[131] On 10 July they attacked on the coast near Nieuwpoort and reduced the British to a tiny bridgehead across the Yser estuary; but further inland they held their front-line trenches so thinly that on 27 July British and French forces occupied them along the Yser canal. This was a warning, however, that much of the high explosive expended in the unprecedented bombardment would be wasted. On the first day of the attack, which began on Tuesday 31 July, the British infantry gained 18 square miles of ground against 3.5 square miles on 1 July 1916, and for 27,000 casualties instead of 60,000,[132] but the resistance was fiercer than at Messines or Vimy, and counter-attacks began on the opening afternoon. Haig's note to his wife—'we have begun very well. As you will know, I am grateful to the Almighty God for this'—proved premature.[133] Although in the centre the British advanced up to 4,000 yards and overran Pilckem ridge, the assault on the Gheluvelt plateau failed. Torrential rain began on the first evening, and would continue for several days. In fact the 127 mm of rain in August was twice the annual average for that month.[134] So far from the hoped-for two to three weeks, there was no window at all. Even on the first day cloud prevented British aircraft from forwarding a single call for emergency artillery support, whereas on the first day at Messines they had forwarded over 200.[135] By 4 August Charteris was noting that the weather 'has killed the attack... If we win through in this battle we can force peace without the Americans. If we can't win through in this battle, we must wait until the American army comes in to counteract the breakdown in Russia, and that means twelve months at least.'[136] On 8 August Kiggell informed Robertson that the increase in the German forces meant any further advance would be confined to less than a mile even when the ground dried out, and 'most unfortunately rain is threatening again and if it comes further delay will be unavoidable'.[137]

For those on the ground, the August fighting was a nightmare of repeated fruitless assaults that gained more territory in the northern half of the salient but not the Gheluvelt plateau.[138] After another abortive attack on 22 August, Haig decided to restore primary responsibility for the offensive to Plumer's Second Army, which proposed to take the plateau through four short-bound offensives of up to 1,500 yards each.[139] In the meantime operations paused, and Rupprecht's COS, Hermann von Kuhl, suspected the British had given up. Yet there was no retreat in ambition. Although Haig had envisaged the coastal landings taking place on 7/8 August, he repeatedly postponed them rather than cancelling them.[140] Whereas Charteris had merely hoped for victory before the Americans arrived, Haig wrote to Robertson that:

> we are convinced that we can beat the enemy, provided units are kept up to strength in men and materials...the war can only be won here in Flanders...I feel we have every reason to be optimistic, and if the war were to end tomorrow, Great Britain would find herself not only the greatest Power in Europe, but in the world. The chief people to suffer would be the Socialists, who are trying to rule us all, at a time when the right minded of the nation are so engaged on the country's battles that they (the Socialists) are left free to make mischief.[141]

It was rare for Haig so to unbutton himself, but both his vision for the Empire and his fears for social order shone through.

Haig had concluded that Gough and his staff were allowing too little preparation, and he gave Plumer three weeks before the next effort.[142] Plumer and Harington 'hated the whole thing',[143] but carried out their task to the best of their considerable abilities. The three weeks were characterized by fine weather, and the ground dried out. Plumer then staged three battles: on the Menin Road (20 September), at Polygon Wood (26 September), and at Broodseinde (4 October), in which he advanced on narrower fronts than Gough and with more circumscribed objectives, but was able mostly to attain them, albeit after bombardments up to three times more intense than Gough's and even so with higher casualties per square yard gained.[144] The Germans had never experienced such concentrated firepower, and for them early October marked the battle's crisis. They changed their tactics for Broodseinde, amassing more men in the front line, but only to suffer even higher losses, after which they reverted to the previous system.[145] At this point they did not know how to prevent further enemy advances and considered withdrawing out of artillery range, Ludendorff describing October as one of the most difficult months of the war.[146] GHQ still hoped to reach the coast and Haig told Pétain that enemy reserves were exhausted and 'great results' still attainable.[147] He asserted retrospectively that 'the possibility of the French army breaking up in 1917 *compelled me to go on attacking*. It was impossible to change sooner from the Ypres front to Cambrai without Pétain coming to press me not to leave the Germans alone for a week, on account of the *awful* state of the French troops.'[148] However, Plumer too was falling victim to impatience, probably partly due to pressure from Haig, and each of his battles was less thoroughly prepared. Although he and Gough both urged a continuing step-by-step approach, Haig overruled them.[149] In addition, in early October the rain returned, impeding aerial observation and artillery supply. Hence the battle of Poelcapelle on 8 October, which marked the failure of Plumer's first effort to seize the Passchendaele ridge, was a turning point, Charteris now recognizing that little more was possible before the winter, and Plumer recommending that operations should cease.[150] Haig, however, was determined to take the ridge, as a basis for renewing the offensive in 1918.[151] Hence fighting continued until 10 November, the Canadian Corps being tasked with taking Passchendaele village, and its commander, General Sir Arthur Currie, accurately predicting a toll of 16,000 casualties. By now it was so difficult to bring up the artillery that the battle had degenerated into infantry charges against machine guns protected by uncut wire, the Germans resisting from pillboxes and flooded craters. And in the final phase, the British casualties escalated.[152] By this stage, even Robertson acknowledged afterwards, 'It is difficult to deny that the campaign was protracted beyond the limits of justification, but a correct decision was not so easy to make at the time as it appears now, and in fact, post-war information shows that G.H.Q. opinion was very near to the truth.'[153] But actually in the final stages German confidence revived, Ludendorff writing to the Rupprecht Army Group that if they held on until the winter 'all is won'.[154]

The casualty bills are disputed. According to the German official history, German Fourth Army losses between 21 July and 31 December were 217,000, including 38,000 dead and 48,000 missing.[155] British casualties for Messines and Third Ypres together were about 275,000; for Third Ypres alone about 245,000.[156] They ran at about the level Haig had predicted to the WPC. Although the ratios were less unfavourable than on the Somme,

Figure 13. Canadian pioneers laying tapes on the road to Passchendaele

the British figures still substantially exceeded the German ones, and were suffered by a smaller army. Almost all the BEF went through Third Ypres, whereas much of the German army did not. This mattered, because participants on both sides testified that the experience was horrific: German observers found the Allied aircraft and artillery more powerful than ever, the BEF firing some 33 million shells,[157] but Allied observers felt much the same.[158] Conditions in the salient were trying enough at any time, the approach roads lying exposed to strafing and bombardment, but now were added a backdrop wilderness of brimming craters, unprecedented quantities of heavy weaponry, less chance for rest at night and in the rear, and mustard gas. Certainly, German morale suffered from the appalling conditions of shell-hole-based defence and the strain of never knowing when the next attack was coming, but eyewitness and postal censorship evidence confirm that Third Ypres harmed British resilience more than had any previous campaign.[159] It is plausible to see a connection with the thousands of British prisoners taken when Ludendorff attacked on 21 March 1918.[160] Yet the advance had failed to cut the railway or reach the ports and had failed to attain even its first objective until after more than three months. The navy's wishes remained unsatisfied, and the Germans ensconced in Ostend. It is true and important that while the campaign continued, the Germans undertook no major action against the French, who not only achieved their objectives at Third Ypres but also carried out successful attacks in August and October on the symbolic battlegrounds of Verdun and the Chemin des Dames. By the winter the French army had regained its capacity at least as a defensive force, which in 1918 would prove to be vital. But even during the Flanders fighting the Germans were pushing back the Russians and threatening Petrograd, as well as helping Austria-Hungary to rout the Italians. The claim that it would deny the initiative to the enemy proved ill-founded. In contrast Britain's 20 November massed tank offensive at Cambrai was initially spectacularly successful, but a German counter-attack soon retook much of the lost ground. By December Haig was preparing in the spring to face a German offensive rather than renew his own,[161] and in April 1918 it fell to Plumer to make the painful decision to abandon Passchendaele. It is hard not to conclude that Third Ypres fell short of almost all its stated objectives and did so at exceptional cost. It altered the balance between Britain and Germany to Germany's benefit. It would have been better, in fact, to do nothing.

During the desperate August fighting, Hankey observed that 'The P.M. is obviously puzzled, as his predecessor was, how far the Government is justified in interfering with a military operation.'[162] It had innumerable other concerns, ranging from bombs on London to enemy peace feelers, declarations to India and the Zionists, and Italian and Russian collapse. The fact remains that ministers failed to keep the offensive under the intended close review. It was not halted (nor was the possibility discussed) after Gough got bogged down in August, or after Plumer did at Poelcapelle. Robertson reported to the War Cabinet on 31 July and on 2, 17, and 22 August without his sanguine prognostications being challenged.[163] Discussion centred not on Flanders but on whether and how to aid Italy. When the French pressed in October for the British to extend their line, which would have terminated the campaign, the War Cabinet refused to do so while it remained in progress. The Cabinet received broadly accurate casualty figures,[164] and even allowing for the time that it was reasonable to grant the generals to get on with the business, it was clear by late August that the operation was replicating the standard pattern of heavy casualties for minor gains. Yet when the WPC reconvened on 18 October and Hankey urged a reconsideration, he found the premier reluctant. Lloyd George confined himself to remarking:

> He would have no hesitation in comparing the present offensive with predictions he had made about it. We had not yet got to the Klercken Ridge, and he had always insisted that the French had promised to fight but had not carried out that promise...they had been guided by the very confident paper they had received from General Haig, and he (the Prime Minister) thought that no-one would have voted for that offensive had they not been considerably influenced by his optimism.[165]

In contrast to Nivelle, Haig was shrewd and well-connected, but his conduct at the February 1917 Calais conference suggests he would have submitted to a Cabinet ruling, as he did in February 1918 when Robertson was removed. Yet Haig was the guiding spirit behind the offensive, and his subordinates deferred to him. Robertson, who wished in retrospect that he had, like Painlevé, seen the army commanders individually,[166] assisted Haig against his better judgement, and the Cabinet was too divided to forbid the operation, while Lloyd George, though always against it, had no convincing alternative. On 14 September Hankey found the premier 'rather despondent at the failure of the year's campaigning, and disgusted at the narrowness of the General Staff, and the inability of his colleagues to see eye to eye with him and their fear of overruling the General Staff. He was also very annoyed at the way the General Staff twist their facts and estimates to suit their arguments.'[167] Yet Lloyd George had weakened himself by the Nivelle affair, and done so further by his espousal of the Trieste plan. If there *was* a viable alternative to Third Ypres it was indeed the 'Pétain tactics' implemented by the French at La Malmaison and by the British at Vimy Ridge, Messines, and Cambrai.[168] But this, more or less, was what Haig and Robertson claimed Third Ypres would be. Such operations could have brought the victories believed necessary to bolster the French, and which Lloyd George reiterated were needed as an antidote to British war weariness,[169] although they too would have claimed thousands of lives, and brought victory no closer. The outstanding 'what if' is whether the battle could have achieved more if started in the spring, entrusted to Plumer, and sustained through weeks of fine weather. But even in these circumstances, assuming an unavoidable delay after Messines, the Allies would have had just two months to clear the ridges before the August deluge. They were running out of options, and without American intervention the consequences of the Chemin des Dames and Passchendaele would have been still graver. Third Ypres can be ascribed in part to a surge of nationalism in the British high command, directed to sloughing off French tutelage and winning before the Americans deployed. To that extent it was a product of hubris. Although it did not end in quite the humiliation and the impotence that Lloyd George feared, the harm to British power and confidence would be lasting.

8

Collapse at Caporetto

On Wednesday 24 October 1917 German and Austrian forces launched one of the most daring attacks of the war. Breaking through Italian positions in the upper Isonzo river valley, within two weeks they had advanced over 100 miles. Almost half the Italian army were killed, wounded, or captured, or discarded their weapons and streamed to the rear. Territory that had taken more than two years and 900,000 casualties to capture was abandoned within hours.[1] Amid the dreary litany of failed offensives and attrition battles, the name of Caporetto stands out, and in Italy has remained a shorthand for rout and fiasco.[2] Even so, for most of the war it had been the Italians, not the Central Powers, who had been on the attack, in conditions often even worse than on the Western Front. In part, the collapse grew out of overstretch. To understand how the Italian army became so exposed, we must consider not only the Twelfth Battle of the Isonzo (as the Italians officially entitled Caporetto), but also the Tenth and Eleventh. It is further necessary to survey the operations themselves, from Austro–German break-through to Italian recovery. Devastating though Caporetto was, in many ways it strengthened Italy's war effort.

Between 1882 and 1914 Italy had regularly renewed its Triple Alliance with Germany and Austria-Hungary. In 1914 it stayed neutral, and in May 1915 it joined the Allies, following the secret Treaty of London concluded with Britain, France, and Russia in April. Italy's nineteenth–century national unification had left some 800,000 Italian-speakers under Austrian rule. But the Allies promised Italy not only the ethnically Italian areas in the Trentino and the environs of Trieste, but also the German-speaking South Tyrol and the Slovenian and Croatian territories of Istria and Dalmatia. And to incorporate any of these areas the Italians would have to conquer them. As France and Britain would enter any peace negotiations handicapped unless they dislodged the German army from France and Belgium, so too would Italy unless it dislodged the Austro-Hungarian army from the areas promised. In both theatres, if the Central Powers defended successfully they would win.

In both, however, they defended with one hand tied behind their backs. The Germans kept on average a third of their field army on the Eastern Front. The Austrian army was smaller, and because of its commitments in the Eastern and Balkan theatres, in 1917 only one-fifth of it faced Italy.[3] Even so, this fifth included some of its best units, and the Italian war, imposed by an aggressor, was less unpopular than were other fronts. The Austrians also benefited from geography. The Front ran for 375 miles from the Swiss border to the Adriatic Sea, but much was so mountainous as to be completely unsuitable for operations (though fighting none the less occurred—trenches being dug in ice fields and thousands perishing in avalanches or freezing to death). The exceptions were the Trentino and the lower stretches of the Isonzo. The Trentino was one of the Italians' target areas, but it was remote from the Austro-Hungarians' urban and industrial centres, and easily defended. Projecting southwards, it formed an obvious jumping-off point for driving into the Po valley and cutting off the main Italian forces. For these reasons the Austrians had attacked there in May 1916, and although the Italians had rallied with assistance from Russia's Brusilov offensive, the Austrians had pushed them closer to the plateau edge. They would be still more vulnerable if Austria-Hungary attacked again.

None the less, the fighting concentrated on the Isonzo. Between May 1915 and September 1917 no fewer than eleven battles were fought there. In rocky terrain, bitterly cold in winter, it was hard to excavate dugouts and trenches, and stone splinters magnified the impact of bombardment, both sides sheltering in cliff-side caves. The quantities of heavy artillery, gas, and aircraft were smaller than in France, and to begin with the Italians were poorly equipped. Only in August 1916 did they achieve their first big success by switching reinforcements rapidly from the Trentino battle, gaining surprise, and taking Gorizia. Three more Isonzo battles that autumn, however, led to no further progress, and left the army exhausted before a prolonged winter pause.

By this stage the Italians held most of the Isonzo except for an Austrian bridgehead round Tolmino. But east of Gorizia a natural 'amphitheatre' of encircling peaks overlooked their positions, and to the north and south lay the limestone plateaux of the Bainsizza, the Ternova, and the Carso. Rising to over 2,000 feet, the plateaux were waterless, treeless, and largely devoid of roads and settlement. But beyond them lay no comparably short and

artillery in July, and the howitzers took part in the Eleventh Battle of the Isonzo.[6] Plans were agreed for transporting French and British divisions, which arrangements would later prove to be invaluable but for the moment remained contingency schemes. More far-reaching cooperation was discussed in June in the British government's War Policy Committee, Lloyd George calling on the chief British military liaison officer in Italy, Charles Delmé-Radcliffe. Radcliffe agreed with the premier that 300 British heavy guns and crews might enable the Italians to reach Trieste.[7] But Robertson insisted that the Italian high command was an unknown quantity; that the Central Powers controlled a better transport infrastructure; that if Trieste were seriously threatened the Germans would send troops; and that committing British forces in Italy offered less chance to shape the war as a whole than would committing them in Flanders.[8] The War Policy Committee's final report largely reproduced these views. It kept open the option of sending heavy guns, but the Allies did not pursue it seriously. The French authorities were also doubtful, and the Italians would stay on their own.

Cadorna's Trentino fears were sincere. He foresaw a repeat of May 1916 but against German as well as Austro-Hungarian troops. As just two single-tracked railways connected Italy with southern France, the French and British could help him quickly only if they pre-positioned units in Italy, which he knew their militaries would be loath to provide.[9] Cadorna warned Prime Minister Paolo Boselli that if Italy were attacked it could not count on Franco-British aid, and he told Robertson that only pre-positioned forces would do.[10] But if Italy could not count on its partners, nor would Cadorna strike on the Isonzo until sure of his Trentino flank. Although Nivelle's offensive spirit pleased him, Cadorna delayed the Tenth Battle of the Isonzo to mid May, starting after the Chemin des Dames attack had failed. When asked at the Allied Paris conference in July to commit to big offensives in August and October, he said he had too few munitions and men, and needed at least three months between major operations.[11] Although he would cite supporting Britain and France as a reason for the Eleventh Battle of the Isonzo in August, it was his final attack of the year. In addition the mood in London changed during Third Ypres, Balfour warning his ambassador that any substantial aid to Italy would mean breaking off in Flanders, which the government could not contemplate unless it was 'absolutely convinced' that 'a really decisive success' and 'a genuine overthrow of the Austrian army...involving at least the fall of Trieste' ensued.[12] To this Cadorna—who whatever his other failings showed a commendable frankness—replied he could not assure this outcome so late in the season. By September Cadorna was so concerned about the Central Powers attacking *him* that he suspended offensive operations anyway: another unilateral action, which the British government viewed 'with equal surprise and concern'.

The record shows Cadorna was quite capable of saying no to Italy's allies. Their opinions came second to his appraisal of what was feasible and desirable. Unlike Nivelle and Haig, he could still devise his strategy with little political interference, and it is on Cadorna, his staff at the *Comando supremo* at Udine, and his senior field commanders that analysis must focus. For good or ill, Cadorna was among the most consistent of First World War commanders. Like Haig, he combined an aggressive strategy with moderation over war aims. Italy's politicians had not consulted him before signing the Treaty of London,[13] and he foresaw that the Dalmatian coast would be indefensible, though felt unable to voice this misgiving.[14] On the other hand, breaking through to Trieste and to Ljubljana had been in his mind since the start of (or even before) Italy's intervention; when Lloyd George suggested a diversion to Pola in return for British assistance, Cadorna demurred.[15] He expected a long war, and his strategy was of repeated attacks along a much narrower active sector than on the Western Front in order to wear down the enemy (attrition—*logoramento*—being among his favourite words). He told his wife that 'This war can only be ended through the exhaustion of men and resources... It's frightful, but that's how it is.'[16] By 1916, with the fall of Gorizia and growing unrest and hardship in Austria–Hungary, he had reason to believe attrition was working. Moreover, his army continued to expand, by calling up both younger and older conscript cohorts, and by early 1917 was at its maximum strength. Organized now in fifty-nine divisions, it had nearly 2 million men (200,000 more than in 1916), and between May 1916 and May 1917 its numbers of medium and heavy guns doubled.[17] Like other armies it had curtailed training, and fewer experienced officers and subalterns remained to oversee it. None the less, Cadorna boasted that he led the biggest Italian army since the Caesars.[18]

Yet time now started to work against him. Whereas the November 1916 Chantilly conference had envisaged him attacking as part of another synchronized effort, alongside Russia in the north and the Salonika armies in the south-east, the February Revolution meant that Italy would attempt to knock out Austria-Hungary single-handed, and must strike before the Austrians brought forces back from Russia, perhaps accompanied by Germans. Given the long interval since Ninth Isonzo, and how Italy had been strengthened in the interim, Premier Paolo Boselli urged Cadorna to make the next battle 'decisive, in the sense that it virtually gives us Trieste',[19] and Cadorna hoped and believed his adversary could be beaten that summer. The Italians impressed on their allies that defeating Austria-Hungary might mean the defeat of Germany, Delmé-Radcliffe reporting that they 'consider a military defeat of Austria there would go a long way towards determining, this year, the issue of the war'.[20] Cadorna, however, blended ambition with apprehension, for he claimed that Russia's paralysis might enable Austria-Hungary to redirect fifty or sixty divisions against him.[21] Hence he wanted a secure defensive position as well as a springboard for further advances. Given that his superiority in manpower and logistics was not matched by comparable superiority in artillery, he envisaged a more complex strategy than previously, starting with a bombardment along the whole of the front to camouflage his intentions. The newly formed Gorizia Zone Command under General Luigi Capello would strike east of Gorizia in order to draw off enemy reserves before the Third Army, under the Duke of Aosta, delivered the main attack further south, against the Carso plateau.[22]

The Austrians knew from wireless intercepts that Italy would not attack before mid April, and they had indeed brought reinforcements from Russia.[23] As usual both sides hailed the Tenth Battle of the Isonzo as a success, but in fact the Italian gains—though bigger than in many previous battles—were disappointing. The bombardment, with 2,150 guns and 980 mortars, began on 1 May and the infantry attack two days later. The Italians captured Hill 383, which had eluded them for two years, after desperate fighting in which the two lead brigades suffered more than 50 per cent casualties. They also took two more peaks, Kuk and Vodice, but not the key to the whole area, the Monte Santo, whose summit they twice reached but twice had to abandon. The Austrians did, however, have to draw on their reserves, and on 23 May the Carso phase began with a barrage of 1 million shells.[24] Once again the infantry made initial progress, capturing three positions and taking several thousand prisoners; but after two days they lost impetus, and on 3 and 4 June the Austrians counter-attacked in both sectors, recapturing much of the ground lost and for the first time finding thousands of Italians discarding their weapons. The battle ended with 43,000 Italians killed, 96,000 wounded, and 27,000 captured, against Austrian casualties of 90,000, some 24,000 of them prisoners.[25] Italian casualties were double those of their enemies, and more attackers surrendered than did defenders, which was an unprecedented indicator of faltering morale. Cadorna had had to ration artillery support, and shortage of munitions was the principal reason he gave for halting the battle. According to a British observer, heavy shells were 'a ruling factor in the plan of operations for the Italian army'.[26] Infantry/artillery liaison was inadequate and the infantry failed repeatedly in unsupported charges against the enemy guns, whereas the artillery neglected counter-battery work (targeting the Austrian front-line trenches rather than their guns) and was not moved forward quickly enough.[27] Yet the weaknesses ran deeper. D'Aosta judged that at this rate it would take ten years to win and the Italian people would say 'enough': he did not see a military solution. Senior officers said that when pushed out of their trenches the men had gone forward, but they had done so weeping.[28] And Cadorna was 'disgusted and nauseated' by the success of the Austrian counter-attack, which he considered 'the most shameful fact of the war'.[29]

Worse followed. The Austrian offensive in May 1916 had taken the Arsiero and Asiago heights, leaving the Italian positions in the Trentino more exposed and needing larger garrisons.[30] Within a week of Tenth Isonzo Cadorna launched the battle of Ortigara, an attempt to push the Austrians back. It cost 25,000 casualties for no gain whatever, Cadorna blaming his troops' lack of 'élan' (slancio) and acknowledging privately the operation was a 'fiasco'.[31] Yet he looked forward already to an eleventh Isonzo battle that would resume where the tenth had left off, but be even bigger.[32] It is true that this time there were doubts. After the end of Tenth Isonzo, Cadorna had told the staff historian Angelo Gatti that he would stage no more big offensives until circumstances altered. He understood that German divisions were coming to Italy, and he considered withdrawing to a more defensible line. Yet he also sensed the war might end soon, and it was urgent to reach Trieste.[33] As Cadorna explained afterwards, his motive for the eleventh battle was to improve on the positions gained in the tenth, given that Russia was likely to cease fighting. He warned Boselli that three Austro-Hungarian divisions had transferred from the Eastern Front, six more were being moved, and a further eight might follow, while the French army's inaction meant Germans might come too.[34] He hoped to overrun the Ternova and Bainsizza plateaux and take Mount Hermada, which dominated the Carso, as well as the remaining heights east of Gorizia. By attacking he could relieve the pressure on Russia and coordinate efforts with France and Britain. To do nothing would mean inaction until the following spring, undermining morale in the army and the country. Finally, although in retrospect he stressed the defensive motives, and he envisaged a further campaign in

1918,[35] he also hoped a new blow could force Vienna to sue for peace. He told Delmé-Radcliffe that he planned 'a great offensive from Tolmein [Tolmino] to the sea, since it was only by an offensive on this scale that he could be sure of obtaining a decisive success'. He could not undertake such an effort 'without a reasonable prospect of success, as, apart from the military disadvantages of non-success, a very serious repercussion might be brought about in the country by a failure'. He therefore understood the risk.[36] He increased the divisions assigned from forty-two to fifty-one, and would strike with 1.2 million men, 3,747 guns, and 1,882 trench mortars.[37] As he had still more men and guns than in the spring, he could keep the Austrians guessing by bombarding the entire Isonzo Front and he refrained from shifting between sectors as in the tenth battle, instead leaving more initiative to his commanders: Capello (who had been promoted to lead the Second Army in the north), and d'Aosta (who remained in charge of the Third). By August 1917 the Italian army would be twice as big as in May 1915, and its supplying railways had twice the capacity of the Austrian ones.[38] The rest of the front was denuded of men in order to concentrate two-thirds of the troops in the attack sector.

Although one rationale for the Eleventh Battle of the Isonzo was to support Third Ypres, the preliminary bombardment started later than in Flanders (on 18 August), before the infantry attack went in that evening. Once again the Third Army on the Carso made little headway, but Capello's elite units crossed the Isonzo and reached the northern edge of the Bainsizza plateau. The Austrians threw in tired and under-strength reserves, and by 22 August the Italians were close to breakthrough. That day the Austrian Emperor Karl was visiting the front (at the same time as King Victor Emmanuel III visited the Italian side), and agreed with the Isonzo commander, Svetozar Boroević, on a tactical withdrawal. Yet this decision was also the immediate origin of Caporetto, as Boroević's agreement was sweetened by the promise of a counter-offensive before the winter. The upshot was that the Austrians retreated out of range of the Italian heavy guns to improvised positions on the plateau's edge. The Italians followed cautiously, and after the first attacks against the new positions failed Cadorna switched his attention to Monte San Gabriele, another of the peaks east of Gorizia, which his troops took but failed to hold. Even so, by early September, the Italians had secured the most significant territorial gains in any of the Isonzo battles, though at the cost of even higher casualties than in May. Their losses totalled 166,000, including 40,000 dead, and 400 of the 660 battalions involved lost half or more of their strength. Austrian casualties of 140,000, in a smaller army, were proportionately even heavier.[39] None the less, the inquiry commission after Caporetto concluded that without Eleventh Isonzo Italy would have been better able to withstand the subsequent enemy attack. Cadorna launched the battle despite Italian politicians' pleas to reconsider, and knowing morale was fragile. As his deputy, Carol Porrò reflected after Caporetto, the country would ask why, if the spirit of the troops was so shaken, had they undertaken Eleventh Isonzo?[40]

Although the Isonzo battles were shorter than the Somme or Third Ypres, the daily casualty rates were even higher; and the numbers of divisions and guns committed were similar. The Italian Front had become extraordinarily destructive, and Italian casualties in 1917 were the highest in any year of the war. Deaths in action totalled 66,000 in 1915; 118,880 in 1916; 152,790 in 1917; and 40,250 in 1918. Wounded in action totalled 190,400 in 1915; 285,620 in 1916; 367,200 in 1917; and 103,240 in 1918.[41] Yet whereas in France and Britain the Chemin des Dames and Third Ypres followed investigation of the alternatives and interrogation of the senior military, in Italy politics and strategy remained largely separate. The Council of Ministers did not concern itself with strategy; nor, until after Caporetto, did it have a war committee. The war minister had less influence than his equivalent in Paris or London, and was normally a general. General Gaetano Giardino, who held the post from June to October, had a low opinion of Cadorna and would have preferred to rest the men. Yet he had no precise information about the upcoming eleventh battle.[42] Both Giardino and Foreign Minister Sidney Sonnino, cautioned Cadorna against the operation, but unavailingly. According to Gatti, 'No one, neither Sonnino, nor Giardino, nor Orlando [minister of the interior], nor me, nor Italy ... will vote for the action. There were a thousand fears, a thousand doubts ... ', but Cadorna defied them all.[43] Nor was there effective opposition even within the *Comando supremo*, where Cadorno's pessimistic deputy, Porrò, was sidelined.[44] In the Caporetto inquiry commission, Orlando was pressed about government supervision of Cadorna. He replied that Cadorna never discussed with the Cabinet his plans for major offensives, and the Cabinet never asked whether it should be consulted: it did not attempt a critical appreciation of the Isonzo offensives, and the war minister did not offer one. Cadorna enjoyed high prestige after halting the Austrian Trentino offensive in 1916, and his right to stay in post was unquestioned, even if after Tenth Isonzo Orlando and others had reservations.[45] Distance also played a part, as Cadorna's headquarters lay 350 miles north-east of Rome, whereas the French GQG lay barely 30 miles north of Paris. Although Cadorna met periodically and corresponded with Boselli and the war minister, his appearances at Cabinet meetings were rare.

The Boselli Cabinet was unlikely to challenge this position. Formed in June 1916, in the emergency after the Austrians' Trentino attack, it was meant to be a government of national unity, though also a safeguard against military dictatorship. The latter possibility was spoken of, but Cadorna, who in some things was meticulous, rejected it, while insisting strategy was his prerogative.[46] Moreover, the ex-socialist, Leonida Bissolati, who had been a prominent interventionist and had served at the front, held special responsibility within the government for liaison with the high command and became a Cadorna enthusiast.[47] Any attempt to clip the commander's wings might break up the Cabinet. Nor was there much pressure to do so from parliament, where the only regular opposition came from the socialist party, the PSI, which had opposed war entry and continued to do so, though not obstructing the war effort by strikes or direct action. It was true that after Tenth Isonzo the government agreed to a secret session, and encountered a storm of criticism. General Murazzi, whom Cadorna had sacked, called for a purely defensive conduct of the war.[48] Boselli—a shrewd intellectual but now over 80—was seen as lacking vigour. None the less, he made support for Cadorna a question of confidence, and with minor concessions the government won through.

Boselli survived in part for lack of a successor. Foreign Minister Sonnino did not wish to replace him; and Interior Minister Orlando, who eventually did, was charged with laxity. Cadorna was increasingly anxious about the army's morale and discipline, and after the mass surrenders during the Austrian counter-attack in June he began a heated correspondence, remonstrating against the interior minister. He told Orlando that most of those who surrendered came from Sicily, where 20,000 deserters and service refusers were at large: he blamed 'poisonous propaganda' and the toleration of 'internal enemies'. To keep order he must respond with summary shootings 'on a vast scale' and with the 'decimation' of infected units.[49] Cadorna told Boselli that he must 'repress with extreme methods every act of indiscipline', even though the soldiers were largely innocent victims of 'a subversive propaganda' whose orchestrators remained safely in the interior.[50] He told his family that he did not wish to 'act the Nero', but he had to keep order.[51] Cadorna's letters implicitly blamed Orlando, who was also targeted by patriotic demonstrations in Milan.[52] In fact the ideological divide of 1917 prefigured the quasi-civil war conditions in Italy during the rise of Fascism.[53] But Orlando defended himself in the June secret session of parliament and in a special meeting of the Council of Ministers.[54] While condemning the anti-war propaganda, he believed the correct response was to contain it rather than simply to repress all opposition.[55] He admitted after Caporetto that 'he had gambled on the war ending this year and therefore managed affairs with a very light hand'.[56] But in any case he contested the assumption that the flow of influence ran from the interior to the army; the problem was also war weariness among the troops, for reasons including inadequate leave and Tenth Isonzo.[57] Cadorna's method (probably reflecting shyness and discomfort with politicians) was to fire off letters but not to discuss problems face to face.[58] However, in the special Cabinet meeting on 28 September Orlando again stressed the demoralization caused by Tenth Isonzo,[59] and while Cadorna maintained that pacifist propaganda had 'polluted' morale, Orlando said the real issue was that 'the supreme command slaughters too many soldiers in too great haste'. Afterwards Cadorna still derided the politicians as 'those idiots', and wrote in 1926 (under Mussolini's dictatorship) that 'if during the war there had been in Italy the present strong government, the disaster would not have happened'.[60]

Conditions in the Italian army were worse than for any force on the Western Front. Part of the reason was social. Two-thirds of the infantry (which suffered 94 per cent of the casualties) were country dwellers—*contadini*. Many were illiterate, spoke dialect rather than standard Italian, and their national consciousness was weak. Away from the north-east, a war for Trieste and the Trentino made little sense, and soldiers' letters identified it as a ruling-class project. Orlando was right that the army was ungenerous with leave: units stayed in the forward trenches for a month or more, and their leave entitlement (not honoured in any case) was only two-thirds of that in the French army before the mutinies and one half of it afterwards.[61] During the war 100,000 soldiers were convicted of desertion, most of them simply being late in returning from home. The high command exacerbated the problems, not least through Cadorna's frenetic purging of officers who were insufficiently committed to the offensive or had failed to achieve their superiors' objectives. By May 1917 regiments had averaged six changes in commanding officers, and some had had as many as eighteen.[62] Such turnover militated against learning from experience and against the men identifying with their units. Italian troops were also subjected to exceptionally ferocious discipline. When Cadorna warned he would resort to 'decimation', or punishing deficient units by selecting men by lot for execution, it was actually practised already, contrary to military law.[63] The demoralization of the Italian army, like the French, was gradual, but disappointment in the seventh, eighth, and ninth Isonzo battles in autumn 1916 came cruelly after the capture of Gorizia, as still more did disappointment in Tenth Isonzo, launched on an unprecedented scale and after months of preparation. Cadorna and Orlando both recognized a morale crisis in summer 1917 (even if they differed over the diagnosis), and disaffection was ascending from individual to unit level. In March 1917 twenty-nine soldiers of the Ravenna Brigade were executed after a minor act of rebellion that caused no casualties.[64] In May executions reached their highest monthly total of the war.[65] In July the Catanzaro Brigade protested against being sent back to the front, and for the only time soldiers used weapons against their superiors.[66] By September over 100,000 fugitives were at large in the interior, and a report to Cadorna indicated that since 1915 the desertion rate had tripled.[67] Indeed, court-martial convictions for desertion rose from 856 per month in 1915–16 to 2,319 in 1916–17 and 4,586 in 1917–18.[68] From early 1917 the *Comando supremo* was monitoring morale, although its evidence suggested an improvement in August and September, following the Bainsizza plateau success.[69] This recovery may have been due, however, to the first troops being released for the winter, and men assuming the year's fighting had ended. Indeed, when Caporetto began 120,000 soldiers were on leave, and the front-line corps were well below strength.[70]

Army indiscipline coincided with a wider malaise. It was remarkable this had not come earlier, given the anomalousness of one section of society forcing another to risk all for purposes of dubious relevance and given also Italy's pre-war restiveness. The authorities had lost control of the province of Emilia-Romagna in June 1914, and by spring 1917 local officials had almost done so again.[71] Real living standards, especially in the countryside, fell from the start, but in late 1916 the combination of Isonzo setbacks with the Central Powers' peace note and the winter cold broke the surface tranquillity. Thousands of women marched in protest, demanding their men back and more food. In 1917 Italy suffered its first serious strikes and the critics grew bolder. The PSI was divided between a more moderate wing under Filippo Turati and a more radical one. After the February Revolution and the failure of the Stockholm conference, it moved from non-support towards active opposition.[72] Much quoted was the slogan of the deputy,

Claudio Treves, 'not another winter in the trenches'.[73] Pope Benedict XV, in his peace note published just before Eleventh Isonzo, called for a return to the status quo ante and an end to the 'useless massacre' (*l'inutile strage*). The Vatican had lost control over Rome and the Papal States in 1870 at the time of Italy's unification, and refused to cooperate with the liberal and secular Italian kingdom; it was also ambivalent about fighting the predominantly Catholic Austria-Hungary. None the less, Benedict had allowed Italian priests to support the war effort,[74] and Cadorna had let them become chaplains. The pope's message and its timing angered members of the officer corps, but his appeal was liable to sway the many in the army who remained observant. Finally Giovanni Giolitti, the pre-war premier, who enjoyed a substantial parliamentary following and was known to have opposed intervention, in a speech at Cuneo characterized the war as 'the greatest catastrophe since the Deluge' and warned that 'profound changes in the conduct of our foreign relations' were needed. The British ambassador could 'seldom remember a period in my long experience of Italy when people in a certain class of society were so prone to speak of the coming revolution',[75] and although he discounted these anxieties, Italy was dangerously dependent on imported coal and wheat, and the shipping crisis reduced its 1917 import tonnage to three-fifths of the 1913 level.[76] In late August the torpedoing of a grain ship precipitated in Turin the worst disorder of the war. The city was a socialist heartland, made tenser by a visit from Petrograd Soviet delegates. In scenes reminiscent of Russia, a protest starting with women queuing fruitlessly outside bakers grew into a strike by armaments workers and martial law was imposed. Unlike in Petrograd, the troops opened fire, and subdued the working-class districts.[77] Enough of the Italian army remained reliable to keep order, even if much of it no longer wanted to hold the line. Perhaps Italian troops were isolated from home conditions, by illiteracy and by leave restrictions as well as by distance, but many knew of the currents of opinion in the interior, if not necessarily responding to socialist propaganda. They hardly needed it, in any case, in order to understand the misery of their lives, the capriciousness of authority, and the slimness of their survival chances.

   Early in September the Italian commanders switched abruptly from an offensive to a defensive stance. How much warning they received and how well prepared they were for the impending attack were major concerns of the Caporetto inquiry commission. Although Cadorna told Gatti on 1 September that they would not reach Trieste that year, and scaled down operations to reduce his casualties and his munitions expenditure, he hoped the Allies would support a joint offensive in the spring.[78] By mid September, he was more pessimistic, partly because of the losses during Eleventh Isonzo, but also due to anxiety about Russia. When the Kornilov coup failed, he went pale, and foresaw big Austrian and even German concentrations against Italy.[79] On 18 September Cadorna warned Capello and d'Aosta that the enemy build-up in the Julian Alps (north of the Isonzo) made 'a serious attack' likely, and he had decided 'to renounce all offensive operational projects and to concentrate all activity on the predispositions for an all-out defence, so that the possible attack finds us appropriately prepared to repulse it'. All troop activities, artillery deployments, and construction priorities should proceed with this principle in mind.[80]

This advice seemed to indicate the priorities clearly, and was issued in good time. But its aftermath was damaging. The Allies had expected continuing operations into the autumn, and were taken aback. A bald statement explained to them that events in Russia (and Austrian reinforcement) had compelled a 'defensive posture'.[81] The British protested that 'the attack in Flanders was undertaken as part of a general plan for putting simultaneous pressure on all enemy fronts'. Porrò told the French that a renewed offensive would cost 2 million shells and 150,000 men, and weaken the army when it was liable to be attacked, thus endangering civilian morale; Cadorna told the British an offensive now would weaken one in 1918.[82] Yet the Western Allies remained unconvinced, and recalled their heavy artillery. By the date of Caporetto most had gone.[83]

A second difficulty was that Cadorna's instructions were not implemented, at any rate not by the Second Army, which would bear the brunt of the blow. Unlike before the Austrian attack in May 1916, he failed to follow up with detailed orders; perhaps because he tended now to delegate more, but also because he did not treat the intelligence reports very seriously. In early October he left headquarters for several days, to visit the positions on the Trentino and take a holiday with his wife.[84] Capello, the Second Army commander, was ruthless: he regretted Italian soldiers were too good-natured, not natural killers. His relations with Cadorna were difficult. He lost some of his artillery after the offensive ended, and he badgered Cadorna for more men, eventually receiving 20,000.[85] Cadorna had promoted Capello as a go-getter. In face-to-face discussions between them Capello could think faster and tended to gain what he wanted,[86] and increasingly he disregarded his superior. The consequences would be serious, as Capello believed the correct response to an enemy attack was a prompt counter-offensive, so most of his infantry and artillery should be well forward. He argued in retrospect that a strategic withdrawal like that to the Hindenburg Line was out of the question as it meant abandoning territory conquered at such cost; furthermore the Italians lacked the depth of terrain for a German-style elastic defence, which in any case would take weeks to prepare whereas the work of moving guns and laying cables for an offensive was largely complete.[87] After receiving Cadorna's 18 September order Capello seems to have done little for a month except withdraw some artillery,[88] though he also sought clarification through an interview. Genuine grounds existed for misunderstanding in that a note from Cadorna's headquarters on 10 October approved Capello's dispositions, and while Cadorna was in the Trentino it was difficult to see him.[89] In instructions Capello issued on 17–18 October he still envisaged a counter-offensive. When the two men finally met on the 19th the discussion was difficult and may have become a shouting match, but in a written directive the next day Cadorna spelled out that the army was too weak for an ambitious counterstroke.[90] By now it was too late to make a difference.

Yet as late as in this 20 October order, Cadorna still suggested the reason for renouncing a counter-offensive now was to be ready for an enemy attack *next* year.[91] On the eve of Caporetto, he underestimated what was about to hit him. Although Capello's disregard of instructions shares the blame, Cadorna's command style, now more than ever, was solitary. He avoided reliance on his staff officers or discussion of the intelligence reports,[92] which was the more regrettable as the intelligence was inconsistent. Admittedly, it was harder to detect the enemy build-up than it might have been on the Western Front. The Italians lacked the Western Allies' customary air superiority, and they had to monitor enemy movements through steep-sided mountain valleys, conducted mainly at night, and often under cloud cover.[93] Hence much depended on prisoners and defectors, but the latter might deliberately serve deception. In fact the Central Powers played on Cadorna's nervousness about the Trentino by placing German contingents there and emitting dummy wireless messages. Although the *Comando supremo* knew an attack was likely, the intelligence picture came into focus too late. During September the only unambiguous warning of something serious was the closure on the 20th of the Austro-Swiss border (presumably to prevent observation by Swiss nationals).[94] On 28 September the *Comando supremo*'s 'Situation Office' (*Uffizione situazione*) correctly estimated that the Trentino activity was a diversion—given the greater height of the terrain there, it was too late for a major operation—and a big attack in 1917 was possible only on the Isonzo. Two days later, however, it said the enemy had abandoned plans for an Isonzo offensive and, on 2 October, that if there was one it would only be local. As of 8 October, it expected an Austrian offensive but with small German involvement, intended to recapture the Bainsizza plateau; on the 10th it said the enemy concentration on the middle Isonzo reflected 'a defensive or counter-offensive concept', and as late as 17 October it still envisaged a Bainsizza counter-offensive.[95] Cadorna apparently accepted the latter analysis, telling Delmé-Radcliffe on 10 October that he expected a big Austro-Hungarian attack using German artillery towards the Bainsizza and Tolmino.[96] The next day he advised Orlando that rumours of an attack were a bluff.[97] Yet the incoming information now confirmed the Austro-Hungarian build-up, and that the upper Isonzo would be the likely attack zone in late October, although precision was still lacking.[98]

Only in the final week did the intelligence picture become unambiguous, by which time Cadorna could no longer make big changes. Deserter information was pivotal—particularly from a Czech on the 20th and two Romanians on the 21st—and an intercepted radio message on 22 October disclosed the date. It was now clear that this would be a major attack with large German participation, centred on the north of the Isonzo Front round the Tolmino bridgehead.[99] On the morning of 24 October itself, Cadorna told Foch and Robertson that it would fall between Plezzo and the sea, though predominantly between Plezzo and Tolmino: four German divisions were in the front line, and the target was the heads of the valleys descending to the plain lying west of the Italians so as to turn their entire position.[100] Although this was mostly accurate, Cadorna still understated what was coming to the *north* of Plezzo, and had sent no extra reconnaissance aircraft to that sector. Until the end he thought reconquering the Bainsizza might be the main goal, and this probably influenced his reserves' disposition. On 21 October he told the British the rugged terrain in the Tolmino sector made it easy to defend and he was therefore holding it lightly.[101]

The combination of flawed intelligence and faulty dispositions meant that on 24 October the Italian army was poorly prepared—even if its enemies' had applied more orthodox tactics. Despite the Central Powers' reinforcements, the Italians retained their numerical advantage, but not in the breakthrough sector: their forces were poorly distributed and unprepared for defence in depth. The Second Army had 231 of its 353 infantry battalions in the front line. The main attack fell on the XXVII and IV Corps, and whereas Cadorna had ordered the bulk of XXVII Corps to stay west of the Isonzo, actually more than half its infantry and much of its medium artillery lay east of the river. The two corps each held three defence lines, but XXVII Corps had a weak second line and IV Corps a weak first line, both systems lacking good dug-outs.[102] Both corps also held long frontages and XXVII Corps' trenches had been dug in 1915 with wooden revetments that were highly visible and would quickly succumb to bombardment; IV Corps had no organized line to withdraw to if the first line fell. Moreover, both corps held broken and partly wooded terrain that lent itself to infiltration. The salient between Plezzo and Tolmino was held more thinly than the Bainsizza further south, being garrisoned by just four mediocre Italian divisions against eight elite Austrian and German ones, and behind the defenders lay very few quickly available reserves. Capello had worked until the last few days on a counter-offensive rather than a defensive plan, and he commanded an unmanageably large army; his VII Corps, which was tasked with supporting IV and XXVII Corps, lay well to the south-west and could not move up rapidly. But the same was even truer of Cadorna's general reserve, which was west and south-west of Gorizia, behind the Third Army rather than the Second. It was too far south, too close there to the front line, composed of poor-quality divisions, and smaller than before the previous emergency in May 1916.[103] But in any case, Cadorna had no contingency plan for using it, and once the crisis erupted he had to improvise.[104]

None the less, the Italian commanders on the eve of battle exhibited equanimity, even complacency, and not least about their men. According to the British ambassador, 'a greater feeling of confidence as regards the military situation on the Austrian front exists today than probably at any time since the beginning of the war'.[105] Cadorna told Robertson and Foch that 'I await the development of events with perfect serenity and complete confidence.'[106] He told his family that he was worried about the defences around Plezzo but had taken steps to strengthen them; 'For the rest I regard the situation with perfect tranquillity and great confidence', and for the last two nights he had slept soundly.[107] He similarly reassured the government. Capello felt more exposed, and nervous about his inability to communicate with Cadorna, but on 23 October he accurately forecast to his corps commanders the location and character of the attack, reassuring them that the Italian troops were efficient, well deployed, technically prepared, and that IV and XXVII Corps were reinforced: 'We have prepared everything and victory will not be lacking.' His commanders, Capello told the inquiry commission, felt 'Olympian serenity' about their troops' morale.[108] On 19 October Cadorna sent officers to interview the front-line chiefs. General Alberto Cavaciocchi, commanding XXVII Corps, reported that while his own preparations were almost complete he saw little evidence of enemy ones and did not expect simultaneous attacks from the Plezzo and Tolmino basins (though precisely this would happen), while morale and discipline were 'in the highest degree satisfactory'. Pietro Badoglio, commanding IV Corps, also said he had carried out his own preparations and saw few by the enemy; his troop morale was 'satisfactory' and apparently raised by the prospect of fighting Germans. When Cadorna personally visited the two generals on 22 and 23 October they confirmed their statements, praising their soldiers' 'excellent spirit'.[109] It seemed that everything was ready.

For the Central Powers to deliver their attack, Austrian and German thinking had to converge. For most of the war, the Austrians in Italy had been on the defensive. The one major exception had been the May 1916 attack, which had not only failed to achieve its objectives but had also exposed the Dual Monarchy to disaster on the Eastern Front and forced it to appeal for German aid. Yet at first that offensive had gone well, and it made lasting gains. The Austro-Hungarian CGS, Franz Conrad von Hötzendorff, who detested the Italians, continued working on attack plans, and early in 1917 Austria-Hungary and Germany discussed the spring campaigning. Conrad proposed precisely what Cadorna most feared: an attack on the Isonzo followed by a decisive assault in the Tyrol, intended to cut off Italy's Isonzo armies and knock it out of the war. At this stage, however, surviving the expected Allied spring offensives was the OHL's first imperative.[110] Hindenburg and Ludendorff hoped the unrestricted submarine campaign could win the war quickly. Failing that, they had long envisaged that Germany must defeat Russia first and then turn to the west, Italy remaining peripheral.[111] During the spring and summer they held off the French and British and halted the Kerensky offensive, while Karl sought peace through the mediation of Prince Sixte de Bourbon.[112] He got nowhere, in the first instance due to Italian objections, and Austrian interest in attacking Italy revived. The defeat of the Kerensky offensive made such an operation feasible, by releasing forces from Russia;[113] and Eleventh Isonzo made it urgent, as the Austrians feared that they had almost lost the last defence line before Trieste and that their faltering infantry might not withstand a twelfth Isonzo battle.

It had been agreed after the Brusilov offensive that the OHL would be the *Oberste Kriegsleitung* (supreme war direction) for the Central Powers in decisive questions, though without command authority over Germany's partners. Karl weakened this arrangement and reserved Austria-Hungary's rights in case of conflict,[114] but it was still prudent to consult Germany before a major offensive in Italy—which without German assistance was now beyond the Habsburg army's strength. Even before the eleventh Isonzo battle, August von Cramon, the German plenipotentiary at the Austro-Hungarian high command (*Armee Oberkommando* or AOK) was considering an operation that would roll up the Italian front from the north: but Ludendorff, who was worried about Third Ypres and would have preferred to follow up the repulse of the Kerensky offensive by finishing off Romania, was unenthusiastic.[115] Cadorna thought Austria-Hungary would be too proud to seek help, and that Eleventh Isonzo had so weakened the Dual Monarchy that it was unlikely to attack before the winter.[116] But in fact during late August the Austro-German discussions went into higher gear. After the Bainsizza evacuation, the Austrians held only an improvised line, and after conferring with Karl, Arthur Arz von Straussenberg (whom Karl had appointed as a more pliable CGS than Conrad while demoting the latter to the Trentino command) decided on a counter-offensive before Italy could attack again. His chosen theatre was the Isonzo as he needed to act quickly and a Tyrol attack would take too long to prepare,[117] and it helped that Arz's Chief of Operations, Alfred von Waldstätten, had already drafted a scheme. Two approaches to the Germans followed. First, Karl wrote to Wilhelm on 26 August, saying that a twelfth Isonzo defensive battle would create 'an extraordinarily difficult situation' and the best response was an offensive; though he did not want to use German troops (except for heavy artillery), preferring that German forces replaced Austrian ones in Russia. Karl said that having Germans on the Italian front would demoralize his soldiers, who considered it 'our war': an unconvincing cover for his fear of indebtedness to his ally.[118] Wilhelm's reply was also guarded: although he agreed an offensive was the best response, he could not agree to replace Austrian forces in the east, and the general situation would determine Germany's decision.[119] This did not shut the door entirely, but it reflected the OHL's coolness, which changed only due to the second prong of the Austrians' approach.

On 29 August Waldstätten met Hindenburg and Ludendorff at Bad Kreuznach. He found Ludendorff still preferred to attack in Moldavia, breaking Romania's resistance and perhaps also Russia's; and because of the

Flanders fighting Ludendorff doubted whether he could release men for Italy. Ludendorff thought the attack sector was too narrow, and that the Italians would bring up reinforcements.[120] But when Waldstätten insisted that the situation was decisively important, Hindenburg sent Lieutenant General Konrad Krafft von Delmensingen, a Bavarian artillery officer with expertise in mountain warfare and previously commander of the Alpenkorps, to visit and report. Unusually, a difference between Hindenburg and Ludendorff had emerged. Hindenburg commented retrospectively that he had little confidence in being able to knock Italy out of the war, but the Austro-Hungarian line protecting Trieste had been stretched to the limit, and the city held great economic and symbolic value as the Dual Monarchy's principal sea access, so that its loss might also mean losing Germany's main ally.[121] Ludendorff was more sceptical about how bad Austria-Hungary's situation really was, as indeed was Krafft.[122] But at the beginning of September two developments brought on a final decision. First, Arz persuaded Karl to accept German troops, Karl writing to Wilhelm that he hoped the two empires' forces would soon engage in victorious operations.[123] Karl was accepting the dependence on Berlin that he had previously resisted.[124] The point was underlined when the Germans learned that Karl's foreign minister, Czernin, had said Austria-Hungary would no longer fight for Germany's war aims. After Karl denied the report and insisted Austria-Hungary remained loyal, Wilhelm refrained from pressing for a written guarantee.[125] Although he passed by an opportunity to tie Karl down, a spectacular joint victory would have similar consequences, especially as the key assault forces would include German infantry and would serve under German command.

    The second development was Krafft's mission. Having visited the prospective battlefront, he met Hindenburg and Ludendorff on 8 September. Ludendorff described this encounter as 'decisive' (maßgebend).[126] Krafft endorsed the Austrians' warnings about their army's parlous state, and considered the proposed operation, although 'at the limits of the possible', was feasible.[127] Krafft was a respected and articulate senior officer, whose nine-page report acknowledged the difficulties and risks.[128] Ludendorff found renouncing his Moldavian operation 'difficult',[129] but after a loaded silence he assented. The AOK and OHL soon reached agreement and on 18 September orders for Operation 'Comradeship in Arms' (Waffentreue) were issued. It was symptomatic that in the decision-making the German civilian leadership had no perceptible role.

German forces had just defeated the Russians at the battle of Riga (1–5 September) and in early September the Flanders fighting paused. These developments may have facilitated the choice. Even so Ludendorff stipulated that unless the attack broke through at once, it must be called off.[130] He was concerned to restrict the operation to a few weeks and to cap the number of German personnel. As he could spare only eight to nine divisions, a two-pronged attack was excluded.[131] Hence the chances of cutting off Italy's Isonzo armies were slim, and the Germans always intended Caporetto to be limited and were uncharacteristically pessimistic about its chances, though if proved mistaken were willing to broaden their goals.

Caporetto originated with Waldstätten's planners in the AOK Operations Division. They intended to strike not on the Bainsizza plateau, as Cadorna supposed, but further north, along the Tolmino–Flitsch portion of the Isonzo sector, driving towards Cividale.[132] Krafft made the scheme more radical: the main weight would be on the right northern flank, and the breakthrough would aim wider, seeking to push back the Italians at least to the River Tagliamento.[133] In this sector a new German Fourteenth Army would spearhead the drive, commanded by General Otto von Below with Krafft as his COS but comprising both German and Austrian units. Its seventeen divisions would include some of the best in both armies, including mountain warfare specialists, though Krafft believed non-specialists, if properly trained, could also acquit the exacting tasks ahead of them, and he considered the Italians less formidable than the French or British.[134] In the chosen sector the opposing defences were weaker than further south, and it was easier to gain surprise, facilitating a breakthrough to the valleys leading down to the north Italian plain. Its main disadvantage was logistical: only two rail routes ran up to it, and the front line lay 30 miles beyond the railheads. In the view of the Austrian General Alfred Krauß, who commanded on the Plezzo sector, the preparation period was 'the hardest and bitterest time of the entire undertaking'.[135] The season was late, and troops and equipment must be transported from the Russian, Romanian, and Western Fronts, 2,400 trainloads for the Fourteenth Army alone. In total 140,000 men, 60,000 horses, and 1.5 million shells were moved up,[136] the final stretch by road being undertaken in darkness due to the proximity of the Italian lines, the men helping the horses draw the guns before hauling them into place up to 1,000 metres above the floors of the valleys. Although the munitioning was completed two days late, the preparations stayed largely secret until deserters belatedly disclosed them, whereas eavesdropping on the Italian wireless gave the Central Powers vital information.[137] After detraining, the Württemberg Mountain Battalion, in which the young Erwin Rommel commanded a company, marched 63 miles at night, mostly in pouring rain and with scanty and monotonous rations, but their morale was sky-high.[138]

After the Eleventh Battle of the Isonzo, the AOK had had twenty-one divisions on the Isonzo Front against forty Italian ones; it reinforced them with eight Austro-Hungarian divisions from the Eastern Front in addition to the German units, and by 24 October the Central Powers equalled the Italians in numbers of divisions and exceeded them in fighting quality and in heavy artillery and machine guns.[139] After two years of a big Italian numerical edge, which before the spring and summer battles had been widening, the advantage abruptly tilted. The Fourteenth Army had instructions to break through as rapidly as possible between Flitsch and Tolmino, secure the valley between them, and sweep round to the edge of the mountains with the emphasis of the advance on their right flank. The Italians must be driven out of the limestone terrain and behind the River Tagliamento. Some of the Austrian commanders wanted to advance beyond the river, although—perhaps to facilitate German assistance—for the time being they suppressed that aspiration. Conversely, Cadorna expected much longer resistance than actually occurred, because he underestimated his men's demoralization and failed to foresee the enemy tactics.[140] Caporetto marked a stage in the evolution of the assault methods that the Germans would soon unleash in the west. The laborious concentration enabled their artillery to deliver a bombardment whose intensity was unprecedented on the Italian Front, guns being positioned at a density of one every 4.4 metres for 45 kilometres. The first phase lasted from 2.00 a.m. to 4.30 a.m., and the second from 6.30 a.m., before the infantry went in at 8.00 a.m. and 9.00 a.m. At Plezzo the Germans fired phosgene gas shells, against which the Italian masks were almost useless, and hundreds of the defenders were asphyxiated; the bombardment was delivered largely without the warning given by ranging shots and directed principally against the command areas and gun batteries rather than the forward trenches.[141] Cable communications were quickly severed, and the Italian counter-barrage petered out with little damage to the attackers. Admittedly its weakness also reflected Cadorna's anxiety to conserve shells for the battle he planned for spring 1918, and Badoglio's advice to his gunners to be sparing as he had only three days' supply.[142] But by the time they realized the scale of the onslaught, the forward areas were already out of contact.

The Germans and Austrians understood the need to break clean through before the Italians brought up reinforcements. Fortunately Capello's nearest reserves were 30 kilometres from Caporetto, and Cadorna's even more distant.[143] The Italian forward defences east of the Isonzo were shallow and in places very thinly held. The attacking unit commanders had orders to advance as rapidly as possible, without worrying about their flanks, and reinforcements would be sent to the points of deepest breakthrough. The veil of dark and rain assisted them, and Krafft reflected that it was very unusual for an operation to run so smoothly.[144] While the outnumbered Italian IV and XXVII Corps on the east bank were overrun, Austrian forces from the north and German forces from the Tolmino bridgehead in the south converged on Caporetto, cutting off the Italian forces beyond the river. Krauß's principle, contrary to staff college doctrine on mountain warfare, was to drive along the valley floors (which the Italians garrisoned more lightly),[145] and he next moved into the Uccea valley, where the Italians abandoned the Saga pass, the route from here on leading to the plains beyond. Von Below, in contrast, had told his forces to use the ridge tops as 'land bridges', an approach adopted most spectacularly by Rommel's Württemberg Mountain Battalion. Over three days it pushed along the Kolowrat ridge to Monte Matajur, capturing 150 officers, 9,000 men, and eighty-one guns for losses of six dead and thirty wounded.[146] Cadorna had visited the ridge a month before and considered it impregnable,[147] but Rommel's account suggests that once the Italian strongpoint garrisons felt cut off and attacked from flank and rear, they surrendered easily, even with their officers, and in groups of up to several hundred men. During the advance as a whole, half a dozen Italian generals and over fifty colonels were captured.[148]

As the collapse unfolded, little help reached the outposts. Badoglio, the IV Corps Commander, was out of touch with his subordinates. VII Corps, under General Luigi Buongiovanni, was supposed to assist him, but by the evening, when Capello told it to advance on Caporetto, the town had already fallen. Capello ordered local counter-offensives during the day, but Cadorna and the *Comando supremo* were almost completely uninformed, the commander-in-chief still uncertain whether the attack was a 'bluff'.[149] Not until 10.00 p.m. was it confirmed that key positions and 20,000 prisoners had been lost. Conferring with his officers the following morning, Cadorna recognized that this was the worst disaster of the war, and more serious because the troops were exhausted and 'corrupted by the propaganda from the interior... I have troops who do not resist, shamefully...' None the less, his instincts were mostly sound: he would break away from contact with the enemy, and prepare a defence along the Tagliamento. He hesitated partly due to under-standable reluctance to abandon territory for which his troops had paid so terrible a price, but also because Capello's substitute as Second Army commander, General Luca Montuori, believed his force could still hold. Not until news came on 26 October of the loss of Monte Maggiore, which was the key to all the intermediate defence lines that Cadorna had envis-aged, did he abandon planning a counterstroke and authorize a retreat to the Tagliamento in the first instance and if necessary to the River Piave. This decision the war and armaments ministers approved.[150]

The general retreat meant that not just the Second Army but also the Third Army to its south would have to fall back. The latter withdrew in good order, taking its equipment with it. D'Aosta, unlike Capello, had moved most of his artillery east of the Isonzo before the battle began, and he and his staff gave clear directions on the routes to follow. In much of the Second Army, however, discipline broke down. The Second Army had been

Figure 14. German lorries passing through an Italian village, November 1917

huge—some 670,000 men—and tens of thousands were now captured, nearly all uninjured and often openly celebrating. Hundreds of thousands more joined the 'disbanded' (*sbandati*), leaving their units and jettisoning their rifles. There was little attempt at traffic management: with only 20,000 motor vehicles before the war, Italy had no experience of such a migration, and the high command had no contingency plans. Some officers and police tried to impose order, but most went with the flow, while the men torched and pillaged civilian homes, sometimes because they were inebriated and sought revenge on the interior, but often because supplies had broken down and they were hungry. Troops moving up were abused as 'betrayers'. Although many were incensed against their superiors, not least in units that had suffered decimation, they were not violent, and when the king, Orlando, and General Roberti Brusati found themselves in a car surrounded by *sbandati* the men were respectful.[151] All the same, they reiterated that the war had ended and they were going home. According to one of Capello's officers, 'It was a tranquil march by tranquil people. Not a face on which lay shame or anger or desperation, not an eye that was not serene.'[152] Cadorna, in contrast, issued a communiqué blaming the defeat on elements that had 'retreated like cowards without fighting or ignominiously surrendered to the enemy'.[153] Although Orlando had tried to tone it down, Austrian propaganda exploited it. It was also alleged—though later refuted—that some troops had collaborated with the enemy to let them through. More accurate was Bissolati's analogy of a 'military strike', though it was not a social revolutionary movement. After two and a half years of oppression, mistreatment, and massacre, the men had had enough. None the less, the phenomenon profoundly disturbed Italy's political and especially military leaders, who wondered if any line could now be held. Cadorna lamented to Orlando that 'the spirit has gone, and is still lacking; and when the soldier's spirit and will to fight are lacking, all is lacking'. They faced 'an irremediable moral crisis ... this pacific rebellion of an inert human mass, morally exhausted, convinced that the war is finished'.[154]

Yet Caporetto transformed rather than terminated Italy's war. The tensest period was late October, when *sbandati* and civilian refugees swarmed over the Tagliamento bridges. By the 31st the main Italian forces were over the river, but four days later the Central Powers crossed it and Cadorna ordered a retreat to the Piave. By 10 November the Italians held the new position and assaults immediately began against it, at the same time as Conrad, belatedly and with much weaker forces, attacked in the Trentino. A further month of fighting followed until the Central Powers, having failed to make significant gains in either sector, wound the campaign down.

The campaign failed, therefore, to knock Italy out, but it was even more successful than the attackers had anticipated. The Italians no longer menaced Trieste, and would launch no further major offensive until October 1918. They withdrew by up to 150 kilometres, and an area normally inhabited by 1.15 million people fell under occupation.[155] The Italians lost 294,000 prisoners (thousands of whom perished), 12,000 battle dead, and 30,000 wounded, as well as half their artillery.[156] Given that over 350,000 became 'disbanded', only half the field army remained operational. In comparison, German and Austrian killed, wounded, and missing totalled some 70,000, of whom about 15,000 were German.[157] Even so, Hindenburg felt 'a sense of dissatisfaction': the triumph was incomplete.[158] Given the ease with which the Italians had crumbled, perhaps the German divisions should have gone to the Trentino rather than the Isonzo, encircling Italy's Second and Third Armies.[159] Alternatively, perhaps Austrian forces should have gone to the Trentino to strengthen and hasten Conrad's attack—which the OHL favoured but hesitated to impose on Arz and Waldstätten, who wanted to finish the job on the Isonzo first, in addition to which the rail links between the two sectors were difficult.[160] Alternatively again, perhaps the leading German units could have wheeled south faster, to reach the coast and bar the Third Army's evacuation. But this had not figured in the original conception, and the Austro-German planning, so thorough for the opening phases, had not designated routes for the advance across the plain.[161] Moreover, the attackers were short of horses and lorries, and such lorries as they did have used steel tyres that rutted the mountain roads, while no rail link to the Tagliamento was reinstated until 20 November.[162] The forward units therefore lacked artillery and munitions, as well as much support from aerial observation (despite their air superiority) due to the poor weather. Nor did they have enough bridging equipment and engineers.[163] Although they captured a mass of 60,000 prisoners east of the prematurely broken Tagliamento bridge at Codroipo and two whole divisions near Longarone, the pursuit—which Below ordered to be 'continued until the Italian army is annihilated'[164]— was surprisingly sluggish. Matters reached decision point in early November, by which time Ludendorff was again under pressure in Flanders and inclining towards a Western Front offensive for spring 1918. On 12 November he was willing to consider extending the objectives as far as the River Adige and

Lake Garda but, as the Piave operations slowed down, the moment passed.[165]
The German infantry left by the end of November and the artillery in the
following month. But even without them Austria-Hungary was now more
tightly bound to Germany, and a separate peace between Vienna and Rome
still harder to achieve.

Given the Central Powers' self-limitation, Italian recovery could come
into play. It began with a change of leadership. Confidence in Boselli had
been ebbing for some time, and the Right denounced Orlando; but the
Giolittians complained the government did not consult parliament enough.[166]
On 26 October it lost a vote of confidence by 315:96, just before news of
the scale of the defeat reached Rome, so that many deputies soon regretted
the vote and wanted to minimize the disruption.[167] It might seem paradoxical
that Orlando emerged as the new premier, but he formed a more inclusive
government of national unity that carried over many ministers from its
predecessor, including Bissolati, Sonnino at Foreign Affairs, and Alfredo
dall'Olio at Armaments, but also brought in the able Francesco Nitti as
finance minister, and replaced Giardino with Lieutenant General Vittorio
Alfieri (an enemy of Cadorna) at the War Ministry. Cadorna still, however,
kept ministers in the dark, to their indignation.[168] Yet the incoming government probably benefited from Caporetto, which encouraged national unity.
Accompanying the political shake-up was a military one, linked to an appeal
for Allied aid. The Italians contacted Britain and France on the first afternoon,
and on 26 October, without consulting the War Cabinet, Lloyd George told
Robertson that Haig must send two divisions without delay, the French supplying four.[169] Haig protested it would jeopardize the situation in Flanders,
but was disregarded.[170] British troops began entraining on 6 November and
detrained near Mantua by the 20th; three more divisions were ordered during November, and the French eventually sent six, the Allied forces entering
the line on 25–27 November.[171] When Lloyd George and Painlevé arrived
to confer with the Italians at the Rapallo conference on 5–7 November,
therefore, the impending arrival of Allied troops, together with the very
poor impression made by Porrò as the high command's representative,
strengthened the visitors' insistence that the *Comando supremo* must change
if French and British soldiers were to fight under it.[172] They would have
been willing to see d'Aosta replace Cadorna, but Victor Emanuel's dynastic
jealousies impeded this solution, and the king and Orlando already had an
alternative in the shape of General Armando Diaz, with Badoglio and

Giardino becoming his deputies. Orlando was determined to remove Cadorna anyway—his and Cadorna's conceptions of the proper relationship between government and high command were completely incompatible—but Allied pressure precipitated the decision, and Diaz proved a good choice.[173] The new commander-in-chief was a southerner, at variance with the army's Piedmontese traditions, and an artillery officer, with both field command and staff experience. He established excellent relations with Orlando—who consulted with him regularly and established a war committee on the French and British model—and made military justice not necessarily more lenient but at least less arbitrary, as well as improving the soldier's lot.[174] Unlike Cadorna also, he erred on the side of caution over big offensives, rather than boldness.

Italy's decision-making structure—supposedly a constitutional monarchy—contrasted with that in France and Britain, although Caporetto led temporarily to a civil–military relationship that was closer to the Western European norm. Cadorna's fall had comparable consequences to Joffre's in 1916 in France and Robertson's in 1918 in Britain. The tortured civil–military deliberations that preceded the Chemin des Dames and Third Ypres had no counterpart in Rome before the tenth and eleventh Isonzo battles, though those battles likewise highlighted the driving forces behind the Allies' commitment to the offensive. Before Tenth Isonzo Cadorna had Boselli's encouragement; but before Eleventh Isonzo he was under no pressure from his government: rather the reverse. Like Nivelle and Haig, he saw one reason for attacking as being to keep the initiative and feared that, unless Italy struck, its opponents would do so. Like Haig, Cadorna was also encouraged by his army's expansion and apparent improvement and by hopes of beating his enemy in 1917 and largely unaided. There was again an element of hubris here, whereas the Central Powers' commanders were more grounded. Certainly Caporetto was risky—that they well understood—but they took a carefully calculated risk and showed a tactical virtuosity of which the Italians seemed incapable.

The new team at the top in Rome would make a difference only gradually, and even the French and British divisions, though doubtless a morale booster,[175] came too late to decide the battle of the Piave. The major part in halting the invasion came from Italian soldiers, whom opponents such as Rommel now found were fighting harder.[176] Orlando told Diaz it was 'absolutely vital for the national interest' to hold the new front, which was 170 kilometres shorter than the old one,[177] from which change the Italians benefited. In addition, the collapse had largely been confined to the Second Army, whereas the Third and Fourth held the Piave line, and the *sbandati* were reintegrated into new units.[178] The government also called up the 1899 conscript cohort, so that before the year ended the army was almost back to pre-Caporetto numbers, while by the spring it would largely recoup its equipment losses. To be sure, British and French deliveries assisted, especially British gas masks, but Italian industry accomplished most of the task.[179] Psychological recovery was harder, as over the winter food supplies remained critical and in several regions the civilian mood was fragile.[180] The army sat out the cold in improvised positions and the military authorities, who continued monitoring troop morale, were nervous. The first two wartime prime ministers, Salandra and Boselli, were among many politicians who now doubted whether it had been right to enter the conflict.[181] None the less, with the Germans gone the Austrians were again on their own, and from now on conditions on their home front and among their troops deteriorated while those of the Italians improved. 1918 would see less fighting than in 1917, much of the action being confined to the unsuccessful Austrian attack on the Piave line in June and the final Italian advance at the battle of Vittorio Veneto. This was a transformed front, and one that became the Austro-Hungarian army's major commitment. Yet although Caporetto in the short term had spectacularly fulfilled the Central Powers' objectives, in a curious way it weakened them in the longer, as Tenth and Eleventh Isonzo had weakened the Italians. Italy's political unity and military morale improved in the aftermath and it received more Allied aid. But in the longer term still, among the consequences were the strengthening of ultra-nationalism and the PSI's move towards extremism, paving the way for the rise of Fascism.

9

Peace Moves and Their Rejection

1917 was a year not only of decisions to act, whatever the obstacles, but also of failure to act: the collapse of initiatives for a compromise peace. The war's most significant peace moves were concentrated in the spring, summer, and autumn, between two periods characterized less by secret contacts than by public declarations (in the winters of 1916/17 and 1917/18), and by all-out combat (the massive spring and summer battles of 1916 and 1918). During 1917 ferocious fighting continued, but was more sporadic. Given that in all the European belligerents labour protest and anti-war opposition were reviving, the circumstances seemed propitious for the diplomatic impasse between the two sides' incompatible political objectives—or war aims—also to loosen. To an extent this indeed happened, but not enough, and even when those conducting them felt close to breakthrough none of the peace feelers came near success. The contacts highlighted the intractability of the points at issue, and strategy and diplomacy must be viewed in conjunction. The diplomatic impasse set the context for decisions to launch offensives, and the military balance shaped responses to the peace bids.

Diplomacy in 1917 was exceptionally intricate. According to the British Foreign Secretary, 'In all belligerent countries everyone was anxious for peace, and everyone had begun to look about to see in what way the war could be brought to an end.'[1] A first wave of initiatives followed the February Revolution, after which the Central Powers sounded out the Provisional Government while the Left pursued the Stockholm conference project. Austria-Hungary and Russia leaned on their stronger partners. By the summer the approaches to the Provisional Government had foundered and Stockholm had been vetoed. But a potentially more fruitful second wave centred on contacts between the belligerent governments, and followed a distinctive pattern: the advances came from the Central Powers, and the Allies rejected them. Whereas in the spring and summer, however, the centre for diplomacy was Vienna, in the summer and autumn it became Berlin. What follows will concentrate on the highest-level soundings. It will consider, on the Austrian side, the Sixte de Bourbon and Armand–Revertera affairs, before turning on the German side to the Reichstag peace resolution, Pope Benedict XV's peace note, the 'Villalobar kite', and the Briand–Lancken episode. In each case the account will focus on why the initiative was launched, and on the reasons for its failure.

Peace feelers had occurred before. The September 1914 Pact of London bound Britain, France, and Russia not to negotiate separately, and the 1915 Treaty of London imposed similar obligations on Italy. None the less, the German leaders soon recognized that victory over all their enemies was improbable, and their best means of extricating themselves was by bringing one or another of the Allies to a separate peace. In 1915 they targeted Russia; in 1916 they hoped Verdun would cripple France's will to resist. Hindenburg and Ludendorff's advent to the army high command left Bethmann and the Foreign Ministry with less manoeuvring room. None the less, the 1916–17 winter was one of open diplomacy, centred on the Central Powers' peace offer and on Woodrow Wilson's peace note.

For most of this period Austria-Hungary neither received approaches nor launched them, in contrast with the prominence it was about to assume. It might have had to reactivate diplomacy anyway, in view of its armies' exhaustion and of worsening shortages of food and fuel. But the precipitant was a change of monarch. In November 1916 and at the age of 29 Karl succeeded Franz Joseph. His writings while undertaking military service in 1914–16 suggest he wanted to free up Austria-Hungary internally, by giving its nationalities more autonomy, and to reorientate it internationally—perhaps reviving an alignment with Russia—although the German alliance would remain the linch-pin of its foreign policy.[2] Karl brought an enquiring mind and a relative, though not total, absence of prejudice (he disliked Italians and Poles). His wife, Zita, was widely credited with decisive influence, although for the Sixte peace initiative the two shared responsibility.[3] Zita's brothers in the Bourbon-Parma family, Sixte and Xavier, were in Austria at the outbreak of war, but returned to France. As members of the former royal dynasty they could not serve in the French army, but they became artillery officers in the Belgian one. Sixte considered himself, in fact, a patriotic

Figure 15. Photograph of Austrian Emperor Karl I and Empress Zita from 1917

Frenchman, and fulfilled his intermediary role accordingly. As early as September 1914 he wrote to Zita that Austria-Hungary should replace its German alliance by one with France. In 1916 President Poincaré awarded Sixte and Xavier the Croix de Guerre, and via William Martin, director of protocol at the Quai d'Orsay (the French Foreign Ministry), Sixte could access senior levels of the French government. In October 1916 he met Charles de Freycinet, one of Briand's ministers, and pressed his ideas for Austria-Hungary to ally with France and absorb South Germany.[4] Although he was more than ready to mediate between Paris and Vienna, however, it was the latter that began the Sixte affair. In the first phase Sixte made contact with the French and tried to clarify Austria-Hungary's terms; in the second Austria-Hungary pursued a general peace by moderating Germany's claims; and in the third any possibility of a general or even an Austro-Hungarian separate peace fell foul of Allied pledges to Italy. Whereas until the end of March Sixte was broadly making progress, thereafter it became evident to all concerned that he was failing.

During the first phase the strategic conjuncture still favoured the Allies. Austria-Hungary had suffered enormous losses in the 1916 Brusilov offensive, and faced new Russian and Italian assaults. The French anticipated a decisive role in the spring campaigning, and took the lead in rejecting the Central Powers' and Woodrow Wilson's peace notes as well as in agreeing with Russia on far-reaching war aims. Sixte's project began with an ostensibly simple invitation from Zita's mother for a family reunion at Neuchâtel in Switzerland. Sixte's and Xavier's visit there required consent from King Albert of the Belgians (whose queen, Elizabeth, was the princes' cousin), as well as the French government.[5] Only two days after Franz Joseph died, Sixte met the Quai d'Orsay secretary-general, Jules Cambon, who warned that Italy, Serbia, and Russia must obtain their promised gains at Austria-Hungary's expense, although Austria-Hungary could compensate by taking Silesia from Germany.[6] At the family gathering on 29 January Sixte received a letter from Zita imploring him to mediate. He had ready a four-point plan: France to regain Alsace-Lorraine with the frontier not of 1870 but of 1814 (so including much of the Saar coalfield), the complete restoration of Belgium and of Serbia (the latter with sea access), and Russia to gain Constantinople. This list became the basis of discussion, and characteristically was drafted by neither principal but by the intermediary. Despite omitting Italy, it favoured the Allies.[7]

For two months the mission centred on this agenda, while Sixte shuttled via Switzerland and made each side seem closer to the other than it was. This was not quite falsification, but he was not particularly scrupulous. On returning from Neuchâtel he told William Martin that Karl was offering a *separate* peace, though this was actually Sixte's own aspiration and is unsupported by the Austrian evidence. Complicating the situation was Karl's delicate relationship with his foreign minister, Ottokar Count Czernin, who agreed the Dual Monarchy must end the war quickly and would do well to avoid losing territory (although both men also favoured Balkan expansion if the opportunity presented). Thus at a 12 January meeting of the Common Ministerial Council, which represented the governments of the Monarchy's Austrian and Hungarian halves and which Karl chaired, the emperor sought to define maximum and minimum aims. It was agreed that the main objective should be simply to preserve the Monarchy's integrity, and ministers were surprisingly willing for concessions to Serbia, though unwilling (in this following Karl's lead) for any to Italy.[8] This outcome was in keeping with the empire's strategy: Austria-Hungary, uniquely, undertaking

no 1917 offensive until Caporetto. It is true that at the start of the year
Conrad von Hötzendorff had planned to attack Italy, but Karl replaced
Conrad with Arz von Straussenberg. Czernin seems not to have known
about the Sixte contact, however, until mid February, and meanwhile
explored separate indications that French representatives sought a meeting.
And although a dinner remark in January suggests that Czernin would have
considered the possibility of a separate peace,[9] once he was drawn into the
Sixte negotiations he ruled it out, even though the Germans heard about the
contact only in May, and even then did not learn the intermediary's name.

   Karl and Czernin displayed their differences in two notes that Sixte
brought to Paris after a second trip to Switzerland in February. Czernin
denied Vienna was under Berlin's 'tutelage', but insisted Austria–Hungary's
alliances with Germany, Turkey, and Bulgaria were 'absolutely indissoluble' and
a separate peace was 'for ever excluded'. However, he accepted Belgium must
be 'restored', would not oppose a German renunciation of Alsace–Lorraine,
and denied seeking Serbia's 'annihilation', though political agitation there
must be banned. He was readier to sacrifice German than Austro-Hungarian
interests. In contrast, supplements from Karl (unknown to Czernin) not only
expressed the 'greatest sympathy' for Belgium, but also promised to support
France over Alsace–Lorraine and apply pressure to Germany, though even
Karl did not suggest a separate peace, support the Alsace-Lorraine of 1814,
or mention Russia's claims.[10] The papers Sixte conveyed, despite emanating
from the top Vienna leaders, seemed neither substantial nor to communicate
a common position. When Poincaré read Czernin's letter he saw no basis
for peace, though after seeing Karl's supplement he was willing to continue
the exchanges, and now he and Jules Cambon spoke belatedly to Briand.[11]
Before Sixte left Paris he was advised France would require not only the
Alsace–Lorraine of 1814 but also 'reparations, indemnities, and guarantees
on the left bank of the Rhine', while offering Austria–Hungary German
territory in Silesia and Bavaria.[12] The precondition for any such arrangement would be a crushing Allied victory and precisely such a reversal of
alliances as Sixte had envisaged; but given that Czernin and Karl had stressed
Austria–Hungary was fighting defensively it is hard to see the French
response as seriously engaging with them. It did, however, match the
expanded French war aims programme adopted in the Cambon letter[13] and
reflected Paris's expansive mood before the doubts about Nivelle set in.

   Sixte was unimpressed: he considered Briand a 'chatterbox' and Poincaré
a coward. But on returning to Switzerland he and Xavier reluctantly

accepted an invitation to Vienna. On 23 and 24 March they met Karl and
Zita at Schloβ Laxenburg, where Czernin joined them. As for most of the
key conversations during the Sixte mediation, we rely primarily on Sixte's
account, which cannot be accepted uncritically.[14] As the talk continued,
with heavy snow outside, Karl said that now the two sides were approxi-
mately balanced the time was ripe for peace, whereas if the war went on
one or other would gain total victory. Again by Sixte's account, Karl said he
would try his hardest with Germany but if necessary would make peace
separately. He agreed with Sixte about Belgium, and Sixte passed on France's
wishes for the 1814 frontier and a neutralized west bank of the Rhine, but
Karl felt that in view of the February Revolution the Constantinople question could be postponed, and he wanted Britain, France, and Russia to
decide for peace with Austria-Hungary before broaching Italy's claims,
which implied that Italy might be sidelined. When Czernin arrived,
nervous and silent, the atmosphere grew tense, Czernin commenting afterwards that this was not really a peace offer. None the less, on 24 March Karl
delivered to Sixte the most significant text of the entire negotiation, in the
shape of a handwritten and autographed letter that he had worked on all
day. Czernin may have been aware of it, but did not see it. Instead Karl
started from a draft from Sixte and worked with an adviser, the Middle East
expert Alois Musil.[15] He supported full restoration of Belgium's sovereignty
and integrity, with compensation. Serbia would gain access to the Adriatic,
though groups wishing to break up Austria-Hungary must be suppressed.
On Russia Karl reserved his position until a legitimate government
emerged; but he went beyond Sixte's wording by promising to use his
influence to support 'the just French claims relative to Alsace-Lorraine'.[16]
Although the phrase caused a sensation when in 1918 the letter was published, it was actually ambiguous: Karl was supporting only what he
defined as 'just'. Once again, moreover, the letter left out Italy, and implicitly these were terms for a general rather than a separate peace, based
largely on the pre-war status quo. They fell well short of meeting France's
claims, though equally short of meeting Germany's, and added little to the
Czernin and Karl notes already communicated. All the same, this document, intended for Sixte to forward to Poincaré, was a remarkable risk for
Karl to run without consulting his allies or even his foreign minister,
and when revealed it would irreparably damage his reputation. Still, it
persuaded the French they must consult their allies, and moved the affair
into its decisive phase.

The initiative had progressed so far because of Sixte's impetuousness and Karl's inexperience. Karl trusted his brother-in-law enough to act boldly. Sixte won Karl's approval for most of his conditions, while warning the Allies would want more. From the French, Sixte had no commitment except for the passports needed to keep the operation running. Yet the Austrians attempted to do business with France and Britain, as their least intransigent enemies, while deferring concessions to Italy and Russia and side-stepping Germany's goals. In fact Sixte had uncovered only exiguous common ground even between Paris and Vienna, let alone any basis for a wider settlement.

The immediate obstacle to a general peace was Germany's demands. Austria-Hungary had supported the Central Powers' December 1916 offer, though wanting in it a list of war aims, which the Germans rejected. Still, they now seemed more flexible. When Czernin invited Bethmann to Vienna on 16 March, the ostensible reason was not the Sixte affair but Czernin's hopes of reaching the French via Count Albert von Mensdorff, the former Austro-Hungarian ambassador in London. Czernin warned Bethmann that Austria-Hungary was 'at the end of her strength': food and manpower were critically short and military raw materials sufficient only to the autumn. Hence it must investigate every peace opportunity. Bethmann agreed to Mensdorff going to Switzerland, provided he was just 'receptive', and although the chancellor warned that Germany could not return Alsace-Lorraine and would want to annex France's Briey-Longwy iron ore basin, he was open to a German–French rapprochement.[17] In fact Bethmann was more interested in expansion against Russia, as indeed was Czernin, who told the Common Ministerial Council he wanted an equivalence between Germany's and Austria-Hungary's gains.[18] Hence when Karl gave his fateful letter to Sixte he knew the Germans were willing to talk to France, though not to concede its full territorial claims.[19]

Bethmann's visit took place when news of the Russian Revolution was just breaking. But once Nicholas II had been overthrown Berlin and Vienna needed to woo the Provisional Government, and Bethmann again saw Russia rather than France as the best peace prospect.[20] At a follow-up conference in Berlin on 26 March, Czernin met Bethmann and Zimmermann. He offered them a rearrangement—if Germany made concessions to France, Austria-Hungary would allow its Polish province of Galicia (which many Vienna leaders would be happy to lose) to transfer into a union of the Polish areas previously governed by Austria-Hungry and Russia. This new entity would form a buffer state under German control, while Austria–Hungary compensated itself in Romania. But the Germans claimed to be constrained by the OHL—which doubted Austria–Hungary's food position was as difficult as Czernin painted—and by hard–line public opinion.[21] Since the January Pless conference (see chapter 1) Bethmann could no longer count on having the final say in Berlin. Hence, although the March conferences established common ground they did not find enough for an early peace, and both Czernin and Karl were impatient, the Austrian premier having warned them that food would run out in six weeks.[22] After the 26 March meeting, therefore, they by–passed Bethmann and tried more drastic methods.[23]

Karl first requested an urgent meeting with Wilhelm, which took place at Bad Homburg on 3 April. Hindenburg and Ludendorff attended, and to the Austrians Wilhelm seemed very much under the generals' influence. Karl again suggested returning Alsace–Lorraine to France in return for Germany controlling Poland and Galicia, but again the suggestion found no favour, and he and Zita left Homburg disappointed.[24] The next step was an apocalyptic Czernin memorandum that Karl forwarded to Wilhelm on 12 April with the warning that 'international revolution', linked to food shortage, was now more dangerous than the Allies. The U–boats would not defeat Britain, and the war should end as soon as the Allies' spring offensives had been repelled, now that Russia was losing striking power and before America's participation took effect. If it continued for another winter the 'waves of revolution will wash away all for which today our sons and brothers still fight and die'.[25] Yet although Karl endorsed this prophecy, he may not have believed it,[26] and Wilhelm doubted its applicability.[27] The Berlin leaders were more sanguine about Germany's situation and unconvinced that even Austria–Hungary's was as grave as Czernin depicted, while the foreign minister's continuing designs on Serbian and Romanian territory put his sincerity in doubt. Ludendorff believed the threat of revolution would be greatest if the Central Powers were beaten. In contrast Bethmann believed that for the foreseeable future Germany could not dictate terms and should seek a negotiated peace before America intervened in strength.[28] But instead, at Bad Kreuznach on 23 April the government and the OHL agreed on the most ambitious German war aims yet.[29] Hence Bethmann's draft for the reply that Wilhelm sent to Czernin drew on Holtzendorff's and Ludendorff's rebuttals: the military situation was favourable, and a general peace would be premature. Like Ludendorff, Bethmann argued that an unfavourable

peace—rather than another war winter—would trigger revolution. The
entire German leadership resisted what Zimmermann dubbed an 'anxiety
peace'.[30] It was true that Czernin was also cultivating the Reichstag opposition, particularly Matthias Erzberger of the Catholic, or Centre, Party, to
whom Karl gave a copy of the alarmist 12 April memorandum; and when
the German socialists called, like the Russians, for a peace without annexations or indemnities Czernin declared that Austria–Hungary was fighting
a defensive war.[31] However, his ambassador in Berlin warned against undermining Bethmann, as any replacement might be less sympathetic. After a
month Czernin called off his 'para–diplomacy' and on 17/18 May Germany
and Austria–Hungary approved a new joint programme of aims. Its terms
were expansionist: Germany would absorb Courland and Lithuania and
dominate Poland, while Austria–Hungary would control western Romania
and become the leading political, economic, and military influence in
Serbia, Montenegro, and Albania. Czernin doubted its attainability, and it
said nothing about Alsace-Lorraine.[32] But neither through conventional nor
unconventional methods had he moderated German claims.

Diplomacy on the Allied side was equally unpromising. It did not help
that when Sixte returned to Paris with Karl's 24 March letter, Briand
had fallen. Whereas hitherto Poincaré and the Quai d'Orsay officials had
taken the lead, now Ribot, who like Briand was both premier and foreign
minister, became central. He had justification for seeing Sixte's message
as being too good to be true.[33] As reported by Poincaré, who met Sixte on
31 March, the Austrians were offering a separate peace and the Alsace-
Lorraine of 1814 but mentioned neither Italy's nor Russia's demands.[34] The
risk in pursuing this opening would be a split not between the Central
Powers but among the Allies. All the same, Ribot believed he should at least
consult the British, and he arranged an urgent meeting with Lloyd George
at Folkestone on 11 April. After Ribot disembarked in the rain, the two
men's reactions were symptomatic: Lloyd George exclaiming this meant
peace, Ribot insisting they must study the documentation. The Austrian
approach ran with the grain of Lloyd George's thinking, given his beliefs
that Britain and France should support an Italian offensive and the Allies
should target Germany's weaker partners.[35] However, he agreed with Ribot
that the immediate stumbling block was Italy (both men being less concerned about Russia or the hapless Serbs and Romanians). He hoped to get
round it by offering Italian Foreign Minister Sonnino a share of Turkish
Anatolia round Smyrna (Izmir). And he consulted neither the Foreign

Office nor his War Cabinet, the only person in the know being Cabinet Secretary Maurice Hankey.[36]

Sonnino was under fire over Turkey in the Italian parliament and press.[37] Britain, France, and Russia had agreed in 1916 on their zones of control and spheres of influence if the Ottoman Empire were partitioned, and the demand was for Italy to have a share. Although Italy had not fought against the Turks, Lloyd George was willing to disregard that objection in order to facilitate an Austrian deal. At the St-Jean de Maurienne conference, however, where the British, French, and Italians met in a railway carriage in the Mediterranean Alps, once more against a backdrop of snow, the plan misfired. Lloyd George and Ribot offered Sonnino the Smyrna region. Sonnino said he had previously been offered more, which his interlocutors duly promised him. He agreed to depose the Greek King Constantine, which would enable Greece to join the Allies.[38] Only now did Lloyd George allude to an Austrian peace offer. Probably Sonnino smelt a rat, even if he did not know the go-between's name and Ribot and Lloyd George had promised Sixte not to mention Karl's letter. Once Lloyd George asked what attitude should be taken if Austria–Hungary sought a separate peace, Sonnino replied that if Italy were asked to sacrifice any of its Treaty of London gains, he would resign and Victor Emmanuel would abdicate. According to one account, Lloyd George threatened that London and Paris could make a separate peace with Vienna 'tomorrow', but he did not insist, while Sonnino denounced the feeler as a 'German manoeuvre'. In effect, the approach was rejected out of hand, and when in July Ribot breached confidence and disclosed Sixte's identity, it made no difference. Lloyd George did not conceal his contempt for the Italians, whom he had supposed he could bribe. He reasoned Sonnino feared for his personal position if he accepted terms on offer in 1915, before tens of thousands of Italian soldiers had died. But prickly though he could be, Sonnino seemed dependably pro-Allied. And although Lloyd George sometimes calculated the Allies would be net beneficiaries if Austria–Hungary and Italy both dropped out, the French disagreed. So far from pressing Sonnino, Ribot and Lloyd George approved with him a secret resolution that 'it would not be opportune to engage in a conversation that in present circumstances would be dangerous and would risk weakening the close union existing between the Allies and which is more necessary than ever'.[39]

After St-Jean de Maurienne, Lloyd George told Sixte that agreement remained possible if Austria–Hungary made concessions,[40] but Ribot warned

that the Allies could not renege on their promises to Rome. As Karl and
Czernin had resisted even mentioning Italy, it might seem that Sixte had
encountered an insuperable obstacle. It was a tribute to his ingenuity that he
persisted for two more months, aided by a bizarre new development. When
he and Xavier returned to Switzerland Zita told them the Italians had
offered to accept peace in return simply for the Italian-speaking areas of
the Trentino. This was quite at variance with Sonnino's line at St-Jean de
Maurienne, and the approach has left no trace in the Austrian or Italian
archives. It may have come from Cadorna or from Victor Emmanuel,[41] if it
happened at all. But more significantly, Karl's position had softened. When
Sixte and Xavier met him on 8 May he suggested he might indeed be
willing to cede the Italian-speaking Trentino (though this excluded both
Gorizia and Trieste). For the only time too, according to Sixte, Karl contemplated a separate peace, perhaps exasperated by German intransigence.
However, in a second autographed letter that Karl handed to Sixte on
9 May, he omitted reference to a separate agreement. He asserted Italy had
offered peace on the basis of getting just the Trentino, and Karl had suspended a decision pending an Anglo-French reply to his earlier proposal.
And again accompanying Karl's letter was a curt missive from Czernin,
refusing any cession of Austria-Hungary's territory without compensation,
and requiring guarantees of its integrity.[42] When Sixte returned to Paris and
London, his reception was still more reserved. Ribot said Italy could not get
less than the Treaty of London; Lloyd George wanted to continue with the
feeler, but in order to divide the Central Powers.[43] Lloyd George proposed
another ruse: that under the cover of a state visit to the Western Front,
King George V and Poincaré would meet Victor Emmanuel and quiz him
on whether a peace approach had been made. Sonnino, perhaps divining
the true purpose, found reasons to defer the visit, and on 25 June Sixte
returned to his regiment. The episode closed until its history came into the
open in April 1918.

   Of all the peace soundings, the Sixte affair was the longest running. Sixte
sustained it by implying to the Allies that Karl was more forthcoming over
Alsace-Lorraine and a separate peace than he really was. Karl wanted a general
peace, though was hampered by Czernin's efforts to expand, not just restore,
the pre-war borders. The Germans wanted to limit any such expansion, the
OHL viewing Austria-Hungary as a potential adversary.[44] Nor were they
interested in exchanging Alsace-Lorraine for a Polish puppet state. They did
not need to control Galicia; they were loath to cede more than token portions

of Alsace and they wanted the Briey-Longwy ore. Although Bethmann was conciliatory, Wilhelm, the OHL, and German nationalism hemmed him in. And on the Allied side, British ministers were willing to talk with the Austrians but not the Germans,[45] the French agreeing until Nivelle's failure and France's internal crises forced a reconsideration.

The obstacles to an Austro-Hungarian separate peace were equally forbidding. Czernin may have toyed with the idea. Karl considered it during May, but he preferred a general settlement and the Allies did little to tempt him.[46] In the absence of an Austrian separate peace, even Britain and France had little to gain and something to lose from exchanges with Karl. It is true they disregarded Russia, which to its irritation was neither represented at Folkestone and St-Jean de Maurienne nor told what had happened there. But Russia's collapse made Italy more important, and Paris and London would abandon neither Rome's claims nor those of Belgrade. Potentially Montenegro and Romania too would need satisfaction at Austria-Hungary's expense. Karl knew Italy wanted German-speaking districts in the Tyrol and South Slav ones in Dalmatia, but he opposed a plebiscite even in the Italian-speaking areas, to discourage separatism in the rest of his domains. Whereas Italy maintained its territorial claims, Karl refused to grant more than a fraction of them. If he had entered a separate negotiation, deprived of German protection, he would likely have been forced into concessions. The process would have deepened friction between the two halves of his monarchy, and stirred a nationalist frenzy among the ethnic groups that did not break away. Czernin suggested later it would have caused civil war.[47] As to whether Germany would have intervened, in summer 1917 Wilhelm threatened Ambassador Hohenlohe with invasion; and Germany had 240 mobilized divisions to Austria-Hungary's seventy-five, though German forces were so stretched elsewhere that they lacked the strength to do much.[48] German and Austrian units were intertwined, however, in the southern portion of the Eastern Front, and this was the biggest practical obstacle to a separate peace.[49] Although Karl and Czernin were right that Austria-Hungary desperately needed to leave the war, separate peace negotiations might have been still more dangerous than the course they pursued. By June, moreover, after the successful counter-attack that terminated the tenth Isonzo battle, and the failure of Italy's Ortigara attack, they had less reason to compromise.

Karl and the French, however, engaged in one more exchange. The Armand–Revertera conversations were shorter and simpler than the Sixte affair, but they too highlighted the obstacles to peace, and had far-reaching after-effects. And although the intermediaries were less prominent than Sixte, again the governments controlled them poorly. The families of Count Nikolaus Revertera (on the Austrian side) and Count Abel Armand (on the French) were connected, and Revertera's mother-in-law knew Zita's mother as well as Karl and Zita themselves. Both Karl and Czernin approved of the contact. Armand, in contrast, had been employed as an army officer and in business. In 1912 he had tried to strengthen Franco-German commerce, in cooperation with Baron Oscar von der Lancken-Wakenitz, the counsellor at the German embassy in Paris and a central figure in another peace contact. By 1917 Armand was working in the Second (Intelligence) Bureau of the French General Staff. His liaison with Revertera was via the doctor to both families, a Swiss, Henry Reymond.[50]

The initiative seems again to have come from Vienna. Neither Armand nor Revertera knew about the Sixte mission. But in June and July the Second Bureau learned that Revertera had asked through Reymond to meet Armand. Armand saw his service chief, Lieutenant Colonel Goubet, whose officers had received reports that Zita was Francophile; that Karl had warned Wilhelm that Austria-Hungary could not survive a fourth war winter; and that the Austrian royal family, aristocracy, and officer corps simmered with anti-German resentment. Goubet, like Sixte, saw an Austro-Hungarian separate peace as an opportunity to win a new ally, compensating for the loss of Russia. It was unsurprising that he approved,[51] as did the CGS Ferdinand Foch, who at this stage in his career shared Pétain's and Painlevé's cautious views. In fact the Armand–Revertera conversations took place at a nadir in French fortunes, when a breakthrough seemed far distant. Painlevé was interested in alternative, non-military, methods of achieving French objectives, and German agents in Switzerland received reports of his interest in peace talks.[52] He won enthusiastic backing for the conversations from Lloyd George.[53] Whereas Ribot agreed only to Armand's being empowered to listen; moreover, Painlevé authorized him to hold out to Austria territorial gains in Poland and even from Germany; and Armand actually offered Revertera Bavaria, Silesia, and Poland in its boundaries of 1772. The Frenchman took the lead, and although the drivers seem to have been Painlevé and Goubet rather than Lloyd George and Ribot, even Painlevé thought Armand was 'too absolute'.[54]

Armand and Revertera met on 7–9 and 22–23 August.[55] At the first meeting the usual cross-purposes surfaced. Revertera had expected to hear conditions for a general peace but actually heard conditions for a separate agreement between Austria–Hungary and the Allies, which Armand justi-fied by referring to American war entry and to evidence that Ludendorff intended any ceasefire to be just a truce while Germany rearmed. His 'terms' astonished Revertera, who would welcome gaining the 1772 Poland, but doubted Bavaria would want to join Austria–Hungary, and was appalled at the prospect of absorbing Silesia. Nor did he take kindly to Italy gaining the Trentino or to Trieste becoming a free city. Fundamentally though, while acknowledging the contact's value and wanting to maintain it, Revertera resisted a 'betrayal' of Germany. At the second meeting Armand therefore brought proposals for a general peace. He said the non-negotiable points were restoring Belgium's independence and returning Alsace–Lorraine with its 1814 frontier to France, perhaps in return for colonial compensation. The west bank of the Rhine should be demilitarized, Germany pay an indemnity, Britain gain Helgoland, and Italy take the Trentino and Trieste. Revertera, unable to keep a straight face, considered the terms completely unacceptable to Germany, while Austria–Hungary refused any concession to Italy. However, he proposed that Czernin and Painlevé should meet, and code messages were agreed for taking matters further. On Revertera's return to Vienna he reported to Czernin and to Karl; the terms also went to the Germans, who responded (as will be seen) by hastening their own approach to the Allies. Ambassador Hohenlohe warned Karl and Czernin that Germany could not accept; but even Austria–Hungary's policy was hardening, as the second Armand–Revertera meeting coincided with Italy's breakthrough in the eleventh Isonzo battle and with Karl's appeal to Wilhelm for assistance, which forced him to reaffirm his loyalty. The Dual Monarchy was returning to the fold, and by September the French were sending disconsolate messages via Henri Reymond about the lack of Austrian response. Armand and Revertera did not meet again until February 1918. The problems that bedevilled the Sixte negotiation still applied: Austria–Hungary resisted cessions to Italy, and France demanded more than Germany would yield. A general peace was off the table, and Karl rejected a separate one. But as Austrian and German troops prepared to fight shoulder to shoulder on the Isonzo, and Russia's eclipse offered the Central Powers new prospects, incentives were growing for Karl to gamble on a German victory. The second Armand–Revertera meeting closed Vienna's most active search for peace, and the locus of initiative shifted to Berlin.

The most obvious change in Germany was the July peace resolution, passed by a Reichstag majority of 212:126. It recalled Wilhelm's 1914 promise that 'we are driven by no lust of conquest', and proclaimed that 'Germany took up arms in defence of its liberty and independence and for the integrity of its territories. The Reichstag labours for peace and mutual understanding and lasting reconciliation among the nations. Forced acquisitions of territory and political, economic, and financial violations are incompatible with such a peace.'[56] The resolution opposed post-war economic blockades, and supported freedom of the seas and 'international political organizations'. It had backing from the SPD, Catholic Centre, National Liberal, and Progressive parties, and has been viewed as the foundation of the Christian, socialist, and liberal combination that underpinned the Weimar and later the West German Republic. The resolution testified to a new assertiveness, and was accompanied by the fall of Bethmann, in whom the Reichstag had lost confidence. It proved, however, to be less significant than its proponents hoped and its critics feared.

The principal mover in the run-up to the resolution was Erzberger. Earlier in the conflict he had supported aggressive war aims, but he became more sceptical. Although he knew nothing of the Sixte affair, he was in touch with Czernin and visited Vienna in April. Czernin's 12 April memorandum warning of 'international revolution' shocked him, and Karl told him that a big peace effort that summer was imperative. It was also pressing because German war finance depended on the Reichstag voting every six months for a new instalment of credits, and Erzberger feared the SPD would no longer do so. But what weighed most with him was evidence that the submarine campaign was failing. He had never found the navy's case convincing, and now Holtzendorff's five-month deadline was approaching, with the spectre beyond it of another war winter. In every belligerent that prospect became a gnawing preoccupation. Erzberger estimated that if global (and not just British) tonnage was factored in, the Allies could meet their requirements throughout 1918. He actually viewed the Allies' prospects more optimistically than did the British themselves, but the German authorities gave him no satisfactory answers. Whereas Bethmann assured him that the OHL believed in the navy's projections, on 10 June Colonel Max Bauer, the OHL's representative in Berlin, admitted to Erzberger that there had been irresponsible optimism, there would be another war winter, the Allies on the Western Front had a 4:1 munitions superiority, and by 1918 it would be 6:1.[57]

On 6 July Erzberger made a sensational speech in the Reichstag's Main
Committee. He said a fourth year of hostilities would cost at least 50 billion
marks, with no prospect of Germany's situation improving. It should therefore seek a compromise, with a Reichstag resolution intended to strengthen
the chancellor's hand and to reunite the nation on the basis of the 1914
principle of self-defence rather than conquest.[58] Erzberger carried conviction because he was known to possess sensitive information, because
of his conversion from previous annexationism, and because he achieved
surprise: the government was unprepared, and an inter-party steering
group of the Centre, SPD, Progressives, and National Liberals was formed
to draft a text.[59]

Erzberger did not intend to oust Bethmann. But his action coincided with
another crisis between the chancellor and the high command. Their relations
had never recovered since the Pless conference, and the OHL thought
Bethmann too conciliatory towards the Austrians and towards internal dissentients. They particularly objected to his promise, via Wilhelm's 'Easter Message',
to democratize the Prussian franchise.[60] On 19 June Hindenburg wrote to the
chancellor about the need to combat war-weariness; Bethmann responded
that 'with all confidence care is needed'; a dictated peace was distant and
uncertain; it would be hard to keep Austria–Hungary fighting longer than the
autumn; and it was unclear when, if ever, the U-boats would bring victory.
He wanted to avoid condemning a peace by negotiation, and he hoped for
discussions with Britain, the 'soul of the war'. Hindenburg wrote in the margin, 'A regrettably dismal appreciation. We do not share it', and replied that
Germany must reject a British compromise peace, continue bombing London,
accept another war winter, and await Britain's collapse in 'foreseeable time'.[61]
Like Nivelle and Cadorna, Hindenburg and Ludendorff saw the home front
as the weak point, and Erzberger's speech signalled that Bethmann no longer
controlled the Reichstag.

Wilhelm resented the OHL's pressure on him, and when Hindenburg
and Ludendorff arrived in Berlin on 6 July he sent them away empty-
handed. But he was indignant about the peace resolution, as an unjustified
display of weakness.[62] Hindenburg told Wilhelm that he viewed it with 'the
most serious reservations': it would undermine the army, and the enemy
would not respond. If he and Ludendorff could not work with the chancellor they could not prosecute the war, and unless Bethmann went they must
resign. This was decisive. Bethmann told Wilhelm the nation trusted
Hindenburg and Ludendorff and it was impossible to let them go. Hence he

must step down, and Wilhelm agreed.[63] Yet although Bethmann's assessment of Germany's situation resembled Erzberger's, he had opposed a Reichstag resolution, probably so as not to tie his hands. When, at the OHL's behest, Crown Prince Wilhelm canvassed the Reichstag party leaders, Bethmann was denounced not only by the right wing but also by Erzberger, on the grounds that as Bethmann had antagonized President Wilson he could never make peace. Hence when Hindenburg and Ludendorff sent their ultimatum they knew the Reichstag had also lost confidence in the chancellor.[64] But Erzberger's preferred candidate—Bethmann's predecessor, Bernhard von Bülow—was unacceptable to Wilhelm, which meant that no one had a viable alternative. The initiative fell to the chief of Wilhelm's Civil Cabinet, Rudolf von Valentini, who came up with Georg Michaelis, a Prussian official who had dealt primarily with food supply. Michaelis was not the OHL's candidate, and had hardly dealt with them, though they accepted the recommendation. Nor was he well known to Wilhelm. But with the emperor and the OHL both willing to agree, he was appointed without consulting the Reichstag parties. Nor was this his only handicap, as he lacked familiarity with foreign and military affairs. He accepted the job on Wilhelm's insistence, but was all too aware of his inadequacies.[65]

Michaelis disliked the draft resolution, and was plunged into negotiations with the Reichstag parties. When it was voted through on 19 July, he responded with a speech that had mostly been agreed with them beforehand. He insisted that:

the territory of the fatherland is inviolable... If we make peace we must in the first line make sure that the frontiers of the German Empire are made secure for all time. We must by means of an understanding and give and take guarantee the conditions of existence of the German Empire upon the continent and overseas... Peace must... provide a safeguard that the league in arms of our opponents does not develop into an economic offensive alliance against us. These aims may be attained within the limits of your resolution as I interpret it [wie ich sie auffasse].

The last qualification, according to Michaelis, was inserted spontaneously as an afterthought.[66] Yet it outraged the Reichstag leaders and created another barrier to working with them, for, as he wrote to the Crown Prince, 'my interpretation has removed the greatest danger from the notorious resolution. One can now, after all, make any peace that one likes under its terms.'[67] Yet actually it did not invalidate his acceptance of the resolution in spirit, and his difference from Erzberger was less than it seemed.[68] Erzberger had deliberately avoided the Petrograd Soviet's formula of 'no annexation or indemnities' and, on the day after the resolution passed, he recommended to Michaelis that Lithuania become a nominally independent duchy with Wilhelm as its duke, in customs union with Germany. Alsace-Lorraine should remain German (though becoming autonomous) and he thought Longwy-Briey might be attainable through an exchange.[69] Under this interpretation the resolution was compatible with the more modest aims that Bethmann had envisaged in his final months, and indeed with those of Michaelis, whose instincts were more conservative than Bethmann's but who also questioned the value of annexations and whether they would merit the extra fighting needed to acquire them.[70] The resolution therefore still permitted indirect expansion by means of buffer states. An ambiguous text, it did not alter government policy, and the Allies dismissed it as window dressing.[71] Arguably its biggest impact came inside Germany, where the xenophobic Pan-German League took the lead in forming the German Fatherland Party (DVP), which campaigned against the resolution and soon had hundreds of thousands of members,[72] while the army launched a propaganda programme of 'Patriotic Instruction' by officers of their men. These were signs, characterizing much of Europe, of how opinion on the war was polarizing.

Michaelis's response to the peace resolution made clear that it was not another peace offer like that of December 1916. The Central Powers felt they had made such an offer and been rebuffed. The Allies felt that in response to President Wilson they had published their war aims, and it was up to the Central Powers to reciprocate, the resolution not filling the gap. These considerations influenced both sides' reactions to the next attempt to end the war by public diplomacy: Pope Benedict XV's Peace Note.

The note was dated 1 August, and forwarded to the belligerents nine days later. It appealed for the 'useless massacre' to stop. It set forth 'concrete and practical proposals': that arbitration, backed by sanctions and accompanied by simultaneous and reciprocal disarmament, should settle international disputes; freedom of the seas; mutual renunciation of reparations claims; German evacuation of France and Belgium 'with guarantees of its [Belgium's] entire political, military, and economic independence toward any Power whatever'. The territorial disputes between Italy and Austria-Hungary and between Germany and France would be settled in a spirit of equity and justice, as would questions relating to Armenia, the Balkans, and Poland. Apart from this hint of possible Polish independence, Russia did not feature.

Essentially Benedict proposed returning to the pre-1914 status quo with negotiated solutions to the thorniest questions, whose outlines, however, remained unspecified.[73]

The Vatican possessed an experienced diplomatic corps and was represented in both camps, although it had official relations with neither the French nor the Italian governments. Since 1914 it had deplored the conflict. The Christian and humanitarian imperative was obvious enough, but in addition the war divided the church's congregations. Benedict (Giaccomo della Chiesa) was an intelligent and strong-willed member of the Genoese aristocracy, who became pope just after war broke out. He selected as his Secretary of State Cardinal Pietro Gasparri, who shared his views.[74] The Vatican offered its services as a mediator, though not an arbiter, as to take a position on specific issues would compromise its impartiality. Yet in the changed diplomatic climate of 1917 it became more activist. It appears to have been unaware of the Sixte initiative, although Sixte had met Benedict and called on him to mediate.[75] Erzberger, who had also met Benedict, urged after visiting Vienna in April 1917 that it was time for the pope to make a peace announcement.[76] One papal concern may have been not to leave the field to the atheistic socialists: and certainly the German liberal politician and publicist Friedrich Naumann urged this consideration. The Vatican felt particularly for Austria-Hungary, the only predominantly Catholic Great Power with which it maintained diplomatic relations, and Cardinal Bisleti, who had officiated at Karl and Zita's wedding, told Zita in May that the pope was willing to act for peace if Karl desired, though he also asked what Austria-Hungary could offer Italy. It seems the answer was little, and Gasparri concluded that no basis existed for negotiation. For this reason (and perhaps also because Germany was the stronger and more influential partner, despite its predominant Protestantism), whereas Sixte had liaised initially with Paris, the Vatican did so primarily with Berlin.[77]

Eugenio Pacelli, one of the most experienced papal diplomats (and later Pius XII during the Second World War) was sent in May as nuncio to Munich, with instructions to seek out German peace conditions. A letter from Benedict to the emperor invited Wilhelm to offer arms limitation, restore Belgian independence, and show 'delicacy' over Alsace-Lorraine, perhaps obtaining a French colony as well as becoming the 'hero of pacification'.[78] On 26 June Pacelli met Bethmann, the day after the latter sent his despondent letter to Hindenburg, and when the chancellor was considering a conciliatory new statement about war aims.[79] Bethmann told Pacelli that Germany could accept reciprocal arms limitation and an international arbitration procedure, completely restore Belgian independence (though with guarantees against Allied domination), and discuss frontier rectifications in Alsace-Lorraine.[80] According to Gasparri, had it not been for Bethmann's assurances—particularly about Belgium, which like Poland was a martyred Catholic country—Benedict would not have gone ahead.[81] Yet Bethmann did not reflect the Kreuznach war aims programmes, and did not speak for his sovereign. On 13 May Wilhelm had stipulated as a minimum that Belgium should be split into Wallonia and Flanders; its fortresses occupied until they were razed; the coast, railways, and banks fall under German control; and that Germany's enemies would pay indemnities.[82] When Pacelli met the emperor on 30 June the conversation was difficult, Wilhelm accusing the Allies of scorning the Central Powers' 1916 peace offer. Only force could bring them to the table. He still encouraged Benedict, not least to avert a socialist monopoly of peace-making,[83] but Pacelli failed to ascertain Germany's terms. In fact the German government seemed in disarray, and still more so after the peace resolution. Regardless, on 24 July Pacelli told Zimmermann that the Vatican wanted agreement on the peace note prior to issuing it, and presented a seven-point memorandum from Gasparri: freedom of the seas; mutual disarmament; international arbitration; Britain to evacuate Germany's colonies; Germany to evacuate France and Belgium (and Belgian independence to be fully restored); and a peace conference to settle economic differences and attend to the Austro-Italian border, Alsace-Lorraine, Poland, Romania, Serbia, and Montenegro. This closely foreshadowed the note's final text, although Zimmermann insisted that Germany must have guarantees in Belgium.[84] He sent no official reply before the Vatican published its appeal, Benedict now hurrying because he sensed that OHL influence was growing and delay would be damaging. But, in addition, the Vatican knew that Karl was willing to cede the Trentino. Finally the moment seemed propitious because of the military deadlock and the menace of a further war winter, as food ran short and the Left gained ground.[85]

Although Benedict professed impartiality, his démarche followed liaison with the Central Powers, whereas with the Allies there was none. It was unsurprising that reaction in the latter camp was icy. In France Georges Clemenceau dubbed Benedict 'the boche Pope', and the press was almost uniformly hostile; in Italy the note came on the eve of the Eleventh Battle of the Isonzo and the 'useless massacre' phrase—on which Benedict insisted—especially stung.[86] Consistent sympathy, ironically, came only from the socialists. The note hardly mentioned Russia, whose foreign minister dismissed it as 'purely pro-German'.[87] Sonnino considered it 'a fine nothing' and calculated to divide Allied public opinion. It was not 'a friendly act towards Italy'.[88] Ribot similarly advised the British that the correct response was simply to acknowledge receipt.[89] As for the Americans, House and Wilson had been discussing how among their most useful contributions would be to encourage 'the German liberals' against the Berlin government, declaring willingness to deal with the German people but not a military autocracy.[90] House told the president it mattered more to establish a 'virile Republic' in Russia than to beat Germany to its knees, recognizing that the war was destabilizing Russian democracy. He recommended answering Benedict in a way that left the door ajar and distinguished between the German people and their rulers. But Wilson adopted just the second part of House's opinion,[91] and for once he followed Lansing's guidance: that the papal note envisaged an unacceptable return to the status quo ante, and its proposals rested on Berlin's good faith. The present military situation favoured the Central Powers, before America had asserted itself, and as a basis for negotiation the note must be rejected.[92] Wilson's reply to Benedict, dated 27 August, explicitly denied that returning to the status quo ante bellum would bring the benefits the pope aspired to. On the contrary, it would leave Germany thrall to 'a vast military establishment controlled by an irresponsible government', which would force the Allies to continue to combine against it. But with a democratic Germany that renounced the search for 'domination' things might be different: 'Punitive damages, the dismemberment of empires, the establishment of selfish and exclusive economic leagues, we deem inexpedient and in the end worse than futile, no proper base for a peace of any kind, least of all for an enduring peace.'[93] Wilson's reply pleaded for German regime change (though he was willing to leave Wilhelm as figurehead), but was vague about what guarantees of good behaviour were needed. It also fired a warning shot against the European Allies, whose secret treaties had perturbed the American leaders. Hence Wilson purposely omitted to confer with his partners before replying, for, as he told House, they would have wanted changes that he could not make.[94] The implications for the European Allies were grave. On the one hand Ribot had advised his Washington ambassador, Jusserand, that 'until the United States has made the decisive effort it is preparing we shall not be in a favourable position to negotiate'. But on the other, Jusserand warned Ribot, the more France depended on American assistance, the more 'a Head of State assuredly well-disposed to us, but... who naturally cannot attach the same importance to our peace terms as we do ourselves, will be free to choose the hour and the circumstances of the ending of the conflict'.[95]

London was caught in the crossfire. Whereas Ribot wanted an Anglo-French reply to Benedict that implicitly dissociated the two governments from Wilson, the British preferred to say nothing, neither endorsing the president's language nor exposing the cracks in trans-Atlantic solidarity.[96] Hence Wilson's note remained the only official Allied and American response to Benedict. But privately the British had already replied, and helped to trigger the most important peace initiative of the war.

The pope's note came to the British War Cabinet on 20 August. The tone of the discussion—held after Third Ypres had degenerated into stalemate—showed how the mood had changed since the Allies' reply to Wilson on 10 January. Ministers felt the earlier declaration had been used to discredit the Allies as 'imperialistic and grasping': it had damaged their reputation in the neutrals and helped the governments of the Central Powers to spur their peoples on. But to replace it by a less ambitious programme would discourage any Allies whose objectives were scaled down. In any case, because last time Britain's opponents had withheld a statement of their terms, it might be better now to let them respond first. 'If these terms included the evacuation of Belgium, it would show a marked advance on the part of the Central Powers towards a settlement. If on the contrary, they showed no such intention it would prove that no basis whatever for discussion existed.' The Cabinet hoped to smoke out the enemy governments and wanted Wilson to delay until they had responded (which in fact he did not). It authorized Balfour to reply to Benedict that Britain would delay a detailed answer until it had received one from the Central Powers, and Balfour should include 'the principle of restoration'.[97] The Foreign Secretary duly telegraphed Count John de Salis, his Vatican representative, that:

> no progress is likely to be made until the Central Powers and their allies have officially announced the objects for which they are carrying on the war, the measures of restoration and reparation they are prepared to concede, and the methods by which the world may be effectively guaranteed against any repetition of the horrors from which it is now suffering. Even as regards Belgium, where they have owned themselves in the wrong, we have no clear intimation of their intentions either to restore its complete independence or to repair the injuries which they have inflicted on it.[98]

Balfour highlighted the territory of greatest British concern, where thousands of British Empire soldiers were being killed and wounded daily, while the French were greatly exercised about Lloyd George's failure unambiguously to support them over Alsace-Lorraine.[99] Whereas at the start of 1917 the Cabinet had shrunk from talking to Germany at all, now it was willing at least to explore the basis for negotiations. It is hard not to see this change as evidence of waning confidence.[100] Moreover, two further developments reinforced the démarche's significance. First, Ribot—with uncharacteristic carelessness—associated his government with the de Salis message, before having read its text. And secondly, de Salis, instead of using Balfour's telegram as guidance when he met Gasparri, actually handed it over and said he personally would support a Vatican approach to the Germans for an official declaration about Belgium.[101] Ribot was tipped off by Camille Barrère, the French ambassador in Rome, and warned the British that they risked being led along 'a dangerous road' where France had no wish to tread.[102] The Foreign Office reprimanded de Salis.[103] None the less, Benedict was grateful for the British message, which Gasparri forwarded to the Germans. He asked them for a formal declaration on Belgium and on guarantees.[104]

When the pope's note reached the Central Powers, Michaelis was caught, like his predecessor, between Czernin and the OHL. Meeting Michaelis on 1 August, shortly before the first Armand–Revertera conversation, Czernin reiterated his proposal that Germany should cede at least part of Alsace-Lorraine, in exchange for a Polish buffer state.[105] For Michaelis, however, an enlarged Poland was unwelcome: Germany would need to annex territory for protection against it, and he hesitated to concede more Polish autonomy. Hence the meeting was inconclusive, and when Michaelis met Hindenburg and Ludendorff, they were willing to abandon at most a few districts of upper Alsace, while Germany must annex Longwy-Briey, dominate Belgium, and control not only Courland, Lithuania, and Poland but also— and this was new—seek a 'silent friendly attachment to us' in the Ukraine.[106] After a further round of talks with Czernin, Michaelis reconsidered. He wanted peace as soon as possible, but felt Germany could last out another year. He rejected Czernin's offer, as Germany would not surrender any sig- nificant portion of Alsace-Lorraine, although it might be content with long-term economic agreements for access to the Briey iron ore, rather than annexing the Briey-Longway basin.[107] Michaelis justified this position in retrospect as illustrating his understanding of a peace compatible with the

Reichstag resolution, and it reflected his distinctive preference for indirect control over incorporating foreign territory into Germany.[108] But it was hardly a recipe for returning to the situation before 1914, and such a return was acceptable neither to the Germans nor to the European Allies, nor to the Americans.

All the same, Michaelis was more inclined than Hindenburg and Ludendorff to a diplomatic solution, as he showed by replacing Zimmermann with Richard von Kühlmann as secretary for foreign affairs. Kühlmann had been counsellor at the German embassy in London before the war, and during it had been minister at The Hague and ambassador at Constantinople. Michaelis gave him a free hand,[109] and in many ways Kühlmann became Bethmann's true heir. Before being appointed he sent a memorandum to the chancellor, who indicated general agreement.[110] Kühlmann believed the OHL had too much influence, and the civil–military boundaries should be re-established, though he and Michaelis hoped to negotiate with Hindenburg and Ludendorff rather than get Wilhelm to override them. Kühlmann also believed that Czernin had excessive leverage over German policy. That being said, he was pessimistic about the prospects. He thought the Central Powers needed peace and would do well to lose no territory, and he saw extensive annexations as unattainable. He thought the French leaders were 'fanatics', and pinned his hopes on Britain. While he opposed concessions over Alsace-Lorraine (beyond greater autonomy within Germany), he was willing to abandon the Belgian coast and even Liège.

A concatenation of circumstances helped Kühlmann move swiftly. The first was the pope's note. Kühlmann preferred to let the Allies reply first, thus taking the blame if they seemed intransigent, or (if they were conciliatory) appearing as the first to speak of peace. His tactics mirrored those of the British, and he did not want Czernin railroading him. If there were negotiations, he wanted to control them.[111] Hence the Germans were in no hurry, and as the government resisted committing itself to specific conditions, it liaised with a group of Reichstag deputies, the Committee of Seven, on the reply. When they pressed for a public commitment fully to restore Belgium's independence, Kühlmann refused, even though privately he believed it would be needed, as he saw this as a trump card to retain until the Allies were shown to be serious.[112] Hence Germany's reply to the pope was belated and vague,[113] but Erzberger, who served on the Committee of Seven, was willing to acquiesce in return for a government undertaking to communicate a private assurance about Belgium.[114] After the war this became a cause célèbre, Erzberger denouncing the authorities for being duplicitous and missing an opportunity for peace with honour.[115] Indeed, a note from Michaelis to Pacelli on 24 September, responding to the de Salis message, said it was too early for a definite declaration of Germany's intentions towards Belgium.[116] Erzberger may well have been right about the duplicity, and the note killed off the papal initiative, at the heart of which had been Bethmann's apparent declaration on 26 June of disinterest in Belgium. Nor did Austria–Hungary give satisfaction, Karl's official reply to Benedict being similarly evasive. A personal letter from Karl to Benedict said Austria had been unable to soften the Germans over Belgium, and opposed any but minor concessions to Italy: another indication of the hardening Austro-Hungarian position as Caporetto approached. Benedict wrote on the envelope 'Important but discouraging', and replied that he had received Karl's letter 'at the bitterest hour of my life'.[117] All sides had now passed over or rejected the Vatican blueprint.

The papal note's repercussions, however, were not over yet. Kühlmann was resolved to make a peace move, though not to let the Vatican or the Austrians lead it. But after the second Armand–Revertera conversation, on 22–23 August, Czernin notified the Germans of his opening to the French. His ambassador in Berlin told Kühlmann that Czernin was willing to meet Painlevé, and described the 'terms' that Armand had communicated. Kühlmann rushed to Vienna, saying this was a very clever and dangerous appeal for Austria-Hungary to make peace at Germany's expense.[118] On his return he drafted a memorandum on 'The Political Situation'. If the Allies were driving a wedge between Germany and Austria-Hungary, Germany must attempt the same between France and Britain. An 'ocean of hatred' separated Germany from France, and no significant concession could be offered to Paris, which, in any case had no leverage over London. But in Britain he believed a movement for compromise was growing, the British were not committed to support France over Alsace-Lorraine, and London could force Paris to make peace. To avoid being taken in tow by Austria-Hungary, Germany should ascertain the Allies' minimum conditions over Belgium, and although complete renunciation of Germany's claims there would not be necessary at first, it might have to follow.[119] By the time the de Salis message reached Berlin, Kühlmann's memorandum had persuaded Michaelis that an inter-departmental discussion of Belgium's future was urgent. Although the Armand–Revertera contact was the key precipitant, the de Salis telegram (which Michaelis treated seriously though Kühlmann viewed more sceptically)[120] confirmed that Britain might be receptive to a declaration—which reports to Kühlmann on British press articles and speeches already indicated.[121]

The first step was a discussion among Prussian government ministers on 4 September. Michaelis had just visited the Western Front, where he found troop morale high and the high command seeing no danger of an Allied breakthrough. The winter would be difficult, though Germany would survive it. But he preferred to be able to take up Allied peace offers, and the lack of agreement about Belgium handicapped him: he wanted to clarify the situation with the army and navy, and he believed that guaranteed access to the iron ore would suffice in Longwy-Briey. By these proposals—which the ministers endorsed—Michaelis hoped to head off the 'ever more forward pressing Democracy'.[122] At a further meeting on 10 September, moreover, Kühlmann pressed Navy Secretary Capelle on when the submarines could force Britain to terms and Capelle could not answer, reinforcing Kühlmann's conclusion that Germany must negotiate.[123]

The meeting with the OHL and the navy was scheduled to take place under Wilhelm's chairmanship at Schloβ Bellevue on Tuesday 11 September. The location was a neoclassical summer residence in Berlin's Lustgarten district. The gathering was the most important since the Pless conference, but now with the navy discredited and a new team running the Chancellery and Foreign Ministry. And this time the civilians believed they had the emperor's backing. After Wilhelm returned on 9 September from the Eastern Front, Michaelis spoke to him in the car from Friedrichstraβe Station. Wilhelm agreed they might be facing a serious British approach and should define their Belgian war aims, bringing the question 'to decision that we could not reject an honourable peace on account of the Flemish coast or other parts of Belgium'. On the same day Kühlmann spent several hours with Bethmann at the latter's estate at Hohenfinow. Late in the night of 10–11 September, however, the foreign minister roused Michaelis to discuss a diatribe he had received from Wilhelm. The emperor felt he had agreed too quickly. Although the Flanders coast should not on its own prevent peace conversations, he had earlier stressed its value for the navy and if they lost it they would gain nothing (and would have fought the Battle of Jutland in vain), leading to a dangerous agitation.[124] He expected another war against Britain, and the navy must be rebuilt with overseas bases: in any event Zeebrugge must be retained.[125] Kühlmann warned that without a favourable decision he would resign, but the chancellor calmed him and on

the morning of the 11th walked with Wilhelm in the park, Wilhelm agreeing
to give Michaelis a free hand and the chancellor assuring Kühlmann that all
would be well. Hence the proceedings were tense but orderly, and tran-
spired as the civilians had hoped. Wilhelm was at his most statesmanlike,
perhaps because over-optimistic. He said Britain's inquiry about Germany's
intentions over Belgium was 'a great success' and a sign 'it was acknowledging it had lost', because of shipping losses, Russia's collapse, the poor harvest,
working-class discontent, and fear of the United States. He no longer
believed it was Germany's interest to annex Belgium, which would mean
absorbing Catholics and Walloons, and if Belgium were abandoned the
Flanders coast must be too, though Germany should have guarantees, which
might entail excluding British economic influence and granting Flemish
self-government. These points, and Liège's future, should be discussed with
Belgium, but the Flanders coast should not prevent an honourable peace.
Michaelis agreed that peace was a real possibility, and the Belgian coast
should not obstruct it; Treasury Secretary Siegfried von Roedern stressed
Germany's financial difficulties, and Hindenburg and Ludendorff said they
were willing to cede the coast though needed control of Liège to protect
the Ruhr. Holtzendorff and Capelle defended the navy's position—Germany
must stay in Flanders to keep the opportunity of attacking England—but
were isolated. As so often in 1917, no minutes were taken, but Kühlmann
understood from Wilhelm's résumé that the government had freedom to act
until the end of the year, Wilhelm shaking his hand warmly and saying 'now
it is a question of showing what he can do to help us to a good peace'.[126]

On the following day, however, 12 September, Michaelis wrote to
Hindenburg in different vein and without Kühlmann's knowledge. As the
chancellor summarized, the OHL wanted Liège as a glacis to cover the
Ruhr, such tight economic bonds as would make it inconceivable for
Belgium to fight Germany, and military sureties (including occupying
Liège) during the many years until that stage of affairs was reached. Germany
would have the use of Belgium's rail and waterways and of the port of
Antwerp, influence over the Flemings, and access to the Briey iron ore, as
well as gains in the east, while its enemies paid for their own reconstruction.
This, felt Michaelis, was no peace of renunciation.[127] In reply, Hindenburg
forwarded a memorandum from Ludendorff that insisted the Central
Powers were more favourably placed than their enemies (above all due to
events in Russia), though peace was worth trying for if it permitted Germany
to develop economically and defend itself in a new war. The Reich needed

eastern agricultural land and protection for its frontier industrial areas in Upper Silesia, the Saar/Lorraine/Luxemburg, and the Ruhr. Hence Ludendorff still wanted to annex Briey and Liège and if not annexing all of Belgium at least to make it an economic dependency. It was vital to maintain a threat against Britain, by dominating Belgium and therefore also dominating the Netherlands and its colonies, as Germany must protect its foreign supply networks in the next conflict.[128] Hindenburg endorsed this chilling analysis, and underlined his need for the Baltic coastline in order to manoeuvre his left flank in a future struggle with Russia, while Wilhelm envisaged a 'Second Punic War' against Britain.[129] All of this contrasted with Bethmann's weary comment in 1916 that no one could fight wars again in Europe for twenty or thirty years after this one,[130] and Lloyd George's *War Memoirs* would reproduce Ludendorff's memorandum as encapsulating what Britain was up against.[131] Indeed Lloyd George inferred that a compromise would have meant renewed fighting in another few years—though he saw this more clearly in retrospect than he did at the time. So far from conducting a war to end war, the OHL and the Admiralty Staff were positioning Germany for the next round. The OHL had not really changed its thinking, and Wilhelm's conciliatoriness over Belgium was heavily qualified. The Bellevue conference outcome was ambiguous.

None the less, immediately after Bellevue, Kühlmann met with a Spanish diplomat, the Marqués de Villalobar, whom he had called to Berlin to act as an intermediary. He authorized Villalobar to tell the British representatives in The Hague that he had authentic information from the German government to communicate about Belgium.[132] Kühlmann's basis was that Germany would lose no territory (and regain its colonies), pay no indemnities, and suffer no economic boycott; but it could restore Belgium's sovereignty and integrity. Essentially he proposed a peace based on the status quo ante in Western Europe, while ignoring the claims both of Britain's and of Germany's allies.[133]

As so often in the story of the 1917 peace contacts, the intermediary failed to act as a simple conduit, and it was unhelpful that the OHL decoded his messages.[134] Villalobar was the Spanish representative in the Low Countries, so well-known to Kühlmann who chose him in a personal capacity and did not envisage that the Spanish *government* would mediate. Villalobar felt the need, however, to contact his foreign minister, the Marqués de Lema, who had opposed him travelling to Berlin. Villalobar concealed both that he had done so and the peace terms Kühlmann had outlined, though disclosing that Kühlmann wanted him as an intermediary. Lema was guarded—particularly due to a general strike and left-wing insurrection in Spain during August—as he feared antagonizing the Allies.[135] Before allowing Villalobar to proceed, he informed Sir Arthur Hardinge, the British ambassador in Madrid, on 18 September that the 'German Government would be glad to make a communication to ourselves relative to peace', and that the message came 'from a very exalted personage'. He gave no details, but asked if Britain was willing to listen.[136]

In this bald form, the German offer reached the Foreign Office. It did so almost simultaneously with news of a parallel approach to the French. It seemed the Allies were the targets for a flurry of approaches, perhaps designed to play them off against each other: and this impression added to their wariness.[137] The Franco-German contact—usually known as the Briand–Lancken affair—was therefore central to France and Britain's response.

The affair grew out of the Belgian diplomatic underworld. Lancken was head of the Political Department of the German occupation administration in Brussels. Before the war he had been counsellor at the German embassy in Paris, and was well known to French politicians and diplomats. He had a reputation as an intriguer. He was also known to the Belgian government, in exile at Le Havre, and headed by Charles de Broqueville, whose role in the affair would be equivocal. King Albert, also in exile, had sounded out Germany in 1915 via the so-called Törring–Waxweiler conversations, but found its terms too severe.[138] The Briand–Lancken episode began with conversations in autumn 1916 between Lancken, the Archbishop of Mechelen (Cardinal Désiré-Joseph Mercier), and Countess Pauline de Mérode, the French widow of a Belgian senator.[139] They planned a meeting between Lancken and a French leader, and from early on Lancken wanted Briand, whom he and de Mérode knew well. According to Lancken, he received the go-ahead when meeting in April 1917 with Bethmann, Zimmermann, Hindenburg, and Ludendorff, the latter being willing to cede fragments of Alsace and Lorraine to get peace.[140] In June the countess called on Briand, who was now out of office, and suggested Alsace-Lorraine might be on offer, but the proposal was vague and Briand did not pursue it.[141] However, in August Briand was approached again, this time by Baron Evence Coppée, who headed the Belgian coal owners' association, and his son.[142] Coppée senior had met Benedict XV in February.[143] He had also met Lancken and told him Germany must be willing to evacuate Belgium entirely, cede Alsace-Lorraine, and pay reparations, Lancken's response being unspecific

but conciliatory. After meeting Coppée senior, Briand dined on 1 September
with both Coppées and with de Broqueville, who warned that a rendezvous
with Lancken might be a trap but none the less believed the approach
sincere and that the minimum conditions should be restoring Belgium,
reparations, and regaining Alsace-Lorraine. He thought the latter might be
on offer in exchange for colonial concessions and no economic boycott
of Germany after the war.[144] Briand was now keen to meet Lancken in
Switzerland, subject to French government approval. According to the
journalist Raymond Recouly, Briand was fired with enthusiasm for a Franco-
German peace on the basis of France gaining all of Lorraine while Alsace
received autonomy within Germany (he said nothing about the other
Allies' claims): 'Continuing the war at the point it has reached is a veritable
folly ... Why not stop as quickly as possible this killing, this carnage ... '[145]

A first obstacle was the German government. Although Ludendorff
remained keen to pursue Lancken's initiative, Michaelis and Kühlmann val-
ued it less than had Bethmann. Kühlmann advised Lancken that his primary
interest was the Villalobar feeler. In any conversation with Briand, Lancken
should 'offer little' and remain dilatory until the situation elsewhere had
clarified.[146] But a bigger obstacle was the French government, which in
September was restructured, Painlevé replacing Ribot as premier but the
latter continuing as foreign minister. The new Cabinet lasted only two months,
and Painlevé was sober about the military prospects and keener than Ribot
on sounding the enemy. When Briand briefed him on 13 September,
Painlevé responded: 'The negotiation should be pursued to the end and the
interview accepted.'[147] He explained to Poincaré that the French army's
situation was not unfavourable (the mutinies had subsided and Pétain was
staging successful offensives), and the Central Powers could not withstand
attrition indefinitely, although Russia's collapse gave them new opportunities. The present was a good moment to talk. Previously Painlevé had
envisaged hanging on for the Americans, but Wilson's indifference to
French war aims may have unsettled him; at all events he believed the
Americans needed convincing about France's viewpoint. And if Painlevé
was willing to explore negotiation, so too was Poincaré, or so Briand's con-
temporaneous notes indicated, although Poincaré's memoirs suggested
otherwise.[148] Ribot's suspicion of any contact with the Germans was becoming
a minority position.

When Briand briefed Ribot on 14 September, the foreign minister feared
a 'snare', but said he must confer with Painlevé. After doing so, he asked

Briand for a written statement to use when consulting France's allies. What Briand actually supplied on 20 September was curious, given that he knew the meeting with Lancken had now been scheduled for two days' time. It said that before a meeting it must be accepted that France would stay loyal to its partners (though their aims went unmentioned), and its occupied territories must be evacuated: France would regain Alsace-Lorraine and receive reparation for damages together with guarantees on the west bank of the Rhine, though not annexing it. There was no possibility of Germany agreeing to these conditions, and Briand (like the Belgians) was always vague about what, if anything, it had accepted. Briand added a postscript that if the Germans publicized the meeting he would shoulder all the blame; but Ribot could hardly consent to such a subterfuge. In fact there was bad blood between the two men, and if Briand's letter was drafted poorly and in bad faith, so too was the circular that Ribot sent to his ambassadors, which implied that Briand had wished to proceed without consulting the Allies. Ribot set up the consultation to elicit a negative response from France's partners, which indeed it did, and on 23 September Ribot told Briand that the government had decided the meeting could not proceed.[149] De Broqueville, whom Ribot also consulted, said he would have advised Briand that although the proposal was genuine it was too dangerous to go (which was directly contrary to the impression he had given Briand). Ribot also saw Painlevé and four other ministers, before vetoing the meeting. He feared that because Briand had greater status than Lancken the project was intended to divide the Allies, and to demoralize French opinion if it were publicized. Actually the German evidence supports neither this nor Briand's view, for Berlin intended no substantial concessions over Alsace-Lorraine, and Lancken's plan seems to have been to get a meeting and take things from there.[150] Most likely if Briand and Lancken had met (and Lancken did actually travel to Switzerland), they would have found little common ground.

When Balfour met the French ambassador Paul Cambon in London, on Friday 21 September, Balfour told him about the Villalobar feeler and Cambon told Balfour about the Briand–Lancken one.[151] Both considered the latter an intrigue designed to divide the Allies by making France appear the barrier to peace. Balfour doubted Germany was yet sufficiently beaten to give up Belgium and Alsace-Lorraine.[152] But over the Villalobar feeler, Balfour had accurately advised Lloyd George that Kühlmann was the originator and the approach was serious. He did not believe that Britain could simply ignore it: to do so would unite German opinion behind the extremists while having the opposite effect in Britain, where public opinion would not support the war if its prolongation seemed unnecessary. However, he wanted to respond that Britain would only hear proposals if it could at once communicate them to the other Allies. He doubted whether the Germans would agree but, if they refused, that might be 'the best thing that could happen to us'.[153]

On Balfour's second principle the Cabinet was divided, and both in Paris and in London the last week of September witnessed a contest between premier and foreign minister. The debate prefigured that over whether to respond to Hitler's peace offer to Britain in May 1940, but unlike on that occasion with the prime minister himself inclining to negotiate.[154] Indeed Winston Churchill (who had entered the government in July as munitions minister) was startled by Lloyd George's vehemence. Part of the explanation was the timing: just as Plumer was beginning his Third Ypres battles. On the results thus far Lloyd George might well feel vindicated in his scepticism about the Flanders operation.[155] The question of how the war could possibly be won without intolerable suffering and wrecking Britain's Great Power status was more pressing than ever. Against this dismal backdrop, the War Cabinet held two sessions on 24 and 27 September, recorded only in Hankey's manuscript notes reserved for exceptionally confidential business. The key issue, however, was not Western Europe but whether to confer with Russia, as the tide of chaos there rose higher. At the first meeting Balfour reported on both the German feelers. As he understood the Lancken approaches, they were so generous—including the return of Alsace-Lorraine—'as to arouse suspicion that their object must be sinister' and intended to lure France out of the war, while Russia and Romania, if they got wind of the terms, would drop out at once. Over the Villalobar 'kite', however, Balfour did not win authority to talk at once to all the major Allies. Bonar Law felt Russia had become 'practically useless'. Lloyd George felt that if 'the Soviet was going to destroy our prospects of success, then Russia ought to pay the penalty', and he believed the Germans preferred expansion in the Baltic rather than in Western Europe. Curzon, Smuts, and Barnes all wanted more information about the Madrid approach before communicating with the Allies, and Balfour found himself isolated. But as the discussion proceeded, ministers had second thoughts about letting the Germans expand in the east. Lloyd George felt that if they controlled Courland and Lithuania 'two great empires would emerge from the war, namely the British Empire and Germany'. Milner said 'it would mean

Germany coming out of the war more powerful than she had entered it, and another war in 10 years' time'; the premier summed up that Britain should carry on, but only if it could 'crush Germany' even if Russia dropped out. Even so, he did not think it necessary to consult the American ambassador: 'At present, we wanted the USA to fight and there was no need to discuss questions of peace with them.' None the less, a decision was postponed until Lloyd George had talked to Painlevé at a meeting scheduled for the following day at Boulogne.[156]

Balfour was unhappy. After the Cabinet he reiterated to Lloyd George how dangerous it would be to communicate with Germany without forewarning Russia. He feared that if disclosed the news would demoralize the Allies' Russian supporters and might release dozens of German Eastern Front divisions.[157] He urged on Paul Cambon that Painlevé should push back against Lloyd George, who was liable to take up the Lancken feeler as he had the Spanish one.[158] But in fact at Boulogne Painlevé told Lloyd George that French ministers had no wish to negotiate until German power was broken; and what worried him was that the Lancken feeler might be genuine. He 'evidently doubted whether France would continue fighting if it were known that the Germans had offered both nine-tenths of Alsace-Lorraine and the whole of Belgium'. Painlevé now agreed with Ribot that it was wisest not to follow Lancken's lead, but for contrasting reasons: he feared France being bought out of the war.[159] According to Painlevé, Lloyd George considered the Lancken affair an effort to divide the Allies and alarm Russia, or to make peace with Britain and France at Russia's expense, and 'the greatest circumspection' was needed. It seemed his colleagues had influenced him. But in addition, Lloyd George took military advice. Robertson was pessimistic about attaining victory if Russia made peace: he was gloomy about the French army and thought Russia virtually finished. But Lloyd George also met Foch (a soldier whose opinions he respected) and Haig (whose opinions he respected more than Robertson's) and both disagreed. According to Lloyd George, Foch confirmed the prime minister's judgement that now the U-boats were contained Allied victory was assured even without Russia, though it might take a long time.[160] The premier told Haig a serious proposal was likely soon for a peace at Russia's expense that gave Britain and France what they wanted, though accepting it would leave Germany stronger.[161] Haig's advice was not to desert Russia but 'go on hammering': the situation at the front was 'very favourable'. According to General Clive, a week earlier Haig believed 'the Germans will make great effort to make peace during the winter before the Americans come into line. Hopes that peace will not come, for he believes we can finish off Germany next year.'[162] Subsequently Haig minuted, 'I can see no prospect of obtaining the peace we seek...[A compromise would mean] not only the almost certain renewal of the war hereafter at a time of Germany's choosing but the entire loss of faith and respect of our Overseas Dominions, America and of our other Allies, and indeed of the entire world, East and West.'[163]

Although Lloyd George was far less bellicose than Haig, he modified his earlier opinion before the second, and decisive, War Cabinet meeting on the 27th. Balfour and the Foreign Office had also been active. Sir Eric Drummond, Balfour's private secretary, had spoken to the leader of the opposition, Asquith, before Asquith gave a speech at Leeds on 26 September: Drummond tipping him off that the Germans were seeking either a compromise so they could expand at Russia's expense, or a separate peace with Russia so that they could concentrate against the Western Allies. Hence Asquith's speech, to Lloyd George's anger, called for evacuation of all *French and Russian* occupied territory as a precondition for negotiation.[164] At the 27 September Cabinet Lloyd George reported Painlevé's opinions and voiced similar doubts on whether the British public would support continued fighting if offered favourable terms. Balfour thought they would do rather than see Germany emerge strengthened; and George Barnes agreed, if the alternative was Germany 'gaining such accession of strength as would enable her to undertake a fresh war in a few years' time with better prospects of success'. Lloyd George held that not only the Russians and Italians but also now the French were scarcely fighting, while the BEF was unlikely to accomplish even the first stage of Haig's Flanders scheme. In these circumstances declarations such as Asquith's were very unwise, and Britain might warn the Russians that it would not fight for them unless they fought for themselves. Milner disagreed, and Balfour warned that such an attitude would make a Russian separate peace more likely. The Foreign Secretary pointed to the enormous effort America was preparing both in shipbuilding and in raising armies. This time it was Lloyd George rather than Balfour who found himself isolated, and ministers finally agreed to consult Britain's allies.[165]

Balfour first checked with his Petrograd ambassador, Buchanan, who confirmed the balance of risks favoured consulting the Russians rather than not.[166] On 6 October Balfour met representatives from America, Russia, France, Italy, and Japan, and told them about the Madrid approach. He considered 'it was extremely doubtful whether it was more than a diplomatic move intended rather to divide the allies than to end the war', but if only for reasons of managing public opinion in Germany and the Allied countries, it should not be rejected or ignored. Hence he proposed to respond in a way that could meet 'the tactics of diplomatists like Herr von Kühlmann', by replying the British government would be prepared to receive any communication that Germany made, and discuss it with Britain's allies.[167] The foreign representatives agreed and a message went back to Sir Arthur Hardinge, and thence via Lema to Villalobar and Kühlmann.[168] It is not known how Kühlmann viewed it. But he never responded, and over the following weeks the diplomatic doors slammed shut. Kühlmann gained the impression that the British would, after all, support the French over Alsace-Lorraine. In the Reichstag on 9 October he said Germany would 'never' return the provinces.[169] Two days later Lloyd George gave his strongest undertaking yet that Britain would stand by France 'until she redeems her oppressed children from the degradation of a foreign yoke'.[170] Speaking in the Chamber of Deputies, and needled by reports from the French postal surveillance that Briand was still in touch with the Coppées, Ribot let slip an aside about German approaches to a 'high political personage' offering Alsace-Lorraine in return for a separate peace. Briand then read out in the parliamentary corridors his 20 September letter, forcing a secret session of the Chamber on 16 October in which he successfully defended his integrity whereas Ribot acquitted himself badly, appearing shifty and to have sabotaged a peace opening. Painlevé reshuffled his Cabinet and replaced Ribot by Louis Barthou, who, however, was no less hard-line than Ribot. And when in November Painlevé's ministry collapsed, Poincaré felt he had to choose between Joseph Caillaux, the disgraced pre-war premier who was widely supposed to be in touch with Germany and to favour a compromise, and Georges Clemenceau, the irascible political veteran who detested the president but was single-mindedly committed to victory. Poincaré chose Clemenceau;[171] and in the opposing camp Karl and Czernin had thrown in their lot with Germany. After the Bolshevik Revolution in November Russia finally made peace, but the divide between the Western Allies and the Central Powers deepened.

The breakdown of the 1917 peace feelers can be explained at different levels. Certainly it demonstrated the perils of amateur diplomacy. An older Catholic, aristocratic, and dynastic Europe, alongside the socialists and portions of the business elite, attempted to transcend divisions, as later it would support continental unification. Yet mediators such as Sixte and the Coppées helped sustain the contacts by over-representing to each party the other's goodwill, and it is hard to see that professionals would have done better. Although the feelers made both sides review their war aims, they remained far apart. Admittedly, there were signs of movement: some French and British leaders were prepared at least to talk to the Germans; and the Germans to renounce the annexation of Longwy-Briey and give up the Belgian coast, while the Austrians considered ceding the Italian-majority areas of the Trentino (though both Central Powers hoped for compensations). But the Allies were less willing to jettison their claims. The British wanted full restoration for Belgium and to retain Germany's colonies, while the German leaders, except for Kühlmann and briefly Bethmann, insisted on continuing control of Belgium. Nor would they cede more than a fraction of the Alsace-Lorraine of 1870, whereas the French wanted all of it, and preferably more. Italy's Treaty of London claims on Austro-Hungarian territory were an equally formidable stumbling block. The territorial controversies really mattered, for economic and strategic reasons as well as on grounds of national self-determination, ethnicity, and international law and morality. But behind the territorial disputes lay a deeper issue: that the peace feelers served as weapons in the struggle, and especially to divide the enemy. The British and French saw the Sixte and Armand–Revertera affairs as such opportunities, as did Kühlmann the Villalobar contact. Both alliances' efforts to shatter the other had been central to pre-1914 diplomacy, and this quest continued during the war.

The belligerent governments were cognizant of the rising threat of revolution and Czernin tried to use it as a lever. But none, except for Russia, stood quite yet on the verge of insurrection. Socialist and labour movements had gained support, but a renewed and strident nationalism rallied against them, and governmental concessions to the Left—such as pledges to support a League of Nations—were cosmetic. The domestic balance in the major belligerents shifted in favour of anti-war forces, but not, until the Bolsheviks seized power, by enough to end the conflict. The Reichstag peace resolution meant less than it seemed. Moreover, if the diplomatic and domestic political elements in Europe's stalemate softened rather than dissolved, the same was true of the military deadlock. By summer 1917 both unrestricted submarine warfare and the Allies' Chantilly offensives had failed to deliver. But by the autumn Russia's collapse opened new prospects for the Central Powers, especially in conjunction with tactical innovations

PART III

Global Repercussions

remaining neutrals); and that Washington had invited others to follow its lead. Moreover, unrestricted submarine warfare created a potential casus belli for any state with merchant ships or coastline. It served at least as a pretext for Siam, China, and Brazil, and contributed to the circumstances that brought in Greece. But each new entrant also had its own particular motives, and the war expanded as a series of parallel conflicts, governments profiting from the turbulence to pursue ambitions and settle scores. Thus, among the pre-1917 entrants Japan had designs on Germany's North Pacific islands and on its leased territory in China, as well as for control over China more broadly; Italy wanted to integrate all Italian speakers into one kingdom, as well as gain strategic frontiers on the Alps and in Dalmatia; Portugal to protect its African colonies; and Romania to incorporate the Romanian speakers under Austro-Hungarian rule. Conversely the Ottoman leaders wanted protection against Russia, though also to recoup their nineteenth-century territorial losses; and the Bulgarians to reverse the outcome of the 1913 Second Balkan War. Decisions to intervene rested on calculations of the security and expansion that might be obtainable, but also on assessments of who was likelier to win, as well as on ideological sympathies with one or other side. The Turks and Bulgarians were impressed by German military prowess, others by the British navy. But after America entered, and despite the February Revolution, no new entrants joined the Central Powers.

In June 1917 the Allies forced into exile the neutralist King Constantine I of Greece and reinstated as prime minister the leader of the country's Liberal party, Eleutherios Venizelos, who promptly joined their side. Modern Greece had emerged from a revolt in 1821–9 against Ottoman Turkish rule. At first it embraced only a portion of the ethnically Greek territories, and nationalists nurtured the *Megali Idea* or 'Great Idea' of uniting all the lands inhabited by Hellenes in the past and present, founding a successor to Byzantium that would dominate the Eastern Mediterranean. Like their Italian counterparts, they sought unification and more. Venizelos, a Cretan lawyer who became premier in 1910, shared these aspirations, and during the Balkan Wars of 1912–13 Greece doubled its size. Venizelos also championed a British alliance.[2] In January 1915 he wanted to take up a British suggestion of gains on the Asia Minor coast, which had a large Greek population round Smyrna/Izmir. The idea proved controversial, and in March he resigned. Constantine, who had considerable prerogative powers over foreign affairs, headed the critics. The appropriate limits to royal authority were one issue in the political divide that became known as the 'National

Schism' (*Ethnikos Dikhasmos*), although the primary debate was over whether to stay neutral or join the Allies. Venizelos's Liberal Party had strongest support in the more recently acquired territories; it was also more radical over questions such as land redistribution and the use of the demotic Greek language. Its opponents included the Army Chief of Staff (Ioannis Metaxas), an older generation of parliamentary politicians, and Constantine and his circle. Constantine had served in the German Imperial Guard and was married to Wilhelm II's sister, Sophia; although sympathetic to the Germans he did not advocate joining the Central Powers, which would make Greece too vulnerable to the Royal Navy and became still less attractive after Turkey and Bulgaria joined Austria–Hungary and Germany. In contrast to Venizelos he favoured a calculated neutrality, sceptical whether Britain would deliver on its promises and judging the Central Powers more likely to win. However, in the August 1915 elections Venizelos's party kept its majority and Constantine reappointed him as premier, just before the September crisis when Germany and Austria–Hungary invaded Serbia from the north while Bulgaria invaded from the east. Although the 1913 Greco-Serb alliance treaty was ambiguous, Venizelos claimed Greece must support Serbia, and he asked France and Britain to assist, which they did by landing an expedition at Salonika. They acted too late to prevent Serbia from being overrun, but stayed, forming a new front in Macedonia, until the end of the war.

The Salonika front took up more time in 1916–17 inter-Allied conferences than almost any other issue.[3] The forces committed to the *Armée d'Orient* were sizeable: by the end of 1916 they included 140,000 British, 130,000 Serbs, 33,000 Italians, and 18,000 Russians.[4] The British General Staff detested dissipating resources in a peripheral campaign. Many British politicians agreed, though Lloyd George was at first supportive of an operation that might offer a cheaper and easier route to success than did the Western Front. British governments also hesitated to force a withdrawal that risked a crisis with the French. The Salonika commander, Maurice Sarrail, was one of the few French generals with a following among the radical and socialist Left. French governments feared that diluting his authority would weaken the pro-war majority in the Chamber of Deputies and they saw a Salonika presence as protecting French interests in the region.[5] They did not necessarily back Venizelos, who was pro-British. Rather they wanted a nominally neutral Greece that would, however, support the *Armée d'Orient* and the Allied war effort.[6] The upshot was that after Venizelos resigned for a second time, in October 1915, the *Armée d'Orient* continued as a heterogeneous and poorly supplied expedition that confronted—in the shape of a Bulgarian army with Austro-Hungarian and German reinforcements—an unexpectedly formidable opponent.

The 1916 Macedonia fighting manoeuvred the royalist government towards confrontation with the Allies. In May the Greek army surrendered the strategically important Fort Rupel, enabling the Central Powers to overrun Eastern Macedonia. Greek officers in Salonika rebelled against Constantine and set up a Committee of Public Safety. Venizelos left Athens to join them, forming a Provisional Government, so that now he controlled the north while Constantine held the centre and south. Sarrail and the French government suspected Constantine of colluding with the Central Powers, and feared the Allies' communication lines were endangered. In December 1916 Allied troops landed in Athens, in pursuance of an agreement whereby the government had agreed to provide weapons to replace those lost at Fort Rupel, but they were fired on and forced to withdraw. In the French parliament pressure built up for forceful action, and after Ribot replaced Briand as premier in March 1917 he was more inclined to respond.[7] In London too the mood was changing, in part due to the submarine crisis. Jellicoe insisted Britain must reduce its overseas obligations in order to supply the home islands and the Western Front. Of 874,000 tons of Allied shipping lost in April 1917, 268,000 went down in the Mediterranean; a total of 411 ships or an average of over thirteen a day.[8] During 1917 British and French shipping involved in supplying the Macedonian army totalled 600,000 and 400,000 tons, Jellicoe estimating the commitment at 160 British vessels. As Robertson put it, shipping 'dominated the whole problem'.[9] Jellicoe's naval arguments emboldened Robertson to insist on troop withdrawals, and Lloyd George was coming to see Palestine as an alternative arena, where British Empire forces could gain territory of paramount strategic value and operate independently, while being supplied via the Cape of Good Hope and the Indian Ocean where sinkings were fewer.[10] Hence by spring 1917 the War Cabinet was preparing to demand that two divisions be transferred from Macedonia to Palestine: another sign that Britain's leverage within the Anglo-French relationship was growing, and it was more inclined to pursue imperial interests.

The decision on Greece emerged from a succession of Anglo-French conferences, at St-Jean de Maurienne in April and at Paris and London in May. Venizelos declared he could no longer work with Constantine, who should abdicate.[11] At St-Jean de Maurienne the Italians accepted a sphere of influence round Smyrna, thus intensifying their rivalry with Greece in the Aegean. In return they withdrew their opposition to deposing Constantine, provided (as the British stipulated) that Greece remained a constitutional monarchy rather than becoming a republic. Even though the treaties establishing Greek independence had made Russia one of the 'Protecting Powers', the other Allies brushed aside its protests.[12] Ribot did assure the Russians, however, that France would 'assume no engagement towards Venizelos in regard to the vast nationalist ambitions of the Greeks'.[13] Although no final agreement was reached at St-Jean de Maurienne, Lloyd George told the War Cabinet that Ribot and Painlevé had been less hostile than he expected to British troop cuts, 'provided that we would assist them to clear up the situation in Greece itself, including, if necessary, the removal of King Constantine from the throne. The prime minister was inclined to the view that a bargain might be made along these lines for the reduction of British forces in the Balkans.'[14]

At the Paris conference on 4–5 May Lloyd George agreed a French high commissioner should present the Allies' demands—which meant sacrificing some of Britain's diplomatic independence but would saddle France with the blame if the plan misfired.[15] Finally, the London conference on 28–29 May agreed a plan of action, based on a French step-by-step scheme but with safeguards to reassure the British that pressure would be gradual, and with precautions to avoid a civil war that might jeopardize the Salonika army and draw in even more men. The key issue was the harvest in Thessaly, a region Venizelist in sympathy but under royalist control. If the royalists gathered its grain they would be less vulnerable to the blockade the Allies had imposed, while the Venizelist regions would be more exposed because all incoming food ships would evidently be for them and therefore submarine targets.[16] A paper for the conference by Lord Robert Cecil, the British Parliamentary Under-Secretary for Foreign Affairs, said the best solution would be to take control of the Thessaly harvest, demand Constantine's abdication, and aim for a continuing constitutional monarchy but with a Venizelist government.[17] The meeting agreed that Constantine must be removed, but the process should be peaceful. Hence after establishing control over the Thessaly harvest the Allies through their High Commissioner, Charles Jonnart, and as Protecting Powers who could no longer tolerate Constantine's alleged unconstitutional conduct or Greece's division, would demand his abdication, if necessary completing the blockade and occupying the Corinth isthmus. The references to the Allies' role as Protecting Powers were largely window dressing, but the key point was that British forces would stay until July in the hope that the issue would be settled quickly. In fact Ribot had no intention of following so leisurely a timetable, and when Jonnart reached Greece in June he moved much faster, the French correctly calculating that if they achieved the objective the methods would be forgiven.[18] When Jonnart demanded Constantine's abdication the king decided resistance would achieve nothing and went into exile, leaving the throne to his second son Alexander. Jonnart then intervened again by requiring the recall of the June 1915 Venizelist-majority parliament, which the Prime Minister Aleksandros Zaimis could not accept, and Zaimis resigned. He was replaced by Venizelos, who at once began purging his opponents from parliament, the civil service, the army, and the church, while French troops occupied Athens' public places.[19] Strictly speaking, in Venizelos's view, the Salonika government was already at war with the Central Powers and that state of belligerency was simply extended to Athens: he recalled the Greek diplomats in the Central Powers' capitals, and by the end of 1917 a Greek army of 100,000 had been recruited for the Macedonian Front, more than enough numerically to replace the British forces transferred.[20]

To the reconvened parliament Venizelos delivered a four-hour justification of his life and actions. Greece would 'regain the national territories we have lost; we shall reassert our national honour; we shall effectively defend our interests at the Peace Congress and secure our national frontier. We will be a worthy member of the family of free nations that the Congress will organize, and hand on to our children the Greece that past generations could only dream of.'[21] Like the other 1917 war entrants (not least Woodrow Wilson), Venizelos saw attending the peace conference as a key benefit, and he pledged that territorial claims including, implicitly, to land that had never belonged to modern Greece would be satisfied. He may not have known that the Allies had secretly assigned Constantinople to Russia and Smyrna to Italy—and he was not the only interventionist to be thus deceived. In the event, in May 1919, while the Italians were boycotting the Paris Peace Conference, the other Allies agreed to Greece occupying Smyrna, thus facilitating the Turkish national revival under Mustafa Kemal and opening the way to Greece's calamitous defeat in the Greco-Turkish war of 1919–22. The domestic repercussions were even longer lasting. Venizelos's return did not heal the 'national schism': on the contrary his purge continued a practice begun in 1915 whereby each side in politics on taking office filled the upper echelons of the public services with their adherents. Competing factions became embedded in the officer corps until Metaxas's 1936–40 dictatorship. In contrast, the military consequences of Greek involvement were more limited and its army, like America's, took a year to build up. None the less by 1918 Greek troops garrisoned the quieter sectors of the Macedonian line, enabling other contingents such as the French and Serbs to concentrate on the offensive that in September 1918 forced Bulgaria out of the war. Their arrival also released two British infantry divisions to advance on Jerusalem. In short, Greece's entry may not have brought what Venizelos hoped, but it largely delivered what the Allies expected of it. It was none the less a flagrant intervention in Greek internal politics.

American intervention was not particularly relevant to Greece's war entry, but for the remaining cases it was much more significant. After the United States broke off relations with Germany, it urged that it would 'make for the peace of the world' if other neutrals followed suit.[22] Among the Latin American countries breaking off relations were Costa Rica in September 1917 and Peru and Uruguay in October, and by November 1918 Bolivia, the Dominican Republic, Salvador, and Ecuador. The governments that declared war, however, were largely confined to Central America, and acted belatedly. Panama and Cuba did so in April 1917, but Guatemala only in April 1918, Costa Rica and Nicaragua in May, and Haiti and Honduras in July.[23] Brazil, in contrast, broke off diplomatic relations with Germany and Austria-Hungary in April 1917 and declared war on the Central Powers in October, the only South American state to do so, and followed up the declaration by—albeit limited—military action.

Brazil had declared independence from Portugal in 1822 and become a republic in 1889. Its population in 1910 was 22 million.[24] Its leading exports were rubber and coffee, especially the latter, of which it was the leading world producer. Most Brazilians lived along the coast between Recife and Porto Alegre, and since the 1880s hundreds of thousands of European immigrants had joined them. Among the newcomers were Germans, going primarily to the three southernmost provinces, where they formed by 1914 a community of 400,000, mostly prosperous but linguistically, culturally, and politically aloof.[25] Although under European (and especially French) cultural influence, Brazil kept out of European power politics, and its diplomacy focused on its neighbours. While the Barón del Río Branco was foreign minister in 1902–12 Brazil staged a naval race against Argentina and Chile, but his successor, Lauro Müller, gave priority to improved relations between the 'ABC' countries, at the expense of Río Branco's rapprochement with the United States.[26]

Müller was unusual in being a German-Brazilian with national prominence. Wenceslau Braz, who became president in 1914, kept Müller on, and allowed him a large say in shaping Brazilian neutrality. Braz lacked a strong party to support him: observers saw him as ineffective and preoccupied with the budget deficit. He and Müller—who may also have harboured presidential ambitions—were potential rivals, and of the Cabinet in place in 1914 only the navy minister was overtly pro-Allied. None the less, British diplomats found Müller efficient and helpful, within a correct definition of neutrality. German merchant ships were allowed to leave the ports only on purely commercial missions, and not to coal offshore German warships; most German wireless stations were closed, handicapping German cruisers in the South Atlantic.[27] Müller may have been influenced by public opinion, whose vocal sections were more pro-Allied than in the United States. The mood reflected pro-French sympathies (Britain was not well known, despite being the pre-eminent foreign investor), as well as outrage over the invasion of Belgium. Italy's entry in 1915 and Portugal's in 1916 added to the Allied camp the biggest sources of pre-war immigration, whereas the German-Brazilians were increasingly isolated. They raised funds for the German Red Cross and some returned to do military service, but they could press at most for continuing neutrality rather than joining the Central Powers.[28] They had no equivalent to the *Liga pelos Aliadas* (League for the Allies) headed by Senator Ruy Barbosa, one of the most distinguished Brazilian intellectuals and jurists. Its purposes were to defend the Allies and protest against German atrocities, but also to help assimilate immigrants and to nurture Brazilian patriotism. The *Liga de Resistencia Nacional*, set up to encourage military preparedness, again resembled counterparts in the United States. In contrast the *Germanische Bund für Süd-Amerika*, intended to rally Germans across the continent, encountered greater opposition, including within the German community (whose leaders feared appearing unpatriotic).[29] That being said, the 1916 blacklisting controversy over Allied sanctions against neutral traders with the Central Powers (see chapter 2) harmed the Allies' reputation in Brazil as well as in the USA, and both the Brazilian government and the press remonstrated, while when Britain tried to save on shipping by banning coffee imports, the São Paulo growing region was hit hard. Thus far, the government was not even considering pro-Allied intervention.

Müller's response to submarine warfare was circumspect. When in 1916 a Brazilian merchantman, the *Rio Branco*, was torpedoed, the government protested and Germany sent a conciliatory reply. In February 1917 Wilson did not consult the Latin American countries before breaking off relations with Germany, and he deliberately avoided a hemispheric response, believing—characteristically—that only the US government was truly disinterested.[30] Although encouraged by the Americans to break off relations (and the *Liga pelos Aliadas* and the Rio papers called for intervention) Brazil confined itself to a carefully worded declaration that it could not accept that the submarine campaign amounted either to an effective or a legal blockade, opposed sinking without warning, and would hold Germany responsible for losses of Brazilian lives, goods, and ships.[31] It went no further until on the night of 4–5 April the Brazilian steamer *Paraná* was torpedoed off the French coast with the loss of three lives. Although the ship was lit up and flying the Brazilian flag as well as an illuminated sign, the U-boat gave no warning, and it fired on the crew in the boats.[32] This time the reaction among Brazilians—whose self-image was of tolerance and non-violence—was sharper. Müller wanted first to see if Germany would punish the submarine commander and compensate the victims' families, but the Cabinet overruled him.[33] A note on 11 April declared that Germany was mounting a blockade, was not providing warning, not assisting the crews and on these and other points contravened international law. Brazil was therefore severing diplomatic relations.[34] The Cabinet acted swiftly because of the forty-six Central Power merchant ships detained in Brazilian harbours, which could be invaluable to Brazil or to the Allies, and which might escape or be sabotaged by their crews. While the authorities impounded the vessels, patriotic demonstrations took place in Rio, São Paulo, and Porto Alegre, which in the latter city led into two days of violence against the German community's shops and clubs and businesses.[35] The *Liga pelos Aliados* and the Rio papers now had Müller in their sights, accusing him of being pro-German and demanding his resignation. He still issued a declaration indicating Brazil's neutrality towards both Germany and the United States, which it would require an Act of Congress to revoke. None the less, in May he decided he was a liability to the government and resigned.[36] His departure removed the main obstacle at official level to Brazil entering the war.

Müller's successor, Nila Peçanha, was a former vice-president with a pro-Allied reputation who had reportedly conferred with Ruy Barbosa before accepting. He had a reputation for decisiveness, and was said to have

President Braz's backing for 'a firm and determined line of action'.[37] Whereas Müller had seemed to drag his feet, delaying and doing the minimum, Peçanha followed the trend of public opinion more emphatically, though still timing his moves in response to German actions, so that ship sinkings punctuated Brazil's path to hostilities. After the news that another Brazilian vessel, the *Tijuca*, had been torpedoed and sunk off Brittany, Congress abrogated the declaration of neutrality between Germany and the United States. This marked a departure from Müller's line, and was justified on the new grounds of friendship and solidarity with Washington as well as upholding international law, Peçanha having told a reporter, 'I am trying to follow a fully American policy.'[38] The practical import was that German vessels in Brazilian ports could be added to Brazil's merchant fleet.[39] After Brazil similarly abrogated its neutrality decree between Germany and the European Allies, it terminated diplomatic relations with the Central Powers, although it took one more outrage to precipitate the final break. After a submarine torpedoed the Brazilian steamer *Macao* 200 miles from the Spanish coast, and took its captain prisoner, Braz asked Congress for a declaration of war, which on 26 October the Chamber of Deputies passed by 149:1 and the Senate unanimously.[40] Only now, in a curious echo of the Zimmermann Telegram, did Peçanha disclose the decrypted 'Luxburg despatches', from the German minister in Argentina, which Lansing had forwarded to Brazil and Argentina and which envisaged 'the reorganization of Brazil'. This was far from an authoritative statement of German policy and Peçanha overstated its significance, but it reinforced the government's unease about the German–Brazilian community and added a supplementary vindication. Indeed, more anti-German rioting in the southern cities followed the declaration of hostilities.

In contrast with Greece, neither European Allied nor American actions precipitated Brazil's war entry. In the British Foreign Office it was minuted that 'Brazil has not yet entered the war and we are not encouraging her to do so—for naval and military reasons.'[41] The service departments thought the confiscated enemy ships might be valuable and control of the Pernambuco wireless station would block communications between Germany and South America; but the Brazilian navy would need British officers (who were not available) to be of use, and an army could neither be transported to Europe nor supplied there.[42] In contrast, the US Navy was more positive, and Lansing keen for Brazil to enter. Yet even under the pro-American Peçanha, Brazil delayed the break.[43]

The official Brazilian justifications referred to Germany's violations of international law and to Brazil's responsibility for Western hemispheric solidarity, but its war entry did not (as Washington had hoped) give a lead to other South American countries. Instead it arguably fractured South American unity. It seemed that Argentina might follow, as Argentinian ships were sunk and pro-Allied demonstrations unfolded in the country's cities. However, pro-neutrality demonstrations counterbalanced them, and the Argentinian government accepted German apologies and maintained diplomatic relations, seeking instead an inter-American conference to reaffirm Latin America's neutrality. After the Americans disclosed the Luxburg telegrams, in which the German minister to Buenos Aires made dismissive remarks about the Argentinian government and called for Argentinian ships to be sunk, resolutions in favour of breaking off relations gained big majorities in the Chamber of Deputies and Senate, but were resisted by President Hipólito Yrigoyen, a Radical who was the first president to be elected by a direct and universal male franchise, and in foreign policy was a neutralist, suspicious of the United States. His position contrasted with that of Braz, who would have preferred neutrality but moved cautiously away from it.[44] Argentina never broke off relations with the Central Powers, although it did adopt a more pro-Allied neutrality, an agreement in January 1918 providing for it to supply 2.5 million tons of cereals a year on credit to Britain and France in return for coal.[45] Argentina prospered from booming demand for its meat and grain, but war entry remained contentious.

In contrast, the Brazilian government may have acted when it did in order to anticipate a similar declaration by Argentina, which in fact did not materialize; and that Brazil (a traditional rival) moved first gave Yrigoyen another reason not to do likewise. In addition Brazil's coffee exports were a luxury product that gave Rio de Janeiro less bargaining power than Buenos Aires. Whereas Britain had traditionally been Brazil's main coal supplier, by 1917 Brazil imported four times as much American as British coal and faced potential catastrophe, with Britain ceasing to import its coffee while American coal, steel, and shipping might now be diverted to Europe. Unprecedented general strikes for higher wages disrupted Rio and São Paulo during July, and economic considerations may have encouraged closer ties with the Allies and the United States.[46] Also important, however, was the kind of war expected. For Brazil, this was a conflict of choice rather than necessity, and Peçanha said before the declaration that it should provide moral and economic support rather than troops.[47] Brazil's finances remained precarious, its currency overvalued, and its navy at low readiness. The army's principal functions were frontier garrisoning and suppressing unrest (in 1914–15 it had fought a major campaign against the Contestado uprising). Conscription was introduced in 1916 and the army was being reorganized when Brazil intervened.[48] Although it doubled from 30,000 men in 1914 to 60,000 in 1918, housing, feeding, and clothing the recruits proved testing.[49] The army forfeited thirty field-gun batteries that it had ordered from Germany; and when a mission visited America it found that supplying Brazil ranked low among Washington's priorities.[50] Still, another mission attended training in France, and some of its members served in the line, while medical personnel staffed a Brazilian hospital near Paris. A report in 1918 to Braz's prospective successor recommended sending an expeditionary force, which might have ensued in 1919. A naval task force of two battleships, two cruisers, and four destroyers patrolled under British command off West Africa, although its crews suffered grievously from Spanish influenza. But Brazil's main contribution remained on its own territory, where it seized enemy ships and suppressed German commerce and communications. After two more Brazilian vessels were torpedoed in November, the authorities took extraordinary powers, proclaiming a state of siege, sequestrating German businesses, banning all German-language publications, and closing German-language schools.[51]

In truth, the American ambassador reported, 'the Brazilian public is not vitally interested in the war'.[52] The government's response to Benedict XV's peace note stressed Brazil's peaceful traditions and that had it not been for German actions it would have kept out.[53] Brazil's involvement proved divisive and unspectacular, despite the initial patriotic enthusiasm. Its story underlines how exceptional was the experience of the United States. The Brazilian government, unlike those of Greece and China, had no far-reaching ambitions for the peace conference, although its representatives served on the commission that drafted the League of Nations Covenant. Yet in many ways the conflict weakened Latin American connections with Europe, as European exports to and investments in South America dried up and the United States supplanted them.[54] Pro-Allied sympathies among commentators and intellectuals became tinged with revulsion against an international system that produced such havoc. The war experience accelerated trends towards separate Latin American identity and cultural emancipation.[55]

In Asia by 1914, if indigenous states had escaped annexation or protectorate status, they had mostly been divided into spheres of interest or subjected to 'unequal treaties', which restricted their freedom to levy customs tariffs on European and American imports and required Western nationals on their territory accused of criminal offences to be tried by the local consuls according to European or American law. The war encouraged revolt against such indirect domination, as well as against colonial rule. Both the Asian countries that entered the conflict in 1917 did so less because of hostility to Germany than in order to use the peace conference as a platform to challenge the unequal treaty system, and they targeted the Allies as well as the Central Powers.

Siam declared war on Germany on 22 July 1917.[56] The 1855 Bowring Treaty had limited its tariffs to 3 per cent and secured extraterritorial jurisdiction for British citizens, soon to be followed by those of other Powers. By 1914 Siam had ceded more than one-third of its territory to French Indochina and to the British Malay states. That its core remained independent owed something to it suiting Britain and France to keep Siam as a buffer, and something to King Rama V (reigned 1868–1910) and his advisors. Rama appointed Prince Dewrawangse as foreign minister, who served for thirty-eight years, and by 1914 was vastly experienced and temperamentally cautious. When Rama VI acceded to the throne in 1910, he kept Dewrawangse on.

Siam was less developed than Greece or Brazil. Its population in 1910 was about 8 million, and Bangkok the one substantial city. Its principal export was rice and most of its foreign trade was managed by the British from Singapore and Hong Kong. Its government was an absolute monarchy, untrammelled by representative institutions, in which members of the royal family held key ministerial portfolios and several hundred foreign advisers worked in royal service. Insofar as public opinion existed, it might have been expected to be hostile to France and Britain; but Europe was distant and Germany and Austria-Hungary could not have aided the country. In fact such considerations were outweighed by the personal outlook of King Rama, who had attended Sandhurst and Oxford and undergone officer training with the Durham Light Infantry. In 1915–16 he made donations to widows and orphans of his former regiment, and he and George V exchanged the titles of 'General' in each other's armies, despite German protests that such behaviour was un-neutral.[57]

Unrestricted submarine warfare and America's appeal to other neutrals to break off relations with Germany started a similar debate in Siam to those in Brazil and China. The initial response to Wilson was that Siam was very remote from the war, and preferred to see how the situation developed.[58] This holding position was primarily due to Dewrawangse, who worked closely with the British minister in Bangkok, Herbert Dering, who in turn advised London that it was best to apply no pressure but let the situation mature, and this recommendation the Foreign Office heeded. Although it might be advantageous to control the nine German steamers in Bangkok harbour and expel the 300 Germans working for the Siamese government, the country had already cooperated in, for example, deporting Indian seditionists, and the advantages from its belligerency were marginal.[59] Dering also feared the Siamese might seek concessions over the unequal treaties. The situation remained unchanged until Rama returned from a visit to the provinces, during which time Dewrawangse (with reluctant acquiescence from an impatient ruler) sounded out Siam's overseas emissaries. In a Cabinet meeting on 28 May Rama intervened decisively. Dewrawangse reported that the diplomats were divided: the representatives in France and Russia recommended breaking off relations (as did the French and Russian governments), but the London envoy considered it unnecessary. The king, however, said Siam should join the Allies. Previously the Central Powers had seemed to be winning, but American entry altered the equation and delaying meant Britain would end the war with greater leverage than it had now. Rama hoped the unequal treaties could be revised or even abrogated, although he forbade his ministers from saying so. Instead Dewrawangse, who was uneasy but went along, drafted a note that blamed Germany's persistence in an illegal method of warfare despite Siam's protests.[60] The government took over the German vessels before their crews could damage them, rounded up the German nationals, and asked the Allies how Siam could help them.[61] When the communications minister voiced concern about running the railways without German experts, Rama replaced him.[62] The kingdom had an army of 12,000–15,000 men, and initially it was not intended to send troops, but in 1918 a contingent of 1,254 volunteers went to France, where nineteen were killed. Siam attended the peace conference and urged amendments to the unequal treaties and recovery of full sovereignty, which America conceded in 1920 and Britain and France in 1925. In relation to the objectives set for it, Siam's was the most successful of the 1917 interventions, despite the war being followed by a financial crisis. The story underlines how the new conditions forged opportunities for dissatisfied nations to press claims.

China's intervention had larger repercussions. Like Siam and the Ottoman Empire it had accepted extraterritorial justice for Western nationals on its soil, and required international consent for tariff increases. It was heavily indebted, and much of its shipping and transport infrastructure was foreign-owned, as was much of its manufacturing and mining. Portions of its coastal territories had been leased to foreign governments. Hong Kong, where the New Territories were leased to Britain until 1997, had set the precedent but wartime diplomacy would revolve around Shandong, a province that was both strategically important as a promontory between Beijing and Shanghai, and—as Confucius's birthplace—charged with historical and religious significance. In 1898 Germany acquired a ninety-nine year lease around the port of Tsingtao (Qingdao) on Kiautschou (Jiaozhou) Bay, the finest anchorage on the China coast, and gained rights to build railways into the interior and to mine coal deposits.[63] The timing was traumatic, following China's defeat by Japan in 1894–5 and before the 1900 Boxer Uprising that culminated in China declaring war on the Western Powers, a siege of the foreign legations in Beijing, and a humiliating treaty that imposed an indemnity of over $330 million. China was not, as had been predicted, partitioned like Africa, but economic spheres of influence were created, while the Chinese reform movement sought through internal change and limited Westernization to rebuild national independence. Diluting its assumptions of cultural superiority, China would recast its future as a nation among other nations. By the twentieth century a revolutionary nationalist movement had emerged, based on the Chinese student community in Japan, where Sun Yat-sen was the most prominent leader. In 1911 a series of pro-vincial uprisings led to the creation of a republic, with Sun briefly serving as its president. The former imperial premier and commander-in-chief, Yuan Shikai, arranged the departure of the last Manchu emperor in return for becoming president himself, and he crushed a rebellion by Sun's party, the Guomindang.[64] Such was the situation—a fledgling republic whose leader was uncommitted to its institutions—when war began.

Two events in the conflict's opening months—the siege of Tsingtao and the Twenty-One Demands—were central to Beijing's decision to become a belligerent. Both involved encroachments by Japan. Although the Chinese government hoped to keep hostilities off its soil by neutralizing the foreign concessions, neither Japan nor America would cooperate.[65] Japan had been allied to Britain since 1902, but was not obliged to assist it in the circumstances in which war broke out, and the British Foreign Secretary, Sir Edward Grey, avoided invoking the alliance when on 7 August he asked the Japanese to declare war on Germany for the limited purpose of helping defend British shipping against enemy cruisers in the Pacific. The Japanese government had no intention of being thus restricted, and it declared war on 23 August with the intention of destroying all German forces in East Asia. One motive cited by the driving force behind the decision, foreign minister Kato Komei, was to overrun the German island possessions in the North Pacific (the Carolines, Marianas, and Marshalls), and Japan quickly did so. But he wanted additionally to take over the Shandong lease, and saw an opportunity while the Europeans were preoccupied to make broader demands.[66]

Japanese control of Shandong would pincer Beijing between the new strongpoint and the existing Japanese occupation zone in southern Manchuria.[67] Japan's war entry therefore created a crisis for Yuan Shikai. Although Yuan's Cabinet agreed unanimously that Japan was the greatest threat to China's sovereignty, War Minster Duan Qirui warned that China had arms and ammunition to resist for only forty-eight hours.[68] Hence the Chinese permitted the belligerents to conduct operations in Shandong by proclaiming it a 'war zone', and by November a primarily Japanese exped-itionary force had captured Tsingtao. 'China', said Kato, 'is not Belgium', and German, British, and Japanese forces all violated China's neutrality, the Japanese looting, raping, and killing civilians, and occupying not just the leased area but also eastern Shandong, ignoring China's annulment of the war zone after fighting ended.[69] They attempted to consolidate their position by requiring in Group I of the secret 'Twenty-One Demands' pre-sented to Beijing in January 1915 that China should accept whatever arrangement Japan and Germany came to about Shandong. Group II required Japan's leases on the harbours of Port Arthur and Dairen and on three railway lines in southern Manchuria to be extended to ninety-nine years. Group III required the Hanyeping Company, which owned the biggest coal and iron deposits in China, to become a joint Sino-Japanese concern. Group IV forbade China to cede or lease any further coastal areas to foreign Powers. Group V (technically 'wishes' rather than demands) asked the Chinese government to employ Japanese political, financial, and military advisers. Again the Chinese government considered war against Japan and again Yuan rejected it, spinning out the negotiations until Japan presented an ultimatum. Once more, however, he got little help. France, Russia, and Germany had jointly intervened in 1895 to limit Japan's gains after the Sino-Japanese War, but all were now preoccupied in Europe, where France wanted Japanese assistance. America was focused on the first German submarine campaign, and although Wilson (who knew little about East Asia) sympathized with China, he and Secretary of State Bryan remained at arm's length.[70] Bryan sent a note that objected to Groups IV and V but acknowledged that between Japan and Eastern Mongolia, South Manchuria, and Shandong 'territorial contiguity creates special relations'.[71] Sir Edward Grey considered 'it would be madness to quarrel with the Japanese while the war lasts, our proper course is to lie low'.[72] Yet the British were exasperated that Kato had not consulted them about the Demands, and Grey warned that Britain would not support Japan in a war against China. The *genro* (Japanese elder statesmen) obliged Kato to compromise. The Japanese ultimatum in May required the Chinese to accept Groups I to IV but not Group V. Hence the Chinese preserved their more general sovereignty at the price of signing a series of bilateral treaties, including for Shandong. The crisis strengthened Japan's legal position and showed that no one else was likely to reverse it, although the United States warned it would recognize no Sino-Japanese agreement that impaired American rights or China's integrity and independence.[73]

Although the Chinese government knew it was too weak to fight, the crisis sparked nationalist demonstrations and a boycott of Japanese goods. 1915 is conventionally dated as the beginning of a 'New Culture Movement', directed to breaking more decisively with traditional thought and practice so that China could remedy its weaknesses. More practically, the Foreign Ministry calculated that the best means of regaining Shandong was to raise it at the peace conference, given that the 1898 agreement had not permitted Germany to reassign its rights.[74] Yuan sought a pretext to enter the war, liaising with an Australian ex-journalist who served as an adviser, George Ernest Morrison. By the end of 1915 the European Allies were keener for China to enter, so that it could expel enemy nationals and deliver supplies to Russia. Morrison proposed that China should cite un-neutral acts by Germans on its territory in order to declare war, in the hope of Allied loans to re-equip its arsenals and of a seat at the peace conference. Yuan was willing to go to war in return for an Allied loan; but when Britain, France, and Russia sounded out Japan the latter objected, guided by military opposition.[75] The Japanese feared intervention would strengthen Chinese nationalism, raise China's diplomatic status, and improve its position at the peace conference; and Grey promised not to discuss concessions to China in return for intervention except in consultation with Tokyo.[76]

Yuan's real preoccupations were domestic. He had long aspired to restore the monarchy, convening a Citizens' Convention in November 1915 to change the form of government. The European Allies warned against it and the Japanese more emphatically, moving warships to the coast and clashing with Chinese forces on the border. None the less, Yuan accepted the convention's offer of the throne, and rebellion broke out. By the time he died in June 1916 much of southern China had declared independence and a separate government had been established at Guangzhou, while the Japanese were determined to remove him. The new president was Li Yuan-hang, a former soldier who was acceptable both to north and south and to the Japanese, with the result that the republican government was nominally reunified, though its dependence on Japan deepened. But if full belligerency remained blocked, China did supply labour. Chinese officials saw the labourers—recruited by private companies to parry charges of non-neutrality—as a means of winning Allied goodwill. Contracts were first signed with the French, and between 1916 and 1918 some 43,000–44,000 men were sent to work behind the Western Front. The Battle of the Somme created a labour shortage for the British, and from autumn 1916 the British government recruited directly, eventually employing up to 100,000 Chinese (35,000 of them by April 1917). Especially under the British, hours and conditions were punishing, discipline rigorous, and pay meagre, and some 5,000 Chinese died on the journey or in Europe. Their contributions to the Allied armies, which desperately needed workers, were very considerable, although the benefit to China at the peace conference is questionable.[77]

From spring 1917 a series of developments finally opened the way to Chinese intervention. The first was that Japan lifted its veto, after General Terauchi Matasake replaced Okuma Shigenobu as premier and Baron Motono Ichirò, the former ambassador in Russia, became foreign minister. Theirs was a non-party administration, which sought consensus by setting up an advisory council on foreign affairs representing the government, the army and navy, and the political parties in the Diet.[78] Motono believed Japan had been too aggressive towards China and insufficiently cooperative with the Allies. A Cabinet resolution in January 1917 approved a policy of maintaining China's independence and integrity and of non-interference in its internal affairs, although it was agreed to exert influence by extending loans.[79] Motono told the British ambassador that Japan wanted protection for its special rights in Manchuria and Mongolia but to work with China as a partner.[80] The change was lasting, the Foreign Office's Far Eastern

Department considering the 'most extraordinary development in last year has been the sudden volte-face of Japanese Government and apparently sincere desire to create a stable government in China'.[81] The new government's broader parliamentary base may have been part of the reason, as may also have been Japan's economic leverage as its exports and investible surpluses expanded with its wartime boom. A further factor perhaps was the increasing likelihood that America would enter the war and the Allies would triumph, whereas in 1915–16 many Japanese feared they had backed the wrong horse and the government had engaged in secret contacts with the Germans.[82] Indeed, fear of the Japanese changing sides had been one reason for Allied reluctance to confront them. But in addition, with Yuan departed, the Japanese had a government in Beijing that was easier to deal with, and in early 1917 they safeguarded themselves by concluding secret agreements with Britain, France, and Russia about Germany's rights. Once again the Admiralty needed Japanese warships—cruisers to patrol the South Atlantic and destroyer escorts in the Mediterranean—and when the Foreign Office forwarded this request to Tokyo, the quid pro quo was a promise of support for Japan's claims to Germany's North Pacific islands and the Shandong lease. The former was relatively straightforward, once the Dominion governments had grudgingly acquiesced, though on the condition that Japan endorsed the British Empire's claims to Germany's South Pacific colonies. Despite its distaste for 'a political deal', the War Cabinet also agreed,[83] and on 14 February Britain promised support at the peace conference for 'Japan's claims in regard to the disposal of Germany's rights in Shantung', the Foreign Office justifying the concession to its Tokyo ambassador by invoking 'the present condition of British political and financial helplessness in the Far East'. Similar assurances came from France (which wanted Japanese assistance in encouraging China to break off relations with Germany), from Russia, and from Italy.[84]

The Japanese had therefore buttressed their position when America broke off relations with Germany and appealed to the other neutrals to do likewise. Motono told the British that Japan would support China breaking off relations and he hoped it would declare war.[85] Yet the Chinese stalled, protesting to Germany on 10 February but not breaking off relations until 14 March (or declaring war until 14 August), while Britain and America equivocated. Wilson feared 'We may be leading China to risk her doom', and Lansing considered it would be an 'immense advantage' to China to raise a big enough army to defend itself, but that Japan was likely to oppose it: America could not give assurances to the Chinese, and they should act with 'prudence' and 'caution'. In any case, Beijing should not be encouraged to declare war.[86] However, the American minister there, Paul Reinsch, a political scientist from Wisconsin who felt vulnerable because his wife and parents were German and who got on poorly with the State Department, seems not to have passed the message on. He urged the Chinese to join the war in order to emancipate their country, and gave financial assurances for which he lacked authority.[87] But the British Foreign Office also questioned the value of war entry if it undermined Chinese stability.[88] According to Baron Hardinge of Penshurst, the permanent under-secretary, the Office was 'naturally suspicious' of Japan's volte-face, but Foreign Secretary Balfour ruled that in 1915 Britain had welcomed Chinese intervention and it would be wrong now to reverse that position.[89] In fact not only was Motono urging the Chinese minister in Tokyo that China must break off relations, but the Japanese chargé in Beijing was also lobbying sympathetic officials, including the CGS, and promising Japanese loans.[90]

As for the Chinese themselves, in addition to President Li the key figures were the vice-president (Feng Guozhang), the prime minster (Duan Qirui)—the former war minister—and the foreign minister, Wu Tingfang. The government treated very seriously America's appeal to break off relations, holding four special meetings in four days, while the legislature deliberated in secret and both the Cabinet and parliament set up study groups. The British chargé, Beilby Alston, reported that most of the Cabinet favoured breaking off relations, and the foreign minister said China would do what the Americans did. Remonstrating against U-boat warfare was straightforward, as the submarines imperilled Chinese seamen and labourers in transit towards Europe. The Foreign Office estimated that up to 19 February forty-two Chinese seamen on eight vessels had lost their lives, and on 21 February three more died when the *Perseus* hit a mine off Colombo,[91] but the biggest loss came when the French steamer *Athos* was torpedoed off Malta on 17 February with 754 dead, 523 of them Chinese labourers. Yet although China's initial protest warned that it would break off relations if Germany persisted, it seems the sinkings, as for Siam, were a pretext for intervention rather than a substantive cause. On 9 February a telegram from the state council to the provincial military governors said the real, secret reasons were that unless China acted it would have no voice at the peace conference, and it could be isolated unless it followed America: a further telegram said China was not hostile to Germany, but wanted 'to avoid an isolated position'.[92]

On 3 March the Cabinet decided to break off relations, though even this step caused a rift between President Li, who was more constitutionally scrupulous and wanted to consult parliament, and Premier Duan. Duan resigned, but was quickly recalled to office, and parliament approved the breach of relations by a large majority, despite Guomindang opposition.[93] The authorities then took over the Central Powers' concessions and ships. Although Duan wanted to declare war without delay, however, a new political deadlock postponed action, and catalysed precisely the internal destabilization that British and American observers had foreseen. Part of the reason was that the Chinese government had a set of conditions (though in the end it took the plunge without being assured of them). It asked the Allies for a ten-year suspension of payments on the Boxer Indemnity and the right to raise the customs tariff to 5 per cent and eventually 12.5 per cent, as well as to occupy at least temporarily Tianjin (the port of Beijing). It also hoped for loans. To the Allies' disquiet, China's government was challenging the system of foreign domination, partly because its slackening control over the provinces was drying up its revenue. Russia, France, and Italy opposed concessions over the Boxer Indemnity, Russia and Japan opposed a tariff increase,[94] and the Americans advised that war entry was of 'secondary importance' compared to national unity and internal peace, and a divided China could give the Allies little assistance. However, the Americans took this position unilaterally (to Japanese irritation), and although Lansing invited America's partners to make similar declarations they held back.[95] Britain and France were polite, but did not agree that Chinese war entry was of secondary importance.

By this stage a process had begun that the Americans could not arrest, and such unity as remained in China was cracking. According to the British chargé, Li was well intentioned and had come to office with support from every faction, but had proved indecisive, shown poor judgement, and been badly advised.[96] Duan, in contrast, whose background was also in the army and had undertaken military studies in Berlin, was more impetuous. He had been willing to fight Japan in 1914 and 1915 but by 1917 was prepared to cooperate with Tokyo and was impatient for war against Germany; he believed intervention could bring national renewal[97] and he chafed at constitutional constraints. Having got his way over breaking off relations by threatening to resign, he was willing for more drastic steps to get China into the war. Unlike Siam, moreover, China had an embryonic public opinion: in 1915 it had 165 Chinese-language newspapers whose readership was 2–4 million in a population of 400 million.[98] Many businessmen were worried about the economic repercussions of intervention and feared China was too weak; others saw Japan, not Germany, as the real enemy; while Sun Yat-sen favoured continuing neutrality, not least because of past encroachments on China's sovereignty by the Allies.[99] Although most of the Guomindang were willing to support a declaration of war, they feared Duan would use it to borrow money and repress opposition or restore the monarchy. The struggle between Li and Duan bore comparison with that between Constantine and Venizelos, and it too reflected uncertainty over the head of state's powers.

Finally Duan took the fateful step of applying pressure on the president and on parliament by convening a conference of the provincial military governors, the *dujun*, many of whom owed him allegiance. With the *dujun* in the background, the Cabinet decided on 1 May to recommend a declaration of war, which the legislature might have approved had it not been for the *dujun* organizing a crowd to surround the parliament building, the protestors demanding a declaration at once. The legislature resolved it would pass a declaration only if the government were reorganized. When Duan called on Li to dissolve parliament the president said he had no power to do so and instead dismissed Duan, turning for support to another military governor, Zhang Xun, who marched on Beijing but in order to reinstate dynastic rule, Li himself then resigning. Duan, now posing as the defender of the republic, regained the premiership in July, while Li was replaced by Li's deputy and on 14 August the restored Duan government finally declared war.[100] The declaration deplored the U-boat campaign and said China was upholding international law and protecting Chinese lives and property,[101] but Duan also disclosed to parliament that intervention would enable higher tariffs and postponement of the Boxer Indemnity, while China supplied labour and raw materials to the Allies: Germany was nearing collapse and China otherwise risked isolation.[102] Regardless, the Guomindang delegation withdrew from parliament and again set up a separate government in the south, which also declared war on the Central Powers, and in September fighting between the two governments began. China entered a phase of endemic civil war—the 'warlord era'—that would last for over a decade.

Both Duan and Li had been willing to go to war against Germany, but both had seen it as not just an international gesture but also an internal move. Allied loans offered an advantage in the domestic struggle,[103] and Japan did, in fact, extend to Duan a 10 million yen credit. The Japanese

Cabinet decided to back him and refuse help to the south, and the British agreed.[104] Yet Duan brought in China on the basis of assurances of goodwill but no definite Allied commitments,[105] and against American advice. And the intervention process proved so divisive that it weakened the Beijing government externally, as a comparison between China's wartime contribution and its recompense makes evident.

Chinese intervention meant, as elsewhere, that the Central Powers' ships in Chinese harbours were impounded and their citizens interned or expelled.[106] Beyond that, China's main contribution remained the labourers until France and Britain ceased recruiting them, primarily due to transport shortages, in spring 1918. The Chinese became one of the biggest contingents in the BEF's workforce, and for the most part executed their arduous and unglamorous duties to their employers' full satisfaction. Unlike Greece, Brazil, or Siam, however, China provided no combat personnel. Its army expanded from 457,000 in 1914 to 850,000 in 1918 and the military budget rose by one-third in 1916–18, but the troops were poorly equipped and trained, and British observers remained unimpressed.[107] Duan, who resigned as premier in November but as head of the War Participation Bureau continued to oversee the war effort, was keen to despatch combat forces and the Cabinet resolved in favour of sending 20,000–30,000 men. However, although the Allies discussed the possibility into early 1918, French enthusiasm was countered by American unwillingness to pay; and by the usual absence of transport. Eventually and reluctantly the French said no.[108] Additionally, the Japanese objected to Chinese troops going to Europe, as they had decided not to go themselves;[109] the Tokyo general staff wanted to keep their forces close to home in order to strengthen 'Japan's position in eastern Asia so that she would be able, after the war, to withstand the competition of the Western Powers in China'.[110] Hence the idea lost impetus, and China's armies found alternative employment in their own land.

China's lack of a military contribution weakened it financially and politically. During the war it received no concessions over tariff autonomy or the Boxer Indemnity, beyond cancellation of Germany's and Austria-Hungary's Boxer payments. Nor did it receive American loans. Instead the Beijing government's biggest creditor was Japan, which demanded in exchange free movement for its troops and a further series of treaties, one of which again recognized its right to Germany's interests in Shandong. Something similar was implicit in the Lansing–Ishii Agreement, signed on 2 November 1917 by Lansing and by Ishii Kikujiro, a former Japanese foreign minister who headed a mission to Washington. The Japanese government was aware of America's growing economic strength and its military and naval build-up, and wanted continuing access to American steel, which threatened to be redirected to home industry and the European Allies. Hence Japan had reason to seek an accommodation; but so did the Americans, who were concerned about Japan but wanted to postpone a confrontation at least until after the war. Lansing may have feared a German–Japanese alliance,[111] and he had long sought an arrangement whereby America would acknowledge Japan's sphere of interest in northern China as long as the independence of the rest of the country and equal economic access to it were respected.[112] Hence according to the public part of the agreement, 'the United States recognizes that Japan has special interests in China, particularly in the part to which her possessions are contiguous', but 'the territorial sovereignty of China remains unimpaired'. The Japanese government had wanted the formula *special interest and influence*', but Ishii warned Tokyo that insisting could cause the talks to collapse. On the other hand, a secret protocol bound both parties to refrain from exploiting the present state of affairs in order to seek 'special rights or privileges in China which would abridge the rights of subjects of other friendly states'.[113] Lansing said the text would leave 'ample room for suitable interpretations on both sides', and after the war he and Ishii publicly disagreed over what it meant.[114] But in the short term he was content with the agreement, which the Japanese represented as a victory, whereas the Chinese government, which was not consulted closely, voiced disappointment and refused to acknowledge it.[115] Lansing argued, disingenuously, that he had deliberately excluded the Chinese so that they would not be bound.[116] None the less, whereas the Chinese government declared war in the hope of representation at the peace conference, the better thereby to challenge Japan over Shandong, the spring 1917 agreements between Japan and the European Allies had strengthened Tokyo's claim before China entered and without Beijing's knowledge. The Japanese had secured treaty acknowledgement of their claims from the Chinese themselves in 1915 and in 1918, and the Lansing–Ishii Agreement implied American willingness to acquiesce in Japan's position in those areas of China—Manchuria and Shandong—to which it lay closest. All of this rendered China's peace conference attendance in 1919 largely meaningless. And although at the conference the Shandong issue did cause a crisis, the European Allies accepted that their 1917 agreements bound them, whereas Wilson's own principle of respecting treaties left him isolated and with his hands tied.[117] He still secured some concessions for China, but its delegates walked out in protest against Germany's Shandong rights being transferred to Japan: an outcome that sparked the 'May Fourth Movement' of nationwide intellectual and popular protest.[118] Although Shandong was eventually returned to China at the Washington Conference of 1921–2, America and the West were discredited in China and Chinese nationalists now sought inspiration from elsewhere.

By the end of 1917 most of the world's population had entered a state of belligerency. Even during the Napoleonic Wars this situation had no precedent. Two impetuses to the process came from the unrestricted submarine campaign and from American entry. The first threatened death and destruction to almost every country; the second made neutrality less attractive and joining the Allies more so. Yet the new belligerents made their own decisions, which were frequently contested. In China intervention led to civil war, and in Greece to something close to it; in Brazil it prompted civil disorder and repression of the German–Brazilians. In China, the issue became embroiled with the contests between Duan and Li and between the northern Chinese warlords and the Guomindang. Intervention became a gambit in a domestic struggle, with Duan holding the advantage. Brazilian public opinion was always pro-Allied in tendency, but it took the submarine sinkings to create a Congress majority for belligerency. Finally, in Siam the government had no legislature to contend with, and once the king insisted on intervention his foreign minister assented.

None of the four countries envisaged an all-out struggle, which makes their interventions easier to comprehend. So does US entry, which made the Allies more likely to win. Indeed, America also initially envisaged a limited commitment, but unlike the other new arrivals it subsequently expanded it. China, Brazil, and Siam were remote from the Central Powers and therefore ran little risk. Greece ran a bigger one, as a fighting front ran through its northern territory, and of the four it made the biggest military contribution. But the costs and risks should be set against the prospective gains. For Brazil these were primarily economic. For Siam and China the additional incentive was gaining traction against the unequal treaties, the Chinese being particularly focused on the Shandong lease. In Greece Venizelos wanted Bulgarian and Turkish territories that might support a glittering future in the Eastern Mediterranean and Aegean. The prize all sought was a voice in the peace settlement.

These objectives would be satisfied unequally and tardily; and in Greece's case scarcely at all. But the widening of the war through new interventions

II

Responsible Government
for India

The policy of His Majesty's Government, with which the Government of India are in full accord, is that of the increasing association of India in every branch of the administration and the gradual development of self-governing institutions with a view to the progressive realization of responsible government in India as an integral part of the British Empire. They have decided that substantial steps in this direction should be taken as soon as possible...I should accept the Viceroy's invitation to proceed to discuss those matters with the Viceroy and the Government of India, to consider with the Viceroy the views of local Governments, and to receive with him the suggestions of representative bodies and others.

(Edwin Montagu, Secretary of State for India,
declaration in the House of Commons, 20 August 1917).[1]

As the European Powers ground each other down, their global predominance withered. In August 1917 the British government committed itself to 'responsible government' in India, a policy for which precedents existed only in the 'white' Dominions of Canada, Newfoundland, South Africa, Australia, and New Zealand. Implicitly the declaration marked the lifting of a colour bar, and recognition that colonial peoples of non-European origin could govern themselves. As Sir Algernon Rumbold put it, 'The British abdication in India, and in particular the statement made in 1917...set the pattern for the dismantlement of the whole British Empire and the Empires of all western democracies.'[2] For this development to occur at the time and in the manner that it did, the precondition was the war.

India had contributed more than any other overseas possession to Britain's global status. Its importance rested primarily on the Indian army, whose size was comparable to the forces in the British Isles. When war broke out it comprised 78,000 European personnel and 158,000 Indians.[3] Between 1857 and 1914 Indian troops served in campaigns from China to Egypt, and on the eve of war they were providing garrisons in Egypt, China, the Indian Ocean, and Singapore. It had been agreed that Indian taxpayers should bear primary financial responsibility for operations where India had a 'direct and substantial interest', including in Egypt, Persia, and Afghanistan.[4] And because since the 1857 rebellion at least a third of the army was European, and Indians were denied officer commissions, it cost much more than an all-Indian force would have done. It added to the 'home charges' that the Government of India (GOI) paid in sterling for the pensions of officers and civil servants who had retired to Britain, as well as for debt interest and for purchases of stores. The burden was onerous, as the GOI feared that raising taxes would stir unrest, and it was denied authority to augment import tariffs. Its 3.5 per cent general tariff was offset by an excise duty levied on Indian-made cotton goods in order to protect the Lancashire cotton industry. India was Britain's largest export market in 1913–14, and the biggest purchaser of British cotton textiles and of iron and steel. It accounted for a tenth of British overseas investment, placed primarily in the railways.[5] In fact, Britain's trade surplus with India went far to compensate for its deficits with other industrialized nations. Its control of India was critical for its staple industries as well as its strategic reach.

The constitutional arrangements for British rule had evolved over a century and a half. After 1857 direct responsibility to the government in London replaced control by the East India Company. The Secretary of State for India answered to the Westminster Parliament (whose attention to Indian affairs was fitful) and was advised by the Council of India, a body composed mainly of former officials. The GOI (which had moved in 1912 from Calcutta to Delhi), came under the Viceroy. His Executive Council, comprising the heads of the administrative departments, included in 1914 just one Indian member; the Legislative Council, which passed all-India legislation, included elected Indians, but most of its members were appointees. One-third of the subcontinent came not under Delhi but remained as princely states linked to British India by treaties and by European advisers. Within British India, the three presidencies of Bombay (Mumbai), Bengal, and Madras (Chennai) had governors and legislative councils, as did some smaller provinces. Under the Morley–Minto reforms, approved in 1909, provincial legislative councils were expanded to include more elected Indians, but neither at central nor at provincial level did the executive depend on a majority in the legislature. On this critical point India resembled Imperial Germany rather than the UK.

In practice much of India's governance was conducted through what its nationalist critics maligned as 'the bureaucracy', and the system remained autocratic, though operating within a framework of law and allowing considerable civil liberties, including for the press, political parties, and religion (the British Raj being officially neutral in matters of faith). It depended on the civil service, the police, and the army, all of whose junior ranks were predominantly Indian. But their senior ranks were not, and the Indian Civil Service, whose members held the key official roles, was overwhelmingly European.

After 1885 the British refrained from territorial expansion. Their rule brought a measure of internal peace, as well as posts and telegraphs and the fourth-largest railway network in the world. Whether it raised living standards is disputed, but the pre-war decade saw generally good harvests and relative prosperity. The regime also brought Western, English-medium education, whose imprint would endure. The Indian National Congress (INC), founded in 1885, campaigned to strengthen a unified national consciousness, extend self-government, and redress grievances, though its agenda fell short of independence and it ruled out illegality and violence. At first it was a decorous lobbying body rather than a continuously organized opposition, and much of its membership came from the high-caste and Western-educated lawyers, teachers, and journalists of the coastal cities. In 1900 the then Viceroy Lord Curzon predicted Congress was 'tottering to its fall, and one of my greatest ambitions while in India is to assist it to a peaceful demise'.[6] Nor had it much reach among the Muslims, who comprised about a quarter of India's 303 million population in 1911, and in Bengal and the Punjab formed the majority.[7] The 1909 reforms allowed them to comprise separate electorates, thus ensuring they could return representatives even in provinces where they were a minority. The All-India Muslim League, established in 1906, worked with Congress down to 1914, despite worsening inter-communal violence at the grass roots. The INC had acquired a more radical wing, led by Bal Gangadhar Tilak and influenced by Hindu revivalism, which wanted self-governing institutions and employed direct action. In 1907, however, at the Surat Congress, the moderates regained control, while Muslim agitation against a British decision to partition Bengal subsided when in 1912 the British annulled the measure. On the eve of war Indian politics seemed quieter than for several years. The Viceroy, now Baron Hardinge of Penshurst, and the Secretary of State, Lord Crewe, made statements apparently debarring India from ever becoming independent or achieving Dominion status, Hardinge writing that 'there can be no question as to the permanency of British rule'.[8] Whereas earlier nineteenth-century liberals such as Thomas Macaulay had envisaged that India would eventually become self-governing, albeit steeped in British cultural borrowings, later commentators assumed the Raj would last indefinitely.[9] Support for independence was confined to radical pressure groups and a handful of British MPs.

At first the war seemed to consolidate British rule, and only as the conflict lengthened did it undermine it. This generalization also applied in Ireland, as indeed in autocracies such as Germany and Russia. At first the INC supported the war effort, and only 850 attended its Congress in December 1914. The GOI felt able to take chances. The chief danger spot lay on the North-West Frontier, where Pathan tribes might rebel with backing from Afghanistan, the British depending on the goodwill of the Amir Habibulla in Kabul. Hardinge kept on the frontier the three divisions normally stationed there, but relinquished nearly all the other regular British units and most of the Indian ones[10]: 'It was a big risk, but I took it, in spite of the repeated and vigorous protests of the Commander-in-Chief and some of the European community, as I trusted the people of India... and my confidence was not misplaced.'[11] India sent two infantry and two cavalry divisions to Europe, and twelve battalions to East Africa; when Turkey became a belligerent, India sent a division to Basra. A third of the British forces on the Western Front in the 1914–15 winter came from the subcontinent. To replace them in India, the authorities shipped out thirty-five territorial field batteries: older men, less well-trained, and with obsolete equipment. In the opinion of the GOI's Army Department, India in late 1916 still fell 'dangerously below the safety level...It is not too much to say that at the present moment the military security of India rests largely on a well-established military prestige and on the trust reposed in a just and paternal administration.'[12] Even in peacetime the European population in India was tiny: in 1921 about 156,000 men, women, and children, or one to every 1,500 Indians,[13] with most of the men serving in the army, civil service, or police. India never became a white-settler colony, and British authority's flimsy foundations should be kept in mind.

The British did not, however, face a physical force challenge like that of 1857. Some 6,000 Sikhs returned to the Punjab in the winter of 1914–15 as part of the *Ghadr* or 'mutiny' movement, and violent protest broke out in 1915, but was quickly put down. A terrorist campaign by Hindu nationalists in Bengal demoralized the local police, whose intelligence officers were murdered, but by 1917 this movement too was being contained.[14] Although unrest among the North-West Frontier tribes did grow, the Amir of Afghanistan did not aid them, and by the end of 1915 the GOI received reinforcements. Given Muslim sepoys' prominence in 1857, the authorities were also concerned about the army. Before 1914 some younger Muslims had begun transferring their allegiance from the Christian British to the Turkish Sultan in his capacity as Muslim caliph. Yet the army generally stayed loyal, even when fighting Ottoman forces. Hankey noted that Britain's eastern empire 'depends on prestige and bluff', but these commodities proved more robust than many had feared.[15]

Instead the challenge to British paramountcy was more subtle, and in some degree a paradoxical by-product of India's contribution to the war effort. Although Indian infantry left the Western Front in summer 1915, for a year they had fought alongside British regulars against the most formidable army in Europe, as well as defending the empire in the Middle East. Over 35,000 men went abroad to work in supply and transport, and military recruitment, which ran to 15,000 annually in peacetime, jumped to 178,700 between 1 August 1914 and 30 June 1916. By early 1917, 67,450 British and 105,300 Indian troops had gone overseas, and Indian killed, wounded, missing, and captured totalled 67,213.[16] Recruitment extended outwards from the Sikh and Pathan 'martial races' to whom the British had increasingly confined it.[17] India was the main supply base for the Mesopotamian campaign, and a principal one for Egypt and Palestine. It manufactured 145,000 rifles and over a million shells, delivering manganese, wolfram, and saltpetre for UK munitions production.[18] By summer 1915 the Calcutta jute mills were producing 50 million sandbags a month, two-thirds of British requirements. India supplied leather for more than 3 million pairs of army boots, as well, by 1917, as 25,000,000 hundredweight of wheat and more than 180,000 pack animals.[19] Whereas the GOI's pre-1914 annual revenue averaged £85–90 million, up to March 1917 it had already remitted to Britain £71.5 million (for war expenditure and for purchasing commodities), as well as spending £35 million on war securities and £11.5 million on expeditionary forces.[20] War finance entailed an increase in the money supply, shortages of basic products such as kerosene, and a rise in the price index from 147 in 1914 to 152 in 1915, 184 in 1916, and 196 in 1917.[21] By the later war years India was becoming a cauldron of discontent, even if the root of its problems—like Russia's—was pressure on resources due to rapid development. None the less, the most immediate internal influence on the Montagu Declaration was the wartime transformation of nationalist politics.

Economic pressures assisted this transformation, but its roots lay deeper. Before 1914 British administrators distinguished between a 'moderate' INC wing led by Gopal Krishna Gokhale and an 'extremist' wing under Tilak. They supported the former against the latter, and after 1914 they tried to do so again. Tilak was detained in Burma and the moderates controlled Congress, but once the conflict proved not to be over within weeks the movement grew more radical. Tilak returned from Burma, and although internment had chastened him, attempts at compromise with Gokhale still ended in disagreement.[22] As fighting extended into 1915, and Indian troops attacked in France at Neuve Chapelle, repelled a Turkish offensive against the Suez Canal, and marched on Baghdad, observers noted a growing sense that India's role should be acknowledged. One expression of that sense was a demand for Dominion status, not least to head off a federation between Britain and the existing Dominions that would relegate India to the second tier. Long-standing grievances such as Indians' inability to become commissioned officers now seemed intolerable.[23] During 1915 the moderates suffered from the deaths of two leaders, Gokhale and Pherozeshah Mehta, and the December 1915 Congress passed resolutions allowing Tilak and his followers to re-enter the movement.[24] Whereas only 856 delegates had attended the 1914 INC annual gathering at Madras, some 2,190 delegates attended at Bombay in 1915 and 2,249 at Lucknow in 1916.[25]

Two further 1916 developments made the situation more menacing: the emergence of the Home Rule Leagues and a Hindu–Muslim rapprochement. Tilak modelled himself on Irish nationalism and established a Home Rule League,[26] as did Annie Besant, who although of Irish descent was a long-standing Indian resident and a political activist with many British well-wishers.[27] Her gender, her age (nearly 70), and her ethnicity made her harder to silence, and she travelled the length of the country, denouncing British rule as exploitative and repressive, while professing loyalty to the Crown and avoiding incitement to violence. Adapting the old Fenian slogan, she saw that 'England's difficulty is India's opportunity', and the two Home Rule Leagues began campaigning in the aftermath of Ireland's Easter Rising. Unlike Congress, they set up local branches and reached social strata and recesses in the interior where nationalism had failed to take root. They formed a permanent opposition with a new vociferousness.[28] They were

Figure 16. Photograph of Annie Besant from 1917

also impatient, Besant demanding Home Rule (which if on the Irish model meant full Indian control over internal affairs) immediately.

Given that Tilak's supporters could now lobby within Congress, it was likely to grow more extreme. But if it did so, the Hindu and Muslim communities might drift apart. Although the INC was supposedly a secular and All-India body, representation of Muslims at its annual sessions (0.81 per cent in 1914 and 3.77 per cent in 1916) was weak;[29] and whereas Gokhale and the 'moderates' wanted to westernize Indian society, Tilak and his followers wished to uphold Hindu traditions. The separate electorates granted to the Muslims in 1909 had shaken moderates' confidence in British rule. No more than the Hindus, however, were the Muslims monolithic, and whereas an older 'conservative' generation of community leaders had shunned participation in Congress, a younger 'nationalist' group was more willing to work alongside it. Muhammad Ali Jinnah, later credited as the father of Pakistan, was a leading example. He and Besant pressed for reconciliation, and at the end of 1915 Congress and the Muslim League agreed to seek a joint programme. In September 1916 nineteen Indian members of the central legislative council published a constitutional reform scheme. Once the Congress side reluctantly agreed to separate electorates, the key question became how many seats the Muslim constituencies should command,

and the proposed solution was fewer than the Hindus wanted in the United Provinces but fewer than the Muslims wanted in the Punjab and Bengal. Although the Muslim League remained comparatively tiny (only 500–800 members in 1915–16),[30] and many Muslims had doubts about cooperation, both bodies' leaders wanted rapid devolution to elected assemblies, with safeguards for minorities. This understanding became known as the Lucknow Pact.

The British response would lead to the Montagu Declaration in 1917, the Montagu–Chelmsford report in 1918, and the Government of India Act in 1919. Its essence was not repression but conciliation, not only over the constitution but also over grievances such as the cotton excise and officer commissions. Certainly repression was feasible: the police numbered 200,000 and the army 250,000, and the administration had the power to pass whatever legislation it wanted; to break up demonstrations; to censor the press; and to imprison, try, and execute its opponents. But the risks were higher once political consciousness was roused, the army's best units were overseas, and its soldiers possibly unreliable; and the authorities had tolerated freedom of organization for activists who remained within the law. British rule depended on willing cooperation by hundreds of thousands of Indians. It rested on a balance between coercion and concession, but as the war progressed it moved first towards the former and then towards the latter. A striking feature in this evolution was how the GOI 'bureaucracy' became reform's strongest advocate, first requesting and then insisting on a home government response. Delhi led the process, and eventually not unanimity but surprisingly wide support formed across Raj officialdom. Controversy and delay were greatest in London.

Before the war Hardinge had dismissed self-government as 'ridiculous and absurd'.[31] But his thinking had altered by the time of his 'Memorandum by H. E. the Viceroy upon Questions likely to arise in India at the End of the War', submitted in October 1915. Hardinge now warned that the conflict had encouraged India's political development and heightened its self-esteem; concessions were needed to maintain faith in British justice, 'the cornerstone of British rule in India', and whereas accommodations would reinforce 'the golden chain' binding India to the empire, to deny legitimate aspirations might have 'far-reaching and disastrous consequences'. The 1909 reforms had 'opened a door to political progress that cannot now be closed': timely concessions were needed to manage the evolution peacefully. They included concrete changes over officer commissions and the cotton excise, but also devolution to the provincial governments and Indian-elected majorities in the provincial legislative councils.[32]

Hardinge's memorandum, printed and bound in red leather, was sent when India remained relatively quiet. It had little immediate impact. The War Office continued to oppose commissions for Indians and Asquith's Cabinet hesitated to confront Lancashire over excise duties.[33] But Viscount Chelmsford, who replaced Hardinge as Viceroy in March 1916, brought a mandate for change. Chelmsford had qualified as a barrister and was a captain in the Dorset Regiment, with which he served in India in 1914–15. He remains enigmatic: a lifelong Conservative and yet a quietly pertinacious reformer. He was affronted by the 'accentuated racial antagonism' that he found in India, considering it 'the most serious problem that we had to face and the one most full of menace to British rule'.[34] Possibly he had learned from being a governor in Australia, where he had resisted a progressive ministry in Queensland but later worked successfully with another in New South Wales; and he had contact with the Round Table group of imperial federationists, which had been debating India's constitutional status. The Asquith coalition government chose him as a liberal Conservative, in this resembling the Secretary of State, Austen Chamberlain. Once in post, Chelmsford promoted progressives onto his Executive Council and as heads of provinces.[35] But his main concern was that the GOI seemed 'aimless', responding to events in a 'hand-to-mouth' fashion, and without a policy for 'the political future'.[36] Hence he asked the Executive Council two questions: '(1) What is the goal of British rule in India? (2) What are the first steps on the road to that goal?'[37] As the same questions had been asked by the Congress Party president, S. P. Sinla (a moderate whom the British frequently consulted), a Congress-led agenda was thus fed into the heart of the Raj.[38] Chelmsford's practice, however, was to consult his Council, often withholding his own opinions, and to move collectively: he found its members very willing to discuss his questions and 'very much concerned about the situation'. He also found them more agreed than he had expected, and by July they could send out a text to the provincial governments:[39]

> The only goal to which we can look forward is to endow India, as an integral part of the British Empire, with the largest measure of Self-Government compatible with the supremacy of British rule...we contemplate her gradual progress towards a larger and larger measure of control by her own people, but the form of Self-Government which she can ultimately enjoy must be evolved on lines which take into account her special circumstances and traditions.

Progress should take place in three directions: devolution of authority (to elected Indian politicians) in local government; increasing numbers of Indians in official positions, including senior ones, to train them in running their affairs; and a larger elected component in the provincial and central legislative councils. After consulting the provinces, the GOI sent its recommendations in a 'Reforms Despatch' to Chamberlain on 24 November.[40] This again emphasized the war, the Indians' loyalty that had enabled troops to move elsewhere, and their resistance to the enemy's siren songs. Better conditions were needed for the Indian army, and specific grievances should be met; but above all Britain must set 'The Goal before India', and whereas before 1914 to have done so might have been premature, wartime developments had 'taken the decision out of our hands'. Even so, the despatch proposed only a ponderous and heavily qualified formulation: 'The goal to which we look forward is the endowment of British India, as an integral part of the Empire, with self-government, but the rate of progress towards the goal must depend upon the improvement and wide diffusion of education, the softening of racial and religious differences, and the acquisition of political experience.' This was hardly a clarion call, nor even unanimous. The majority of the Executive Council felt that India's constitution should not yet be determined, and the Dominions were not necessarily a model. The provincial legislative councils would have an increased elected element, but not necessarily the central council; and although the provincial (but not central) executive councils would be half Indian, their chairmen would remain British. Sir Reginald Craddock, the most conservative member of the Executive Council, appended a memorandum of dissent. But Sir Sankaran Nair, the Council's one Indian member, felt the proposals fell short, and disagreed with his colleagues' decision to retain separate Muslim electorates. Nair had been influenced by a memorandum from the Indian members of the Imperial Legislative Council, who wanted substantial majorities of elected representatives on all legislative councils and for India to receive something close to Dominion status. Even though foreign and defence policy would remain with London, Chelmsford thought this document 'preposterous'.[41]

Several points stand out. The first is the leisurely pace: the GOI took six months to complete its consultation. The starting impulse came from Chelmsford (probably encouraged by London), and although in a general sense the war determined the timing, the Executive Council did not feel it was responding to India's demands: on the contrary, Chelmsford hoped to head off agitation.[42] Sir James Meston, the Lieutenant Governor of the United Provinces, saw the purpose as 'the rewarding of India's loyalty and the timely grant of concessions to India's aspirations', so as to strengthen the moderates against the extremists and to guide the country through a difficult period *after* the war.[43] One of Chelmsford's signature characteristics, however, was that he opposed delaying until the war ended, and his proposals not only incorporated Hardinge's ideas but also went further and faster.[44] Convinced that 'we cannot stand still',[45] he wanted not just to deal ad hoc with grievances, but also to set an overall objective of preparing Indians for greater self-government, albeit as continuing members of the empire and with not only defence and foreign policy but also key domestic functions remaining under British control.

The Reform Despatch presented proposals. But *decisions*, especially constitutional decisions, must be taken in London. By August 1917 a decision in principle had been taken, but the process was slow and contentious. When the Reform Despatch arrived in December 1916 Lloyd George had replaced Asquith, and although the new prime minister had no particular interest in Indian constitutional issues (not even mentioning the Montagu Declaration in his War Memoirs), he had reformist instincts, wanted to get things done, and to get more for the war effort from India and the Dominions. As Austen Chamberlain put it, whereas Asquith had never pushed or driven, Lloyd George was quite the reverse, determined not to fail on the same grounds. He wanted Empire troops to replace British ones in the Middle East, and had exaggerated notions of what India could do.[46] When Meston visited London he found gratitude, but also 'a feeling that India does not realize the gravity of the situation, or the need for casting aside its customary caution and reserve, in the face of a tremendous Imperial crisis'.[47]

In 1917–18 India's economic and manpower contributions indeed expanded; and the imperial government was forced to address the grievances that Hardinge and Chelmsford had identified, at the same time as it clawed towards 'responsible government'. The grievances involved finance, officer commissions, and India's imperial status, as well as its constitution. Under the first heading, the GOI offered in October 1916 to take over £50 million of British government war debt, but Asquith and Bonar Law warned that £100 million was expected.[48] The GOI estimated it could find that sum if it exploited all available revenues, primarily by borrowing but also by slashing civil expenditure and by raising taxes on the highest incomes.[49] India was a very poor country and Chelmsford did not want to help 'extremists and agitators' by increasing land or salt tax, but the GOI insisted on raising the tariff on imported cotton goods to 7.5 per cent and wanted a pledge to end the excise on Indian–produced cotton goods as soon as funds permitted.[50] Chelmsford believed he could carry his Legislative Council for the financial contribution because of the rise in the cotton tariff; but the corollary was a fierce parliamentary struggle in London, where Chamberlain noted the 'violence and unanimity' in Lancashire, whose MPs lobbied him and Lloyd George. The Cabinet was willing to call an election if defeated in the Commons, and Lloyd George was very firm, but the opposition did not press the issue and resistance collapsed, an indication of how the new premier would fight battles that his predecessor had shrunk from.[51]

The new government also wanted extra soldiers. By the second half of the war manpower was a critical variable for all the belligerents, and India became the British Empire's biggest reserve, providing more and more of Mesopotamia's and Palestine's requirements so that British and Dominion forces could concentrate on the Western Front. But to expand, the Indian army needed more officers. In November 1915 Hardinge had reported that he and his Executive Council believed at least a limited number of Indian commissions were needed to maintain the army's 'loyalty, contentment, and good-will', and although the commander–in–chief, Sir Beauchamp Duff, objected, Hardinge considered Duff's position no longer tenable 'in the face of all that is happening around us'.[52] Duff considered that Indian troops' physical bravery did not mean that Indians had the moral courage needed in officers, and demand for commissions would come from far beyond the martial races. British troops in wartime would not accept commands from an Indian, and Indian troops might resist an officer of a different faith. Hardinge considered the problem was not getting British soldiers to accept an Indian's orders, but British *officers*. None the less, for the moment the issue drifted.

The new element under Lloyd George was a recruitment drive. Although Chelmsford's Reforms Despatch mentioned Indian officer commissions, it was Chamberlain who wanted practical recommendations. He warned the Viceroy that the Cabinet assumed the war would last 'throughout 1918', and it would expect 'considerable extra help from India next year'.[53] Chelmsford replied that recruiting another 100,000 would be challenging. Duff's successor as commander–in–chief, Sir Charles Monro, considered the officer problem the most serious restraint, as officers should be conversant with their soldiers' languages and customs, such knowledge took time to acquire; and many officers had died.[54] Chamberlain acknowledged that 'the difficulty about officers is the chief limiting factor in your military effort'.[55] In fact Monro was more accommodating than his predecessor. He feared discouraging applications from families that had hereditarily applied for officer service in the Indian army and who represented 'the best type of English gentlemen', but he accepted the need to admit a limited number of 'carefully selected' applicants from the martial races, 'who by their character, upbringing and family traditions, are likely to develop, with training, into officers of a type capable of association with English gentlemen on terms of social equality'.[56] This commentary confirmed that the difficulty lay in placing Indians in authority over (and sharing a mess with) British officers. But even if Monro moved a little, the War Office did not. On 1 June Chamberlain urged on Derby, the Secretary of State for War, that 'In view of the difficulty of employing sufficient officers of pure European descent to the Indian army, of the effect on recruiting of the racial bar, of the Government of India's strong recommendation, of the widespread demand in India for higher military employment for Indians, and of India's services to the Empire during the war...the time has come when the principle of granting commissions to Indians must be admitted.' He put forward the names of nine men, all having served overseas since 1914 and two holding the Military Cross. Five weeks later the War Office responded tersely that the proposal 'would entail a great risk from a military point of view, in that it involves placing native Indian officers in a position where they would be entitled to command European officers': the matter should be deferred until after the war. Chamberlain forwarded the correspondence to the War Cabinet for a ruling, presenting the issue as integral to the 'partnership' with the empire desired by moderate Indian politicians.[57] By the time it came to the Cabinet on 2 August, Edwin Montagu had replaced Chamberlain, but the two men were agreed. Montagu told the Cabinet it was untenable to say an Indian could exert authority over Europeans if he were a judge or a civilian official, but never in the army: the matter was causing 'the profoundest dissatisfaction' and 'very gravely hampering recruiting'. He was supported by Lord Curzon, who as a former Viceroy carried authority as the War Cabinet's Indian expert, and who during his own time in India had prepared proposals that the then commander, Lord Kitchener, had blocked. Milner and Smuts and Bonar Law also backed the proposal, as did the Labour War Cabinet members, Arthur Henderson and George Barnes. The colonial secretary, Walter Long, concurred, though warned of 'trouble' if

Indians commanded Australian or Canadian troops. Derby was therefore outnumbered. Not only was he himself 'strongly against' the proposal, but he believed the 'vast majority' of the British serving in the Indian army agreed with him, so recruitment of both officers and men would suffer. But backing for the War Office position came only from Carson, who warned that Indian students admitted to the British bar had mostly failed and had returned to India 'disgusted, resentful, and hostile', going on to support 'seditionary movements'. Still, the Cabinet majority was decisive, even though Lloyd George himself stayed out of the debate.[58] Perhaps it helped that this was a change in principle rather than of substance, with little immediate impact. But given the balance of risks between displeasing the Indians in the Indian army and displeasing the British, the Cabinet had opted for the latter.

The third issue on which the government acted was India's imperial status. One of Lloyd George's earliest steps was to convene an Imperial War Conference, which met between March and May 1917, the Dominion leaders travelling to London for briefings on the war effort as well as attending the expanded War Cabinet. Once again, behind this initiative lay concern for more resources and troops.[59] Whereas at pre-1914 imperial conferences the GOI had not been represented, this time it was,[60] and the conference discussed bars by other Dominions on Indian immigrants. Canada, for example, excluded Indian women almost completely, as their admission would 'make perpetual in their midst a colony of an alien race who do not, and cannot, assimilate as do peoples of the European stock'. Although the British government did not press the principle sought by Indian nationalists of their unqualified right to settle anywhere in the empire, the Dominions did agree not to treat Indians worse than other 'Asiatics'.[61] Furthermore, the GOI consented to prohibit except under licence the export by sea of indentured Indian labourers, which campaigners had condemned as inhumane; although here too there was an ulterior motive of prioritizing 50,000 Indian labourers whom Lloyd George had requested for service in Europe.[62]

On the central, constitutional issues raised in Chelmsford's Reform Despatch, however, progress was slower, a response being delayed first at the India Office and then in the War Cabinet, while the Indian political position deteriorated and Chelmsford's patience ran out. The despatch took five weeks to reach London by sea. Chamberlain felt inexperienced to judge it, and referred it to a committee at the India Office under Sir William Duke.[63] At this stage Chelmsford said there was no hurry, given how long the GOI had taken to prepare it.[64] The committee was favourable, but thought the proposed declaration too vague and restrictive.[65] Chamberlain told Chelmsford on 29 March that 'the opinion of the vocal classes is moving very fast... The fact is that all the world is in a state of revolution... Opinion cannot but be excited by the Russian revolution, by the congratulations showered upon the revolutionaries from England and elsewhere, and by the constant appeals to the spirit of liberty and nationality...' Yet having acknowledged the urgency, he wanted to refer the question to another committee or even a royal commission, and still withheld his own views. Meston reported from London that 'there is a good deal of hesitation about a decision', and 'The atmosphere here is very conservative.' The king opposed a pronouncement, and 'any form of declaration seems to be viewed with apprehension by the India Office';[66] while Chamberlain pleaded that he had to attend meetings every day and needed time to consider. A month later, on 7 May, Chelmsford still knew little of Chamberlain's views and, although the Viceroy had heard rumours that the dispatch was seen as ultra-progressive, 'I can only say having regard to the pace [at] which the world is moving, it almost appears to me as reactionary.' His Council opposed a commission, which would waste more time;[67] they preferred Chamberlain to come to India. But Chamberlain rejected such a journey. As an objective he suggested 'the development of free institutions with a view to ultimate self-government', though the latter was 'a distant goal'. None the less, because of the Russian Revolution, the claims that the Allies were fighting for liberty and nationality, and the effect on public opinion in both India and Britain, they must be prepared for 'bold and radical measures', not just for Indian representation in the legislative councils but also giving the councils real powers in order to train the Indians in self-government: 'this is the real crux of the question'. By now Chamberlain largely agreed with the Duke Committee, and was now sufficiently decided to go to the Cabinet, but he found no clear morning or afternoon on its agenda, and during June, while the WPC deliberated, the issue was repeatedly postponed.[68] Chelmsford was content with Chamberlain's reformulation of the policy goal, but warned 'a catastrophic change may be forced upon us'.

Whereas hitherto the GOI had moved gradually, now its leaders felt foreboding. The danger was not bloodshed, but embitterment that made India harder to govern.[69] The Lucknow Pact and the Home Rule Leagues were part of the cause. The February Revolution set a precedent for overthrowing autocracy. American entry and Wilson's War Message were reported in the nationalist press, and seen as complementing events in Russia. Annie Besant mentioned Russia and cited the War Message, while other nationalists invoked America's administration of the Philippines as a model.[70] But rather than any specific event forming a turning point, the key development was the GOI's perception that conditions were worsening and that deadlock in London inhibited action. Meston, one of the most progressive heads of provinces, had reported in May 1916 that 'at present, in the United Provinces, all is extremely well', but after the Lucknow Pact he considered that 'The situation is ... one of considerable seriousness', that 'I have never taken a gloomy view of our political situation, but I regard the position now as one of considerable gravity', and finally that 'the air has never been thicker with suspicion and mistrust of us than it is today. Whatever the reasons, the anti-Government and almost the anti-British feeling among the advanced party is stronger than I have ever seen it.'[71] According to Sir Benjamin Robertson in the previously quiet Central Provinces, Home Rule agitation was spreading fast and he too had never known such feeling behind any movement or such impatience with the GOI, while according to Lord Willingdon in Bombay (a nationalist heartland), Annie Besant gained adherents daily and the moderates were losing hope: he saw 'a very serious danger in all this'. Although Willingdon was a conservative, he led the pressure for a declaration.[72] Some heads of provinces wanted to tighten repression and issue warnings, but Chelmsford hesitated to set a common line, citing the delay in London. However, a GOI circular on 26 March authorized pre-censorship of the press, and on 16 June the Madras Presidency prohibited Annie Besant from attending meetings or publishing, which action Chelmsford and Chamberlain approved although it stirred the agitation even more.[73] By now the provincial governments were nearly unanimous that a declaration on India's political future was vital. Chelmsford considered it would be sufficiently authoritative only if it came from London, although he became so desperate that he requested permission for a statement of his own, which the India Office refused. He complained that he had never imagined that 'days would slip into weeks and weeks into months without a decision being reached ... We are a government which does not govern, and inasmuch as I took up this question now some 15 months ago with the very object of not being caught napping, it is the irony of fate that, when the crisis comes, I have perforce to remain silent.'[74]

Chamberlain picked up on the urgency. He advised the Cabinet on 26 June that they had been sitting on his reform papers for more than a month,

while 'the Viceroy's telegrams betray a growing uneasiness as to the situation
in India. I share this feeling...The situation is daily becoming more difficult and a declaration of the intentions of H. M. Government is urgently
required.'[75] When the matter reached the War Cabinet three days later, however, as item 13 on a crowded agenda, it made little headway. Chamberlain
reported that 'the present situation was causing grave anxiety' both to himself and to the GOI; that national self-consciousness was growing fast and
would soon spread down to the masses; and that without a British commitment to self-government the moderate Indians would fade away or join the
extremists. He still disliked the GOI's formula, as a cumbersome committee
compromise, and wanted in devolved areas (such as public works and sanitation) to see real power, including financial power, delegated to the legislative councils, as well as a broader franchise and more elected members. His
preference remained, however, to proceed through a royal commission. Any
concessions would *not* be a reward for India's wartime services but made
because on wider grounds the British government believed they were
appropriate; although the situation 'fomented by the Russian Revolution
and the ideas adopted by the Allies in the war' made the moment ripe, with
the risk otherwise of 'the gravest possibilities'.

Chamberlain elicited two substantive responses, from Curzon and from
Balfour. Curzon felt India had not yet made a disproportionate contribution,
given the size of its population and its wartime prosperity. If concessions
were made, it was:

> because in the course of the war forces have been let loose, ideas have found
> vent, aspirations have been formulated, which were either dormant before or
> which in a short space of time have received almost incredible development.
> We are really making concessions to India...because of the free talk about
> liberty, nationality, democracy, and self-government which have become the
> common shibboleths of the Allies, and because we are expected to translate in
> our own domestic household the sentiments which we have so enthusiastically
> preached to others. The Russian Revolution has lent an immense momentum
> to this tide, and will...be recognised in the future as a landmark in history
> comparable with and even more disturbing than the French Revolution.

He none the less accepted that self-government within the British Empire
should be the goal, and that if they did not take the lead, the Home Rule
movement would do so.[76] Whereas Curzon proposed a different rationale
for reaching a similar conclusion, however, Balfour was more intransigent,
as he considered granting self-government would make India a political

unit, which it was not and had never been, being rather 'a congeries of Oriental communities or races'. More self-government was possible locally, but above that should remain 'a benevolent, sympathetic, and wise suzerainty'. The opposing views being thus set out, the rest of the Cabinet contributed little, and left Chamberlain to return with a suitable formula.[77] When the Cabinet reconsidered India, however, this time as agenda item 18 on 5 July, it broke off almost at once in order to discuss UK beer output. Chamberlain still had not produced a formula, and Balfour suggested 'Our policy is to increase the share of natives in Indian administration as rapidly and to as great an extent as circumstances will permit.' According to Hankey's minutes, 'It was further suggested that it was impossible for His Majesty's Government, in the midst of a great war, to give adequate time and thought to the proper and full consideration of so important and complex a question.'[78] At this point it seemed as if Indian reform would drop off the agenda. Moreover, ministers were preoccupied with the report from the Mesopotamia Commission, an inquiry into the surrender in 1916 by a besieged British army to the Turks at Kut-al-Amara. The document was replete with damning criticisms of the GOI's failure to provision and assure medical care for an army largely composed of Indian soldiers. When the Cabinet published the report and it became evident that legal proceedings might follow, Chamberlain judged he must resign in case he had to defend his officials in court, which gesture was, perhaps, over-scrupulous, and he may have welcomed an opportunity to step down. Chelmsford was mortified at the prospect of further delay, and urged Lloyd George to ask Chamberlain to reconsider.[79] But the prime minister intervened more effectively, by bringing in Edwin Montagu.

Montagu was 38 and a rising Liberal star, whom Lloyd George wanted in his government to strengthen its Liberal component and to deprive Asquith of an ally. Montagu courted the premier with little subtlety, although the post he actually wanted was minister of reconstruction. However, he had been Under-Secretary of State for India in 1910–14, had spent time there, and maintained an interest. He was known as a critic of the Raj, which in the Commons debate on the Mesopotamia Commission he described as 'too wooden, too inelastic, too ante-diluvian to be of any use for the modern purposes we have in view'. He favoured more Indian self-government, though in the form of 'not one great Home Rule country, but a series of self-governing Provinces and Principalities, federated by one Central Government'. Montagu protested subsequently that Chamberlain's resignation

surprised him, and the speech had not been a bid for the India Office. None
the less, when Chamberlain stood down Lloyd George offered him the job,
and said he wanted Montagu to take it even though Curzon and Balfour
did not. This showed Lloyd George wanted to maintain the reform momentum, although the speech's notes of caution also impressed the premier. In
his acceptance letter, Montagu said he would take it that his speech bound
the government, and the ultimate objective was a system of self-governing
provinces united to each other and to the princely states by a central government; although 'many generations' would be needed to attain it and he
would not urge 'precipitate action'.[80]

Perhaps Montagu was being disingenuous. He proved far more decisive
than his predecessor. On 2 August he scored a first success in Cabinet, by
carrying the principle of officer commissions. On the broader constitutional question he was further pressured by Chelmsford, who issued something tantamount to an ultimatum: that if there were still no declaration
when his Legislative Council reconvened on 5 September, he would speak
his mind. But Montagu assured the Viceroy that he wanted 'an announcement...at the earliest possible moment' and 'bold and radical measures'.[81]
Assisted by the ultimatum, Montagu persuaded Lloyd George to restore the
item to the agenda, even though Curzon wanted further delay. On 14
August Indian reforms therefore came back to the War Cabinet and this
time with only brief items preceding, Lloyd George having assured Montagu
at breakfast that if necessary he would back him.[82]

The preliminaries set the tone for the debate, in which Lloyd George
again participated little. Montagu had prepared a memorandum urging that
not only the Viceroy and the GOI but also the heads of provinces wanted a
declaration now:

> The Russian Revolution, the activities of Mrs Besant and her friends, the issue
> of the Mesopotamian Commission Report, the improved status given to India
> by her representation at the Imperial War Conference and the War Cabinet,
> seem to have produced a situation in which, unless a certainty of substantial
> reform is at once conceded to India, the Indian Government and its friends
> have reason to fear a considerable recruitment to the extreme party from the
> moderate party, and a general feeling of discouragement and pessimism which
> would be very grave in its results.[83]

Ireland, where since the Easter Rising support had drained from the Irish
Parliamentary Party towards Sinn Feín, was much in ministers' minds,
Chamberlain having warned of 'a second Ireland' in India.[84] Montagu felt

Britain must acknowledge 'ultimate self-government within the Empire' as 'a legitimate aspiration'. This did not mean Home Rule now, or eventual independence, and his personal view remained that the ultimate destination would be 'a commonwealth of self-governing provinces or countries united to the Home Government, to one another and to the Native States', and evolving at differing speeds. But the plan submitted in the Reform Despatch he felt was untenable, and further work was needed, which he judged best done if he accepted Chelmsford's invitation to go to India. In the interim he proposed the wording that 'His Majesty's Government and the Government of India has in view the gradual development of free institutions in India with a view to self-government within the Empire.' He reiterated the urgency and necessity of giving the moderates a lead, insisting that the phrase 'self-government' had become a 'shibboleth' and must be included.[85]

In addition to a paper from Chamberlain supporting Montagu, the Cabinet had received two contrasting memoranda from Balfour and Curzon. Balfour focused on the phrase that Montagu deemed indispensable. Everyone would understand 'self-government' as meaning 'parliamentary government on a democratic basis', as in the Dominions, which was 'totally unsuitable' for India and probably always would be: 'East is East and West is West.' Balfour divided humanity into a hierarchy of races, and in 'negro states' such as Liberia and San Domingo parliamentary democracy had failed disastrously. India was more complex, with great ethnic variety and blurred interracial distinctions, but still the differences 'are quite sufficient to make real Parliamentary institutions unworkable in the future, as they are admittedly unworkable in the present'. However, he had no objection to developing 'a system under which India should be more and more governed by Indians', and his vision differed less from Montagu's than it might seem.[86] But Curzon's new memorandum would be more influential. Like Balfour, Curzon doubted India could ever 'in any future that can reasonably be predicted... become a singly autonomous or quasi-autonomous political unit, in which Indians will be universally substituted for British administrators, and the 250 millions of Indian peoples of every race, religion, and state of development—outside the Native States—will constitute a self-governing Dominion under the suzerainty, either more or less effective, of the British Crown'. This prospect he dismissed as 'the wildest of dreams' but, unlike Montagu, he rejected even 'an organised federation of autonomous States under the control of a Federal Government' as also 'an impractical ideal'.

What 'self-government' meant was that 'the areas in which self-government exists shall be extended step-by-step, that the process of self-government shall be enlarged, that the number of Indians who participate in self-government shall steadily increase until a time comes when Indian representative opinion, trained and moulded by experience, will have a predominant influence in the administration of the country'. The 'Protecting Power', however, must still play an essential role, or Indian unity and such liberties and rights as had been gained would be endangered. Indian parliamentary institutions must strike much deeper roots, and the country be capable from its own resources of maintaining internal order and defending its frontiers before it could claim to be a 'self-governing nation'. Until that 'distant goal' was reached Britain must maintain 'the responsibility we have assumed for the guidance of India on the path of moral and material advancement'.[87]

In the 14 August Cabinet meeting Balfour, having made his point in writing, stayed silent. Instead discussion centred on Montagu and Curzon. Like other British politicians, Curzon had paternal feelings towards India, as to an unruly child. He was wary of the Western-educated urban and professional elite as unrepresentative of the agricultural and aristocratic interior. In Montagu's draft, Curzon disliked the phrase 'free institutions', which Indians would interpret as meaning free from British interference and control. He also, like Balfour, disliked 'ultimate self-government', which Indians might think meant in a generation, whereas the Cabinet 'probably contemplated an intervening period that might extend to 500 years'. Of India's 315 million inhabitants 295 million were illiterate and only 1.75 million had any knowledge of English. Self-government now 'would simply mean setting up a narrow oligarchy of clever lawyers... England must continue to rule unless India were to relapse into chaos or be dominated by some other nation less qualified to guide her destinies.' Hence the formula adopted, and largely drafted by Curzon, became 'The policy of His Majesty's Government is that of increasing association of Indians in every branch of the administration, and the gradual development of self-governing institutions, with a view to the progressive realisation of responsible government in India under the aegis of the British Crown', and the War Cabinet agreed that Montagu should go to India to discuss how the policy should be implemented.[88]

Chelmsford's Executive Council accepted the formula with the proviso that 'under the aegis of the British Crown' should be replaced by 'as an integral part of the British Empire' and the clarification that this was Indian government policy as well as British.[89] In this final form Montagu unveiled it to the Commons on 20 August. Writing in retrospect about the 14 August Cabinet, Montagu mused 'It was a strange discussion', largely revolving round terminology. He had pressed for 'self-government', as the phrase desired by the GOI and current on the subcontinent, but he did not see how 'responsible government' differed from it, and if anything it promised more.[90] He had, however, included the word 'progressive', which would later prove important. Moreover, at the breakfast meeting before the Cabinet Lloyd George had warned that Curzon's 2 July memorandum had adequately defined 'self-government' and he did not want to quarrel about words.[91] At the Cabinet meeting itself the premier's sole intervention was in the same sense—he believed the Cabinet's views were generally represented by Curzon's paragraph defining self-government as meaning that its area should be extended, its powers enlarged, and more and more Indians participate until they had the predominant influence in administering their country.[92] This suggested that the Cabinet was being less ambitious than Montagu had envisaged, though Montagu was pleased with the declaration and the GOI thought it sufficient. Indeed, Montagu felt Curzon had accepted a very liberal formula, while Curzon viewed himself as occupying a middle position between Montagu and the 'very stubborn and reactionary' Balfour.[93]

Actually the phrase 'responsible government' came from a speech by the India Office Under-Secretary of State, Lord Islington, at Oxford, which was also circulated to the Cabinet.[94] Islington had been anxious to forestall the anarchy and extremism of Russia and, in his personal opinion, 'the essence of responsible government' was that the Indians on the Legislative Councils should be responsible to the electorate and the voters could remove them; and if in deference to their opinions the government changed policy, they should share responsibility for the results. Indians should be trained to think responsibly and not just criticize.[95] The phrasing recalled Curzon's anxiety that Indian institutions should not represent an oligarchy of lawyers, and similar thinking had been developed by the Round Table group.[96] Implicitly it looked ahead towards the post-1919 model of 'dyarchy' in which elected Indian politicians took responsibility for certain aspects of policy but other aspects remained reserved business. It implied a gradual evolution, as Indian politicians and officials were trained up and the electorate broadened and educated. Britain would remain in place for many

years and even indefinitely to guarantee an orderly and impartial domestic
framework and to conduct defence and foreign policy. Indeed, not even the
Dominions, at this stage in the empire's history, ran their own foreign affairs.
In any case, Dominion status was not discussed in detail and the Colonial
Office not consulted about it.[97] The Cabinet envisaged real but carefully
circumscribed concessions (and that Britain would determine the rate of
progress) but it left the intermediate steps and the final objective to emerge
from Montagu's Indian visit. It issued the declaration first in order to head
off what seemed a dangerous, even desperate, situation. Perhaps the GOI
overstated the threat—Congress and the Home Rule Leagues were still
essentially constitutional and peaceful, and India lacked an equivalent to the
Easter Rising paramilitaries. None the less, both Ireland and Russia provided
warnings: the men on the spot feared India was getting out of hand and it
was hard for London to second-guess them.

The declaration won greater significance in retrospect. By sending the
new Secretary of State to India the Cabinet cut slack for a declared radical
(Montagu) to work alongside a covert one (Chelmsford). Immediately,
however, the GOI had warned that what would have sufficed six months
ago would not do so now, and the reaction in India was muted. The conservative Lord Pentland and his council in Madras protested that the effects
would be disastrous but Chelmsford told Pentland he was isolated and that
most of the provinces had been demanding a declaration for months.[98] In
the Indian press, Chelmsford reported, the reception was 'favourable, but
not very enthusiastic'—the moderate newspapers welcoming the declaration and the extremist ones minimizing it.[99] Congress greeted it with
'grateful satisfaction', but still wanted the Lucknow Pact implemented as
soon as possible.[100] Annie Besant was released from internment on Montagu's
initiative and with Chelmsford's agreement, which indicated the GOI
would be more tolerant of opposition.[101] But any honeymoon was short-
lived. By October the British community in India was losing confidence in
Montagu and Chelmsford, and protesters demonstrated in Calcutta and
London. Hindu landlords in the district of Arrah orchestrated a week of
attacks on Muslim villagers: a warning that as Britain disengaged communal
violence would worsen.[102] Chelmsford was disappointed at the moderates'
failure to assert themselves as he had hoped.[103] Montagu also was worried
that younger educated Indians had lost faith in the government, and the
moderates did not stand up to the extremists or were going over to them.[104]
He had confided to Chelmsford that 'the world has moved … since a year

ago. It would be a strangely inanimate world if this horrible year with its revolutions and war left it unmoved.'[105]

It seemed the declaration had failed to halt the drift, and the auspices when Montagu reached India were unpromising. None the less, his mission proceeded calmly and he and Chelmsford got on well, although he felt overwhelmed by the volume of petitions as he progressed from Delhi to Calcutta, Madras, Bombay, and back. The 'Report on Indian Constitutional Reforms' that the two men submitted in April 1918 was formidable, drafted with speed and eloquence by the classicist William Marris.[106] In disregard of the Cabinet, it employed 'self-governing' as shorthand for 'responsible government as an integral part of the British Empire', and it described the declaration as 'the most momentous utterance ever made in India's chequered history'. The war 'had become the predominant factor in the present political situation... the war and the sentiments to which the war has given expression have made political reform loom larger in India'. Britain could not easily deny the self-determination that British and American statesmen claimed to be fighting for in Europe, and the Russian Revolution had galvanized India's aspirations: 'we have a richer gift for her people than any that we have yet bestowed on them; that nationhood within the Empire represents something better than anything India has hitherto attained; that the placid, pathetic contentment of the masses is not the soil in which Indian nationhood will grow, and that in deliberately disturbing it we are acting for her higher good'. This was a notably idealist framing, invoking an Indian nationhood that Curzon and Balfour had negated, and in addition to such staples as officer commissions, more Indians in the civil service, and greater freedom to set tariffs, the Report recommended generous measures of devolution and democratization. Local government should as far as possible be under complete popular control; the provincial governments would take over more and more responsibilities; and the central Legislative Council would become more representative and gain more influence. In the provinces there would be dyarchy: one legislature but two executives, one Indian and responsible to the legislature and one mostly British and dealing with reserved subjects; separate Muslim electorates would continue; governments would need majorities in provincial legislatures but the Viceroy could still veto legislation. In the central legislature, Montagu insisted on an elected majority, though there would also be a second chamber.[107] Even though the report excluded any 'transfer of power' at central level in the foreseeable future,[108] it adopted Montagu's rather than Curzon's understanding of what the 1917 declaration meant.

The reception was again divided and lukewarm. The moderates and extremists in Congress were now drifting apart, and to an extent the declaration and what followed it did disrupt the united front against the Raj.[109] But Curzon was alarmed and wanted to delay the report's appearance, though the government published it without committing itself to the recommendations. None the less, in November the Cabinet approved the bill that would become the 1919 Government of India Act. Since the declaration the political dynamics had changed. Chamberlain had re-entered (as minister without portfolio) into what was now a largely Unionist Cabinet, and he rather than Montagu or Lloyd George kept up the momentum. Curzon feared the process was getting out of hand. 'Why is it necessary', he asked, 'to proceed at a breakneck speed in a case that constitutes a revolution, of which not one person in a thousand realises the magnitude, and which will probably lead by stages of increasing speed to the ultimate disruption of the Empire?' Curzon had hoped this package would be final, whereas for Montagu and Chelmsford it was a down payment. Even so, Curzon accepted that the declaration committed the government to legislate, and objected more to the speed of the advance than to its direction.[110] Conversely, Chamberlain was persuaded by the Report's contention that 'the time has come when it is necessary to make a real advance in spite of all the dangers or abuses to which it may give rise'. Implicitly self-government was better than good government, and it was necessary to 'give real power and responsibility in respect of a limited field of political activity'. Looking back, Chamberlain felt 'in one sense I think we had no choice. We were not in a position of suitable equilibrium and we could not continue for an indefinite time balancing on the point on which the Morley–Minto reforms left us.' Yet he still hoped the experiment with dyarchy could save the Raj:[111] 'I think it of great importance that we should lead the movement for reform, for... only by leading it, can we adequately control it.'[112]

In fact before the situation eased it got much worse. During 1917–18 India's military contribution intensified as Lloyd George had wanted. Indian recruitment rose from 113,000 combatants in 1916–17 to 276,000 in 1917–18, and the 1918–19 goal was 500,000.[113] Although officer recruitment remained a bottleneck, in 1918 the Cabinet agreed to 200 additional Indian commissions.[114] By the Armistice over half the British Empire forces in Mesopotamia and over a third of those in Palestine were Indian, and Indians were serving with the British contingent in Macedonia.[115] In 1917–18 the Indian army doubled in size, recruitment extending far beyond the traditional 'martial races', but still falling heaviest on the Punjab, where local leaders received bounties for recruits and applied considerable coercion.[116] GOI military spending rose from £37.48 million in 1916–17 to £43.56 million in 1917–18 and £66.72 million in 1918–19;[117] the price index rose from 196 in 1917 to 225 in 1918 and 276 in 1919.[118] Coal normally shipped from Bengal to Bombay by sea was diverted overland and, as in Russia, railway congestion aggravated shortages.[119]

Mohandas Gandhi, who had returned to India from South Africa in 1915, already had a formidable reputation as a political organizer, but he followed the advice of his mentor, Gokhale, to begin cautiously. In 1914 he had supported the war effort; in 1917 he still argued India's best interest was to abstain from nationalist activism,[120] and as late as 1918, despite his philosophy of non-violence, he conducted a personal recruitment campaign for the British army, declaring that the Montagu–Chelmsford report demanded 'sympathetic handling rather than summary rejection'. All the same, according to his biographer, 'The First World War transformed Gandhi into a political leader in his native land', and the years 1919–20, during which Tilak died and Besant became marginal, saw his rise to ascendancy in Congress politics.[121] In March 1919 the Rowlatt Act extended the government's wartime powers of press censorship, arrest without warrant, detention without trial, and trial without juries, and Gandhi's civil disobedience campaign against the measure led on to an uprising in the Punjab and culminated in the Amritsar (Jallianwala Bagh) Massacre, when troops opened fire and killed hundreds of peaceful protestors. The Afghans then attacked across the North-West Frontier: precisely the combination of rebellion with invasion that the British military had long dreaded. Although they repelled the Afghans and regained control, the Raj's vulnerability arguably strengthened it in dealing with London, for a further consequence of the Montagu–Chelmsford process was a reconsideration of India's fiscal and military contribution. Under dyarchy the previously highly centralized arrangements began to be dismantled: the provinces taking the receipts from the land, excise, and stamp taxes, the GOI those from the opium, salt, and income taxes, as well as customs revenues. Delhi gained more tariff autonomy, which it used to raise duties. It also cut the army budget at a moment when London had deployed Indian troops along an arc running from the Mediterranean and the Turkish Straits through the Middle East to Malaya and China. It was agreed the army would henceforth not be used for big permanent overseas garrisons unless at London's expense. And as lobbying from Indians in the provincial assemblies for social spending grew, and they resisted financial transfers to the centre, pressure for further readjustment mounted.[122] In 1929 India was promised Dominion status, at the same time as the Dominions were winning the right to decide for themselves on whether to declare war, and in 1935 a further round of devolution followed. Meanwhile recruitment of British officials to the Indian Civil Service fell dramatically. In short the British were now, as Curzon had predicted, on an inclined plane where each concession laid the basis for more while India became less of an asset and more a liability. And once the Raj's days seemed numbered, the religious divide that Montagu and Chelmsford had identified as the greatest obstacle to their project also sharpened, as demands emerged for a separate Muslim homeland.[123] Whereas Montagu and Chelmsford, like Chamberlain and Hardinge, hoped concessions would strengthen Anglo-Indian bonds, their critics seemed more prescient, even if Balfour's insistence that India could never be governed as a parliamentary unit proved excessive. On the other hand, Chelmsford was right that it would have been better to act sooner, rather than creating the impression of a grudging concession extracted under duress. What all agreed on, however, was the war's significance for supercharging Indian political development, and unsettling the old combination of conciliation with repression. As Reginald Craddock, the Executive Council's diehard, wrote to Curzon, 'Nothing hitherto done gave away *control* though it afforded opportunities for advice and, incidentally, for opposition.'[124] The Montagu Declaration thus remains the starting indicator for processes that led to independence not only for India but also for the rest of the British Empire, and even for the Western colonial empires as a whole.

12

A Jewish National Home

O n Friday 2 November 1917 the British Foreign Secretary informed
Walter, Baron Rothschild that the Cabinet had approved a statement
for communication to the Zionist Federation:

> His Majesty's Government view with favour the establishment in Palestine of
> a national home for the Jewish people, and will use their best endeavours to
> facilitate the achievement of this object, it being clearly understood that noth-
> ing shall be done which may prejudice the civil and religious rights of existing
> non-Jewish communities in Palestine, or the rights and political status enjoyed
> by Jews in any other country.[1]

On 9 November the declaration appeared in *The Times*. On 31 October,
three days before Balfour sent it, British Empire forces had launched an
offensive that took them to Jerusalem. Simultaneously with issuing the
declaration, the British government won the ability to implement it and,
after conquering the rest of Palestine in 1918, it administered the territory
until in 1922 it received authority to continue doing so as a League of
Nations mandatory power, the Balfour Declaration being incorporated into
the mandatory treaty.[2] During the mandate the *Yishuv*, or Jewish community, not only expanded its numbers but also built up institutions that
in 1948–9 would provide the basis for the state of Israel. The declaration
exemplified how the Russian Revolution and American intervention transformed the war. It was the precursor to one of the twentieth and twenty-first
centuries' most intractable conflicts. Its story can be analysed in five stages: the
situation before 1914; developments in 1914–16; the Zionist 'breakthrough'
in 1917; the Cabinet struggle for the declaration; and the statement's
reception and impact.

Palestine before 1914 belonged to the Ottoman Empire. It was not an
administrative unit. What became the British mandate was divided between

the two northern districts, or sanjaks, of Acre and Nablus, which came under the vilayet of Beirut, and the south which fell within the sanjak of Jerusalem.³ A boundary with Egypt was agreed in 1906, but to the north and east there were no distinct demarcation lines.⁴ Palestine compared in size with Lloyd George's Welsh homeland, comprising a coastal plain (with a natural harbour at Haifa), the Judaean hills, and the Jordan Valley. Except for the semi-arid area in the south, the land was largely settled. The population was mostly Arabic-speaking and Sunni Muslim, although it included sizeable Christian Arab and Jewish minorities. The Ottomans conducted no censuses, although they incompletely enumerated the male inhabitants for purposes of taxation and conscription. Their statistics suggest the total population of Ottoman citizens rose from 452,000 in 1879–80 to 712,000 in 1913–14, of whom 80,000 were Christian. The Jewish population is difficult to measure, because since 1881 immigrants had swelled it, but not all had stayed and many who had stayed had not taken Ottoman citizenship. Figures cited by modern writers vary between 60,000 and 85,000,⁵ although papers to the British Cabinet at the time suggested totals between 90,000 and 125,000. Most lived in the cities, especially Jerusalem, which had a Jewish majority, but Jews had also established agricultural settlements, primarily on the coastal plain and in Galilee. By the turn of the century such settlement was causing friction, as Arab farmers lost their grazing rights or labouring jobs after property changed hands. Following the Young Turk Revolution in 1908 that brought to power a more nationalist Ottoman regime, attacks took place on Jewish colonists and those in Galilee formed a self-defence league. Opposition to Jewish settlement came from Arab representatives in the Constantinople parliament and from the emergent Arab-language press.⁶

Palestine would become a cockpit for Zionism and for Arab nationalism. A distinctly Palestinian-Arab consciousness remained embryonic before 1914, but a broader Arab national movement for freedom from the Turks (found most strongly in Syria) was more developed. A division emerged between reformists who believed the Muslim world should borrow from Western practices, and conservatives who feared that doing so would dilute Islam. After the Young Turk Revolution, Ottoman authority in some ways grew more oppressive while in others allowing greater freedom to organize. An Arab nationalist congress convened in Paris in 1913, and groups of intellectuals and army officers sought not just autonomy within the Ottoman Empire but complete separation from it, though most Arabs remained loyal to the regime and tens of thousands would soon fight in Turkey's armies.⁷

Jewish separate identity was centuries-old, but under the impact of the Enlightenment and the French Revolution it had seemed to be diminishing and by the mid-nineteenth century the relatively small and well-assimilated Jewish populations of Western Europe had gained equal rights and civil liberties. From 1881, however, pogroms and intensified persecution in tsarist Russia encouraged a surge of emigration from present-day Poland, Lithuania, and Belarus, alongside another from the similarly persecuted community in Romania. Most of those departing went outside Europe, especially to the United States, though also to Germany, France, and Britain, where the immigration helped rekindle traditional anti-Semitism, now accompanied by racist and Social Darwinian overtones. Theodore Herzl, the Viennese journalist who was the principal founder of the Zionist movement, considered that complete assimilation was unattainable and the Jews needed their own home: in the words of the resolution at the 1897 Basle Congress establishing the Zionist Organization, 'the creation in Palestine of a home for the Jewish people secured by public law'.[8] Herzl was not religious and not necessarily committed to Palestine as the location, but he saw creating a national home as needing a political agreement. When his approaches to the Turkish authorities proved fruitless, he found Britain willing to entertain a Jewish settlement in East Africa. This offer, however, split the movement. After Herzl's death his successors insisted Palestine was the only acceptable homeland, though some retreated from 'political' to 'practical' or 'cultural' Zionism, whose goals were assisting and enlarging the *Yishuv* and developing it as a cultural and spiritual focus rather than as necessarily a political entity. Given Palestine's Turkish rulers' resistance to the latter, and the increasing obstacles to immigration and to agricultural settlement, Zionism seemed to be pursuing an unrealizable objective. In the pre-war years its adherents formed small minorities among the Jewish diaspora, and the movement was in decline.[9]

The British case exemplified these generalities. The Suez Canal was pivotal to imperial communications and the British had been the predominant power in Egypt since 1882, extending their control in 1906 to the Sinai Peninsula, but neither the Cairo nor the London governments envisaged further expansion. Britain had a tradition of gentile Zionism, which peaked in 1840–1, when *The Times* advocated a Jewish state and Foreign Secretary Palmerston pressed Turkey to allow unrestricted immigration. The sultan resisted, however, and after the 1870s gentile interest waned.[10] On the other hand, some 150,000 Jewish immigrants reached the British Isles after 1881, and by 1914 British Jews may have totalled 250,000. Although immigration fell after the Aliens Act of 1905, it fuelled tension between, on the one hand, the 'cousinhood' of old-established families who ran the banks and Jewish political institutions of the capital and, on the other, the foreign-born populations in the provinces and London's East End, among whom Zionism was strongest. It was not particularly strong, however: before the war the English Zionist Federation (EZF) had 9,000 members, and it has been estimated that in 1914 less than 6 per cent of the community supported the movement.[11] When Nahum Sokolov, from the World Zionist Organization, sought a Foreign Office interview in 1913, he had to wait three months, and then found no willingness to intervene on the Zionists' behalf. British policy was to keep Turkey-in-Asia intact.[12]

The outbreak of war certainly altered that policy, but not at first to Zionism's benefit. The key development was Turkey's adherence to the Central Powers. During 1915, while British Empire and French forces tried to overrun the Gallipoli peninsula and a largely Indian army pushed up the Tigris, the search for partners became a leitmotiv of British Middle Eastern policy, and one pursued none too scrupulously. In March–April, France and Britain concluded the Straits Agreement, secretly promising that Russia could annex Constantinople and the Bosphorus in return for supporting French and British claims elsewhere. Respect for Ottoman integrity was abandoned, and bidding could now open.

The most relevant consequences for Palestine were the McMahon–Hussein correspondence and the Sykes–Picot Agreement. The first was a clandestine exchange of letters between the British High Commissioner in Egypt, Sir Henry McMahon, and the Sharif Hussein of Mecca, the ruler of the Hejaz, who governed semi-autonomously under Turkish suzerainty. In early 1914 Hussein had sent one of his sons to contact the British as an insurance against the Ottomans trying to regain control, though the British showed no interest. But once Turkey entered the conflict, Kitchener (McMahon's predecessor in Cairo and now Secretary of State for War) favoured sounding out the Sharif, while Hussein entered into perilous contacts with the nationalist societies that had formed among the Arab officers serving with the Turkish forces in Syria. These latter drew up the Damascus Protocol, which envisaged cooperating with Britain if it recognized Arab independence in an area corresponding to the present Saudi Arabia, Iraq, Syria, Jordan, and Israel. If Hussein obtained such a British promise, the secret societies would recognize him as their spokesman and lead their army divisions into revolt.[13] When Hussein put these demands to the British, they thought them exorbitant. But by September 1915 the situation at Gallipoli was worsening and the Turks were moving Arab divisions to the Dardanelles. At this point a Kurdish defector, al-Faruqi, briefed the British in Cairo that a well-organized Arab nationalist movement indeed existed but that unless they responded to Hussein it might throw in its lot with Germany. Without attempting to corroborate the report, McMahon obtained authority from Foreign Secretary Grey to 'promise whatever necessary', while respecting French interests. Hence the letter that McMahon sent Hussein on 24 October 1915 pledged to 'recognize and support the independence of the Arabs in all the regions within the limits demanded by the Sharif of Mecca', on condition that any European advisers and officials used to govern the territories would be British. Britain would enjoy 'special administrative arrangements' in the vilayets of Basra and Baghdad; the areas where France had an interest were reserved; and 'the two districts of Mersina and Alexandretta and portions of Syria lying to the west of the districts of Damascus, Homs, Hama, and Aleppo cannot be said to be purely Arab, and should be excluded from the limits demanded'.[14] McMahon omitted to check his wording with the Foreign Office, and the translation into Arabic was imprecise, but in any case, he acknowledged afterwards, his priority was to get the Arabs in and the content was 'largely a matter of words'.[15] The letter formed part of a continuing correspondence, and full agreement was still pending when in June 1916 Hussein unfurled the banner of the Arab Revolt. The British failed to specify what they expected in return for their offers and, although Hussein confirmed he would not demand Mersina and Alexandretta, the status of the coastal area west of the Damascus–Aleppo districts remained obscure. The wording certainly excluded the area of present-day Lebanon, but appeared not to exclude Palestine as well (although McMahon said later that he had so intended).[16] Hussein seems to have assumed that Palestine fell within his sphere; the British that they remained free to dispose of it. But the correspondence never became a formal agreement; it failed to mention Palestine by name, and nor was it even accompanied by a map.

The prospect of an Arab rising prompted Britain to pursue what became the Sykes–Picot Agreement. The British negotiators were led by Sir Mark Sykes, a Yorkshire baronet and Unionist MP who had impressed the Asquith Cabinet as a Middle East expert, if with less than solid credentials (he had travelled widely there but did not know the local languages).[17] His sympathies lay with Arab nationalism and with British imperial interests: he felt little loyalty to the accord that bore his name. François Georges-Picot, in contrast, the former French Consul General at Beirut, belonged to the Comité de l'Asie française, a lobbying group for French interests in the Ottoman Empire that sought control of Syria and the Lebanon. Under the secret May 1916 agreement (this time accompanied by a celebrated map, albeit small-scale), Britain would rule directly a 'red' area in southern and central Mesopotamia and France a 'blue' area in Cilicia and along the Syrian and Lebanese coast, whereas the Arab state in the interior would be divided into a northern 'Area A' and southern 'Area B' in which France and Britain respectively would enjoy exclusive rights to appoint advisers and priority in seeking economic concessions and making loans. Russian spheres of influence and annexation were added later in Kurdistan and Armenia, and—at the St-Jean de Maurienne conference in 1917—an Italian zone in southern Anatolia. In the Holy Land itself, the coastal region round Haifa and Acre, where the British envisaged termini for a railway and an oil pipeline, would form another British-ruled red area; the northern part would fall within the French 'blue area'; and the central and southern parts including Jerusalem would become a 'brown' area under an international administration whose form would be decided in conjunction with the other Allies. The international zone was an alternative to the French demand to rule the whole of Palestine, and acknowledged the Jerusalem Holy Places' special status, though its governance arrangements were never more closely specified.[18] But none of the Holy Land would come under the independent Arab state, and that state's northern and southern segments would become French and British zones of influence. None of this was communicated to Hussein before he rebelled, and it was compatible with the McMahon–Hussein correspondence only if 'independent' meant liberated from the Turks rather than truly sovereign. Sykes–Picot, with its Russian and Italian extensions, was a project for partitioning Turkey-in-Asia in disregard of its inhabitants and for redrawing boundaries on a largely arbitrary basis. Although it did not, in fact, precisely anticipate the borders of the inter-war Middle East, its logic came from the European Powers' strategic, economic, and prestige imperatives.

In February 1915 Ottoman forces had crossed the Sinai peninsula and attacked the Suez Canal. Although Indian soldiers repelled them, the episode showed that the Sinai afforded the waterway insufficient protection. In 1916 the Ottomans reinforced their troops in the Sinai, while the British transferred evacuated forces from Gallipoli, expanding their garrison to 275,000. After a second assault on the canal was defeated in August, the British began a two-year-long advance that by November 1918 would reach Aleppo. If they decided to remain in Palestine as a forward defence screen for the canal, the Ottoman obstacle to Zionist objectives would be removed. Within the Asquith government, Herbert Samuel, the president of the Local Government Board and the first practising Jew to serve in a British Cabinet, first raised with Grey the possibility of a Jewish state: although Samuel had not previously been a Zionist, the situation had 'profoundly altered'. Grey said he felt a 'strong, sentimental attraction' to the idea, and Lloyd George was 'very keen'.[19] When in March 1915 the subject came to the Cabinet, however, Lloyd George was virtually Samuel's sole supporter. Samuel contended that after the war Palestine should not stay under the Turks, who had failed to develop it; but nor should it go to France, which would threaten the Suez canal. He feared that because of Jewish pro-German sympathies an international administration would end up as a German protectorate, and a state run by the Jewish minority could neither command obedience from the Arabs nor defend itself externally: hence the only alternative was a British protectorate and 'carefully regulated' immigration until the Jews attained a majority.[20] He estimated that of a worldwide Jewish population of 9 million (2 million in the United States) Palestine contained 90,000–100,000 Jews as against 500,000–600,000 Muslim Arabs. But despite Samuel's attempt to appeal to British interests, Asquith was indifferent, Edwin Montagu, the other Jewish member of the government, opposed the plan as he would in 1917, and Grey shrank from the responsibilities of a British protectorate.[21] Britain was uncertain about its allies' attitudes, and its army in Egypt still so small and unprepared as to make the discussion hypothetical. The inter-departmental de Bunsen Committee on the future of the Middle East, which reported in June 1915, did not mention Zionism and was indecisive about Palestine, preferring Turkey-in-Asia to be decentralized but to remain in being.[22]

Samuel feared that Germany would outbid Britain. Although the bulk of Zionism's rank-and-file support came from Russian Jews, its pre-war headquarters was in Berlin. Concerned to maintain neutrality, its leaders moved to Copenhagen,[23] but France and Britain still laboured at an immense disadvantage from being partnered with the tsarist regime, which during the 1915 'great retreat' from Poland deported some 1.5 million Jews to the east.[24] In fact the Russian government was not necessarily hostile to Zionism, if only to provide an outlet for its Jewish population. But the German Foreign Ministry repeatedly interceded at Constantinople for the Jews, notably during the 1914–15 winter when the Ottomans threatened to expel all foreign Jews from Jaffa, ban the use of Hebrew, and confiscate weapons from Jewish hands while leaving them in Arab ones. The Germans got the expulsions cancelled, in part because the Ottomans were worried almost as much about the Arabs as about the Jews. In November 1915 German consuls were instructed to show a 'friendly attitude' to Zionist organizations, and the Berlin Foreign Ministry hoped 'international Jewry' would reciprocate, especially in the United States.[25] However, the Zionist leaders' commitment to neutrality, German reluctance to press Turkey, and the Turks' ability to defy their ally all set limits to this partnership, and the absence of an imminent danger from Germany reduced the incentive for Britain to act.

Even so, the British government and the Zionists began to come together. British Zionism increased its popular following, a 1915 petition in favour of a 'publicly recognized, legally secure home for the Jewish people in Palestine' attracting 50,000 signatures.[26] Chaim Weizmann, who would become the most influential Zionist leader, had come from Russia to work as a chemistry researcher at Manchester University and developed a process for fermenting acetone (a key ingredient in cordite) from grain rather than wood.[27] It brought him to Lloyd George's notice as minister of munitions, and to Balfour's as First Lord of the Admiralty, though Weizmann and the Manchester and London Zionists were at odds with the Jewish community's established leadership. The Board of Deputies of British Jews and the Anglo-Jewish Association, both with British-born and assimilated leaders, had established the Conjoint Foreign Committee (CFC), whose secretary was Lucien Wolf, as their vehicle for Foreign Office liaison and their mouthpiece on foreign affairs. It was Wolf rather than the Zionists who first seized on the Foreign Office's perception of a propaganda opportunity among what its officials commonly referred to as 'world Jewry'.[28] According to Lord Robert Cecil, the Foreign Office's Parliamentary Under-Secretary, 'I do not think it is easy to exaggerate the international power of the Jews.'[29] Yet concern was growing that Russia's behaviour would alienate American Jews, imperilling Britain's financial and political influence in the United States. Although Britain could do little to restrain its ally, embracing the Zionist cause might limit the damage. Such arguments came from Professor Horace Kallen at the University of Wisconsin; from Edgar Soares, the head of the Alexandria Jewish community; and from the Russian Zionist Vladimir

Jabotinsky, who wanted to found a Jewish Legion.[30] Wolf understood that the French were also worried about Russia and were setting up a French Committee for Neutral Jews. The field should not be abandoned to them,[31] and early in 1916 he urged Cecil for a declaration promising 'reasonable facilities' for immigration, colonization, and local autonomy in post-war Palestine. This position resembled that of the pre-1914 'cultural Zionists', and Soares in Alexandria warned that in the absence of an Allied declaration the Jews might seek a German protectorate. This danger tipped Grey into action.

On 11 March a Foreign Office cable to the British ambassadors in Paris and Petrograd suggested that a declaration on behalf of Jewish aspirations in Palestine might 'bring over to our side the Jewish forces in America, the East and elsewhere which are now largely, if not preponderantly, hostile to us', offering 'the prospect that when in course of time the Jewish colonists in Palestine grow strong enough to cope with the Arab population they may be allowed to take the management of the internal affairs of Palestine (with the exception of Jerusalem and the Holy Places) into their own hands ... Our sole object is to find an arrangement which would be so attractive to the majority of Jews as to enable us to strike a bargain for Jewish support.' Well before British forces entered Palestine, therefore, and before the government made contact with the British Zionists, the Foreign Office proposed a statement more radical than the Balfour Declaration. The Russian foreign minister, Sergei Sazonov, was willing to support it, Russia having no territorial claims in Palestine. The scheme foundered on French objections, Briand doubting it would influence Jewish opinion and foreseeing that it would antagonize the Arabs. The French may also have feared that it would undermine their Middle Eastern position and tie their hands with Turkey.[32] The French Jewish community, seared by the Dreyfus affair, was wary of Zionism and Briand considered Grey's proposal 'could not be usefully taken up until after question of creation of Arab Empire has been solved'.[33]

Despite its failure, the March 1916 initiative was revealing. Wolf was the nearest thing to an official spokesman for Anglo-Jewry, but the Foreign Office disliked him, modified his formula, and resisted immediate action. Yet it accepted that the Allies should appeal to Jewish sympathies, if possible without antagonizing France and Russia. All of this prefigured the concatenation of forces that in the following year led to the Balfour Declaration. However, in 1916 the Foreign Office's formula did not go to the Cabinet, which would probably have been hostile, while the United States was still neutral and France opposed. In contrast, the first six months of 1917 have been characterized as the Zionist 'breakthrough'. The British army approached Palestine's borders; the British government resolved to revise the Sykes–Picot Agreement; and objections both from Britain's allies and from the anti-Zionists in the Anglo-Jewish community were muted.

A crucial development was the formation of Lloyd George's coalition ministry, with its War Cabinet of imperialists and Balfour as Foreign Secretary. Balfour had met Weizmann in 1906 and 1915. Despite his notorious indolence and metaphysical scepticism, he was a religious man and eventually persuaded of the justice underlying Zionist claims, if slow to throw his weight behind them. Lloyd George himself, though a non-believer, found Palestine 'the one really interesting part of the war'.[34] Brought up in a secessionist Baptist sect, the premier wrote later that the declaration was 'undoubtedly inspired by natural sympathy, admiration, and also by the fact that, as you must remember, we had been trained even more in Hebrew history than in the history of our own country'.[35] Like many politicians and officials of the day (including Balfour), Lloyd George was disparaging about individual Jews and their supposed collective characteristics, but he seems sincerely to have sympathized with the Zionist project, and inherited Gladstone's detestation of the Turks. His sympathy, however, was neither unconditional nor devoid of self-interest. In his way the prime minister was no less imperialist than Curzon or Milner, convinced of the British Empire's civilizing mission and his obligation to protect it. Additionally, the issue became entangled in his conflicts over strategy with Haig and Robertson. When the new Cabinet took over, the Middle East fighting was turning in the Allies' favour. During 1917 the British in Mesopotamia and in Egypt-Palestine and the Arabs in the Hejaz all moved forward, the region's interwar political boundaries crystallizing as they did so.

After the disaster at Kut, Russian operations in Armenia and Persia distracted the Turks, while the British reorganized their supply lines and reinforced the Mesopotamia Expeditionary Force (MEF), placing it under an aggressive new commander, General Sir Frederick Maude. Robertson advised in September 1916 that the MEF should confine itself to protecting the oilfields and pipelines at the head of the Persian Gulf: it remained too weak to take Baghdad, whose capture would anyway have little broader effect.[36] Maude was told not to advance without authorization, but to stay as far forward as was possible without heavy losses, and to improve his position without requesting reinforcements, which Maude interpreted as permitting an attack.[37] In the Third Battle of Kut between December and February his forces destroyed their outnumbered opponents. The War Cabinet, which had long wanted Baghdad not least for symbolic and psychological reasons, was quick to approve when Robertson agreed that Maude should continue. The city fell on 11 March, and the Cabinet confirmed that Britain's presence in the Baghdad vilayet should be permanent, partly for fear that otherwise Russia would take over.[38] The proclamation that Sykes drafted appeared to promise independence and unity, and ministers and officials agreed that Baghdad should come under a 'façade' Arab government with British advisers.[39] With the General Staff expecting a complementary Russian offensive, on the eve of the February Revolution it seemed momentarily possible to drive Turkey out of the war.

The Egyptian Expeditionary Force (EEF) stayed on the defensive until summer 1916. But that July the Cabinet authorized General Sir Archibald Murray to advance across the Sinai, disrupt Ottoman communications between Syria and the Hejaz, and encourage the Arab Revolt to spread.[40] In contrast to Maude, Murray was a cautious leader who was unpopular with the EEF and commanded it from Cairo, but his troops built a railway and a water pipeline as they went, and once the hot weather ended they advanced to El Arish on 21 December and Rafah on 9 January. They reached the edge of the Sykes–Picot 'brown area' of international administration. The War Cabinet agreed to reassure the French that the objective was to defeat the Turks (rather than stake out territorial claims) and that Britain would welcome political cooperation, though the Cabinet shared Robertson's objections to French troops, a small detachment of whom—in fact Muslims—none the less participated.[41] Although Robertson still described the operation as intended to secure Egypt, its purpose was broadening.[42] In a 29 December memorandum he recognized the value of an advance on Jerusalem, though wanted to delay it until autumn 1917, after the hot season and after giving priority to the Western Front over the summer. On 2 January the Cabinet accepted this advice.[43] From Robertson's perspective, operations during the winter were anyway not feasible in France and Belgium; and Middle Eastern victories might raise 'our prestige particularly in the east', distract the Turks from other fronts, and even, if combined with a Russian offensive, destroy the Ottoman Empire in Asia. Hence, although the Jaffa–Jerusalem–Jericho line should be the first objective, beyond that the targets should include Acre–Lake Tiberias, and subsequently Beirut and Damascus.[44] On 26 March, Murray attacked Gaza, attempting to seize it before his assault forces, who had to traverse an arid wadi, ran out of water. By the time the attack was called off the Turks were evacuating their positions, but because the British failed to appreciate the situation their opponents re-established themselves and the First Battle of Gaza was a set-back.

Even so, Murray's reporting was upbeat, and this, coupled with the fall of Baghdad and the hope that Russia might also advance inspired the Cabinet to order a drive on Jerusalem *now*, despite Murray's protests that he had too few men.[45] Hence on 17 April he attempted a Second Battle of Gaza, against a line the Turks had reinforced. Murray used heavy artillery, gas shells, and eight tanks, staging a Western Front battle in miniature on the shores of the Mediterranean, but this time he could not disguise a costly defeat. For the rest of the summer the EEF confronted the Turks along the Gaza–Beersheba line, while Murray was replaced by Sir Edmund Allenby. Before Allenby left London, Lloyd George told him the War Cabinet expected 'Jerusalem before Christmas' and a determined attack that would expel the enemy from Palestine; a series of defeats might knock the Turks out of the war, and Allenby was to ask for the supplies and reinforcements that he needed. Allenby had a reputation for temper, and scared his staff officers, but he moved his HQ forward, was more visible than Murray to the dejected troops, and worked hard to raise morale and improve supplies.[46] He prepared with care, but he intended to attack.

Strategy set the context for war aims. It was agreed that a political mission should accompany the EEF, and Sykes and Picot were selected as its members. But as British troops approached the Palestine border, the mood grew more assertive. Lloyd George told his ambassador in Paris, 'We shall be there by right of conquest, and shall remain.'[47] Before Sykes left for the Middle East he met Lloyd George, Curzon, and Hankey at Downing Street on 3 April. The premier, who that morning had seen Weizmann, 'laid stress on the importance, if possible, of securing the addition of Palestine to the British area', and warned Sykes to make no understandings with the Arab 'tribes' that would prejudice British interests. Curzon thought 'the French had got much the better of the bargain' in the Sykes–Picot Agreement. 'They impressed on Sir Mark Sykes the difficulty of our relations with the French in this region and the importance of not prejudicing the Zionist movement and the possibility of its development under British auspices.'[48] The day before, the War Cabinet had instructed Murray to advance 'with all energy',[49] and even after Second Gaza official thinking little altered. At the St-Jean de Maurienne conference on 19 April, Lloyd George was 'very coldly received' when he suggested Britain should control the Holy Land. Undeterred, the War Cabinet subjected Sykes–Picot to 'considerable criticism, more particularly from the point of view of the proposed internationalization of Palestine which was felt to be impossible'.[50] Similarly, when a subcommittee of the Imperial War Cabinet on territorial war aims discussed the Middle East, Curzon (who chaired) said 'the only safe settlement' in Palestine was a British protectorate, and the Zionists would oppose any other arrangement. Smuts agreed that *any* other Power controlling Palestine would be 'a very serious menace to our communications'. The Curzon Committee advised that 'from the military and strategic point of view it is of primary importance to the safety of the Empire to retain control of Palestine and Mesopotamia'.[51] In reaching this conclusion it acknowledged a remarkable memorandum by its secretary, Leo Amery (a Unionist MP and friend of Milner), who warned the war might end with continuing German domination of a Continental European land mass unified by railways, while U-boats menaced Britain's sea lanes. The future empire should be bound by land communications, which holding Palestine, Mesopotamia, and German East Africa would ensure, thus safeguarding 'the great southern half of the British Empire which lies in an irregular semi-circle round the Indian Empire'.[52] The committee, chastened by military set-backs, was guarded in its recommendations for Europe, but was determined to protect Britain's global position.[53] When the Curzon Committee's report came to the Imperial War Cabinet on 1 May, however, Lloyd George cautioned that it embodied the desirable in the event of complete victory but might not be feasible in a negotiation where Germany still held French and Russian territory. Implicitly he was more pessimistic, and the Cabinet (barring its Labour member, Arthur Henderson) accepted the report as an indication of the objects to be pursued by the British peace conference delegates, rather than as 'definite instructions from which they are not intended in any circumstances to depart'.[54] But even if the war ended in a draw, the Holy Land was moving up the priority list. On 17 May Lloyd George told Curzon and Robertson that if the French suspended their Western Front offensive, Britain should also stop attacking and instead reinforce Palestine. 'If, as assumed, the defensive were adopted on the Western Front it would mean a general stalemate, and therefore we should endeavour to secure more territory for the purposes of bargaining at peace negotiations. He considered that our possession of Palestine would be a very great asset.'[55]

In the 3 April Downing Street meeting, Lloyd George reserved the Zionist claims, while Curzon told his committee that the Zionists wanted British control of Palestine. These statements reflected the contact that had now been made with the Zionists by British officials. The initiative had come from Sykes, acting for Lloyd George and without Foreign Office involvement: a sign of how under Lloyd George the Cabinet secretariat and the prime minister's private secretariat would intervene in foreign relations.[56] Sykes was working in the secretariat to the Cabinet's Committee of Imperial Defence when on 28 January 1917 he first met Weizmann.[57] At a second meeting, with Herbert Samuel and others including Walter Rothschild and Nahum Sokolov, the Zionists handed over a memorandum on their aims. Sykes wanted backing against France, and they confirmed their preference for a British protectorate. On 13 March Weizmann met Lloyd George and Balfour at a dinner, and subsequently more officially. He urged on Balfour a British protectorate: Balfour foresaw difficulties with France and Italy but agreed, while Lloyd George believed 'it is of great importance to Great Britain to protect Palestine'. The premier confirmed this view to Weizmann at breakfast on 3 April, saying he opposed an Anglo–French condominium, though neither he nor Sykes (on the day after Woodrow Wilson's War Message) excluded an Anglo-American one.[58]

Weizmann and Sokolov were executive members of the Zionist Organization, though had not attended its meetings since 1914. In July a meeting of the Zionist executive reaffirmed that it should maintain neutrality in the war and criticized Weizmann and Sokolov for acting too independently.[59] But Weizmann was indeed pursuing an Anglo–Zionist alliance, and in February had been elected president of the English Zionist Federation (EZF). In Manchester he had a circle of younger Zionist colleagues, including Harry Sacher who worked for the *Manchester Guardian*, whose editor (C. P. Scott) Weizmann knew. But Weizmann also cultivated contacts with the Rothschilds, who in addition to their international connections were the leading Anglo-Jewish family. His network extended from the provinces to the London cousinhood. For all his lobbying skills, however, the Zionists' moment came when the government sought them out, Sykes seeing an opportunity to undermine Palestine's internationalization. It is less clear that other British leaders saw the matter in this light, though Lloyd George did,[60] and it seems no coincidence that at the moment when links were established British forces seemed on the verge of invading.

Before the Zionists and the British could start the negotiations leading to the Balfour Declaration, obstacles had to be cleared on both sides. It was necessary to square Britain's allies—especially the French—and to overcome the anti-Zionists within the Jewish community. Whereas the first task proved unexpectedly straightforward, the second not only delayed the declaration but threatened to sink it altogether.

Sykes had been working on France and Italy. On 28 February he told Picot that the Zionists would oppose both an international administration and a condominium. The areas the Jews wanted to settle, moreover, extended well beyond where their colonies clustered now, to take in the arable land east of the Jordan and south and west of Jerusalem. He foresaw 'no great difficulties' with the Arabs, as most of these areas were 'practically uninhabited'. Although the Holy Places could come under a 'special administration', Sykes warned that 'If the great force of Judaism feels that its aspirations are not only considered but in a fair way towards realisation, then there is hope of an ordered and developed Arabic and Middle East... if that force feels that its aspirations will be thwarted... You will find that we will be hampered at every turn by intangible hindrances which it will be beyond our power to remove.'[61] Sykes overstated Zionism's influence as a hidden, manipulative element. But his contact with Picot lent the Zionists access to senior French governmental levels. Picot invited Sokolov to Paris, where the Quai d'Orsay sought backing for a *French* protectorate in Palestine. This aspiration was largely confined to the French Foreign Ministry, as although France had a Jewish population of 100,000, Zionism there was weak and the main Jewish organization, the Alliance israélite universelle, opposed it.[62] However, the Quai hoped to influence Jewish opinion in Russia and America, and when Sokolov met Picot and Pierre de Margerie (the Quai d'Orsay political director) with Jules Cambon on 9 April the French were agreeable in principle to a Jewish national home with local autonomy. Both sides at the meeting evaded the issue of who would be the protecting power, thus allowing the French to hope they remained in contention while Sokolov concealed his preference for the British.[63] He then continued to Rome, where Sykes had again prepared the way. In the Vatican, Sokolov met Pacelli, Gasparri, and Benedict—who voiced sympathy if assurances were given about the Holy Places—and subsequently he met Italian premier Boselli, who said Italy would not take the lead but nor would it oppose an initiative.[64] On his way back Sokolov returned to Paris, where Picot was advising that the British were committed to the Zionists and France could best retain some influence by also supporting their claims. In the midst of strikes, mutinies and France's gravest internal crisis of the war, Sokolov received a confidential letter from Jules Cambon dated 4 June. Noting Sokolov's opinion that 'if the circumstances permit it and the independence of the Holy Places were assured... it would be a work of justice and reparation to aid the rebirth of the Jewish nation, through the protection of the Allied Powers, on this land whence the people of Israel were chased so many centuries ago', it declared that 'The French Government, which entered the war to defend a people that had been unjustly attacked and which pursues the struggle to ensure the triumph of right over might, cannot but feel sympathy for your cause, the triumph of which is bound up with that of the Allies.'[65]

The 'Cambon Declaration' lifted the biggest diplomatic barrier to a British commitment. In addition to France and Italy, Russia's Provisional Government was also sympathetic to the Zionist case, as too was Woodrow Wilson, though he held back from an announcement.[66] The Cambon Declaration also alleviated a major embarrassment: that the London Zionists had got wind of the Sykes–Picot Agreement. On 25 April Weizmann had a difficult meeting with Robert Cecil. He objected to what amounted to a partition of Palestine, with Galilee included in the French area. American Jews, he warned, would view a French administration as 'a third destruction of the temple'.[67] Yet although the Zionists felt deceived, they concluded that a public commitment now mattered all the more. Indeed, although Ronald Graham in the Foreign Office (who now took over from Sykes as the British government liaison) believed the government had *already* committed itself, nothing official had yet been communicated.[68] Cecil, among others, still questioned how far Weizmann represented Jewish opinion,[69] and this issue was about to be tested.

By 1917 the rivalry between Zionists and anti-Zionists had developed into a pamphlet war. Lucien Wolf impressed on Balfour that only the CFC could speak for British Jews, and the Zionists were a minority led by foreigners; Milner promised to Claude Montefiore (the president of the Anglo-Jewish Association) that the Foreign Office would consult the CFC before deciding, while warning that Lloyd George was 'impressed by and sympathetic to many of the ideas of the Zionists'.[70] Although the two sides' immediate proposals for Palestine were not that far apart, Wolf feared that a national home would intensify anti-Jewish prejudice and hinder integration by the millions in the diaspora who could never move to the Holy Land: a fear the Zionists considered unfounded.[71] The CFC, Wolf told the Foreign

Office, could not stay silent; they were being misrepresented and their constituents demanded to know their views.[72] On 24 May a letter appeared in *The Times*, signed by David Alexander for the Board of Deputies and Claude Montefiore for the Anglo-Jewish Association, neither having consulted their executive committees. They said they had tried to negotiate with the Zionist organizations on the basis of 'cultural' Zionism: making Palestine a spiritual centre and setting its political future aside. Agreement had been unattainable, and the CFC stood by its 1916 proposal that the Jews in Palestine should enjoy civil and religious liberty, equal political rights, 'reasonable facilities' for immigration and colonization, and some local self-government. The Jews in Britain were primarily a religious community, and establishing a national home in Palestine could undermine their status. Conversely, the Zionist programme of political nationalism envisaged special rights for the Jews in Palestine that exceeded those of the rest of the population, with the danger of 'the bitterest feuds with their neighbours of other races and religions, which would seriously retard their progress, and would find deplorable echoes throughout the Orient'. The 'eventual preponderance' of the Jews in the Holy Land might still come, but if an unforced process it would rest on far firmer foundations.[73]

The letter anticipated the position that Edwin Montagu would put to the War Cabinet. It elicited a blizzard of responses far exceeding what *The Times* could publish, mostly taking strong exception and denying that the signatories spoke for their parent organizations or for the great majority of Jews. Among the correspondents were Weizmann, Lord Rothschild, and the chief rabbi Joseph Hertz, Weizmann refuting the charge that the Zionists sought exclusive privileges. *The Times* ran a pro-Zionist editorial, as did the *Jewish Chronicle*, which denounced the letter as a 'great betrayal'.[74] In the face of this chorus, the other members of the CFC executive wrote to *The Times* to support Alexander and Montefiore, and the Council of the Anglo-Jewish Association voted by a big majority in their favour; but at the larger and more representative Board of Deputies a resolution voicing 'profound disapproval' passed on 18 June by 56:51. It was true the vote could be interpreted as a provincial rebellion against metropolitan high-handedness. Subsequently the Board's constitution became more representative, but its submission to the 1919 peace conference still denied the Jews were 'a separate political nationality', and although the CFC was wound up, a Joint Foreign Committee replaced it, with Wolf continuing as secretary.[75] Even so, Rothschild became a vice-president of the Board of Deputies, and it was hard to discount the Zionist triumph, the Foreign Office concluding that Wolf and the CFC were losing influence.[76] Weizmann had urged a pro-Zionist declaration when British forces entered Palestine, and in June an (unfounded) rumour that German Foreign Minister Zimmermann was about to approach the Zionists spurred Weizmann to meet with Ronald Graham, who believed 'Our best card in dealing with the Russo–German proletariat is now Zionism.'[77] Graham contacted Balfour but found the Foreign Secretary still doubtful and inclined towards an American protect-orate, Graham highlighting the situation in Russia and suggesting something similar to the Cambon Declaration. Immediately after the Board of Deputies vote, however, Balfour changed tack. On 20 June he asked Weizmann and Rothschild 'to submit to him a declaration which would be satisfactory to us, which he would try and put before the War Cabinet for sanction'.[78] The Weizmann group had won the initiative.

The draft that Rothschild sent to Balfour was brief: '1. His Majesty's Government accepts the principle that Palestine should be reconstituted as the National Home of the Jewish people. 2. His Majesty's Government will use its best endeavours to secure the achievement of this object and will discuss the necessary methods and means with the Zionist Organisation.'[79] The Foreign Office had helped prepare this wording, Balfour having rejected previous versions. Sokolov led the drafting on the Zionist side, although many hands produced the text, which was a compromise, tactical wording. Its outstanding feature was the deliberately ambiguous 'national home', which derived from the German term 'Heimstätte' in the 1897 Basle Declaration, but whose meaning the political and cultural wings of the movement had contested. The first draft came from Harry Sacher, who dis-trusted Sykes and Lloyd George and asked for a 'Jewish state' as well as a national home. But Rothschild was more cautious, as was the cultural Zionist Ahad Ha'am—a leading influence on Weizmann[80]—while Sokolov believed that 'If we want too much we shall get nothing; on the other hand, if we get some sympathetic declaration, I hope we will gradually get more and more.' Sokolov envisaged an equivalent to the Cambon Declaration: not an 'agreement' or a 'full programme' (though those might follow) but 'a *general* approval of Zionist aims—as short and pregnant as possible'.[81] On 12 July a meeting at the Imperial Hotel tried to reconcile the differences by specifying the goal as a national home, with internal autonomy, free immi-gration, and a Jewish National Colonizing Corporation for resettlement and economic development, but on further British advice this was rejected as too detailed and the final very bald statement substituted.[82] It seems clear that the Zionists understated their objectives, under guidance from the Foreign Office and their own sense of the possible. In a speech to the EZF on 20 May Weizmann had warned that 'the conditions are not yet ripe for the setting up of a state *ad hoc*' in Palestine: 'States must be built up slowly, gradually, systematically and patiently'. While 'the creation of a Jewish commonwealth in Palestine is our final ideal', it must be achieved through 'a series of intermediary stages', one of which was a Great Power protectorate, ideally by Britain, during which 'while not interfering with the legitimate interests of the non-Jewish population', they would be able to 'set up the administrative machine which … would enable us to carry out the Zionist scheme'.[83]

The Zionists expected that their draft—after its repeated rewordings—would be accepted quickly. In fact the process took over three months and entailed major amendments. Once again the military context must be remembered. When Allenby reached the Palestine Front on 27 June, Lloyd George and much of the War Cabinet were anxious to invade not only for strategic reasons but also to boost public morale. They reached agreement with the French on redirecting the 10th Infantry Division from Salonika, and on 10 August the War Office instructed Allenby that it was of the 'highest importance' to 'strike the Turks as hard as possible'.[84] The Cabinet did not set specific objectives, some ministers thinking the order too cautious whereas others feared Allenby would overextend himself.[85] Allenby's interpretation, however, was that if he took the Gaza–Beersheba line the next one he could hold with reasonable security was Jaffa–Jerusalem. He had inherited a plan prepared by Sir Philip Chetwode to break through by taking Beersheba, at the inland (eastern) end of the line, after a feint at Gaza. Success hinged on seizing Beersheba's wells and water, which required meticulous preparation and concealment, though regaining air superiority with new Bristol fighters facilitated the task.[86] On 20 August Allenby told his corps commanders that he preferred to wait for reinforcements and until the 10th Division was ready,[87] but as Third Ypres dragged on towards its dismal conclusion the War Cabinet invested greater hopes in the Middle East. On 5 October Robertson advised Allenby that the Cabinet believed the capture of the Jaffa-Jerusalem line might enable diplomacy to get Turkey out of the war.[88] Allenby opposed any peace that left the Arabs under Turkish rule, as this would jeopardize the Arab Revolt and endanger his communications.[89] But on 31 October he launched the Beersheba operation anyway, and with a big numerical preponderance. From now on, in fact, the British overestimated the Turks rather than under-estimating them. The wells fell rapidly and intact, and on 6 November the Turks evacuated Gaza. By the middle of the month the British had progressed up to 60 miles and Allenby resolved to press on to Jerusalem, his men now crossing hill country in cold and rain against defenders who still fought hard, but with outdated equipment and clothing in tatters. Jerusalem was enveloped from the west and fell, without fighting within the city, on 9 December, just a month after the Balfour Declaration was published. Allenby established a defence line to the north, and his progress halted.

Jewish intelligence as well as the Arab Revolt—which was striking against Turkish communication lines in the interior—had assisted Allenby. Yet the War Cabinet was slow to consider the Zionist draft declaration, and when it finally did so considerations far from Palestine were uppermost. Balfour submitted it at the beginning of August,[90] and the Cabinet debated it three times—on 3 September, and on 4 and 31 October. Balfour's text differed little from what Rothschild had sent: 'His Majesty's Government accepts the principle that Palestine should be reconstituted as the national home of the Jewish people and will use their best endeavours to secure the

Figure 17. British troops by the Wailing Wall, Jerusalem

achievement of this object and will be ready to consider any suggestions on this subject which the Zionist Organisation may decide to lay before them.' What came to the Cabinet on 3 September, however, was both this and an alternative by Milner: 'His Majesty's Government accepts the principle that every opportunity should be afforded for the establishment of a home for the Jewish people in Palestine and will use its best endeavours to facilitate the achievement of this object and will be ready to consider any suggestions on the subject which the Zionist organizations may decide to lay before them.'[91] Although Milner was one of the government's most consistent Zionist sympathizers, he put 'home' rather than 'national home' and implied it might occupy only part of Palestine; in addition Britain would commit itself only to facilitating such a home rather than attempting to secure it. Moreover, a third document before the Cabinet was an ironically entitled memorandum by Edwin Montagu on 'The Anti-Semitism of the Present Government'. Montagu was not a member of the War Cabinet, but it allowed him to attend the discussion. As Secretary of State for India he had a departmental interest in the Middle East, and he was the only Jewish Cabinet minister. He had criticized Samuel in 1915 and now was more outspoken. His starting point was that the Jews were a religion, not a nation, and he was a 'Jewish Englishman'. 'I view with horror the acquisition of national unity', and if the Cabinet accepted the text he would have to resign his office and declare his neutrality in the war.[92] Although Montagu could be extremely cogent, his preoccupation with his personal position weakened him, as did his exaggeration of the implications for diaspora Jews. None the less, he made an impact. Zionism he dismissed as 'a mischievous political creed' and a reaction to state discrimination against Jews in Russia: a discrimination that the revolution had ended. He did not know what a 'national home' meant, but he presumed that Palestinian Muslims and Christians must make way for Jews and would be treated as foreigners. If Jews were told Palestine was their national home, every other country would try to get rid of them, and three times more Jews lived in the world than Palestine could accommodate even if its entire non-Jewish population departed. It would 'become the world's Ghetto' and all Jews foreign Jews. Hence the government should seek complete freedom of settlement for Jews in Palestine and equality with inhabitants of other faiths, but go no further.[93] The phrase 'the home of the Jewish people ... vitally prejudiced the position of every Jew elsewhere'.[94]

The 3 September Cabinet was unusual in that Lloyd George was ill and Balfour on holiday.[95] Even so, Montagu did not have things all his way. It was countered that 'the existence of a Jewish state or autonomous community in Palestine' might improve the lot of Jews in Eastern Europe and would have little effect in Britain. A small and influential section of British Jews opposed the idea, but many others supported it. Cecil (who spoke for Balfour) and the Foreign Office had 'very strongly pressed for a long time on this... There was a very strong and enthusiastic organization, more particularly in the United States, who were zealous in this matter, and his belief was that it would be of most substantial assistance to the Allies to have the earnestness and enthusiasm of these people enlisted on our side. To do nothing was to risk a direct breach with them...' Given that Britain was about to invade Palestine, Zionism was now less necessary to subvert Sykes–Picot. Hence the argument centred on propaganda and publicity, and was led by the Foreign Office, which looked to Zionism in Russia and America and feared that unless the Allies embraced Zionism, Germany would. It was significant that the Cabinet agreed, before any declaration, to consult Woodrow Wilson. Whereas previously France especially needed to be cleared, now it was America.[96]

Ministers had many reasons to seek influence over the American public and the Wilson administration. During October they rejected a peace with Germany by negotiation, and in a struggle extending into 1919 or 1920 US assistance would be vital. Yet Zionism was of questionable efficacy. Hankey briefed the Cabinet that in 1916–17 the number of dues payers in the American Zionist Federation and its affiliated bodies had risen from 200,000 to 320,000. Zionism had financial power, the Provisional Executive Committee for General Zionist Affairs set up in 1914 under the chairmanship of Louis Brandeis (the first Jewish Supreme Court Justice) having raised vast sums to aid the Jews in Palestine.[97] Modern studies of American Zionist organizations place the membership much lower, however, and suggest the main growth followed the Balfour Declaration: from 7,500 in 1914 to 30,000 in 1918.[98] This compared with an American Jewish population of over 2 million and, although the Zionists had successes in the elections to the American Jewish Congress in June 1917, opposition came from the liberal and Reform synagogue movement and also from the trade unions and socialists who were strongest among the 1.5 million, often working-class and Yiddish-speaking, Jews of New York City.[99] The Provisional Committee focused on helping Palestine now rather than on its future, maintaining neutrality for fear the Turks would obstruct its work or slaughter the Jews as they had the Armenians (see Introduction). Only in May 1917, after America had declared war (although not on Turkey), did Brandeis and his adviser Jacob de Haas tell Rothschild and Weizmann that the American Zionists shared their counterparts' aims, including a British protectorate, but they did not publicize this view and concentrated instead on high-level lobbying. Brandeis's colleague, Rabbi Stephen Wise, met Colonel House, who seemed supportive (as House did to most of his interlocutors) but actually had reservations.[100] In contrast, Wilson told Brandeis that he was sympathetic to a publicly guaranteed homeland for the Jewish people under British protection and would publicize this view when the time came. There matters rested until after the 3 September War Cabinet meeting Cecil cabled House to ask whether Wilson would favour a declaration. House replied that he had spoken with the president and 'In his opinion the time is not yet opportune for any definite statement further perhaps than one of sympathy provided it can be made without conveying any real commitment. Things are in such a state of flux at the moment that he does not consider it advisable to go further.'[101] This message came just after Wilson's reply to Benedict XV had disassociated the president from extreme Allied war aims; and the United States still remained at peace with Turkey, which was trying to avoid provocation. It was therefore unsurprising that the Americans were unforthcoming in response to what was, after all, a fairly informal approach.[102] But discouragement from Washington, following Montagu's assault in Cabinet, stalled consideration for a month. Balfour told Weizmann and Rothschild the case had been 'decided against the Zionists', and he minuted that 'as this question was (in my absence) decided by the Cabinet against the Zionists I cannot do anything till the decision is reversed'.[103] It returned to the agenda only when Lloyd George put it there, after Weizmann used Scott of the *Manchester Guardian* to intercede with the premier. Palestine was discussed again on 4 October, and this time Balfour and Lloyd George attended.

In the run-up to the second meeting, both sides prepared. Weizmann and Rothschild complained that the Cabinet listened to Montagu but not to the majority view.[104] A Foreign Office memorandum contested Montagu's claims. It doubted a national home would endanger Jews in Britain, whereas it would improve their status in Palestine and allow Jews elsewhere to escape persecution. Moreover, the Allies had proclaimed 'the peace settlement must be based on the principle of nationality. It would be a strange and glaring anomaly if, while professing to observe that principle, we were to deny or ignore the claims of nationality in the case of the people who throughout history have clung to them more tenaciously than any other.'[105] Rothschild warned that the German press was urging the Central Powers to demand at the peace conference that Palestine become a Jewish settlement under German protection, while Ronald Graham told Hankey that the British Zionists had virtually suspended propaganda in Russia, and Sokolov and Weizmann would do no more until the declaration was settled. He too cited the 'evidently inspired' campaign in the German press.[106] In fact Zimmermann, the leading Zionist sympathizer in the German Foreign Ministry, feared Britain might outbid Germany, and the German biochemist Otto Warburg together with Victor Jacobson (who headed the Zionist Copenhagen office) had submitted proposals for freedom of immigration and cultural autonomy for Jews in Palestine. Kühlmann, however, who until August was the German ambassador in Constantinople, advised caution, especially now that Palestine was threatened and Germany wanted Turkey to break relations with the United States. The Turks feared Palestinian autonomy would set a dangerous precedent, and the German Foreign Ministry feared pushing Turkey towards a separate peace. It was true that when in April the Turks ordered 9,000 Jews to leave Jaffa and warned that Jerusalem would be next the OHL interceded with the Turkish war minister, Enver Pasha, to halt the evacuations. But when Kühlmann replaced Zimmermann he deferred discussion of the Zionist proposals to 'a more opportune moment'. So although German newspapers indeed called for Palestinian autonomy, the British Foreign Office was wrong to think a German pro-Zionist declaration was imminent.[107] As for Russia, the Provisional Government had granted Jews full citizenship and equal rights. The number of Zionist dues payers there rose from 25,000 in 1914 to 146,000 after the revolution.[108] The War Cabinet was briefed that out of 6 million Russian Jews, 2.4 million were under enemy occupation. In the occupied area the leading Jewish papers were pro-Zionist, and Zionists were being elected to town councils. In non-occupied Russia, the Jewish press was also Zionist and foreign minister Tereschchenko wished success to the all-Russian Zionist Conference when it met in May.[109] But at the same conference, Yechiel Tchlenov, the most prominent Russian Zionist, avoided calling for a British protectorate and praised the Jews who were serving in the Ottoman army, thus preserving a measure of neutrality even though Russia and Turkey were at war. The reporting from British diplomats was ambiguous (and Ambassador Buchanan denied Zionism had influence), but

nothing shall be done which may prejudice the civil and religious rights of existing non-Jewish communities in Palestine, or the rights and political status enjoyed in any other country by such Jews who are fully contented with their existing nationality.[112]

This 'Milner–Amery draft', like the final declaration, was both balanced and potentially contradictory, Milner having asked Amery for 'something which would go a reasonable distance to meeting the objections both Jewish and pro-Arab without impairing the substance of the proposed declaration'.[113] The national home might not include all Palestine, and the Zionist organization no longer featured. Above all, the declaration became subject to two provisos, the second meant to mollify Montagu and the first (though Amery in later life was unsure of this) to mollify Curzon.[114] However, the first proviso referred only to the civil and religious rights of non-Jews in Palestine and, given that the second referred to 'political status', the absence from the first of political rights appears no oversight. By implication the non-Jews within Palestine were being less completely safeguarded than were the Jews outside and in neither case were the protection mechanisms specified. None the less, it was on this revised draft that the War Cabinet agreed to consult the Zionists and anti-Zionists and to clarify the American government's views. For a second time a decision was deferred. Even so, by authorizing the consultation the War Cabinet made it hard to follow Montagu's opposition to any declaration at all.

The first requirement was to clarify matters in Washington. The 4 October Cabinet had conflicting information, as House's 10 September cable saying Wilson opposed a commitment was offset by a telegram from Brandeis to Weizmann on 26 September that 'from talks I have had with the president and from expressions of opinion given to closest advisers, I feel I can answer you that he is in entire sympathy with declaration quoted in yours of the 19th as approved by Foreign Office and Prime Minister'.[115] But now the approach to the Americans was more direct. Balfour sent the Milner–Amery draft to House with the gloss that 'in view of reports that the German Government are making great efforts to capture the Zionist movement, the question of a message of sympathy with the movement from His Majesty's Government has again been considered by the Cabinet'. On 13 October Wilson wrote to House that he 'concurred' with the text, the Foreign Office being informed of the president's 'approval' but asked not to publicize it as he would make a later announcement to the American Jews. As usual, the decision-making process was very different from that in

London. Brandeis and Wise had less continuous contact with the authorities than did their British counterparts, and the State Department appears to have been by-passed. House laced his correspondence with anti-Semitic innuendos, saw 'many dangers', and feared Britain would use America to assist its plans to block the road to Egypt. However, he acknowledged that the president was more supportive than he was, both because of the self-determination principle and because of Wilson's Protestant upbringing in the household of a Presbyterian minister, steeped in the Old Testament scriptures. 'To think', Wilson told Wise, 'that I as the son of the manse should be able to restore the Holy Land to its people.' The British message to him of 6 October, unlike that of 3 September, was a pressing official démarche that included a draft declaration, and he responded accordingly.[116]

By the time the Cabinet held its third discussion on 31 October, it knew the American president had approved a similar text to the final version. It also knew the outcome from the consultation of British Jews. Weizmann arranged an impressive petitioning movement among synagogues and friendly societies: not only in London but also in Manchester, Leeds, Liverpool, Birmingham, Glasgow, Northampton, and Sheffield. The phenomenon, Graham reported, was 'rather remarkable', and 'almost unanimously favourable to the Zionist idea'.[117] In addition Hankey sought out nine community leaders recommended by Weizmann and Montagu. This was hardly an attempt at a representative sample, but it included many key political and religious figures, of whom six broadly favoured the Milner–Amery draft and only three did not. Claude Montefiore, who had written to *The Times*, held to his views: the Jews were not a nation; if the Russian Revolution succeeded the Jewish problem would be solved and a national home not needed; and such a home, were it to exist, would be a hotbed of German intrigue. L. L. Cohen, chairman of the Jewish Board of Guardians, agreed Jews were not a nation and not homeless: the declaration would stimulate anti-Semitism everywhere but only some could move to Palestine. Finally Sir Philip Magnus disliked the phrase 'national home' and wanted Palestine to be a Jewish cultural centre, or opposition from other communities might mean Jews suffering the fate of the Armenians. In contrast, Herbert Samuel recapitulated the strategic threat to Egypt if Turkey or any Continental Power controlled Palestine. The chief rabbi agreed with Samuel that a British protectorate would be welcomed worldwide, and approved of the protection for Palestine's existing inhabitants. Lord Rothschild, with curious precision, said 10 million of the 12 million Jews in the world were

Zionists, and all but 10,000–15,000 of the Jews in Britain. The Jews in Palestine would have their own language and civil, religious, and educational institutions under Allied protection, and he was optimistic they would have cordial relations with the Arabs, whose rights would be respected. Sir Stuart Samuel, the new president of the Board of Deputies, said British Jews had tended to stay aloof from Zionism, but a large majority would favour a national home, even if not wanting to go there themselves, and the Jews of the world would pay for its economic development. Finally, both Weizmann and Sokolov insisted on the massive welcome the declaration would receive, and Sokolov did not oppose the provisos. Whereas the critics still denied the Jews were a race, the supporters concentrated on the breadth of support across the global Jewish community.[118]

In the run-up to the final meeting Montagu, Curzon, Sykes, and Graham also reiterated their positions.[119] Montagu questioned the appeal of Zionism in America, reporting that the central conference of American rabbis had issued an anti-Zionist statement; but he focused on Palestine. The Jews numbered less than a quarter of the population and the rest were mostly Muslim Arabs who would not accept Jewish authority; and, further, Jerusalem should not be controlled by just one faith. Nor was there scope for a big increase in population: so who should be dispossessed?[120] And Curzon, in a memorandum for which the meeting was delayed, took a similar tack. The Jewish people globally, he wrote, numbered 12 million, of whom 9.25 million were in Europe (6 million in Russia), 2 million in North America, and 245,000 in Britain. Before the war 125,000 had lived in Palestine, in a total population of 600,000–700,000. The territory had no natural resources; even to be developed for agriculture it needed irrigation and afforestation and during the war the Turks had wreaked further destruction. The Arabs and their forefathers had been there for over 1,500 years, they owned the land, and 'they will not be content either to be expropriated for Jewish immigrants, or to act merely as hewers of wood and drawers of water to the latter'. He acknowledged the arguments of 'political expediency' in favour of a declaration, and the need to head off the Germans, but he proposed that while a European administration kept order in the Holy Places the Jews should have equal civil and religious rights with those of other faiths and a scheme should help them to purchase and settle land. The essence of his argument was that Palestine could not support a massive Jewish immigration (and would need expensive investment to take extra numbers at all), and implicitly he opposed a 'national home' if meaning a Jewish state.[121]

The principal riposte came from Sykes. He countered that Palestine only seemed barren because of misgovernment, over-dependence on religious orders and the seasonal tourist trade, and neglect by the 'naturally idle and indolent race who lived there'. Orange production round Jaffa had grown fiftyfold in ten years, and abundant potential existed for olives and wine as well as for subtropical crops in the Jordan Valley: irrigation was possible along the coast and the interior enjoyed plenty of rain. Over a forty-year period the population could quadruple or quintuple.[122] In addition to addressing Curzon's economic arguments, he mentioned new contacts between German diplomats, the Young Turks, and Zionists, while Graham once more stressed the urgency.[123] In fact by the final Cabinet meeting the proceedings (as with the final discussion of the Montagu Declaration) appeared a matter of form. Ministers had Curzon's memorandum and Hankey's collation of Jewish opinion, as well as notes on Zionism in Russia and the United States. Balfour said he gathered everyone now agreed that 'from a purely diplomatic and political point of view, it was desirable some declaration favourable to the aspirations of the Jewish nationalists should now be made'. The 'vast majority' of Jews in Russia and America and the world over seemed favourable to Zionism, and a declaration would enable 'extremely useful propaganda'. He did not believe a declaration would hinder Jewish assimilation in Western countries, and although opinions differed he was informed that if Palestine were 'scientifically developed' it could support many more inhabitants. He understood a 'national home' to mean:

> some form of British, American, or other protectorate, under which full facilities would be given to the Jews to work out their own salvation and to build up, by means of education, agriculture, and industry, a real centre of national culture and forum of national life. It did not necessarily involve the early establishment of an independent Jewish state, which was a matter for gradual development in accordance with the ordinary laws of political evolution.[124]

According to Lloyd George's memoirs Balfour was heard attentively and without dissent.[125] Montagu had warned Lloyd George about Weizmann that 'you are being misled by a foreigner, a dreamer and idealist...who sweeps aside all practical difficulties'[126] but, with Montagu now absent on his mission to India, Curzon was isolated and more moderate. He said he disagreed with Montagu, accepted the 'bulk' of Jews held Zionist opinions, and admitted the force of the diplomatic and propaganda considerations. But he did not share the prevailing optimism about Palestine's future, and 'feared that by the suggested declaration we should be raising false expectations which could never be realised'. None the less, he supported it, while recommending its language should be guarded, and on this note the Cabinet approved the text.

In some ways the process had been commendably thorough. The Zionist draft had been diluted and qualified. Knowing the French were sympathetic, the Cabinet waited to clarify Wilson's attitude, and to ascertain the

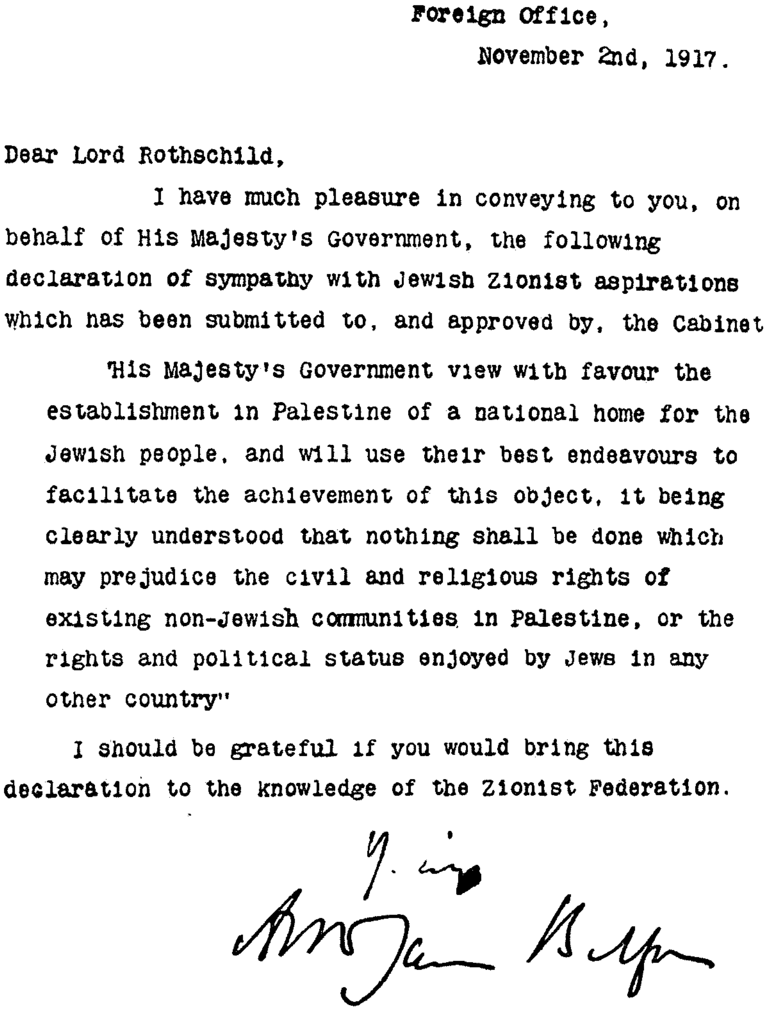

Foreign Office,

November 2nd, 1917.

Dear Lord Rothschild,

      I have much pleasure in conveying to you, on behalf of His Majesty's Government, the following declaration of sympathy with Jewish Zionist aspirations which has been submitted to, and approved by, the Cabinet

    "His Majesty's Government view with favour the establishment in Palestine of a national home for the Jewish people, and will use their best endeavours to facilitate the achievement of this object, it being clearly understood that nothing shall be done which may prejudice the civil and religious rights of existing non-Jewish communities in Palestine, or the rights and political status enjoyed by Jews in any other country"

    I should be grateful if you would bring this declaration to the knowledge of the Zionist Federation.

Figure 18. A facsimile of the Balfour Declaration (Arthur Balfour to Lord Rothschild, 2 November 1917)

views of British Jewish leaders as well as being briefed about American and Russian opinion. Sykes had given assurances about Palestine's economic potential while the Foreign Office emphasized the situation in Russia and the risk of German pre-emption. Lloyd George had been sympathetic all along, perhaps for biblical reasons but more from his determination to control Palestine, although now Allenby was invading Palestine anyway. Whereas the premier had been more proactive in April, in the final stages he intervened little, except to return the issue to the agenda after the 3 September Cabinet. In his memoirs he said the declaration was driven primarily by propagandist motives, at a very dark moment in the war, and 'we had every reason at that time to believe that in both countries [Russia and America] the friendliness or hostility of the Jewish race might make a considerable difference'.[127] Balfour similarly, though preoccupied with propaganda and diplomacy rather than Palestine's strategic significance, drafted in August a much less qualified commitment than the one eventually adopted. Of the remaining Cabinet members Milner—perhaps the closest to the premier—was supportive, if willing to acknowledge potential objections. Smuts was impressed by Weizmann and accepted the propaganda arguments, but also was convinced of the justice of the Zionist cause, which for the rest of his life he defended. In August Labour had passed a resolution in favour of the Jews forming 'a free State under international guarantee' in Palestine, and Barnes, the War Cabinet's Labour member, went along with the declaration, despite harbouring doubts in retrospect.[128] In contrast, Bonar Law was more guarded, as was habitual with him, though he did not press his views.[129] Curzon intervened forcefully on 4 October but having registered his dissent for posterity he deferred to his colleagues. Montagu was the most important obstacle, but would probably have been overridden on 31 October even if he had attended. At first he brought the Cabinet up short, but he weakened his credibility by dwelling on the supposed threat to Jewish assimilation, which case his critics eventually rejected.

The drawn-out process of gaining agreement helped clarify what the declaration meant. The British government was not committed to more than facilitating the establishment of a Jewish national home, though by the time the declaration was published it was likely to have more say in Palestine's future than would anyone else. The declaration had no accompanying boundary map[130] and the national home would not necessarily embrace the whole of Palestine. Balfour was not even committed to a *British* protectorate (and the declaration did not specify it should be British), though it is reasonable to assume his colleagues were. All could agree on an initial programme of assisting Jewish immigration and colonization, and of eco- nomic and cultural development. Beyond that, according to Lloyd George's peace conference memoirs, the Cabinet did not intend to establish a Jewish state without reference to Arab wishes, but if representative institutions were established and the Jews attained a majority, Palestine would become a 'Jewish Commonwealth'.[131] This more or less matches with Balfour's statement at the 31 October Cabinet: that conditions were being created in which Jews might attain a majority in all (or part of) Palestine, but achieving this would be up to the Jews themselves.[132] As Balfour told the intelligence officer, Richard Meinertzhagen, 'My personal hope is that the Jews will make good in Palestine and eventually found a Jewish State. It is up to them now; we have given them their great opportunity.' Both he and Lloyd George confirmed to Meinertzhagen in 1919 and 1921 that they envisaged a Jewish sovereign state would emerge from the declaration, which the Palestine Royal Commission report in 1937 interpreted as 'the outcome of a compromise between those Ministers who contemplated the ultimate establishment of a Jewish State and those who did not'.[133]

Back in the spring, Sykes (whose sympathies lay more with Arab than with Jewish nationalism) had opened contacts with the Zionists in the belief that they could block Palestine's internationalization; Lloyd George, who wanted to 'grab' Palestine and Mesopotamia, probably held a similar view. Yet Curzon, who also wanted to control the two territories, was the most reluctant War Cabinet member to approve the declaration, and eventually did so on different grounds. After two failures at Gaza, the British could not be sure that Allenby would succeed, but there were grounds for saying that military superiority made the declaration less necessary for their strategic objectives. The declaration also built a further obstacle against a negotiated peace with Turkey.[134] Its key incentives were its diplomatic and propaganda advantages, which the Foreign Office urged so strongly and feared Germany would pre-empt. Yet actually the arguments that the Cabinet found com- pelling were misleading, and the immediate consequences of the Balfour Declaration, as of the Montagu Declaration, were disappointing. Perhaps both statements betrayed an overestimation of such pronouncements, reflecting waning Whitehall confidence in Britain's military prowess. Thus the German danger proved exaggerated and the evidence for it largely based on hearsay and assumptions that German newspapers were officially inspired. In fact after the declaration was published Kühlmann refused to meet the

German Zionists. Although the press called for an equivalent German statement, all that materialized (in January 1918) was German backing for a Turkish declaration in support of 'a flourishing Jewish settlement in Palestine' to be obtained through controlled immigration and colonization 'within the absorptive capacity of the country', local self-government, and free development of Jewish civilization. The Turks were unlikely to recapture Jerusalem, and now would have to curry Jewish favour.[135] The boot was on the other foot.

The Foreign Office also overestimated Zionist influence in Russia, where the declaration coincided with the Bolshevik Revolution (and the Cabinet knew that Jews were prominent in the Bolshevik leadership),[136] while Tchlenov and the Russian Zionists considered Weizmann and Sokolov too close to the British.[137] News of the declaration circulated slowly. It did elicit welcoming demonstrations and editorials, but the Bolsheviks were determinedly anti-Zionist, and forbade the meeting in March 1918 of a Russian Jewish Congress in which the Zionists would have been the largest element. The declaration failed to keep Russia in the war, or to influence Lenin.[138] In America, the Provisional Executive Committee for General Zionist Affairs welcomed the declaration, as did a Zionist Convention in Baltimore, while in August 1918 a public letter from Wilson to Stephen Wise followed Balfour's wording almost verbatim.[139] Yet Weizmann was disappointed by the lack of cooperation with Brandeis, some American Jewish organizations remained wary,[140] and there is no evidence that the declaration made American policy more pro-Allied. The declaration must be seen, however, within two contexts. The first was the enthusiasm of British ministers, not least Lloyd George himself, for propaganda, and their (unjustified) fear that the Germans were better at it. In late 1917 Lloyd George was preparing to reorganize Britain's propaganda machinery in order to campaign more aggressively.[141] Secondly, foremost among the Central Powers' weaknesses was perceived to be their multinational composition. The Allies were cautious in embracing national self-determination as a battle-cry, partly because they hoped for separate ceasefires with Vienna and Constantinople, but also from fear of blow-back in their own empires (and one of the arguments for the Montagu Declaration was the inconsistency of supporting self-determination externally but not within). During 1917, however, the Allies deepened their engagement with the Polish, Czech, and South Slav exiled nationalist movements, and self-determination as a principle figured in their 10 January 1917 reply to the Central Powers' peace note and increasingly in British and

American leaders' rhetoric. In the Foreign Office, Graham highlighted what he considered the anomaly of supporting infant national movements but not the oldest one of all, and in the 31 October Cabinet Balfour referred to the Zionists as 'nationalists'. The national sovereignty they pursued, how-ever, lay in a territory where they formed a minority, Balfour later writing to Lloyd George that:

> The weak point of our position of course is that in the case of Palestine we deliberately and rightly decline to accept the principle of self-determination ... if the present inhabitants were consulted they would unquestionably give an anti-Jewish verdict. Our justification for our policy is that we regard Palestine as being absolutely exceptional; that we consider the question of the Jews outside Palestine as of world importance, and that we consider the Jews to have an historic claim to a home in their ancient land, provided that home can be given them without either dispossessing or oppressing the present inhabitants.[142]

A final miscalculation therefore related to the Palestinian Arabs. Sykes had given reassurance that 'the Arabs could be managed'.[143] Lloyd George wrote afterwards that the British could not communicate with them because they were fighting for the Turks.[144] Montagu had raised them as a concern, but as a secondary concern to that of assimilated Jews in the West. Curzon had been more forceful, but had not pressed the case. At the end of the discussion process, Sykes's memorandum drew attention primarily to the Holy Land's economic potential, of which he correctly took a more sanguine view than Curzon, albeit on an impressionistic basis. Balfour could there-fore tell the Cabinet that Palestine could support substantially greater numbers (and although the necessary investment would be costly, diaspora communities might contribute). In addition the Milner–Amery draft pro-vided for the civil and religious rights of the non-Jewish population to be respected. Fundamental here was that whereas Montagu and the anti-Zionists denied the Jews were a nation, the Cabinet by approving the declaration accepted Weizmann's contention that they were a national and not just religious community. Nothing suggests the Cabinet thought similarly of the Palestinian Arabs. They were acknowledged to be part of the larger Arabic-speaking world, but that world was not deemed ready for political independence, as the Sykes–Picot Agreement testified. As for Hussein, it was questionable how far he had accepted that agreement, which he was told about only when Sykes and Picot met him and his son Feisal at Jeddah in May 1917. At the meeting Hussein strongly objected to foreign direct rule and to foreign officials as opposed to advisers, and particularly objected to French administration, although eventually accepting it in principle in Syria if exercised on a similar basis to that by the British in Baghdad. However, Sykes neither left him with a copy of the agreement, nor mentioned possible plans for the Jews in Palestine.[145] After the Balfour Declaration, Hussein received a new British assurance, in the shape of the 'Hogarth Message' of 4 January 1918. It provided for a 'return of Jews to Palestine' in so far as was 'compatible with the freedom of the existing population both economic and political', thus mentioning political rights where the declaration itself had not, but thereby adding further potential contradictions to the web of Britain's undertakings. Hussein accepted the statement with the proviso that it might have to be reconsidered after the war,[146] and indeed by November 1918 it was already harder than a year earlier to imagine Arab and Jewish aspirations being reconciled.[147] During 1918 the British administration in southern Palestine circulated Arabic-language and Hebrew-language newspapers, recruited Arabs for Feisal's Northern Arab Army and Jews for the Jewish Legion, and facilitated ceremonial acts such as funerals for Arab leaders killed by the Turks and the inauguration of the Hebrew University of Jerusalem. By the end of the year the two communities were mobilizing against each other, and in 1920–1 the first widespread rioting followed. By this stage many in London were having second thoughts, but Britain accepted the mandate in 1922 and after a Whitehall review persisted with it. The propaganda arguments now carried little weight, but Palestine remained strategically important, it was hoped that worldwide Jewish financial aid would make its development less burdensome, and Colonial Secretary Winston Churchill as well as Balfour and Lloyd George accepted that Britain must honour its commitment.[148]

If in retrospect the declaration seemed more significant than at the time, its makers understood it was momentous. Lloyd George told the Commons on 20 December that:

> It would be rather interesting looking at the year 1917, if it were possible to project ourselves into the year 2017 and to observe the events of this particular year...when the history of 1917 comes to be written...these events in Mesopotamia and Palestine will hold a much more conspicuous place in the minds and in the memories of the people than many an event which looms much larger for the moment in our sight.[149]

The Balfour Declaration would have been unthinkable without the war and Turkey's intervention. But equally crucial was the 1917 turning point, when

Britain's prospects of victory dwindled, and the Russian Revolution and American intervention meant that over two of its partners it had little diplomatic purchase and must appeal to public opinion. Sympathy with Zionism carried less weight, unsurprisingly, than perceptions of national and imperial interest. The same applied to France's Cambon Declaration, which paved the way for the British one, although American support appears to have derived more simply from Wilson's idealism. The British hoped to use the Zionists, as the Zionists hoped to use the British, and both sides overestimated what the partnership might bring. But for all the opportunism that surrounded it, after other 1917 legacies had receded the declaration's consequences would endure.

PART IV

Conclusion

Towards 1918

Lenin's Revolution, the Ludendorff Offensives, and Wilson's Fourteen Points

World politics in 1917 was framed by the German submarine offensive and the American and Allied response, and by revolution in Russia. World politics in 1918 played out against a German land offensive, a stepping up of the American commitment, and a second Russian Revolution. In the east, the Bolshevik seizure of power took Russia out of the conflict. In the west, Britain, France, and Italy hoped to accomplish with American assistance a victory they were now too weak to gain alone, while Austria-Hungary, Bulgaria, and Turkey staked their futures on a German triumph. Increasingly the struggle became a contest between Washington and Berlin. The transition during the 1917–18 winter will be considered under three main heads: the Bolshevik Revolution; Germany's commitment to an all-out spring attack; and the escalation of America's war effort.

The first step in the transition was the Bolshevik decision to seize power, with the 'October' Revolution (24–25 October/7–8 November) as the consequence. It was one of the outstanding events of 1917 and Lenin was one of the year's outstanding victors. Yet the leader's fiat did not yet determine party policy, which was set at the Seventh All-Russian Party Congress in April and the Sixth Bolshevik Party Congress in July–August, and in between primarily by majority vote in an elected Central Committee. Lenin had to fight to have his positions adopted, and did not always prevail.[1] None the less, in many ways this was indeed his revolution and his leadership was vital: in rejecting any compromise with the Provisional Government; in driving for the takeover; and in steering the new government towards peace with the Central Powers. The international context is sometimes lacking from the Bolshevik Revolution's story, yet none the less was critical to it.

Figure 19. Photograph of Lenin from 1917

Like Kerensky, Lenin came from a family of minor aristocrats. By 1917 he had reached the age of 46 having spent most of his life as a professional agitator and much of it in exile, conspiring, pamphleteering, and progressing from meeting to meeting. The Socialist Revolutionary Viktor Chernov, like so many of Lenin's opponents, under-estimated him. Yet he penned an acute portrait:

> By his endowments Lenin is an outstanding figure, cruelly hollowed, distorted by the abnormal conditions... Lenin possesses a devotion to the revolutionary cause which permeates his entire being. But to him revolution is embodied in his person. Lenin possesses an outstanding mind, but it is a mind that embraces things not with three dimensions; it is a mind of one dimension—more than that a unilinear mind... he is a man of one-sided will and consequently a man with a stunted moral sensitivity... All that is important for him is the correctness of the basic direction... As for the choice of methods, this is sheer particulars and details.[2]

Only the combination of Lenin's leadership with extraordinary circumstances made possible the revolution: 'the first "breach of the front" on a world-wide scale', as Lenin put it; a fracture in the chain of global imperialism.[3] He was conscious of belonging to a worldwide, not just Russian, movement, whose doctrine taught that revolution could forge a socialist society only when historical development was ripe. Georgi Plekhanov, the first important Russian Marxist theoretician, who became another of Lenin's enemies, had argued that given Russia's backwardness its first stage of revolution would be bourgeois and anti-feudal, establishing conditions in which the country could modernize and a mass movement emerge. Seeking to accelerate the process would be dangerously utopian. After the 1905 Russian Revolution, however, Lenin contended that it could indeed be telescoped, that a peaceful transition was impossible, and a 'revolutionary democratic dictatorship of the proletariat and the peasantry' would act not in conjunction with the Russian liberals but against them, laying by force the basis for socialism.[4] This, and his insistence on a tightly knit, conspiratorial party differentiated him from the Mensheviks and from the non-Marxist Socialist Revolutionaries, even before the schism of 1914 pushed him to the fringe of the Russian and global movement. He was appalled by patriotic socialists' willingness to compromise with bourgeois governments in order to support the war effort. On the contrary his exegesis, set out in his *Imperialism, the Highest Stage of Capitalism*, written in Zurich in 1916, was that the war was an imperialist enterprise on both sides, whose true character became discernible not through diplomatic history but through objective analysis of the ruling classes' position. Since 1900 global capitalism had entered a new and more aggressive phase, characterized by concentration of ownership, cartels, the export of capital rather than of goods, and a strategic role for the banks. The war was 'imperialist (that is, an annexationist, predatory war of plunder) on the part of both sides ... a war for the division of the world, for the partition and repartition of colonies and spheres of finance capital, etc.'[5] The working class were dying for a cause that formed no part of their interest.

Lenin therefore possessed an analytical framework when the tsarist regime (to his surprise and his exhilaration) collapsed, and when also (to his consternation) the Bolshevik leaders within Russia were willing to cooperate with the Provisional Government. That government's class composition and expansionist war aims made it, in his view, no better than Nicholas II. His first 'Letter from Afar', written in March 1917, spelled out that the 'imperialist world war' had hastened the historical process, overthrowing tsarism and intensifying the bourgeois/proletarian struggle that would transform the conflict into an international civil war. The February

Revolution he interpreted as a conspiracy between a portion of the Russian bourgeoisie and the British and French embassies:

> to seize power *for the purpose of continuing the imperialist war*...more ferociously and obstinately, for the purpose of *slaughtering fresh millions* of Russian workers and peasants in order that the [Russian capitalists] might obtain Constantinople, the French capitalists Syria, the British capitalists Mesopotamia, and so on. This on the one hand. On the other there was a profound proletarian and mass popular movement of a revolutionary character...for *bread*, for *peace*, for *real freedom*.[6]

It was understandable that he should strain to return to Russia and direct the party into intransigent opposition, the first of his celebrated 'April Theses' insisting that Russia's war under the Provisional Government remained 'a predatory imperialist war' and opposing even 'the slightest concession to "revolutionary defencism"'. Instead power must transfer from the bourgeoisie to the proletariat and the poorest peasantry. The new regime would replace the tsarist and the bourgeois state machines by an administration via the soviets, the police, army, and bureaucracy being abolished and all land and banks being nationalized. Only through overthrowing capital globally, however, could a truly democratic peace ensue.[7] 'Marxism', Lenin had warned, 'is not pacifism.'[8]

By the time Lenin issued the April Theses he was back in Petrograd. This precondition for his later actions was arranged by Germany, and figured not least among the international contributions to the revolution. Both sides in the war attempted to destabilize their opponents by backing national separatist and social revolutionary movements, but the Central Powers were first off the mark. By 1915 their representatives in Switzerland were monitoring the Russian exiles and seeking contact, through a variety of intermediaries of whom the most important was the German socialist Parvus Helphand, whom, however, Lenin shunned.[9] German finance—in what quantities remains uncertain—was channelled to the Bolsheviks, and helped to fund their newspapers and pamphlets. Kühlmann told the OHL that 'The Bolshevik movement could never have attained the scale or the influence which it has today without our continual support.'[10] As even Lenin's critics acknowledged, however, though willing to use the Germans he was in no sense beholden to them. This point was borne out by the circumstances of his return via the notorious 'sealed train' from Zurich via Berlin and Sweden to Finland, and on to Petrograd. The German authorities endorsed the scheme, including the OHL, Wilhelm, and Bethmann, and the decision was rapid and uncontroversial (as also for the supposedly neutral Swedish government). Ludendorff justified it as necessary for the war, and most of the difficulties came from the revolutionaries, Lenin fearing that he and his companions would be viewed as traitors and arrested on arrival. The train was sealed not to protect the German population from the Bolshevik virus, but so that the Russian travellers avoided contact with German personnel, all interactions being conducted by the accompanying Swiss socialist, Fritz Platten. That they were playing with fire seems not to have crossed the German leaders' minds.[11] Yet on the other hand, the non-Bolshevik socialists in the Petrograd Soviet had no thought of arresting Lenin for treasonable transactions with the enemy, and the chair of the Soviet, Nikolay Chkheidze, greeted him on his arrival at the Finland Station on 3/16 April, urging him to respect political unity. The refusal codified in the April Theses was Lenin's response.

It is true that on reaching Russia—a country from which he had been absent for a decade and knew about through letters and the press—Lenin made concessions. He recognized the Bolsheviks were too weak for insurrection now, and backed land redistribution to the peasantry.[12] Over the war, however, he did not relent; and although his programme seemed outlandish to the party's internal leadership (the Central Committee on 6/19 April rejecting the April Theses), by tireless agitation he won support at the grassroots.[13] Hence the Bolsheviks were well positioned to garner members once their Menshevik and Socialist Revolutionary competitors joined forces with the liberals in the second Provisional Government. The new coalition was slow to grant concessions to peasant land hunger and to the nationalist movements in Finland and the Ukraine; it hesitated to call elections for a Constituent Assembly, and economic conditions went from bad to worse. Although the eight-hour day was widely granted, price rises wiped out early wage gains, and between April and July half a million Russians went on strike.[14] Above all, the Provisional Government not only failed to negotiate peace but also authorized the Kerensky offensive, from whose failure the events leading through the July Days to the Kornilov Affair were the more or less direct consequence.

Although the July Days damaged the Bolsheviks, and Lenin took refuge in Finland, the party structures remained largely intact. After the Kornilov Affair most detainees were released, while 40,000 rifles had been distributed to the hitherto largely unarmed Petrograd workers.[15] During September evidence mounted that public opinion was radicalizing. Bolsheviks won majorities in more and more soldiers' committees in the northern and central sectors of the front.[16] Officers' relations with their men became more strained, and many were murdered. Between March and October perhaps a million troops deserted, and from June the desertion rate rose.[17] British observers predicted that in no circumstances would the troops remain once the cold set in: winter clothing was lacking, and it was difficult even to keep the men fed.[18] Aleksandr Verkhovsky, who became war minister after the Kornilov episode, recognized Russia could not maintain the army at its present size. He decided to release all men over 40 and to disband sixty divisions. He promised the Allied military attachés that the front-line fighters would not be reduced, though warned that the Kornilov Affair had damaged discipline.[19] Eventually he declared that peace was needed at once, with or without Allied agreement.[20]

As the soldiers regained their villages, land seizures multiplied and became more violent. Across central and southern Russia, gentry homes were ransacked.[21] But this, to complete the circle, made food supply still more precarious, and in its final weeks the Provisional Government prepared to relocate Petrograd's inhabitants. Foreign observers reported continuing disruption on the railways, and Lenin predicted famine.[22] After the summer crises the government had forfeited respect, and Kerensky repeatedly reorganized it. He became more idiosyncratic, inhabiting the Winter Palace and sleeping in the tsars' bedroom, and allegedly entering a liaison with Nicholas's daughter. The scandal and incompetence that had tarnished the tsarist regime now discredited its successor, and between Kerensky and the Bolsheviks much of the officer corps would stay neutral.[23] Once the offensive failed and Russia's partners refused to scale down their war aims, the government had run out of ideas for restoring peace or doing more than clutch to such authority as it retained. It was unsurprising that Bolshevik support expanded, not only in the soldiers' committees but also in the trade unions, in municipal elections, and in the Moscow and Petrograd Soviets, where the Bolsheviks had been small minorities after the February Revolution but during September became the majority.

On the other hand, the Germans, who during the spring had been deliberately inactive, and during the summer had focused on the Kerensky offensive, now redirected their attention to the Baltic. They took Riga on 20 August/3 September, and in amphibious operations during October they captured the islands of Ösel, Moon, and Dago, driving the Russian fleet into the Gulf of Finland. The campaign stemmed from Ludendorff's long-standing

The Bolshevik Party still permitted freedom of debate. It was in the Central Committee on Tuesday 10/23 October that Lenin took the biggest step to carrying the party leadership. Only a summary record has survived from the meeting, which took place at a secret location in the Vyborg district, and which only twelve out of twenty-six members attended, Lenin himself arriving in disguise. Of all the 1917 meetings this was among the strangest, remote from the official conference chambers and from gilt and chandeliers. It lasted two hours, the plotters regaling themselves on sausage and rye bread, as Lenin confronted opposition from Lev Kamenev and Grigory Zinoviev, long-standing associates whose attitude grieved him. He spoke for nearly an hour, reiterating that the international situation impelled decisive action, still more if the Provisional Government intended ceding territory as far as Narva and even Petrograd. Whereas in July a coup would have failed, now the situation was ready, not least because of the rural upheaval. To await the Constituent Assembly was ill-advised, as the Bolsheviks would be a minority.[31] Zinoviev and Kamenev summarized their objections in a paper they wrote afterwards, and on many points were prescient. They denied the Bolsheviks commanded a majority: in the Constituent Assembly elections most peasants would vote for the Socialist Revolutionaries (as indeed they did), while most of the soldiers who now supported Bolshevism would run away rather than fight a revolutionary war. Nor, despite the unrest in Germany and Italy, did they expect much external support, and if the Bolsheviks were defeated the international revolutionary cause would falter. Lenin overestimated both Bolshevik strength and government weakness, as this time—unlike during the Kornilov crisis— the Bolsheviks would lack allies. Only on this last point were Kamenev and Zinoviev mistaken: actually the government was so completely isolated that a coup would be easy. The difficulties would follow.[32] But finally other committee members reported on the mood in Petrograd, Moscow, and elsewhere, and although not all shared Lenin's confidence, all supported him. The meeting ended with a resolution, drafted in Lenin's handwritten notebook, which ten of the twelve members approved. It cited the international situation, including the danger of the capitalist powers combining to crush the revolution (Lenin feared a British–German separate peace), the gaining of a Bolshevik majority in the Soviet, the peasant rebellion, and the government's plans to replace the Petrograd garrison and surrender the city. All of this 'places the armed uprising on the order of the day' and, although no date was set, the focus now must be on practical planning.[33]

This was still therefore a decision in principle for revolution rather than on precisely when and where to start one, a meeting of the party's Petrograd Committee on 15/28 October judging preparations still incomplete.[34] Already, however, news of Lenin's *Letters from Afar* was circulating among the Bolshevik lower echelons, and the resolution would do likewise, while a cover had been created on 9/22 October when the Petrograd Soviet set up a Military Revolutionary Committee (MRC). Chaired by Leon Trotsky, who had joined the Bolsheviks during the summer, the MRC served ostensibly to organize Petrograd's defence against the Germans and against counter-revolution, but actually was soon steered towards organizing a coup in the Soviet's name. It was Trotsky's idea to seize power simultaneously with the convening of the Second All-Russian Congress of Soviets on 20 October/2 November, so as to gain legitimacy but also present the Congress with a fait accompli.[35] At a further Central Committee on 16/29 October Lenin again prevailed over Kamenev and Zinoviev, this time gaining nineteen votes against two, with four abstentions. The arguments deployed were similar, Lenin delivering one of his most impassioned orations: 'History will not forgive us if we do not take power now!'[36] By this stage rumours of the preparations were circulating widely, and Kerensky seems to have believed that if he drew his enemies into open rebellion he could crush them as he had in July.[37] In an atmosphere this tense, exactly who started the showdown might seem trivial, but on the one hand Kamenev and Zinoviev publicized their opposition in the press (thus compromising secrecy), and on the other from 21 October/3 November Trotsky and the MRC were defying the authorities in the Petrograd Military District by appointing commissars over the city garrison, nearly all of whose members were willing to stay neutral or assist the insurrection. De facto the Provisional Government had lost control of Petrograd before the October Revolution began.[38] When it tried to close down the Bolshevik press and move in suburban troops before sealing off the city centre by raising the bridges, the Bolshevik Red Guard kept them lowered and started seizing public buildings during the night of 24–25 October/6–7 November. Lenin hastened to party headquarters during the small hours and insisted on faster action before the Congress of Soviets assembled—belatedly—on the following day.[39] Unlike in February, there was little mass mobilization: perhaps 25,000–30,000 Red Guards and garrison members, later reinforced by·Kronstadt sailors, took over key positions and isolated the government in the Winter Palace. A women's detachment and some officer cadets were the only force available to Kerensky, and they refused to fight.[40] Hence on 25 October/ 7 November he fled the city, leaving his ministers to be arrested. Damage and casualties were small, and Petrograd life continued much as normal in so far as wartime conditions permitted.

At the All-Russian Congress Lenin and Trotsky could proclaim the overthrow of the Provisional Government and their seizure of power in the name of the soviets, while the Mensheviks and most of the Socialist Revolutionaries walked out. The new regime was not a socialist coalition but all-Bolshevik, although later the Left Socialist Revolutionaries temporarily joined it. The first stage of Lenin's prognosis had been more or less borne out, and his government promptly issued a peace decree. It called for an immediate ceasefire and negotiations for 'a just, democratic peace', without annexations or indemnities. The Soviet government would publish all secret treaties ratified or concluded by the Provisional Government and it would conduct its own diplomacy in the open.[41] Although addressing the 'class-conscious workers' of Britain, France, and Germany, the decree was more liberal than Marxist, and seemed a calculated appeal to the Americans and the Allied Left.[42] As none of the Allied governments would recognize the new regime, however, it was with the Central Powers that the Bolsheviks, after overcoming token resistance from their officer corps, opened negotiations that produced a ceasefire on 2/15 December. It would run for a month in the first instance, and be complemented by peace negotiations. While it lasted the front-line troops would neither be augmented nor moved elsewhere, though the latter was permitted if movements had already begun and in fact Germany continued its troop transfers.[43] Moreover, the ceasefire was the signal for a mass departure by the remnants of the Russian army, and along much of the front the soldiers' committees went Bolshevik.[44]

With the ceasefire a new phase therefore opened, and it was finally clear which of the tendencies competing since the February Revolution had prevailed. The liberals and moderate socialists were out of office; the officer corps beleaguered, and threatened both by the new government and by their own men.[45] The Bolsheviks had at last halted the imperialist war, realizing one of their key pledges. Yet well before October Britain and France had practically written Russia off. The year 1918 would be militarily very different from 1917 as the Western Front grew still more central and first the Germans and then their enemies attacked with all their strength.

Hindenburg and Ludendorff had made their names in the east. During their struggle with their predecessor, Falkenhayn, their interest lay in querying

Figure 20. Captain addressing soldiers in Kronstadt, 7 December 1917

whether the Western Front would determine the war as a whole. Once
they took over the OHL their perspective altered. As early as 17 April
1917, the day after the Nivelle offensive, Ludendorff discussed with the
Eastern Front COS Max Hoffmann a scenario in which the Russian
Revolution released forces for a decisive western attack. Ludendorff understood a western breakthrough would be 'infinitely more difficult' than an
eastern one and he envisaged successive blows where Allied defences were
weakest. For the moment, however, he pinned his faith on the U-boats.
When they failed to starve out Britain, the success of the defence in
Flanders heartened him, and he hoped Kühlmann could end the war on
favourable terms.[46] Meeting the chiefs of staff of the Western Front army
groups on 20 September, Ludendorff ruled out a big western offensive,
pointing out that Britain and France had been unable to break through
and that since May French morale had recovered. Despite Germany's
economic difficulties, the Allies too faced shortages. Overall, he told a
newspaper publisher, 'Our position despite Austria-Hungary is better than
that of the Entente... We have every reason to keep our nerve ten minutes
longer than our enemies.'[47]

Even before the Bolshevik Revolution this viewpoint began to alter. One reason was Kühlmann's inability to secure peace. Ludendorff and Hindenburg believed that Germany must triumph or go under: a compromise ending would be tantamount to defeat.[48] Against their preferences, they had agreed at the 11 September Bellevue conference not to press for Flanders naval bases. But once it emerged that Kühlmann was getting nowhere, they withdrew the concession, and insisted on Germany keeping permanent access to Belgian territory and on barring it to the Allies. Their 14 September memorandum portrayed a dismal cycle of future wars in which the Reich must safeguard its supply of food and raw materials against blockade and bombing.[49] In a further memorandum two weeks later, Colonel Georg Wetzell, Ludendorff's Chief of Operations, likewise foresaw a second round, in which Britain, France, America, and Russia would reunite against Germany, Austria-Hungary would be unreliable, and London and Paris connected by a Channel tunnel while British and American conscript armies stood poised to intervene. All of Belgium, and not just the Meuse line in the east, must therefore be accessible for German military purposes.[50]

One source of Ludendorff's change of heart was the failure of the submarines and of peace feelers. A second was that the status quo seemed unsustainable. He understood the strain on Germany's economy from interlocking shortages of coal, steel, transport, and labour.[51] However, economic factors did not cause the reorientation of strategy, and nor did domestic politics, the Reichstag peace resolution being countered by the OHL-backed Fatherland Party, *Deutsche Vaterlandspartei*. But at the front the high command knew even before Passchendaele that troop morale was wavering, and Allied artillery was by now far more destructive than on the Somme. Endless defensive combat dispirited the men, and both Plumer's successes at Ypres and Pétain's at La Malmaison suggested the German infantry's ability to repel more heavily armed attackers was nearing its limit. Such at any rate was the headquarters view from the Fourth Army, which bore the brunt of the Flanders fighting.[52] The Germans expected the British in 1918 to renew their drive towards the coast, while the French army had recovered and the American Expeditionary Force (AEF) would join them. The Germans had a poor impression of the Americans' fighting qualities, and correctly predicted that their build-up would be slow, but for 1918 they foresaw a faster deployment, and even if poorly trained and disciplined the AEF would be fresh, energetic, and well-equipped.[53] In fact the OHL overestimated the

AEF expansion plans, and by attacking it actually hastened the massive deployment that it dreaded. Unrestricted submarine warfare was partially a by-product of the Somme, and Ludendorff's 1918 offensives were partially a by-product of Third Ypres; so that Germany's greatest strategic errors were unexpected consequences of apparently frustrated Allied efforts.

Certainly the need to strike before the AEF became formidable was central to the planning that took shape from October.[54] The process was largely one of consultation within the army, between the OHL and the commanders and staff chiefs of the Western Front armies and army groups, conducted via position papers and conferences. Only after it concluded did the chancellor and emperor ratify the outcome. Nothing comparable occurred to the civilian interrogations of the French and British generals before the Chemin des Dames and Third Ypres; or even to the Crown Councils before the unrestricted submarine campaign. The army was the senior service and politicians were less likely to second-guess its recommendations than they were the navy's; but also the power balance had altered. Count Georg von Hertling, who replaced Michaelis as chancellor in September 1917, was 74 and his eyesight was failing. Although not completely passive, he was less assertive than Bethmann, while Hindenburg and Ludendorff had become more practised in challenging and removing civilian critics and Wilhelm was more reclusive and disengaged.

Wetzell had already advocated German intervention in Italy as a means of showing the Allies their position was hopeless and they should make peace before the Americans arrived. Caporetto was launched partly with this aim in mind.[55] Its military success, following on the victories in Galicia and at Riga, suggested new tactics might restore the viability of an offensive strategy. In minutes on morale reports from his Western Front army groups, Ludendorff inclined to agree that a pure defensive had no prospect, and to consider a spring counterstroke against a renewed British advance in Flanders.[56] He now accepted that Germany would have to fight a 1918 campaign. Wetzell predicted that Russia would stay in the war and between ten and fifteen American divisions would be in the line next spring. He envisaged that another attack on the Russians and another strategic withdrawal in the west could release thirty German divisions for a decisive early offensive against the southern flank of the Ypres salient, directed towards the BEF railway junction at Hazebrouck, or (which Wetzell preferred) against a more dangerous opponent, the French, via a surprise attack on Verdun. Typically, Wetzell built in a complex sequence of operations before the culminating blow, Germany shifting forces rapidly by rail and exploiting its interior communication lines while long-range artillery and aerial strafing hampered Allied reinforcements.[57] Yet Wetzell was a controversial figure with a knack of making enemies, who was out on a limb among Ludendorff's advisers.[58] His isolation was evident at the first staff conference devoted to 1918 planning, held at Mons on 11 November 1917, just after the Bolshevik Revolution and precisely a year before the war came to an end.

The participants at Mons included Ludendorff, Wetzell, and Colonel Max Bauer from the OHL, as well as Crown Prince Rupprecht; his Chief of Staff, Hermann von Kuhl; and Crown Prince Wilhelm's Chief of Staff, Friedrich von der Schulenburg. No civilians were present. Ludendorff opened by expressing great satisfaction with operations during 1917: the Western Front had held, they had succeeded in Italy, and the Bolshevik Revolution promised German control over Eastern Europe. The revolution would also release forces for the west, where he insisted on first hitting the BEF: 'The British must be knocked out of the war.'[59] He wanted to strike early—in late February or early March—and therefore did not share Kuhl's preference for attacking towards Hazebrouck in order to cut off the British and drive them on the Channel ports, as the seasonal flooding of the River Lys might delay operations until April. But if Germany followed Wetzell and chose Verdun the British were unlikely to send reinforcements to help their allies, so a second assault in Flanders would still be needed. As a third option, Bauer and Schulenburg mooted an attack in Picardy, near St-Quentin, which Kuhl disliked, as here the British were further from the sea and had more manoeuvring room, while the French could threaten the Germans' left flank. The meeting ended without a resolution, but a subsequent memorandum concluded that developments in Italy and Russia would permit an offensive in late February or early March, before strong US forces arrived. Yet Germany would enjoy only numerical equality, and resources for just one big attack, which underlined the venture's hazards.

Further memoranda were exchanged for two more months, while Ludendorff let the argument run. The Russian ceasefire enabled nearly forty divisions to be moved from the Eastern to the Western Front, while smaller contingents returned from Macedonia and Italy. Now the attackers would possess a small numerical advantage. Yet Wetzell feared an advance in Picardy would lose momentum when it crossed the old Somme battlefield, and he shared Kuhl's preference (if the British were the target) for a drive towards Hazebrouck. He still envisaged this as coming last in a sequence of blows, all the more after the British attack at Cambrai on 20 November, which initially succeeded not just because the British committed over 400 tanks after a surprise bombardment but also because the bulk of Germany's reserves lay to the north, in Flanders. If the Germans similarly drew off Allied reserves in preliminary diversions, their decisive onslaught might destabilize the entire British front, thus delivering the elusive breakthrough. However, Wetzell still believed that capturing Verdun could knock the French army out of the war, and Schulenberg agreed an attack in the hilly Verdun terrain could start earlier and was likelier to gain surprise, and that a French collapse might force Britain to come to terms.[60] In contrast, Kuhl continued to favour a drive on Hazebrouck, to protect the U-boat bases, and ideally as a counterstroke once Haig had resumed operations, in order to cut off the maximum number of British forces. Kuhl and Wetzell were unimpressed by British tactical proficiency, and Kuhl had noticed that Portuguese troops held the Lys first line.[61] Even though an attack here must wait until April, the Rupprecht Army Group preferred it to St-Quentin, the Sixth Army commander pointing out that a Picardy advance would entail crossing not only the old Somme battlefield but also the terrain devastated in the retreat to the Hindenburg line, which Germany's emaciated horses could not negotiate, while the men would have to recapture territory that they had voluntarily relinquished. None the less, the Second Army, which also faced the St-Quentin sector, now planned in detail to attack there.[62]

On 14 December Krafft von Delmensingen, the architect of Caporetto, visited the OHL and spoke out against Wetzell, insisting the British should be the primary target and that a second Verdun was a waste of time. Ludendorff was moving in the same direction. A meeting at Bad Kreuznach on 27 December between the staff chiefs of the Western Front army groups narrowed the differences. Its covering documents advised that the balance was moving in Germany's favour and an attack would be possible in March. Not just paper planning but also preparations on the ground were authorized for a portfolio of operations, including the Hazebrouck plan ('Georg'); an Arras attack ('Mars'); three variants of the St-Quentin ('Michael') scheme; and blows in the Argonne, Champagne, Alsace, and at Verdun, although the latter was now being relegated and in January Ludendorff rejected it.[63] He was also losing interest in preliminary diversions and inclining towards one massive blow, which Krafft argued should be 'Michael' whereas Kuhl still favoured 'Georg'. Finally, after a tour round the Western Front headquarters, Ludendorff met Kuhl and Schulenburg at Avesnes on

21 January and ruled for 'Michael'. 'Georg' would start too late, and the local commanders felt it would be too difficult, while 'Mars' faced very strong British defences. 'Michael' could start early on drier, undisturbed ground, and promised rapid opening success—a consideration Ludendorff emphasized—although the British could withdraw more easily and momentum might dissipate. None the less, in Western Front conditions the initial breakthrough was vital, even if the strategic objectives remained undefined.[64] The sector commanders envisaged progressing along the Somme Valley before swinging northwards, in a mirror image of the Allies' 1916 Somme plan. Yet capturing the Amiens railway junction, which was even more significant than Hazebrouck, was not specified.

The deliberations before the 'Michael' decision proceeded almost solely in the German army's upper echelons. Discussion centred on the timing and location; the principle of a spring offensive was hardly questioned. Hindenburg played little part, and even Ludendorff kept his distance, though steering the process after the Mons and before the Kreuznach conferences, and again at Avesnes. In the end he followed Krafft rather than Wetzell or Kuhl, though keeping 'Georg' as a second option, and warning Wilhelm that unlike in Italy and Russia a succession of attacks would be needed. But he had always felt the main target should be the British (on whom the French depended) and operations should come as early as possible, so his starting assumptions shaped the outcome. In fact the critics of 'Michael' accurately foresaw its drawbacks: that it would lose momentum, the British withdraw, and the French attack the left flank, leaving the Germans short of Amiens in a distended and militarily valueless bulge. In contrast even the weakened version of 'Georg' delivered in April 1918, with fewer and wearier attacking troops, caused the Allies acute anxiety. Ludendorff should probably have heeded Kuhl, as the Americans came later than predicted, and the Lys sector offered major assets—Hazebrouck and the ports—at shorter distance. Distance was critical as the OHL knew Germany was far inferior in draught animals and motor vehicles, and faced formidable logistical challenges.[65] Its new assault tactics would help in the early stages but not the exploitation. As everyone from Ludendorff downwards acknowledged, Britain and France had failed with greater margins of superiority to gain a breakthrough and Germany could not conduct a prolonged *Materialschlacht* (battle of materiel) like the Somme or Third Ypres.[66] The offensive was a wager with highly uncertain prospects that risked drastically curtailing Germany's ability to sustain the war.

The decision cried out for sceptical scrutiny. It was lacking. Within three days of the Avesnes conference, Wilhelm authorized 'Michael'.[67] Hertling had told Hindenburg that 'If therefore with God's gracious help the intended new offensive under Your Excellency's proven leadership, supported by our soldiers' heroism and will to victory, leads to the hoped for breakthrough successes, we will be in a position in a peace with the Western Powers to establish those conditions demanded for the security of our frontiers, our economic interests, and our international status after the war.'[68] The offensive was necessary to make the enemy submit to Germany's terms. Since the Bellevue conference Germany's leaders had hardened against compromise, Wilhelm minuting in January that peace with London was no longer on the table, and one or other of Britain and Germany must go under. He told Ludendorff that they must gain victory before dictating conditions.[69] Ludendorff similarly had compromised at Bellevue only on the misunderstanding that Britain would accept German domination of Belgium. He agreed with Wetzell that any peace must safeguard Germany in a future war, and he feared that a disappointing outcome would undermine internal order. But as the enemy had rejected compromise anyway, Ludendorff had an activist temperament and was drawn to taking the initiative. Germany should break the European Allies before America could help them. The OHL had thought much about peace terms, including outside Europe, where it wanted control of Central Africa for food, raw materials, and a colonial army, and to strengthen Turkey as a means of pressure on the Suez Canal.[70] Within Europe it wanted annexations and buffer states in the east, and the Briey-Longwy iron ore field as well as Luxemburg and Belgium in the west. But even if Germany's demands on Belgium had been conceded, a long list of further points divided Berlin from the Allies, and nor was negotiation welcome to Ludendorff, who feared that Britain would offer inadequate terms and the German civilians jump at them.[71] Given these premises, his choice in winter 1917–18, as in winter 1916–17, was between slow asphyxiation (while American divisions resuscitated his opponents) and striking out. He chose the latter, telling the Bundesrat Foreign Affairs Committee on 2 January that there was a prospect of ending the war victoriously and the military situation was better than ever.[72]

The Bolshevik Revolution and Russia's ceasefire helped commit the Germans to an all-out spring offensive. But for the OHL an armistice was not enough: it wanted a peace treaty. The armistice was temporary and provided for peace talks, which began in Brest-Litovsk on 7/20 December.[73]

The Bolshevik delegation, at first headed by Adolph Joffe, came determined to negotiate in open session, as Lenin's decree on peace had provided, and to publish at once the records of proceedings. It also came committed to the national self-determination doctrine, which Lenin had sketched out in 1915–16 and the Soviet government reasserted in its Declaration of the Rights of the Nations of Russia, following which Finland, Lithuania, Latvia, Estonia, the Ukraine, and Transcaucasia declared independence.[74] In principle Lenin had favoured national groupings being free to determine their future by plebiscite, across Europe and globally. This had made tactical sense as a means of undermining tsarism and the warring coalitions, even if its compatibility with Marxism was debatable. At Brest-Litovsk Joffe set out the preconditions of no annexations and indemnities and called for any region that had shown nationalist discontent since the later nineteenth century to be able to decide its future by referendum. But for a time the Central Powers seemed willing to go along. Their tactics derived from a letter from Czernin to Hertling on 10 November 1917 that urged the key imperative was to draw the Bolsheviks into a separate peace by seemingly renouncing annexations and indemnities, while creating faits accomplis by stage-managing declarations of independence among the nationalities under German and Austrian occupation.[75] Kühlmann's approach was similar, and the Central Powers exploited self-determination to consolidate a zone of nominally autonomous buffer states. In their 'Christmas Declaration', they accepted the Bolshevik peace programme on condition that the Allies did likewise. Czernin and Kühlmann assessed correctly that the Allies would remain aloof; and indeed the Allies disregarded the Christmas Declaration and the Bolshevik programme, enabling the Central Powers to revoke their acceptance. But Kühlmann had approved the declaration without consulting Hindenburg and Ludendorff, who never forgave him. They had little sympathy for the foreign minister's subtleties, and wanted sweeping annexations on Poland's borders as well as guaranteed control over the Baltic provinces. Further, they demanded 'clarity' in the shape of a peace treaty that unambiguously terminated hostilities with Russia and freed up forces for the west.[76]

Early in 1918 the situation was indeed clarified after a crisis over the Ukraine. Ukrainian resources had been fundamental to the tsarist empire's pre-war economic build-up, and to supplying Petrograd and Moscow with grain and coal. During 1917 a council, or Rada, in Kiev, led by moderate socialists and Ukrainian nationalists, won increasing autonomy, especially after the counterstroke against the Kerensky offensive brought German forces into the region. After negotiations at Brest-Litovsk resumed in January 1918 a delegation arrived from a self-proclaimed independent Rada, while pro-Bolshevik forces invaded eastern Ukraine. The Central Powers were desperate for Ukrainian food and horses, the Austrians so much that they agreed to transfer the predominantly Polish region of Cholm, triggering mass protests across the Dual Monarchy's Polish-inhabited districts.[77] On 9 February the Central Powers signed a separate peace with the Rada. They also demanded that Russian sovereignty terminate over all territory west of a line between Brest-Litovsk and the Gulf of Riga.[78] Negotiations with the Bolsheviks, now led by Trotsky, who had become the People's Commissar for Foreign Affairs, were deadlocked even before the Russians retaliated by walking out.

Lenin's aspiration before October had been for the revolution to spread, and initially to Germany.[79] If the revolution made a forthright peace offer and published the secret treaties, he foresaw a 99 per cent chance that the capitalists could not prevent peace.[80] When the revolution failed to spread, and Allied resistance ruled out a general settlement, he was forced into a reappraisal. According to his 'Twenty-One Theses' of January 1918, the priority was to consolidate socialism within Russia and settle accounts with the bourgeoisie: 'Our tactics ought to rest on the principle of how to ensure that the socialist revolution is best able to consolidate itself and survive in one country until such time as other countries join in.'[81] Renewing hostilities would stake the Russian Revolution's fate on the outbreak of a German one. Moreover, when he had spoken to soldiers' delegates he found an appetite not for further fighting but for peace at any price. Russia had to sign because it had no army.

Once again the issue was thrashed out in the Central Committee, and once again Lenin started in a small minority, whereas most, following Nikolai Bukharin, preferred a 'revolutionary war' to accepting enemy terms. Trotsky, however, offered a middle road of proclaiming 'no war, no peace' and abandoning the peace conference, in the hope the Central Powers would acquiesce rather than renew hostilities. Lenin did not share this expectation, and accurately predicted that following Trotsky's course would lose Russia more of the Baltic provinces, but a bare majority of the Central Committee was willing to try out the tactic, and after the treaty with the Ukraine it went into effect.[82]

The Germans and Austrians responded by terminating the armistice and moving forward. At the Bad Homburg Crown Council on 13 February

Kühlmann had indeed argued that the Central Powers should accept the walk-out. Imposing a treaty would antagonize Russia far into the future, and occupying more territory would achieve nothing. Friedrich von Payer, Hertling's deputy, feared inflaming Russian nationalism. But Hindenburg and Ludendorff insisted Germany must stop the Bolsheviks overrunning the Ukraine and barring access to its food. A new advance would bring a peace treaty.[83] Kühlmann found little support from Wilhelm, who was absent from much of the meeting but found the Bolsheviks repugnant and was tempted to suppress them. Hertling feared strikes in Germany (which Ludendorff discounted) and defended his foreign minister, but eventually deferred to the military view.[84] Hence Kühlmann—like Bethmann a year earlier—became committed to a policy he disagreed with. He also found his judgement discredited, as when the Central Powers moved forward the Soviet government immediately requested a new ceasefire. On 3/16 March it signed a treaty that surrendered sovereignty over Poland, the Baltic coast, and the Ukraine (adding Livonia and Estonia to the abandoned area), and that left it to the Central Powers to decide these regions' fate. Russia would pay what in all but name was an enormous indemnity, and demobilize its army. It lost 34 per cent of the tsarist empire's population, 32 per cent of its agricultural land, 73 per cent of its iron ore, and 89 per cent of its coal.[85] It was true that most of the territory ceded was not ethnically Great Russian, and partly for this reason the SPD abstained in the Reichstag, only the breakaway independent socialists, the USPD, voting against ratification. In many ways the treaty was a provisional, framework document. Yet it marked just a beginning, as during 1918 the OHL drove deeper into former tsarist territory, in June prevailing on Wilhelm to remove Kühlmannn after the foreign minister had the temerity to declare that Germany could not win by military means alone. At Brest-Litovsk, none the less, the peace diplomacy that had characterized 1917 came to an end. Instead the war would be decided by a new trial of strength, which the peace process had prepared for both by allowing Germany to reinforce the Western Front and by convincing Woodrow Wilson that scope for diplomacy was exhausted. Russia had completed its long disengagement, and its withdrawal obliged America to redress the balance.

In Milner's words, 'the entrance of America into the war has introduced a new factor, of great ultimate promise but small immediate value'.[86] The Bolshevik Revolution and Ludendorff's spring offensive brought forward America's advance to primacy in the anti-German coalition. This process was incremental, and it is harder to identify key decision points. Wilson dealt with his Cabinet officers individually, and delegated liberally to them, viewing Abraham Lincoln's more interventionist style during the American Civil War as an anti-model.[87] He left not only recruitment and supply but also strategy to Baker and Daniels, his War and Navy Secretaries, and war finance to McAdoo, though endorsing their actions. Wide authority was also left with John J. Pershing, the commander of the American Expeditionary Force, and Rear Admiral William Sims, who became senior naval representative in London and commanded American ships in European waters. Still, by April 1918, a year after America's entry, Wilson and his officials had transformed its war effort from a relatively modest contribution—calibrated just to give the Allies the edge—into a much larger endeavour. If the Allies seemed weaker than expected and the Central Powers more formidable, the United States responded by deepening its involvement.[88]

Wilson understood the need to rouse American opinion, and among his earliest acts was to establish the Committee on Public Information under George Creel. In August 1917 the secretary of the Council of National Defense wrote to Creel that 'this country is not awake', and the underlying reasons for the war had still to be explained.[89] Tumulty warned Wilson that the 'general mass of the people' remained indifferent,[90] and the British ambassador reported that the United States lay thousands of miles from the Front, its homeland was undamaged, and its people had little interest in European territorial questions. War enthusiasm was largely confined to the east, and most Americans did not understand why they might be called to fight, although now they were in the war they were determined to win it. A pacifist and anti-war lobby stayed vocal, though grew increasingly unpopular.[91] Yet during this period resources were marshalled that would enable more decisive action. McAdoo had hoped to avoid the inflationary Civil War financial practices and cover half of war expenditure through taxation. But whereas he estimated in April that the first year would cost $3 billion, by July the figure was already $15 billion and the tax yield less than $2 billion.[92] More successful was his propaganda for government borrowing, the first Liberty Loan bringing in over $3 billion. However, about half the proceeds were lent to the Allies to finance their American purchases, and it became clear when Allied missions visited Washington that their needs would be greater and the consequent US spending even more 'prodigious' than the Treasury secretary had anticipated.[93] Although the Americans also lent to Russia and Italy, the main recipients were France and Britain. In summer 1917 Britain experienced a still more acute payments crisis than at the end of 1916, as a result of which a reluctant McAdoo (with Wilson's acquiescence) doubled his monthly subsidies.[94] The United States not only funded Allied purchases but also supported the sterling–dollar exchange rate of £1 = $4.76, which if left to plummet, the British warned, would force them to restrict their buying, harming American producers as well as the war effort.[95] Shaken though McAdoo was by the mounting cost, he saw the Allies' indebtedness as giving America leverage, to insist on them centralizing and prioritizing their purchases, although Wilson held back on using financial dependence to moderate Allied war aims until after the war ended.[96] None the less, in November McAdoo advised that:

> we are facing the time when America must take the responsibilities of leadership. We alone have the power to impose our decisions on the Allies, first because we control the essential resources for the conduct of the war and secondly because we have no selfish purpose in view and, therefore, our decisions will be regarded as impartial. The responsibilities of American leadership are very grave—I realize that fully—but, on the other hand, I think the responsibilities of a failure on our part to take that leadership are even greater.[97]

A basic decision was to give priority to delivering the orders made by America's partners during the neutrality period.[98] It forced up wheat prices in the Chicago commodities market, where the Allies competed for grain. The federal government guaranteed a price to farmers in order—very successfully—to stimulate production,[99] while Herbert Hoover at the head of the United States Food Administration led a publicity campaign urging households to restrict consumption. By these means America helped overcome French and Italian grain shortages in the autumn and winter, as well as stepping up food shipments to Britain and sending oil to alleviate a Royal Navy fuel shortage. But American industry converted slowly to military production, and the United States contributed dollars, grain, fuel, and steel, rather than arms. In late 1917 the 'international ordnance agreement' confirmed this emerging division of labour,[100] with the result that when the AEF arrived it would be largely equipped by France and to a lesser extent by Britain, indispensable though American finance and raw materials were becoming to both countries.

American industry was more successful in supplying the naval war effort than that on land. Here the key decision was to suspend the battleship building programme that Congress had approved in 1916 and to concentrate on merchant ships and anti-submarine vessels.[101] This matched the direction of American naval strategy, which (from Wilson downwards) was to encourage convoys, and provide the escorts that enabled them to operate.[102] Although Sims took the lead, Daniels and Wilson acquiesced, and by September 1917 thirty-five American destroyers had crossed the Atlantic, with battleships following in 1918.[103] For the duration of the war, the American battleship build-up against Japan and potentially Britain took second place to keeping the North Atlantic corridor open for combatants and supplies.

Before the combatants were sent, they had to be recruited, and mostly by conscription. The immediate stimulus was Wilson's concern to head off a proposal by his predecessor and Republican rival, Theodore Roosevelt, to lead a division of volunteers to Europe, but the president was also trying to learn from British experience and retain workers in key sectors, following 'scientific' principles of manpower allocation.[104] Wilson wanted Baker to use National Registration Day on 5 June 1917 as a patriotic and unifying demonstration, which largely it was, nearly 10 million registering their liability for service. Potentially the military authorities controlled a larger manpower pool than any European belligerent, though the men lacked officers, equipment, and training.[105] The initial contingent that arrived in September in hastily constructed camps numbered 687,000, and the General Staff intended first to bring the regular army up to strength and reinforce the National Guard before creating the all-conscript divisions of the new 'National Army'. They envisaged that the whole of 1917 would be needed for preparation and training, and that the existing regular soldiers and officers should be held back to assist.[106] The Operations Section at AEF GHQ expected to be ready for a victorious offensive only in 1919.[107]

Events would not wait so long. If the British mission to Washington brought home the scale of Britain's financial requirements, the French mission brought home not only France's manpower shortage but also its psychological exhaustion.[108] Under Painlevé and Pétain waiting for the Americans became integral to French strategy, and under Clemenceau it continued to be. In the first French plan, communicated prior to the April offensive, Nivelle envisaged some 90,000 US personnel would serve mainly in transport, telegraphy, and wood chopping; after the Chemin des Dames disaster Pétain intended a much larger US role.[109] Haig warned the Americans that 'the French are flagging' and for 'moral effect' even a small contingent should be sent without delay. Joseph Kuhn, the head of the War College Division, advised the American COS that 'great importance attaches to the necessity of relieving the critical situation now existing in France, by the despatch to that country of a substantial armed force'. Men and material must be 'shipped to the war theatre at the earliest practical date and in the largest practicable quantity'.[110] In fact the first American division reached France in June, sent primarily as a morale booster. It entered the front line only in October, and no second division followed for months. In some ways more important for shaping the American commitment was the arrival of the AEF commander, John J. Pershing, who met Wilson just once before departing and received remarkably unprescriptive guidelines. He was expected to support the French, but also to maintain his force's independence, and this to maintain America's political influence as well as focus its patriotic loyalties.[111] French and British pressure to 'amalgamate' American soldiers by incorporating them into units under Allied senior command would be resisted. However, Pershing and his staff soon lobbied for a much faster build-up,[112] in which they were supported both by the French and by the General Staff in Washington.[113] Whereas only 175,000 American troops had reached France by the end of 1917, an inter-Allied conference at Paris in November approved a goal of twenty-five divisions (477,050 men) by June 1918.[114] Wilson's War Message had envisaged raising an extra 500,000, but Congress voted $3 billion on 5 June to provide arms for a million, and $3.7 billion on 6 October for a second million.[115]

Not only were larger forces being readied, but by autumn 1917 the authorities were clarifying how to use them. The AEF was deployed in Lorraine, which the French welcomed because it would adjoin French sectors on both flanks rather than the British, but did not guard the shortest route to Paris and could release French troops to operate elsewhere. But it also suited Pershing and the administration, which preferred to be seen as cooperating with France, Wilson telling his predecessor, William Howard Taft, that the United States 'must not be put in a position of seeming, in any way, involved in British policy'.[116] Before February only a defensive war plan against Germany had existed, but by May 1917 Baker, Pershing, and Assistant CGS Tasker H. Bliss had agreed on France as the desired theatre. Pershing and his staff saw Lorraine (with its connecting railways from the French Atlantic ports that circumvented Paris) as a jumping-off point against the German stronghold at Metz, the steel plants and iron ore of northern Lorraine, and the trunk railway running behind and parallel to the opposing Front.[117] Here the AEF might unleash a war-winning offensive, with political as well as strategic pay-offs, and Pershing was determined to train his

Figure 21. US troops on Western Front, 1917

infantry in open warfare tactics such as sharpshooting. None of this seems
to have been discussed, however, with Wilson, who in October still considered sending substantial forces elsewhere. At this point Baker asked the
General Staff to justify the selection of the Western Front for the primary
deployment. The reasons, he was advised, were that Britain and France
had urged it and 'this is the nearest, quickest, and safest point from which
to attack the enemy and success here will have a direct bearing on the
primary objective of the Germans, which is the crushing of France'.
From here too, America could launch 'our great air campaign' against the
U-boat bases and 'the vitals of Germany'. A supplementary memorandum
acknowledged that expelling the Germans would take years, but they
were already suffering 100,000 casualties a month and as Allied strength
increased that figure would rise. The United States had the manpower and
supplies for only one military effort, and France was where it should centre.[118] This exposition apparently satisfied Baker and the president, who
did not raise the issue again. Foreshadowing US strategy in the Second
World War, the American military wanted to concentrate in Western
Europe and conduct an air offensive and a battle of attrition alongside
the French and British, in their view the most effective Allied forces.
The strategy was first adopted by the army and then justified to the civilians,
and little controversy attended it.

It helped that fighting in France would bring the greatest political influence. Wilson lacked interest in strategy, being preoccupied with the home front and with diplomacy. American entry widened the circle of neutrals that broke off relations with the Central Powers, and increased the pressure on the remainder to cooperate with the Allied blockade.[119] It much assisted Allied public relations to have American backing for the Balfour Declaration, for resisting the Stockholm Conference, and rejecting Benedict XV's peace note. Yet the president remained ambivalent. Even after America entered he was willing to explore a mediated settlement, warning a British MP that he would remain 'detached from the Allies'.[120] After Balfour visited Washington in May and disclosed the details of the inter-Allied war aims agreements, even House, who was less fastidious than Wilson, found the Ottoman partition arrangements 'all bad'.[121] Although Wilson did not back the Russians' pressure for war aims revision, his reply to Benedict was sent without consulting his European partners and with the intention of firing a shot across their bows. According to British diplomatic reporting, the American newspapers welcomed it, most rejecting a return to the pre-1914 status quo that they blamed for causing the conflict.[122] The reply showed a new assertiveness, and soon afterwards Wilson authorized House to establish the 'Inquiry', a committee of academics and experts, to investigate and prepare the issues at the peace conference.[123]

At this point the Bolshevik Revolution intervened. The Russians' publication of the inter-Allied secret treaties—which were soon available in the British and American press and included texts such as the Doumergue Agreement that even the British had been unaware of—was a disaster for the Allied governments, which had claimed the moral high ground of fighting defensively. Italy had already been unsettled by Benedict's note and the Turin riots; France by the breakdown of the 'sacred union', or political truce. The Clemenceau government formed in November faced outright Socialist hostility. The mortifying disappointments of the Chemin des Dames, Third Ypres, and Caporetto raised once more the question of how, with dwindling manpower, the Allies could ever win, a new and fraught debate which preoccupied Lloyd George's War Cabinet during November.[124] Lord Lansdowne, who had written privately to the Cabinet in the previous winter, openly queried in a letter to the *Daily Telegraph* whether victory at the cost that now seemed likely would be justified,[125] while the Labour Party approved a 'Memorandum on War Aims' that

condemned annexations and indemnities and made a League of Nations a
primary objective.[126]

Such was the backdrop when House, as Wilson's emissary, attended an
inter-Allied conference in Paris in November–December, predicting it
would be 'the turning point in the war even though the fortunes of the
Allies have never seemed so low'.[127] The Americans pressed with some
success for greater strategic and economic coordination, but when House
sought a joint declaration on war aims, the Italians and French resisted and
the British gave him little backing.[128] Immediately on his return he and
Wilson started working on a unilateral statement, which the Central Powers'
Christmas Declaration made more urgent. The outcome was the president's
celebrated Fourteen Points address of 8 January, drafted by House and
Wilson on the basis of a submission from the Inquiry, while Wilson's
Cabinet, with the partial exception of Lansing, was once more by-passed.
The American media welcomed the speech as satisfying a need for greater
certainty about US objectives. Creel's propaganda gave the Fourteen Points
worldwide notoriety, even the Bolsheviks plastering them over the walls of
Moscow, and they were aimed at multiple audiences: not only to orientate
American opinion and hearten socialists and liberals in Western Europe,
but also to undermine the autocracies in the Central Powers as well as
distancing Washington from Allied imperialism and outlining a sanitized
programme on which the Bolsheviks might, after all, continue in the war.
Their impact dwarfed that of Lloyd George's Caxton Hall speech on
5 January, which resembled them in some respects but was more concerned
to open the door to separate peace negotiations with Austria-Hungary and
Turkey and seemed to abandon Russia to its fate.[129] In contrast Wilson urged
that Russia should be free to develop politically in its own way, and reasserted earlier principles—open diplomacy, freedom of the seas, arms limitation, reduction of tariff barriers, and an 'impartial adjustment of colonial
claims'. And for the first time he backed key Allied territorial objectives,
including restoring Belgium, righting the wrong done to France over
Alsace-Lorraine, and Italy's objectives in so far as was compatible with the
nationality principle. These endorsements remained qualified and cautious,
and did not constitute a blanket approval of national self-determination, a
term the speech avoided.[130] Wilson looked to self-government supple-
mented by stronger international organization, rather than to rearranging
sovereignty on the basis of ethnicity, as the basis of a stable peace. Even the

League of Nations that he envisaged in Point Fourteen was more flexible and conciliatory, rather than legal and judicial, than the model favoured by its American supporters in the League to Enforce Peace.[131]

Drafted in the closing days of 1917, the Fourteen Points were among the year's most potent bequests. In autumn 1918 they became the basis on which Germany sought an armistice and America and the Allies acceded. Yet the Points failed to keep the Bolsheviks in the war, and initially the German chancellor rejected them. Austria–Hungary opened new secret contacts with Washington, but Karl and Czernin eventually followed Germany's lead, while anti-war strike waves in Berlin and Vienna were broken and the Reichstag ratified the Brest-Litovsk peace. As Wilson concluded, at Baltimore on 6 April, 'force without stint or limit' must now decide the issue, and during the summer he presided over a spectacular expansion in trans-Atlantic troop shipments and the growth of the AEF to nearly 2 million combatants, who now took on a major share in operations. For the time being, peace feelers were at an end and months of desperate fighting passed before the Germans tried to end a struggle that now seemed hopeless by seeming after all to accept Wilson's peace programme. They struggled with one hand tied behind their backs, in that over half a million troops remained until the end on the Eastern Front, where they intervened in Finland, overran the Ukraine, and advanced as far as the Crimea and Georgia, despite the peace with the Bolsheviks remaining nominally in place. On all these grounds, the war's concluding phase proved very different from the long months of uncertainty which it succeeded.

On 12 December 1917 the new French premier, Georges Clemenceau, testified to the Chamber of Deputies Army Commission. He told his listeners that 120,000 Americans were in France. By June 1918 he expected 350,000; and by June–July 1919, 2 million. 'Consequently, in the military situation that will be created for us, with a ferocious and desperate push by Germany, at several points, against our front, in order to finish things by obtaining an immediate peace, after having tried to terrify us, to break through, to dislocate us, to hustle us, because we know well that we will hold we have no other option than to wait for the Americans...' But once the Germans were exhausted, he would not be surprised if they sued for peace: 'I have the idea that the Americans will not have the opportunity to strike an immense blow that would be completely decisive.'[132] By the end of 1917 the future was becoming clearer, and the exit routes from Europe's war trap more discernible. Following the first transition in 1914 from a war of

movement to one of stalemate, a second and more far-reaching transformation started with Russia's February Revolution and with American
intervention. Both the pattern of campaigning and Europe's political geography were remoulded. Before 1917 the Central Powers were aptly named,
squeezed between Allied forces on all sides. After March 1918 the Allies tried
but largely failed to reconstruct an Eastern Front, whereas French and
British soldiers now fought in Italy under the aegis of the newly formed
Supreme War Council. Hence while during the summer and autumn of
1918 the Germans, Austrians, and Turks drove deeper into Eurasia, the
Allied-American coalition counter-attacked from the west and south. The
coordinated onslaught attempted in summer 1916—and which fell apart in
spring 1917—was renewed. The war was also transformed ideologically, as
more or less liberal democracies now confronted autocracies, while Russia's
socialist regime remained detached: an alignment foreshadowing that of
1939. In the east the struggle that had begun in 1914 ended through the
creation of a Bolshevik regime that prioritized above all else its own survival
and would accept dictated terms. But in the west the Central Powers
rejected the Fourteen Points and staked everything on new offensives that
would force the European Allies to negotiate before the Americans arrived.
Conversely, as Clemenceau summarized, France, Britain, and Italy must
hold on until that juncture, and this perspective simplified matters. During
the winter of 1917–18 Pétain prepared the French defences and built up a
mobile, lorry-borne reserve, while Haig and GHQ shelved their projects for
renewed attacks in Flanders and accepted that the first imperative was to
repel the enemy.[133] If the Allies could withstand Germany's assaults their
prospects were good, although a big American contribution, with the
associated political price, was now unavoidable.

Until late 1916 the pre-war pattern of European domestic and international politics, if terribly strained, remained intact. But by spring 1918 a
Bolshevik dictatorship had replaced the tsarist autocracy and had jettisoned
Russia's alliance with the West, while the Left had strengthened across
Europe and a new and intransigent nationalist Right was stirring. These
trends would intensify during the chaos after the armistice.[134] Even before
the ceasefire a further year of ruinous campaigning would claim hundreds
of thousands more lives, and propel both sides towards economic and social
collapse. Europe's global pre-eminence was also crumbling. Not only did
Russia loosen its grip on its subject nationalities, but even within the British
Empire, although apparently never so united in a common cause, centrifugal

tendencies gathered momentum. In India each concession whetted appetites for more, yet its rulers feared inaction was still riskier. Similarly the Balfour Declaration reflected fears that if Britain failed to harness Zionism, Germany would. Zionist influence was overestimated, but in such a hard-fought contest it might constitute the critical margin that brought victory at a lower cost.

The precondition for these developments was that the war did not end in 1917 but was extended and intensified. Underlying its transformation lay decisions: to intervene, to repudiate compromise, and to attack. The intervention decisions continued a process that had begun in 1914. Most of the Powers that joined the war—even big ones such as Japan, Turkey, and Italy—intended not to plunge into the carnage on the Western Front but rather through parallel efforts to settle scores and satisfy ambitions in their immediate vicinities. Venizelos's Greece fitted this pattern, while Siam and China hoped to end the unequal treaties, and China to gain ground against Japan. Both the latter cases (and still more Brazil's) showed how global were the ramifications of unrestricted submarine warfare and American entry. They also highlighted America's distinctiveness. The United States had no territorial claims, and its trading and investment stake in Allied victory played little part in the decision to come in. Nor did Washington calculate closely which side was likelier to triumph, as American entry could grant victory to either. In fact the Wilson administration conducted astonishingly little prior strategic appraisal, although the evidence suggests its leaders judged Allied victory to be near, and expected American intervention to bring disproportionate influence at modest cost. Between April 1917 and April 1918 the outlook darkened and the US contribution expanded, while Wilson and House advanced towards diplomatic leadership. In contrast to other intervening governments, the Americans planned a war-winning contribution on the Western Front. By spring 1918 they had formulated a peace programme that superficially resembled but also countered Allied goals; and they were fashioning the AEF in order to compel German compliance.

Although Wilson was jealous of his diplomatic independence, he now sought peace through victory (albeit a qualified and moderate victory) rather than peace without it. Like Ribot and Lloyd George, he opposed negotiating until the military balance had moved against the Central Powers. And the hope the United States represented gave the Allies vital encouragement, despite their litany of military disaster. Without American belligerency, in fact—given that the February Revolution, Nivelle's defeat and the French army mutinies, and a British financial and shipping crisis were all likely to have happened anyway—it is difficult to see how the Allies could have salvaged more than, at best, an unfavourable draw. Neither the British nor the French were strong enough to expel the German army from France and Belgium. The Italians were somewhat stronger relative to the Austrians, but not if Germany came to Austria-Hungary's aid. The Allies made substantial progress only against Germany's colonies and in the Middle East. Especially after Russia collapsed it was unclear, without American assistance, how they could ever attain a favourable bargaining position. Even so, when during 1917 Austria-Hungary and Germany sought negotiations the Allies refused. No peace move led to round-table discussion but, if one had done so, the two sides would have found each other far apart. In spring and summer 1917 war aims were still expanding—Britain wanted Palestine and Mesopotamia, France a Rhineland buffer state, and Germany to control the Ukraine. By the autumn the Germans were briefly willing to relinquish Flanders naval bases, and Lloyd George to explore peace at Russia's expense; but both sides still sought to divide their enemies rather than negotiate a general settlement. To be sure, socialists, Catholics, and progressives pressed for a compromise, as the Reichstag Peace Resolution, the French Dumont resolution, and the Labour Party's Memorandum on War Aims testified; but their impact was slight. Instead, during 1917–18 in Britain, France, Germany, and Italy state or state-backed agencies like the Fatherland Party 'remobilized' patriotic opinion. The home fronts became more polarized but not necessarily anti-war.[135] Even in Austria-Hungary, Karl would settle for a return to the frontiers of 1914 but wanted more if obtainable, and after the Sixte disappointment and the Italian breakthrough in August he and Czernin closed ranks with Berlin. In Petrograd the Provisional Government reduced its war aims after Milyukov fell, but after the failure of the Stockholm conference and of the Kerensky offensive it too relaxed the pressure on its partners. Inability or unwillingness to make peace unilaterally helped cause both the Provisional Government's and the Habsburg monarchy's demise. The 1917 peace moves failed for many reasons: compromise between two coalitions was harder than between two governments; pressure from the Right and Centre offset pressure from the Left; and the two sides' war aims remained irreconcilable. But above all, both still had grounds to hope that military and naval operations could gain more than could negotiation; the Central Powers looking first to the submarines and then to Russia's disengagement, the Allies first to the spring 1917 campaigning and then to the AEF.

Both sides also sanctioned new offensives. In Italy Cadorna bore prime responsibility for the tenth and eleventh Isonzo battles (and he and his generals for the dispositions before Caporetto). Only after the retreat did Italy—under Allied pressure—appoint a more compliant commander. In Germany politicians interrogated the Holtzendorff plan, but neither that for Caporetto nor that for 'Michael': an indication of how civilian influence on strategy weakened while military influence over war aims grew. Germany was on a different trajectory from the Western countries, including America (where Wilson delegated liberally but kept the final say) as well as France and Britain. After Joffre was ousted Nivelle lacked his predecessor's authority: not only was his project scrutinized but his generals were set against him. In Britain, in contrast, after the failure of the spring offensives Haig forged ahead. Lloyd George failed to divide him from Robertson, whereas the generals benefited from the War Cabinet's disarray. As in Germany, British politicians could prevail more easily over the navy than over the army; but unlike in Germany at least questions were asked. Even so, although neither Ribot nor Lloyd George felt confidence in their high commands' attack plans, neither felt able to veto them: they lacked alternatives, they hoped to manage the operations so as to avoid another Somme, and they feared that unless they struck first Germany would. Similar considerations weighed with Kerensky. Like American leaders during the war in Vietnam, the Allied statesmen expanded military operations after weighing the alternatives and with little optimism.[136] In Germany, too, submarine warfare was approved, for all its imponderables, partly because the civilians had run out of counter-arguments and partly to offset the expected Allied spring offensives. And when deciding 'Michael', Ludendorff feared that unless he attacked he would face new enemy blows—and now with American reinforcements—while defensive warfare was losing its edge. Certainly, the essence of warfare is competition, a war cannot be won by doing nothing, and by attacking both sides meant to wrest the initiative. Yet in fact in the conditions of 1917 the German army still profited from staying on the defensive, whereas attacking wore down the Allies. In 1918, conversely, it was the Central Powers' infantry that went over the top, and by doing so exhausted their ability to carry on. Sometimes standing still may actually be the wisest course, though appearing the most hazardous.

This book has analysed a transition, running in a larger sense from December 1916 to March 1918 although the key decisions fell during 1917 and between January and November. It coincided not quite exactly with

one of the twelve-month intervals into which we parcel the expanses of the
past. Framing the exposition within a calendar year is not entirely arbitrary,
as it highlights the seasonal rhythms of which contemporaries were acutely
aware. Air conditioning and central heating remained comforts of the
privileged, and millions of combatants lived and died on the high seas or
in open country and at the mercy of the elements. The war described a
distinctive cycle, from winter preparations through spring and summer
campaigning to autumnal taking stock. And as with any historical sub-
division, decisions taken in 1917 developed from others in 1916, and foreshadowed those of 1918. None the less, between spring 1917 and spring 1918
the conflict's outcome went far to being determined. In January 1917 it still
remained Germany's to lose. Yet by launching unrestricted submarine
warfare Berlin brought in a reluctant United States, and thereby virtually
precluded the Central Powers' triumph. By deciding on the 1918 offensives,
it largely set the timing and the manner of its defeat. Conversely in early
1917 it had seemed—in fact misleadingly—that the Allies were finally making headway, and that a renewal of their 1916 strategy might bring victory
without American aid. By early 1918 that victory was actually closer than
they realized, but now only with Wilson's cooperation. In short, in January
1917 the range of possibilities had been greater. A year later Eastern Europe
was already emerging from the war (if only to plunge into successor conflicts), and Western Europe's exit route had been delineated. The destination
would be a peace that America and the Western European Allies were too
divided to uphold jointly and yet that neither could uphold alone.

    1914–18 decision-making is stereotypically a tale of Abraham and Isaac:
of old men consigning young men to oblivion. We see the leaders in metrop-
olises and in Rhineland spas, in country houses and in railway carriages,
repairing after their deliberations to brandy and to schnapps. They set the
context for the lives of millions to be uprooted and a continent turned
upside down. Yet many in authority were among the ablest that their countries had to offer: vigorous, experienced, and reflective. By 1917 the shock
and novelty of authorizing slaughter had worn off, and many were inured
to it, but Clemenceau, Orlando, Pétain, Lloyd George, Wilson—as also Karl
and even Wilhelm—remained cognizant of the human toll. They still felt it
must continue to be paid. In fact the decisions recounted here were far from
uniformly disastrous, but almost none delivered on expectations. Their
authors did not resolve, however, to terminate the conflict. Instead they
searched for quicker and less sanguinary exits—a little more war for an

Notes

PRELIMS

1. David Lloyd George, *War Memoirs* (1938), I, p. 517.
2. *The Times*, 31 July 1917. The declaration features in Pat Barker, *Regeneration* (1991), p. 5.
3. Stephen Kotkin, *Stalin*, I: *Paradoxes of Power, 1878–1928* (2015), p. 151; Jean Moorcroft Wilson, *Siegfried Sassoon: The Making of a War Poet* (1998), p. 373.
4. Ian Kershaw, *Fateful Choices: Ten Decisions that Changed the World, 1940–1941* (2008).

INTRODUCTION

1. The phrase comes from the Soviet writer Ilya Ehrenburg: Richard Overy, *Why the Allies Won* (1995), p. 63.
2. Stephen Broadberry and Mark Harrison (eds), *The Economics of World War I* (2005), pp. 44, 216.
3. David Stevenson, *1914–1918: The History of the First World War* (2004), pp. 198–206.
4. Lloyd George, *War Memoirs*, I, p. 517.
5. Keith Jeffery, *1916: A Global History* (2015), pp. 55, 243–4.
6. Recent accounts include Christopher Clark, *The Sleepwalkers: How Europe Went to War in 1914* (2013); Margaret Macmillan, *The War that Ended Peace: How Europe Abandoned Peace for the First World War* (2013); Gordon Martel, *The Month that Changed the World: July 1914* (2014); Thomas Otte, *July Crisis: The World's Descent into War, Summer 1914* (2014).
7. The Conservative Party was normally referred to as the Unionists, because it opposed Home Rule for Ireland.
8. Mobilization meant bringing an army up to war strength; concentration its deployment on the frontiers.
9. See ch. 10 of this volume.
10. Haig MSS, NLS, Box 196, diary, 19 August 1915.
11. Timothy Dowling, *The Brusilov Offensive* (2008), p. 160.
12. John Paul Harris, *Douglas Haig and the First World War* (2008), p. 271. Generally, William Philpott, *Bloody Victory: The Sacrifice on the Somme and the Making of the Twentieth Century* (2009).
13. Alexander Watson, *Ring of Steel: Germany and Austria-Hungary at War, 1914–1918* (2014), p. 423.
14. Adam Tooze, *The Deluge: The Great War, America, and the Remaking of the Global Order, 1916–1931* (2015), p. 39.
15. Donald Bloxham, *The Great Game of Genocide: Imperialism, Nationalism, and the Destruction of the Ottoman Armenians* (2007); Ronald Suny, '*They Can Live in the Desert but Nowhere Else*': a History of the Armenian Genocide (2013).
16. Fritz Fischer, *Germany's Aims in the First World War* (1967), pp. 103–6.
17. Marvin Fried, *Austro-Hungarian War Aims in the Balkans during World War I* (2014).
18. Angelo Gatti, *Caporetto: dal Diario di Guerra Inedito (Maggio-Dicembre 1917)* (1964), p. 93 Cf. Bruce Bueno de Mesquita, *The War Trap* (1981).

CHAPTER I

1. Walter Görlitz (ed.), *Regierte der Kaiser? Kriegstagebücher, Aufzeichnungen und Briefe des Chefs des Marine-Kabinetts Admiral Georg Alexander von Müller, 1914–1918* (1959), p. 196.
2. John Williamson, *Karl Helfferich, 1872–1924: Economist, Financer, Politician* (1971), p. 165.
3. Karl Erdmann (ed.), *Kurt Riezler: Tagebücher, Aufsätze, Dokumente* (1972), p. 326.
4. RMA to AA, 9 Feb. 1919, AK R/904/502.
5. Carl-Axel Gemzell, *Organization, Conflict, and Innovation: A Study of German Naval Strategic Planning, 1888–1940* (1973), p. 140.
6. Ernest May, *The World War and American Isolation, 1914–1917* (1959), p. 115.
7. See Isabel Hull, *A Scrap of Paper: Breaking and Making International Law during the Great War* (2014), p. 213.
8. RMA to AA, 9 Feb. 1919, AR R/905/502.
9. May, *World War*, pp. 120–3.
10. Joachim Schröder, *Die-U-Boote des Kaisers: die Geschichte des deutschen U-Boot-Krieges gegen Großbritannien im Ersten Weltkrieg* (2000), p. 407.
11. Görlitz (ed.), *Regierte?*, pp. 155, 169.
12. Dirk Steffen, 'The Holtzendorff Memorandum of 22 December 1916 and Germany's Declaration of Unrestricted U-Boat Warfare', *Journal of Military History* 68, no. 1 (2004), p. 216.
13. Schröder, *U-Boote*, p. 428.
14. Herbert Michaelis and Ernst Schraepler (eds), *Ursachen und Folgen. Vom deutschen Zusammenbruch 1918 und 1945 bis zur Staatlichen Neuordnung Deutschlands in der Gegenwart* (1958), I, p. 70.
15. Görlitz (ed.), *Regierte?*, p. 149.
16. Erdman (ed.), *Riezler*, p. 328.
17. Görlitz (ed.), *Regierte?*, p. 147.
18. Holger Afflerbach, 'Wilhelm II as Supreme Warlord in the First World War', *War in History* 5, no. 4 (1998), p. 438.
19. Williamson, *Helfferich*, pp. 151–2, 158–9.
20. Michaelis (ed.), *Ursachen*, I, pp. 107ff.
21. Erdmann (ed.), *Riezler*, p. 337; Görlitz (ed.), *Regierte?*, p. 169.
22. Karl Birnbaum, *Peace Moves and U-Boat Warfare: A Study of Imperial Germany's Policy towards the United States, April 18, 1916–January 9, 1917* (1958), pp. 75–91.
23. Gerhard Granier (ed.), *Die Deutsche Seekriegsleitung im Ersten Weltkrieg* (2000), IV, p. 302; Reinhard Scheer, *Deutschlands Hochseeflotte im Weltkrieg: Persönliche Erinnerungen* (1920), p. 349.
24. Granier (ed.), *Seekriegsleitung*, IV, p. 328.
25. Scheer, *Hochseeflotte*, p. 329.
26. Granier (ed.), *Seekriegsleitung*, IV, pp. 339–43, 348–6.
27. Schröder, *U-Boote*, p. 279.
28. Granier (ed.), *Seekriegsleitung*, IV, pp. 354–6.
29. Marc Frey, 'Bullying the Neutrals: The Case of the Netherlands', in *Great War, Total War: Combat and Mobilization on the Western Front, 1914–1918*, eds Roger Chickering and Stig Förster (2000), pp. 235–6.
30. Deputy Commanding General reports, 15 July, 8 Aug. 1916, BA-MA PH2/62.
31. May, *World War*, p. 259.

32. Schröder, *U-Boote*, pp. 264–5.

33. Görlitz (ed.), *Regierte?*, p. 169.

34. Schröder, *U-Boote*, p. 271.

35. May, *World War*, pp. 254–5.

36. Ibid., p. 253; Williamson, *Helfferich*, p. 160.

37. May, *World War*, p. 259; Klaus Epstein, *Matthias Erzberger and the Dilemma of German Democracy* (1959), p. 159.

38. Granier (ed.), *Seekriegsleitung*, IV, p. 339.

39. Afflerbach, 'Wilhelm II', p. 441; Wolfgang Steglich, *Die Friedenspolitik der Mittelmächte, 1917/18*, I, p. xi.

40. Wolfram Pyta, *Hindenburg: Herrschaft zwischen Hohenzollern und Hitler* (2007), p. 229.

41. Reichsarchiv, *Der Weltkrieg 1914 bis 1918* (1925–56) [henceforth *WK*], XI, p. 478.

42. Günter Wollstein, *Theobald von Bethmann Hollweg* (1995), p. 142.

43. Granier (ed.), *Seekriegsleitung*, IV, pp. 365–8.

44. *WK*, XII, p. 1.

45. 'Hindenburg-Program und Hilfsdienstgesetz', BA-MA W-10/50397.

46. Görlitz (ed.), *Regierte?*, p. 235.

47. Erdmann (ed.), *Riezler*, pp. 383, 386.

48. Schröder, *U-Boote*, p. 437.

49. Ibid., pp. 184–6, 241; see Gary Weir, 'Tirpitz, Technology, and Building U-Boats, 1897–1916', *International History Review* 6, no. 2 (1984), pp. 186–8.

50. Schröder, *U-Boote*, pp. 428–9.

51. Stevenson, *1914–1918*, p. 255; Paul Halpern, *A Naval History of World War I* (1994), p. 335.

52. Granier (ed.), *Seekriegsleitung*, IV, p. 431.

53. Ibid., p. 408.

54. Schröder, *U-Boote*, p. 430.

55. Wollstein, *Bethmann Hollweg*, p. 135.

56. May, *World War*, pp. 387–93.

57. André Scherer and Jacques Grünewald (eds), *L'Allemagne et les problèmes de la paix pendant la Première Guerre Mondiale* (1962), I, pp. 405–7, 438.

58. Ibid., p. 465.

59. Ibid., pp. 469–71, 475–6.

60. Ibid., pp. 491, 517–19.

61. Ibid., pp. 477–81, 486.

62. Stephen, Count Burián, *Austria in Dissolution* (1925), pp. 196–9.

63. Lamar Cecil, *Wilhelm II*, II: *Emperor and Exile, 1900–1941* (1996), p. 242.

64. John Röhl, *Wilhelm II: Into the Abyss of War and Exile, 1900–1941* (2014), p. 1134.

65. *WK*, XI, p. 455.

66. Ibid., pp. 453, 456.

67. Scherer and Grünewald (eds), *L'Allemagne*, I, pp. 542–3, 548, 550–2.

68. Ibid., pp. 633–7.

69. James Scott (ed.), *Official Statements of War Aims and Peace Proposals, December 1916–November 1918* 1921), pp. 26–9.

70. See Granier (ed.), *Seekriegsleitung*, IV, p. 433.

71. Ibid., pp. 415–16.

72. Ibid., pp. 447–51.

73. *WK*, XI, p. 464.

74. Granier (ed.), *Seeleitung*, IV, p. 441.
75. Michaelis and Shraepler (eds), *Ursachen*, I, p. 144.
76. Erich Ludendorff, *My War Memories, 1914–1918* (1919), p. 316.
77. Ibid., p. 136.
78. *WK*, XI, pp. 457–9.
79. Williamson, *Helfferich*, p. 190.
80. *WK*, XI, p. 461.
81. Granier (ed.), *Seeleitung*, IV, p. 467.
82. *WK*, XI, pp. 446–7.
83. Epstein, *Erzberger*, p. 159.
84. *WK*, XI, p. 466.
85. Ibid., p. 467.
86. Manfred Nebelin, *Ludendorff: Diktator im Ersten Weltkrieg* (2011), p. 300.
87. Joachim-Heinrich, Count von Bernstorff, *The Memoirs of Count Bernstorff* (1936), p. 129.
88. Afflerbach, 'Wilhelm II', p. 443.
89. Görlitz (ed.), *Regierte?*, p. 246.
90. Birnbaum, *Peace Moves*, p. 6; May, *World War*, p. 93.
91. Gerhard Granier (ed.), *Magnus von Levetzow: Seeoffizier, Monarchist, und Wegbereiter Hitlers: Lebensweg und Ausgewählte Dokumente* (1982), p. 26.
92. Görlitz (ed.), *Regierte?*, p. 246; Granier (ed.), *Seekriegsleitung*, IV, p. 474.
93. Williamson, *Helfferich*, pp. 192ff.
94. Granier (ed.), *Seekriegsleitung*, IV, pp. 476–8.
95. Görlitz (ed.), *Regierte?*, p. 247.
96. Michaelis and Schraeple (eds), *Ursachen und Folgen*, I, p. 146.
97. Görlitz (ed.), *Regierte?*, p. 248.
98. Michaelis and Schraepler (eds), *Ursachen und Folgen*, I, pp. 146–7.
99. Ibid., doc. 85, p. 148; Bernhard Schwertfeger (ed.), *Kaiser und Kabinettschef: nach eigenen Aufzeichnungen und dem Briefwechsel des Wirklichen Geheimen Rats Rudolf von Valentini* (1931), p. 144.
100. Görlitz (ed.), *Regierte?*, p. 248.
101. Theobald von Bethmann Hollweg, *Betrachtungen zum Weltkriege* (1919), II, p. 137.
102. Schwertfeger (ed.), *Kabinettschef*, pp. 146–9.
103. Afflerbach, 'Wilhelm II', p. 440.
104. Michaelis and Schraepler (eds), *Ursachen und Folgen*, I, p. 49.
105. Görlitz (ed.), *Regierte?*, p. 249.
106. Cecil, *Wilhelm II*, II, p. 243.
107. Budget Commission, 31 Jan. 1917, AR R/1501/212498.
108. Williamson, *Helfferich*, p. 196.
109. Budget Commission, 31 Jan. 1917, AR R/1501/212498.
110. Granier (ed.), *Seeleitung*, IV, pp. 448, 481.
111. Schroeder, *U-Boote*, p. 321.
112. Ibid., p. 320; Watson, *Ring of Steel*, p. 431.
113. Erdmann (ed.), *Riezler*, p. 395.
114. Michaelis and Schraepler (eds), *Ursachen und Folgen*, I, p. 147.
115. *WK*, XI, p. 480.
116. Ibid., p. 479.
117. Ibid., pp. 478–9.

118. Ibid., p. 470; Theobald von Bethmann Hollweg, *Betrachtungen zum Weltkriege* (1919), II, p. 135; Erich Ludendorff (ed.), *Urkunden der Obersten Heeresleitung über ihre Tätigkeit, 1916/18* (1920), p. 308.

119. Bernstorff, *Memoirs*, p. 104.

120. Schröder, *U-Boote*, p. 407.

121. Ibid., pp. 371, 409; see Granier (ed.), *Seekriegsleitung*, IV, pp. 339–40.

122. Wollstein, *Bethmann Hollweg*, p. 137.

CHAPTER 2

1. John Thompson, *Woodrow Wilson* (2002), p. 107.

2. Stephen Gwynn (ed.), *The Letters and Friendships of Sir Cecil Spring Rice* (1929), II, p. 370.

3. Thompson, *Wilson*, p. 8.

4. Robert Osgood, *Ideals and Self-Interest in American Foreign Relations: The Great Transformation of the Twentieth Century* (1953), p. 161.

5. John Milton Cooper, Jr, *The Vanity of Power: American Isolationism and the First World War, 1914–1917* (1969), p. 20.

6. André Kaspi, *Le Temps des Américains: le concours américain à la France en 1917–1918* (1976), p. 2.

7. Frederick C. Luebke, *Bonds of Loyalty: German-Americans and World War I* (1974), pp. 29–30.

8. Gwynn (ed.), *Spring Rice*, p. 245.

9. May, *World War*, p. 48.

10. David Houston, *Eight Years with Wilson's Cabinet, 1913–1920* (1920), I, p. 137.

11. Edward Buehrig, *Woodrow Wilson and the Balance of Power* (1955), p. 88.

12. Ross Gregory, *The Origins of American Intervention in the First World War* (1971), p. 43.

13. Halpern, *A Naval History of World War I*, p. 65.

14. John Cooper, 'The Command of Gold Reversed: American Loans to Britain, 1915–1917', *Pacific Historical Review* 45, No. 2 (1976), p. 215; see McAdoo to Wilson, 17 Sept. 1915, LOC McAdoo MSS 520.

15. Yves-Henri Nouailhat, 'La France et les Etats-Unis, août 1914–avril 1917' (Doctoral dissertation, University of Paris, 1975), pp. 872, 809.

16. Hull, *Scrap of Paper*, ch. 1; *PWW*, XXXVI, p. 214.

17. *FRUS LP, 1914–1920* (1939), I, p. 421.

18. *FRUS 1914 Supplement I*, p. 219.

19. Patrick Devlin, *Too Proud to Fight: Woodrow Wilson's Neutrality* (1974), pp. 199–204.

20. John Coogan, *The End of Neutrality: The United States, Britain, and Maritime Rights, 1899–1915* (1981).

21. Dr Jan Lemnitzer is carrying out important research on this topic.

22. Gwynn (ed.), *Spring Rice*, p. 23; Charles Seymour (ed.), *The Intimate Papers of Colonel House* (1926), I, p. 310.

23. Edward Grey, *Twenty-Five Years, 1892–1916* (1925), II, p. 105.

24. May, *World War*, p. 18.

25. Nouailhat, 'La France', p. 232; Braughan interview with Wilson, 14 Dec. 1914, LOC McAdoo MSS 523.

26. *FRUS 1915 Supplement I*, p. 99.

27. John M. Cooper, *Woodrow Wilson: A Biography* (2011), p. 285.

28. Ibid.; Cooper, *Vanity*, p. 34.

29. *FRUS LP*, I, p. 439.
30. Devlin, *Too Proud*, p. 15.
31. Joseph Tumulty, *Woodrow Wilson As I Know Him* (1970), p. 250.
32. *FRUS LP*, I, p. 406.
33. Thompson, *Wilson*, p. 113.
34. May, *World War*, p. 335.
35. *FRUS 1915 Supplement I*, pp. 393–6.
36. Ibid., pp. 436–7, 480–2.
37. Devlin, *Too Proud*, p. 312.
38. *FRUS 1915 Supplement I*, p. 482.
39. Devlin, *Too Proud*, pp. 325, 328.
40. Ibid., p. 440.
41. Ibid., pp. 474–6; *PWW*, XXXVI, pp. 371–3, 387–9.
42. *FRUS 1916 Supplement I*, pp. 232–4.
43. Ibid., p. 263.
44. *PWW*, XXXVI, p. 597.
45. Chad Fulwider, *German Propaganda and US Neutrality in World War I* (2016).
46. Seymour (ed.), *House*, I, p. 437.
47. John W. Chambers, II, *To Raise an Army: The Draft Comes to Modern America* (1987), pp. 73–97, 107–10; see David M. Kennedy, *Over Here: The First World War and American Society* (1980), pp. 30–5.
48. Thompson, *Wilson*, p. 115; Spring-Rice to Grey, 4 Sept. 1916, FO 371/2800.
49. McAdoo to Wilson, 6 Oct. 1915, LOC McAdoo MSS, 520.
50. Josephus Daniels, *The Wilson Era: Years of Peace—1910–1917* (1974), p. 322.
51. Spring-Rice to Grey, 4 Sept. 1916, FO 371/2800.
52. *PWW*, XXXVI, pp. 644–5.
53. Chambers, *To Raise an Army*, pp. 116–17.
54. Charles Neu, *Colonel House: A Biography of Woodrow Wilson's Silent Partner* (2015), ch. 18.
55. Seymour (ed.), *House*, II, p. 200.
56. Spring-Rice to Grey, 19 May 1916, FO 800/242.
57. Cooper, *Wilson*, p. 317.
58. Lawrence Martin, *Peace Without Victory: Woodrow Wilson and the British Liberals* (1958), p. 101.
59. Cooper, *Wilson*, p. 318.
60. David Stevenson, *French War Aims against Germany, 1914–1919* (1982), pp. 14–15.
61. Daniel Larsen, 'War Pessimism in Britain and an American Peace in Early 1916', *International History Review* 34, No. 4 (2012), pp. 795–817.
62. Daniel Larsen, 'British Intelligence and the 1916 Mediation Mission of Colonel Edward M. House', *Intelligence and National Security* 25, No. 5 (2010), pp. 682–704.
63. Larsen, 'War Pessimism', pp. 811–12.
64. Devlin, *Too Proud*, pp. 483–91.
65. Thomas Knock, *To End All Wars: Woodrow Wilson and the Quest for a New World Order* (1992), p. vii.
66. Kathleen Burk, *Britain, America, and the Sinews of War, 1914–1918* (1985), p. 40.
67. Ibid., p. 80; Devlin, *Too Proud*, pp. 502–17.
68. Devlin, *Too Proud*, p. 518.
69. S. Lovell, *The Presidential Election of 1916* (1980), p. 134.
70. Lovell, *Presidential Election*, pp. 56–7; Knock, *To End All Wars*, p. vii.

71. Lovell, *Presidential Election*, p. 98.
72. Daniels, *Wilson Era*, p. 579.
73. Spring-Rice to Grey, 24 Nov. 1916, FO 800/242.
74. Birnbaum, *Peace Moves*, pp. 151–65.
75. Seymour (ed.), *House*, II, pp. 393–4.
76. Robert Lansing, *War Memoirs of Robert Lansing* (1935), pp. 179–80.
77. Devlin, *Too Proud*, pp. 575–6.
78. Spring-Rice despatch, 10 Dec. 1916, FO 371/2800.
79. McAdoo to Wilson, 3 Jan. 1917, LOC, McAdoo MSS 521.
80. Lamont to McAdoo, 21 Feb. 1917, LOC McAdoo MSS 175.
81. Thompson, *Wilson*, p. 128.
82. Burk, *Sinews*, pp. 77–8; War Office memorandum, 22 Dec. 1916, CAB 37/162/1.
83. Burk, *Sinews*, p. 81.
84. Ibid., p. 82.
85. Ibid., p. 85; Nouailhat, 'La France', pp. 788–9.
86. Spring-Rice telegram, FO to Spring-Rice and Bertie, 29 Nov. 1916, FO 371/2800.
87. War Cabinet, 9 Dec. 1916, CAB 23/1/1.
88. *PWW*, XL, pp. 273–7.
89. *PWW*, XLI, p. 277.
90. Nouailhat, 'La France', p. 818.
91. Ibid., p. 809.
92. Scott (ed.), *Official Statements*, pp. 35–8.
93. Birnbaum, *Peace Moves*, pp. 272, 293–4.
94. *PWW*, XLI, p. 55; Thompson, *Wilson*, pp. 133–4.
95. Martin, *Peace Without Victory*, p. 123.
96. *PWW*, XLI, p. 36.
97. Devlin, *Too Proud*, pp. 609–12; see Wilton Fowler, *British–American Relations, 1914–1918: The Role of Sir William Wiseman* (1969).
98. Martin, *Peace Without Victory*, p. 123; Lansing, *War Memoirs*, p. 193.
99. Seymour (ed.), *House*, II, pp. 417–18; Devlin, *Too Proud*, pp. 600–1.
100. *FRUS 1917 Supplement I*, pp. 24–9.
101. Cooper, *Wilson*, pp. 371–2.
102. *The Literary Digest*, 3 Feb. 1917.
103. James W. Gerard, *My Four Years in Germany* (1917), p. 268.
104. *PWW*, XLI, p. 4.
105. Ibid., p. 3.
106. Gerard, *Four Years*, pp. 265–6.
107. *PWW*, XLI, p. 95.
108. Devlin, *Too Proud*, p. 666.
109. *PWW*, XLI, p. 73.
110. May, *World War*, pp. 416, 421.
111. *PWW*, XLI, p. 107.
112. Ibid., pp. 87, 89.
113. Ibid., pp. 120–1.
114. Ibid., pp. 120, 122.
115. Seymour (ed.), *House*, II, p. 415.
116. *PWW*, XLI, p. 87.

117. Ibid., pp. 90, 103.
118. Ibid., p. 89.
119. Ibid., pp. 94, 183.
120. Houston, *Eight Years*, p. 229.
121. *PWW*, XLI, p. 123.
122. Houston, *Eight Years*, p. 229.
123. *PWW*, XLI, pp. 94, 123–4.
124. *FRUS 1917 Supplement I*, pp. 109–12.
125. General Board, 30 Jan. 1917, NARA M1493, Roll 4.
126. *PWW*, XLI, p. 87.
127. Ibid., p. 122.
128. Ibid., pp. 160 and 66.
129. Arthur S. Link, *Wilson: Campaigns for Progressivism and Peace, 1916–1917* (1965), p. 298.
130. John A. Garraty, *Henry Cabot Lodge: A Biography* (1953), p. 333; Cooper, *Vanity of Power*, p. 169.
131. Spring-Rice to Grey, 9 Feb 1917, FO 371/3709; *Literary Digest*, 10 Feb. 1917.
132. PWW, XLI, pp. 151, 114.
133. Scott to Hardin, Rushmore, and Slocum, 6, 6, and 12 Feb. 1917, LOC Scott MSS 4.
134. General Board, 3, 4, 5, 17 Feb. 1917, NARA M1493, Roll 4.
135. Benson to Winslow, 31 Mar. 1917, LOC Benson MSS 3.
136. *PWW*, XLI, pp. 204–5.
137. See Václav Horčička, 'Austria-Hungary, Unrestricted Submarine Warfare, and the United States' Entrance into the First World War', *International History Review* 34, No. 2 (2012), p. 245.
138. *PWW*, XLI, p. 129.
139. *FRUS 1917 Supplement I*, pp. 40–3, 55–7, 63–5.
140. *PWW*, XLI, p. 115.
141. Ibid., p. 175; see ch. 10 of this volume.
142. *PWW*, XLI, p. 212; *FRUS 1917 Supplement I*, pp. 41–4.
143. *PWW*, XLI, pp. 315–16; Kaspi, *Temps*, pp. 11–12; see Baker to Balfour, 2 Apr. 1917, LGP F/3/2/16.
144. Nouailhat, 'La France', pp. 635, 871; Kaspi, *Le Temps*, p. 15.
145. Spring-Rice to Balfour, 2, 9, 16 Feb. 1917, FO 371/3109.
146. FO to Spring-Rice, 3 Feb. 1917, ibid.; Spring-Rice to FO, 19 Feb. 1917, *PWW*, XLI, pp. 256–7.
147. CND, 28 Feb., Bliss memorandum, 17 Mar. 1917, NARA M1069.
148. Johnston note, 11 May 1917, NARA M1024, Roll 311.
149. Scott to Rushmore, 6 Feb. 1917, LOC Scott MSS 4.
150. Link, *Wilson*, p. 410.
151. McAdoo to Francis, 3 Jan. 1917, LOC McAdoo MSS 172.
152. Scott to Brewster, 9 Mar. 1917, LOC Scott MSS 4.
153. *PWW*, XLI, pp. 117, 190.
154. Spring-Rice telegram, 12 Feb. 1917, FO 371/3109.
155. Spring-Rice to Balfour, 2 Feb. 1917, ibid.
156. Devlin, *Too Proud*, p. 644; Spring-Rice telegram, 16 Feb. 1917, FO 371/3709.
157. Thompson to Willard, 16 Feb., FRB to McAdoo, 17 Feb. 1917, LOC McAdoo MSS 174.
158. *Literary Digest*, 3 Mar. 1917.

159. Houston, *Eight Years*, p. 233.
160. Ibid., p. 234; *PWW*, XLI, p. 239.
161. *PWW*, XLI, p. 266.
162. Houston, *Eight Years*, pp. 235–7.
163. *PWW*, XLI, p. 281.
164. Houston, *Eight Years*, p. 237; Spring-Rice telegrams, 19, 22 Feb. 1917, FO 371/3109.
165. *PWW*, XLI, pp. 283–6.
166. Spring-Rice telegrams, 21, 23 Feb. 1917, FO 371/3109.
167. Friedrich Katz, *The Secret War in Mexico: Europe, the United States, and the Mexican Revolution* (1981), ch. 9.
168. Thomas Boghardt, *The Zimmermann Telegram: Intelligence, Diplomacy, and America's Entry into World War I* (2012), p. 245.
169. Ibid., pp. 66–74.
170. Ibid., pp. 119–20.
171. *PWW*, XLI, p. 280.
172. Ibid., p. 296.
173. Ibid., pp. 288, 305.
174. Ibid., p. 297.
175. Ibid., p. 392.
176. Boghardt, *Zimmermann Telegram*, p. 136.
177. *PWW*, XLI, pp. 354–5; Nouailhat, 'La France', pp. 871, 635.
178. *PWW*, XLI, p. 346.
179. Spring-Rice telegram, 7 Mar. 1917, FO 371/3109.
180. *PWW*, XLI, pp. 336–7.
181. Ibid., p. 349n; Nouailhat, 'La France', p. 859.
182. William McAdoo, *Crowded Years: The Reminiscences of William G. McAdoo* (1931), p. 372.
183. *PWW*, XLI, p. 323.
184. Cooper, *Vanity of Power*, p. 179; Devlin, *Too Proud*, p. 677.
185. Cooper, *Vanity of Power*, pp. 179–81.
186. *PWW*, XLI, pp. 315–16.
187. Ibid., p. 403.
188. Boghardt, *Zimmermann Telegram*, p. 147.
189. *Literary Digest*, 17 Mar. 1917.
190. Gwynn (ed.), *Spring-Rice*, p. 384.
191. Boghardt, *Zimmermann Telegram*, p. 180.
192. *PWW*, XLI, p. 448.
193. Link, *Wilson*, pp. 393–4.
194. Justus D. Doenecke, *Nothing Less than War: A New History of America's Entry into World War I* (2011), pp. 278–9.
195. Barclay telegram, 18 Mar. 1917, FO 371/3109.
196. Doenecke, *Nothing Less*, p. 279.
197. Barclay telegrams, 16, 20 Mar. 1917, FO 371/3109.
198. Barclay telegram, 20 Mar. 1917, ibid.
199. *PWW*, XLI, p. 430.
200. Ibid., pp. 425–6, 436–7.
201. Ibid., p. 429.
202. Cooper, *Wilson*, pp. 381, 642n.

203. Link, *Wilson*, p. 400.

204. *PWW*, XLI, pp. 426–7.

205. Ibid., p. 440.

206. Ibid., pp. 444; Houston, *Eight Years*, p. 244.

207. William Sims, *The Victory at Sea* (1920), p. 1.

208. Chambers, *To Raise an Army*, p. 144.

209. *PWW*, XLI, p. 500; Scott to Slocum, 12 Feb. 1917, LOC Scott MSS 27.

210. *PWW*, XLI, pp. 134, 146.

211. Ibid., p. 416.

212. Ibid., pp. 498, 528.

213. Seymour (ed.), *House*, II, pp. 470–1.

214. Houston, *Eight Years*, p. 247.

215. *FRUS 1917 Supplement I*, pp. 195–201.

216. Doenecke, *Nothing Less*, p. 240.

217. Ibid., pp. 291–6; Cooper, *Vanity*, pp. 198–204.

218. Cooper, *Vanity*, p. 233.

219. Thwaites report, 20 Apr. 1917, FO 115/2185.

220. Doenecke, *Nothing Less*, p. 297.

221. Tumulty, *Woodrow Wilson*, pp. 253–4, 257; *PWW*, XLI, p. 534.

222. David Cronon (ed.), *The Cabinet Diaries of Josephus Daniels, 1913–1921* (1963), p. 118.

223. *Literary Digest*, 7 Apr. 1917.

224. Knock, *To End All Wars*, p. 118.

225. Gwynn (ed.), *Spring-Rice*, p. 382; Cooper, *Vanity of Power*, p. 192; Knock, *To End All Wars*, p. 118.

226. *PWW*, XLI, p. 483.

227. Ibid., pp. 409, 376, 428.

228. Seymour (ed.), *House*, II, p. 444.

229. May, *World War*, p. 41; Devlin, *Too Proud*, p. 337.

230. Devlin, p. 672.

231. Cronon (ed.), *Daniels*, p. 117.

232. Kaspi, *Temps*, p. 19.

233. Mark Grotelueschen, *The AEF Way of War: The American Army and Combat in World War I* (2007), pp. 11–14.

234. Reports by Robertson, 29 Apr., CAB 24/13/17; and General Staff, 17 May 1917, CAB 24/13/46.

235. *PWW*, XLI, p. 305.

236. Hoover to House, 13 Feb., 1917, LOC Baker MSS 3.

237. *PWW*, XLI, p. 66.

238. Thompson, *Wilson*, p. 151.

239. Daniels, *Wilson Era*, p. 582.

240. Seymour (ed.), *House*, II, p. 467.

241. Cooper, *Wilson*, p. 322.

CHAPTER 3

1. Philip Lundeberg, 'The German Naval Critique of the U-Boat Campaign, 1915–1918', *Military Affairs* 27, No. 3 (1964), p. 113.

2. Maurice Hankey, *The Supreme Command* (1961), II, p. 640.
3. Alfred Temple Patterson (ed.), *The Jellicoe Papers: Selections from the Private and Official Correspondence of Admiral of the Fleet Lord Jellicoe* (1968), II, p. 88.
4. John Jellicoe, *The Crisis of the Naval War* (1920), p. x.
5. Lloyd George, *War Memoirs*, I, p. 676.
6. Margaret Barnett, *British Food Policy during the First World War* (1985), pp. 2–4.
7. Board of Trade memorandum, 1 Jan. 1918, CAB 24/38/27.
8. Lloyd George, *War Memoirs*, I, p. 719; Hawkins memorandum, 29 Dec. 1916, NMM BTY 13/23.
9. Arthur Salter, *Allied Shipping Control: An Experiment in International Administration* (1921), p. 77.
10. Board of Trade memorandum, 1 Jan. 1918, CAB 24/38/27.
11. Devonport memorandum, 20 Apr. 1917, CAB 24/11/41; Barnett, *Food Policy*, p. 90.
12. Beale to Devonport, 16 Apr. 1917, PRO 30/68/5.
13. Arthur J. Marder, *From the Dreadnought to Scapa Flow: The Royal Navy in the Fisher Era, 1904–1919* (1969), IV, p. 90; Lloyd George, *War Memoirs*, I, p. 713.
14. Marder, *Dreadnought*, IV, pp. 73–4.
15. Sims, *Victory at Sea*, p. 27.
16. Jellicoe to Beatty, 2 Apr. 1917, NMM BTY/13/23.
17. Henry Newbolt, *Naval Operations* (1920–31), V, p. 36; Sims, *Victory at Sea*, p. 24.
18. Sims, *Victory at Sea*, p. 28.
19. Jellicoe memorandum, 14 July 1917, CAB 24/20/8; see John Jellicoe, *The Submarine Peril: The Admiralty Policy in 1917* (1934), p. xi.
20. Sims, *Victory at Sea*, p. 80.
21. Newbolt, *Naval Operations*, IV, p. 523.
22. Marder, *Dreadnought*, IV, p. 70.
23. Newbolt, *Naval Operations*, IV, pp. 333–7.
24. Ibid., p. 547; Newbolt, *Naval Operations*, V, p. 54.
25. Sims, *Victory at Sea*, pp. 31, 21.
26. Technical History, 'Atlantic Convoy System, 1917–1918', ADM 137/3048, p. 16.
27. Ibid., p. 29; Sir Norman Hill memorandum, 21 June 1917, CAB 24/17/30.
28. Technical History, p. 30; Marder, *From the Dreadnought*, IV, p. 92.
29. Charles Ernest Fayle, *History of the Great War Based on Official Documents: Seaborne Trade* (1924), III, pp. 1–2.
30. Temple Patterson (ed.), *Jellicoe Papers*, pp. 88–92.
31. Barnett, *Food Policy*, p. 87.
32. Lloyd George, *War Memoirs*, I, pp. 673, 670.
33. Barnett, *Food Policy*, p. 85.
34. Liners provided scheduled services; tramps went in search of ad hoc consignments.
35. Hankey diary, 18, 28 March, HNKY/1/1.
36. John Grigg, *Lloyd George: War Leader, 1916–1918* (2003), pp. 11–18.
37. Jellicoe to Duff, 27 Nov. 1916, NMM DFF/1.
38. David French, *The Strategy of the Lloyd George Coalition, 1916–1918* (1995), p. 74; Hankey, *Supreme Command*, II, p. 641.
39. Fayle, *Seaborne Trade*, III, p. 81.
40. Hankey memorandum, 19 Feb. 1917, CAB 24/6/36.
41. Marder, *Dreadnought*, IV, p. 54.

42. Admiralty minute, 9 Feb.; Hunter to Minister, 20 Apr. 1917, ADM 167/52.
43. Fayle, *Seaborne Trade*, III, ch. 8.
44. Ibid., p. 92.
45. R. H. Gibson and Maurice Prendergast, *The German Submarine War, 1914–1918* (1931), p. 354.
46. Terraine, *Business in Great Waters*, pp. 39, 43.
47. Fayle, *Seaborne Trade*, III, p. 96; Marder, *Dreadnought*, IV, p. 52.
48. Archibald Hurd, *The Merchant Navy* (1921–9), III, pp. 7–23.
49. Fayle, *Seaborne Trade*, III, pp. 53, 52.
50. Marder, *Dreadnought*, IV, p. 177.
51. Temple Patterson (ed.), *Jellicoe Papers*, pp. 88–92.
52. Tupper, 23 Oct. and Webb, 26 Dec. 1916, ADM 137/1322.
53. Lloyd George, *War Memoirs*, I, pp. 678–9.
54. 'The Protection of British Sea Borne Trade', n.d., ADM 137/2771; Marder, *Dreadnought*, IV, p. 129.
55. Anderson letter, Webb minute, 10, 20 Jan. 1917, ADM 137/1322.
56. Hankey diary, 8, 9 Feb 1917, HNKY 1/1.
57. Ibid., 11, 13 Feb.; Jellicoe to Duff, 12 May 1933, NMM DFF/1; Hankey, *Supreme Command*, II, p. 647.
58. Newbolt, *Naval Operations*, V, pp. 10–14.
59. Hankey, *Supreme Command*, II, p. 648.
60. Minutes of meeting, 23 Feb. 1917; Kenrick minute 10 Feb. 1918, ADM 137/2753; Sims, *Victory at Sea*, p. 89.
61. Hankey diary, 30 Mar., 22 Apr. 1917, HNKY 1/1.
62. Halpern, *Naval History*, p. 351.
63. Elizabeth Greenhalgh, *Victory through Coalition: Britain and France during the First World War* (2005), p. 105.
64. Armin Triebel, 'Coal and the Metropolis', in Jay Winter and Jean-Louis Robert (eds), *Capital Cities at War: Paris, London, Berlin, 1914–1919* (1997), ch. 12.
65. Greenhalgh, *Victory through Coalition*, p. 114.
66. Ibid., p. 117.
67. French embassy, 20 Feb. 1917; Vandier note, 30 Dec. 1916, ADM 137/1392.
68. Duff memorandum, 1931, NMM DFF/6.
69. Fayle, *Seaborne Trade*, III, ch. 2.
70. Marder, *Dreadnought*, IV, p. 142.
71. Ruddock memorandum, 2 Apr. 1917, ADM 137/1322.
72. Longhope conference minutes, 4 Apr., 1917, ibid.; Marder, *Dreadnought*, IV, p. 142.
73. Duff minute, 14 Apr. 1917, ADM 137/1322.
74. Nicholas Black, *The British Naval Staff in the First World War* (2009), p. 12.
75. Duff memorandum, 1931, NMM DFF/6.
76. Jellicoe to Beatty, 12 Apr. 1917, NMM BTY 13/23/9.
77. Sims, *Victory at Sea*, pp. 67, 318.
78. Ibid., p. 3.
79. Bertram Smith memorandum, 4 Jan. 1917, ADM 137/1322; Black, *Naval Staff*, pp. 174–5.
80. Technical History, p. 22, ADM 137/3048; Lloyd George, *War Memoirs*, I, p. 692.
81. Marder, *Dreadnought*, IV, p. 152.
82. Ibid., pp. 150, 162, 165.

83. Lloyd George, *War Memoirs*, I, p. 698.
84. Jellicoe to Lady Duff, 29 Sept. 1934, NMM DFF/8.
85. Jellicoe, *Submarine Peril*, p. 36.
86. Lloyd George, *War Memoirs*, I, pp. 697–8; Grigg, *War Leader*, p. 61.
87. Fayle, *Seaborne Trade*, III, p. 90.
88. *British Vessels Lost at Sea, 1914–1918* (1977), p. 40.
89. Fayle, *Seaborne Trade*, III, p. 92; Salter, *Shipping Control*, p. 348.
90. Maclay to Hankey, n.d., CAB 24/10/3.
91. Jellicoe memorandum, 22 Apr. 1917, CAB 24/11/19.
92. Temple Patterson (ed.), *Jellicoe Papers*, pp. 160–2.
93. Beale to Devonport, 12 Apr. and 29 Mar. 1917, PRO 30/68/5.
94. Devonport memorandum, 20 Apr. 1917, CAB 24/11/41; Royal Commission, 24 Apr. 1917, CAB 24/11/61.
95. Hankey diary, 22 Apr. 1917, HNKY/1/1.
96. Marder, *Dreadnought*, IV, p. 158; Lloyd George, *War Memoirs*, I, p. 691.
97. Temple Patterson (ed.), *Jellicoe Papers*, p. 157.
98. War Cabinet, 25 Apr. 1917, CAB 23/2/44; Lloyd George, *War Memoirs*, I, p. 691.
99. Duff minute, 26 Apr. 1917, ADM 137/1322.
100. Temple Patterson (ed.), *Jellicoe Papers*, pp. 157–60.
101. Duff to Jellicoe, n.d, Jellicoe to Duff, 13 Aug. 1928, NMM DFF/1.
102. Duff to Bethell, 17 May 1917, NMM DFF/1.
103. Imperial War Cabinet, 26 Apr. 1917, CAB 23/40/12.
104. Hankey diary, 30 Apr. 1917, HNKY 1/3.
105. Lloyd George memorandum, 30 Apr. 1917, CAB 24/12/4.
106. Duff to Newbolt draft, NMM DFF/9.
107. Lloyd George memorandum, 30 Apr. 1917, CAB 24/12/4.
108. Temple Patterson (ed.), *Jellicoe Papers*, p. 181.
109. Arno Spindler, *Der Handelskrieg mit U-Booten* (1964), IV, p. 205.
110. Marder, *Dreadnought*, IV, pp. 186–8.
111. Lloyd George, *War Memoirs*, I, p. 693.
112. Hill memorandum, 21 June 1917, CAB 24/17/30.
113. Hill to Hankey, 6 July 1917, CAB 24/19/8.
114. Maclay to Lloyd George, 27 June 1917, CAB 24/18/8.
115. Duff to Bethell, 26 June 1917, 204A, 51, NMM DFF/3.
116. Marder, *Dreadnought*, IV, pp. 275, 258; Sims, *Victory at Sea*, pp. 331–2.
117. Duff to Bethell, 21 July 1917, NMM DFF/3.
118. Jellicoe to Cabinet, 14 July 1917, CAB 24/20/8; Jellicoe, n.d., BTY 13/23/18.
119. Anderson to Hankey, 21 July 1917, CAB 24/20/78.
120. Marder, *Dreadnought*, IV, p. 29; Lloyd George, *War Memoirs*, I, p. 712.
121. Duff memorandum, 1931, NMM DFF/6.
122. Fayle, *Seaborne Trade*, III, ch. 10; Shipping Ministry, 'Neutral Tonnage', 15 Nov. 1917, MT 25/5.
123. Salter note, 5 May 1917, ADM 137/1322; French, *Strategy*, p. 78.
124. Fayle, *Seaborne Trade*, III, p. 170.
125. Shipping Ministry, 8 June 1917, MT 25/5; Fayle, *Seaborne Trade*, III, p. 131.
126. Barnett, *Food Policy*, p. 110.
127. French, *Strategy*, pp. 90, 80–1.

128. Fayle, *Seaborne Trade*, III, p. 172.

129. Shipping Ministry, 17 Aug. 1917, MT 25/5; Fayle, *Seaborne Trade*, III, ch. 11.

130. Fayle, *Seaborne Trade*, III, pp. 175–6.

131. Beatty to Jellicoe, 27 Jan. 1917, NMM BTY 123/5/3; Sims, *Victory at Sea*, p. 34.

132. Fayle, *Seaborne Trade*, III, p. 175; Tothill to Hankey, 10 July 1917, CAB 24/19/58.

133. Duff to Bethell, 26 Aug. 1917, NMM DFF/3.

134. Terraine, *Business in Great Waters*, p. 131; Marder, *Dreadnought*, V, p. 81.

135. Spindler, *Handelskrieg*, IV, p. 224.

136. *Daily Telegraph*, 18 Nov. 1931, NMM DFF/6.

137. Sims, *Victory at Sea*, p. 95.

138. Ibid., pp. 6, 11–12.

139. Jellicoe to Beatty, 12 Apr. 1917, NMM BTY 13/24/9.

140. Lloyd George, *War Memoirs*, I, pp. 683, 685.

141. Marder, *Dreadnought*, IV, pp. 124–6.

142. Ibid., p. 289.

CHAPTER 4

1. Until 1918 Russia remained on the Julian calendar, thirteen days behind the Gregorian calendar followed in the West. Double dates are given. After the war began St Petersburg was retitled as the less Germanic-sounding Petrograd.

2. Tsuyoshi Hasegawa, *The February Revolution: Petrograd, 1917* (1981), pp. 215–18.

3. Stephen Smith, *Red Petrograd: Revolution in the Factories, 1917–1918* (1983), pp. 23–5.

4. Orlando Figes, *A People's Tragedy: The Russian Revolution, 1891–1924* (1997), p. 300.

5. Barbara Engel, 'Not by Bread Alone: Subsistence Riots in Russia during World War I', *Journal of Modern History* 69, No. 4 (1997), pp. 697–8, 703, 710.

6. Raymond Pearson, *The Russian Moderates and the Crisis of Tsarism, 1914–1917* (1977), pp. 107, 111; Hasegawa, *February Revolution*, p. 217.

7. Robert Browder and Alexander Kerensky (eds), *The Russian Provisional Government, 1917: Documents* (1961), I, p. 27.

8. Lars Lih, *Bread and Authority in Russia, 1914–1921* (1990), p. 1.

9. Norman Stone, *The Eastern Front, 1914–1917* (1975), p. 295 (1 pood = 16.38 kg).

10. Ibid., p. 296.

11. Richard Pipes, *The Russian Revolution, 1899–1919* (1999), p. 234.

12. Stone, *Eastern Front*, p. 288; Peter Bark at Petrograd Conference, 25 Jan./7 Feb. 1917, CAB 28/2.

13. Hasegawa, *February Revolution*, p. 199; Lih, *Bread and Authority*, pp. 30–55.

14. Pipes, *Russian Revolution*, p. 207.

15. A. Senin, *Zheleznodorozhny Transport Rossii v Epoxy Voini i Revolyutsii (1914–1922gg)* (2009), pp. 160ff; A. Sidorov, 'Zheleznodorozhny Transport Rossii v Pervoi Mirovoi Voine i Obostrenie Ekonomicheskogo Krizisa v Strane', *Istoricheskie Zapiski* 26 (1948), p. 3.

16. Roger Pethybridge, *The Spread of the Russian Revolution: Essays on 1917* (1972), p. 6.

17. Anthony Heywood, 'Spark of Revolution? Railway Disorganisation, Freight Traffic, and Tsarist Russia's War Effort, July 1914–March 1917', *Europe-Asia Studies* 65, No. 4 (2013), pp. 753–72.

18. Pethybridge, *Spread*, p. 6.

19. Peter Gatrell, *Russia's First World War: A Social and Economic History* (2005), p. 170.

20. Stone, *Eastern Front*, p. 296; see Gatrell, *Russia's First World War*, p. 166; Lih, *Bread*, p. 159.

21. Hasegawa, *February Revolution*, p. 199; Bagge report, 8 Dec. 1916, FO371/2995.

22. Mark Steinberg and Vladimir Khrustalev (eds), *The Fall of the Romanovs: Political Dreams and Personal Struggles in a Time of Revolution* (1995), p. 45; Hasegawa, *February Revolution*, pp. 200–1.

23. Pipes, *Russian Revolution*, pp. 272–4.

24. Hasegawa, *February Revolution*, pp. 222, 238, 247.

25. Robert McKean, *St Petersburg between the Revolutions: Workers and Revolutionaries, June 1907–February 1917* (1990), pp. 340, 327.

26. Ibid., p. 240; Smith, *Red Petrograd*, pp. 25, 34.

27. Smith, *Red Petrograd*, p. 10.

28. Diane Koenker and William Rosenberg, *Strikes and Revolution in Russia, 1917* (1989), p. 25.

29. Ibid., p. 59.

30. Hasegawa, *February Revolution*, ch. 6.

31. The Russian forces facing the Central Powers were divided into the Northern Front, the Western Front, the South-Western Front, and the Romanian Front: the equivalent of Army Groups in the German and French armies.

32. Hasegawa, *February Revolution*, pp. 160–5.

33. B. Maklakoff (ed.), *La Chute du regime tsariste* (1927), pp. 208–9.

34. Hasegawa, *February Revolution*, pp. 387, 225, 253–4, 263.

35. Maklakoff (ed.), *Chute*, p. 387.

36. Ibid., p. 388.

37. Hasegawa, *February Revolution*, pp. 272, 279, 292.

38. Stone, *Eastern Front*, p. 213; Pipes, *Russian Revolution*, p. 205.

39. Pipes, *Russian Revolution*, p. 205.

40. Allan Wildman, *The End of the Russian Imperial Army* (1980–7), p. 95.

41. Stone, *Eastern Front*, p. 216.

42. Joshua Sanborn, *Imperial Apocalypse: the Great War and the Destruction of the Russian Empire* (2014), pp. 175–83.

43. Dowling, *The Brusilov Offensive*, p. 160.

44. Wildman, *End*, I, pp. 97–8.

45. Irina Davidian, 'The Russian Soldier's Morale from the evidence of Military Censorship', in Hugh Cecil and Peter Liddle (eds), *Facing Armageddon: The First World War Experienced* (1996), ch. 12.

46. Bruce Lockhart to Buchanan, 21, 26 Dec. 1916, FO 371/2995.

47. Wildman, *End*, I, p. 115.

48. Lih, *Bread and Authority*, p. 48.

49. Wildman, *End*, I, p. 115.

50. Maurice Paléologue, *La Russie des tsars pendant la Grande Guerre* (1927), III, pp. 67, 74.

51. Hasegawa, *February Revolution*, pp. 167–8.

52. Peter Kenez, 'Changes in the Social Composition of the Officer Corps during World War I', *Russian Review* 31, No. 4 (1972), pp. 369–75.

53. Hasegawa, *February Revolution*, pp. 258, 315.

54. Ibid., chs. 17, 20–1.

55. Semion Lyandres, *The Fall of Tsarism: Untold Stories of the February 1917 Revolution* (2013), p. 229.

56. Hasegawa, *February Revolution*, p. 227; Pearson, *Russian Moderates*, p. 122.

57. Bruce Lockhart to Buchanan, 16 Jan. 1917, FO 371/2995; George Buchanan, *My Mission to Russia and Other Diplomatic Memories* (1923), II, p. 27.
58. Hubertus Jahn, *Patriotic Culture in Russia during World War I* (1995).
59. Bruce Lockhart to Buchanan, 5 Jan. 1917, FO 371/2995.
60. Pearson, *Russian Moderates*, pp. 49–70.
61. Buchanan, *My Mission*, II, p. 18; Maklakoff, ed, *La Chute*, p. 243.
62. Knox despatch, 20 Jan. 1917, WO 106/1088.
63. Buchanan, *My Mission*, II, p. 28; Bruce Lockhart to Buchanan, 30 Oct. 1916, CAB 37/160.
64. Buchanan to Balfour, 22 Dec. 1916, FO 371/2995; Knox despatch, 20 Jan 1917, WO 106/1088.
65. Bruce Lockhart to Buchanan, 16 Jan. 1917, FO 371/2995.
66. Buchanan to Balfour, 22 Dec. 1916, ibid.
67. Buchanan to Balfour, 18 Jan. 1917, ibid.
68. Buchanan to Balfour, 16 Feb. 1917, ibid.
69. Hasegawa, *February Revolution*, ch. 10; Pearson, *Russian Moderates*, pp. 128–31.
70. Paléologue, *La Russie*, III, p. 22.
71. Ibid., p. 149; Maklakoff (ed.), *La Chute*, p. 530.
72. Steinberg and Khrustalev (eds), *Fall*, pp. 65, 73.
73. Browder and Kerensky (eds), *Provisional Government*, I, p. 83.
74. Ibid., pp. 85–7, 89.
75. Ibid., p. 84.
76. Steinberg and Khrustalev (eds), *Fall*, pp. 6–7.
77. Bruce Lockhart to Buchanan, 16 Jan. 1917, FO 371/2995.
78. Paléologue, *La Russie*, III, p. 99.
79. Hasegawa, *February Revolution*, pp. 447–9.
80. Ibid., p. 476.
81. Ibid., p. 477.
82. Browder and Kerensky (eds), *Provisional Government*, I, p. 91.
83. Brian Taylor, *Politics and the Russian Army: Civil–Military Relations, 1609–2000* (2003), pp. 87–8.
84. Hasegawa, *February Revolution*, pp. 473, 477, 493.
85. Lyandres, *Fall*, p. 106.
86. Hasegawa, *February Revolution*, pp. 443–5.
87. Browder and Kerensky (eds), *Provisional Government*, I, pp. 92–3.
88. Ibid., p. 94.
89. Ibid., pp. 94–5.
90. Ibid., pp. 96–7.
91. Ibid., pp. 95–6.
92. Hasegawa, *February Revolution*, p. 502.
93. Steinberg and Khrustalev (eds), *Fall*, p. 107.
94. Ibid., pp. 96–9; Maklakoff (ed.), *Chute*, pp. 557–71.
95. Maklakoff (ed.), *Chute*, pp. 399–400.
96. Steinberg and Khrustalev (eds), *Fall*, p. 107.
97. Browder and Kerensky (eds), *Provisional Government*, I, pp. 104–5.
98. Horst Linke, *Das Zarische Rußland und der Erster Weltkrieg: Diplomatie und Kriegsziele, 1914–1917* (1982), pp. 235–42; see Paléologue, *La Russie*, III, pp. 40, 148; Milner to Lloyd George, 7 Feb. 1917, CAB 37/2.

99. Buchanan, *My Mission*, II, p. 25–6.
100. Stone, *Eastern Front*, pp. 227–9.
101. *The Times,* 22 Jan. 1917, FO 371/2995.
102. Stone, *Eastern Front*, p. 282.
103. Knox despatch, 20 Jan. 1917, WO 106/1088.
104. Knox despatch, 31 Mar. 1917, WO 106/1090.
105. Louise Heenan, *Russian Democracy's Fatal Blunder: The Summer Offensive of 1917* (1987), ch. 2.
106. Milner note, 13 Mar. 1917, CAB 28/2.
107. Session of 7/20 Feb. 1917, ibid.
108. Heenan, *Fatal Blunder,* p. 33.
109. Milner note, 13 Mar. 1917, CAB 28/2.
110. Buchanan to Balfour, 18 Jan. 1917, FO 371/2995; Dominic Lieven, *Nicholas II: Emperor of All the Russias* (1993), p. 230.
111. Buchanan telegram, 13 Mar. 1917, FO 371/2995.
112. Lyandres, *Fall*, p. 109.
113. Pearson, *Russian Moderates*, p. 144.
114. Browder and Kerensky (eds), *Provisional Government*, I, pp. 78–9.
115. Ibid., pp. 125–6.
116. Lyandres, *Fall*, p. 238.
117. Pipes, *Russian Revolution*, p. 296.
118. Hasegawa, *February Revolution*, p. 54.
119. Ibid., ch. 18.
120. Browder and Kerensky (eds), *Provisional Government*, I, p. 62.
121. Ronald Kowalski (ed.), *The Russian Revolution, 1917–1921* (2006), p. 177; see Hasegawa, *February Revolution*, pp. 396–403; Wildman, *End*, I, pp. 182–92.
122. Wildman, *End*, I, pp. 228ff.
123. Marc Ferro, *La Révolution de 1917: la chute du tsarisme et les origines d'Octobre* (1967), pp. 170–202.

CHAPTER 5

1. Roger Chickering and Stig Förster (eds), *Great War, Total War: Combat and Mobilization on the Western Front, 1914–1918* (2000), p. 325.
2. Harris, *Douglas Haig*, p. 281.
3. *AFGG*, 5(1), Annexes 1, pp. 97–8, 176–88.
4. Paul Painlevé, *Comment j'ai nommé Foch et Pétain: la politique de guerre de 1917; le commandement unique interallié* (1923), p. 4.
5. *AFGG*, 5(1), Annexes 1, pp. 217–18.
6. Raymond Poincaré, *Au service de la France: neuf années de souvenirs* (1926–31), IX, pp. 21–2, 53.
7. Stevenson, *French War Aims against Germany, 1914–1919*, ch. 2.
8. Lloyd George, *War Memoirs*, I, p. 851.
9. Robert Doughty, *Pyrrhic Victory: French Strategy and Operations in the Great War* (2005), p. 317.
10. French, *Strategy*, p. 53. The cohort comprised the able-bodied young men who reached military age in that year.

11. Doughty, *Pyrrhic Victory*, p. 317.
12. Undated Kiggell notes, LHCMA Kiggell MSS 5.
13. Davidson to Spears, 19 Mar. 1933, LHCMA Spears MSS 2/3/8–10 (Spiers changed the spelling of his name to Spears in 1918).
14. William Philpott, *Anglo-French Relations and Strategy on the Western Front, 1914–1918* (1996), p. 129.
15. Painlevé, *Comment*, p. 6.
16. Edward Spears, *Prelude to Victory* (1939), p. 472.
17. Georges Bonnefous, *Histoire politique de la Troisième République*, II: *La Grande Guerre (1914–1918)* (1967), pp. 170ff.
18. Jere King, *Generals and Politicians: Conflict between France's High Command, Parliament, and Government, 1914–1918* (1950), pp. 136–9; Doughty, *Pyrrhic Victory*, pp. 314–21.
19. Edmond Herbillon, *De la Meuse à Reims: le Général Alfred Micheler (1914–1918)* (1934), p. 119.
20. Pierre Miquel, *Le Chemin des Dames* (1997), pp. 28–30.
21. Lloyd George, *War Memoirs*, II, p. 876.
22. Painlevé, *Comment*, pp. 6–8.
23. Brugère Commission Report, p. 5, SHAT 5.N.255.
24. Painlevé, *Comment*, p. 8.
25. Alexandre Ribot (ed.), *Journal d'Alexandre Ribot et correspondances inédites 1914–1922* (1936), pp. 36–7.
26. Spears, *Prelude*, p. 129.
27. Jean de Pierrefeu, *GQG Secteur I* (1922), I, pp. 237–41.
28. Georges Suarez, *Briand: sa vie—son oeuvre* (1940), IV, p. 101.
29. Spears, *Prelude*, pp. 66, 69.
30. Guy Pédroncini, *Les Mutineries de 1917* (1967), pp. 32–4.
31. 'Conditions dans lesquelles ont été décidées des operations offensives du 9 avril 1917' [*sic*]; SHAT 5.N. 255; Nivelle to Thomas, 11 Mar. 1917, SHAT 10.N. 12.
32. *AFGG*, 5(1), pp. 162–3; Poincaré, *Au service*, IX, p. 58.
33. *AFGG*, 5(1), p. 160; Doughty, *Pyrrhic Victory*, p. 324.
34. *AFGG*, 5(1), pp. 163–5.
35. Painlevé, *Comment*, p. 20.
36. Pierrefeu, *GQG*, pp. 243–53.
37. Gary Sheffield and John Bourne (eds), *Douglas Haig: War Diaries and Letters, 1914–1918* (2005), p. 261.
38. Lloyd George, *War Memoirs*, I, pp. 881–3.
39. French, *Strategy*, p. 54.
40. Robertson to Kiggell, 5 July 1916, LHCMA Kiggell MSS 3/3.
41. Grigg, *War Leader*, p. 52.
42. Stephen Kotkin, *Stalin*, I: *Paradoxes of Power, 1878–1928* (2015), p. 152.
43. Sheffield and Bourne (eds), *Haig*, pp. 259–60.
44. Ibid., p. 267.
45. Spears, *Prelude*, p. 49.
46. French, *Strategy*, p. 50.
47. Painlevé, *Comment*, p. 19.
48. *AFGG*, 5(1), Annexes 1, p. 775.
49. Lloyd George, *War Memoirs*, I, pp. 889–90.
50. *AFGG*, 5(1), Annexes 1, pp. 777–84.

51. Spears, *Prelude*, p. 46.
52. Sheffield and Bourne (eds), *Haig*, p. 268.
53. Miquel, *Chemin*, p. 115; French, *Strategy*, p. 55.
54. Haig to Kiggell, 18 Jan. 1917, LHCMA Kiggell MSS 1/47.
55. Sheffield and Bourne (eds), *Haig*, p. 269.
56. Greenhalgh, *Victory through Coalition*, p. 141; Spears to Armitage, 28 Jan. 1917, LHCMA Spears MSS 1/8.
57. Miquel, *Chemin*, pp. 117–18.
58. Lloyd George, *War Memoirs*, I, p. 892.
59. Grigg, *War Leader*, p. 43.
60. GQG, 21 Feb. 1917, SHAT 16.N.1711.
61. Ibid.
62. Doughty, *Pyrrhic Victory*, p. 240.
63. French, *Strategy*, p. 49.
64. *WK*, XII,, pp. 1–4.
65. Ibid., pp. 38–47.
66. Ibid., pp. 61–3.
67. Ibid., pp. 279–83.
68. Painlevé, *Comment*, pp. 27–8.
69. Spears, *Prelude*, chs. 12–14.
70. See French Embassy note, 7 Mar. 1917, LHCMA Spears MSS 2/1/14.
71. Doughty, *Pyrrhic Victory*, pp. 337–8.
72. Nivelle to Haig, 27 Feb., Balfour to Paul Cambon, 9 Mar. 1917, LHCMA Spears MSS, 2/1/4, 2/1/18.
73. Poincaré, *Au service*, IX, pp. 66–7.
74. Haig to Kiggell, 6 Mar. 1917, LHCMA Kiggell MSS 1/48.
75. Haig memorandum, 2 Mar.; Nivelle to Haig, 6 Mar., French Embassy note, 7 Mar. 1917 LHCMA Spears MSS 2/1/6, 12, 14.
76. Robertson to Haig, 6 Mar. 1917, ibid. 2/1/11.
77. Spears, *Prelude*, ch. 11.
78. Philpott, *Anglo-French Relations*, p. 134.
79. Doughty, *Pyrrhic Victory*, pp. 334–5.
80. Poincaré, *Au service*, IX, p. 59.
81. Painlevé, *Comment*, pp. 32–5; Spears, *Prelude*, p. 251.
82. *AFGG*, 5(1), Annexes, pp. 809–10.
83. Ribot, *Journal*, p. 48; Poincaré, *Au service*, IX, p. 9.
84. King, *Generals and Politicians*, pp. 151–2.
85. Miquel, *Chemin des Dames*, p. 61.
86. Painlevé, *Comment*, pp. 8, 41.
87. Spears, *Prelude*, p. 338; Painlevé, *Comment*, p. 42.
88. GQG 3rd Bureau memoranda, 16, 18 Mar. 1917, SHAT 16.N. 1711; Herbillon, *Micheler*, p. 159.
89. Painlevé, *Comment*, pp. 338–40.
90. *AFGG*, 5(1), Annexes 2, p. 193.
91. Ibid., pp. 259–60, 422–3.
92. Spears, *Prelude*, p. 492.
93. Doughty, *Pyrrhic Victory*, p. 347.

94. Herbillon, *Micheler*, pp. 157–8.
95. Ibid., pp. 161–2; Spears, *Prelude*, pp. 343–4.
96. Doughty, *Pyrrhic Victory*, p. 339.
97. Spears, *Prelude*, p. 348.
98. Ribot, *Journal*, p. 76.
99. Alexandre Ribot, *Lettres à un ami: souvenirs de ma vie politique* (1924), pp. 187–8.
100. Poincaré, *Au service*, IX, pp. 95–9.
101. Charles Mangin, *Comment finit la guerre* (1920), p. 122.
102. Ribot, *Lettres*, p. 186; Poincaré, *Au service*, IX, p. 101.
103. Edmond Herbillon, *Du général en chef au Gouvernement. Souvenirs d'un officier de liaison pendant la Guerre mondiale* (1930), II, p. 49.
104. Ibid., p. 50.
105. Ibid.; Poincaré, *Au service*, IX, p. 99.
106. Ribot, *Journal*, p. 75; *Lettres*, p. 187.
107. Painlevé, *Comment*, pp. 46–7.
108. Ibid., pp. 48–50; Spears, *Prelude*, pp. 350–4.
109. Spears, *Prelude*, pp. 356–7; Painlevé, *Comment*, pp. 50–1.
110. Herbillon, *Micheler*, pp. 164–5; Ribot, *Journal*, pp. 76–7.
111. Ribot, *Journal*, p. 52; Poincaré, *Au service*, IX, pp. 105–6.
112. Poincaré, *Au service*, IX; Herbillon, *Du général*, pp. 52–3.
113. Spears, *Prelude*, p. 364.
114. Herbillon, *Du général*, p. 4.
115. *AFGG*, 5(1), p. 562.
116. Spears, *Prelude*, p. 379.
117. Ibid., p. 361; Nicolas Offensatadt (ed.), *Le Chemin des Dames: de l'événement à la mémoire* (2004), p. 80.
118. Franchet to Brugère, AFGG, 209A, 27–8; *AFGG*, 5(1), Annexes 2, No. 1947.
119. Spears, *Prelude*, pp. 365–6; Brugère report, Annex C, SHAT 5.N. 255; *AFGG*, 5(1), p. 563.
120. Franchet to Brugère, AFGG, 209A, 27–8; *AFGG*, 5(1), Annexes 2, No. 1947.
121. Spears, *Prelude*, p. 367; King, *Generals and Politicians*, p. 157.
122. Thomas to Nivelle, 5 Apr. 1917, SHAT 10.N.12.
123. *AFGG*, 5(1), p. 364.
124. Brugère report, annexes, 1ère fascicule, p. 22, SHAT 5.N. 255.
125. Spiers, *Prelude*, pp. 368–9.
126. Castelnau statement, 23 Sept. 1917, SHAT 5.N.255.
127. Ibid.; Painlevé, *Comment*, p. 58.
128. Spiers, *Prelude*, p. 372.
129. Painlevé, *Comment*, p. 52.
130. Herbillon, *Micheler*, p. 170.
131. Poincarè, *Au service*, IX, p. 107.
132. *AFGG*, 5(1), p. 566.
133. Herbillon, *Micheler*, p. 170.
134. Herbillon, *Du Général*, pp. 55–6.
135. Ribot, *Journal*, p. 79.
136. Miquel, *Chemin des Dames*, p. 74; *WK*, XII, p. 307.
137. Spears, *Prelude*, p. 41.
138. GQG 3rd Bureau, 13, Mar. 1917, SHAT 16.N. 1711.

139. *AFGG*, 5(1), p. 569.
140. Spiers report, 17 Apr. 1917, LHCMA Spears MSS 1/8; *WK*, XII, p. 288.
141. *WK*, XII, pp. 294–5.
142. Ibid., pp. 282–3, 288; *AFGG*, 5(1), Annexes 2, pp. 826–8.
143. *AFGG*, 5(1), Annexes 2, p. 841.
144. Spears, *Prelude*, p. 483.
145. Ibid., pp. 458–9.
146. Ibid., p. 326.
147. AFGG 5(1), pp. 568–70; Spiers, *Prelude*, p. 494.
148. Spiers, *Prelude*, p. 454.
149. Harris, *Douglas Haig*, pp. 299–315.
150. Spears, *Prelude*, p. 451.
151. Offenstadt (ed.), *Chemin des Dames*, pp. 78–80.
152. Guy Pedroncini, 'La France et les négociations secrètes de paix en 1917', *Guerres mondiales et conflits contemporains* 42, No. 170 (1993), p. 132.
153. Spiers reports, 20, 30 Apr. 1917, LHCMA Spears MSS 1/8.
154. Pierrefeu, *GQG*, p. 288.
155. Poincaré, *Au service*, IX, pp. 113–15.
156. Ribot, *Journal*, p. 80.
157. Painlevé, *Comment*, pp. 207–11.
158. Guy Pedroncini, *Pétain: Général en chef 1917–1918* (1974), pp. 88ff.
159. Painlevé, *Comment*, p. 211.
160. André Loez and Nicolas Mariot, *Obéir/désobéir: les mutineries de 1917 en perspective* (2008); Pedroncini, *Les Mutineries de 1917*.
161. Pedroncini, *Les Mutineries de 1917*, pp. 62, 98, 308.
162. Benjamin Ziemann, 'Le Chemin des Dames dans l'historiographie militaire allemande', in Nicolas Offenstadt (ed.), *Le Chemin des Dames: de l'événement à la mémoire* (2004), p. 348.
163. EMA 2nd Bureau monthly bulletins, SHAT 6.N/147.
164. King, *Generals and Politicians*, pp. 187–8.
165. Doughty, *Pyrrhic Victory*, p. 354.
166. *WK*, XII, p. 76.

CHAPTER 6

1. Louise Heenan, *Russian Democracy's Fatal Blunder: The Summer Offensive of 1917* (1987), p. xiii.
2. Kotkin, Stalin, I, p. 180.
3. Heenan, *Fatal Blunder*, ch. 2.
4. Ibid.; Conference minutes of 7/20 Feb. 1917, CAB 28/2.
5. General Staff memorandum, 20 Mar. 1917, CAB 24/8/29.
6. M. Frenkin, *Russkaya armiya i revolutsiya 1917–18* (1978), pp. 304, 307.
7. Knox despatch, 20 Feb. 1917, CAB 24/1/90.
8. Browder and Kerensky (eds), *Provisional Government*, II, pp. 926–8.
9. Robert Feldman, 'The Russian General Staff and the June 1917 Offensive', *Soviet Studies*, 19, No. 4 (1968), p. 529; Heenan, *Fatal Blunder*, p. 39.
10. Heenan, *Fatal Blunder*, p. 44; Frenkin, *Russkaya armiya*, pp. 183–4; Feldman, 'General Staff', pp. 529–30.

11. Browder and Kerensky (eds), *Provisional Government*, II, p. 924; Heenan, *Fatal Blunder*, p. 42.
12. Heenan, *Fatal Blunder*, p. 44.
13. Erich Ludendorff, *Meine Kriegserinnerungen, 1914–1918* (1919), p. 327.
14. Paul von Hindenburg, *Aus Meinem Leben* (1920), pp. 247–8.
15. *WK*, XII, p. 484.
16. On the sealed train, Werner Hahlweg, *Lenins Rückekhr nach Rußland* (1957); Catherine Merridale, *Lenin on the Train* (2016). On fraternization, Mark Cornwall, *The Undermining of Austria-Hungary: The Battle for Hearts and Minds* (2000), ch. 3.
17. *WK*, XII, pp. 489–93.
18. Alfred Knox, *With the Russian Army, 1914–1917* (1921), II, p. 124.
19. Smith, *Red Petrograd*, pp. 54–68; Figes, *People's Tragedy*, pp. 367–71.
20. Browder and Kerensky (eds), *Provisional Government*, II, pp. 848, 851–2.
21. Neilson report, 31 Mar. 1917, WO 106/1129.
22. Heenan, *Fatal Blunder*, p. 49.
23. Knox despatch, 10 July 1917, CAB 24/21/54.
24. Frenkin, *Russkaya armiya*, pp. 194–5.
25. Graeme Gill, *Peasants and Government in the Russian Revolution* (1979), pp. 112–13.
26. Frenkin, *Russkaya armiya*, p. 191.
27. Buchanan telegram, 18 Mar. 1917, FO 371/2995.
28. Titus Komarnicki, *Rebirth of the Polish Republic: A Study in the Diplomatic History of Europe, 1914–1920* (1957), p. 156.
29. Buchanan telegram, 20 Mar. 1917, FO 371/2998; Browder and Kerensky (eds), *Provisional Government*, II, p. 1042; Heenan, *Fatal Blunder*, p. 35.
30. Browder and Kerensky (eds), *Provisional Government*, II, pp. 1044–5.
31. Buchanan telegram, 14 May 1917, FO 371/2998; Browder and Kerensky (eds), *Provisional Government*, II, p. 1057.
32. Browder and Kerensky (eds), *Provisional Government*, II, pp. 1045–6.
33. Ibid., pp. 1077–8, 1083.
34. Oliver Radkey, *The Agrarian Foes of Bolshevism: Promise and Default of the Russian Socialist Revolutionaries, February to October 1917* (1958), p. 156.
35. Sean McMeekin, 'Enter Lenin', in Tony Brenton (ed.), *Historically Inevitable? Turning Points of the Russian Revolution* (2016), ch. 5. See 'Conclusion' in this volume.
36. Browder and Kerensky (eds), *Provisional Government*, II, p. 1098.
37. Lindley letter, 20 Mar. 1917, FO 371/2996.
38. Rex Wade, 'Why October? The Search for Peace in 1917', *Soviet Studies* 20, No. 1 (1968), pp. 36ff.
39. Buchanan telegram, 17 May 1917, FO 371/2998.
40. Buchanan telegrams, 14, 16 May 1917, ibid.
41. Buchanan telegram, 19 May 1917, ibid.
42. Rex Wade, *The Russian Search for Peace, February–October 1917* (1969), p. 68.
43. Ian Thatcher, Memoirs of the Russian Provisional Government 1917', *Revolutionary Russia* 27, No. 1 (2014), p. 5.
44. See ch. 9 of this volume.
45. Steglich, *Friedenspolitik*, I, p. 59.
46. Ibid., p. 65; Scherer and Grünewald (eds), *L'Allemagne*, II, pp. 94–6.
47. Scherer and Grünewald (eds), *L'Allemagne*, I, pp. 132–4; Steglich, *Friedenspolitik*, I, pp. 67–8.
48. Steglich, *Friedenspolitik*, I, p. 53.

49. Scherer and Grünewald (eds), *L'Allemagne*, II, pp. 149–51.

50. Ibid., pp. 133–4, 194–5.

51. Steglich, *Friedenspolitik*, I, p. 70.

52. Ibid., pp. 95–9; Scherer and Grünewald (eds), *L'Allemagne*, II, pp. 204–6.

53. Steglich, *Friedenspolitik*, I, pp. 100–1.

54. *WK*, XII, pp. 498–9.

55. Scherer and Grünewald (eds), *L'Allemagne*, II, pp. 222–3.

56. Wade, *Russian Search*, p. 52.

57. Scherer and Grünewald (eds), *L'Allemagne*, II, pp. 158, 163, 166–7.

58. David Kirby, *War, Peace, and Revolution: International Socialism at the Crossroads, 1914–1918* (1986), p. 91.

59. Wade, *Russian Search*, p. 55.

60. Kirby, *War, Peace*, pp. 58–61.

61. Jay Winter, 'Arthur Henderson, the Russian Revolution, and the Reconstruction of the Labour Party', *The Historical Journal* 15, No. 4 (1972): p. 753.

62. Jürgen Stillig, *Die Russische Februarrevolution 1917 und die Sozialistische Friedenspolitik* (1977), pp. 280–2.

63. Kirby, *War, Peace*, p. 109; Paléologue, *La Russie*, III, pp. 308–37.

64. Kirby, *War, Peace*, p. 153.

65. Ribot, *Journal*, p. 138; Poincaré, *Au service*, IX, p. 149.

66. Bonnefous, *Histoire politique*, II, p. 265.

67. Wade, *Russian Search*, p. 62.

68. *FRUS LP*, II, p. 17.

69. Lloyd George, *War Memoirs*, II, ch. 58.

70. Browder and Kerensky (eds), *Provisional Government*, II, pp. 1109–10.

71. Ibid., pp. 1106–8.

72. See ch. 12 of this volume.

73. Browder and Kerensky (eds), *Provisional Government*, II, pp. 1120–1; Wade, *Russian Search*, pp. 85–8.

74. Wade, *Russian Search*, p. 88; Heenan, *Fatal Blunder*, p. 52.

75. Heenan, *Fatal Blunder*, p. 50; David Stone, *The Russian Army in the Great War: The Eastern Front, 1914–1917* (2015), p. 287.

76. Knox despatch, 18 May 1917, WO 106/1091.

77. Lyandres (ed.), *Fall of Tsarism*, p. 224.

78. Richard Abraham, *Alexander Kerensky: The First Love of the Revolution* (1987), chs. 5–6.

79. Buchanan telegram, 19 Mar. 1917, FO 371/2995; 8, 9 April 1917, FO 371/2996.

80. Heenan, *Fatal Blunder*, p. 52.

81. See Alexander Kerensky, *Russia and History's Turning Point* (1965), p. 296.

82. Browder and Kerensky (eds), *Provisional Government*, II, pp. 880–3.

83. Taylor, *Russian Army*, pp. 100–1.

84. Aleksei Brusilov, *A Soldier's Notebook, 1914–1918* (1971), p. 290; Blair despatch, 20 Apr. 1917, WO 106/1033.

85. Cornwall, *Undermining*, pp. 45, 48–9.

86. Frenkin, *Russkaya Armiya*, p. 347.

87. Blair to Buckley, 7 June 1917, WO 106/5128.

88. Barter despatch, 17 June 1917, CAB 24/16/90; Frenkin, *Russkaya Armiya*, p. 345.

89. Browder and Kerensky (eds), *Provisional Government*, II, pp. 932–8.

90. Heenan, *Fatal Blunder*, p. 55.
91. Abraham, *Kerensky*, p. 208; Wade, *Russian Search*, pp. 68–71.
92. Heenan, *Fatal Blunder*, pp. 55–6.
93. Alexander Kerensky, *The Catastrophe: Kerensky's Own Story of the Russian Revolution* (1977), ch. 9.
94. Heenan, *Fatal Blunder*, p. 52.
95. Knox despatch, 9 July 1917, CAB 24/19/88; *WK*, XIII, p. 152.
96. *WK*, XIII, p. 148.
97. Ibid., pp. 162–70.
98. Ibid., pp. 178–9.
99. Wade, *Russian Search*, pp. 94–5.
100. Alexander Rabinovitch, *The Bolsheviks come to Power: The Revolution of 1917 in Petrograd* (2004), chs. 1 and 2.
101. Anton Denikin, *La Décomposition de l'armée et du pouvoir (février-septembre 1917)* (1922), pp. 278ff.
102. Wildman, *End of the Russian Imperial Army*, II, ch. 7.
103. Pedroncini, *Pétain*, pp. 112–16; French, *Strategy*, pp. 102, 171.
104. Wade, *Russian Search*, pp. 108–12.
105. See chs. 10 and 11 of this volume.
106. See ch. 10 of this volume.

CHAPTER 7

1. Hankey, *Supreme Command*, II, pp. 703–4.
2. Andrew Wiest, 'The Planned Amphibious Assault', ch. 13 in Peter Liddle (ed.), *Passchendaele in Perspective: The Third Battle of Ypres* (1997), pp. 201–2.
3. Andrew Wiest, *Passchendaele and the Royal Navy* (1995), p. 36; Kiggell to Falls, 9 Mar. 1936, CAB 45/115.
4. Unsigned note, 4 Jan. 1934, CAB 43/24/10; James Edmonds, *History of the Great War Based on Official Documents: Military Operations: France and Belgium 1917* (1933–48) [henceforward *MOFB*], II, pp. 3–7, 396–400; Wiest, *Royal Navy*, p. 60.
5. Draft letter, 21 Nov. 1916, Lloyd George, *War Memoirs*, II, pp. 1251–2.
6. Robertson in WPC, 11 June 1917, CAB 27/6.
7. Admiralty memorandum, 16 Nov. 1916, CAB 24/2/51.
8. Meeting of 23 Nov. 1916, WO 158/22.
9. Robertson to Joffre, 1 Dec. 1916, ibid.
10. GQG memorandum, 7 Dec. 1916, SHAT 16.N.1683; Haig to Joffre, 18 Dec. 1916, WO 158/214.
11. Temple Patterson (ed.), *The Jellicoe Papers*, II, pp. 137, 183.
12. Wiest, 'Amphibious Assault', p. 205.
13. *MOFB*, II, p. 9.
14. Kiggell letter, 6 Jan. 1917, WO 158/38; *MOFB*, II, pp. 406–7.
15. Davidson to Macmullen, 8 Jan. 1917, WO 158/39.
16. Macmullen note, 15 Jan. 1917, WO 158/214.
17. Plumer plan, 30 Jan. 1917, WO 158/38; *MOFB*, II, pp. 15–16.
18. *MOFB*, II, pp. 18–19, 410–16.
19. Philpott, *Anglo-French Relations*, pp. 131ff.

20. Spears, *Prelude*, pp. 65–6.
21. Philpott, *Anglo-French Relations*, pp. 131–5.
22. Ibid., p. 133; John Turner, 'Lloyd George, the War Cabinet, and High Politics', in Peter Liddle (ed.) *Passchendaele in Perspective: The Third Battle of Ypres* (1997), p. 18.
23. Philpott, *Anglo-French Relations*, pp. 135–6.
24. Robertson memorandum, 17 Apr. 1917, CAB 24/10/77; Haig to Robertson 15 Apr., Robertson to Haig, 17 Apr. 1917, LHCMA Robertson MSS 7/7/19–20.
25. Robertson to Haig, 20, 28 Apr. 1917, ibid., 21, 23.
26. Turner, 'High Politics', p. 17–18.
27. David Woodward, *Lloyd George and the Generals* (1983), p. 160.
28. Grigg, *War Leader*, p. 159; Haig diary, 19 June 1917, LHCMA Haig MSS, I, 97.
29. Smuts to Robertson, 13 Apr. 1917, CAB 24/11/49.
30. Robertson to Haig, 28 Apr. 1917, LHCMA Robertson MSS 7/7/23; Robertson memorandum, 30 Apr. 1917, CAB 24/11/99.
31. Smuts memorandum, 29 Apr. 1917, CAB 24/11/97.
32. War Cabinet, 1 May 1917, CAB 23/13/3.
33. See ch. 10 of this volume.
34. Robertson statement, 5 May 1917, CAB 24/12/57.
35. Minutes of 4 May 1917, CAB 28/2.
36. Clive diary, 4 May 1917, CAB 45/201; *MOFB*, II, p. 23.
37. Haig to Doris, 5 May 1917, NLS Haig MSS 147.
38. *MOFB*, II, pp. 20–1.
39. Haig to Nivelle, 5 May 1917, WO 158/48.
40. *MOFB*, II, pp. 24–5.
41. Haig diary, 14 May 1917, LHCMA Haig MSS, I, 97.
42. Amiens conference minutes, 18 May 1917, WO 158/48.
43. Haig diary, 26 May 1917, LHCMA Haig MSS, I, 97.
44. Haig order, 5 June 1917, Haig MSS 215.
45. Jim Beach, *Haig's Intelligence: GHQ and the German Army, 1916–1918* (2013), pp. 239ff.
46. Haig diary, 2 June 1917, LHCMA Haig MSS, I, 97.
47. Harris, *Douglas Haig*, p. 341.
48. Guns on a reverse slope are positioned behind the crest of a ridge, so as to be invisible to the attackers.
49. *WK*, XII, pp. 261, 271, 429–67; *MOFB*, II, ch. 3.
50. Beach, *Haig's Intelligence*, pp. 242–4.
51. Haig memorandum, 12 June 1917, CAB 27/7.
52. *MOBF*, II, pp. 98–9.
53. Geoffrey Powell, *Plumer: The Soldier's General* (2004), p. 229; Harington to Edmonds, 3 Nov. 1934, CAB 45/114.
54. Haig diary, 9 June 1917, LHCMA Haig MSS, I, 97.
55. Haig diary, 25 May 1917, ibid.
56. Milner memorandum, 7 June 1917, CAB 23/16/1.
57. War Cabinet, 8 June 1917, ibid.
58. Harris, *Douglas Haig*, p. 349.
59. WPC Report, 10 Aug. 1917, CAB 27/6.
60. Bridges report, 14 June 1917, CAB 27/7.
61. French, *Lloyd George Coalition*, p. 102.

62. Ibid., pp. 84–90; Chris Wrigley, *David Lloyd George and the British Labour Movement: Peace and War* (1976), ch. 12; Lloyd George, *War Memoirs*, II, pp. 1149–52.

63. Derby to Haig, 27 May 1917, Haig MSS, NLS 347.

64. Robertson to Haig, 26 May 1917, LHCMA Robertson MSS 7/7/27.

65. WPC, 11 June 1917, CAB 27/6.

66. Hankey, *Supreme Command*, II, p. 674.

67. Woodward, *Lloyd George and the Generals*, p. 174.

68. Pedroncini, *Pétain* (1974), pp. 133–4; Lloyd George, *War Memoirs*, II, pp. 1266–7.

69. David French, 'Who Knew What and When? The French Army Mutinies and the British Decision to Launch the Third Battle of Ypres', in Lawrence Freedman et al. (eds), *Strategy and International Politics: Essays in Honour of Sir Michael Howard* (1992), pp. 133–53.

70. Sheffield and Bourne (eds), *Douglas Haig*, p. 297; Haig to Pétain, 6 June 1917, WO 158/48; Debeney/Haig conversation, 3 June 1917, LHCMA Benson MSS B/38.

71. French, 'Who Knew What', p. 146; John Charteris, *At GHQ* (1931), p. 275; War Cabinet, 6 June 1917, CAB 23/3/13.

72. War Cabinet, 8 June 1917, CAB 23/16/1.

73. WPC, 1 June 1917, CAB 27/6.

74. Robertson memorandum, 12 June 1917, CAB 27/7.

75. Haig to Robertson, 16 May 1917, ibid.

76. Haig diary, 2 June 1917, LHCMA Haig MSS, I, 97.

77. Haig to Robertson, 12 June 1917, CAB 27/7.

78. Haig to Robertson, 16, 17 June 1917, CAB 27/7.

79. WPC, 11, 12 June 1917, CAB 27/6.

80. Lloyd George, *War Memoirs*, II, pp. 1272, 1277.

81. Woodward, *Lloyd George and the Generals*, p. 167.

82. WPC, 19 June 1917, CAB 27/6.

83. See ch. 9 of this volume.

84. Lloyd George, *War Memoirs*, II, p. 1289.

85. WPC, 20 June 1917, CAB 27/6.

86. Marder, *Dreadnought*, IV, p. 204; Hankey, *Supreme Command*, II, pp. 701–2: Wiest, *Royal Navy*, pp. 109–15.

87. WPC, 20 June 1917, CAB 27/6.

88. Charteris, *At GHQ*, p. 233; Haig diary, 20 June 1917, LHCMA Haig MSS.

89. Geoffrey Till, 'Passchendaele: the Maritime Dimension', in Peter Liddle (ed.), *Passchendaele in Perspective: The Third Battle of Ypres* (1997), pp. 75–6; Marder, *Dreadnought*, IV, p. 206.

90. Haig to Doris, 7 May 1917, NLS Haig MSS 147; Haig to Robertson, 15 July 1917, LHCMA Robertson MSS 7/7/37.

91. WPC, 21 June 1917, CAB 27/6.

92. Haig diary, 21 June 1917, LHCMA I 97; William Robertson, *Soldiers and Statesmen 1914–1918* (1926), II, p. 242n.

93. Hankey, *Supreme Command*, II, p. 671.

94. Ibid., p. 683.

95. WPC, 22 June 1917, CAB 27/6.

96. WPC, 25 June 1917, ibid.

97. Haig diary, 25 June 1917, LHCMA Haig MSS I 97.

98. WPC, 3 July 1917, CAB 27/6; Robertson to Haig, 30 June 1917, LHCMA Robertson MSS 7/7/33.

99. WPC, 4 July 1917, CAB 27/6.
100. WPC, 6 July 1917, ibid.; Robertson to Haig, 6 July 1917, LHCMA Robertson MSS 7/7/34.
101. Hankey, *Supreme Command*, II, p. 683; WPC report, 10 August 1917, CAB 27/6.
102. Sheffield and Bourne (eds), *Douglas Haig*, p. 304.
103. Robertson to Haig, 18, 21 July 1917, LHCMA Robertson MSS 7/7/38, 40; *MOFB*, II, pp. 105–6.
104. Gough to Edmonds, 18 Mar. 1944, CAB45/140; Robin Prior and Trevor Wilson, *Passchendaele: The Untold Story* (1996), p. 50.
105. Wynne/Jacob interview, 17 June 1944, CAB 45/114.
106. *MOFB*, II pp. 107–8.
107. Kiggell to Gough, 13 May 1917, WO 158/249.
108. Hubert Gough, *The Fifth Army* (1931), p. 198; Corps commanders' conference and Malcolm memorandum, 16, 30 June 1917, WO 95/519; see *MOFB*, II, pp. 127–8, 432.
109. *MOFB*, II, pp. 436–42; Gough to Edmonds, 2 Feb. 1944, CAB 45/140.
110. Malcolm to Gough, 7 May 1944, CAB 45/140; Kiggell to Falls, 9 Mar. 1936, CAB 45/115.
111. Powell, *Plumer*, p. 204; *MOFB*, II, p. 129.
112. Haig order, 5 July 1917, WO 158/48.
113. Haig diary, 28, 29 June, LHCMA Haig MSS, I, 97.
114. Leon Wolff, *In Flanders Fields: Passchendaele 1917* (1979), p. 175.
115. Charteris, *At GHQ*, p. 237.
116. Ibid.
117. John Hussey, 'The Flanders Battleground and the Weather in 1917', in Peter Liddle (ed.), *Passchendaele in Perspective: The Third Battle of Ypres* (1997), ch. 10.
118. Charteris, *At GHQ*, p. 237; *MOBF*, II, p. 133.
119. *MOBF*, II, pp. 107–9; Prior and Wilson, *Passchendaele*, p. 78.
120. *MOFB*, II, pp. 130, 134, 138.
121. Ibid., pp. 125, 148.
122. *WK*, XII, pp. 265–6, 429–30.
123. Ibid., pp. 22, 24.
124. Ibid., pp. 23, 26; Heinz Hagenlücke, 'The German High Command', in Peter Liddle (ed.), *Passchendaele in Perspective: The Third Battle of Ypres* (1997), p. 47; Hew Strachan, 'The Morale of the German Army, 1917–18', in Hugh Cecil and Peter Liddle (eds), *Facing Armageddon: The First World War Experienced* (1996), pp. 387–8.
125. *WK*, XIII, pp. 28, 33–4.
126. Hagenlücke, 'German High Command', p. 50.
127. *WK*, XIII, p. 54; Jack Sheldon, *The German Army at Passchendaele* (2007), p. x; see *MOFB*, II, pp. 142–6.
128. Hagenlücke, 'German High Command', p. 51.
129. Franky Bostyn et al., *Passchendaele 1917: The Story of the Fallen and Tyne Cot Cemetery* (2007), p. 14.
130. Beach, *Haig's Intelligence*, p. 247.
131. *MOFB*, II, p. 137.
132. Prior and Wilson, *Passchendaele*, p. 95.
133. Haig to Doris, 31 July 1917, Haig MSS, NLS 147.
134. Hussey, 'The Flanders Battleground and the Weather in 1917', p. 149.

135. Charteris, *At GHQ*, p. 238.
136. Ibid., pp. 241–2.
137. Kiggell to Robertson, 8 Aug. 1917, LHCMA Robertson MSS 7/7/41.
138. Lyn MacDonald, *Passchendaele: The Story of the Third Battle of Ypres, 1917* (2013), Part 3.
139. Prior and Wilson, *Passchendaele*, p. 113.
140. Wiest, *Royal Navy*, pp. 154–64.
141. Haig to Robertson, 13 Aug. 1917, LHCMA Robertson MSS 7/7/44.
142. Sheffield and Bourne (eds), *Douglas Haig*, pp. 318, 320; Robertson to Edmonds (n.d. but 1944?), CAB 45/115.
143. Harington to Edmonds, 3 Nov. 1934, CAB 45/114.
144. Powell, *Plumer*, p. 211; Grigg, *War Leader*, p. 261; Prior and Wilson, *Passchendaele*, pp. 119–23.
145. Sheldon, *German Army*, pp. 226–33.
146. *MOFB*, II, p. xiii; Ludendorff, *Kriegserinnerungen*, p. 389.
147. Haig to Pétain, 28 Sept. 1917, WO 158/48.
148. Haig to Charteris, 5 Mar. 1927, CAB WO 256/21.
149. Harris, *Douglas Haig*, p. 374.
150. Charteris, *At GHQ*, p. 259.
151. Haig to Pétain, 17 Oct. 1917, WO 158/48.
152. Bostyn, et al., *Passchendaele 1917*, p. 199.
153. Robertson, *Soldiers and Statesmen*, II, pp. 262–3.
154. *WK*, XIII, p. 325.
155. Ibid., p. 96.
156. Bostyn et al., *Passchendaele 1917*, pp. 5, 199.
157. Paddy Griffith, 'The Tactical Problem: Infantry, Artillery, and the Salient', in Peter Liddle (ed.), *Passchendaele in Perspective: The Third Battle of Ypres* (1997), p. 69.
158. Guy Chapman, *A Passionate Prodigality: Fragments of Autobiography* (1967), p. 149.
159. *MOFB*, II, p. 209; S. P. Mackenzie, 'Morale and the Cause: The Campaign to Shape the Outlook of Soldiers in the British Expeditionary Force, 1914–1918', *Canadian Journal of History* 25, 1990), pp. 215–32.
160. Martin Middlebrook, *The Kaiser's Battle: 21 March 1918 the First Day of the German Spring Offensive* (1978), p. 101.
161. Prior and Wilson, *Passchendaele*, p. 181.
162. Hankey, *Supreme Command*, II, p. 693.
163. Prior and Wilson, *Passchendaele*, p. 144.
164. Ibid., p. 186.
165. WPC, 3 Oct. 1917, CAB 27/6.
166. Spears, *Prelude*, p. 342.
167. Hankey, *Supreme Command*, II, p. 697.
168. Such tactics were expensive: during the Messines bombardment between 26 May and 6 June, Second Army fired 3,561,530 shells at a cost of £17.5 million, *MOBF*, II, p. 49; the shells fired at La Malmaison cost twice as much as all French tank construction during the war, Michel Goya, *La Chair et l'acier: l'invention de la guerre moderne (1914–1918)* (2004), p. 388.
169. WPC, 24 Sept. 1917, CAB 27/6.

CHAPTER 8

1. Mario Morselli, *Caporetto 1917: Victory or Defeat?* (2001), p. viii.
2. Ibid., p. 4; Nicola Labanca, *Caporetto: storia di una disfatta* (1997), p. 7.
3. Morselli, *Caporetto*, p. 130.
4. Lloyd George, *War Memoirs*, I, pp. 849–57; James Edmonds, *History of the Great War. Military Operations: Italy, 1915–1919* (1949) [henceforth *MOI*], pp. 25–7.
5. Balfour to Rodd, 5 Apr. 1917, CAB 24/10/7.
6. *MOI*, pp. 28–31; Hugh Dalton, *With British Guns in Italy: A Tribute to Italian Achievement* (1919), p. 72.
7. WPC, 12 June 1917, CAB 27/6.
8. WPC, 20 June 1917, ibid.
9. Luigi Cadorna, *La Guerra alla Fronta Italiana: fino all'arresto sulla line della Piave e del Grappa (24 Maggio 1915–9 Novembre 1917)* (1921), II, p. 34.
10. Ibid., pp. 40–4.
11. Ibid., p. 78.
12. Balfour to Rodd, 26 Aug.; Rodd telegram, 6 Sept.; Balfour to Erskine, 21 Sept. 1917, FO 371/ 2947.
13. Gatti, *Caporetto*, p. 3.
14. Raffaelo Cadorna (ed.), *Luigi Cadorna, Lettere famigliari* (1967), p. 182.
15. Lloyd George, *War Memoirs*, I, p. 853.
16. *MOI*, p. 13; Mark Thompson, *The White War: Life and Death on the Italian Front, 1915–1919* (2008), p. 219.
17. Thompson, *White War*, p. 245; Hermann Wendt, *Die Italienische Kriegsschauplatz im Europäischen Konflikten* (1936), p. 337.
18. Gianna Rocca, *Cadorna* (1990), p. 3.
19. Thompson, *White War*, p. 248.
20. Rodd to Balfour, 4 Aug. 1917, FO 371/2947; Delmé-Radcliffe report, 31 May 1917, WO 106/762.
21. Imperiali telegram, 23 May 1917, FO 371/2946.
22. Cadorna, *La Guerra*, II, pp. 52–3.
23. *WK*, XII, p. 515; Edmond Glaise von Horstenau and Rudolf Kiszling (eds), *Österreich-Ungarns Letzter Krieg, 1914–1918* (1929–35) [henceforth *ÖULK*], VI, p. 183.
24. John Schindler, *Isonzo: The Worst Sacrifice of the Great War* (2001), p. 212.
25. John Gooch, *The Italian Army and the First World War* (2014), p. 211.
26. Delmé-Radcliffe reports, 31 May 1917, WO 106/761, WO 106/762
27. Ibid; and M.O. 2 report, 24 June 1917, WO 106/777.
28. Gatti, *Caporetto*, pp. 40, 61.
29. Cadorna, *Lettere famiglieri*, pp. 202–3.
30. *ÖULK*, VI, p. 133; Cadorna, *La Guerra*, II, p. 71.
31. Thompson, *White War*, pp. 258–60; Cadorna, *Lettere famiglieri*, p. 267.
32. Cadorna, *La Guerra*, II, p. 79.
33. Gatti, *Caporetto*, pp. 84–6.
34. Cadorna, *La Guerra*, II, pp. 86–7.
35. War Policy Committee, 3 July 1917, CAB 27/6.

36. Delmé-Radcliffe, 4 July 1917, CAB 24/18/95.
37. Cadorna, *La Guerra*, II, pp. 82–3; Gooch, *Italian Army*, p. 224.
38. Schindler, *Isonzo*, p. 223; Cadorna, *La Guerra*, II, p. 85.
39. Thompson, *White War*, p. 282.
40. Cadorna, *La Guerra*, II, p. 76; Gatti, *Caporetto*, p. 282.
41. Gooch, *Italian Army*, p. 193.
42. Gatti, *Caporetto*, pp. 108, 162–3.
43. Ibid., p. 178.
44. Ibid., p. 148.
45. Vittorio Orlando, *Memorie (1915–1919)* (1960), pp. 526–9.
46. Danilo Veneruso, *La Grande Guerra e l'unità nazionale: il ministero Boselli, giugno 1916–ottobre 1917* (1996), pp. 114, 300.
47. Cadorna, *Lettere famiglieri*, p. 200.
48. Rodd to Balfour, 12 June, 1 July 1917, FO 371/2945; Veneruso, *Grande Guerra*, pp. 336–8.
49. Cadorna to Orlando, 6 June 1917, Archivio centrale dello Stato, Rome, Orlando MSS 67/1560.
50. Orlando, *Memorie*, p. 58.
51. Cadorna, *Lettere famiglieri*, pp. 202–3.
52. Rodd to Balfour, 13 June 1917, FO 371/2945.
53. Mussolini article forwarded by Rodd to Balfour, 21 Aug. 1917, ibid.
54. Rodd to Balfour, 1 July 1917, ibid.
55. Orlando, *Memorie*, pp. 512–13.
56. MacDonagh to Campbell, 6 Nov. 1917, FO 371/2948.
57. Orlando, *Memorie*, pp. 59–63.
58. Ibid., p. 515.
59. Ibid., pp. 63–4.
60. Cesare de Simone, *L'Isonzo Mormorava: Fronti e Generali a Caporetto* (1995), p. 103.
61. Fayolle report, 26 Dec. 1917, WO 106/805.
62. MacGregor Knox, *To the Threshold of Power, 1922/33*, I: *Origins and Dynamics of the Fascist and National Socialist Dictatorships* (2007), pp. 200–10.
63. Thompson, *White War*, pp. 267–9.
64. Ibid., pp. 263–5.
65. Cadorna, *Lettere famiglieri*, p. 205.
66. Giovanna Procacci, *Soldati e Prigionieri Italiani nella Grande Guerra* (2000), pp. 98–101.
67. Report by Riparto disciplino, 25 Oct. 1917, Archivio centrale di stato, Rome, Nitti MSS 17/35/1.
68. Knox, *To the Threshold*, p. 209.
69. Luigi Capello, *Caporetto Perchè? La 2° Armata e gli avennimenti dell'ottobre 1917* (1967), pp. 41–2; Cadorna, *La Guerra*, II, p. 157.
70. Piero Melograni, *Storia politica della Grande Guerra, 1915–1918* (1969), pp. 392–3.
71. Gooch, *Italian Army*, p. 220.
72. Rodd to Balfour, 15 Sept. 1917, FO 371/2944; see Milan Prefect to Orlando, 15 Oct. 1917, Archivio central di stato, Rome, Orlando MSS B.50. F.1495. Sf. 4.
73. Vanda Wilcox, 'Generalship and Mass Surrender during the Italian Defeat at Caporetto', in Ian Beckett (ed.), *1917: Beyond the Western Front* (2009), p. 42.
74. Rodd to Balfour, 10 Mar. 1917, FO 371/2944.
75. Rodd to Balfour, 17 Aug., 29 July 1917, FO 371/2945.

76. Rodd to Balfour, 9 Sept. 1917, FO 371/2947; Knox, *To the Threshold*, p. 211.
77. Rodd to Balfour, 25, 26 Aug. 1917, FO 371/2947.
78. Gatti, *Caporetto*, p. 211; Capel, *Caporetto Perchè?*, p. 269; Rodd telegram, 6 Sept. 1917, FO 371/2947.
79. Gatti, *Caporetto*, p. 271; Cadorna, *La Guerra*, II, pp. 111–12.
80. Cadorna, *La Guerra*, II, p. 112.
81. Italian Embassy note, 27 Sept. 1917, FO 371/2947.
82. Balfour to Erskine, and Spiers report, 21 Sept. 1917, FO 371/2947; *MOI*, p. 42.
83. Promemoria, 2 Oct. 1917, FO 371/2947; *MOI*, pp. 40–2.
84. Roberto Bencivenga, *La Sorpresa strategica di Caporetto* (1932), pp. 31–2; Rocca, *Cadorna*, pp. 263, 265.
85. Capello, *Caporetto Perchè?*, pp. 33–7, 245–6, 171.
86. Gatti, *Caporetto*, pp. 12–13.
87. Luigi Capello, *Note di Guerra* (1920), pp. 137–46.
88. Capello, *Caporetto*, pp. 217, 222.
89. Rocca, *Cadorna*, p. 269.
90. Capello, *Caporetto*, pp. 253–5, 280; Cadorna, *La Guerra*, II, pp. 153–5.
91. Capello, *Caporetto Perchè?*, p. 280.
92. Rocca, *Cadorna*, p. 267.
93. Bencivenga, *Sorpresa strategica*, p. 47.
94. Arz memorandum, 18 Jan. 1918, WO 106/847.
95. Bencivenga, *Sorpresa strategica*, pp. 37–9, 40–8.
96. Delmé-Radcliffe letter, 12 Oct. 1917, WO 106/786.
97. Melograni, *Storia politica*, p. 396.
98. Cadorna, *La Guerra*, II, pp. 119–22.
99. Ibid., pp. 123–6; Bencivegna, *Sorpresa Strategica*, pp. 48–9.
100. Cadorna to Robertson, 24 Oct. 1917, WO 106/787.
101. Cadorna, *La Guerra*, II, p. 126; *MOI*, p. 45.
102. *MOI*, pp. 47–8.
103. Benivenga, *Sorpresa Strategica*, pp. 100–5, 111–20.
104. Labanca, *Caporetto*, pp. 23–33.
105. Rodd to Balfour, 9 Sept. 1917, FO 371/2947.
106. Cadorna to Robertson, 24 Oct. 1917, WO 106/787.
107. Cadorna, *Lettere famigliari*, pp. 226–7.
108. Capello, *Caporetto Perchè?*, pp. 259–62, 41–2.
109. Cadorna, *La Guerra*, II, pp. 157–62.
110. Wendt, *Italienische Kriegsschauplatz*, pp. 333–4; *WK*, XII, p. 515.
111. Wendt, *Italienische Kriegsschauplatz*, p. 341.
112. See ch. 9 of this volume.
113. *ÖULK*, VI, p. 493.
114. Wendt, *Italienische Kriegsschauplatz*, p. 321.
115. August von Cramon, *Unser Österreich-Ungarischer Bundesgenosse im Weltkriege.* (1920), p. 126; *ÖULK*, VI, p. 494.
116. Bencivenga, *Sorpresa strategica*, p. 27.
117. *ÖULK*, VI, p. 495.
118. Ibid.; Arthur Arz von Straußenberg, *Zur Geschichte des Großen Krieges 1914–1918* (1969), p. 171.

119. Arz, *Großen Krieges*, pp. 172–3.
120. Konrad Krafft von Delmensingen, *Der Durchbruch am Isonzo Teil 1. Die Schlacht von Tolmein und Flitsel (24 bis 27 Oktober 1917)* (1926), p. 14.
121. Hindenburg, *Aus meinem Leben*, pp. 259–61.
122. Krafft, *Durchbruch*, pp. 13–14.
123. *WK*, XIII, p. 219; *ÖULK*, VI, p. 497; Arz, *Großen Krieges*, p. 173.
124. Gary Shanafelt, *The Secret Enemy: Austria-Hungary and the German Alliance, 1914–1918* (1985), p. 150.
125. Cramon, *Bundesgenosse*, pp. 127–8.
126. Ludendorff, *Kriegserinnerungen*, p. 387; *WK*, XIII, p. 219.
127. Krafft, *Durchbruch*, p. 18.
128. Martin Müller, *Vernichtungsgedanke und Koalitionskriegführung: Das Deutsche Reich und Österreich-Ungarn in der Offensive 1917/1918. Eine Clausewitz-Studie* (2005), pp. 191–4.
129. Ludendorff, *Kriegserinnerungen*, p. 284.
130. Müller, *Vernichtungsgedanke*, p. 94.
131. Ludendorff, *Kriegserinnerungen*, p. 386; Hindenburg, *Aus Meinem Leben*, pp. 261–2.
132. *ÖULK*, VI, p. 495.
133. *WK*, XIII, p. 222.
134. Thompson, *White War*, p. 296; Krafft, *Durchbruch*, p. 18.
135. Alfred Krauß, *Das 'Wunder von Karfreit' im besonderen der Durchbruch bei Flitsch und die Bezwingung der Tagliamento* (1926), p. 16.
136. Ibid., p. 18; Thompson, *White War*, p. 297.
137. Krauß, *'Wunder von Karfreit'*, pp. 18–22; Krafft, Durchbruch, p. 180; Cyril Falls, *Caporetto 1917* (1965), p. 63.
138. Erwin Rommel, *Infantry Attacks* (1990), p. 172.
139. Morselli, *Caporetto*, pp. 13–14.
140. Melograni, *Storia politica*, p. 434.
141. Ibid., p. 405.
142. Gooch, *Italian Army*, p. 234; Thompson, *White War*, pp. 299, 301.
143. Gooch, *Italian Army*, p. 233.
144. Krafft, *Durchbruch*, p. 181.
145. Melograni, *Storia politica*, p. 408.
146. Rommel, *Infantry Attacks*, pp. 225–6.
147. Cadorna, *Lettere famigliari*, p. 223.
148. Wilcox, 'Generalship', p. 35.
149. Gooch, *Italian Army*, pp. 239–40.
150. Gatti, *Caporetto*, pp. 255–74; Bencivenga, *Sorpresa Strategica*, pp. 133ff.
151. Melograni, *Storia politica*, pp. 423, 427–8, 432.
152. Capello, *Caporetto Perchè?*, p. 189; see Simone, *L'Isonzo*, pp. 75–6.
153. Gooch, *Italian Army*, p. 244.
154. Cadorna to Orlando, 3 Nov. 1917, Archivio Centrale dello Stato, Rome, Orlando MSS 67/1560.
155. Wilcox, 'Generalship', p. 27.
156. Thompson, *White War*, p. 324.
157. *ÖULK*, VI, p. 713.
158. Hindenburg, *Aus Meinem Leben*, p. 263.
159. Cadorna, *La Guerra*, II, p. 177; see *WK*, XIII, p. 274.

160. Cramon, *Bundesgenosse*, p. 130.

161. Morselli, *Caporetto*, p. 29.

162. Falls, *Caporetto*, p. 75; Wendt, *Italienische Kriegsschauplatz*, p. 356.

163. Falls, Caporetto, p. 75; *WK*, XIII, p. 26; Morselli, *Caporetto*, p. 26.

164. *MOI*, p. 69.

165. Wendt, *Italienische Kriegsschauplatz*, pp. 353–5.

166. Rodd to Balfour, 13 Sept., Erskine to Balfour, 18 Oct. 1917, FO 371/2945.

167. Erskine to Balfour, 28 Oct. 1917, ibid.

168. Rodd to Balfour, 31 Oct. 1917, ibid; Gatti, *Caporetto*, pp. 290, 314.

169. *MOI*, p. 58.

170. Robertson memorandum, 14 Nov. 1917, WO 106/796.

171. *MOI*, pp. 88–102.

172. Lloyd George, *War Memoirs*, II, p. 1397.

173. Orlando, *Memorie*, p. 75.

174. Procacci, *Soldati e prigionieri*, p. 155.

175. Ibid.

176. Wilcox, 'Generalship', p. 45; Rommel, *Infantry Attacks*, p. 264.

177. Orlando to Diaz, 9 Nov. 1917, Archivio Centrale dello Stato, Rome, Orlando MSS 67/1562; Thompson, *White War*, p. 328.

178. Procacci, *Soldati e prigionieri*, p. 90.

179. Andrea Curami, 'L'industria bellica italiana dopo Caporetto', in Giampetro Berti and Piero del Negro (eds), *Al di qua e al di là del Piave: l'ultimo anno della Grande Guerra* (2001), pp. 549ff.

180. Orlando to Lloyd George, 16 Dec. 1917, Archivio Centrale dello Stato, Orlando MSS 54/1507.

181. Melograni, *Storia politica*, pp. 461–2.

CHAPTER 9

1. Balfour to Rodd, 26 May 1917, FO 371/2946.

2. Christopher Brennan, 'Reforming Austria-Hungary: Beyond His Control or Beyond His Capacity? The Domestic Policies of Emperor Karl I, November 1916–May 1917' (PhD dissertation, London School of Economics, 2012), ch. 1.

3. Tamar Griesser-Pečar, *Die Mission Sixtus: Österreichische Friedensversuch im Ersten Weltkrieg* (1988), p. 20.

4. Ibid., p. 62.

5. Ibid., p. 58; Steglich, *Die Friedenspolitik der Mittelmächte 1917/18*, I, p. 15.

6. Griesser-Pečar, *Mission Sixtus*, p. 64.

7. Ibid., p. 72.

8. Miklós Komjáthy (ed.), *Protokolle des Gemeinsamen Ministerrates der Österreichisch-Ungarischen Monarchie (1914–1918)* (1986), pp. 440ff.

9. Wolfdieter Bihl, 'La Mission de médiation des princes Sixte et Xavier de Bourbon-Parme en faveur de la paix', *Guerres mondiales et conflits contemporains* 43 (1993), p. 36.

10. Sixte de Bourbon, *L'Offre de paix séparée de l'Autriche (5 décembre 1916–12 octobre 1917)* (1920), pp. 58–60.

11. Ibid., pp. 64–6.

12. Stevenson, *French War Aims*, p. 58.

13. See ch. 5 of this volume.

14. Griesser-Pečar, *Mission Sixtus*, p. 133.

15. Bihl, 'La Mission', p. 46.

16. Griesser-Pečar, *Mission Sixtus*, p. 139.

17. André Scherer and Jacques Grünewald (eds), *L'Allemagne et les problèmes de la paix pendant la Première Guerre Mondiale* (1966–78), II, pp. 32–9.

18. Komjáthy (ed.), *Protokolle*, p. 483.

19. Griesser-Pečar *Mission Sixtus*, pp. 107–14.

20. Scherer and Grünewald (eds), *L'Allemagne*, II, p. 115.

21. Ibid., pp. 54, 57, 75.

22. Steglich, *Friedenspolitik*, p. 46.

23. Robert Hopwood, 'Czernin and the Fall of Bethmann Hollweg', *Canadian Journal of History* 2 (1967), pp. 51ff.

24. Griesser-Pečar, *Mission Sixtus*, pp. 163–7; Bethmann Hollweg, *Betrachtungen*, II, p. 202.

25. Scherer and Grünewald (eds), *L'Allemagne*, II, p. 106.

26. Matthias Erzberger, *Erlebnisse im Weltkrieg* (1920), p. 118.

27. Scherer and Grünewald (eds), *L'Allemagne*, II, pp. 105, 106.

28. Ibid., p. 126; Bethmann Hollweg, *Betrachtungen*, II, pp. 207–10.

29. Scherer and Grünewald (eds), *L'Allemagne*, II, pp. 149–51; see ch. 6 of this volume.

30. Scherer and Grünewald (eds), *L'Allemagne*, II, pp. 169–72, 122, 130–1.

31. Hopwood, 'Czernin', p. 52.

32. Scherer and Grünewald (eds), *L'Allemagne*, II, pp. 204–6, 212.

33. Griesser-Pečar, *Mission Sixtus*, p. 232.

34. Ibid., p. 177; Ribot, *Journal*, p. 62.

35. Ribot, *Journal*, p. 63; Lloyd George, *War Memoirs*, II, p. 1185.

36. Roberta Warman, 'The Erosion of Foreign Office Influence in the Making of Foreign Policy, 1916–1918', *The Historical Journal* 15 (1972), p. 142.

37. Delmé-Radcliffe memorandum, 23 Mar. 1917, FO 371/ 2946.

38. See ch. 10 of this volume.

39. Sidney Sonnino, *Diario 1916–22*, ed. Pietro Pastorelli (1922), III, pp. 120–1; Mario Toscano, *Gli Accordi di San Giovanni di Moriana—Storia diplomatica dell'intervento italiano*: II *1916–1917* (1936), pp. 270–9.

40. Griesser-Pečar, *Mission Sixtus*, p. 188.

41. Ibid., p. 194.

42. Ibid., pp. 201–3.

43. Lloyd George, *War Memoirs*, II, p. 1200; Lloyd George to Ribot, 14 May 1917, LGP, F/50/1/6.

44. Richard von Kühlmann, *Erinnerungen* (1948), p. 516.

45. Victor Rothwell, *British War Aims and Peace Diplomacy, 1914–1918* (1971), pp. 77–80.

46. Grieser-Pečar, *Mission Sixtus*, p. 77.

47. Ottokar Czernin, *In the World War* (1919), pp. 19, 23, 27.

48. Martin Vogt, 'L'Allemagne et les négociations de paix en 1917: réflexions sous form d'esquisse sur un sujet qui a failli tomber dans l'oubli', *Guerres mondiales et conflits contemporains* 43, No. 170 (1993), pp. 95, 97.

49. Steglich, *Friedenspolitik*, I, p. 54.

50. Wolfgang Steglich (ed.), *Die Friedensversuche der Kriegführenden Mächte im Sommer und Herbst 1917. Quellenkritische Untersuchungen, Akten, und Vernehmsprotokolle* (1984), pp. xxi, xxv–xxvii.

51. Michèle Bourlet, 'Le Deuxième Bureau et la diplomatie secrète: les négociations Armand–Revertera de 1917', *Guerres mondiales et conflits contemporains* 221 (2006), p. 34.
52. Stevenson, *French War Aims*, pp. 33–4.
53. Steglich, *Friedenspolitik*, I, p. 148.
54. Stevenson, *French War Aims*, pp. 74–5.
55. Records of conversation in *L'Opinion*, 10, 24 July 1920; see Steglich (ed.), *Friedensversuche*, pp. 10–27.
56. Scott (ed.), *Official Statements*, p. 114.
57. Erzberger, *Erlebnisse*, pp. 115–18, 224–7, 252.
58. Ibid., pp. 255–7.
59. Epstein, *Matthias Erzberger*, pp. 190–2.
60. Martin Kitchen, *The Silent Dictatorship: the Politics of the German High Command under Hindenburg and Ludendorff* (1976), p. 129.
61. *WK*, XIII, pp. 5–6, 8.
62. Georg Michaelis, *Für Staat und Volk: eine Lebensgeschichte* (1922), p. 323.
63. *WK*, XIII, pp. 10–11.
64. Epstein, *Erzberger*, pp. 195–206; Kitchen, *Dictatorship*, p. 134.
65. Michaelis, *Für Staat*, pp. 319–25.
66. Scott (ed.), *Official Statements*, pp. 115–16; Michaelis, *Für Staat*, p. 323.
67. Epstein, *Erzberger*, p. 206.
68. Steglich, *Friedenspolitik*, I, p. 128.
69. Scherer and Grünewald (eds), *L'Allemagne*, II, pp. 269–71; Epstein, *Erzberger*, pp. 202–4.
70. Michaelis, *Für Staat*, p. 331.
71. Lloyd George speech, Scott (ed.), *Official Statements*, pp. 117–18.
72. Heinz Hagenlücke, *Die Deutsche Vaterlandspartei: die nationale Rechte am Ende des Kaiserreiches* (1997).
73. Scott (ed.), *Official Statements*, pp. 129–31.
74. Francis Latour, *La Papeauté et les problèmes de la paix pendant la Première Guerre mondiale* (1996), pp. 18–35.
75. Ibid., p. 151; Steglich, *Friedenspolitik*, I, p. 15.
76. Erzberger, *Erlebnisse*, p. 272.
77. Latour, *La Papeauté*, pp. 152–8.
78. Gabriele Paolini, *Offensive di pace: la Santa Sede e la prima guerra mondiale* (2008), pp. 156–7.
79. Steglich, *Friedenspolitik*, I, p. 126.
80. Wolfgang Steglich (ed.), *Der Friedensappel Papst Benedikts XV vom 1. August 1917 und die Mittelmächte* (1970), pp. 640–1.
81. Latour, *La Papeauté*, p. 184.
82. Scherer and Grünewald (eds), *L'Allemagne*, II, pp. 194–5.
83. Ibid., pp. 250–3.
84. Ibid., pp. 285–7.
85. Paolini, *Offensive*, pp. 158–60.
86. Ibid., pp. 162–4.
87. Buchanan telegram, 17 Aug. 1917, FO 371/3083.
88. Sonnino, *Diario*, III, p. 182.
89. Paul Cambon note, 17 Aug. 1917, FO 371/3083.
90. Seymour (ed.), *House*, III, pp. 60, 130–6; Neu, *House*, p. 313.
91. Seymour (ed.), *House*, III, p. 157.

92. Dragan Živojinović, 'Robert Lansing's Comments on the Pontifical Peace Note of August 1, 1917, *Journal of American History* 56 (1969), pp. 570–1.

93. Scott (ed.), *Official Statements*, pp. 133–5.

94. Seymour (ed.), *House*, III, p. 172.

95. Stevenson, *French War Aims*, pp. 80, 82.

96. Balfour to Bertie, 1 Sept. 1917, BL Balfour MSS Add 49699.

97. War Cabinet, 21 August, 1917, CAB 23/3/69.

98. Balfour to de Salis, 21 Aug. 1917, FO 371/3083.

99. See Cecil to Balfour, 19 July 1917, LGP F/3/2/27; Bertie to Lloyd George, 24 Sept. 1917, LGP 51/4/40.

100. Rothwell, *British War Aims*, pp. 80, 104.

101. De Salis telegram, 24 Aug. 1917, FO 371/3083.

102. Ribot, *Journal*, p. 188.

103. Foreign Office to de Salis, 26 Aug. 1917, FO 371/3083.

104. Paolini, *Offensive*, p. 168; Latour, *La Papeauté*, p. 184.

105. Steglich (ed.), *Friedensversuche*, p. xxxii.

106. Scherer and Grünewald (eds), *L'Allemagne*, II, pp. 296–308, 339–43.

107. Ibid., pp. 346–9.

108. Michaelis, *Für Staat*, pp. 335, 331.

109. Kühlmann, *Erinnerungen*, p. 475.

110. Ibid., pp. 469–73; Steglich, *Friedenspolitik*, I, p. 138.

111. Steglich, *Friedenspolitik*, I, pp. 152, 154; Kühlmann, *Erinnerungen*, p. 476.

112. Steglich (ed.), *Friedensappell*, p. 19; Wilhelm Michaelis, 'Der Reichskanzler Michaelis und die päpstliche Friedensaktion 1917: neue Dokumente', *Geschichte in Wirtschaft und Unterricht* 12 (1961), p. 432.

113. Scott (ed.), *Official Statements*, pp. 139–41.

114. Erzberger, *Erlebnisse*, pp. 279–82.

115. Steglich (ed.), *Friedensappell*, pp. 1–6.

116. Scherer and Grünewald (eds), *L'Allemagne*, II, pp. 454–6.

117. Latour, *La Papeauté*, pp. 188–92.

118. Scherer and Grünewald (eds), *L'Allemagne*, II, pp. 378–84.

119. Ibid., pp. 387–90.

120. Michaelis, *Für Staat*, p. 344; Steglich (ed.), *Friedensversuche*, p. lxv.

121. Steglich, *Friedenspolitik*, I, pp. 166–7.

122. Scherer and Grünewald (eds), *L'Allemagne*, II, pp. 391–400.

123. Kühlmann, *Erinnerungen*, p. 480.

124. Lancelot Farrar, Jr, 'Opening to the West: German Efforts to Conclude a Separate Peace with England, July 1917–March 1918', *Canadian Journal of History* 10 (1975), p. 81.

125. Michaelis, 'Der Reichskanzler Michaelis', p. 435.

126. Michaelis, *Für Staat*, pp. 344–51; Kühlmann, *Erinnerungen*, p. 480–2.

127. Kühlmann, *Erinnerungen*, p. 482; Michaelis, *Für Staat*, pp. 352–3; Scherer and Grünewald (eds), *L'Allemagne*, II, p. 421.

128. Scherer and Grünewald (eds), *L'Allemagne*, II, pp. 429–35; Ludendorff, *Kriegserinnerungen*, pp. 414–17.

129. Kühlmann, *Erinnerungen*, p. 517; Michaelis, 'Der Reichskanzler Michaelis', p. 435.

130. Steglich, *Friedenspolitik*, I, p. xi.

131. Lloyd George, *War Memoirs*, II, pp. 1223–31.

132. Kühlmann, *Erinnerungen*, p. 485.

133. Steglich, *Friedenspolitik*, I, pp. 189–90.
134. Kühlmann, *Erinnerungen*, p. 486.
135. Steglich (ed.), *Friedensversuche*, p. xxiii.
136. Appendix to Balfour to Lloyd George, 24 Sept. 1917, FO 800/214.
137. Steglich, *Friedenspolitik*, I, p. 213.
138. Fischer, *Germany's Aims*, pp. 215–24.
139. Guy Pedroncini, *Les Négociations secrètes pendant la Grande Guerre* (1969), p. 68.
140. Oscar Freiherr von der Lancken-Wakenitz, *Meine dreissig Dienstjahre 1888–1918: Potsdam–Paris–Brüssel* (1931), pp. 253, 258.
141. Suarez, *Briand*, IV, pp. 240–2; Poincaré, *Au service*, IX, p. 167.
142. Steglich (ed.), *Friedensversuche*, p. xlviii.
143. Stelich, *Friedenspolitik*, I, p. 125.
144. Suarez, *Briand*, IV, pp. 257–60.
145. Raymond Recouly, *Les Négociations secrètes Briand–Lancken* (1933), p. 20.
146. Scherer and Grünewald (eds), *L'Allemagne*, II, pp. 346, 442.
147. Suarez, *Briand*, IV, p. 267.
148. Ibid., p. 243; Poincaré, *Au service*, IX, pp. 287ff.
149. Ribot, *Journal*, pp. 203–14.
150. Lancken, *Dienstjahre*, p. 251.
151. Steglich, *Friedenspolitik*, I, p. 213.
152. Ribot, *Journal*, p. 212.
153. Balfour memorandum, 20 Sept. 1917, BL Balfour MSS Add. 49699.
154. Grigg, *War Leader*, pp. 236–44.
155. David Woodward, 'David Lloyd George, a Negotiated Peace with Germany, and the Kühlmann Peace Kite of September 1917', *Canadian Journal of History* 6 (1971), p. 81.
156. War Cabinet, 24 Sept. 1917, CAB 23/16/2.
157. Balfour to Lloyd George, 24 Sept. 1917, FO 800/214.
158. Ribot, *Journal*, p. 216.
159. Lloyd George, *War Memoirs*, II, p. 1242; War Cabinet, 27 Sept. 1917, CAB 23/16/3; Pedroncini, *Négociations secrètes*, p. 136.
160. Lloyd George, *War Memoirs*, II, pp. 1242–3.
161. Woodward, 'David Lloyd George', pp. 87–8; Steglich (ed.), *Friedensversuche*, p. lxxxii.
162. Clive diary, 16 Sept. 1917, CAB 45/201/4.
163. French, *Strategy*, p. 155.
164. Steglich (ed.), *Friedensversuche*, p. lxxv; Rothwell, *British War Aims*, p. 106.
165. War Cabinet, 27 Sept. 1917, CAB 23/16/3.
166. Buchanan to Balfour, 8 Oct. 1917, FO 800/214.
167. Balfour circular telegram, 8 Oct. 1917, ibid.
168. Steglich (ed.), *Friedensversuche*, p. lxxx.
169. Steglich, *Friedenspolitik*, I, p. 215; Kühlmann (ed.), *Erinnerungen*, p. 494.
170. Scott (ed.), *Official Statements*, p. 161.
171. John Keiger, *Raymond Poincaré* (1997), pp. 233–4.

CHAPTER 10

1. Francisco Romero, *Spain, 1914–1918: Between War and Revolution* (1999); Hans Schmitt (ed.), *Neutral Europe between War and Revolution, 1917–23* (1988).
2. Michael Llewellyn Smith, *Ionian Vision: Greece in Asia Minor 1919–1922* (1973), pp. 9–11, 35–6.

3. David Dutton, *The Politics of Diplomacy: Britain and France in the Balkans in the First World War* (1998), chs. 4, 5.
4. Yannis Mourelos, 'British Policy towards King Constantine's Dethronement and Greece's Entry into the War', in *Greece and Great Britain during World War I*, ed. Institute for Balkan Studies (1985), p. 134.
5. Dutton, *Politics of Diplomacy*, ch. 6.
6. Alexander Mitrakos, *France in Greece during War I: A Study in the Politics of Power* (1982), p. 179.
7. Ibid., p. 161.
8. Gérard Fassy, *Le Commandement français en Orient (octobre 1915–novembre 1918)* (2003), p. 182.
9. Mourelos, 'British Policy', p. 133; 28 May 1917 conference, CAB 28/2/4.
10. Dutton, *Politics of Diplomacy*, ch. 5; see ch. 12 of this volume.
11. Cyril Falls, *History of the Great War Based on Official Documents. Military Operations: Macedonia* (1933–5) [henceforth *MOM*] I, p. 348.
12. George Leon, *Greece and the Great Powers 1914–1917* (1974), p. 474.
13. Mitrakos, *France in Greece*, p. 164.
14. Leon, *Greece*, p. 475; War Cabinet, 23 Apr. 1917, CAB 23/2/124.
15. David Dutton, 'The Deposition of King Constantine of Greece: An Episode in Anglo-French Diplomacy', *Canadian Journal of History* 12 (1978), pp. 336–8.
16. *MOM*, I, p. 349.
17. Cecil memorandum, n. d., CAB 28/2/4.
18. *MOM*, I, pp. 355–61; Dutton, 'Deposition', p. 344.
19. Smith, *Ionian Vision*, p. 58.
20. *MOM*, II, p. 341.
21. Andrew Dalby, *Eleutherios Venizelos: Greece* (2010), p. 71.
22. Andrew Boyle (ed.), *The Brazilian Green Book* (1918), p. 21.
23. Ibid., pp. 80–4; Olivier Compagnon, *L'Adieu à l'Europe: l'Amérique latine et la Grande Guerre (Argentine et Brésil, 1914–1939)* (2013), p. 329.
24. Joseph Smith and Francisco Vinhosa, *History of Brazil, 1500–2000: Politics, Economy, Society, Diplomacy* (2003), p. 119.
25. Frederick Luebke, *Germans in Brazil: A Comparative History of Cultural Conflict during World War I* (1987), pp. 10ff.
26. Smith and Vinhosa, *History of Brazil*, pp. 129–34.
27. George Philip (ed.), *British Documents on Foreign Affairs: Reports and Papers from the Confidential Print, Part II, Series D, Latin America, 1914–1939* (1989), I, pp. 13, 26–9.
28. Luebke, *Germans in Brazil*, pp. 84–99.
29. Ibid., pp. 105–8.
30. Joseph Smith, *Unequal Giants: Diplomatic Relations between the United States and Brazil, 1889–1930* (1991), p. 109.
31. Luebke, *Germans in Brazil*, p. 121; Boyle (ed.), *Green Book*, pp. 18, 19, 22.
32. Boyle (ed.), *Green Book*, pp. 24–5.
33. Luebke, *Germans in Brazil*, p. 125.
34. Boyle (ed.), *Green Book*, p. 27.
35. Luebke, *Germans in Brazil*, pp. 155, 129–35.
36. Peel to Balfour, 4 May 1917, FO 371/2901.
37. Peel to Balfour, 10 May 1917, ibid.; Luebke *Germans in Brazil*, p. 151.

38. Boyle (ed.), *Green Book*, pp. 39–46; Peel to Balfour, 10 May 1917, FO 371/2901.
39. Luebke, *Germans in Brazil*, p. 154.
40. Boyle (ed.), *Green Book*, pp. 74, 87–8; Luebke, *Germans in Brazil*, p. 159.
41. Minute, 28 July 1917, FO 371/2901.
42. War Office to Foreign Office, 19 July 1917, ibid.
43. Spring-Rice telegram, 7 August 1917, ibid.; Smith, *Unequal Giants*, pp. 114–17.
44. Pedro Cavalcanti, *A Presidência Wenceslau Braz (1914–1918)* (1983), ch. 9.
45. Compagnon, *L'Adieu*, p. 143.
46. Smith, *Unequal Giants*, pp. 103, 113.
47. Luebke, *Germans in Brazil*, p. 152.
48. Frank McCann, *Soldiers of the Pátria: A History of the Brazilian Army, 1889–1937* (2004), ch. 4.
49. Luebke, *Germans in Brazil*, pp. 198–9; McCann, *Soldiers of the Pátria*, p. 176.
50. McCann, *Soldiers of the Pátria*, p. 181.
51. Luebke, *Germans in Brazil*, pp. 172–81.
52. Smith, *Unequal Giants*, p. 118.
53. Doyle (ed.), *Green Book*, pp. 120–2.
54. Olivier Compagnon, 'Latin America', in Jay Winter (ed.), *The Cambridge History of the First World War* (2014), I, pp. 550–1.
55. Compagnon, *L'Adieu*, pp. 14, 322.
56. Thailand was known as Siam until 1939.
57. Stephen Greene, *Absolute Dreams: Thai Government under Rana VI, 1910–1925* (1994), pp. 102–5.
58. Dering to Balfour, 16 Feb. 1917, FO 371/3027.
59. J. H. Lyons docket note, c.12 Feb. 1917, ibid.
60. Greene, *Absolute Dreams*, pp. 106–9.
61. Dering to Balfour, 8, 21 June 1917, FO 371/3027.
62. Greene, *Absolute Dreams*, p. 107.
63. Russell Fifield, *Woodrow Wilson and the Far East: The Diplomacy of the Shantung Question* (1952), pp. 5–6.
64. Madeleine Chi, *China Diplomacy, 1914–1918* (1970), pp. 62–3.
65. Ibid., pp. 1–3; Stephen Craft, 'Angling for an Invitation to Paris: China's Entry into the First World War', *International History Review* 16, No. 1 (1994), p. 3; Xu Guqui, *China and the Great War: China's Pursuit of a New National Identity and Internationalization* (2005), p. 88.
66. Ian Nish, *Alliance in Decline: A Study in Anglo-Japanese Relations, 1908–1923* (1972), ch. 8; Frederick Dickinson, *War and National Reinvention: Japan in the Great War, 1914–1919* (1999), ch. 2; Chi, *China Diplomacy*, ch. 4.
67. Bruce Elleman, *Wilson and China: a Revised History of the Shandong Question* (2002), p. 4.
68. Craft, 'Angling', p. 4.
69. Ibid., p. 7; Chi, *China Diplomacy*, pp. 19–28.
70. Chi, *China Diplomacy*, pp. 33, 36.
71. Thomas La Fargue, *China and the World War* (1937), pp. 64–5.
72. Chi, *China Diplomacy*, p. 38.
73. Ibid., pp. 55–9.
74. Craft, 'Angling', pp. 5–6, 11; Xu, *China and the Great War*, pp. 96, 98–9.
75. Xu, *China and the Great War*, pp. 106–12; Ian Nish, 'Dr Morrison and China's Entry into the World War, 1915–1917', in Ragnhild Hatton and Matthew Anderson (eds), *Studies in Diplomatic History: Essays in Memory of David Bye Horn* (1970), ch. 17, esp. pp. 323–8.

76. Chi, *China Diplomacy*, pp. 72–4.

77. Xu, *China and the Great War*, ch. 4.

78. Ian Nish, *Japanese Foreign Policy, 1869–1942: Kasumigaseki to Miyakezaku* (1977), pp. 111–12.

79. Nish, *Alliance in Decline*, pp. 197–9.

80. Greene to Balfour, 7, 28 Jan. 1917, FO 405/222; Chi, *China Diplomacy*, pp. 115–16.

81. Maclay to Jordan, 1 Oct. 1917, FO 350/16.

82. Frank Iklé, 'Japanese-German Peace Negotiations during World War I', *American Historical Review* 71 (1965), pp. 62–76; General Staff note, 18 Mar. 1917, WO 106/36.

83. War Cabinet, 29 Jan. 1917, CAB 23/1/47; 1 Feb. 1917, CAB 23/1/51; 12 Feb. 1917, CAB 23/1/63.

84. Chi, *China Diplomacy*, pp. 99–101.

85. Greene to Foreign Office, 18 Feb. 1917, WO 106/35.

86. Thomas La Fargue, 'The Entrance of China into the World War', *Pacific Historical Review* 5 (1936), p. 227.

87. Chi, *China Diplomacy*, pp. 110–19.

88. J. H. Lyons minute, 6 Feb. 1917, FO 371/2190.

89. Hardinge to Robertson, 13 Mar. 1917, WO 106/36.

90. Chi, *China Diplomacy*, p. 120.

91. Foreign Office to Jordan, 19 Feb. and to Alston, 23 Feb. 1917, WO 106/35.

92. Xu, *China and the Great War*, p. 162.

93. Chi, *China Diplomacy*, p. 12.

94. Ibid., p. 130; Xu, *China and the Great War*, pp. 171–7; Alston to Foreign Office, 15 Mar. and 2 Apr. 1917, WO 106/35.

95. *FRUS 1917*, pp. 48–9, 57; Chi, *China Diplomacy*, pp. 124–7.

96. Alston to Balfour, 6 Aug. 1917, FO 405/222.

97. Xu, *China and the Great War*, p. 213.

98. Ibid., pp. 51–2.

99. Robertson letter, 17 May 1917, WO 106/35.

100. Xu, *China and the Great War*, ch. 6; *FRUS 1917*, pp. 63ff.

101. Chi, *China Diplomacy*, p. 128; Declaration of war, 14 Aug. 1917, WO 106/35.

102. Annual Report, 1 Mar. 1920, FO 405/229.

103. La Fargue, *China*, p. 110; La Fargue, 'Entrance of China', pp. 222–3.

104. *Foreign Relations of the United States 1917* (*FRUS*), p. 89; Nish, *Alliance in Decline*, p. 224.

105. Foreign Office to Greene, 18 May 1917, WO 106/35.

106. Xu, *China and the Great War*, pp. 192–6.

107. Ibid., pp. 234–5, 185–6; MI2C report, 24 Feb. 1917, WO 106/35.

108. Xu, *China and the Great War*, pp. 187, 190–1; Folder, 'Chinese Combatant Troops for France', WO 106/35.

109. Xu, *China and the Great War*, p. 188.

110. Chi, *China Diplomacy*, p. 86.

111. Iklé, 'Japanese-German Peace Negotiations', p. 76; Burton Beers, *Vain Endeavour: Robert Lansing's Attempts to End the American-Japanese Rivalry* (1962), p. 103.

112. Burton Beers, *Vain Endeavour*, p. 11.

113. Roy Curry, *Woodrow Wilson and Far Eastern Policy, 1913–1921* (1968), p. 161.

114. Kikujiro Ishii, *Diplomatic Commentaries* (1936), pp. 124–9.

115. Chi, *China Diplomacy*, pp. 110–13; Jordan to Balfour, 13 Nov. 1917, FO 371/3176.

116. Lansing, *War Memoirs*, p. 303.
117. Elleman, *Wilson and China*, p. 5.
118. Erez Manela, *The Wilsonian Moment: Self-Determination and the International Origins of Anticolonial Nationalism* (2007), ch. 9.

CHAPTER 11

1. Bishwa Pandey (ed.), *The Indian Nationalist Movement, 1885–1947: Select Documents* (1979), p. 105.
2. Algernon Rumbold, *Watershed in India, 1914–1922* (1979), p. 322.
3. India Office memorandum, 11 Mar. 1917, AC 21/2/16.
4. Keith Jeffery, *The British Army and the Crisis of Empire, 1918–1922* (1984), pp. 2–3.
5. Brian Tomlinson, *The Political Economy of the Raj, 1919–1947: The Economics of Decolonization in India* (1979), pp. 28, 2–4.
6. Ian Copland, *India, 1885–1947: The Unmaking of an Empire* (2001), p. 93.
7. Rumbold, *Watershed*, p. 9.
8. Peter Robb, 'The British Cabinet and Indian Reform, 1917–1919', *The Journal of Imperial and Commonwealth History* 4 (1976), p. 331; Rumbold, *Watershed* p. 7; Copland, *India, 1885–1947*, p. 19.
9. Francis Hutchins, *The Illusion of Permanence: British Imperialism in India* (1967), pp. xi–xii.
10. Rumbold, *Watershed*, pp. 31, 21–3.
11. Pandey (ed.), *Nationalist Movement*, p. 37.
12. GOI memorandum, 6 Oct. 1916, AC 21/1/26.
13. Copland, *India, 1885–1947*, p. 3.
14. Rumbold, *Watershed*, pp. 31–3, 40–3.
15. David French, 'The Dardanelles, Mecca, and Kut: Prestige as a Factor in British Eastern Strategy, 1914–1916', *War and Society* 5, No. 1 (1987), pp. 48–51.
16. GOI memorandum, 6 Oct. 1916, AC 21/1/26.
17. David Omissi, *The Sepoy and the Raj: the Indian Army, 1860–1940* (1994), pp. 38–9.
18. Krishan Saini, 'The Economic Aspects of India's Participation in the First World War' in DeWitt Ellinwood and S. Pradhan (eds), *India and World War I* (1978), p. 149.
19. India Office memorandum, 5 Mar. 1917, AC 21/1/66; Copland, *India, 1885–1947*, p. 21.
20. Meston in Imperial War Cabinet, 3 Apr. 1917, AC 21/1/69.
21. Ellinwood and Pradhan (eds), *India and World War I*, p. 29.
22. Stanley Wolpert, *Tilak and Gokhale: Revolution and Reform in the Making of Modern India* (1962), pp. 264–6.
23. India Office memorandum, 11 Mar. 1917, AC 21/2/16; Rumbold, *Watershed*, pp. 33–4.
24. Rumbold, *Watershed*, p. 35; Wolpert, *Tilak and Gokhale*, pp. 271–4.
25. Hugh Owen, 'Negotiating the Lucknow Pact', *Journal of Asian Studies* 31, No. 3 (1972), p. 565.
26. Wolpert, *Tilak and Gokhale*, pp. 265, 275.
27. Montagu to Chelmsford, 3 Aug. 1917, BL Chelmsford MSS Eur. E. 264/3.
28. Pentland to Chamberlain, 7 July 1916, AC 63/2/52; Rumbold, *Watershed*, pp. 46–7.
29. Owen, 'Negotiating', p. 565.
30. Judith Brown, *Gandhi's Rise to Power: Indian Politics, 1915–1922* (1974), p. 30.
31. Ibid., p. 125.
32. Hardinge memorandum, Oct. 1915, AC 22/2.
33. Chamberlain to Hardinge, 21 Jan. 1916, AC 21/1/14.

34. Chelmsford to Chamberlain, 11 Jan. 1917, BL Chelmsford MSS Eur. E. 264/3.
35. Peter Robb, *The Government of India and Reform, Policies towards Politics and the Constitution, 1916–1921* (1976), pp. 14–15, 52.
36. Chelmsford to George V, 23 Oct. 1916, BL Chelmsford MSS Eur. E. 264/1; Chelmsford to Chamberlain, 23 Sept. 1916, BL Chelmsford MSS Eur. E. 264/2.
37. Chelmsford to Meston, 20 July 1916, BL Meston MSS Eur. F. 136/1.
38. Robb, *Government of India*, p. 53.
39. Chelmsford to Chamberlain, 23 Sept. 1916, BL Chelmsford MSS Eur. E. 264/2; Chelmsford circular, 20 July 1916, BL Chelmsford MSS Eur. E. 264/51.
40. Chelmsford to Chamberlain, 24 Nov. 1916, ibid.
41. Robb, *Government of India*, pp. 58–61; Chelmsford to Chamberlain, 24 Nov. 1916, BL Chelmsford MSS Eur. E. 264/2.
42. Chelmsford to Chamberlain, 7 July 1917, BL Chelmsford MSS Eur. E. 264/3.
43. Meston to Chelmsford, 17 Aug. 1916, BL Meston MSS Eur. F. 136/1.
44. Robb, *Government of India*, pp. 57, 63.
45. Chelmsford to Meston, 14 Oct. 1916, BL Meston MSS Eur. F. 136/1.
46. Chamberlain to Chelmsford, 2 Feb. 1917, BL Chelmsford MSS Eur. E. 264/3.
47. Meston to Chelmsford, 5 Apr. 1917, BL Meston MSS Eur. F. 136/1.
48. Chelmsford telegram, 21 Oct. 1916, Chamberlain to Chelmsford, 29 Nov. 1916, AC 21/1/30, 38.
49. Memorandum for Chelmsford, 6 Jan. 1917, AC 21/1/43.
50. Memorandum for Chelmsford, 7 Jan. 1917, Chamberlain memorandum, 25 Jan. 1917, AC 21/1/44, 59.
51. Chelmsford telegram, 11 Mar. 1917, AC 21/2/14; Chamberlain to Chelmsford, 2, 10, 15 Mar. 1917, BL Chelmsford MSS Eur. E. 264/3; Tomlinson, *Political Economy*, p. 62.
52. Hardinge memorandum, n.d., Hardinge to Chamberlain, 17 Nov. 1915, AC 21/3/2, 3.
53. Chamberlain to Chelmsford, 14 Feb., 29 Mar. 1917, BL Chelmsford MSS Eur. E. 264/3.
54. Monro to Chelmsford, 4 Apr. 1917, BL Chelmsford MSS, Eur. E. 264/3.
55. Chamberlain to Chelmsford, 29 May 1917, ibid.
56. Army Department despatch, 3 Aug. 1917, AC 21/3/6.
57. India Office to War Office, 1 June; War Office to India Office, 5 July; Chamberlain memorandum, 10 July 1917, AC 21/3/4.
58. War Cabinet, 2 Aug. 1917, CAB 23/3/51.
59. Robert Holland, 'The British Empire and the Great War, 1914–1918', in Judith Brown and Roger Louis (eds), *The Oxford History of the British Empire* (2001), IV, p. 125.
60. Meston to Chelmsford, 20 Apr. 1917, BL Meston MSS Eur. F. 136/1.
61. Chamberlain to Chelmsford, 27 Apr., 15 May 1917, BL Chelmsford MSS Eur. E. 264/3.
62. Chamberlain to Chelmsford, 29 Mar. 1917, ibid.; Rumbold, *Watershed*, p. 65.
63. Robb, *Government of India,* pp. 64–5; Chamberlain to Chelmsford, 10 Jan., 2 Feb. 1917, BL Chelmsford MSS Eur. E. 264/3.
64. Chelmsford to Chamberlain, 1 Mar. 1917, BL Chelmsford MSS Eur. E. 264/3.
65. Rumbold, *Watershed*, p. 69.
66. Chamberlain to Chelmsford, 29 Mar. 1917, BL Chelmsford MSS Eur. E. 264/3; Meston to Chelmsford, 5 Apr. 1917, BL Meston MSS Eur. F. 136/1.
67. Chelmsford to Chamberlain, 7, 13, 19, 26 May 1917, BL Chelmsford MSS Eur. E. 264/3.
68. Chamberlain to Chelmsford, 2, 15, 29 May and 27 June 1917, Chelmsford to Chamberlain, 7 June 1917, ibid.

69. Meston to Chelmsford, 6 June 1917, BL Meston MSS Eur. F. 136/1.
70. Chelmsford to Chamberlain, 22 June 1917, BL Chelmsford MSS Eur. E. 264/3; Manela, *Wilsonian Moment*, p. 92.
71. Meston to Chelmsford, 8 May 1916, 11 Jan., 20 June, 25 July 1917, BL Meston MSS Eur. F. 136/1.
72. Robertson to Chelmsford, 15 July 1917, BL Chelmsford MSS Eur. E. 264/3; Willingdon to Chamberlain, 15 June 1917, AC 63/3/112; Robb, *Government of India*, p. 319.
73. Rumbold, *Watershed*, pp. 74–8; Peter Robb, 'The Government of India and Annie Besant', *Modern Asian Studies* 10, No. 1 (1976), pp. 110–16.
74. Rumbold, *Watershed*, p. 77; Chelmsford to Chamberlain, 7 July 1917, BL Chelmsford MSS Eur. E. 264/3.
75. Chamberlain to Cabinet, 16 June 1917, AC 21/4/20.
76. Curzon memorandum, 27 June 1917, CAB 24/17/99.
77. War Cabinet, 29 June 1917, CAB 23/3/20.
78. War Cabinet, 5 July 1917, CAB/3/24.
79. Chelmsford to Lloyd George, 16 July 1917, BL Chelmsford MSS Eur. E. 264/51.
80. David Waley, *Edwin Montagu: A Memoir and an Account of His Visits to India* (1964), pp. 127, 128, 130–1.
81. Chelmsford to Montagu, 2 Aug. 1917, BL Chelmsford MSS Eur. E. 264/51; Chelmsford to Montagu, 8 Aug.; Montagu to Chelmsford, 3 Aug. 1917, BL Chelmsford MSS Eur. E. 264/3.
82. Robb, 'British Cabinet', p. 320; Waley, *Montagu*, p. 134.
83. Montagu memorandum, 30 July 1917, CAB 24/22/15.
84. Rumbold, *Watershed*, p. 71.
85. Montagu memorandum, 30 July 1917, CAB 24/22/15; War Cabinet, 14 Aug. 1917, CAB 23/3/62.
86. Balfour memorandum, 7 Aug. 1917, CAB 24/22/96.
87. Curzon memorandum, 2 July 1917, CAB 24/18/52.
88. War Cabinet, 14 August 1917, CAB 23/3/62.
89. Chelmsford to Montagu, 15 Aug. 1917, BL Chelmsford MSS Eur. E. 264/151.
90. Montagu to Chelmsford, 21 Aug. 1917, BL Chelmsford MSS Eur. E. 264/3.
91. Waley, *Montagu*, p. 135.
92. War Cabinet, 14 August 1917, CAB 23/3/62.
93. Waley, *Montagu*, p. 135; Richard Danzig, 'The Announcement of August 20th, 1917', *The Journal of Asian Studies* 28, No. 1 (1968), p. 30.
94. Danzig, 'The Announcement of August 20th, 1917', p. 28.
95. Islington speech, 8 Aug. 1917, BL Chelmsford MSS Eur. E. 264/51.
96. Robb, 'British Cabinet', p. 324.
97. Rumbold, *Watershed*, p. 94.
98. Chelmsford to Pentland, 24 Aug. 1917, BL Chelmsford MSS Eur. E. 264/51.
99. Chelmsford to Montagu, 29 Aug. 1917, ibid.
100. Brown, *Gandhi's Rise*, p. 132.
101. Robb, 'Annie Besant', pp. 120–4.
102. Rumbold, *Watershed*, pp. 103–4.
103. Brown, *Gandhi's Rise*, p. 132.
104. Montagu to Chelmsford, 4 Oct. 1917, BL Chelmsford MSS Eur. E. 264/3.
105. Montagu to Chelmsford, 21 Sept. 1917, ibid.
106. BL Chelmsford MSS Eur. E. 264/42.

107. Rumbold, *Watershed*, pp. 108–14.
108. Chelmsford to George V, 27 Feb. 1918, BL Chelmsford MSS, Eur. E. 264/1.
109. Rumbold, *Watershed*, pp. 120–1; Brown, *Gandhi's Rise*, p. 134.
110. Robb, *Government of India*, pp. 329–30.
111. Chamberlain to Lethbridge, 25 June 1918, AC 21/5/17; Chamberlain to Butler, 17 Dec. 1918, AC 321/5/3.
112. Chamberlain to Chelmsford, 20 June 1918, BL Chelmsford MSS Eur. E. 264/15.
113. Rumbold, *Watershed*, pp. 29–30.
114. War Cabinet, 23 June 1918, CAB 23/6.
115. Jeffery, *British Army*, p. 4.
116. Omissi, *Sepoy and the Raj*, p. 124.
117. Tomlinson, *Political Economy*, p. 109.
118. Brown, *Gandhi's Rise*, p. 125.
119. Chelmsford to Chamberlain, 13 Apr. 1917, BL Chelmsford MSS Eur. E. 264/3; Islington to Montagu, 29 Mar. 1918, BL Chelmsford MSS Eur. E. 264/15; Rumbold, *Watershed*, p. 128.
120. Sonya Rose, 'The Politics of Service and Sacrifice in WWI Ireland and India', *Twentieth Century British History* 25, No. 3 (2014): p. 380.
121. Brown, *Gandhi's Rise*, pp. 146–50, 123.
122. Brian Tomlinson, 'India and the British Empire, 1880–1935', *Indian Economic and Social History Review* 12 (1975), pp. 354–8.
123. Montagu–Chelmsford Report, 22 Apr. 1918, BL Chelmsford MSS Eur. E.264/42; Copland, *India, 1885–1947*, pp. 59–61.
124. Robb, *Government of India*, p. 78.

CHAPTER 12

1. Leonard Stein, *The Balfour Declaration* (1961), p. ii.
2. David Lloyd George, *The Truth about the Peace Treaties* (1938), II, p. 1194.
3. Justin McCarthy, *The Population of Palestine: Population History and Statistics of the Late Ottoman Period and the Mandate* (1990), pp. 5–6.
4. Gideon Bigar, *The Boundaries of Modern Palestine, 1940–1947* (2004), p. 13.
5. McCarthy, *Palestine*, pp. 10, 17–24; Jonathan Schneer, *The Balfour Declaration: The Origins of the Arab-Israeli Conflict* (2011), p. 11; Rashid Khalidi, *Palestinian Identity: The Construction of Modern National Consciousness* (1997), p. 96.
6. Khalidi, *Palestinian Identity*, p. 122.
7. Michael Cohen, *The Origins and Evolution of the Arab-Israeli Conflict* (1987), pp. 1–9.
8. Stein, *Balfour Declaration*, p. 3.
9. David Vital, *Zionism: The Crucial Phase* (1987), ch. 2.
10. Abigail Green, 'The British Empire and the Jews: An Imperialism of Human Rights?', *Past & Present* 199, No. 1 (2008), pp. 177, 194; Eitan Bar-Yosef, *The Holy Land in English Culture, 1799–1917: Palestine and the Question of Orientalism* (2005), ch. 2.
11. Geoffrey Alderman, *Modern British Jewry* (1992), pp. 119–20, 221–5; Schneer, *Balfour Declaration*, pp. 110–11.
12. Schneer, *Balfour Declaration*, pp. 107–9.
13. Cohen, *Origins*, pp. 11–13.
14. Ibid., pp, 139–40; Elie Kedourie, *In the Anglo-Arab Labyrinth: The MacMahon–Husayn Correspondence and its Interpretations, 1914–1939* (1976), p. 97.

15. Kedourie, *In the Anglo-Arab Labyrinth*, p. 120.
16. Cohen, *Origins*, pp. 18–24.
17. James Barr, *A Line in the Sand: Britain, France, and the Struggle for the Mastery of the Middle East* (2012), pp. 8–11.
18. Ibid., pp. 30–1.
19. Samuel note, 9 Nov. 1914, MECA Samuel MSS Box 1.
20. Samuel memorandum, March 1915, ibid.
21. Samuel, 2 Feb. 1915, ibid.
22. De Bunsen Committee report, 30 June 1915, CAB 27/1.
23. Vital, *Crucial Phase*, p. 129.
24. Isiah Friedman, *Germany, Turkey, and Zionism, 1897–1918* (1998), p. xi.
25. Ibid., pp. 213–22, 265, 270.
26. Alderman, *British Jewry*, p. 229.
27. Schneer, *Balfour Declaration*, p. 155.
28. Ibid., p. 152; James Renton, *The Zionist Masquerade: The Birth of the Anglo-Zionist Alliance, 1914–1918* (2007), ch. 1.
29. Schneer, *Balfour Declaration*, p. 168.
30. Renton, *Zionist Masquerade*, pp. 40–51; Trumpeldor to Sykes, 5 Feb. 1917, MECA Sykes MSS Box 1.
31. Isaiah Friedman, *The Question of Palestine, 1914–1918: British–Jewish–Arab Relations* (1973), pp. 48–9.
32. Ibid., pp. 57–62.
33. Ibid., p. 60.
34. Schneer, *Balfour Declaration*, p. 209.
35. Bar-Yosef, *Holy Land*, p. 182.
36. Robertson memorandum, 20 Sept. 1916, WO 106/310; Charles Townshend, *When God Made Hell: The British Invasion of Mesopotamia and the Creation of Iraq 1914–1921* (2010), p. 340.
37. Townshend, *When God Made Hell*; Robertson, 2 Jan. 1917, WO 106/311.
38. Townshend, *When God*, pp. 360–75; Eugene Rogan, *The Fall of the Ottomans: The Great War in the Middle East, 1914–1920* (2015), p. 324.
39. Victor Rothwell, 'Mesopotamia in British War Aims, 1914-1918', *Historical Journal* 13, No. 2 (1970), p. 280; see Sykes telegram, 29 Apr. 1917, MECA Sykes MSS Box 1.
40. Rogan, *Fall*, p. 316.
41. War Cabinet, 15 Dec. 1916, CAB 23/1/8.
42. Robertson notes, 14 Dec. 1916, WO 106/310; and 2 Jan 1917, WO 106/311.
43. War Cabinet, 2 Jan. 1917, CAB 23/1/25.
44. Robertson note, 29 Dec. 1916, WO 106/310; George MacMunn and Cyril Falls, *Military Operations: Egypt and Palestine from the Outbreak of War with Germany to June 1917* (1928), p. 272.
45. MacMunn and Falls, *Military Operations*, p. 322, 329; Robertson note, 23 Apr. 1917, WO 106/311.
46. Matthew Hughes, *Allenby and British Strategy in the Middle East, 1917–1919* (1999), ch. 1.
47. Christopher Andrew and Sidney Kanya-Forstner, *France Overseas: The Great War and the Climax of French Imperial Expansion* (1981), p. 124.
48. 3 Apr. 1917 conference, CAB 24/9/75.
49. MacMunn and Falls, *Military Operations*, p. 322.

50. War Cabinet, 25 Apr. 1917, CAB 23/2/44.
51. Curzon Committee report, 24 Apr. 1917, CAB 21/77.
52. Amery note, 11 Apr. 1917, CAB 24/10/48.
53. See Brock Millman, *Pessimism and British War Policy, 1916–1918* (2001), pp. 123ff.
54. Imperial War Cabinet, 1 May 1917, CAB 23/40/13.
55. Robertson note, 17 May 1917, WO 106/311.
56. D. Gillon 'The Antecedents of the Balfour Declaration', *Middle Eastern Studies* 5, No. 2 (1969), p. 138.
57. Schneer, *Balfour Declaration*, pp. 170–6.
58. Ibid., pp. 196, 208–10.
59. Friedman, *Question*, p. 198.
60. Gillon, 'Antecedents', pp. 121–5.
61. Sykes to Picot, 28 Feb. 1917, MECA Sykes MSS Box 1.
62. Andrew and Kanya-Forstner, *France Overseas*, p. 127.
63. Ibid., p. 129; Schneer, *Balfour Declaration*, p. 212; Sykes to Balfour 9 Apr. 1917, LGP F/51/4/18.
64. Vital, *Crucial Phase*, pp. 247–9.
65. Ibid., pp. 254–6; Balfour to Rothschild, 19 July 1917, FO 371/3083.
66. Richard Lebow, 'Woodrow Wilson and the Balfour Declaration', *Journal of Modern History* 40, No. 4 (1968), pp. 567–8.
67. Cecil minute, 25 Apr. 1917, FO 371/3053; Barnet Litvinoff (ed.), *The Letters and Papers of Chaim Weizmann*, I: *Series B, August 1898–July 1931* (1983), pp. 146–9.
68. Graham minute, 21 Apr. 1917, FO 371/3052; Wingate to Graham, 23 July 1917, FO 371/3083.
69. Cecil minute, 25 Apr. 1917, FO 371/3053.
70. Schneer, *Balfour Declaration*, pp. 305–8.
71. Friedman, *Question*, pp. 227–8.
72. Wolf to Oliphant, 18 May 1917, FO 371/3053.
73. *The Times*, 24 May 1917, FO 371/3053.
74. *The Times*, 25, 29 May 1917, ibid.
75. Alderman, *British Jewry*, pp. 247–9.
76. Friedman, *Question*, pp. 239–40.
77. Graham minute, c.27 June 1917, FO 371/3053; see Stein, *Balfour Declaration*, p. 464.
78. Friedman, *Question*, pp. 244–7; Stein, *Balfour Declaration*, p. 465; Andrew and Kanya-Forstner, *France Overseas*, p. 130.
79. Stein, *Balfour Declaration*, p. 470.
80. Jehuda Reinharz, 'The Balfour Declaration and its Maker: A Reassessment', *Journal of Modern History* 64, No. 3 (1992), pp. 400–1.
81. Stein, *Balfour Declaration*, pp. 466–7.
82. Reinharz, 'Balfour Declaration', pp. 462–3.
83. Livinoff (ed.), *Chaim Weizmann*, I: *Series B*, p. 158.
84. Anthony Bruce, *The Last Crusade: The Palestine Campaign in the First World War* (2002), p. 116; Lloyd George, *War Memoirs*, II, pp. 1089–90.
85. Bruce, *Last Crusade*, p. 117; Robertson to Allenby, 10 Aug. 1917, WO 158/611.
86. Hughes, *Allenby*, pp. 45–6.
87. Allenby command conference, 20 Aug. 1917, WO 158/612.
88. French, *Strategy*, pp. 154–7.

89. Allenby to Robertson, 9 Oct. and Robertson to Allenby, 1 Nov. 1917, WO 158/611.
90. Stein, *Balfour Declaration*, p. 473.
91. Ibid., p. 664.
92. Waley, *Montagu*, pp. 139–40.
93. Montagu memorandum, 23 Aug. 1917, CAB 24/24/71.
94. War Cabinet, 3 Sept. 1917, CAB 21/58.
95. Lebow, 'Woodrow Wilson', p. 509.
96. War Cabinet, 3 Sept. 1917, CAB 21/58.
97. Hankey note, 17 Oct. 1917, CAB 24/4/14.
98. Renton, *Zionist Masquerade*, p. 131.
99. Ibid., pp. 132–3.
100. Lebow, 'Woodrow Wilson', pp. 502–4, 506; Neu, *House*, p. 587n.
101. Lebow, 'Woodrow Wilson', p. 510; House to Drummond, 10 Sept. 1917, CAB 21/58.
102. Reinharz, 'Balfour Declaration', pp. 469–74.
103. Lebow, 'Woodrow Wilson', p. 510; Balfour minute, *c*.24 Sept. 1917, FO 371/3083.
104. Rothschild to Balfour, 1 Oct. 1917, FO 371/3083.
105. Note by 'R. McN', n.d., ibid.
106. Rothschild to Balfour, 22 Sept.; Graham minute, 24 Sept. 1917, ibid.
107. Friedman, *Germany*, chs. 14–16.
108. Ibid., p. 324.
109. Hankey note, 17 Oct. 1917, CAB/4/14.
110. Vital, *Crucial Phase*, pp. 256–61; Mark Levene, 'The Balfour Declaration: A Case of Mistaken Identity?', *English Historical Review* 107, No. 422 (1992), pp. 73–4.
111. War Cabinet, 4 Oct. 1917, CAB 21/58.
112. Stein, *Balfour Declaration*, p. 521.
113. Ibid., p. 520; Leopold Amery, *My Political Life*, II, pp. 116–17.
114. Stein, *Balfour Declaration*, p. 522.
115. Brandeis to Weizmann, 26 Sept. 1917, CAB 21/58.
116. Lebow, 'Woodrow Wilson', pp. 512–22.
117. Weizmann to Graham, 23 Oct. 1917, FO 371/3054.
118. Hankey note, 17 Oct. 1917, CAB 24/4/14.
119. Balfour to Lloyd George, 25 Oct. 1917, LGP F/3/2/34.
120. Montagu memorandum, 9 Oct. 1917, CAB 21/58.
121. Curzon memorandum, 26 Oct. 1917, CAB 24/30/6.
122. Sykes memorandum, forwarded 30 Oct. 1917, FO 371/3083.
123. Sykes memorandum, 11 Oct. 1917, CAB 24/144/12; Goodhart to Balfour, 2 Oct. 1917, CAB 21/58; Graham to Balfour, 24 Oct. 1917, FO 371/3054; see Reinharz, 'Balfour Declaration', p. 485.
124. War Cabinet, 31 Oct. 1917, CAB 21/58.
125. Lloyd George, *The Truth*, II, pp. 1138–9.
126. Waley, *Montagu*, p. 140.
127. Lloyd George, *Peace Treaties*, II, pp. 1119–20.
128. Stein, *Balfour Declaration*, ch. 32.
129. Steed to Northcliffe, 14 Oct. 1917, MECA Balfour Declaration MSS.
130. Bigar, *Boundaries*, p. 46.
131. Lloyd George, *The Truth*, II, p. 1139.
132. Friedman, *Question*, p. 315.

133. Ibid., pp. 319, 321, 322.
134. For Weizmann's contribution to the failure of the mission by the American diplomat Henry Morgenthau to achieve a peace with Turkey, see ibid., ch. 13.
135. Friedman, *Germany, Turkey*, pp. 339–45, 380–1.
136. Lloyd George, *The Truth*, II, pp. 1121–22.
137. Vital, *Crucial Phase*, pp. 305–11.
138. Stein, *Balfour Declaration*, pp. 569–75.
139. Friedman, *Question*, p. 301.
140. Stein, *Balfour Declaration*, pp. 576–85; Renton, *Zionist Masquerade*, pp. 138–48.
141. Philip Taylor, 'The Foreign Office and British Propaganda during the First World War', *The Historical Journal* 23, No. 4 (1980), p. 890.
142. Friedman, *Question*, p. 325.
143. Schneer, *Balfour Declaration*, p. 198.
144. Lloyd George, *The Truth*, II, pp. 1119, 1140.
145. Schneer, *Balfour Declaration*, pp. 227–36.
146. Kedourie, *Anglo-Arab Labyrinth*, pp. 188–90.
147. James Renton, 'The Age of Nationality and the Origins of the Zionist–Palestinian Conflict', *International History Review* 35, No. 3 (2013), pp. 585ff.
148. Michael Cohen, *Britain's Moment in Palestine: Retrospect and Perspectives, 1917–1948* (2014), ch. 7.
149. Bar-Yosef, *Holy Land*, p. 292.

CONCLUSION

1. Rabinowitch, *The Bolsheviks Come to Power*, pp. xx, 312.
2. Browder and Kerensky (eds), *Russian Provisional Government*, III, p. 1209.
3. Jonathan Frankel, 'Lenin's Doctrinal Revolution of April 1917', *Journal of Contemporary History* 4, No. 2 (1969), p. 133.
4. Ibid., pp. 119–23.
5. Vladimir Lenin, preface to 'Imperialism: The Highest Stage of Capitalism', in James Connor (ed.), *Lenin on Politics and Revolution: Selected Writings* (1968), p. 112.
6. Lenin, 'First Letter from Afar', in Connor (ed.), *Lenin*, pp. 151–5. Italics in original.
7. Ibid., pp. 158–60.
8. Bernard Semmel (ed.), *Marxism and the Science of War* (1981), p. 169.
9. Zbyněk Zeman (ed.), *Germany and the Revolution in Russia, 1915–1918: Documents from the Archives of the German Foreign Ministry* (1958), p. x.
10. Ibid., p. 70; Kotkin, *Stalin*, I, p. 202.
11. Hahlweg, *Lenins Rückkehr nach Rußland 1917*, p. 25.
12. Rabinowitch, *Bolsheviks*, p. xxiv.
13. Kotkin *Stalin*, I, pp. 191–2.
14. Figes, *People's Tragedy*, p. 367.
15. Rabinowitch, *Bolsheviks*, chs. 4, 9.
16. Wildman, *End*, II, p. 108.
17. Figes, *People's Tragedy*, p. 379; Wildman, *End*, I, p. 370.
18. Blair reports, 20 Aug., 15 Sept. 1917, WO 106/1036.
19. Blair report, 29 Sept. 1917, WO 106/1037.
20. Leon Trotsky, *History of the Russian Revolution*, III (1933), p. 66.

21. Gill, *Peasants and Government*, p. 164.
22. David Stevenson (ed.), *British Documents on Foreign Affairs: Reports and Papers from the Confidential Print*, Part II, Series H, 3 (1989), pp. 203–5, 247; Connor, *Lenin*, pp. 168–9.
23. Taylor, *Politics and the Russian Army*, pp. 116–19.
24. *WK*, XIII, pp. 189–90, 198–200, 206–7; Stone, *Russian Army*, pp. 293–4.
25. Rabinowitch, *Bolsheviks*, p. 179.
26. Trotsky, *Russian Revolution*, III, p. 130.
27. Trotsky, *Russian Revolution*, III, pp. 129–30.
28. Robert Service, *Lenin: A Political Life* (1991), II, pp. 241–5.
29. Kotkin, *Stalin*, I, p. 186.
30. Trotsky, *Russian Revolution*, III, p. 130.
31. Browder and Kerensky (eds), *Russian Provisional Government*, III, pp. 1762–3.
32. Figes, *People's Tragedy*, pp. 478–9; Rossiyskaya sotsial-demokraticheskaya robochaya partiya (bolshevikov), *Protokoly Tsentralnogo Komiteta RSDRP: avgust 1917–fevral' 1918* (1958), pp. 83–92.
33. Browder and Kerensky (eds), *Russian Provisional Government*, III, p. 763.
34. Rabinowitch, *Bolsheviks*, p. 227.
35. Kotkin, *Stalin*, I, p. 215.
36. Rabinowitch, *Bolsheviks*, p. 220; *Protokoly Tsentralnogo Komiteta*, pp. 93–104.
37. Figes, *People's Tragedy*, pp. 476–8.
38. Ibid., pp. 480–1; Rabinowitch, *Bolsheviks*, p. 241.
39. Orlando Figes, 'The "Harmless Drunk": Lenin and the October Insurrection', in Tony Brenton (ed.), *Historically Inevitable? Turning Points of the Russian Revolution* (2016), ch. 7.
40. Ibid., pp. 268–9; Figes, *People's Tragedy*, p. 492; Ronald Suny, 'Towards a Social History of the October Revolution', *American Historical Review* 88, No. 1 (1988), p. 50.
41. Vladimir Lenin, *Collected Works* (1960–78), XXIV, pp. 249–53.
42. Service, *Lenin*, II, pp. 266–9.
43. John Wheeler-Bennett, *Brest-Litovsk: The Forgotten Peace, March 1918* (1938), pp. 379–82.
44. Wildman, *End*, II, pp. 400, 310.
45. Taylor, *Politics of the Russian Army*, p. 124.
46. Müller, *Vernichtungsgedanke*, pp. 56–7.
47. *WK*, XIII, pp. 323–4.
48. Jörg Duppler and Gerhard Groß (eds), *Kriegsende 1918: Ereignis, Wirkung, Nachwirkung* (1994), pp. 46, 48.
49. Ch. 9 of this volume.
50. Wetzell memorandum, 30 Sept. 1917, NARA RG65, Entry 320, Box 11.
51. Memorandum on German economic situation in 1917–18, n.d., BA-MA W-10/50400.
52. *WK*, XIII, pp. 327–8.
53. Gregory Martin, 'German Strategy and Military Assessments of the American Expeditionary Force (AEF)', *War in History* 1, No. 2 (1994), pp. 171–9.
54. *WK*, XIII, pp. 318–19.
55. Ibid., p. 318.
56. Ibid., pp. 328–9; *WK*, XIV, p. 51; Müller, *Vernichtungsgedanke*, pp. 109–10.
57. Wetzell memoranda, 23 Oct., 9 Nov. 1917, NARA RG65, Entry 320, Box 11.
58. David Zabecki, *The German 1918 Offensives: A Case Study in the Operational Level of War* (2006), p. 76.
59. Ibid., p. 99.

60. Wetzell memoranda, 12, 25 Dec.; Schulenburg to Crown Prince, 12 Nov. 1917, NARA RG65, Entry 320, Box 11.
61. Kuhl memorandum, 20 Nov. 1917, ibid.
62. Müller, *Vernichtungsgedanke*, pp. 133–5.
63. Ibid., pp. 149, 161–2.
64. Dieter Störz, '"Aber was hätte anders geschehen sollen?"': Die Deutschen Offensiven and den Westfront 1918', in Jörg Duppler and Gerhard Groβ, eds, *Kriegsende 1918: Ereignis, Wirkung, Nachwirkung* (1999) pp. 63–4.
65. Zabecki, *1918 Offensives*, pp. 84, 87–8; Störz, 'Deutschen Offensiven', pp. 68–9.
66. Störz, 'Deutschen Offensiven', p. 57.
67. Müller, *Vernichtungsgedanke*, p. 167.
68. Rüdiger Schütz, 'Einführende Bemerkungen', in Duppler and Groβ (eds), *Kriegsende 1918*, p. 46.
69. Ibid., p. 45; Bruno Thoβ, 'Militärische Entscheidung und politisch-gesellschaftlich Umbruch. Das Jahr 1918 in der neueren Weltkriegforschung', in Jörg Duppler and Gerhard Groβ (eds), *Kriegsende 1918: Ereignis, Wirkung, Nachwirkung* (1994), p. 27.
70. Hindenburg to Kühlmann, 23 Dec. 1917, BA-MA RM5/2651.
71. Störz, 'Deutschen Offensiven', pp. 54–5.
72. Winfried Baumgart and Konrad Repgen (eds), *Brest-Litowsk* (1969), p. 32.
73. Wheeler-Bennett, *Brest-Litovsk*, p. 111.
74. Borislav Chernev, 'The Brest-Litovsk Moment: Self-Determination Discourse in Eastern Europe before Wilsonianism', *Diplomacy and Statecraft* 22, No. 3 (2011), pp. 370–1; Figes, *People's Tragedy*, p. 503.
75. Zeman (ed.), *Revolution in Russia*, pp. 78–83.
76. Ludendorff, *Meine Kriegserinnerungen*, p. 436.
77. Clifford Wargelin, 'A High Price for Bread: the First Treaty of Brest-Litovsk and the Break-Up of Austria-Hungary, 1917–1918', *International History Review* 19, No. 4 (1997), pp. 757ff.
78. Wheeler-Bennett, *Brest-Litovsk*, p. 173.
79. Service, *Lenin*, II, p. 243.
80. Richard Debo, *Revolution and Survival: The Foreign Policy of Soviet Russia, 1917–1918* (1979), p. 3.
81. Figes, *People's Tragedy*, p. 539.
82. Baumgart and Repgen (eds), *Brest-Litowsk*, pp. 108–16.
83. Ludendorff, *Meine Kriegserinnerungen*, pp. 431, 443.
84. Ibid., p. 449; Baumgart and Repgen (eds), *Brest-Litowsk*, pp. 50–62.
85. Wheeler-Bennett, *Brest-Litovsk*, pp. 269, 403–7.
86. Neu, *House*, p. 298.
87. Timothy Nenninger, 'American Military Effectiveness in the First World War', in Alan Millett and Williamson Murray (eds), *Military Effectiveness*, I: *The First World War* (1988), p. 117; Cooper, *Woodrow Wilson*, p. 340.
88. See Neu, *House*, p. 327.
89. CND Secretary to Creel, 14 Aug. 1917, NARA RG62, Entry 3-B1, Box 172.
90. Neu, *House*, p. 306.
91. Stevenson (ed.), *British Documents on Foreign Affairs*, Part II, Series H, 3, pp. 156–7, 199–200.
92. Kennedy, *Over Here*, pp. 108–10, 100.

93. Burk, *Sinews of War*, p. 162; McAdoo to Wilson, 12 May 1917, LOC, McAdoo MSS 522.
94. McAdoo to Wilson, 5 July 1917, ibid.; Foreign Office to Spring-Rice, 29 June, Spring-Rice to Foreign Office, 3 July 1917, FO 371/3115; see Burk, 'J. M. Keynes and the Exchange Rate Crisis of July 1917', 405–16.
95. Foreign Office to Spring-Rice, 30 July 1917, FO 371/3115.
96. McAdoo to Wilson, 30 Apr. 1917, LOC McAdoo MSS (522); Stephen Schuker, 'The Rhineland Question:West European Security at the Paris Peace Conference of 1919' in Manfred Boemeke, Gerald Feldman, and Elisabeth Glaser (eds), *The Treaty of Versailles: A Reassessment after 75 Years* (1998), p. 276.
97. McAdoo to Wilson, 15 Nov. 1917, LOC McAdoo MSS 523.
98. Nenninger, 'American Military Effectiveness', p. 120.
99. Kennedy, *Over Here*, p. 119.
100. Benedict Crowell, *America's Munitions, 1917–1918* (1919), pp. 14–15.
101. Nenninger, 'American Military Effectiveness', p. 116; William Williams, 'Josephus Daniels and the US Navy's Shipbuilding Program during World War I', *Journal of Military History* 60, No. 1 (1996), pp. 7ff.
102. Cooper, *Woodrow Wilson*, p. 403.
103. Edward Coffman, *The War to End All Wars: The American Military Experience in World War I* (1998), ch. 4.
104. David Stevenson, *With Our Backs to the Wall: Victory and Defeat in 1918* (2011), p. 246.
105. Coffman, *War to End All Wars*, pp. 38–42, 54–8.
106. Johnston memorandum, 11 May 1917, NARA M 1024, Roll 311.
107. Martin, 'German Strategy', p. 176.
108. Neu, *House*, p. 301.
109. French General Staff note, 11 Apr.; Pétain note, 26 Apr. 1917, NARA M1024, Roll 311.
110. Meeting with Haig, 27 Apr. 1917, Kuhn memorandum, 7 June 1917, ibid.
111. John Pershing, *My Experiences in the World War* (1931), pp. 46–7.
112. Nenninger, 'American Military Effectiveness', p. 125; Coffman, *To End All Wars*, p. 126.
113. Réquin note, 29 June, Kuhn memorandum, 7 July 1917, NARA M1024, Roll 311.
114. Kennedy, *Over Here*, p. 169; Neu, *House*, p. 327.
115. Nenninger, 'American Military Effectiveness', p. 119.
116. Neu, *House*, p. 328.
117. Nenninger, 'American Military Effectiveness', pp. 124–5.
118. Lochridge memoranda, 17 Oct. 1917 and n.d., NARA M1024, Roll 311.
119. Spring-Rice to Foreign Office, 23 May 1917, FO 382/1236.
120. Cooper, *Woodrow Wilson*, p. 395.
121. Neu, *Colonel House*, p. 299.
122. Spring-Rice to Balfour, 31 Aug. 1917, FO 371/3083.
123. Lawrence Gelfand, *The Inquiry: American Preparations for Peace, 1917–1919* (1963).
124. French, *Strategy*, pp. 183–6.
125. Douglas Newton, 'The Lansdowne "Peace Letter" of 1917 and the Prospect of Peace by Negotiation with Germany', *Australian Journal of Politics and History* 48, No. 1 (2002), pp. 16–39.
126. Arno Mayer, *Political Origins of the New Diplomacy, 1917–1918* (1959), pp. 315–21.
127. Neu, *House*, p. 326.
128. Seymour (ed.), *House*, III, pp. 284–91.
129. Lloyd George, *War Memoirs*, II, pp. 1490–3.

130. Trygve Throntveit, 'The Fable of the Fourteen Points: Woodrow Wilson and National Self-Determination', *Diplomatic History* 35, No. 3 (2011), pp. 445ff.

131. Scott (ed.), *Official Statements*, pp. 234–9.

132. Clemenceau, 12 Dec. 1917, Archives nationales, Paris, C7499.

133. Winston Churchill, *The World Crisis, 1916–1918* (1927), II, p. 377.

134. Robert Gerwarth, *The Vanquished: Why the First World War Failed to End, 1917–1923* (2016).

135. John Horne (ed.), *State, Society, and Mobilization in Europe during the First World War* (1997), chs. 12–14.

136. Leslie Gelb and Richard Betts, *The Irony of Vietnam: The System Worked* (1979), p. 3.

137. Painlevé, *Comment j'ai nommé*, pp. 1, 9–10. '*Celui-là a beaucoup appris qui a bien connu l'angoisse'*: the quotation comes from the *Song of Roland*.

138. Charteris, *At GHQ*, p. 236.

139. John Maynard Keynes, *The Economic Consequences of the Peace* (1920), p. 31.

Bibliography

The bibliography is not intended as a comprehensive guide to the literature on 1917. It is meant to assist with further reading and in identifying the items listed in the endnotes.

Abraham, Richard, *Alexander Kerensky: The First Love of the Revolution* (1987)

Afflerbach, Holger, *Falkenhayn: Politisches Handeln und Denken im Kaiserreich* (1996)

Afflerbach, Holger, 'Wilhelm II as Supreme Warlord in the First World War', *War in History* 5, No. 4 (1998), p. 427

Albert, Bill and Henderson, Paul, *South America and the First World War: The Impact of the War on Brazil, Argentina, Peru, and Chile* (1988)

Alderman, Geoffrey, *Modern British Jewry* (1992)

Amery, Leopold, *My Political Life* (1953–5)

Andrew, Christopher and Kanya-Forstner, Sidney, *France Overseas: The Great War and the Climax of French Imperial Expansion* (1981)

Arz von Straußenberg, Arthur, *Zur Geschichte des Großen Krieges 1914–1918* (1969)

Bar-Yosef, Eitan, *The Holy Land in English Culture, 1799–1917: Palestine and the Question of Orientalism* (2005)

Barnett, Margaret, *British Food Policy during the First World War* (1985)

Barr, James, *A Line in the Sand: Britain, France, and the Struggle for the Mastery of the Middle East* (2012)

Baumgart, Winfried and Repgen, Konrad (eds), *Brest-Litowsk* (1969)

Beach, Jim, *Haig's Intelligence: GHQ and the German Army, 1916–1918* (2013)

Beckett, Ian (ed.), *1917: Beyond the Western Front* (2009)

Beers, Burton, *Vain Endeavour: Robert Lansing's Attempts to End the American-Japanese Rivalry* (1962)

Bencivenga, Roberto, *La Sorpresa strategica di Caporetto* (1932)

Bernstorff, Joachim-Heinrich, Count von, *The Memoirs of Count Bernstorff* (1936)

Bethmann Hollweg, Theobald von, *Betrachtungen zum Weltkriege* (1919)

Bigar, Gideon, *The Boundaries of Modern Palestine, 1940–1947* (2004)

Bihl, Wolfdieter, 'La Mission de médiation des princes Sixte et Xavier de Bourbon-Parme en faveur de la paix', *Guerres mondiales et conflits contemporains* 43, No. 170 (1993), p. 31

Birnbaum, Karl, *Peace Moves and U-Boat Warfare: A Study of Imperial Germany's Policy towards the United States, April 18, 1916–January 9, 1917* (1958)

Black, Nicholas, *The British Naval Staff in the First World War* (2009)

Bloxham, Donald, *The Great Game of Genocide: Imperialism, Nationalism, and the Destruction of the Ottoman Armenians* (2007)

Boghardt, Thomas, *The Zimmermann Telegram: Intelligence, Diplomacy, and America's Entry into World War I* (2012)

Bonnefous, Georges, *Histoire politique de la Troisième République*, II: *La Grande Guerre (1914–1918)* (1967)

Bostyn, Franky et al., *Passchendaele 1917: The Story of the Fallen and Tyne Cot Cemetery* (2007)

Bourlet, Michèle, 'Le Deuxième Bureau et la diplomatie secrète: les négociations Armand–Revertera de 1917', *Guerres mondiales et conflits contemporains* 221, No. 1 (2006), p. 33

Boyle, Andrew (ed.), *The Brazilian Green Book* (1918)

Brennan, Christopher, 'Reforming Austria-Hungary: Beyond His Control or Beyond His Capacity? The Domestic Policies of Emperor Karl I, November 1916–May 1917' (PhD dissertation, London School of Economics, 2012)

Brenton, Tony (ed.), *Historically Inevitable? Turning Points of the Russian Revolution* (2016)

British Vessels Lost at Sea, 1914–1918 (1977)

Broadberry, Stephen and Harrison, Mark (eds), *The Economics of World War I* (2005)

Browder, Robert and Kerensky, Alexander (eds), *The Russian Provisional Government, 1917: Documents* (1961)

Brown, Judith, *Gandhi's Rise to Power: Indian Politics, 1915–1922* (1974)

Brown, Judith and Louis, Roger (eds), *The Oxford History of the British Empire*, IV: *The Twentieth Century* (1999)

Bruce, Anthony, *The Last Crusade: The Palestine Campaign in the First World War* (2013)

Brusilov Aleksei, *A Soldier's Notebook, 1914–1918* (1971)

Buchanan, George, *My Mission to Russia and Other Diplomatic Memories* (1923)

Buehrig, Edward, *Woodrow Wilson and the Balance of Power* (1955)

Burián, Stephen, Count, *Austria in Dissolution* (1925)

Burk, Kathleen, 'J. M. Keynes and the Exchange Rate Crisis of July 1917', *Economic History Review* 32, No. 3 (1979), p. 405

Burk, Kathleen, *Britain, America, and the Sinews of War, 1914–1918* (1985)

Cadorna, Luigi, *La Guerra alla Fronta Italiana: fino all'arresto sulla line della Piave e del Grappa (24 Maggio 1915–9 Novembre 1917)* (1921), II

Cadorna, Raffaelo (ed.), *Luigi Cadorna, Lettere famigliari* (1967)

Calder, Kenneth, *Britain and the Origins of the New Europe, 1914–1918* (1976)

Capello, Luigi, *Note di Guerra* (1920)

Capello, Luigi, *Caporetto Perchè? La 2° Armata e gli avennimenti dell'ottobre 1917* (1967)

Cavalcanti, Pedro, *A Presidência Wenceslau Braz (1914–1918)* (1983)

Cecil, Hugh and Liddle, Peter (eds), *Facing Armageddon: The First World War Experienced* (1996)

Cecil, Lamar, *Wilhelm II*, II: *Emperor and Exile, 1900–1941* (1996)

Chambers, John, *To Raise an Army: The Draft Comes to Modern America* (1987)

Chapman, Guy, *A Passionate Prodigality: Fragments of Autobiography* (1967)

Charteris, John, *At GHQ* (1931)

Chernev, Borislav, 'The Brest-Litovsk Moment: Self-Determination Discourse in Eastern Europe before Wilsonianism', *Diplomacy and Statecraft* 22, No. 3 (2011), p. 369

Chi, Madeleine, *China Diplomacy, 1914–1918* (1970)

Chickering, Roger and Förster, Stig (eds), *Great War, Total War: Combat and Mobilization on the Western Front, 1914–1918* (2000)

Churchill, Winston, *The World Crisis, 1916–1918* (1927)

Coffman, Edward, *The War to End All Wars: The American Military Experience in World War I* (1998)

Cohen, Michael, *The Origins and Evolution of the Arab-Israeli Conflict* (1987)

Cohen, Michael, *Britain's Moment in Palestine: Retrospect and Perspectives, 1917–1948* (2014)

Compagnon, Olivier, *L'Adieu à l'Europe: l'Amérique latine et la Grande Guerre (Argentine et Brésil, 1914–1939)* (2013)

Compagnon, Olivier, 'Latin America', in Jay Winter (ed.), *The Cambridge History of the First World War* (2014), I, ch. 20

Connor, James (ed.), *Lenin on Politics and Revolution: Selected Writings* (1968)

Coogan, John, *The End of Neutrality: The United States, Britain, and Maritime Rights, 1899–1915* (1981)

Cooper, John, 'The Command of Gold Reversed: American Loans to Britain, 1915–1917', *Pacific Historical Review* 45, No. 2 (1976), p. 209

Cooper, John, *Woodrow Wilson: A Biography* (2011)

Cooper, John Milton, *The Vanity of Power: American Isolationism and the First World War, 1914–1917* (1969)

Copland, Ian, *India, 1885–1947: The Unmaking of an Empire* (2001)

Cornwall, Mark, *The Undermining of Austria-Hungary: The Battle for Hearts and Minds* (2000)

Craft, Stephen, 'Angling for an Invitation to Paris: China's Entry into the First World War', *International History Review* 16, No. 1 (1994), p. 1

Cramon, August von, *Unser Österreich-Ungarischer Bundesgenosse im Weltkriege* (1920)

Cronon, David (ed.), *The Cabinet Diaries of Josephus Daniels, 1913–1921* (1963)

Crowell, Benedict, *America's Munitions, 1917–1918* (1919)

Curami, Andrea, 'L'industria bellica italiana dopo Caporetto', in Giampetro Berti and Piero del Negro (eds), *Al di qua e al di là del Piave: l'ultimo anno della Grande Guerra* (2001), p. 549

Curry, Roy, *Woodrow Wilson and Far Eastern Policy, 1913–1921* (1968)

Czernin, Ottokar, *In the World War* (1919)

Dalby, Andrew, *Eleutherios Venizelos: Greece* (2010)

Dalton, Hugh, *With British Guns in Italy: A Tribute to Italian Achievement* (1919)

Daniels, Josephus, *The Wilson Era: Years of Peace—1910–1917* (1974)

Danzig, Richard, 'The Announcement of August 20th, 1917', *The Journal of Asian Studies* 28, No. 1 (1968), p. 19

Davidian, Irina, 'The Russian Soldier's Morale from the Evidence of Military Censorship', in Hugh Cecil and Peter Liddle (eds), *Facing Armageddon: The First World War Experienced* (1996), ch. 12

Debo, Richard, *Revolution and Survival: The Foreign Policy of Soviet Russia, 1917–1918* (1979)

Denikin, Anton, *La Décomposition de l'armée et du pouvoir (février-septembre 1917)* (1922)

Devlin, Patrick, *Too Proud to Fight: Woodrow Wilson's Neutrality* (1974)

Dickinson, Frederick, *War and National Reinvention: Japan in the Great War, 1914–1919* (1999)

Doenecke, Justus, *Nothing Less than War: A New History of America's Entry into World War I* (2011)

Doughty, Robert, *Pyrrhic Victory: French Strategy and Operations in the Great War* (2005)

Dowling, Timothy, *The Brusilov Offensive* (2008)

Duppler, Jörg and Groß, Gerhard (eds), *Kriegsende 1918: Ereignis, Wirkung, Nachwirkung* (1994)

Dutton, David, 'The Deposition of King Constantine of Greece: An Episode in Anglo-French Diplomacy', *Canadian Journal of History* 12, No. 3 (1978), p. 325

Dutton, David, *The Politics of Diplomacy: Britain and France in the Balkans in the First World War* (1998)

Edmonds, James, *History of the Great War Based on Official Documents: Military Operations: France and Belgium 1917* (1933–48), II

Edmonds, James, *History of the Great War Based on Official Documents: Military Operations: Italy 1915–1919* (1949)

Elleman, Bruce, *Wilson and China: A Revised History of the Shandong Question* (2002)

Ellinwood, DeWitt and Pradhan, S. (eds), *India and World War I* (1978)

Engel, Barbara, 'Not by Bread Alone: Subsistence Riots in Russia during World War I', *Journal of Modern History* 69, No. 4 (1997), p. 696

Epstein, Klaus, *Matthias Erzberger and the Dilemma of German Democracy* (1959)

Erdmann, Karl (ed.), *Kurt Riezler: Tagebücher, Aufsätze, Dokumente* (1972)

Erzberger, Matthias, *Erlebnisse im Weltkrieg* (1920)

Falls, Cyril, *History of the Great War Based on Official Documents: Military Operations: Macedonia* (1933–5)

Falls, Cyril, *Caporetto 1917* (1965)

Farrar, Lancelot, Jr, 'Opening to the West: German Efforts to Conclude a Separate Peace with England, July 1917–March 1918', *Canadian Journal of History* 10, No. 1 (1975), p. 73

Fassy, Gérard, *Le Commandement français en Orient (octobre 1915–novembre 1918)* (2003)

Fayle, Ernest, *History of the Great War Based on Official Documents: Seaborne Trade* (1924)

Feldman, Robert, 'The Russian General Staff and the June 1917 Offensive', *Soviet Studies* 19, No. 4 (1968), p. 526

Ferro, Marc, *La Révolution de 1917: la chute du tsarisme et les origines d'Octobre* (1967)

Ferro, Marc, *La Révolution de 1917: Octobre. Naissance d'une société* (1976)

Fifield, Russell, *Woodrow Wilson and the Far East: The Diplomacy of the Shantung Question* (1952)

Figes, Orlando, *A People's Tragedy: The Russian Revolution, 1891–1924* (1997)

Figes, Orlando, 'The "Harmless Drunk": Lenin and the October Insurrection', in Tony Brenton (ed.), *Historically Inevitable? Turning Points of the Russian Revolution* (2016), ch. 7

Fischer, Fritz, *Germany's Aims in the First World War* (1967)

Fowler, Wilton, *British-American Relations, 1914–1918: The Role of Sir William Wiseman* (1969)

Frankel, Jonathan, 'Lenin's Doctrinal Revolution of April 1917', *Journal of Contemporary History* 4, No. 2 (1969), p. 117

French, David, 'The Dardanelles, Mecca, and Kut: Prestige as a Factor in British Eastern Strategy, 1914–1916', *War and Society* 5, No. 1 (1987), p. 45

French, David, 'Who Knew What and When? The French Army Mutinies and the British Decision to Launch the Third Battle of Ypres', in Lawrence Freedman et al. (eds), *War, Strategy, and International Politics: Essays in Honour of Sir Michael Howard* (1992), p. 133

French, David, *The Strategy of the Lloyd George Coalition, 1916–1918* (1995)

Frenkin, M., *Russkaya armiya i revolyutsiya 1917–18* (1978)

Frey, Marc, 'Bullying the Neutrals: The Case of the Netherlands', in Roger Chickering and Stig Förster (eds), *Great War, Total War: Combat and Mobilization on the Western Front, 1914–1918* (2000), ch. 12

Fried, Marvin, *Austro-Hungarian War Aims in the Balkans during World War I* (2014)

Friedman, Isaiah, *The Question of Palestine, 1914–1918, British–Jewish–Arab Relations* (1973)

Friedman, Isaiah, *Germany, Turkey, and Zionism, 1897–1918* (1998)

Fulwider, Chad, *German Propaganda and US Neutrality in World War I* (2016)

Garraty, John, *Henry Cabot Lodge: A Biography* (1953)

Gatrell, Peter, *Russia's First World War: A Social and Economic History* (2005)

Gatti, Angelo, *Caporetto: dal Diario di Guerra Inedito (Maggio-Dicembre 1917)* (1964)

Gelfand, Lawrence, *The Inquiry: American Preparations for Peace, 1917–1919* (1963)

Gemzell, Carl-Axel, *Organization, Conflict, and Innovation: A Study of German Naval Strategic Planning, 1888–1940* (1973)

Gerard, James, *My Four Years in Germany* (1917)

Gerwarth, Robert, *The Vanquished: Why the First World War Failed to End, 1917–1923* (2016)

Gibson, R. H. and Prendergast, Maurice, *The German Submarine War, 1914–1918* (1931)

Gill, Graeme, *Peasants and Government in the Russian Revolution* (1979)

Gillon, D., 'The Antecedents of the Balfour Declaration', *Middle Eastern Studies* 5, No. 2 (1969), p. 131

Gooch, John, *The Italian Army and the First World War* (2014)

Görlitz, Walter (ed.), *Regierte der Kaiser? Kriegstagebücher, Aufzeichnungen und Briefe des Chefs des Marine-Kabinetts Admiral Georg Alexander von Müller, 1914–1918* (1959)

Gough, Hubert, *The Fifth Army* (1931)

Goya, Michel, *La Chair et l'acier: l'invention de la guerre moderne (1914–1918)* (2004)

Granier, Gerhard (ed.), *Magnus von Levetzow: Seeoffizier, Monarchist, und Wegbereiter Hitlers: Lebensweg und Ausgewählte Dokumente* (1982)

Granier, Gerhard (ed.), *Die Deutsche Seekriegsleitung im Ersten Weltkrieg* (2000)

Green, Abigail, 'The British Empire and the Jews: An Imperialism of Human Rights?', *Past & Present* 199, No. 1 (2008), p. 175

Greene, Stephen, *Absolute Dreams: Thai Government under Rana VI, 1910–1925* (1994)

Greenhalgh, Elizabeth, *Victory through Coalition: Britain and France during the First World War* (2005)

Greenhalgh, Elizabeth, *The French Army in the First World War* (2014)

Gregory, Ross, *The Origins of American Intervention in the First World War* (1971)

Grey, Edward, *Twenty-Five Years, 1892–1916* (1925), II

Griesser-Pečar, Tamar, *Die Mission Sixtus: Österreichische Friedensversuch im Ersten Weltkrieg* (1988)

Griffith, Paddy, 'The Tactical Problem: Infantry, Artillery, and the Salient', in Peter Liddle (ed.), *Passchendaele in Perspective: The Third Battle of Ypres* (1997), ch. 5

Grigg, John, *Lloyd George: War Leader, 1916–1918* (2003)

Grotelueschen, Mark, *The AEF Way of War: The American Army and Combat in World War I* (2007)

Guoqi, Xu, *China and the Great War: China's Pursuit of a New National Identity and Internationalization* (2005)

Gwynn, Stephen (ed.), *The Letters and Friendships of Sir Cecil Spring Rice* (1929)

Hagenlücke, Heinz, *Die Deutsche Vaterlandspartei: die Nationale Rechte am Ende des Kaiserreiches* (1997)

Hagenlücke, Heinz, 'The German High Command', in Peter Liddle (ed.), *Passchendaele in Perspective: The Third Battle of Ypres* (1997), ch. 4

Hahlweg, Werner, *Lenins Rückkehr nach Rußland 1917: die deutschen Akten* (1957)

Halpern, Paul, *A Naval History of World War I* (1994)

Hankey, Maurice, *The Supreme Command, 1914–1918* (1961)

Harris, John Paul, *Douglas Haig and the First World War* (2008)

Hasegawa, Tsuyoshi, *The February Revolution: Petrograd, 1917* (1981)

Heenan, Louise, *Russian Democracy's Fatal Blunder: The Summer Offensive of 1917* (1987)

Herbillon, Edmond, *Du général en chef au gouvernement. Souvenirs d'un officier de liaison pendant la Guerre mondiale* (1930)

Herbillon, Edmond, *De la Meuse à Reims: le Général Alfred Micheler (1914–1918)* (1934)

Heywood, Anthony, 'Spark of Revolution? Railway Disorganisation, Freight Traffic, and Tsarist Russia's War Effort, July 1914–March 1917', *Europe-Asia Studies* 65, No. 4 (2013), p. 753

Hindenburg, Paul von, *Aus Meinem Leben* (1920)

Holland, Robert, 'The British Empire and the Great War, 1914–1918', in Judith Brown and Roger Louis (eds), *The Oxford History of the British Empire* (2001), IV

Hopwood, Robert, 'Czernin and the Fall of Bethmann Hollweg', *Canadian Journal of History* 2, No. 2 (1967), p. 49

Horěiěka, Václav, 'Austria-Hungary, Unrestricted Submarine Warfare, and the United States' Entrance into the First World War', *International History Review* 34, No. 2 (2012), p. 245

Horne, John (ed.), *State, Society, and Mobilization in Europe during the First World War* (1997)

Houston, David, *Eight Years with Wilson's Cabinet, 1913–1920* (1920)

Hughes, Matthew, *Allenby and British Strategy in the Middle East, 1917–1919* (1999)

Hull, Isabel, *A Scrap of Paper: Breaking and Making International Law during the Great War* (2014)

Hurd, Archibald, *History of the Great War Based on Official Documents: The Merchant Navy* (1921–9), III

Hussey, John, 'The Flanders Battleground and the Weather in 1917', in Peter Liddle (ed.), *Passchendaele in Perspective: The Third Battle of Ypres* (1997), ch. 10

Hutchins, Francis, *The Illusion of Permanence: British Imperialism in India* (1967)

Iklé, Frank, 'Japanese–German Peace Negotiations during World War I', *American Historical Review* 71, No. 1 (1965), p. 62

Ishii, Kikujiro, *Diplomatic Commentaries* (1936)

Jahn, Hubertus, *Patriotic Culture in Russia during World War I* (1995)

Jeffery, Keith, *The British Army and the Crisis of Empire, 1918–1922* (1984)

Jeffery, Keith, *1916: A Global History* (2015)

Jellicoe, John, *The Crisis of the Naval War* (1920)

Jellicoe, John, *The Submarine Peril: The Admiralty Policy in 1917* (1934)

Kaspi, André, *Le Temps des Américains: le concours américain à la France en 1917–1918* (1976)

Katz, Friedrich, *The Secret War in Mexico: Europe, the United States, and the Mexican Revolution* (1981)

Kedourie, Elie, *In the Anglo-Arab Labyrinth: The MacMahon–Husayn Correspondence and its Interpretations, 1914–1939* (1976)

Keiger, John, *Raymond Poincaré* (1997)

Kenez, Peter, 'Changes in the Social Composition of the Officer Corps during World War I', *Russian Review* 31, No. 4 (1972), p. 369

Kennedy, David, *Over Here: The First World War and American Society* (1980)

Kerensky, Alexander, *Russia and History's Turning Point* (1965)

Kerensky, Alexander, *The Catastrophe: Kerensky's Own Story of the Russian Revolution* (1977)

Keynes, John Maynard, *The Economic Consequences of the Peace* (1920)

Khalidi, Rashid, *Palestinian Identity: The Construction of Modern National Consciousness* (1997)

King, Jere, *Generals and Politicians: Conflict between France's High Command, Parliament, and Government, 1914–1918* (1950)

Kirby, David, *War, Peace, and Revolution: International Socialism at the Crossroads, 1914–1918* (1986)

Kitchen, Martin, *The Silent Dictatorship: The Politics of the German High Command under Hindenburg and Ludendorff* (1976)

Knock, Thomas, *To End All Wars: Woodrow Wilson and the Quest for a New World Order* (1992)

Knox, Alfred, *With the Russian Army, 1914–1917* (1921)

Knox, MacGregor, *To the Threshold of Power, 1922/33, I: Origins and Dynamics of the Fascist and National Socialist Dictatorships* (2007)

Koenker, Diane and Rosenberg, William, *Strikes and Revolution in Russia, 1917* (1989)

Komarnicki, Titus, *Rebirth of the Polish Republic: A Study in the Diplomatic History of Europe, 1914–1920* (1957)

Komjáthy, Miklós (ed.), *Protokolle des Gemeinsamen Ministerrates der Österreichisch-Ungarischen Monarchie (1914–1918)* (1986)

Kotkin, Stephen, *Stalin, I: Paradoxes of Power, 1878–1928* (2015)

Kowalski, Ronald (ed.), *The Russian Revolution, 1917–1921* (2006)

Krafft von Delmensingen, Konrad, *Der Durchbruch am Isonzo Teil 1. Die Schlacht von Tolmein und Flitsel (24 bis 27 Oktober 1917)* (1926)

Krauβ, Alfred, *Das 'Wunder von Karfreit' im besonderen der Durchbruch bei Flitsch und die Bezwingung der Tagliamento* (1926)

Kühlmann, Richard von, *Erinnerungen* (1948)

La Fargue, Thomas, 'The Entrance of China into the World War', *Pacific Historical Review* 5, No. 3 (1936), p. 222

La Fargue, Thomas, *China and the World War* (1937)

Labanca, Nicola, *Caporetto: storia di una disfatta* (1997)

Lancken-Wakenitz, Oscar Freiherr von der, *Meine dreißig Dienstjahre 1888–1918: Potsdam–Paris–Brüssel* (1931)

Lansing, Robert, *War Memoirs of Robert Lansing* (1935)

Larsen, Daniel, 'British Intelligence and the 1916 Mediation Mission of Colonel Edward M. House', *Intelligence and National Security* 25, No. 5 (2010), p. 682

Larsen, Daniel, 'War Pessimism in Britain and an American Peace in Early 1916', *International History Review* 34, No. 4 (2012), p. 795

Latour, Francis, *La Papeauté et les problèmes de la paix pendant la Première Guerre mondiale* (1996)

Lebow, Richard, 'Woodrow Wilson and the Balfour Declaration', *Journal of Modern History* 40, No. 4 (1968), p. 501

Lenin, Vladimir, *Collected Works* (1960–78)

Leon, George, *Greece and the Great Powers 1914–1917* (1974)

Levene, Mark, 'The Balfour Declaration: A Case of Mistaken Identity?', *English Historical Review* 107, No. 422 (1992), p. 54

Lieven, Dominic, *Nicholas II: Emperor of All the Russias* (1993)

Lieven, Dominic, *Towards the Flame: Empire, War, and the End of Tsarist Russia* (2015)

Lih, Lars, *Bread and Authority in Russia, 1914–1921* (1990)

Link, Arthur, *Wilson: Campaigns for Progressivism and Peace, 1916–1917* (1965)

Linke, Horst, *Das Zarische Rußland und der Erste Weltkrieg: Diplomatie und Kriegsziele, 1914–1917* (1982)

Litvinoff, Barnet (ed.), *The Letters and Papers of Chaim Weizmann*, I: *Series B, August 1898–July 1931* (1983)

Llewellyn Smith, Michael, *Ionian Vision: Greece in Asia Minor 1919–1922* (1973)

Lloyd George, David, *The Truth about the Peace Treaties* (1938)

Lloyd George, David, *War Memoirs* (1938)

Loez, André and Mariot, Nicolas, *Obéir/désobéir: les mutineries de 1917 en perspective* (2008)

Lovell, S., *The Presidential Election of 1916* (1980)

Ludendorff, Erich, *Meine Kriegserinnerungen, 1914–1918* (1919)

Ludendorff, Erich, *My War Memories, 1914–1918* (1919)

Ludendorff, Erich (ed.), *Urkunden der Obersten Heeresleitung über ihre Tätigkeit, 1916/18* (1920)

Luebke, Frederick, *Bonds of Loyalty: German-Americans and World War I* (1974)

Luebke, Frederick, *Germans in Brazil: A Comparative History of Cultural Conflict during World War I* (1987)

Lundeberg, Philip, 'The German Naval Critique of the U-Boat Campaign, 1915–1918', *Military Affairs* 27, No. 3 (1964), p. 105

Lyandres, Semion, *The Fall of Tsarism: Untold Stories of the February 1917 Revolution* (2013)

McAdoo, William, *Crowded Years: The Reminiscences of William G. McAdoo* (1931)

McCann, Frank, *Soldiers of the Pátria: A History of the Brazilian Army, 1889–1937* (2004)

McCarthy, Justin, *The Population of Palestine: Population History and Statistics of the Late Ottoman Period and the Mandate* (1990)

MacDonald, Lyn, *Passchendaele: The Story of the Third Battle of Ypres, 1917* (2013)

McKean, Robert, *St Petersburg between the Revolutions: Workers and Revolutionaries, June 1907–February 1917* (1990)

McMeekin, Sean, 'Enter Lenin', in Tony Brenton (ed.), *Historically Inevitable? Turning Points of the Russian Revolution* (2016), ch. 5

MacKenzie, S. P., 'Morale and the Cause: The Campaign to Change the Outlook of Soldiers in the British Expeditionary Force, 1914–1918', *Canadian Journal of History* 25, No. 2 (1990), p. 215

MacMunn, George and Falls, Cyril, *History of the Great War Based on Official Documents: Military Operations: Egypt and Palestine from the Outbreak of War with Germany to June 1917* (1928)

Maklakoff, B. (ed.), *La Chute du regime tsariste* (1927)

Manela, Erez, *The Wilsonian Moment: Self-Determination and the International Origins of Anticolonial Nationalism* (2007)

Mangin, Charles, *Comment finit la guerre* (1920)

Marder, Arthur, *From the Dreadnought to Scapa Flow: The Royal Navy in the Fisher Era, 1904–1919* (1961–70)

Martin, Gregory, 'German Strategy and Military Assessments of the American Expeditionary Force (AEF)', *War in History* 1, No. 2 (1994), p. 160

Martin, Lawrence, *Peace Without Victory: Woodrow Wilson and the British Liberals* (1958)

May, Ernest, *The World War and American Isolation, 1914–1917* (1959)

Mayer, Arno, *Political Origins of the New Diplomacy, 1917–1918* (1959)

Melograni, Piero, *Storia politica della Grande Guerra, 1915–1918* (1969)

Merridale, Catherine, *Lenin on the Train* (2016)

Michaelis, Georg, *Für Staat und Volk: eine Lebensgeschichte* (1922)

Michaelis, Herbert and Schraepler, Ernst (eds), *Ursachen und Folgen. Vom deutschen Zusammenbruch 1918 und 1945 bis zur Staatlichen Neuordnung Deutschlands in der Gegenwart* (1958), I

Michaelis, Wilhelm, 'Der Reichskanzler Michaelis und die päpstliche Friedensaktion 1917: neue Dokumente', *Geschichte in Wirtschaft und Unterricht* 12, No. 7 (1961), p. 418

Middlebrook, Martin, *The Kaiser's Battle: 21 March 1918 the First Day of the German Spring Offensive* (1978)

Millett, Alan and Murray, Williamson (eds), *Military Effectiveness*, I: *The First World War* (1988)

Millman, Brock, 'A Counsel of Despair: British Strategy and War Aims, 1917–18', *Journal of Contemporary History* 36, No. 2, (2001), p. 241

Millman, Brock, *Pessimism and British War Policy, 1916–1918* (2001)

Miquel, Pierre, *Le Chemin des Dames* (1997)

Mitrakos, Alexander, *France in Greece during War I: A Study in the Politics of Power* (1982)

Morselli, Mario, *Caporetto 1917: Victory or Defeat?* (2001)

Mourelos, Yannis, 'British Policy towards King Constantine's Dethronement and Greece's Entry into the War', in *Greece and Great Britain during World War I*, ed. Institute for Balkan Studies (1985)

Müller, Martin, *Vernichtungsgedanke und Koalitionskriegführung: Das Deutsche Reich und Österreich-Ungarn in der Offensive 1917/1918. Eine Clausewitz-Studie* (2005)

Nebelin, Manfred, *Ludendorff: Diktator im Ersten Weltkrieg* (2011)

Nenninger, Timothy, 'American Military Effectiveness in the First World War', in Alan Millett and Williamson Murray (eds), *Military Effectiveness*, I: *The First World War* (1988), ch. 4

Neu, Charles, *Colonel House: A Biography of Woodrow Wilson's Silent Partner* (2014)

Newbolt, Henry, *Naval Operations* (1920–31)

Newton, Douglas, 'The Lansdowne "Peace Letter" of 1917 and the Prospect of Peace by Negotiation with Germany', *Australian Journal of Politics and History* 48, No. 1 (2002), p. 16

Nish, Ian, 'Dr Morrison and China's Entry into the World War, 1915–1917', in Ragnhild Hatton and Matthew Anderson (eds), *Studies in Diplomatic History: Essays in Memory of David Bye Horn* (1970), ch. 17

Nish, Ian, *Alliance in Decline: A Study in Anglo-Japanese Relations, 1908–1923* (1972)

Nish, Ian, *Japanese Foreign Policy, 1869–1942: Kasumigaseki to Miyakezaku* (1977)

Nouailhat, Yves-Henri, 'La France et les Etats-unis, août 1914–avril 1917' (Doctoral dissertation, University of Paris, 1975)

Offenstadt, Nicolas (ed.), *Le Chemin des Dames: de l'événement à la mémoire* (2004)

Omissi, David, *The Sepoy and the Raj: The Indian Army, 1860–1940* (1994)

Orlando, Vittorio, *Memorie (1915–1919)* (1960)

Osgood, Robert, *Ideals and Self-Interest in American Foreign Relations: The Great Transformation of the Twentieth Century* (1953)

Owen, Hugh, 'Negotiating the Lucknow Pact', *Journal of Asian Studies* 31, No. 3 (1972), p. 561

Painlevé, Paul, *Comment j'ai nommé Foch et Pétain: la politique de guerre de 1917; le commandement unique interallié* (1923)

Paléologue, Maurice, *La Russie des tsars pendant la Grande Guerre* (1927)

Pandey, Bishwa (ed.), *The Indian Nationalist Movement, 1885–1947: Select Documents* (1979)

Paolini, Gabriele, *Offensive di pace: la Santa Sede e la prima guerra mondiale* (2008)

Pearson, Raymond, *The Russian Moderates and the Crisis of Tsarism, 1914–1917* (1977)

Pedroncini, Guy, *Les Mutineries de 1917* (1967)

Pedroncini, Guy, *Les Négociations secrètes pendant la Grande Guerre* (1969)

Pedroncini, Guy, *Pétain: Général en chef, 1917–18* (1974)

Pedroncini, Guy, 'La France et les négociations secrètes de paix en 1917', *Guerres mondiales et conflits contemporains* 43, No. 170 (1993), p. 131

Pershing, John, *My Experiences in the World War* (1931)

Pethybridge, Roger, *The Spread of the Russian Revolution: Essays on 1917* (1972)

Philip, George (ed.), *British Documents on Foreign Affairs: Reports and Papers from the Confidential Print, Part II, Series D, Latin America, 1914–1939* (1989)

Philpott, William, *Anglo-French Relations and Strategy on the Western Front, 1914–1918* (1996)

Philpott, William, *Bloody Victory: The Sacrifice on the Somme and the Making of the Twentieth Century* (2009)

Philpott, William, *Attrition: Fighting the First World War* (2014)

Pierrefeu, Jean de, *GQG Secteur I* (1922)

Pipes, Richard, *The Russian Revolution, 1899–1919* (1999)

Poincaré, Raymond, *Au service de la France: neuf années de souvenirs* (1926–31)

Powell, Geoffrey, *Plumer: The Soldier's General* (2004)

Prior, Robin and Wilson, Trevor, *Passchendaele: The Untold Story* (1996)

Procacci, Giovanna, *Soldati e Prigionieri Italiani nella Grande Guerra* (2000)

Pyta, Wolfram, *Hindenburg: Herrschaft zwischen Hohenzollern und Hitler* (2007)

Rabinowitch, Alexander, *The Bolsheviks Come to Power: The Revolution of 1917 in Petrograd* (2004)

Radkey, Oliver, *The Agrarian Foes of Bolshevism: Promise and Default of the Russian Socialist Revolutionaries, February to October 1917* (1958)

Recouly, Raymond, *Les Négociations secrètes Briand–Lancken* (1933)

Reinharz, Jehuda, 'The Balfour Declaration and its Maker: A Reassessment', *Journal of Modern History* 64, No. 3 (1992), p. 455

Renton, James, *The Zionist Masquerade: The Birth of the Anglo-Zionist Alliance, 1914–1918* (2007)

Renton, James, 'The Age of Nationality and the Origins of the Zionist–Palestinian Conflict', *International History Review* 35, No. 3 (2013), p. 576

Ribot, Alexandre, *Lettres à un ami: souvenirs de ma vie politique* (1924)

Ribot, Alexandre (ed.), *Journal d'Alexandre Ribot et correspondances inédites 1914–1922* (1936)

Robb, Peter, 'The British Cabinet and Indian Reform, 1917–1919', *The Journal of Imperial and Commonwealth History* 4, No. 3 (1976), p. 318

Robb, Peter, 'The Government of India and Annie Besant', *Modern Asian Studies* 10, No. 1 (1976), p. 107

Robb, Peter, *The Government of India and Reform, Policies towards Politics and the Constitution, 1916–1921* (1976)

Robertson, William, *Soldiers and Statesmen, 1914–1918* (1926)

Rocca, Gianna, *Cadorna* (1990)

Rogan, Eugene, *The Fall of the Ottomans: The Great War in the Middle East, 1914–1920* (2015)

Rogger, Hans, *Russia in the Age of Modernisation and Revolution, 1881–1917* (1983)

Röhl, John, *Wilhelm II: Into the Abyss of War and Exile, 1900–1941* (2014)

Romero, Francisco, *Spain, 1914–1918: Between War and Revolution* (1999)

Rommel, Erwin, *Infantry Attacks* (1990)

Rose, Sonya, 'The Politics of Service and Sacrifice in WWI Ireland and India', *Twentieth Century British History* 25, No. 3 (2014), p. 368

Rossiyskaya sotsial-demokraticheskaya robochaya partya (bol'shevikov), *Protokoly Tsentral'nogo Komiteta RSDRP, Avgust 1917-fevral' 1918* (1958)

Rothwell, Victor, 'Mesopotamia in British War Aims, 1914–1918', *Historical Journal* 13, No. 2 (1970), p. 273

Rothwell, Victor, *British War Aims and Peace Diplomacy, 1914–1918* (1971)

Rumbold, Algernon, *Watershed in India, 1914–1922* (1979)

Saini, Krishan, 'The Economic Aspects of India's Participation in the First World War' in DeWitt Ellinwood and S. Pradhan (eds), *India and World War I* (1978)

Salter, Arthur, *Allied Shipping Control: An Experiment in International Administration* (1921)

Sanborn, Joshua, *Imperial Apocalypse: The Great War and the Destruction of the Russian Empire* (2014)

Scheer, Reinhard, *Deutschlands Hochseeflotte im Weltkrieg: Persönliche Erinnerungen* (1920)

Scherer, André and Grünewald, Jacques (eds), *L'Allemagne et les problèmes de la paix pendant la Première Guerre Mondiale* (1966–78)

Schindler, John, *Isonzo: The Worst Sacrifice of the Great War* (2001)

Schmitt, Hans (ed.), *Neutral Europe between War and Revolution, 1917–23* (1988)

Schneer, Jonathan, *The Balfour Declaration: The Origins of the Arab-Israeli Conflict* (2011)

Schröder, Joachim, *Die-U-Boote des Kaisers: die Geschichte des deutschen U-Boot-Krieges gegen Großbritannien im Ersten Weltkrieg* (2000)

Schuker, Stephen, 'The Rhineland Question: West European Security at the Paris Peace Conference of 1919' in Manfred Boemeke, Gerald Feldman, and Elisabeth Glaser (eds), *The Treaty of Versailles: A Reassessment after 75 Years* (1998), ch. 12

Schütz, Rüdiger, 'Einführende Bemerkungen', in Jörg Duppler and Gerhard Groß (eds), *Kriegsende 1918: Ereignis, Wirkung, Nachwirkung* (1994), p. 41

Schwertfeger, Bernhard (ed.), *Kaiser und Kabinettschef: nach eigenen Aufzeichnungen und dem Briefwechsel des Wirklichen Geheimen Rats Rudolf von Valentini* (1931)

Scott, James (ed.), *Official Statements of War Aims and Peace Proposals, December 1916–November 1918* (1921)

Semmel, Bernard (ed.), *Marxism and the Science of War* (1981)

Senin, A., *Zheleznodorozhny Transport Rossii v Epoxy Voini i Revolyutsii (1914–1922gg)* (2009)

Service, Robert, *Lenin: A Political Life* (1991), II

Seymour, Charles (ed.), *The Intimate Papers of Colonel House* (1926–8)

Shanafelt, Gary, *The Secret Enemy: Austria-Hungary and the German Alliance, 1914–1918* (1985)

Sheffield, Gary and Bourne, John (eds), *Douglas Haig: War Diaries and Letters, 1914–1918* (2005)

Sheldon, Jack, *The German Army at Passchendaele* (2007)

Sidorov, A., 'Zheleznodorozhny Transport Rossii v Pervoi Mirovoi Voine i Obostrenie Ekonomicheskogo Krizisa v Strane', *Istoricheskie Zapiski* 26 (1948), p. 3

Simone, Cesare de, *L'Isonzo Mormorava: Fronti e Generali a Caporetto* (1995)

Sims, William, *The Victory at Sea* (1920)

Sixte de Bourbon, Prince, *L'Offre de paix séparée de l'Autriche (5 décembre 1916–12 octobre 1917)* (1920)

Smith, Joseph, *Unequal Giants: Diplomatic Relations between the United States and Brazil, 1889–1930* (1991)

Smith, Joseph and Vinhosa, Francisco, *History of Brazil, 1500–2000: Politics, Economy, Society, Diplomacy* (2003)

Smith, Stephen, *Red Petrograd: Revolution in the Factories, 1917–1918* (1983)

Sonnino, Sidney, *Diario 1916–22*, ed. Pietro Pastorelli (1922)

Spears, Edward, *Prelude to Victory* (1939)

Spindler, Arno, *Der Handelskrieg mit U-Booten* (1964), IV

Steffen, Dirk, 'The Holtzendorff Memorandum of 22 December 1916 and Germany's Declaration of Unrestricted U-Boat Warfare', *Journal of Military History* 68, No. 1 (2004), p. 215

Steglich, Wolfgang, *Die Friedenspolitik der Mittelmächte 1917/18* (1964), I

Steglich, Wolfgang (ed.), *Der Friedensappel Papst Benedikts XV vom 1. August 1917 und die Mittelmächte* (1970)

Steglich, Wolfgang (ed.), *Die Friedensversuche der Kriegführenden Mächte im Sommer und Herbst 1917. Quellenkritische Untersuchungen, Akten, und Vernehmsprotokolle* (1984)

Stein, Leonard, *The Balfour Declaration* (1961)

Steinberg, Mark and Khrustalev, Vladimir (eds), *The Fall of the Romanovs: Political Dreams and Personal Struggles in a Time of Revolution* (1995)

Sterba, Christopher, *Good Americans: Italian and Jewish Immigrants during the First World War* (2003)

Stevenson, David, *French War Aims against Germany, 1914–1919* (1982)

Stevenson, David (ed.), *British Documents on Foreign Affairs: Reports and Papers from the Confidential Print, Part II, Series H, 3* (1989)

Stevenson, David, *1914–1918: The History of the First World War* (2004)

Stevenson, David, *With Our Backs to the Wall: Victory and Defeat in 1918* (2011)

Stibbe, Matthew, *German Anglophobia and the Great War, 1914–1918* (2001)

Stillig, Jürgen, *Die Russische Februarrevolution 1917 und die Sozialistische Friedenspolitik* (1977)

Stone, David, *The Russian Army in the Great War: The Eastern Front, 1914–1917* (2015)

Stone, Norman, *The Eastern Front, 1914–1917* (1975)

Störz, Dieter, '"Aber was hätte anders geschehen sollen?": Die Deutschen Offensiven and den Westfront 1918', in Jörg Duppler and Gerhard Groβ (eds), *Kriegsende 1918: Ereignis, Wirkung, Nachwirkung* (1994), p. 51

Strachan, Hew, 'The Morale of the German Army, 1917–18', in Hugh Cecil and Peter Liddle (eds), *Facing Armageddon: The First World War Experienced* (1996), ch. 28

Suarez, Georges, *Briand: sa vie—son oeuvre* (1940), IV

Suny, Ronald, 'Towards a Social History of the October Revolution', *American Historical Review* 88, No. 1 (1988), p. 31

Suny, Ronald, *'They Can Live in the Desert but Nowhere Else': A History of the Armenian Genocide* (2013)

Taylor, Brian, *Politics and the Russian Army: Civil–Military Relations, 1609–2000* (2003)

Taylor, Philip, 'The Foreign Office and British Propaganda during the First World War', *The Historical Journal* 23, No. 4 (1980), p. 890

Temple Patterson, Alfred (ed.), *The Jellicoe Papers: Selections from the Private and Official Correspondence of Admiral of the Fleet Lord Jellicoe* (1968)

Terraine, John, *Business in Great Waters: The U-Boat Wars, 1916–1945* (1999)

Thatcher, Ian, 'Memoirs of the Russian Provisional Government 1917', *Revolutionary Russia* 27, No. 1 (2014), p. 1

Thompson, John, *Woodrow Wilson* (2002)

Thompson, Mark, *The White War: Life and Death on the Italian Front, 1915–1919* (2008)

Thoβ, Bruno, 'Militärische Entscheidung und politisch-gesellschaftlich Umbruch. Das Jahr 1918 in der neueren Weltkriegforschung', in Jörg Duppler and Gerhard Groβ (eds), *Kriegsende 1918: Ereignis, Wirkung, Nachwirkung* (1994), p. 17

Thronweit, Tryge, 'The Fable of the Fourteen Points: Woodrow Wilson and National Self-Determination', *Diplomatic History* 35, No. 3 (2011), p. 445

Till, Geoffrey, 'Passchendaele: The Maritime Dimension', in Peter Liddle (ed.), *Passchendaele in Perspective: The Third Battle of Ypres* (1997), ch. 6

Tomlinson, Brian, 'India and the British Empire, 1880–1935', *Indian Economic and Social History Review* 12 (1975), p. 337

Tomlinson, Brian, *The Political Economy of the Raj, 1919–1947: The Economics of Decolonization in India* (1979)

Tooze, Adam, *The Deluge: The Great War and the Remaking of Global Order, 1961–1931* (2015)

Toscano, Mario, *Gli Accordi di San Giovanni di Moriana—Storia diplomatica dell'intervento italiano*: II *1916–1917* (1936)

Townshend, Charles, *When God Made Hell: The British Invasion of Mesopotamia and the Creation of Iraq 1914–1921* (2010)

Triebel, Armin, 'Coal and the Metropolis', in Jay Winter and Jean-Louis Robert (eds), *Capital Cities at War: Paris, London, Berlin, 1914–1919* (1997), ch. 12

Trotsky, Leon, *History of the Russian Revolution* (1933)

Tumulty, Joseph, *Woodrow Wilson as I Know Him* (1970)

Turner, John, 'Lloyd George, the War Cabinet, and High Politics', in Peter Liddle (ed.), *Passchendaele in Perspective: The Third Battle of Ypres* (1997), ch. 2

Veneruso, Danilo, *La Grande Guerra e l'unità nazionale: il ministero Boselli: giugno 1916–ottobre 1917* (1996)

Vital, David, *Zionism: The Crucial Phase* (1987)

Vogt, Martin, 'L'Allemagne et les négociations de paix en 1917: réflexions sous forme d'esquisse sur un sujet qui a failli tomber dans l'oubli', *Guerres mondiales et conflits contemporains* 43, No. 170 (1993), p. 79

Wade, Rex, 'Why October? The Search for Peace in 1917', *Soviet Studies* 20, No. 1 (1968)

Wade, Rex, *The Russian Search for Peace, February–October 1917* (1969)

Waley, David, *Edwin Montagu: A Memoir and an Account of His Visits to India* (1964)

Wargelin, Clifford, 'A High Price for Bread: The First Treaty of Brest-Litovsk and the Break-Up of Austria-Hungary, 1917–1918', *International History Review* 19, No. 4 (1997), p. 757

Warman, Roberta, 'The Erosion of Foreign Office Influence in the Making of Foreign Policy, 1916-1918', *The Historical Journal* 15, No. 1 (1972), p. 133

Watson, Alexander, *Ring of Steel: Germany and Austria-Hungary at War, 1914–1918* (2014)

Weir, Gary, 'Tirpitz, Technology, and Building U-Boats, 1897-1916', *International History Review* 6, No. 2 (1984), p. 174

Weir, Gary, *Rebuilding the Kaiser's Navy: The Imperial Navy and German Industry in the Tirpitz Era, 1890–1919* (1990)

Wendt, Hermann, *Die Italienische Kriegsschauplatz im Europäischen Konflikten* (1936)

Wheeler-Bennett, John, *Brest-Litovsk: The Forgotten Peace, March 1918* (1938)

Wiest, Andrew, *Passchendaele and the Royal Navy* (1995)

Wiest, Andrew, 'The Planned Amphibious Assault', in Peter Liddle (ed.), *Passchendaele in Perspective: The Third Battle of Ypres* (1997) ch. 13

Wilcox, Vanda, 'Generalship and Mass Surrender during the Italian Defeat at Caporetto', in Ian Beckett (ed.), *1917: Beyond the Western Front* (2009), ch. 2

Wildman, Allan, *The End of the Russian Imperial Army* (1980–7)

Williams, William, 'Josephus Daniels and the US Navy's Shipbuilding Program during World War I', *Journal of Military History* 60, No. 1 (1996), p. 7

Williamson, John, *Karl Helfferich, 1872–1924: Economist, Financer, Politician* (1971)

Winter, Jay, 'Arthur Henderson, the Russian Revolution, and the Reconstruction of the Labour Party', *The Historical Journal,* 15, No. 4 (1972), p. 753

Winter, Jay (ed.), *The Cambridge History of the First World War* (2013)

Winter, Jay and Robert, Jean-Louis (eds), *Capital Cities at War: Paris, London, Berlin, 1914–1919* (1997–2007)

Wolff, Leon, *In Flanders Fields: Passchendaele 1917* (1979)

Wollstein, Günter, *Theobald von Bethmann Hollweg* (1995)

Wolpert, Stanley, *Tilak and Gokhale: Revolution and Reform in the Making of Modern India* (1962)

Woodward, David, 'David Lloyd George, a Negotiated Peace with Germany, and the Kühlmann Peace Kite of September 1917', *Canadian Journal of History* 6, No. 1 (1971), p. 75

Woodward, David, *Lloyd George and the Generals* (1983)

Wrigley, Chris, *David Lloyd George and the British Labour Movement: Peace and War* (1976)

Zabecki, David, *The German 1918 Offensives: A Case Study in the Operational Level of War* (2006)

Zeman, Zbyněk (ed.), *Germany and the Revolution in Russia, 1915–1918: Documents from the Archives of the German Foreign Ministry* (1958)

Ziemann, Benjamin, 'Le Chemin des Dames dans l'historiographie militaire allemande', in Nicolas Offenstadt (ed.), *Le Chemin des Dames: de l'événement à la mémoire* (2004), p. 348

Živojinović, Dragan, 'Robert Lansing's Comments on the Pontifical Peace Note of August 1, 1917, *Journal of American History* 56, No. 3 (1969), p. 566

Image Credits

1. Print Collector/Getty Images
2. Hulton Archive/Stringer/Getty Images
3. © Imperial War Museums (Q 70000)
4. © Imperial War Museums (Q 69404)
5. Fine Art Images/HIP/TopFoto
6. © TopFoto
7. © Imperial War Museums (Q 4997)
8. © Imperial War Museums (Q 64693)
9. © Imperial War Museums (Q 106243)
10. © Imperial War Museums (Q 91670)
11. National Motor Museum/HIP
12. © TopFoto
13. © Imperial War Museums (CO 2253)
14. © Imperial War Museums (Q 86164)
15. Imagno/Getty Images
16. Henry Guttmann/Stringer
17. © Imperial War Museums (Q 12663)
18. World History Archive/TopFoto
19. Print Collector/Getty Images
20. © Imperial War Museums (Q 103662)
21. © Imperial War Museums (HU 56409)

Index

Note: Tables and figures are indicated by an italic *t* and *f* following the page number.